Lecture Notes in Artificial  51

Subseries of Lecture Notes in Computer Science
Edited by J. G. Carbonell and J. Siekmann

Lecture Notes in Computer Science

Edited by G. Goos, J. Hartmanis and J. van Leeuwen

**Springer**

*Berlin*
*Heidelberg*
*New York*
*Barcelona*
*Budapest*
*Hong Kong*
*London*
*Milan*
*Paris*
*Tokyo*

Klaus P. Jantke  Steffen Lange (Eds.)

# Algorithmic Learning for Knowledge-Based Systems

GOSLER Final Report

Springer

Series Editors

Jaime G. Carbonell
School of Computer Science, Carnegie Mellon University
Pittsburgh, PA 15213-3891, USA

Jörg Siekmann
University of Saarland, German Research Center for AI (DFKI)
Stuhlsatzenhausweg 3, D-66123 Saarbrücken, Germany

Volume Editors

Klaus P. Jantke
Steffen Lange
Hochschule für Technik, Wirtschaft und Kultur Leipzig
Fachbereich Mathematik, Informatik und Naturwissenschaften
Postfach 66, D-04251 Leipzig, Germany

Cataloging-in-Publication Data applied for

Die Deutsche Bibliothek - CIP-Einheitsaufnahme

**Algorithmic learning for knowledge-based systems** : GOSLER
final report / Klaus P. Jantke ; Steffen Lange (ed.). - Berlin ;
Heidelberg ; New York ; Barcelona ; Budapest ; Hong Kong ;
London ; Milan ; Paris ; Tokyo : Springer, 1995
  (Lecture notes in computer science ; 961 : Lecture notes in artificial
  intelligence)
  ISBN 3-540-60217-8
NE: Jantke, Klaus P. [Hrsg.]; GT

CR Subject Classification (1991): I.2.6, I.2.1, I.2.3-4, I.2.8, F.4.1, F.4.3

ISBN 3-540-60217-8 Springer-Verlag Berlin Heidelberg New York

© Springer-Verlag Berlin Heidelberg 1995
Printed in Germany

Typesetting: Camera ready by author
SPIN 10486575      06/3142 – 5 4 3 2 1 0      Printed on acid-free paper

# Preface

The present book partially reflects the results of a comprehensive basic research project named GOSLER on "Algorithmic Learning for Knowledge-Based Systems". GOSLER was supported by the German Federal Ministry of Research and Technology (BMFT, nowadays BMBF) under grant no. 413-4001-01 IW 101 during 1991–1994. Within GOSLER, research teams at Humboldt University Berlin, Chemnitz University of Technology, University of Kaiserslautern, and Leipzig University of Technology did cooperative basic research on algorithmic learning theory. Among the 10 research projects in the field of artificial intelligence supported by the German Federal Ministry of Research and Technology during the early 1990s, GOSLER was clearly the most theoretically oriented one. It was particularly focused on the study of fundamental learnability problems integrating theoretical research with the development of research tools and experimental investigations.

The GOSLER project has had remarkable repercussions on the scientific communication in the field of algorithmic learning theory. A large number of common research results achieved by the cooperative work of GOSLER participants and scientists all over the world have been documented by a score or more of technical reports, by a series of conference contributions presented at the international workshops on Analogical and Inductive Inference (AII), Algorithmic Learning Theory (ALT), and Computational Learning Theory (COLT), and by a number of journal papers published during these years. The present book summarizes an essential part of this research work in a form not published elsewhere. Besides documenting the success of GOSLER, its main intention is to give an impression of prototypical problems, techniques, and solutions in algorithmic learning theory. It may well serve as an introduction to the area emphasizing a number of issues motivated and outlined below. The work of 11 GOSLER participants is naturally complemented by contributions due to 23 colleagues from Australia, Austria, Japan, Latvia, Singapore, and the USA.

Machine learning is a computer science area currently attracting a steadily growing interest. This tendency is clearly based on the need for computer systems which are more flexible, more robust, and more autonomous than nowadays. The growing number of computer installations, the wider scope of applications addressed, and the larger community of naive users involved bears abundant evidence of the need for truly learning computer systems. Like every computer science discipline, machine learning has more theoretically oriented as well as more application oriented subareas. Algorithmic learning theory (or computational learning theory, synonymously) is the more theoretically oriented and mathematically based branch of machine learning putting emphasis on algorithms, on their power and limitations, and on their complexity including the tradeoffs among fundamental properties. In algorithmic learning theory, learning from incomplete information is deemed to be essential. The standard technical term to denote learning from usually incomplete information is inductive inference. In Dana Angluin's words, "*Inductive inference is to computational learning theory as computability theory is to complexity and analysis of algorithms. Inductive inference and computability theory are historically and logically prior to and part of their polynomially-obsessed younger counterparts, share a body of techniques from recursion theory, and are a source of potent ideas and analogies in their respective fields.*" Intentionally, the investigations undertaken within GOSLER have been focused on learning from incomplete information, i.e. on *inductive inference*. It has been a guideline of the overall project to contribute to the field as a whole by doing disciplinary work both theoretically as well as experimentally, by extracting and communicating insights into basic phenomena of learning, by analysing learning algorithms which have an architecture and a behaviour motivated by artificial intelligence research, and, last but not least, by establishing new hopefully fruitful relations between different subareas. The following two instances should fairly illustrate these overall intentions.

The unavoidable incompleteness of information underlying learning processes causes a number of difficulties. Essentially, learning results must be hypothetical, in general, as particular information provided may turn out later to be insufficient for extracting the target phenomenon to be learned. Due to this unavoidable uncertainty of hypotheses generated during learning, users of learning systems are usually interested in trustability properties of those intermediate hypotheses. A fundamental property deemed important in learning, especially in application-oriented systems, is consistency. A learning algorithm or program is said to learn consistently, exactly if every hypothesis built during learning reflects the amount of information it is built upon. Consistency depends on a precise relationship between hypotheses and information fragments possibly presented. When formal languages are to be learned from positive and negative examples, this may be formalized via membership. Other formalisms require other approaches. It is immediately clear that certain decidability problems are fundamental for consistency. Recall, for instance, that there is no universal method to decide whether or not some particularly given partial recursive function admits any given input/output example. Thus, checking consistency turns out to be a non-trivial problem. Barzdin and the Blums show that there are learning problems which are only solvable if inconsistent intermediate hypotheses are allowed. This seems to contradict common sense. The paper by Wiehagen and Zeugmann gives an impressive overview on the problem of consistency. In particular, it illustrates the need for and the power of inconsistent learning algorithms both in function and language learning. It is the editors' strong belief that presentations of this type carry a lot of messages useful in wider areas of learning.

Recently, there have been enormously many approaches and applications of case-based reasoning and learning techniques. In case-based reasoning, knowledge is represented in the form of particular cases with an appropriate similarity measure rather than any form of rules. The main task of case-based learning is to collect good cases which will be stored in the case base for describing knowledge and classifying unknown examples. Thus, case-based learning algorithms do not construct explicit generalizations from examples which most other supervised learning algorithms derive. Besides this particular architecture and behaviour, the main intention is the design of algorithms that are suitable for learning from incomplete information. Thus, it is quite natural to relate case-based learning to other approaches focusing on learning from incomplete information. This may help to gain deeper insights into both the power as well as the limitations of case-based learning, to elaborate essential features of case-based learning algorithms, and to show how these parameters influence their learning capabilities. The paper by Globig and Wess follows this line and extends previously obtained insights into the relations between inductive and case-based learning.

Despite GOSLER's emphasis on theoretical research, there has been a remarkable investment in developing and using experimental systems. The motivation for the experimental work within GOSLER has been twofold: First, experiments are deemed fundamental for guiding theoretical investigations through the huge amount of possible approaches. Second, prototypical implementations are understood as a testbed for theoretically developed algorithmic ideas. The two main experimentation-oriented developments of the GOSLER project are reflected in the final two contributions of the present volume. The paper by Grieser describes an experimental system $T_{\!I}P^S$ for inductive program synthesis within a term rewriting framework. $T_{\!I}P^S$ provides a suitable environment for synthesizing toy-size term rewriting programs. The paper by Beick and Stankov describes a meta-programming activity extending and tuning Prolog towards a flexible environment for implementing and testing learning algorithms. The resulting system GOSLERP supports logic programming for deriving and handling hypothetical knowledge including backtracking of knowledge base manipulations, i.e. meta-programming. Both systems have been the basis of further still ongoing experiments.

We gratefully acknowledge the support by the German Federal Ministry of Research and Technology which provided both a firm basis for the research work within GOSLER and a launching pad for a fruitful international cooperation. During the long period of preparations for the present volume, our colleague Oksana Arnold did a very important and responsible job in editorial management including long e-mail conversations with the authors. The Algorithmic Learning Group at Leipzig University of Technology with our colleagues Oksana Arnold, Ralf Böhme, Katy Börner, Ulf Goldammer, Erwin Keusch, Jürgen Koch, Uwe Metzner, Ingo Müller, Eberhard Pippig, Takeshi Shinohara, Elisabeth-Ch. Tammer, and Phil Watson has provided a stimulating atmosphere which made our work as well as a couple of results presented in this book possible.

Leipzig, June 1995

Klaus P. Jantke
Steffen Lange

# Table of Contents

## 1    Inductive Inference Theory

## 1.1    Inductive Inference of Recursive Functions

## 1.2    Inductive Inference of Formal Languages

## 2 Inductive Inference for Artificial Intelligence

## 2.1 Theoretical Approaches

## 2.2 Systems

# Learning and Consistency

### Rolf Wiehagen

University of Kaiserslautern

Department of Computer Science

P.O. Box 3049

67653 Kaiserslautern

Germany

wiehagen@informatik.uni-kl.de

### Thomas Zeugmann

Research Institute of

Fundamental Information Science

Kyushu University 33

Fukuoka 812

Japan

thomas@rifis.sci.kyushu-u.ac.jp

### Abstract

In designing learning algorithms it seems quite reasonable to construct them in such a way that all data the algorithm already has obtained are correctly and completely reflected in the hypothesis the algorithm outputs on these data. However, this approach may totally fail. It may lead to the unsolvability of the learning problem, or it may exclude any efficient solution of it.

Therefore we study several types of consistent learning in recursion-theoretic inductive inference. We show that these types are not of universal power. We give "lower bounds" on this power. We characterize these types by some versions of decidability of consistency with respect to suitable "non-standard" spaces of hypotheses.

Then we investigate the problem of learning consistently in polynomial time. In particular, we present a natural learning problem and prove that it can be solved in polynomial time if and only if the algorithm is allowed to work inconsistently.

## 1. Introduction

The phenomenon of learning has attracted much attention of researchers in various fields. When dealing with learning computer scientists are mainly interested in studying the question whether or not learning problems may be solved algorithmically. Nowadays, algorithmic learning theory is a rapidly emerging science, cf. Angluin and Smith (1983, 1987), Osherson, Stob and Weinstein (1986). Nevertheless, despite the enormous progress having been made since the pioneering papers of Solomonoff (1965) and of Gold (1965, 1967), there are still many problems that deserve special attention. The global question we shall deal with may be posed as follows: Are all data of equal importance a learning algorithm is fed?

First we study this question in the setting of inductive inference. Then we ask whether the insight obtained may be important when one has to solve learning problems that are in a sense closer to potential applications. For that purpose we consider a domain that has recently attracted attention, namely the learnability of indexed families (cf., e.g., Zeugmann, Lange and Kapur, 199x, and the references therein). We consider the particular indexed family of all the pattern languages and show the superiority of inconsistent learning strategies over consistent ones for this particular family. Next, we want to explain all this in some more detail.

One main problem of algorithmic learning theory consists in synthesizing "global descriptions" for the objects to be learned from examples. Thus, one goal is the following. Let $f$ be any computable function from $\mathbb{N}$ into $\mathbb{N}$. Given more and more examples $f(0), f(1), ..., f(n), ...$ a learning strategy is required to produce a sequence of hypotheses $h_0, h_1, ..., h_n, ...$ the limit of which is a correct global description of the function $f$, i.e., a program that computes $f$. Since at any stage $n$ of this learning process the strategy knows exclusively the examples $f(0), f(1), ..., f(n)$, it seems reasonable to construct the hypothesis $h_n$ in a way such that for any $x \leq n$ the "hypothesis function" $g$ described by $h_n$ is defined and computes the value $f(x)$. Such a hypothesis is called *consistent*. In other words, a hypothesis is consistent if and only if all information obtained so far about the unknown object is completely and correctly encoded in this hypothesis. Otherwise, a hypothesis is said to be *inconsistent*. Consequently, if the hypothesis $h_n$ above is inconsistent, then there must be an $x \leq n$ such that $g(x) \neq f(x)$. Note that there are two possible reasons for $g$ to differ from $f$ on argument $x$; namely, $g(x)$ may be not defined, or the value $g(x)$ is defined and does not equal $f(x)$. Hence, if a hypothesis is inconsistent then it is not only wrong but it is wrong on an argument for which the learning strategy does already know the correct value. At first glance we are tempted to totally exclude strategies producing inconsistent hypotheses from our considerations. It might seem that *consistent strategies*, i.e., strategies that produce always consistent hypotheses, are the only reasonable learning devices.

Surprisingly enough this is a misleading impression. As it turns out, in a sense learning seems to be *the art of knowing what to overlook*. Barzdin (1974a) first announced that there are classes of recursive functions that can be learned in the limit but only by strategies working inconsistently. This result directly yields the following questions:

(1) Why does it make sense to output inconsistent hypotheses?
(2) What kind of data, if any, the strategy should overlook?

As we shall see below the first question finds its preliminary answer in the fact that, in general, there is no algorithm detecting whether or not a hypothesis is consistent. Consequently, in general, a strategy has no chance to effectively verify the consistency of its previous guess with the new data it has been fed. On the other hand, a strategy cannot overcome this drawback by simply searching any consistent hypothesis, since it has to converge in the limit, too. Therefore, in order to be really successful in the limit a strategy cannot take care whether all the information it is provided with is actually correctly reflected by its current hypotheses. Answering the second question is more complicated. However, an intuitively satisfying answer is provided by a characterization of identification in the limit in terms of computable numberings (cf. Wiehagen (1978), Theorem 8). This theorem actually states that a class $U$ of recursive functions can be learned in the limit iff there are a space of hypotheses containing for each function at least one program, and a computable "discrimination" function $d$ such that for any two programs $i$ and $j$ the value $d(i,j)$ is an upper bound for an argument $x$ on which program $i$ behaves differently than program $j$ does. The key observation used in constructing the strategy that infers any function from $U$ is the following. Let $i$ be the strategy's last guess and let $f(0),...,f(n)$ be the data now fed to it. If the strategy finds a program $j$ such that for all inputs $x \leq d(i,j)$ its output equals $f(x)$, then program $i$ *cannot be a correct one* for function $f$. Then the strategy changes its mind from $i$ to $i+1$. In other words, the strategy uses the data up to $d(i,j)$ for the purpose to find a *proof* for the possible *incorrectness* of its actual hypothesis $i$ via some global property the space of all hypotheses possesses. Just for achieving this reasonable purpose the learning strategy may ignore all the data $f(x)$ where $d(i,j) < x \leq n$, thus trading off consistency of the new hypothesis (unachievable, in general, anyway) for an incorrectness proof concerning the former hypothesis.

Summarizing the above discussion we see that the main reason for the superiority of inconsistent strategies in the setting of inductive inference of recursive functions is caused by the undecidability of consistency. As we shall see further, consistent learning is also sensitive with respect to additional requirements that a learning strategy might be supposed to fulfil, e.g. the order in which the input data are provided or the domain on which a strategy is required to behave consistently.

However, it remained open whether this inconsistency phenomenon is of epistemological importance, only, but of almost no practical relevance. Dealing with the latter problem requires a different approach. It might be well conceivable that consistency is often decidable if one restricts itself to learning problems that are of interest with respect to potential applications. Consequently, the superiority of inconsistent strategies in this setting, if any, can only be established in terms of complexity theory. What we present in the sequel is a partial solution to this problem. As it turned out, there are natural learning problems having the following property: Though consistency is decidable in the corresponding domain, these learning problems can be solved by a polynomial-time strategy if and only if the strategy may work inconsistently.

Hence the inconsistency phenomenon does survive also in domains where consistency *is* decidable. Moreover, the reason for the eventual superiority of inconsistent strategies is in both settings in some sense the same. In both cases the learning algorithms cannot handle the problem of finding/constructing consistent hypotheses. On the one hand, this inability has been caused by the provable absence of any algorithm solving it, while, on the other hand, this problem may be computationally intractable.

As far as we know the result above is the first one formally proving the existence of learning problems that cannot be solved in polynomial time by any consistent strategy in a setting where consistency is decidable. Moreover, in our opinion it strongly recommends to take *inconsistent* learning strategies seriously into consideration. This requires both, the elaboration of "intelligent" inconsistent techniques as well as finding criteria with the help of which one can decide whether or not fast consistent strategies are unavailable. The inconsistency technique we have used just consists in ignoring data unnecessary for the strategy in order to fulfil its learning task. Of course, this might not be the only such technique.

The paper is structured as follows. Section 2 presents notation and definitions. Section 3 deals with the inconsistency phenomenon in the setting of inductive inference of recursive functions. The problem whether the inconsistency phenomenon is of any relevance in the world of polynomial time learning is affirmatively exemplified in Section 4. In Section 5 we discuss the results obtained and present open problems. All references are given in Section 6. Note that Wiehagen and Zeugmann (1992) and Wiehagen (1992) dealt already with the inconsistency phenomenon in inductive inference and in exact learning in polynomial time. Furthermore, part of the present paper has been published in Wiehagen and Zeugmann (1994).

## 2. Preliminaries

Unspecified notations follow Rogers (1967). $\mathbb{N} = \{0, 1, 2, ...\}$ denotes the set of all natural numbers. The set of all finite sequences of natural numbers is denoted by $\mathbb{N}^*$. The classes of all partial recursive and recursive functions of one, and two arguments over $\mathbb{N}$ are denoted by $P$, $P^2$, $R$, and $R^2$, respectively. $R_{0,1}$ denotes the set of all $0 - 1$ valued recursive functions. Sometimes it will be suitable to identify a recursive function with the sequence of its values, e.g., let $\alpha = (a_0, ..., a_k) \in \mathbb{N}^*$, $j \in \mathbb{N}$, and $p \in R_{0,1}$; then we write $\alpha j p$ to denote the function $f$ for which $f(x) = a_x$, if $x \leq k$, $f(k+1) = j$, and $f(x) = p(x - k - 2)$, if $x \geq k + 2$. Furthermore, let $g \in P$ and $\alpha \in \mathbb{N}^*$; we write $\alpha \sqsubset g$ iff $\alpha$ is a prefix of the sequence of values associated with $g$, i.e., for any $x \leq k$, $g(x)$ is defined and $g(x) = a_x$. If $U \subseteq R$, then we denote by $[U]$ the set of all prefixes of functions from $U$.

Any function $\psi \in P^2$ is called a numbering. Moreover, let $\psi \in P^2$, then we write $\psi_i$ instead of $\lambda x \psi(i, x)$ and set $P_\psi = \{\psi_i \mid i \in \mathbb{N}\}$ as well as $R_\psi = P_\psi \cap R$. Consequently, if $f \in P_\psi$, then there is a number $i$ such that $f = \psi_i$. If $f \in P$ and $i \in \mathbb{N}$ are such that $\psi_i = f$, then $i$ is called a $\psi$-program for $f$. A numbering $\varphi \in P^2$ is called a Gödel numbering (cf. Rogers (1967)) iff $P_\varphi = P$, and for any numbering $\psi \in P^2$, there is a $c \in R$ such that $\psi_i = \varphi_{c(i)}$ for all $i \in \mathbb{N}$. $Göd$ denotes the set of all Gödel numberings.

Using a fixed encoding $\langle ... \rangle$ of $\mathbb{N}^*$ onto $\mathbb{N}$ we write $f^n$ instead of $\langle (f(0), ..., f(n)) \rangle$, for any $n \in \mathbb{N}$, $f \in R$. Furthermore, the set of all permutations of $\mathbb{N}$ is denoted by $\Pi(\mathbb{N})$. Any element $X \in \Pi(\mathbb{N})$ can be represented by a unique sequence $(x_n)_{n \in \mathbb{N}}$ that contains each natural number precisely ones. Let $X \in \Pi(\mathbb{N})$, $f \in P$ and $n \in \mathbb{N}$. Then we write $f^{X,n}$ instead of $\langle (x_0, f(x_0), ..., x_n, f(x_n)) \rangle$ provided $f(x_k)$ is defined for all $k \leq n$. Finally, a sequence $(j_n)_{n \in \mathbb{N}}$ of natural numbers is said to converge to the number $j$ iff all but finitely many numbers of it are equal to $j$. A sequence $(j_n)_{n \in \mathbb{N}}$ of natural numbers is said to finitely converge to the number $j$ iff it converges in the limit to $j$ and for all $n \in \mathbb{N}$, $j_n = j_{n+1}$ implies $j_k = j$ for all $k \geq n$. Now we are ready to define some concepts of learning.

**Definition 1. (Gold, 1965)** Let $U \subseteq R$ and let $\psi \in P^2$. The class $U$ is said to be learnable in the limit with respect to $\psi$ iff there is a strategy $S \in P$ such that for each function $f \in U$,

(1) for all $n \in \mathbb{N}$, $S(f^n)$ is defined,

(2) there is a $j \in \mathbb{N}$ such that $\psi_j = f$ and the sequence $(S(f^n))_{n \in \mathbb{N}}$ converges to $j$.

If $U$ is learnable in the limit with respect to $\psi$ by a strategy $S$, we write $U \in LIM_\psi(S)$. Let $LIM_\psi = \{U \mid U$ is learnable in the limit w.r.t. $\psi\}$, and let $LIM = \bigcup_{\psi \in P^2} LIM_\psi$.

Some remarks are mandatory here. Let us start with the semantics of the hypotheses produced by a strategy $S$. If $S$ is defined on input $f^n$, then we always interpret the number $S(f^n)$ as a $\psi$-number. This convention is adopted to all the definitions below. Furthermore, note that $LIM_\varphi = LIM$ for any Gödel numbering $\varphi$. In the above definition $LIM$ stands for "limit." Moreover, in accordance with the definition of convergence, only finitely many data of the graph of a function $f$ were available to the strategy $S$ up to the unknown point of convergence. Therefore, some form of learning must have taken place. Thus, the use of the term "learn" in the above definition is indeed justified. As we have mentioned, in general it is not decidable whether or not a strategy has already converged when successively fed some graph of a function. With the next definition we consider a special case where it has to be decidable whether or not a strategy has already learned its input function.

**Definition 2. (Gold, 1967; Trakhtenbrot and Barzdin, 1970)** *Let $U \subseteq R$ and let $\psi \in P^2$. The class $U$ is said to be finitely learnable with respect to $\psi$ iff there is a strategy $S \in P$ such that for any function $f \in U$,*

(1) *for all $n \in \mathbb{N}$, $S(f^n)$ is defined,*

(2) *there is a $j \in \mathbb{N}$ such that $\psi_j = f$ and the sequence $(S(f^n))_{n \in \mathbb{N}}$ finitely converges to $j$.*

*If $U$ is finitely learnable with respect to $\psi$ by a strategy $S$, we write $U \in FIN_\psi(S)$. Let $FIN_\psi = \{U \mid U$ is finitely learnable w.r.t. $\psi\}$, and let $FIN = \bigcup_{\psi \in P^2} FIN_\psi$.*

Next we formally define different models of consistent learning.

**Definition 3. (Barzdin, 1974a)** *Let $U \subseteq R$ and let $\psi \in P^2$. The class $U$ is called consistently learnable in the limit with respect to $\psi$ iff there is a strategy $S \in P$ such that*

(1) *$U \in LIM_\psi(S)$,*

(2) *$\psi_{S(f^n)}(x) = f(x)$ for all $f \in U$, $n \in \mathbb{N}$ and $x \leq n$.*

*$CONS_\psi(S)$, $CONS_\psi$ and $CONS$ are defined analogously as above.*

Intuitively, a consistent strategy does correctly reflect all the data it has already seen. If a strategy does not always work consistently, we call it inconsistent.

Next, we add a requirement to the definition of the learning type $CONS_\psi$ that is often implicitly assumed in applications, namely, that the strategy is defined on every input, cf. Michalski et al. (1984, 1986).

**Definition 4. (Jantke and Beick, 1981)** *Let $U \subseteq R$ and let $\psi \in P^2$. The class $U$ is called R-consistently learnable in the limit with respect to $\psi$ iff there is a strategy $S \in R$ such that $U \in CONS_\psi(S)$.*

*$R\text{-}CONS_\psi(S), R\text{-}CONS_\psi$ and $R\text{-}CONS$ are defined analogously as above.*

The latter definition has a peculiarity that should be mentioned. Although the strategy is required to be recursive, consistency is only demanded for inputs that correspond to some function $f$ from the class to be learned. With the next definition we model the scenario in which consistency is required on all inputs. In order to distinguish the resulting learning type from the latter defined one, we use the prefix $T$. Informally, $T$ points to *total* consistency.

**Definition 5. (Wiehagen and Liepe, 1976)** *Let $U \subseteq R$ and let $\psi \in P^2$. The class $U$ is called $T$-consistently learnable in the limit with respect to $\psi$ iff there is a strategy $S \in R$ such that*

(1) $U \in CONS_\psi(S)$,

(2) $\psi_{S(f^n)}(x) = f(x)$ *for all $f \in R$, $n \in \mathbb{N}$ and $x \leq n$.*

$T - CONS_\psi(S)$, $T - CONS_\psi$ *and* $T - CONS$ *are defined in the same way as above.*

Finally, looking at potential applications it is often highly desirable to make no assumptions concerning the *order* in which input data should be presented. Therefore, we sharpen Definitions 3 through 5 by additionally demanding a strategy to behave consistently independently of the order of the input.

**Definition 6. (Blum and Blum, 1975)** *Let $U \subseteq R$ and let $\psi \in P^2$. $U \in T - CONS_\psi^{arb}$ iff there is a strategy $S \in R$ such that*

(1) *for all $f \in U$ and every $X \in \Pi(\mathbb{N})$, there is a $j \in \mathbb{N}$ such that $\psi_j = f$, and $(S(f^{X,n}))_{n \in \mathbb{N}}$ converges to $j$,*

(2) $\psi_{S(f^{X,n})}(x_m) = f(x_m)$ *for every permutation $X \in \Pi(\mathbb{N})$, $f \in R$, $n \in \mathbb{N}$, and $m \leq n$.*

$T - CONS_\psi^{arb}(S)$ *as well as* $T - CONS^{arb}$ *are defined in analogy to the above.*

Furthermore, appropriately incorporating the requirement to learn from arbitrary input directly yields the learning types $LIM^{arb}, FIN^{arb}, CONS^{arb}$, and $R - CONS^{arb}$. Therefore, the formal definition of these learning models is omitted here. Note that $LIM = LIM^{arb}$ as well as $FIN = FIN^{arb}$, cf. Jantke and Beick (1981). Moreover, for all learning types $LT \in \{FIN, FIN^{arb}, T - CONS, T - CONS^{arb}, R - CONS, R - CONS^{arb}, CONS, CONS^{arb}\}$ we have $LT_\varphi = LT$ for every Gödel numbering $\varphi$. In the following section we aim to compare the learning power of the different models of consistent learning to one another as well as to the other models of learning that we have defined. Note that in the following $\subseteq$ denotes subset and $\subset$ denotes *proper* subset. Finally, incomparability of sets is denoted by $\#$.

# 3. The Inconsistency Phenomenon in Inductive Inference

The main goal of this section is a thorough study of the learning power of the different models of consistent learning. Our first subsection deals with the learning type $CONS$ and compares it to learning in the limit.

## 3.1. The General Inconsistency Phenomenon

The inconsistency phenomenon has been discovered independently by Barzdin (1974a) and the Blums (1975). They observed that there are classes of recursive functions that are inferable in the limit but which cannot be learned by any consistent strategy. Since both papers do not contain a proof of this assertion, we present here a proof from Wiehagen (1976) actually showing a somewhat stronger result than the one formulated in the next theorem. We shall discuss this issue below.

**Theorem 1. (Barzdin, 1974a)** $CONS \subset LIM$

*Proof.* Let $U = \{f \in R \mid f = \alpha j p, \; \alpha \in \mathbb{N}^*, \; j \geq 2, \; p \in R_{0,1}, \; \varphi_j = f\}$, where $\varphi \in G\ddot{o}d$. Obviously, $U \in LIM(S)$, where $S(f^n)$ is equal to the last value $f(x) \geq 2$ from $(f(0), ..., f(n))$ and $0$, if no such value exists. For the purpose to prove that $U \notin CONS$ we need the following claim.

*Claim.* For every $\alpha \in \mathbb{N}^*$, there is an $f \in U$ such that $\alpha \sqsubset f$.

Indeed, by an implicit use of the Recursion Theorem, cf. Rogers (1967), it is easy to see that for every $\alpha \in \mathbb{N}^*$ and every $p \in R_{0,1}$, there is a $j \geq 2$ such that $\varphi_j = \alpha j p$.

Now, suppose that there is a strategy $S \in P$ such that $U \in CONS_\varphi(S)$. By the claim, we get $S \in R$ and for every $\alpha \in \mathbb{N}^*$, $\alpha \sqsubset \varphi_{S(\alpha)}$. Thus, on every $\alpha \in \mathbb{N}^*$, $S$ always produces a consistent guess. Then, again by an implicit use of the Recursion Theorem, let $j \geq 2$ be any $\varphi$ number of the function $f$ defined as follows: $f(0) = j$, and for any $n \in \mathbb{N}$,

$$f(n+1) = \begin{cases} 0, & \text{if } S(f^n 0) \neq S(f^n) \\ 1, & \text{if } S(f^n 0) = S(f^n) \text{ and } S(f^n 1) \neq S(f^n). \end{cases}$$

In accordance with the claim and the assumption that $S$ works consistently one straightforwardly verifies that $S(f^n 0) \neq S(f^n)$ or $S(f^n 1) \neq S(f^n)$ for any $n \in \mathbb{N}$. Therefore the function $f$ is everywhere defined and we have $f \in U$. On the other hand, the strategy $S$ changes its mind infinitely often when successively fed $f$, a contradiction to $U \in CONS_\varphi(S)$. q.e.d.

Note that the class from the proof of Theorem 1 is even *iteratively* learnable in the limit. We call a class $U$ of recursive functions iteratively learnable iff there is a strategy that learns any $f \in U$ as follows: In step $n$ the strategy exclusively gets its previous guess produced in step $n-1$ as well as the new value $f(n)$. By IT we denote the collection of all classes $U$ which can be learned iteratively. In Wiehagen (1976) $CONS \subset IT \subset LIM$ has been proved. Recent papers give new evidence for the power of iterative learning (cf., e.g., Porat and Feldman (1988), Lange and Wiehagen (1991), Lange and Zeugmann (1992)).

A closer look to the proof above shows that, in general, a strategy attempting to learn functions consistently has to overcome two difficulties. First, it should avoid to change too often its current guess that is eventually no longer consistent, to a definitely consistent hypothesis, since this behavior may force the strategy to diverge. Second, trusting that its current guess is consistent may eventually lead to an actually inconsistent hypothesis, since the strategy cannot effectively prove consistency. Indeed, it turns out that a class $U$ is consistently learnable iff there is a suitable space of hypotheses $\psi$ such that the consistency problem restricted to $U$ and $\psi$ is effectively decidable. More precisely, let $U \subseteq R$ and let $\psi$ be any numbering. We say that $U$-consistency is decidable with respect to $\psi$ iff there is a predicate $cons \in P^2$ such that for every $\alpha \in [U]$ and all $i \in \mathbb{N}$, $cons(\alpha, i)$ is defined, and $cons(\alpha, i) = 1$ if and only if $\alpha \sqsubset \psi_i$.

**Theorem 2.** $U \in CONS$ *iff there is a numbering* $\psi \in P^2$ *such that*

(1) $U \subseteq P_{\psi}$,

(2) $U$-*consistency with respect to* $\psi$ *is decidable.*

Theorem 2 is a consequence of Theorem 9 from Wiehagen (1978). Note that for an arbitrary Gödel numbering, $U$-consistency is undecidable for any non-empty class $U \subseteq R$.

Next we provide deeper insight to the problem whether or not consistent learning is sensitive with respect to the domain of the allowed strategies.

## 3.2. Consistent Learning in Dependence on the Domain of the Strategies

As already mentioned, in machine learning it is often assumed that learning algorithms are defined on all inputs. On the one hand, this requirement is partially justified by a result of Gold (1967). He proved that learning in the limit is insensitive with respect to the requirement to learn exclusively with recursive strategies, i.e., if $U \in LIM(S)$, then there is a strategy $\hat{S} \in R$ such that $U \in LIM(\hat{S})$. One the other hand, consistency is a common requirement in machine learning. Therefore, it is natural to ask whether or not the power of consistent learning algorithms further decreases if one restricts itself to recursive strategies. The answer to this question is provided by our next theorem.

**Theorem 3.** $T-CONS \subset R-CONS \subset CONS$.

*Proof.* By definition, $T - CONS \subseteq R - CONS \subseteq CONS$. In order to show $R - CONS \setminus T - CONS \neq \emptyset$ let $U = \{f \mid f \in R, \ \varphi_{f(0)} = f\}$ where $\varphi \in G\ddot{o}d$. Obviously, $U \in R-CONS_{\varphi}(S)$ by the strategy $S(f^n) = f(0)$ for all $n \in N$.

Now assume that $U \in T-CONS_{\varphi}(S)$. Hence $S \in R$ and $\varphi_{S(f^n)}(x) = f(x)$ for any $f \in R, n \in N$ and $x \leq n$. By an implicit use of the Recursion Theorem, let $f = \varphi_i$ be the following function.

$$f(0) = i,$$

$$f(n+1) = \begin{cases} 0, & \text{if } S(f^n 0) \neq S(f^n) \\ 1, & \text{if } S(f^n 0) = S(f^n) \text{ and } S(f^n 1) \neq S(f^n). \end{cases}$$

Clearly, $f \in U$ (note that one of the two cases in the definition of $f$ must happen for all $n \geq 1$). On the other hand, $S(f^n) \neq S(f^{n+1})$ for all $n \in \mathbb{N}$, contradicting $U \in T-CONS_{\varphi}(S)$. Hence $U \notin T-CONS$. This completes the proof of $T-CONS \subset R-CONS$.

In order to prove $CONS \setminus R-CONS \neq \emptyset$ we use a class similar to the class above, namely $U = \{f \mid f \in R, \text{ either } \varphi_{f(0)} = f \text{ or } \varphi_{f(1)} = f\}$. First we show that $U \in CONS$. The wanted strategy is defined as follows. Let $f \in R$ and $n \in \mathbb{N}$.

$S(f^n) = $ "Compute in parallel $\varphi_{f(0)}(x)$ and $\varphi_{f(1)}(x)$ for all $x \leq n$ until (A) or (B) happens.

(A) $\varphi_{f(0)}(x) = f(x)$ for all $x \leq n$.

(B) $\varphi_{f(1)}(x) = f(x)$ for all $x \leq n$.

If (A) happens first, then output $f(0)$. If (B) happens first, then output $f(1)$. If neither (A) nor (B) happens, then $S(f^n)$ is not defined."

By the definition of $U$, it is obvious that $S(f^n)$ is defined for all $f \in U$ and all $n \in \mathbb{N}$. Moreover, $S$ is clearly consistent. Hence, it suffices to prove that $(S(f^n))_{n \in \mathbb{N}}$ converges for all $f \in U$. But this is also an immediate consequence of the definition of $U$, since either $\varphi_{f(0)} \neq f$ or $\varphi_{f(1)} \neq f$. Hence $S$ cannot oscillate infinitely often between $f(0)$ and $f(1)$. Consequently, $U \in CONS_\varphi(S)$.

Next we show that $U \notin R-CONS$. Suppose there is a strategy $S \in R$ such that $U \in R-CONS_\varphi(S)$. Applying Smullyan's Recursion Theorem, cf. Smullyan (1961), we construct a function $f \in U$ such that either $S(f^n) \neq S(f^{n+1})$ for all $n \in \mathbb{N}$ or $\varphi_{S(f^x)}(y) \neq f(y)$ for some $x, y \in \mathbb{N}$ with $y \leq x$. Since both cases yield a contradiction to the definition of $R-CONS$, we are done. The wanted function $f$ is defined as follows. Let $h$ and $s$ be two recursive functions such that for all $i, j \in \mathbb{N}, \varphi_{h(i,j)}(0) = \varphi_{s(i,j)}(0) = i$ and $\varphi_{h(i,j)}(1) = \varphi_{s(i,j)}(1) = j$. For any $i, j \in \mathbb{N}, x \geq 2$ we proceed inductively.

Suspend the definition of $\varphi_{s(i,j)}$. Try to define $\varphi_{h(i,j)}$ for more and more arguments via the following procedure.

(T) Test whether or not (A) or (B) happens (this can be effectively checked, since $S \in R$):

(A) $S(\varphi_{h(i,j)}^x 0) \neq S(\varphi_{h(i,j)}^x)$,

(B) $S(\varphi_{h(i,j)}^x 1) \neq S(\varphi_{h(i,j)}^x)$.

If (A) happens, then let $\varphi_{h(i,j)}(x+1) = 0$, let $x := x+1$, and goto (T).
In case (B) happens, set $\varphi_{h(i,j)}(x+1) = 1$, let $x := x+1$, and goto (T).
If neither (A) nor (B) happens, then define $\varphi_{h(i,j)}(x') = 0$ for all $x' > x$, and goto (*).

(*) Set $\varphi_{s(i,j)}(n) = \varphi_{h(i,j)}(n)$ for all $n \leq x$, and $\varphi_{s(i,j)}(x') = 1$ for all $x' > x$.

By Smullyan's Recursion Theorem, there are numbers $i$ and $j$ such that $\varphi_i = \varphi_{h(i,j)}$ and $\varphi_j = \varphi_{s(i,j)}$. Now we distinguish the following cases.

*Case* 1. The loop in (T) is never left.

Then we directly obtain that $\varphi_i \in U$, since $\varphi_j = ij$, and hence a finite function. Moreover, in accordance with the definition of the loop (T), on input $\varphi_i^n$ the strategy $S$ changes its mind for all $n > 0$.

*Case* 2. The loop in (T) is left.

Then there exist an $x$ such that $S(\varphi_{h(i,j)}^x 0) = S(\varphi_{h(i,j)}^x 1)$. Hence $S(\varphi_i^{x+1}) = S(\varphi_j^{x+1})$, since $\varphi_{h(i,j)} = \varphi_i$, $\varphi_{s(i,j)} = \varphi_j$, $\varphi_i(n) = \varphi_j(n)$ for all $n \leq x$ by (*), as well as $\varphi_i(x+1) = 0$ and $\varphi_j(x+1) = 1$. Furthermore, $\varphi_i, \varphi_j \in R$. Since $\varphi_i(x+1) \neq \varphi_j(x+1)$, we get $\varphi_i \neq \varphi_j$. On the other hand, $\varphi_i(0) = i$ and $\varphi_j(1) = j$. Consequently, both functions $\varphi_i$ and $\varphi_j$ belong to $U$. But $S(\varphi_i^{x+1}) = S(\varphi_j^{x+1})$ and $\varphi_i(x+1) \neq \varphi_j(x+1)$, hence $S$ does not work consistently on input $\varphi_i^{x+1}$ or $\varphi_j^{x+1}$. This contradiction completes the proof. q.e.d.

Note that even $T-CONS$, the most stringent type of consistent identification considered above, is of remarkable power. Therefore, let $NUM = \{U | \text{ there is } \psi \in R^2$ such that $U \subseteq P_\psi\}$ denote the set of all recursively enumerable classes of recursive functions. Then in Wiehagen and Liepe (1976) the following result was proved.

**Theorem 4.** $NUM \subset T-CONS$

*Proof.* Every class $U \in NUM$ can be learned T-consistently by a slightly modified version of Gold's identification-by-enumeration strategy.

A class witnessing $T-CONS \setminus NUM \neq \emptyset$ can be defined as follows. Let $\varphi \in G\ddot{o}d$. Let $\Phi$ be any complexity measure associated with $\varphi$, cf. Blum (1967). Then $\{\Phi_i | i \in \mathbb{N}, \varphi_i \in R\} \in T-CONS \setminus NUM$. We omit the details. q.e.d.

The next result provides a more subtle insight into the different power of $T-CONS$ and $R-CONS$.

**Theorem 5.**

(1) $FIN \# T-CONS$

(2) $FIN \subset R-CONS$

*Proof.* (1) $T-CONS \setminus FIN \neq \emptyset$ is proved in Wiehagen and Liepe (1976). Note that the class $\{\Phi_i | i \in \mathbb{N}, \varphi_i \in R\}$ where $\Phi$ is a complexity measure associated with $\varphi \in G\ddot{o}d$ in the sense of Blum (1967) also witnesses $T-CONS \setminus FIN \neq \emptyset$.

Let now $U = \{f | f \in R, \varphi_{f(0)} = f\}$. Obviously, $U \in FIN$. On the other hand, $U \notin T-CONS$, cf. proof of Theorem 3. Hence $T-CONS \setminus FIN \neq \emptyset$. This proves (1).

Next, we prove Assertion (2). Since $T-CONS \subset R-CONS$, $R-CONS \setminus FIN \neq \emptyset$ is an immediate consequence of (1). The proof of $FIN \subseteq R-CONS$ mainly relies on the decidability of convergence of any finite learning algorithm. Let $U \in FIN$, and let $S$ be any strategy witnessing $U \in FIN_\varphi(S)$. Furthermore, let $s \in R$ be any function such that $\varphi_{s(\alpha)} = \alpha 0^\infty$ for all $\alpha \in \mathbb{N}^*$. The wanted strategy $\hat{S}$ is defined as follows. Let $f \in R$ and $n \in \mathbb{N}$. Then

$\hat{S}(f^n) = $ "In parallel, try to compute $S(f^0), ..., S(f^n)$ for precisely $n$ steps. Let $k \geq 1$ be the least number such that all values $S(f^0), ..., S(f^k)$ turn out to be defined, and $S(f^{k-1}) = S(f^k)$.
In case this $k$ is found, output $S(f^k)$. Otherwise, output $s(f^n)$."

It remains to show that $U \in R-CONS(\hat{S})$. Obviously, $\hat{S} \in R$. Now, let $f \in U$. We have to show that $\hat{S}$ consistently learns $f$.

*Claim 1.* $\hat{S}$ learns $f$.

Since $f \in U$, the strategy $S$ is defined for all inputs $f^n$, $n \in \mathbb{N}$. Moreover, since $S$ finitely learns $f$, the sequence $(S(f^n))_{n \in \mathbb{N}}$ finitely converges to a $\varphi$-program of $f$.

Hence, $\hat{S}$ eventually has to find the least $k$ such that $S(f^{k-1}) = S(f^k)$, and all values $S(f^0), ..., S(f^k)$ are defined. By the definition of $FIN$, $\varphi_{S(f^k)} = f$. Hence, $\hat{S}$ learns $f$.

*Claim 2.* For all $f \in U$ and $n \in \mathbb{N}$, $\hat{S}(f^n)$ is a consistent hypothesis.

Clearly, as long as $\hat{S}$ outputs $s(f^n)$, it is consistent. Suppose, $\hat{S}$ outputs $S(f^k)$ for the first time. Then it has verified that $S(f^{k-1}) = S(f^k)$. Since $f \in U$, and $U \in FIN_\varphi(S)$, this directly implies $\varphi_{S(f^k)} = f$. Therefore, $\hat{S}$ again outputs a consistent hypothesis. Since this hypothesis is repeated in any subsequent learning step, the claim is proved. q.e.d.

The next result points out another difference between the types $CONS, R{-}CONS$, on the one hand, and $T{-}CONS$, on the other hand.

**Theorem 6.**

(1) *$CONS$ and $R{-}CONS$ are not closed under finite union.*

(2) *$T{-}CONS$ is closed under recursively enumerable union.*

*Proof.* (1) is a direct consequence of a more general result of Barzdin (1974b). Let $U = \{f \mid f \in R, \varphi_{f(0)} = f\}$ and let $V = \{\alpha 0^\infty \mid \alpha \in \mathbb{N}^*\}$. It is easy to see that $U, V \in R{-}CONS$, and hence $U, V \in CONS$. On the other hand, $U \cup V \notin LIM$ as shown in Barzdin (1974b).

In order to prove (2), we restate this assertion more formally. Let $(S_i)_{i\in\mathbb{N}}$ be a recursive enumeration of $T{-}$consistent strategies. Then there exists a strategy $S$ such that $T{-}CONS(S) = \bigcup_{i\in\mathbb{N}} T{-}CONS(S_i)$.

Without loss of generality, we may assume that all the strategies $S_i$ output as hypotheses programs in some fixed Gödel numbering $\varphi$. Note that the following proof mainly uses a proof technique of Minicozzi (1976). Let $f \in R$. Then two cases are possible. Either there is a strategy $S_i$ that learns $f$ or all strategies fail to learn it. However, in the latter case each of the strategies $S_i$ has to change its mind infinitely often. On the other hand, if $f$ is learned by some $S_i$ then at least one strategy stabilizes its output. The wanted strategy $S$ searches for an enumerated machine that might learn $f$ as follows.

The strategy $S$ dovetails the computation of more and more outputs of the enumerated strategies. For each strategy $S_i$ that is already included in its dovetailed computations, it counts the number of equal outputs. This number is called weight. As long as a strategy repeats its actual guess on the next input, the weight increments. If a strategy performs a mind change, its weight reduces to zero. After having read the initial segment $f^k$ of the function $f$ the strategy $S$ favors from the first $k + 1$ strategies $S_0, ..., S_k$ that one which actually has the greatest weight. In case there are two strategies $S_i$ and $S_j$ taking the greatest weight the strategy $S$ chooses that one having the smallest index.

We formally define $S$ as follows. Let $f \in R$, and $k \in \mathbb{N}$.

$S(f^k) = $ "Compute in parallel

$$S_0(f^0), ..., S_0(f^k),$$

$$S_1(f^0), ..., S_1(f^k),$$

$$-$$

$$-$$

$$-$$

$$S_k(f^0), ..., S_k(f^k),$$

and assign to each strategy $S_i$, $i \leq k$, its weight, i.e., the greatest number $m \leq k - i$ satisfying the condition that $S_i(f^{k-i-m}) = S_i(f^{k-i-m+1}) = ... = S_i(f^{k-i})$. Note that we calculate the weights in a triangular fashion. This is necessary in order to achieve convergence of $S$. Choose $w(k)$ to be the smallest $i \leq k$ such that the strategy $S_i$ has the greatest weight.

In case all considered machines have weight zero, output a $\varphi$–program of $f(0) \cdot \cdots f(k)0^\infty$.

If $w(k) = w(k-1)$, then output $S_{w(k)}(f^k)$. Otherwise, output a $\varphi$–program of $f(0) \cdots f(k)0^\infty$ that is different from $S(f^{k-1})$."

It remains to show that $T\text{--}CONS_\varphi(S) = \bigcup_{i \in \mathbb{N}} T\text{--}CONS_\varphi(S_i)$. Obviously, $S$ works consistently on any initial segment it is fed, since all of the strategies $S_i$, $i \in \mathbb{N}$, do so. Now, let $f \in R$ and suppose that $f$ is learned by some strategy $S_i$. Consequently, there exists numbers $j$, $n_0$ such that $S_i(f^n) = j$ for all $n \geq n_0$, and $\varphi_j = f$. Hence, for any strategy that learns $f$ its weight increases after some point in each step of $S$'s computation. Therefore, for almost all $k$ the strategy $S$ must favor exactly one of the strategies $S_i$ that learns $f$ and, after some point, $S$ outputs always $S_i(f^k)$. Note that the computation of weights in a triangular fashion really ensures the desired convergence, since any new strategy included in $S$'s computation initially gets weight zero.

On the other hand, if none of the strategies $S_i$, $i \in \mathbb{N}$, learns $f$, then each strategy $S_i$ has to perform infinitely many mind changes. This is ensured by our assumption that each $S_i$ is $T$–consistent. Hence, the case $w(k) \neq w(k-1)$ occurs infinitely often. But each occurrence of this case forces $S$ to perform a mind change. Consequently, $S$ cannot converge. q.e.d.

We finish this subsection with characterizations of $T\text{--}CONS$ and $R\text{--}CONS$ which are similar to that of $CONS$ presented in Theorem 2. Therefore let $\psi \in P^2$ be any numbering. Then we say that consistency with respect to $\psi$ is decidable iff there is a predicate $cons \in R^2$ such that for every $\alpha \in \mathbb{N}^*$ and all $i \in \mathbb{N}$, $cons(\alpha, i) = 1$ if and only if $\alpha \sqsubset \psi_i$.

**Theorem 7.** $U \in T\text{--}CONS$ iff there is a numbering $\psi \in P^2$ such that

(1) $U \subseteq P_\psi$,

(2) consistency with respect to $\psi$ is decidable.

*Proof.* Necessity. Let $U \in T\text{--}CONS_\varphi(S)$ where $\varphi \in P^2$ is any numbering and $S$ is a $T$–consistent strategy. Let $M = \{(z,n) | z, n \in \mathbb{N}, \varphi_z(x)$ is defined for any $x \leq n$, $S(\varphi_z^n) = z\}$ be recursively enumerated by a function $e$. Then define a numbering $\psi$ as follows. Let $i, x \in \mathbb{N}$, $e(i) = (z, n)$.

$$\psi_i(x) = \begin{cases} \varphi_z(x), & \text{if } x \le n \\ \varphi_z(x), & \text{if } x > n \text{ and, for any } y \in \mathbb{N} \text{ such that } n < y \le x, \\ & \varphi_z(y) \text{ is defined and } S(\varphi_z^y) = z \\ \text{undefined}, & \text{otherwise.} \end{cases}$$

In order to show (1) let $f \in U$ and $n, z \in \mathbb{N}$ be such that for any $m \ge n$, $S(f^m) = z$. Clearly, $\varphi_z = f$. Furthermore, $(z, n) \in M$. Let $i \in \mathbb{N}$ be such that $e(i) = (z, n)$. Then, by definition of $\psi$, $\psi_i = \varphi_z = f$. Hence $U \subseteq P_\psi$.

In order to prove (2) we define $cons \in R^2$ such that for any $\alpha \in \mathbb{N}^*$, $i \in \mathbb{N}$, $cons(\alpha, i) = 1$ iff $\alpha \sqsubset \psi_i$. Let $\alpha = (\alpha, \ldots, \alpha_x) \in \mathbb{N}^*$ and $i \in \mathbb{N}$. Let $e(i) = (z, n)$. Then define

$$cons(\alpha, i) = \begin{cases} 1, & \text{if } x \le n \text{ and, for any } y \le x, \alpha_y = \psi_i(y) \\ 1, & \text{if } x > n, \alpha_y = \psi_i(y) \text{ for any } y \le n, \text{ and,} \\ & \text{for any } y \in \mathbb{N} \text{ such that } n < y \le x, S(\alpha_0, \ldots, \alpha_y) = z \\ 0, & \text{otherwise.} \end{cases}$$

It is not hard to see that $cons \in R^2$ and, for every $\alpha \in \mathbb{N}^*$, $i \in \mathbb{N}$, we have $cons(\alpha, i) = 1$ iff $\alpha \sqsubset \psi_i$.

Sufficiency. Let $\psi \in P^2$ be any numbering. Let $cons \in R^2$ be such that for all $\alpha \in \mathbb{N}^*$, $i \in \mathbb{N}$, $cons(\alpha, i) = 1$ iff $\alpha \sqsubset \psi_i$. Let $U \subseteq P_\psi$. In order to consistently learn any function $f \in U$ it suffices to define $S(f^n) = min\{i | \, cons(f^n, i)\}$. However, $S$ is undefined if, for $f \notin U$, $n \in \mathbb{N}$, there is no $i \in \mathbb{N}$ such that $f^n \sqsubset \psi_i$. The following more careful definition of $S$ will circumvent this difficulty. Let $\varphi \in G\ddot{o}d$. Let $aux \in R$ be such that for any $\alpha \in \mathbb{N}^*, \varphi_{aux(\alpha)} = \alpha 0^\infty$. Finally, let $c \in R$ be such that for all $i \in \mathbb{N}, \psi_i = \varphi_{c(i)}$. Then, for any $f \in R$, $n \in \mathbb{N}$, define a strategy $S$ as follows.

$$S(f^n) = \begin{cases} c(j), & \text{if } I = \{i | \, i \le n, \, cons\,(f^n, i) = 1\} \ne \emptyset \text{ and } j = min\, I \\ aux(f^n), & I = \emptyset. \end{cases}$$

Clearly, $S \in R$ and $S$ outputs only consistent hypotheses. Now let $f \in U$. Then, obviously, $(S(f^n))_{n \in \mathbb{N}}$ converges to $c(min\{i | \, \psi_i = f\})$. Hence, $S$ witnesses $U \in T\text{-}CONS_\varphi$. $\qquad$ q.e.d.

Finally, let $U \subseteq R$ and $\psi \in P^2$ be any numbering. Then we say that $U$–consistency with respect to $\psi$ is $R$–decidable iff there is a predicate $cons \in R^2$ such that for every $\alpha \in [U]$ and all $i \in \mathbb{N}$, $cons(\alpha, i) = 1$ if and only if $\alpha \sqsubset \psi_i$.

**Theorem 8.** $U \in R\text{-}CONS$ iff there is a numbering $\psi \in P^2$ such that

(1) $U \subseteq P_\psi$,

(2) $U$–consistency with respect to $\psi$ is $R$–decidable.

The proof of Theorem 8 is similar to that of Theorem 7.

The characterizations of $T\text{-}CONS$, $R\text{-}CONS$ and $CONS$ give rise to point out some relationship between the problem of deciding consistency and the halting problem. As it follows from Theorem 3 and Theorem 4, for any of the learning types $LT \in \{T{-}CONS, R{-}CONS, CONS\}$, we have $NUM \subset LT$. On the other hand, as it was shown in Wiehagen and Zeugmann (1994), for any class $U \subseteq R$ and any numbering $\psi \in P^2$, if $U \notin NUM$ and $U \subseteq P_\psi$, then the halting problem with respect to $\psi$ is undecidable, i.e., there is no $h \in R^2$ such that for any $i, x \in \mathbb{N}, h(i, x) = 1$ iff $\psi_i(x)$ is defined.

Consequently, for any $U \in LT \setminus NUM$ and any numbering $\psi \in P^2$ from the corresponding theorem above characterizing $LT$, the halting problem with respect to $\psi$ is undecidable. On the other hand, the corresponding version of consistency with respect to $\psi$ is decidable. Hence this version of consistency *cannot* be decided by firstly deciding the halting problem and secondly, if possible, computing the desired values of the function under consideration in order to compare these values with the given ones. More formally, in general, $cons(f^n, i)$ *cannot* be evaluated by deciding whether or not $\psi_i(x)$ is defined for all $x \leq n$ and, if it is, then computing $\psi_i^n$ and comparing it with $f^n$.

Informally, though consistency is decidable in the "characteristic" numberings of Theorems 2, 7, 8 it is not decidable in a "straightforward way."

## 3.3. Consistent Learning on Arbitrary Input Order

In applications it is often highly desirable to make no assumption concerning the *order* in which input data should be presented. Therefore, we now state a characterization of the type $T{-}CONS^{arb}$ due to Blum and Blum (1975). This characterization easily yields a "lower bound" on the power of $T{-}CONS^{arb}$.

**Definition 7.** *A numbering $\psi \in P^2$ is said to be measurable iff the predicate "$\psi_i(x) = y$" is uniformly recursive in $i, x, y$.*

**Theorem 9. (Blum and Blum, 1975)**

$U \in T{-}CONS^{arb}$ *iff there is a measurable numbering $\psi \in P^2$ such that $U \subseteq P_\psi$.*

Note that the measurability of $\psi$ allows deciding consistency with respect to $\psi$ in a "straightforward way."

**Corollary 10.** $NUM \subset T{-}CONS^{arb}$

*Proof.* $NUM \subseteq T{-}CONS^{arb}$ can easily be proved by a slight modification of Gold's identification by enumeration.
For proving the proper inclusion, let $\varphi \in G\ddot{o}d$ and $\Phi \in P^2$ be a complexity measure associated with $\varphi$, cf. Blum (1967). Let $U = \{\Phi_i \mid i \in \mathbb{N}, \varphi_i \in R\}$. Then $U \notin NUM$, since otherwise $R \in NUM$ could be proved, a contradiction. On the other hand, $U \in T{-}CONS^{arb}$ via Theorem 9, since $\Phi \in P^2$ is a measurable numbering.     q.e.d.

As far as we now, it is still an open problem whether $T{-}CONS^{arb}$ is a *proper* subset of $T{-}CONS$. But, of course, any solution to this problem will not influence the "lower bound" on the power of $T{-}CONS^{arb}$ by Corollary 10.

The reader is encouraged to consult Jantke and Beick (1981), Zeugmann (1983) and Fulk (1989) for further investigation concerning consistent identification.

# 4. Exact Learning in Polynomial Time and Inconsistency

The results presented in the previous section may lead to the impression that the inconsistency phenomenon may be far beyond any practical relevance, since it has been established in a setting where the consistency problem is undecidable in general. Therefore now we ask whether the inconsistency phenomenon does survive in settings where consistency is decidable. Moreover, we additionally restrict ourselves to deal exclusively with learning strategies that are polynomial time computable. Then, of course, the superiority of inconsistent strategies, if any, has to be established in terms of complexity theory. We present a learning problem which is generally consistently solvable but which *cannot be solved consistently in polynomial time* unless $\mathcal{P} \neq \mathcal{NP}$. The desired goal is achieved by elaborating an algorithm *inconsistently* solving the same learning problem in *polynomial time*. As far as we know this is the first learning problem for which the announced properties are rigorously proved. In our opinion, this result gives strong evidence of seriously taking inconsistent learning strategies into consideration.

The setting we want to deal with is the learnability of pattern languages introduced by Anghuin (1980). Subsequently, Shinohara (1982) dealt with polynomial time learnability of subclasses of pattern languages. Nix (1983) outlined interesting applications of pattern inference algorithms. Recently, Jantke (1991) and Lange and Zeugmann (1993) as well as Zeugmann, Lange and Kapur (199x) dealt with the learnability of pattern languages under monotonicity constraints. Moreover, Kearns and Pitt (1989), Ko, Marron and Tzeng (1990) and Schapire (1990) intensively studied the learnability of pattern languages in the PAC–learning model; thus, Schapire (1990) proved that the class *PAT* of all pattern languages is not PAC-learnable unless $\mathcal{P}_{/poly} = \mathcal{NP}_{/poly}$.

So let us define pattern languages. Let $\Sigma = \{a, b, ..\}$ be any non–empty finite alphabet containing at least two elements. Furthermore, let $X = \{x_i | \ i \in \mathbb{N}\}$ be an infinite set of variables such that $\Sigma \cap X = \emptyset$. *Patterns* are non–empty strings from $\Sigma \cup X$, e.g., $ab$, $ax_1ccc$, $bx_1x_1cx_2x_2$ are patterns. $L(p)$, the language generated by pattern $p$ is the set of strings which can be obtained by substituting non–null strings from $\Sigma^*$ for the variables of the pattern $p$. Thus $aabbb$ is generable from pattern $ax_1x_2b$, while $aabba$ is not. *Pat* and *PAT* denote the set of all patterns and of all pattern languages over $\Sigma$, respectively. In order to deal with the learnability of pattern languages we have to specify from what information the learning strategies should do their task. Following Gold (1967) we distinguish between learning from text and from informant. Formally, let $L \subseteq \Sigma^*$; we call a mapping $I : \mathbb{N} \to \Sigma^* \times \{+, -\}$ *informant* of $L$ iff

(1) For every $w \in \Sigma^*$, there are an $n \in \mathbb{N}$ and $\lambda \in \{+, -\}$ such that $I(n) = (w, \lambda)$,

(2) for every $n \in \mathbb{N}$, $w \in \Sigma^*$, and $\lambda \in \{+, -\}$, if $I(n) = (w, \lambda)$ then $w \in L$ iff $\lambda = +$.

Let *Info(L)* denote the set of all informants of $L$. Furthermore, for $I \in Info(L)$ and $n \in \mathbb{N}$, let $I^n = cod(I(0), ..., I(n))$, where *cod* denotes an effective and bijective mapping from the set of all finite sequences of elements from $\Sigma^* \times \{+, -\}$ onto $\mathbb{N}$.

Finally, we set $I_n = \{w \in \Sigma^* |$ there are $i \leq n,\ \lambda \in \{+, -\}$ s.t. $I(i) = (w, \lambda)\}$, and $I_n^+ = I_n \cap L$, $I_n^- = I_n \setminus I_n^+$.

Any mapping $T$ from $\mathbb{N}$ onto $L$ is called a *text* for L. By *Text(L)* we denote the set of all texts for $L$. The sets $T_n$, $T_n^+$ as well as $T_n^-$ are analogously defined as above.

Intuitively, a text for $L$ generates the language $L$ without any information concerning the complement of $L$, whereas an informant of $L$ decides $L$ by informing the strategy whether or not any word from $\Sigma^*$ belongs to $L$. Note that we allow a text and an informant to be non–effective.

**Definition 8.** *PAT is called learnable in the limit from informant (abbr. PAT $\in$ LIM $-$INF) iff there is an effective strategy S from $\mathbb{N}$ into Pat such that for all $L \in PAT$ and every $I \in Info(L)$,*

(1) *for all $n \in \mathbb{N}$, $S(I^n)$ is defined,*

(2) *there is a $p \in Pat$ such that $L(p) = L$ and for almost all $n \in \mathbb{N}$, $S(I^n) = p$.*

**Definition 9.** *PAT is called consistently learnable in the limit from informant (abbr. PAT $\in$ CONS$-$INF) iff there is an effective strategy S from $\mathbb{N}$ into Pat such that*

(1) *PAT $\in$ LIM$-$INF by S,*

(2) *for all $L \in PAT$, $I \in Info(L)$ and $n \in \mathbb{N}$, $I_n^+ \subseteq L(S(I^n))$ and $I_n^- \cap L(S(I^n)) = \emptyset$.*

Note that a consistent learning strategy is required to correctly reflect both the positive as well as the negative data it has already seen. Next we sharpen Definition 8 and 9 by additionally requiring polynomial time computability of $S$.

**Definition 10.** *PAT is called (consistently) learnable in the limit from informant in polynomial time (abbr. PAT $\in$ Poly$-$LIM$-$INF (PAT $\in$ Poly$-$CONS$-$INF)) iff there are a strategy S and a polynomial pol such that*

(1) *PAT $\in$ LIM$-$INF (PAT $\in$ CONS$-$INF) by S,*

(2) *for all $L \in PAT$, $I \in Info(L)$ and $n \in \mathbb{N}$,*
   *time to compute $S(I^n) \leq pol(length(I^n))$.*

Learning from text is analogously defined in replacing everywhere "informant" by "text." However, one point should be stated more precisely, namely that consistent learning from text does only require consistency with the data contained in the text. In order to have an example illuminating the difference we could define a strategy that initially outputs $x_1$. Since $L(x_1)$ contains every string over $\Sigma$ but the empty one, this hypothesis is consistent on text for every finite input. However, since the strategy has to converge, it cannot maintain this hypothesis *ad infinitum*. Finally, we use $LIM-TXT$, $CONS-TXT$, $Poly-LIM-TXT$ as well as $Poly-CONS-TXT$ to denote the corresponding learning types from text.

Now we can state the result mentioned above.

**Theorem 11.**

(1) $PAT \in CONS-INF$,

(2) $PAT \notin Poly-CONS-INF$, provided $\mathcal{P} \neq \mathcal{NP}$,

(3) $PAT \in Poly-LIM-INF$.

*Proof.* Assertion (1) is proved in applying Gold's (1967) enumeration technique. Therefore, let $(p_i)_{i \in \mathbb{N}}$ be any fixed effective enumeration of *Pat*. Let $L \in PAT$, let $I \in Info(L)$ be any informant, and let $n \in \mathbb{N}$. Define $S(I^n)$ to be the first pattern $p$ in the enumeration of *Pat* satisfying $I_n^+ \subseteq L(p)$ and $I_n^- \cap L(p) = \emptyset$. Since membership for pattern languages is uniformly decidable, cf. Angluin (1980), $S$ is computable. Due to the definition of $S$, consistency is obvious. Moreover, the strategy converges to the first pattern in the enumeration that generates the language $L$ to be learned. Note that $S$ cannot be computed in polynomial time, unless $\mathcal{P} = \mathcal{NP}$, since membership for pattern languages is $\mathcal{NP}$-complete, cf. Angluin (1980).

Next we have to show that there is no strategy at all consistently learning *PAT* from informant that is computable in polynomial time, if $\mathcal{P} \neq \mathcal{NP}$. This part of the proof is done by showing the $\mathcal{NP}$-hardness of an appropriate problem defined below. For any information concerning reducibility as well as $\mathcal{NP}$-complete problems the reader is referred to Garey and Johnson (1979). First we define the following decision problem *SEP*. Let $W^+, W^- \subseteq \Sigma^*$. We say that $W^+, W^-$ are *separable* iff there is a pattern $p$ such that $W^+ \subseteq L(p)$ and $W^- \cap L(p) = \emptyset$. *SEP* denotes the problem of *deciding* whether any $W^+, W^- \subseteq \Sigma^*$ are separable. Moreover, by *CSEP* we denote the problem of *constructing* a separating pattern $p$ for any given $W^+, W^-$ that are separable. The proof of Assertion (2) is completed via the following lemmata.

**Lemma A. (Ko, Marron, Tzeng, 1990)**
$3-SAT$ is polynomial time reducible to *SEP*.

**Lemma B.** *CSEP* is $\mathcal{NP}$-*hard*.

*Proof of Lemma B.* Let $C3-SAT$ denote the problem to construct a satisfying assignment to any satisfiable instance from $3-SAT$.

*Claim 1.* $C3-SAT \in \mathcal{P}$ implies $3-SAT \in \mathcal{P}$.

Assume there is an algorithm $\mathcal{A}$ having a running time that is bounded by some polynomial *pol* in the length of its input, and that, moreover, on input $C$ returns a satisfying assignment of $C$, if $C$ is satisfiable. Now let $C$ be any instance of $3-SAT$. Start $\mathcal{A}$ on input $C$. Since any polynomial is time constructible, we may combine $\mathcal{A}$ with a clock, i.e., we can efficiently stop $\mathcal{A}$ on input $C$ after at most $pol(length(C))$ steps of computation. Then two cases are possible. Either $\mathcal{A}$ returns nothing. Consequently, $C$ cannot be satisfiable. Otherwise $\mathcal{A}$ outputs an assignment *ass* within the given time bound. Then one can check in polynomial time whether or not *ass* indeed satisfies $C$. In case it does, we know that $C$ is satisfiable. In case it does not $C$ is again not satisfiable, since otherwise $\mathcal{A}$ would fail.

Note that we *cannot* prove the $\mathcal{NP}$-hardness of *CSEP* in the same manner as in showing Claim 1, since membership for pattern languages is $\mathcal{NP}$-complete. Hence, one cannot check in polynomial time whether a pattern eventually returned on input

$(W^+, W^-)$ does indeed separate these sets. However, we overcome this difficulty by showing the following claim.

*Claim* 2. *CSEP* $\in \mathcal{P}$ implies $C3-SAT \in \mathcal{P}$.

In accordance with Lemma A let *red* be any polynomial time reduction of $3-SAT$ to *SEP*. Suppose, there is an algorithm $\mathcal{B}$ solving *CSEP* in polynomial time. Now let $C$ be any satisfiable instance of $3-SAT$. The wanted satisfying assignment may be computed as follows. First, compute $red(C) = (W^+, W^-)$. Since $C$ is satisfiable, we get that $(W^+, W^-)$ are separable. Next compute $p = \mathcal{B}(W^+, W^-)$. Finally, let *ass* be the assignment constructed to $p$ in the proof of the "only–if" direction of Lemma A. Since *red* is computable in time bounded by a polynomial in the length of $C$, the length of $(W^+, W^-)$ is bounded by a polynomial in the length of $C$, too. Consequently, *ass* is polynomial time computable. Hence, $C3-SAT \in \mathcal{P}$, if $CSEP \in \mathcal{P}$.

Finally, Claim 1 and Claim 2 directly yield Lemma B.

The proof of Assertion (2) is completed by showing the next claim.

*Claim* 3. *PAT* $\in$ *Poly*$-CONS-INF$ implies *CSEP* $\in \mathcal{P}$.

Suppose *PAT* $\in$ *Poly*$-CONS-INF$ by some strategy $S$. Let $W^+$, $W^-$ be any two separable sets, and let $p$ be any pattern separating them. Let $I \in Info(L(p))$ be an arbitrary informant such that, for some $n$, $I_n^+ = W^+$ and $I_n^- = W^-$. In accordance with the definition of separability, $I$ obviously exists. Consequently, $S(I^n)$ has to be defined, and furthermore, $q = S(I^n)$ has to be a pattern separating $W^+$, $W^-$. Finally, $S$ is polynomial time computable. Hence we get $CSEP \in \mathcal{P}$.

It remains to prove Assertion (3). In Lange and Wiehagen (1991) $PAT \in Poly-LIM-TXT$ has been shown. The corresponding strategy witnessing $PAT \in Poly-LIM-TXT$ works by "overlooking" data, namely it ignores all but the actually shortest strings of the language to be learned. It turns out that sufficiently many really shortest strings of a pattern language do suffice to learn it. From these remaining strings a hypothesis is generated in time that is even polynomial in the length of these strings. However, this hypothesis may be inconsistent, while being correct in the limit. Let $S$ denote the strategy from Lange and Wiehagen (1991) proving $PAT \in Poly-LIM-TXT$. We define a strategy $\tilde{S}$ witnessing $PAT \in Poly-LIM-INF$ as follows. On any input $I^n$ we set $\tilde{S}(I^n) = S(I_n^+)$. This proves (3) and hence the theorem.

Note that $\tilde{S}$ even works semi–consistently, since $I_n^- \cap L(\tilde{S}(I^n)) = \emptyset$ is valid for all $n \in \mathbb{N}$. Moreover, $\tilde{S}$ works iteratively as $S$ does. q.e.d.

At this point some remarks are mandatory. It should be mentioned that any consistent strategy $S$, independently of how complex it is, may be trivially converted into an inconsistent one that works in quadratic time. This is done as follows. On input $I^n$, one simulates $S$ on input $I^1$, $I^2$,...,$I^n$ no more than $n$ steps, and outputs $S(I^k)$, where $k$ is the largest number $y \leq n$ for which $S(I^y)$ is computable within at most $n$ steps.

However, it is obvious that this simulation technique does not yield any advantage. It does neither increase the efficiency of the learning algorithm, if one sums up all steps of computation until the learning task is successfully solved; nor does it enlarge the learning power. What we are looking for are "intelligent" inconsistent techniques.

In our opinion, Lange and Wiehagen's (1991) refined strategy behaves thus by the following reasons. First, it avoids membership tests at all. Second, it iteratively computes its current hypothesis. Third, the test whether or not it should eventually change its mind is extremely simple and may be executed in linear time. Moreover, the algorithm yielding an eventually new hypothesis performs exclusively syntactical or formal manipulations over strings.

Finally, let $Poly-CONS-LEXINF$ ($Poly-CONS-LEXTXT$) be the learning type obtained from $Poly-CONS-INF$ ($Poly-CONS-TXT$) by restricting the information presentation from any informant $I \in Info(L)$ (any text $T \in Text(L)$) to the lexicographically ordered one. Furthermore, let $S$ be a strategy such that $PAT \in LIM-INF$ ($LIM-TXT$) by $S$. Then, for any $L \in PAT$ and $D \in Info(L) \cup Text(L)$, let

$$Conv(S, D) = \text{the least number } m \text{ such that for all } n \geq m, S(D^n) = S(D^m)$$

denote the *stage of convergence* of $S$ on $D$.

The following theorem actually states that the inconsistent learning strategy of Lange and Wiehagen (1991) may behave both consistently and efficiently, if it receives the crucial information on the language to be learned in an appropriate order.

**Theorem 12.**

(1) *There are a strategy $\tilde{S}$ and a polynomial pol such that*

(i) *$PAT \in Poly-CONS-LEXINF$ by $\tilde{S}$,*

(ii) *for every $p \in Pat$, there are uncountably many informants $I \in Info(L(p))$ such that*

      – *$\tilde{S}$ works consistently on $I$,*

      – *$\Sigma_{n=0}^{Conv(\tilde{S}, I)}$ time to compute $\tilde{S}(I^n) \leq pol(length(p))$.*

(2) *There are a strategy $S$ and a polynomial pol such that*

(i) *$PAT \in Poly-CONS-LEXTXT$ by $S$,*

(ii) *for every $p \in Pat$, there are uncountably many texts $T \in Text(L(p))$ such that*

      – *$S$ works consistently on $T$,*

      – *$\Sigma_{n=0}^{Conv(S, T)}$ time to compute $S(T^n) \leq pol(length(p))$.*

*Sketch of proof.* Assertion (1), part (i) is proved using the strategy $\tilde{S}$ from the proof of Theorem 11, Assertion (3) above. Then part (i) follows by Lemma 2 of Lange and Wiehagen (1991). Part (ii) directly follows from Theorem 2, Assertion (3) of Lange and Wiehagen (1991).

The first part of Assertion (2) is an immediate consequence of the proof of Theorem 1 in Lange and Wiehagen (1991), while the second follows as above.       q.e.d.

We conjecture that Theorem 11 remains valid after replacing $INF$ by $TXT$. The corresponding Assertion (1) has been proved by Angluin (1980). As already mentioned above, the strategy from Lange and Wiehagen (1991) directly yields (3). Consequently, the only part not yet proved is (2). One reason why (2) seems to be easier provable for informant than for text is the following. A strategy working consistently on informant has to work "hard" at *any* step of the learning process in order to build its actual "biconsistent" hypothesis, while a consistent strategy on text may output the trivially consistent hypothesis $x_1$ for an "unbounded" number of steps.

# 5. Conclusions

We have investigated the problem of consistent versus inconsistent learning. In spite of the remarkable power of consistent learning it turns out that this power is not universal. There are learning problems which can exclusively be solved by inconsistent strategies, i.e., by strategies that do temporarily incorrectly reflect the behavior of the unknown object on data for which the correct behavior of the object is already known at the current stage of the learning process. This phenomenon has been investigated in a "highly theoretical" setting, namely in inductive inference of recursive functions. In this setting the seemingly senseless work of inconsistent strategies could be completely explained by the undecidability of consistency.

However, it turned out that the inconsistency phenomenon is also valid in more realistic situations, namely in domains where consistency is always decidable and the learning strategies have to work in polynomial time. The reason is quite analogous to that in the setting of arbitrary recursive functions. Providing $\mathcal{P} \neq \mathcal{NP}$, the $\mathcal{NP}$-hardness of problems can prevent learning strategies from producing consistent hypotheses in polynomial time. Note that the validity of our main result, Theorem 11, crucially depends on the fact that membership testing for pattern languages (hence also deciding consistency for hypotheses patterns, in general) is $\mathcal{NP}$-complete.

On the other hand, inspired by Wiehagen and Zeugmann (1992), Kummer (1992) has proved that the inconsistency phenomenon also holds in domains where the membership problem is even decidable in polynomial time for any single object to be learned, but *not uniformly* decidable in polynomial time with respect to the whole class of objects to be learned.

Finally, one can easily show that in domains where the membership problem is *uniformly* decidable in polynomial time, under weak assumptions any polynomial time learning algorithm can be effectively transformed into a polynomial time algorithm possessing at least the same learning power and being even consistent. Nevertheless, just in these domains we conjecture that there are learning problems solvable consistently in polynomial time, but solvable inconsistently (much) faster.

Moreover, we conjecture that our results may be extended to incremental learning of *finite* classes of *finite* objects such as Boolean functions, too.

In any case, we regard the results obtained as giving strong evidence to take fast *inconsistent* strategies seriously into account.

Finally, the presented results do suggest directions of further research such as

– finding fast inconsistent learning techniques,

– deriving conditions yielding that a given learning problem has no fast consistent solution, but it has a fast inconsistent one.

## Acknowledgements

The first author has been supported by the German Ministry for Research and Technology (BMFT) within the joint project (BMFT–Verbundprojekt) GOSLER under grant 01 IW 101 B9 and E7.

Substantial part of this work has been performed while the first author was visiting TH Darmstadt. He is grateful indebted to Rüdiger Reischuk and Wolfgang Bibel for providing inspiring working conditions.

Both authors heartily acknowledge many enlightening discussions with Steffen Lange (HTWK Leipzig) and with Andreas Jakoby and Christian Schindelhauer (TH Darmstadt).

# 6. References

ANGLUIN, D. (1980), Finding patterns common to a set of strings, *Journal of Computer and System Sciences* **21**, 46 – 62.

ANGLUIN, D., AND SMITH, C.H. (1983), Inductive inference: theory and methods, *Computing Surveys* **15**, 237 – 269.

ANGLUIN, D., AND SMITH, C.H. (1987), Formal inductive inference, *in* "Encyclopedia of Artificial Intelligence" (St.C. Shapiro, Ed.), Vol. 1, pp. 409 – 418, Wiley-Interscience Publication, New York.

BARZDIN, J. (1974a), Inductive inference of automata, functions and programs, *in* "Proceedings International Congress of Math.," Vancouver, pp. 455 – 460.

BARZDIN, J. (1974b), Две теоремы о предельном синтезе функций, *in* "Теория Алгоритмов и Программ," (J. Barzdin, Ed.), Vol.1, pp.82 – 88, Latvian State University.

BLUM, L., AND BLUM, M. (1975), Toward a mathematical theory of inductive inference, *Information and Control* **28**, 122 – 155.

BLUM, M. (1967), Machine independent theory of complexity of recursive functions, *Journal of the Association for Computing Machinery* **14**, 322 – 336.

FULK, M. (1988), Saving the phenomena: requirements that inductive inference machines not contradict known data, *Information and Computation* **79**, 193 – 209.

GAREY, M.R., AND JOHNSON, D.S. (1979), "Computers and Intractability. A Guide to the Theory of $\mathcal{NP}$–completeness," San Francisco, Freeman and Company.

GOLD, M.E. (1965), Limiting recursion, *Journal of Symbolic Logic* **30**, 28 – 48.

GOLD, M.E. (1967), Language identification in the limit, *Information and Control* **10**, 447 – 474.

JANTKE, K.P. (1991a), Monotonic and non-monotonic inductive inference, *New Generation Computing* **8**, 349 – 360.

JANTKE, K.P., AND BEICK, H.R. (1981), Combining postulates of naturalness in inductive inference, *Journal of Information Processing and Cybernetics (EIK)* **8/9**, 465 – 484.

KEARNS, M., AND PITT, L. (1989), A polynomial-time algorithm for learning $k$-variable pattern languages from examples, *in* "Proceedings 1st Annual Workshop on Computational Learning Theory," (D. Haussler and L. Pitt, Eds.), pp. 196 –205, Morgan Kaufmann Publishers Inc., San Mateo.

KO, KER-I, MARRON, A., AND TZENG, W.G. (1990), Learning string patterns and tree patterns from examples, *in* "Proceedings 7th Conference on Machine Learning," (B.W. Porter, and R.J. Mooney, Eds.), pp. 384 – 391, Morgan Kaufmann Publishers Inc., San Mateo.

KUMMER, M. (1992), personal communication to T. Zeugmann.

LANGE, S., AND WIEHAGEN, R. (1991), Polynomial-time inference of arbitrary pattern languages, *New Generation Computing* **8**, 361 – 370.

LANGE, S., AND ZEUGMANN, T. (1992), Types of monotonic language learning and their characterization, *in* "Proceedings 5th Annual ACM Workshop on Computational Learning Theory," (D. Haussler, Ed.), pp. 377 – 390, ACM Press, New York.

LANGE, S., AND ZEUGMANN, T. (1993), Monotonic versus non-monotonic language learning, *in* "Proceedings 2nd International Workshop on Nonmonotonic and Inductive Logic," (G. Brewka, K.P. Jantke and P.H. Schmitt, Eds.), Lecture Notes in Artificial Intelligence Vol. 659, pp. 254 – 269, Springer-Verlag, Berlin.

MICHALSKI, R.S., CARBONELL, J.G., AND MITCHELL, T.M. (1984), "Machine Learning, An Artificial Intelligence Approach," Vol. 1, Springer-Verlag, Berlin.

MICHALSKI, R.S., CARBONELL, J.G., AND MITCHELL, T.M. (1986), "Machine Learning, An Artificial Intelligence Approach," Vol. 2, Morgan Kaufmann Publishers Inc., San Mateo.

MINICOZZI, E. (1976), Some natural properties of strong-identification in inductive inference, *Theoretical Computer Science* **2**, 345 – 360.

NIX, R.P. (1983), Editing by examples, Yale University, Dept. Computer Science, Technical Report 280.

OSHERSON, D., STOB, M., AND WEINSTEIN, S. (1986), "Systems that Learn, An Introduction to Learning Theory for Cognitive and Computer Scientists," MIT-Press, Cambridge, Massachusetts.

PORAT, S., AND FELDMAN, J.A. (1988), Learning automata from ordered examples, in "Proceedings 1st Workshop on Computational Learning Theory," (D. Haussler and L. Pitt, Eds.), pp. 386 – 396, Morgan Kaufmann Publishers Inc., San Mateo.

ROGERS, H.JR. (1967), "Theory of Recursive Functions and Effective Computability," McGraw–Hill, New York.

SCHAPIRE, R.E. (1990), Pattern languages are not learnable, in "Proceedings 3rd Annual Workshop on Computational Learning Theory," (M.A. Fulk and J. Case, Eds.), pp. 122 – 129, Morgan Kaufmann Publishers, Inc., San Mateo.

SHINOHARA, T. (1982), Polynomial time inference of extended regular pattern languages, in "Proceedings RIMS Symposia on Software Science and Engineering," Lecture Notes in Computer Science 147, pp. 115 – 127, Springer-Verlag, Berlin.

SMULLYAN, R.M. (1961), Theory of formal systems, Annals of Math. Studies 47.

SOLOMONOFF, R. (1964), A formal theory of inductive inference, Information and Control 7, 1 – 22, 234 – 254.

TRAKHTENBROT, B.A., AND BARZDIN, J. (1970) "Конечные Автоматы (Поведение и Синтез)," Наука, Москва,
English translation: "Finite Automata–Behavior and Synthesis, Fundamental Studies in Computer Science 1," North-Holland, Amsterdam, 1973.

WIEHAGEN, R. (1976), Limes–Erkennung rekursiver Funktionen durch spezielle Strategien, Journal of Information Processing and Cybernetics (EIK) 12, 93 – 99.

WIEHAGEN, R. (1978), Characterization problems in the theory of inductive inference, in "Proceedings 5th Colloquium on Automata, Languages and Programming," (G. Ausiello and C. Böhm, Eds.), Lecture Notes in Computer Science 62, pp. 494 – 508, Springer-Verlag, Berlin.

WIEHAGEN, R. (1992), From inductive inference to algorithmic learning theory, in "Proceedings 3rd Workshop on Algorithmic Learning Theory," (S. Doshita, K. Furukawa, K.P. Jantke and T. Nishida, Eds.), Lecture Notes in Artificial Intelligence 743, pp. 3 – 24, Springer-Verlag, Berlin.

WIEHAGEN, R., AND LIEPE, W. (1976), Charakteristische Eigenschaften von erkennbaren Klassen rekursiver Funktionen, Journal of Information Processing and Cybernetics (EIK) 12, 421 – 438.

WIEHAGEN, R., AND ZEUGMANN, T. (1992), Too much information can be too much for learning efficiently, in "Proceedings 3rd International Workshop on Analogical and Inductive Inference," ( K.P. Jantke, Ed.), Lecture Notes in Artificial Intelligence 642, pp. 72 – 86, Springer-Verlag, Berlin.

WIEHAGEN, R., AND ZEUGMANN, T. (1994), Ignoring data may be the only way to learn efficiently, Journal of Theoretical and Experimental Artificial Intelligence 6, 131 – 144.

ZEUGMANN, T. (1983), A-posteriori characterizations in inductive inference of recursive functions, *Journal of Information Processing and Cybernetics (EIK)* **19**, 559 – 594.

ZEUGMANN, T., LANGE, S., AND KAPUR, S. (199x), Characterizations of monotonic and dual monotonic language learning, *Information and Computation*, to appear.

# Error Detecting in Inductive Inference

Rūsiņš Freivalds and Efim B. Kinber*

Institute of Mathematics and Computer Science

University of Latvia

Raiņa bulvāris 29, LV-1459 Riga, Latvia

Rolf Wiehagen

Department of Computer Science

University of Kaiserslautern

P.O.Box 3049, D-67653 Kaiserslautern, Germany

### Abstract

Several well-known inductive inference strategies change the actual hypothesis only when they discover that it "provably misclassifies" an example seen so far. This notion is made mathematically precise and its general power is characterized. In spite of its strength it is shown that this approach is not of universal power. Consequently, then hypotheses are considered which "unprovably misclassify" examples and the properties of this approach are studied. Among others it turns out that this type is of the same power as monotonic identification. Then it is shown that universal power can be achieved only when an unbounded number of alternations of these dual types of hypotheses is allowed. Finally, a universal method is presented enabling an inductive inference strategy to verify the incorrectness of any of its incorrect intermediate hypotheses.

## 1. Introduction

The theory of inductive inference developed quite well in recent years, cf. (Angluin and Smith, 1983), (Klette and Wiehagen, 1980), (Osherson, Stob, and Weinstein, 1986), (Theory of Algorithms and Programs, 1974, 1975, 1977), provides an appropriate mathematical description of many aspects of human thinking. Identification of classes of recursive functions is one of the simplest inductive processes, but it simulates many of its main features.

---

*Current address: Department of Computer and Information Science, University of Delaware, Newark, Delaware 19716

However, there is an aspect in which the theory has not discovered the real mechanisms of human thinking, but it has discovered something artificial instead. This aspect is: How an inductive inference strategy discovers that its actual hypothesis is incorrect (and hence this hypothesis has to be changed at some moment).

We wish to show that a proper answer to this problem does influence the power of the strategies very much and, therefore, cannot be disregarded.

The moment when the identification strategy performs a mind change is relatively free. In general, it may be delayed for some time. However, there can be some restrictions on the identification strategy. These restrictions, in fact, define new types of identification which may be more restrictive than the standard type EX. Thus the identification type CONS requires that if, for some $x$, the value $f(x)$ of the function $f$ to be identified differs from the value $h(x)$ where $h$ is the "hypothesis function" produced by the strategy when fed $f(0), f(1), \ldots, f(x-1)$, then the hypothesis $h$ *must* be changed *immediately* to a new one which has to be consistent with all values $f(0), f(1), \ldots, f(x)$. This restrictive type CONS may be compared with the absolutely non-restrictive type EX or with less severely restrictive types.

Our research started by considering the well-known duality between must and may, duty and right, restriction and permission. We tried to construct the counterpart of the identification type CONS dual to it according to the notion of duality above. We focussed on the following definition. The hypothesis $h$ *may* be changed only if there is an $x$ such that $f(x)$ and $h(x)$ are defined and different. We call the functions $f$ and $h$ *convergently different* and the corresponding identification type "identification with convergently incorrect intermediate hypotheses" (abbreviated: CEX). The type CEX may be compared with other types where the strategy has not always a definite proof of the incorrectness of its current hypothesis, but more or less justified "suspicions", only.

Perhaps, the property to be convergently different from the function to be identified yields the most natural way to prove the incorrectness of the current hypothesis.

Of course, one can imagine other ways to prove the inconsistency of a hypothesis with the function to be identified. For instance, the strategy may try to prove the function $h$ not being total within Peano arithmetics or within some other reasonable consistent recursively enumerable logic system. However, (Kummer, 1992) has shown that no such logic system can increase the identification power.

Another reason to study the power of identification with "convergently justified" mind changes is the simple observation that practically all known identification strategies do work in this manner. Gold's identification-by-enumeration strategy identifying any enumerable class of recursive functions may serve as a classical example (Gold, 1967). Furthermore, any Popperian inference strategy producing only numbers of recursive functions belongs to this class of strategies (Case and Ngo Manguelle, 1979), (Case and Smith, 1983); cf. Section 3. Also the strategy of Barzdin and Freivalds achieving the best possible bound of $\log_2 n$ mind changes on the $n$-th function of any enumerable class of recursive functions, possesses this property (Barzdin and Freivalds, 1974).

There may be a different motivation for an identification strategy to perform a mind change, namely, if the current hypothesis is a program of a partial function which is a proper subfunction of the function to be identified. Then no convergently justified mind change is possible, but this case may be considered as a dual one, in a sense, to the case of convergently justified mind changes. We use the terms "divergently different", "divergently incorrect hypothesis", "identification with divergently incorrect intermediate hypotheses" for this case. Clearly, if a function class cannot be identified with convergently incorrect intermediate hypotheses, only, then any strategy identifiying this class has to produce infinitely many divergently incorrect intermediate hypotheses. Thus, convergently justified mind changes and "divergently justified" mind changes are, in a sense, two extremes.

We now summarize our main results.

The first one concerns identification with convergently incorrect intermediate hypotheses. This restriction still leaves much freedom to the strategy how to accomplish the corresponding requirement. A wide spectrum of different natural strategies is possible, and it seems likely that this wide spectrum is inevitable. Quite surprisingly, we were able to prove that there is a natural type of strategies (called temporarily conform hereafter) such that every class identifiable with convergently incorrect intermediate hypotheses can be identified by a strategy of this type. Moreover, the converse is also true (Theorem 20).

However, it turns out that identification with convergently incorrect intermediate hypotheses is not of universal power (Theorem 27). We even show that no finite number of alternations between convergently justified and divergently justified mind changes suffices to identify every class of recursive functions identifiable at all (Theorem 40).

Nevertheless, there is a uniform and universal method by the help of which inductive inference strategies can discover their errors, i.e., they can prove the incorrectness of any incorrect intermediate hypothesis (Theorem 42).

The paper is organized as follows.

Section 2 contains some notation and definitions.

In Section 3 following a suggestion of M. Fulk (Fulk, 1991) we define temporarily conform identification. Intuitively, a strategy is working temporarily conform if it always takes the minimal hypothesis which does not contradict the unknown function within a certain time bound. We characterize the power of this approach by giving a pure numbering-theoretic characterization of the corresponding identification type and by comparing this type with other types. In Section 4 we show that temporarily conform identification is not only *one* way of making precise the intuition of convergently incorrect intermediate hypotheses but, in a sense, it is the *most powerful* one. Moreover, this result provides us with the technical possibilities to show that this natural approach is not universal. There are identifiable function classes which cannot be identified with convergently incorrect intermediate hypotheses, only. Note that in (Angluin, 1980) a similar result was proved for identification of classes of recursive languages with uniformly decidable membership problem from positive data.

In Section 5 we consider the dual situation where none of the hypotheses differs convergently from the function to be identified. Consequently, all hypotheses have to describe *subfunctions* of the unknown function. We show that the resulting identification type working with "divergently incorrect" intermediate hypotheses is equivalent to monotonic identification introduced in (Jantke, 1991), where the hypotheses have to be changed such that the corresponding subfunctions converge monotonically to the unknown function. Furthermore, this identification type turns out to be set-theoretically incomparable with that of convergently incorrect intermediate hypotheses.

In Section 6 we present a hierarchy result yielding that for identification of *all* identifiable classes of recursive functions we have to allow an unbounded number of alternations of convergently and divergently incorrect intermediate hypotheses.

In Section 7 we prove that there is a uniform method enabling inductive inference strategies to verify the incorrectness of any of its incorrect intermediate hypotheses. Using this method any class of recursive functions identifiable at all is shown to be identifiable by a strategy never changing its first correct hypothesis.

In Section 8 we discuss the results obtained.

For the proofs not contained in this paper the reader is referred to (Freivalds, Kinber, and Wiehagen, 199x).

## 2. Notation–Definitions

$N$ denotes the set of natural numbers $\{0, 1, 2, \ldots\}$. For $y \in N$, let $\bar{y} = 1$, iff $y = 0$ and $\bar{y} = 0$, otherwise. For a set $A$, card$A$ denotes the cardinality of $A$. For sets $A$, $B$, we sometimes write $A \nsubseteq B$ instead of $A - B \neq \emptyset$. $A \subset B$ denotes the proper inclusion. $P, P^2$ denotes the set of all partial recursive functions of one argument, two arguments, respectively. $R$ denotes the set of all recursive functions of one argument. $R_{0,1}$ denotes the set of all $0, 1$-valued functions from $R$.

Any function $\psi \in P^2$ is called a *numbering*. We write $\psi_i$ instead of $\lambda x(\psi(i, x))$. Let $P_\psi = \{\psi_i \mid i \in N\}$ denote the class of all partial recursive functions enumerated by $\psi$. For a numbering $\psi$ and $f \in P_\psi$, let $\min_\psi f$ denote the least $i \in N$ such that $\psi_i = f$. $\varphi \in P^2$ is called a *Gödel numbering* (Rogers, 1967) iff $P_\varphi = P$ and for any numbering $\psi$, there is a function $c \in R$ such that for any $i$, $\psi_i = \varphi_{c(i)}$. Let $G$ denote the set of all Gödel numberings.

Let $f, g \in P$, $n \in N$. Then $f =_n g$ iff $\{(x, f(x)) \mid x \leq n \text{ and } f(x) \text{ is defined}\} = \{(x, g(x)) \mid x \leq n \text{ and } g(x) \text{ is defined}\}$. Now let $f \in R$. We call $g$ a proper subfunction of $f$ (abbreviated: $g \subset f$) iff $\{(x, g(x)) \mid x \in N \text{ and } g(x) \text{ is defined}\} \subset \{(x, f(x)) \mid x \in N\}$. We say that $g$ *differs convergently* from $f$ iff there is $x \in N$ such that $g(x)$ is defined and $g(x) \neq f(x)$. We say that $g$ *differs divergently* from $f$ iff $g \subset f$.

Let $\psi$ be any numbering, $f \in R$ and $i \in N$. Then $i$ is called *incorrect* for $f$ with respect to $\psi$ iff $\psi_i \neq f$. Futhermore $i$ is called *convergently incorrect* for $f$ with respect to $\psi$ iff $\psi_i$ differs convergently from $f$. We say that $i$ is *divergently incorrect* for $f$ with respect to $\psi$ iff $\psi_i$ differs divergently from $f$. Clearly, if $i$ is incorrect for $f$ then $f$ is either convergently or divergently incorrect.

For a function $f \in R$ and $n \in N$, let $f^n = \mathrm{cod}(f(0), f(1), \ldots, f(n))$ where cod denotes a computable and bijective mapping from the set $N^*$ of all finite sequences of natural numbers onto $N$. Sometimes, for the sake of simplicity of notation, we identify $\alpha \in N^*$ with $\mathrm{cod}(\alpha)$. If $\alpha = (y_0, \ldots, y_n) \in N^*$ and $\beta = (y'_0, \ldots, y'_m) \in N^*$, then $\alpha\beta = (y_0, \ldots, y_n, y'_0, \ldots, y'_m)$. For $\alpha \in N^*$, $|\alpha|$ denotes the length of $\alpha$. Let $\{0, 1\}^*$ denote the set of all $0, 1$-tuples of finite length.

A function $g \in P$ is called *initial* iff there is $n \in N$ such that $\mathrm{domain}(g) = \{0, 1, \ldots, n\}$. At several places we identify an initial or a recursive function with the sequence of its values. Thus, for $j \in N$ and $\alpha = (y_0, \ldots, y_n) \in N^*$, $j\alpha$ denotes the following initial function $g$:

$$g(x) = \begin{cases} j & \text{if } x = 0 \\ y_{x-1} & \text{if } 1 \le x \le n + 1 \\ \text{undefined} & \text{otherwise.} \end{cases}$$

Analogously, $j\alpha 0^\infty$ denotes the following recursive function $g$:

$$g(x) = \begin{cases} j & \text{if } x = 0 \\ y_{x-1} & \text{if } 1 \le x \le n + 1 \\ 0 & \text{otherwise.} \end{cases}$$

If $p \in R_{0,1}$, then $j\alpha p$ denotes the following function $g \in R$:

$$g(x) = \begin{cases} j & \text{if } x = 0 \\ y_{x-1} & \text{if } 1 \le x \le n + 1 \\ p(x - n - 2) & \text{if } x \ge n + 2. \end{cases}$$

A function $g \in P$ is called *finite* iff $\mathrm{domain}(g)$ is finite.

We now define some basic identification types which will be used in the sequel.

**Definition 1** (Gold, 1967; Barzdin, 1971; Blum and Blum, 1975) Let $U \subseteq R$ and let $\psi$ be any numbering. $U$ is called *identifiable* with respect to $\psi$ iff there is $S \in P$ such that
1) for any $n \in N$, $S(f^n)$ is defined,
2) there is $j \in N$ such that $\psi_j = f$ and for almost all $n \in N$, $S(f^n) = j$.

Thus, on any function $f \in U$ the strategy $S$ produces a sequence of hypotheses converging to a correct $\psi$-number of $f$. We note that no restriction is made that we should be able to algorithmically determine whether the sequence of hypotheses has already stabilized itself. This identification type is also referred to as identification in the limit or explanatory correct identification, elsewhere.

Let
$EX_\psi = \{U \mid U$ is identifiable with respect to $\psi\}$,
$EX = \bigcup_{\psi \in P^2} EX_\psi$.
By $U \in EX_\psi(S)$ we denote the fact that $U$ is identifiable with respect to $\psi$ by the strategy $S$.

**Definition 2** (Barzdin, 1974; Blum and Blum, 1975; Wiehagen, 1976; Fulk, 1988)
Let $U \subseteq R$ and let $\psi$ be any numbering. $U$ is called *consistently* identifiable with respect to $\psi$ iff there is $S \in P$ such that
1) $U \in EX_\psi(S)$,
2) for any $f \in U$ and any $n \in N$, $\psi_{S(f^n)} =_n f$.

Thus, a consistent hypothesis coincides with the unknown function on the initial segment seen so far.

Let
$CONS_\psi = \{U \mid U$ is consistently identifiable with respect to $\psi\}$,
$CONS = \bigcup_{\psi \in P^2} CONS_\psi$.

**Definition 3** (Wiehagen, 1978; Fulk, 1988) Let $U \subseteq R$ and let $\psi$ be any numbering. $U$ is called *conformly* identifiable with respect to $\psi$ iff there is $S \in P$ such that
1) $U \in EX_\psi(S)$,
2) for any $f \in U$ and any $x, n \in N$ such that $x \leq n$, $\psi_{S(f^n)}(x) = f(x)$ or $\psi_{S(f^n)}(x)$ is undefined.

Thus, a conform hypothesis does not "contradict" the unknown function on the initial segment seen so far; for $x \leq n$, it is not allowed that $\psi_{S(f^n)}(x)$ is both defined and different from $f(x)$.

Let
$CONF_\psi = \{U \mid U$ is conformly identifiable with respect to $\psi\}$,
$CONF = \bigcup_{\psi \in P^2} CONF_\psi$.

In (Wiehagen, 1978a) $CONS \subset CONF \subset EX$ was proved.

The reader is referred to (Fulk, 1988) and (Wiehagen and Zeugmann, 1994) for further investigation of CONS and CONF.

**Definition 4** (Case and Smith, 1983) Let $U \subseteq R$, $\psi$ be any numbering and $m \in N$. $U$ is called identifiable with respect to $\psi$ *after no more than $m$ mind changes* iff there is $S \in P$ such that
1) $U \in EX_\psi(S)$,
2) for any $f \in U$, $\text{card}\{n \mid S(f^n) \neq S(f^{n+1})\} \leq m$.

Let
$EX_\psi^m = \{U \mid U$ is identifiable with respect to $\psi$ after no more than $m$ mind changes$\}$,
$EX^m = \bigcup_{\psi \in P^2} EX_\psi^m$.

In (Case and Smith, 1983) the following result is proved:
$$EX^0 \subset EX^1 \subset \ldots \subset EX^m \subset EX^{m+1} \subset \ldots \subset EX.$$

An easy possibility to provide an inference strategy with the ability to detect whether its actual hypothesis differs convergently from the function to be identified consists in producing only numbers of recursive functions. In (Case and Ngo Manguelle, 1979) such a strategy is called Popperian following Karl Popper's principle that scientific explanation ought to be subject to refutation (Popper, 1968). For a more detailed discussion of Popper's refutation principle and its significance for inductive inference the reader is referred to (Case and Smith, 1983).

**Definition 5** (Case and Ngo Manguelle, 1979; Case and Smith, 1983) Let $U \subseteq R$ and let $\psi$ be any numbering. $U$ is called identifiable with respect to $\psi$ *by a Popperian strategy* iff there is $S \in R$ such that
1) $U \in EX_\psi(S)$,
2) for any $f \in R$ and any $n \in N$, $\psi_{S(f^n)} \in R$.

Let
$PEX_\psi = \{U \mid U \text{ is identifiable with respect to } \psi \text{ by a Popperian strategy}\}$,
$PEX = \bigcup_{\psi \in P^2} PEX_\psi$.

Hence a Popperian strategy always outputs numbers of recursive functions.

The so-called total strategies are allowed to output arbitrary numbers on initial segments of functions not belonging to the class to be identified. Of course, this does not injury the strategy's ability to detect that the hypothesis and the unknown function differ convergently if this is the case.

**Definition 6** (Case and Ngo Manguelle, 1979) Let $U \subseteq R$ and let $\psi$ be any numbering. $U$ is called identifiable with respect to $\psi$ *by a total strategy* iff there is $S \in R$ such that
1) $U \in EX_\psi(S)$,
2) for any $f \in U$ and any $n \in N$, $\psi_{S(f^n)} \in R$.

Let
$TEX_\psi = \{U \mid U \text{ is identifiable with respect to } \psi \text{ by a total strategy}\}$,
$TEX = \bigcup_{\psi \in P^2} TEX_\psi$.

In (Case and Ngo Manguelle, 1979) the following result is proved: $PEX \subset TEX$.

As we shall see in Section 3, there are more powerful identification strategies than Popperian and total ones which nevertheless satisfy Popper's refutation principle in that any incorrect hypothesis produced by these strategies differs convergently from the function to be identified.

# 3. Temporarily conform identification–a special case of identification with convergently incorrect intermediate hypotheses

Following a suggestion of M. Fulk (Fulk, 1991) we define an identification type where always the strategy takes the minimal hypothesis which does not contradict the unknown function within a certain time bound.

Therefore we need an auxiliary predicate $\text{tconf}_\psi(i, f^n)$ where $\psi$ is a numbering, $i, n \in N$ and $f \in R$. Intuitively, $\text{tconf}_\psi(i, f^n)$ is true iff within the time bound of $n$ steps of computation the function $\psi_i$ does not contradict the function $f$ for all $x \leq n$. More exactly:

$\text{tconf}_\psi(i, f^n)$ iff for any $x \leq n$, either 1) or 2) holds:
    1) $\psi_i(x)$ is defined within $n$ steps of computation and $\psi_i(x) = f(x)$,
    2) $\psi_i(x)$ is not defined within $n$ steps of computation.

**Definition 7** Let $U \subseteq R$ and let $\psi$ be any numbering. $U$ is called *temporarily conformly identifiable* with respect to $\psi$ iff
$U \in \text{EX}_\psi(\text{TC}_\psi)$ where for any $f \in R$ and any $n \in N$,
$\text{TC}_\psi(f^n) = \min\{i \mid \text{tconf}_\psi(i, f^n)\}$.

Hence a temporarily conform strategy is allowed to change its mind only if the former hypothesis differs convergently from the function to be identified within the given time bound. Thus, temporarily conform identification is a natural way of making precise the approach of identification with convergently incorrect intermediate hypotheses.

Define
$\text{TCONF}_\psi = \{U \mid U \text{ is temporarily conformly identifiable with respect to } \psi\}$,
$\text{TCONF} = \bigcup_{\psi \in P^2} \text{TCONF}_\psi$.

Hence $U \in \text{TCONF}$ iff there is a suitable numbering $\psi$ such that $U$ is temporarily conformly identifiable with respect to $\psi$ by $\text{TC}_\psi$.

We now derive an easy but useful characterization of TCONF in terms of numbering theory.

**Theorem 8** $U \in \text{TCONF}$ iff there is a numbering $\psi$ such that
1) $U \subseteq P_\psi$,
2) for any $f \in U$, there is no $i < \min_\psi f$ such that $\psi_i \subset f$.

Clearly, any $i < \min_\psi f$ such that $\psi_i \subset f$ forces a temporarily conform strategy to converge to an "undergeneralized" hypothesis—by the way, a dual difficulty to that of "overgeneralization" in language identification from positive data (Angluin, 1980).

Theorem 8 yields some consequences. One of them shows that Gödel numberings are extremely weak for temporarily conform identification. The simple reason is that they enumerate *all* partial recursive functions among them the empty function which is always "temporarily conform".

**Corollary 9**
(1) For any $\varphi \in G$, if $U \in \text{TCONF}_\varphi$ then $U$ is finite.
(2) There is $\varphi \in G$, such that $\text{TCONF}_\varphi = \{\emptyset\}$.

Our next results show that for suitable numberings, temporarily conform identification is more powerful than identification by Popperian and by total strategies which are also working with convergently incorrect intermediate hypotheses as mentioned above.

**Definition 10** (Barzdin and Freivalds, 1972; Podnieks, 1974; Blum and Blum, 1975)
Let $U \subseteq R$. $U$ is called *next-value predictable* iff there is $S \in P$ such that for any $f \in U$,
1) for any $n \in N$, $S(f^n)$ is defined,
2) for almost all $n \in N$, $S(f^n) = f(n+1)$.

Let $\text{NV}' = \{U \mid U \text{ is next-value predictable}\}$.
Note that NV "without dash" is defined as NV' with the only difference that the prediction strategy $S$ is required to be from $R$. (Podnieks, 1974) proved that $\text{NV} \subset \text{NV}'$.

**Theorem 11** $\text{NV}' \subseteq \text{TCONF}$.

Actually, the proper inclusion $\text{NV}' \subset \text{TCONF}$ holds, as it quite easily follows below (Corollary 24).

**Corollary 12**
(1) $\text{PEX} \subset \text{TCONF}$.
(2) $\text{TEX} \subset \text{TCONF}$.

Thus, temporarily conform strategies also satisfying Popper's refutation principle are more powerful than Popperian and total strategies.

We now want to locate the place of TCONF within the "world" of identification types more exactly. Therefore we define two types which are very closely related to CONS, and then we state that these types are fully contained in TCONF. These results turn out to be tight in that CONS itself is *not* fully contained in TCONF, as we shall see in Section 4.

**Definition 13** Let $U \subseteq R$. $U \in \text{CONS}^{+1}$ iff there is $\varphi \in G$ and $S \in P$ such that
1) $U \in \text{CONS}_\varphi(S)$,
2) for any $f \in U$ and any $n \in N$, $\varphi_{S(f^n)}(n+1)$ is defined.

Clearly, the definition of $\text{CONS}^{+1}$ does not depend on the choice of the Gödel numbering $\varphi$.

**Theorem 14** $\text{CONS}^{+1} \subseteq \text{TCONF}$.

Our next definition confines the identification type CONS to classes of recursive predicates.

**Definition 15** $\text{CONS}_{0,1} = \{U \mid U \subseteq R_{0,1} \text{ and } U \in \text{CONS}\}$.

**Theorem 16** $\text{CONS}_{0,1} \subseteq \text{TCONF}$.

In Section 4 we will present yet another result indicating the power of TCONF, namely $\text{TCONF} - \text{CONS} \neq \emptyset$ (Corollary 23). This result also easily yields that all the inclusions of Theorems 11, 14 and 16 are proper.

On the other hand, concerning the *full* containment of identification types in TCONF Theorem 14 and Theorem 16 are in a sense the best possible results, since it turns out that they do not remain valid for CONS itself. Actually, below we derive that $\text{CONS} \not\subseteq \text{TCONF}$. Of course, this will prove that temporarily conform identification is not of universal power, $\text{TCONF} \subset \text{EX}$.

Here we want to mention a technical difficulty in proving $\text{CONS} \not\subseteq \text{TCONF}$ directly. Indeed, such a proof would require to find a class $U \in \text{CONS}$ such that for *all* numberings $\psi$, $U \notin \text{TCONF}_\psi$ has to be proved. But in an arbitrary numbering the usual recursion-theoretic means such as the $s$-$m$-$n$-theorem and the recursion theorem, cf. (Rogers, 1967), which are essential for proving many results in inductive inference, are not available in general. We present a solution to this problem in the next section. Informally, it consists in the following. We first define the general type of identification with convergently incorrect intermediate hypotheses, CEX. Then we prove $\text{TCONF} = \text{CEX}$ and $\text{CEX} = \text{CEX}_\varphi$ for any Gödel numbering $\varphi$. Hence in order to prove $\text{CONS} \not\subseteq \text{TCONF}$ it suffices to prove $\text{CONS} \not\subseteq \text{CEX}_\varphi$ for an arbitrary $\varphi \in G$. But in a Gödel numbering all the recursion-theoretic means mentioned above *are* available.

# 4. Identification with convergently incorrect intermediate hypotheses–the general case

Now we give the general definition of identification with convergently incorrect intermediate hypotheses.

**Definition 17** Let $U \subseteq R$ and let $\psi$ be any numbering. $U$ is called identifiable with respect to $\psi$ *with convergently incorrect intermediate hypotheses* iff there is $S \in P$ such that
1) $U \in \text{EX}_\psi(S)$,
2) for any $f \in U$ and any $n \in N$, if $\psi_{S(f^n)} \neq f$, then $\psi_{S(f^n)}$ and $f$ differ convergently.

Hence a strategy of the type above is allowed again to change its mind only if the former hypothesis differs convergently from the function to be identified. In contrast to temporarily conform identification there is no requirement concerning the way of how to find the new hypothesis.

Define

$CEX_\psi = \{U \mid U$ is identifiable with respect to $\psi$ with convergently incorrect intermediate hypotheses$\}$,

$CEX = \bigcup_{\psi \in P^2} CEX_\psi$.

First we want to show that any strategy working with convergently incorrect intermediate hypotheses can really be thought as a strategy working with "convergently justified mind changes" in the following sense.

**Definition 18** Let $U \subseteq R$ and let $\psi$ be any numbering. $U$ is called identifiable with respect to $\psi$ *with convergently justified mind changes* iff there is $S \in P$ such that
1) $U \in EX_\psi(S)$,
2) for any $f \in U$ and any $n \in N$, if $i := S(f^n) \neq S(f^{n+1})$, then there is $x \leq n$ such that $\psi_i(x)$ is defined within $n$ steps and $\psi_i(x) \neq f(x)$.

Let

$CJM_\psi = \{U \mid U$ is identifiable with respect to $\psi$ with convergently justified mind changes$\}$.

**Lemma 19** For any numbering $\psi$, $CEX_\psi = CJM_\psi$.

Note that any CJM-strategy (as well as any TCONF-strategy and CEX-strategy) has the following property: When it outputs a correct hypothesis for the first time, then this hypothesis will never be changed. This reasonable and desirable property is non-trivial, because in general there is no way to algorithmically determine whether a given hypothesis is correct.

We now state that any strategy working with convergently incorrect intermediate hypotheses can be replaced with a temporarily conform strategy of the same power. Hence temporary conformity is not only one possibility of working with convergently incorrect intermediate hypotheses but, in a sense, it is the most powerful one.

**Theorem 20** CEX = TCONF.

From Theorem 20 and Corollary 12 we get immediately that Popperian as well as total identification is strictly less powerful than identification with convergently incorrect intermediate hypotheses.

**Corollary 21**
(1) PEX $\subset$ CEX.
(2) TEX $\subset$ CEX.

We proceed in deriving some more results concerning the strength of CEX (as well as TCONF via Theorem 20).

**Theorem 22**
CEX − CONS $\neq \emptyset$.

Theorem 22 yields some more consequences concerning the power of TCONF.

**Corollary 23** TCONF − CONS $\neq \emptyset$.

**Corollary 24**
(1) NV' $\subset$ TCONF.
(2) CONS$^{+1}$ $\subset$ TCONF.
(3) CONS$_{0,1}$ $\subset$ TCONF.

**Corollary 25**
(1) NV' $\subset$ CEX.
(2) CONS$^{+1}$ $\subset$ CEX.
(3) CONS$_{0,1}$ $\subset$ CEX.

It turns out that Corollary 24, (2)&(3) and Corollary 25, (2)&(3) are the best possible results in that CONS is *not* fully contained in TCONF, CEX. This follows from the proof of Theorem 27 below. The main consequence is that CEX-strategies are not of universal power, CEX $\subset$ EX. Of course, the same is true for TCONF-strategies.

Formally, to prove a result of the type $U \notin$ CEX, it requires to prove that $U \notin$ CEX$_\psi$ for *all* numberings $\psi$. But Lemma 26 implies that it suffices to show $U \notin$ CEX$_\varphi$ for an arbitrary $\varphi \in G$.

**Lemma 26** For any $\varphi \in G$, CEX$_\varphi$ = CEX.

Note that Lemma 26 does not remain valid for TCONF instead of CEX, though TCONF = CEX. This easily follows from Corollary 9. Hence to prove $U \notin$ TCONF "directly", actually, it would be necessary to prove $U \notin$ TCONF$_\psi$ for *all* numberings $\psi$.

**Theorem 27** CEX $\subset$ EX.

*Proof of Theorem 27.*
CEX $\subseteq$ EX is obvious.
Since CONS $\subseteq$ EX, CEX $\subset$ EX follows via Lemma 26 by proving that CONS $\setminus$ CEX$_\varphi \neq \emptyset$ where $\varphi \in G$. Therefore define $U_0, U_1 \subseteq R$ as follows:

$$U_0 = \{f = jp \mid j \in N \,\&\, p \in R_{0,1} \,\&\, \varphi_j = f\},$$
$$U_1 = \{f = j\alpha k0^\infty \mid j,k \in N \,\&\, k \geq 2 \,\&\, \alpha \in \{0,1\}^* \,\&\, \varphi_j = j\alpha \,\&\, \varphi_k = f\}.$$

Let $U = U_0 \cup U_1$. We show that $U \in$ CONS and $U \notin$ CEX$_\varphi$.

$U \in$ CONS. Note that if $f = j\alpha k 0^\infty \in U_1$, then $j$ is a consistent hypothesis for the initial function $j\alpha$. Hence $U \in$ CONS$_\varphi(S)$, where informally, on a function $f$ the strategy $S$ outputs $f(0)$, the $j$, and then checks whether there is $x > 0$ such that $f(x) \geq 2$, the $k$, in which case $S$ changes its hypothesis from $j$ to $k$ forever.

$U \notin$ CEX$_\varphi$. Assume to the contrary that $U \in$ CEX$_\varphi(S)$. Then we show that there is a function $f \in U$ which $S$ cannot CEX-identify with respect to $\varphi$. Therefore, by an implicit use of the recursion theorem, we define a function $g := \varphi_j \in P$. The function $g$ will be recursive (then $g \in U_0$ and $f := g$) or initial (then $g = j\alpha$ where $\alpha \in \{0,1\}^*$, and $f := j\alpha k 0^\infty$ where $k \geq 2$ is such that $\varphi_k = f$; hence $f \in U_1$).

Definition of $g := \varphi_j$.

The definition of $g$ proceeds by stages. We name these stages by $\alpha$'s where $\alpha \in \{0,1\}^*$. The definition of $g$ starts with stage $\alpha$ where $\alpha =$ empty. We now describe the general stage $\alpha$.

Stage $\alpha$, $\alpha = (y_1, \ldots, y_n) \in \{0,1\}^*$, $|\alpha| \geq 0$.

At the beginning of stage $\alpha$ the function $g$ is defined as follows:

$$
\begin{aligned}
g(0) &= j, \\
g(x) &= y_x \text{ for } 1 \leq x \leq n.
\end{aligned}
$$

Now in parallel do both (A) and (B).

(A) Define, step by step, $g(x) = 0$ for $x = n+1, n+2, \ldots$
(B) Compute $S(g^n)$.

Comment: $S(g^n)$ must be defined, since otherwise, by (A), $g = \varphi_j = j\alpha 0^\infty \in U_0$. But for a function $g \in U_0$ and any $n \in N$, $S(g^n)$ is defined.

As soon as $i := S(g^n)$ has been defined, suspend defining $g$ by (A). Let $m \in N$ be the maximal argument such that $g(m)$ has been defined so far. Then in parallel check whether Case 1 or Case 2 happens.

*Case 1.* There is $y \leq m$ such that $\varphi_i(y)$ is defined and $\varphi_i(y) \neq g(y)$.
    Then in parallel do both (C) and (D).
    (C) Define, step by step, $g(x) = 0$ for $x = m+1, m+2, \ldots$
    (D) Search for $z > n$ such that $S(g^z)$ is defined and $S(g^z) \neq i$.
        Comment: $z$ must exist (hence it will be found effectively), since otherwise, by (C), $g = \varphi_j = j\alpha 0^\infty \in U_0$ and $S(g^{n'}) = i$ for all $n' \geq n$. But $\varphi_i \neq g$ by Case 1, a contradiction.
        As soon as $z \in N$ corresponding to (D) has been found, suspend defining $g$ by (C). Let $m' \in N$ be the maximal argument such that $g(m')$ has been defined so far. Go to stage $\alpha = (g(1), \ldots, g(m'))$.

*Case 2.* There is $y > m$ such that $\varphi_i(y)$ is defined.

Then define

$$g(x) = \begin{cases} 0 & \text{if } m < x < y \\ \overline{\varphi_i(y)} & \text{if } x = y. \end{cases}$$

Comment: $i$ is an incorrect hypothesis for any function coinciding with $g$ up to $y$.

Go to stage $\alpha = (g(1), \ldots, g(y))$.

*Case 3.* Neither Case 1 nor Case 2.

Then $g$ will not be defined at any further arguments.

Now in order to define $f \in U$ which cannot be $\text{CEX}_\varphi$-identified by $S$ we consider two cases.

*Case A.* At any stage during the definition of $g$ Case 1 or Case 2 happens.

Then $g \in U_0$. Clearly, at least one of the Cases 1 and 2 must happen at infinitely many stages.

If Case 1 happens infinitely often, then on the function $g$ the strategy $S$ changes its hypotheses infinitely often.

If Case 2 happens infinitely often, then on the function $g$ the strategy $S$ produces an incorrect hypothesis infinitely often.

Hence, in Case A it suffices to set $f := g$.

*Not Case A.* Let $\alpha = (y_1, \ldots, y_n)$, $n \geq 0$, be the last stage reached during the definition of $g$. Hence $g = j\alpha\beta$ where $\beta \in \{0\}^*$. Let $i := S(g^n)$. Since during stage $\alpha$ neither Case 1 nor Case 2 happens, we easily get $\varphi_i \subseteq g$. Furthermore, since $j$ is a $\varphi$-number of $g$, by use of the recursion theorem the function $g$ can be extended to a function $f = j\alpha\beta k 0^\infty \in U_1$. Since $f =_n g$, we have $S(f^n) = S(g^n) = i$. Furthermore, since $\varphi_i \subseteq g$ and $g \subset f$, we get $\varphi_i \subset f$. But $S(f^n) = i$ and $\varphi_i \subset f$ where $f \in U$, contradicts condition (2) of a CEX-strategy. Consequently, the function $f$ cannot be $\text{CEX}_\varphi$-identified by the strategy $S$.  Q.E.D.

Theorem 27 and its proof have several consequences concerning limitations of the power of TCONF and CEX.

**Corollary 28** TCONF $\subset$ EX.

Thus, the natural way of temporarily conform identification is not of universal power for identifying all classes from EX (or even from CONS) though the spaces of hypotheses, i.e. the numberings with respect to which the identification must be done, can be chosen in an appropriate way. More exactly: For any class $U \notin$ TCONF and for any numbering $\psi$ such that $U \subseteq P_\psi$, there are infinitely many functions $f \in U$ such that $\psi_i \subset f$ for some $i < \min_\psi f$. This follows easily from Theorem 8 and Corollary 28. The resulting danger of "undergeneralization" turns out to be a real one not only for any temporarily conform strategy but also for any strategy at all working with convergently incorrect intermediate hypotheses, only.

Note that Theorem 27 as well as Corollary 28 disprove the following conjecture in (Fulk, 1990):

For every class $U \in$ EX and any numbering $\varphi \in G$, there exists an effective sequence of programs $p_0, p_1, \ldots$ such that for all $i \neq j$, $\varphi_{p_i}$ and $\varphi_{p_j}$ differ convergently and $U \subseteq \{\varphi_{p_i} \mid i \in N\}$.

Actually, let $\psi_i = \varphi_{p_i}$ for any $i$. Then it immediately follows from the conjecture that $U \in$ TCONF$_\psi$(TC$_\psi$). Hence EX = TCONF, a contradiction.

**Corollary 29**
(1) EX$_1 \not\subseteq$ CEX.
(2) CONS $\not\subseteq$ CEX.
(3) CONS $\not\subseteq$ TCONF.
(4) CONF $\not\subseteq$ TCONF.

In Section 4 we have seen that identification with *convergently* incorrect intermediate hypotheses, only, is not of universal power for identifying all classes from EX. Consequently, in order to achieve universal power the dual type of *divergently* incorrect intermediate hypotheses has to be permitted. In the next section we study the case that *only* such hypotheses are allowed.

# 5. Identification with divergently incorrect intermediate hypotheses

The dual case to that considered in Sections 3 and 4 consists in that the strategy is allowed to output only such incorrect intermediate hypotheses which differ *divergently* from the function to be identified, DEX-identification. Consequently, any such hypothesis describes a proper subfunction of the unknown function.

In this section we present some results concerning the strength of this approach of identification. Then we state that it coincides with the type of monotonic identification from (Jantke, 1991). From this result we derive a considerable weakness of identification with divergently incorrect intermediate hypotheses. Finally, we present a numbering-theoretic characterization of DEX which to some extent answers the question how in general strategies can work when they are allowed to produce only hypotheses describing subfunctions of the functions to be identified.

**Definition 30** Let $U \subseteq R$ and let $\psi$ be any numbering. $U$ is called identifiable with respect to $\psi$ *with divergently incorrect intermediate hypotheses* iff there is $S \in P$ such that
1) $U \in$ EX$_\psi(S)$,
2) for any $f \in U$ and any $n \in N$, if $\psi_{S(f^n)} \neq f$, then $\psi_{S(f^n)}$ and $f$ differ divergently.

Let
DEX$_\psi = \{U \mid U$ is identifiable with respect to $\psi$ with divergently incorrect intermediate hypotheses$\}$,
DEX = $\bigcup_{\psi \in P^2}$ DEX$_\psi$.

In order to demonstrate the power of DEX we need the definition of one more type of identification, finite identification.

**Definition 31** Let $U \subseteq R$. $U$ is called *finitely* identifiable iff there is a numbering $\psi$ and $S \in P$ such that for any $f \in U$, there is $n \in N$ with
1) $S(f^x) = ?$ for any $x < n$,
2) $S(f^n) \in N$ and $\psi_{S(f^n)} = f$.

Here "?" is a special symbol the output of which can be interpreted as saying by the strategy "I don't know yet". It is required that the first "real" hypothesis be a correct $\psi$-number for the function $f$.

Let
FIN $= \{U \mid U$ is finitely identifiable$\}$.

**Theorem 32**
(1) FIN $\subset$ DEX.
(2) DEX $-$ CEX $\neq \emptyset$.
(3) DEX $-\bigcup_{m \in N}$EX$^m \neq \emptyset$.

Thus, in spite of the strong demand on the hypotheses the approach of identification with divergently incorrect intermediate hypotheses is of remarkable power.

On the other hand, this approach has also its weaknesses, as it will follow from Theorem 34 below.

**Definition 33** (Jantke, 1991) Let $U \subseteq R$ and let $\psi$ be any numbering. $U$ is called *monotonically* identifiable with respect to $\psi$ iff there is $S \in P$ such that
1) $U \in$ EX$_\psi(S)$,
2) for any $f \in U$ and any $n \in N$, $\psi_{S(f^n)} \subseteq \psi_{S(f^{n+1})}$.

Hence a function is identified monotonically if the hypotheses produced by the strategy converge monotonically to the unknown function.

Let
MON$_\psi = \{U \mid U$ is monotonically identifiable with respect to $\psi\}$,
MON $= \bigcup_{\psi \in P^2}$MON$_\psi$.

**Theorem 34** DEX $=$ MON.

In (Jantke, 1991) it is shown that for any class $U \in$ MON, $U$ does not contain any accumulation point. A function $g \in R$ is called an *accumulation point* of $U \subseteq R$ iff for any $n \in N$, there is $f \in U$ such that $f =_n g$ and $f \neq g$.
Let us call a class $U \subseteq R$ *discrete* iff $U$ does not contain any of its accumulation points. Then we get immediately the following result.

**Corollary 35** For any class $U \in$ DEX, $U$ is discrete.

It follows easily that CEX and DEX are incomparable.

**Corollary 36** CEX and DEX are incomparable.

Since there are many classes $U \in$ EX containing some of their accumulation points or even consisting of accumulation points only, by Corollary 35 all these classes are not identifiable with divergently incorrect intermediate hypotheses. Hence, obviously, DEX $\subset$ EX. However, we get a stronger result which is tight in some sense.

**Theorem 37** DEX $\subset$ CONF.

Note that Theorem 37 is tight in that DEX $\subseteq$ CONS is not valid. This follows from (Jantke, 1991) where MON and CONS are shown to be incomparable. Hence, via Theorem 34, DEX and CONS are incomparable.

Finally, we derive a numbering-theoretic characterization of DEX.

**Theorem 38** $U \in$ DEX iff there is a numbering $\psi$ such that
(1) $U \subseteq P_\psi$,
(2) there is $d \in R$ such that for any $f \in U$,
$I_f := \{i \mid \psi_i =_{d(i)} f\}$ is finite, and
for any $i, j \in I_f$, if $d(i) \leq d(j)$ then $\psi_i \subseteq \psi_j \subseteq f$.

The proof of the sufficiency of Theorem 38 points out a general way of successful work of DEX-strategies. The main problem for these strategies is to detect that an actual hypothesis, say $i$, is incorrect for the function $f$ to be identified with respect to the underlying numbering $\psi$. Actually, this implies $\psi_i$ being a proper subfunction of $f$. But this cannot be recognized by computing $\psi_i$ at the divergent arguments. Moreover, this cannot be recognized by solving the halting problem in $\psi$ directly, since in general the halting problem in $\psi$ is undecidable. The solution suggested by the sufficiency proof of Theorem 38 consists in the following. Intuitively, the strategy changes its hypothesis if it finds an alternative hypothesis which coincides with the unknown function on a "much larger" initial segment than the actual hypothesis seems to do. Note that the existence of such an alternative hypothesis does not prove that the former one is really incorrect (this contrasts with the sufficiency proof of Lemma 43 below). Nevertheless, if the underlying numbering $\psi$ possesses the properties (1) and (2) above, then the strategy's behavior described leads to successful DEX-identification.

# 6. Alternations of convergently and divergently incorrect intermediate hypotheses

In the previous sections we have seen that universal power, i.e. identification of all classes from EX, cannot be achieved by allowing either convergently or divergently incorrect intermediate hypotheses alone. Hence, in order to identify any class from EX both types of hypotheses must be available to the strategies. More exactly, we will see that only an arbitrary finite number of alternations of these dual types of hypotheses can guarantee universal power of identification.

Let $\psi$ be any numbering and let $f \in R$.

Define
$C_{\psi,f} = \{i \mid \psi_i$ and $f$ differ convergently$\}$,
$D_{\psi,f} = \{i \mid \psi_i$ and $f$ differ divergently$\}$.

**Definition 39** Let $U \subseteq R$, $\psi$ be any numbering and $a \in N$. $U$ is called identifiable with respect to $\psi$ *after no more than $a$ alternations* iff there is $S \in P$ such that
1) $U \in EX_\psi(S)$,
2) for any $f \in U$, $\text{card}\{n \mid (S(f^n) \in C_{\psi,f}$ & $S(f^{n+1}) \in D_{\psi,f})$ or $(S(f^n) \in D_{\psi,f}$ & $S(f^{n+1}) \in C_{\psi,f})\} \leq a$.

Let
$\text{AEX}^a_\psi = \{U \mid U$ is identifiable with respect to $\psi$ after no more than $a$ alternations$\}$,
$\text{AEX}^a = \bigcup_{\psi \in P^2} \text{AEX}^a_\psi$.

**Theorem 40**
$\text{CEX} \cup \text{DEX} = \text{AEX}^0 \subset \text{AEX}^1 \subset \ldots \subset \text{AEX}^b \subset \text{AEX}^{b+1} \subset \ldots \subset \bigcup_{a \in N}\text{AEX}^a \subset \text{EX}$.

# 7. Identification with verifiably incorrect intermediate hypotheses

In Sections 3 and 4 we have shown that a natural approach to provide inference strategies with the ability to discover their errors is not always realizable. Actually, it turned out that, for some classes from EX, there is no strategy proving its incorrect hypotheses to be incorrect by exhibiting a point of convergent difference between the hypothesis function and the function to be identified. Naturally the question arises whether a *universal* method of proving the incorrectness of incorrect hypotheses does exist at all. In this section we will answer this question affirmatively.

A first attempt to make this problem mathematically precise could consist in the following. Let $U \subseteq R$ and $\psi \in P^2$. Call $U$ identifiable with respect to $\psi$ by a strategy $S$ equipped with an incorrectness prover iff $U \in EX_\psi(S)$, and there is an incorrectness prover inc $\in P$ such that, for any $f \in U$ and any $n \in N$, $\psi_{S(f^n)} \neq f$ iff $\text{inc}(S(f^n)) = 1$.

But this definition seems to be unrealistic, in general. The incorrectness prover should be allowed to take into account *further* values of $f$, i.e., $f^m$ for some $m \geq n$, in order to prove the incorrectness of $S(f^n)$ (if any).

**Definition 41** Let $U \subseteq R$ and let $\psi$ be any numbering. $U$ is called identifiable with respect to $\psi$ *with verifiably incorrect intermediate hypotheses* iff there is $S \in P$ such that

(1) $U \in \mathrm{EX}_\psi(S)$,

(2) there is $inc \in P$ such that, for any $f \in U$ and any $n \in N$, $\psi_{S(f^n)} \neq f$ iff there is $m \geq n$ such that $inc(S(f^n), f^m) = 1$.

Note that no requirement is made that the incorrectness prover should be able to determine whether an incorrect hypothesis differs convergently or divergently from the function to be identified.

Let
$\mathrm{VEX}_\psi = \{U \mid U$ is identifiable with respect to $\psi$ with verifiably incorrect intermediate hypotheses$\}$,
$\mathrm{VEX} = \bigcup_{\psi \in P^2} \mathrm{VEX}_\psi$.

As our next result shows, any class from EX can be identified with verifiably incorrect intermediate hypotheses.

**Theorem 42** $\mathrm{VEX} = \mathrm{EX}$.

*Proof of Theorem 42.*
$\mathrm{VEX} \subseteq \mathrm{EX}$ is obvious.
In order to show $\mathrm{EX} \subseteq \mathrm{VEX}$ we need a result which was proved in (Wiehagen, 1978b).

**Lemma 43** $U \in \mathrm{EX}$ iff there is a numbering $\psi \in P^2$ such that
(1) $U \subseteq P_\psi$,
(2) there is $d \in R$ such that, for any $i, j \in N$ with $i \neq j, \psi_i \neq_{d(i,j)} \psi_j$.

Hence, for any different $\psi$-indices $i$ and $j$, the "discriminating function" $d$ computes an upper bound of some argument $x$ such that $\psi_i(x) \neq \psi_j(x)$. Note that $\psi_i$ and $\psi_j$ may differ convergently or divergently.

*Proof of Lemma 43.*
Necessity. Let $U \in \mathrm{EX}$. Let $\varphi \in P^2$ be any numbering and let $S \in P$ be any strategy such that $U \in \mathrm{EX}_\varphi(S)$. Assume without loss of generality that $S \in R$.
Let $Z = \{(z, n) \mid z, n \in N \ \& \ \forall x \leq n(\varphi_z(x)$ is defined$) \ \& \ S(\varphi_z^{n-1}) \neq S(\varphi_z^n) = z\}$.

Intuitively, the set $Z$ contains all the initial segments $\varphi_z^n$ of functions $\varphi_z$ such that, on $\varphi_z^n$, the strategy $S$ produces its final hypothesis on $\varphi_z$. Let $Z$ be recursively enumerated without repetitions (the case that $Z$ is a finite set and, consequently, $U$ is finite, is trivial) by a computable, total function $e$. In order to define the desired numbering $\varphi$ let $i \in N$. Let $e(i) = (z, n)$. Let $g \in R$ be an auxiliary function defined as $g(i) = n$. Define

$$
\psi_i(x) = \begin{cases}
\varphi_z(x), & \text{if } x \leq n \\
\varphi_z(x), & \text{if } x > n \text{ and, for any } y \text{ such that } n < y \leq x, \text{ both } \varphi_z(y) \text{ is} \\
& \text{defined and } S(\varphi_z^y) = z \\
\text{undefined}, & \text{otherwise.}
\end{cases}
$$

Finally, let $d(i, j) = \max(g(i), g(j))$. Then (1) and (2) can easily be shown.

Sufficiency. Let the numbering $\psi$ and the discriminating function $d$ be given such that (1) and (2) hold. Then a strategy $S \in P$ identifying any function $f \in U$ with respect to $\psi$ works as follows.

Go to stage 0.

Stage $i$. Output the $\psi$-number $i$ as actual hypothesis.
Check whether there is $j > i$ such that $\psi_j =_{d(i,j)} f$ in which case go to stage $i + 1$.

We will show that, on any function $f \in U$, the strategy $S$ produces a sequence of hypotheses of the following structure:

$$
0, 0, 0, \ldots, 1, 1, 1, \ldots, 2, 2, 2, \ldots, (\min_\psi f)^\infty. \tag{$*$}
$$

Therefore let $i$ denote the actual hypothesis produced by $S$ on $f$ and let $i < \min_\psi f$. Clearly, there is $j > i$, namely $j = \min_\psi f$, such that $\psi_j =_{d(i,j)} f$. Hence, eventually, $S$ changes its mind from $i$ to $i + 1$. Moreover, the existence of a number $j$ such that $\psi_j =_{d(i,j)} f$ yields $\psi_i \neq f$. Indeed, from $\psi_i \neq_{d(i,j)} \psi_j$, cf. (2), and $\psi_j =_{d(i,j)} f$ it follows immediately that $\psi_i \neq_{d(i,j)} f$; hence $\psi_i \neq f$. Consequently, the strategy $S$ will eventually reach stage $i = \min_\psi f$. On the other hand, it will never leave this stage, since in that case $\psi_i \neq f$ would follow as above, a contradiction to $\psi_i = \psi_{\min_\psi f} = f$. This proves($*$). Q.E.D. Lemma 43

Now let $U \in$ EX. Let $\psi \in P^2$ and $d \in R$ be given according to Lemma 43. Let $S \in P$ be the strategy from the sufficiency proof of Lemma 43.

Then define
$inc(S(f^n), f^m) = 1$ iff there is $j > S(f^n)$ such that $d(S(f^n), j) \leq m$ and $\psi_j =_{d(S(f^n),j)} f$.

Obviously, the strategy $S$ identifies the class $U$ with respect to the numbering $\psi$ with verifiably incorrect intermediate hypotheses using the incorrectness verifier $inc$. Hence EX $\subseteq$ VEX. Q.E.D.

Intuitively, the incorrectness verifier of Theorem 42 works as follows. In order to disprove a hypothesis $i := S(f^n)$ it searches for a $\psi$-number $j$ such that $\psi_j$ coincides with $f$ "much more" than $\psi_i$ seems to do. Condition (2) of Lemma 43 then guarantees that finding $j$ really implies $\psi_i \neq f$. Thus, via Lemma 43, the intuitive idea behind Theorem 38, the characterization of DEX, can be generalized in an appropriate way to any class from EX even yielding the necessary incorrectness proofs.

Finally, we want to derive explicitly that the existence of an incorrectness verifier is equivalent to the existence of a strategy never changing its mind after having produced a correct hypothesis.

**Definition 44** Let $U \subseteq R$ and let $\psi$ be any numbering. $U$ is called *semantically finitely* identifiable with respect to $\psi$ iff there is $S \in P$ such that
1) $U \in EX_\psi(S)$,
2) for any $f \in U$ and any $n \in N$, if $\psi_{S(f^n)} = f$, then, for any $m \geq n, S(f^m) = S(f^n)$.

Let
$SFEX_\psi = \{U \mid U$ is semantically finitely identifiable with respect to $\psi\}$,
$SFEX = \bigcup_{\psi \in P^2} SFEX_\psi$.

Recall that it is not evident that any identifiable class is even semantically finitely identifiable, since, of course, the relation $\psi_{S(f^n)} = f$, i.e., the correctness of a hypothesis, is undecidable, in general.

**Theorem 45** SFEX = VEX.

**Corollary 46** SFEX = EX.

Note that in an analogous manner for various identification types $I$ among them $I$ = CONS, DEX one can show that SFI = I. Hence, for any of these types, there is a uniform and universal method to prove the incorrectness of incorrect intermediate hypotheses.

# 8. Conclusions

In inductive inference one natural way to detect that the actual hypothesis is incorrect consists in finding out some argument at which the hypothesis is defined and differs from the function to be identified. Since several well-known and powerful strategies are working just in this manner, we were interested in characterizing the genereal power of this approach of identification with convergently incorrect intermediate hypotheses, CEX-identification.

We started with a particular realization of CEX-identification, the temporarily conform identification. A temporarily conform strategy takes always the minimal hypothesis which does not contradict the unknown function on the initial segment seen so far within a given time bound. We gave a pure numbering-theoretic characterization of temporarily conform identification. This characterization yields a better understanding of the danger of "undergeneralization" in temporarily conform identification. Furthermore, the extremely limited possibilities of Gödel numberings for temporarily conform identification are easily derived. On the other hand, using suitable non-Gödel numberings as spaces of hypotheses temporarily conform identification can be shown to be strictly more powerful than several established identification types.

Then we stated that CEX-identification and temporarily conform identification are of the same power. This enabled us to show that CEX-identification (hence temporarily conform identification, too) is not of universal power, CEX ⊂ EX, which disproves a conjecture by M. Fulk.

Consequently, inductive inference has also to take into consideration the dual type of intermediate hypotheses which only differ divergently from the function to be identified, hence describing proper subfunctions of them, DEX-identification.

We compared DEX-identification with other identification types among them CEX establishing incomparability in the latter case. Again we derived a numbering-theoretic characterization of DEX-identification which yields a way of how DEX-strategies can work in general. Furthermore, DEX-identification turned out to coincide in power with monotonic identification. This implies that DEX-identification is also not of universal power.

We then presented a hierarchy result from which it follows immediately that universal power can be achieved only by allowing an unbounded finite number of alternations of CEX-style and DEX-style hypotheses. Note that there is some analogy between this alternation's hierarchy and the Kleene-Mostowski hierarchy. It seems to be interesting to study the corresponding problems in more detail.

The results above lead to the question whether or not there is a uniform and universal method which would enable inductive inference strategies to discover their errors. We gave an affirmative answer to this question for all EX-identifiable function classes. Any such class $U$ can be embedded into a suitably constructed numbering $\psi$ such that while identifying $f \in U$ with respect to $\psi$, a strategy is able to prove the incorrectness of a hypotheses $i$ by finding out an "alternative hypotheses" $j$ such that $\psi_j$ coincides with $f$ on an initial segment the length of which can be computed only from $i$ and $j$. If $i$ is really incorrect, then such a $j$ does always exist and, consequently, $j$ can effectively be found. Note that though $\psi_j$ coincides with the function $f$ to be identified "very much", the index $j$ will *not* be used as the next hypothesis produced by the strategy. Instead the existence of $j$ will be used as a proof of the incorrectness of the current hypothesis $i$, i.e., $\psi_i \neq f$. Observe that this approach does always succeed independently of whether $\psi_i$ differs convergently or divergently from $f$. We will not exclude that the ideas behind this method of checking the incorrectness of programs can also be applied in the field of program verification.

# Acknowledgements

We would like to thank Mark Fulk for suggesting the definition of temporarily conform identification.

The research of the two first authors was supported by the grant No. 93.599 from the Latvian Science Council.

The third author was supported by the German "Bundesministerium für Forschung und Technologie" under Grant GOSLER 01 IW 101 B9 and E7.

# References

ANGLUIN, D. (1980), Inductive inference of formal languages from positive data, *Information and Control* 45; 117–135.

ANGLUIN, D., and SMITH, C. H. (1983), Inductive inference: Theory and methods, *Computing Surveys* 15, 237–269.

BARZDIN, J. (1971), Complexity and frequency solution of some algorithmically unsolvable problems, Doct. Diss., Novosibirsk State Univ. (Russian).

BARZDIN, J. (1974), Inductive inference of automata, functions and programs, *in* "Proceedings, International Congress of Mathematicians" pp.455–460.

BARZDIN, J., and FREIVALDS, R. (1972), On the prediction of general recursive functions, *Soviet Math. Dokl.* 13, 1224–1228.

BARZDIN, J., and FREIVALDS, R. (1974), Prediction and limit synthesis of recursively enumerable function classes, *Theory of algorithms and programs,* vol. 1, 100–111 (Russian).

BLUM, L., and BLUM, M. (1975), Toward a mathematical theory of inductive inference, *Information and Control* 28, 125–155.

CASE, J., and NGO MANGUELLE, S. (1979), Refinements of inductive inference by Popperian machines, Technical Report Nr. 152, Dept. of Computer Science, State Univ. of New York at Buffalo.

CASE, J., and SMITH, C. (1983), Comparison of identification criteria for machine inductive inference, *Theoretical Computer Science* 25, 193–220.

FREIVALDS, R., and BARZDIN, J. (1975), Relations between predictability and identifiability in the limit, *Theory of algorithms and programs,* vol.2, 26–34 (Russian).

FREIVALDS, R., KINBER, E. B., and WIEHAGEN, R. (199x), How inductive inference strategies discover their errors, *Information and Computation* (to appear)

FULK, M. A. (1988), Saving the phenomena: Requirements that inductive inference machines not contradict known data, *Information and Computation* 79, 193–209.

FULK, M. A. (1990), Robust separations in inductive inference, *in* "Proceedings, 31st IEEE Symposium on Foundations of Computer Science" pp.405–410.

FULK, M. A. (1991), personal communication to R. Wiehagen.

GOLD, E. M. (1967), Language identification in the limit, *Information and Control* 10, 447–474.

JANTKE, K. P. (1991), Monotonic and non-monotonic inductive inference, *New Generation Computing* 8, 349–360.

KLETTE, R., and WIEHAGEN, R. (1980), Research in the theory of inductive inference by GDR mathematicians—a survey, *Information Sciences* 22, 149–169.

KUMMER, M. (1992), personal communication to E. B. Kinber.

OSHERSON, D. N., STOB, M., and WEINSTEIN, S. (1986), "Systems that learn: An introduction to learning theory for cognitive and computer scientists", MIT Press, Cambridge, Mass.

PODNIEKS, K. (1974), Comparing various types of limit synthesis and prediction of functions, *Theory of algorithms and programs*, vol.1, 68–81 (Russian).

POPPER, K. (1968), "The logic of scientific discovery", 2nd ed. Harper Torch, New York.

ROGERS, H. (1967), "Theory of recursive functions and effective computability", McGraw-Hill, New York.

"Theory of algorithms and programs", vol.1, 2, 3 (1974, 1975, 1977), J. Barzdin, Ed., Latvian State Univ., Riga (Russian).

WIEHAGEN, R. (1976), Limes-Erkennung rekursiver Funktionen durch spezielle Strategien, *Elektronische Informationsverarbeitung und Kybernetik* 12, 93–99 (German).

WIEHAGEN, R. (1978a), Zur Theorie der algorithmischen Erkennung, Diss. B, Sektion Mathematik, Humboldt-Univ. Berlin (German).

WIEHAGEN, R. (1978b) Characterization problems in the theory of inductive inference, *in* "Proceedings, Int. Coll. on Automata, Languages and Programming", G. Ausiello, C. Böhm, Eds., *Lecture Notes in Computer Science* 62, 494–508.

WIEHAGEN, R. (1991), A thesis in inductive inference, *in* "Proceedings, First International Workshop Nonmonotonic and Inductive Logic" 1990, J. Dix, K. P. Jantke, P. Schmitt, Eds., *Lecture Notes in Artificial Intelligence* 543, 184–207.

WIEHAGEN, R., and ZEUGMANN, T. (1994), Ignoring data may be the only way to learn efficiently, *Journal of Experimental and Theoretical Artificial Intelligence* 6, 131–144.

# Learning From Good Examples

Rūsiņš Freivalds and Efim B. Kinber[*]

Institute of Mathematics and Computer Science

University of Latvia

Raiņa bulvāris 29, LV-1459 Riga, Latvia

## Rolf Wiehagen

Department of Computer Science

University of Kaiserslautern

P.O.Box 3049, D-67653 Kaiserslautern, Germany

### Abstract

The usual information in inductive inference for the purposes of learning an unknown recursive function $f$ is the set of *all* input/output examples $(n, f(n))$, $n \in \mathbb{N}$. In contrast to this approach we show that it is considerably more powerful to work with *finite* sets of "good" examples even when these good examples are required to be effectively computable. The influence of the underlying numberings, with respect to which the learning problem has to be solved, to the capabilities of inference from good examples is also investigated. It turns out that nonstandard numberings can be much more powerful than Gödel numberings.

We then show that similar effects can be achieved for learning pattern languages and finite automata from good examples in polynomial time essentially using the "structure" of these objects. Here the number of the good examples is *polynomially bounded* by the size of the objects to be learnt (length of pattern, number of states, respectively).

# 1 Introduction

We present a phenomenon which was discovered in pure recursion-theoretic inductive inference, namely learning from good examples, cf. (Freivalds, Kinber and Wiehagen, 1989) and (Freivalds, Kinber and Wiehagen, 1993).

The main problem in recursion-theoretic inductive inference is the following. Let $f$ be any recursive function, and let $\psi$ be any numbering of some class of partial recursive functions containing $f$. Then the task is to synthesize an index (a "program") of $f$ with respect to $\psi$ solely from the sequence $((n, f(n))_{n \in N}$. Thus, an inductive inference strategy can use the sequence of *all* input/output examples of the unknown function

---

[*]Current address: Department of Computer and Information Science, University of Delaware, Newark, Delaware 19716

as standard information. In the sequel we refer to this approach as inductive inference from all examples (abbreviated: aex-inference).

In this paper we investigate inductive inference from "good" examples (abbreviated: gex-inference). Informally, good examples
– are considerably less examples than all examples, but they are "important",
– can be computed effectively from the objects to be learnt,
– are intended to be sufficient for learning rich classes of objects.
In gex-inference of recursive functions only *finitely many* examples are allowed as good examples. Hence, formally, a gex-inference strategy misses almost all examples in comparison with an aex-inference strategy. Nevertheless, it turns out that from good examples considerably more classes of recursive functions can be learnt than from all examples. Consequently, gex-inference is much more powerful than aex-inference.

Now it is natural to ask where this additional power comes from. A preliminary answer for gex-inference of recursive functions is that this power comes from two sources. It comes from the knowledge of the function to be learnt when computing the good examples to that function. And, in a sense simultaneously, it comes from the possibility to build the "space of hypotheses" $\psi$ in such a manner that the good examples allow to learn $f$ just with respect to that numbering $\psi$. Note that the additional power does *not* come from some "artificial tricks" of encoding an index of $f$ into the good examples. We shall come back to the latter problem after presenting the formal definition of learning from good examples.

Another reasonable question is whether a similar effect of increasing the power when providing the learning strategy with good examples only, can be exhibited for other object classes which should even be learnt in polynomial time. We give an affirmative answer to this question by stating finite ("one shot") learnability of
– the class of all pattern languages,
– a class of "almost all" finite automata
in polynomial time from good examples. Here the good examples are also computable in polynomial time, and hence their number is bounded by a polynomial in the size (length of the pattern, number of states of the automaton) of the object to be learnt. But in contrast to gex-inference of recursive functions now the "structure" of the objects to be learnt will be used in order to compute the good examples. As a consequence the corresponding learning strategies build their hypotheses "constructively" from these good examples, whereas the strategies for learning recursive functions from good examples typically find their hypotheses by an enumerative search through the space of hypotheses.

The paper is organized as follows. Section 2 gives notation, definitions and some basic results concerning aex-inference of recursive functions. Section 3 presents the approach of inductive inference of recursive functions from good examples. In Section 4 we deal with learning of objects "with structure" in polynomial time from good examples. Finally, in Section 5 we discuss the results obtained.

# 2  Preliminaries

$\mathbb{N} = \{0, 1, 2, \ldots\}$ denotes the set of natural numbers. The set of all finite sequences of natural numbers is denoted by $\mathbb{N}^*$. For a finite set $A$, let $card(A)$ denote the number of elements of $A$.

The classes of all partial recursive, recursive functions of one, two arguments are denoted by $P$, $P^2$, $R$, $R^2$, respectively.

A function $\psi \in P^2$ is called a numbering. We write $\psi_i$ instead of $\lambda x \psi(i, x)$. Let $P_\psi = \{\psi_i \mid i \in \mathbb{N}\}$ denote the class of all partial recursive functions enumerated by $\psi$, and let $R_\psi = P_\psi \cap R$. A numbering $\varphi \in P^2$ is called a Gödel numbering, cf. (Rogers, 1967) iff $P_\varphi = P$ and, for any numbering $\psi \in P^2$, there is $c \in R$ such that, for any $i \in \mathbb{N}, \psi_i = \varphi_{c(i)}$. Let $G$ denote the set of all Gödel numberings.

For a function $f \in R$ and $n \in \mathbb{N}$, let $f^n = cod(f(0), f(1), \ldots, f(n))$ where $cod$ denotes an effective and bijective mapping from $\mathbb{N}^*$ onto $\mathbb{N}$.

We now define three basic types of inductive inference of recursive functions.

**Definition 1** Let $U \subseteq R$ and let $\psi \in P^2$ be any numbering.
$U$ is called *finitely* learnable with respect to $\psi$ iff
there is a strategy $S \in P$ such that, for any function $f \in U$, there is $n \in \mathbb{N}$ such that
    (1) for all $x < n$, $S(f^x) = ?$,
    (2) $\psi_{S(f^n)} = f$.

Here ? is a special symbol the output of which can be interpreted as saying by the learning strategy $S$ "I don't know yet." It is required that the first "real" hypothesis ("one shot") be a correct $\psi$-program for the function $f$.
    Let
    $\text{FIN}_\psi = \{U \mid U \text{ is finitely learnable with respect to } \psi\}$,
    $\text{FIN} = \bigcup_{\psi \in P^2} \text{FIN}_\psi$.
    Finite learnability was introduced in (Gold, 1967). The reader is also referred to (Freivalds, 1979), (Jain and Sharma, 1990) and (Daley, Pitt, Velauthapillai and Will, 1991).

**Definition 2** Let $U \subseteq R$ and let $\psi \in P^2$ be any numbering.
$U$ is called learnable *in the limit* with respect to $\psi$ iff
there is a strategy $S \in P$ such that, for any function $f \in U$, there is $i \in \mathbb{N}$ such that
    (1) $\psi_i = f$,
    (2) $S(f^n) = i$ for almost all $n \in \mathbb{N}$.

Thus the sequence of hypotheses produced by the strategy $S$ on the function $f$ converges to a correct $\psi$-program of $f$. We note that no restriction is made that we should be able to algorithmically determine whether the sequence of hypotheses has already stabilized. It is easy to see that such a restriction would lead to the concept of finite learning.
    Define
    $\text{LIM}_\psi = \{U \mid U \text{ is learnable in the limit with respect to } \psi\}$,
    $\text{LIM} = \bigcup_{\psi \in P^2} \text{LIM}_\psi$.
    As to some fundamental papers concerning learnability in the limit the reader is referred to (Gold, 1967), (Blum and Blum, 1975) and (Case and Smith, 1983).

**Definition 3** Let $U \subseteq R$ and let $\psi \in P^2$ be any numbering.
$U$ is called *behaviorally correct* learnable with respect to $\psi$ iff
there is a strategy $S \in P$ such that, for any function $f \in U$ and for almost all $n \in \mathbb{N}$,
$\psi_{S(f^n)} = f$.

Thus on the function $f$ the strategy $S$ produces a sequence of $\psi$-programs almost all
of which compute $f$.
  Define
  $BC_\psi = \{U \mid U$ is behaviorally correct learnable with respect to $\psi\}$,
  $BC = \bigcup_{\psi \in P^2} BC_\psi$.
  Behaviorally correct learnability was studied among others in (Barzdin, 1974),
(Podnieks, 1974) and (Case and Smith, 1983).

In (Barzdin, 1974), (Podnieks, 1974) and (Case and Smith, 1983) the following theorem was proved giving an insight into the possibilities of finite, limit and behaviorally
correct inference. Here $pR$ denotes the set of all subsets of $R$.

**Theorem 4** $FIN \subset LIM \subset BC \subset pR$.

Another remarkable fact about aex-inference is pointed out by the following obvious
lemma.

**Lemma 5** Let $I \in \{FIN, LIM, BC\}$. Then, for any $\varphi \in G, I = I_\varphi$.

  Hence, if a function class is aex-inferable at all, then it is always aex-inferable
with respect to an arbitrary Gödel numbering. In this sense Gödel numberings are
the "most powerful" numberings for aex-inference. Moreover, this seems to imply
that the only kind of numberings which are "interesting" for inductive inference are
just the Gödel numberings. However, we are convinced that in this strong sense this
implication is not justified even for aex-inference. In (Freivalds, Kinber and Wiehagen,
1982) it is shown that one-one numberings, a special kind of non-Gödel numberings,
are very helpful in characterizing the function classes from FIN and LIM in terms
of pure numbering theory. In (Freivalds, Kinber and Wiehagen, 1988) it is shown
that probabilistic inference strategies may have extreme advantages over deterministic
ones for FIN, LIM-, BC-learning just with respect to suitable non-Gödel numberings.
Moreover, below we shall see that also for gex-inference, which we will define now,
non-Gödel numberings can be more powerful than Gödel numberings.

For survey papers on inductive inference the reader is referred to (Barzdin, ed., 1974,
1975, 1977), (Klette and Wiehagen, 1980), (Anguin and Smith, 1983) and (Osherson,
Stob and Weinstein, 1986).

# 3   Inductive inference from good examples

The idea of inductive inference of recursive functions from good examples is to use
*finite* sets of "well chosen" examples instead of the infinite sets of *all* examples to
learn the unknown functions.

**Definition 6** (Freivalds, Kinber and Wiehagen, 1989, 1993)

Let $U \subseteq R$ and let $\psi \in P^2$ be any numbering.

$U$ is called *finitely learnable from good examples* with respect to $\psi$ iff there is a numbering $ex \in P^2$, a strategy $S \in P$, and a function $z \in P$ such that $U \subseteq P_\psi$ and, for any $i \in \mathbb{N}$ with $\psi_i \in U$,

(1) $ex_i$ is a finite subfunction of $\psi_i$, $z(i)$ is defined, and $z(i) = card(ex_i)$,

(2) for any finite subfunction $\varepsilon$ of $\psi_i$, $\psi_{S(ex_i \cup \varepsilon)} = \psi_i$.

Let us neglect the $\varepsilon$ for a moment, i.e., take the special case $\varepsilon = \emptyset$. Then it follows from condition (2) above that, for any function $\psi_i$ from the class $U$, the strategy $S$ "finitely" produces a correct $\psi$-program of $\psi_i$ (which may be different from $i$) solely from $ex_i$, the finite set of good examples.

Furthermore it follows from condition (1) that, for any $i$ such that $\psi_i \in U$, $ex_i$ is effectively computable from $i$.

The $\varepsilon$ we need in order to avoid "unfair coding tricks" such as $ex_i = \{(i, \psi_i(i))\}$ or $card(ex_i) = i$ which would lead to trivial learning of the whole class $R$. Note that bounding $card(\varepsilon)$ uniformly would not suffice to avoid such tricks, (Nessel, 1993).

On the other hand, in "real life" it seems to be seldom to get such a pure set $ex_i$ of good examples. Often one gets additional correct, but non-necessary information (just the $\varepsilon$) and then one has to deal with the union of all the information, yielding another interpretation of the $\varepsilon$ in the definition above. But note that the inference strategy receives exclusively the examples from $ex_i \cup \varepsilon$ in order to learn the function $\psi_i$.

A possible scenario of learning from good examples is the relationship between teacher and pupil. As a rule the teacher will not tell the pupil only the correct and final answer, and s/he will not present her/him all s/he knows about the phenomenon to be learnt, say $\psi_i(0), \psi_i(1), \psi_i(2), \ldots$. Actually, s/he will offer some typical information, just "good examples", in order to enable the pupil to learn the unknown phenomenon by processing the good examples.

Other authors have also dealt with (variations of) the approach above.

(Shinohara and Miyano, 1991) consider the problem of teaching from a finite set of examples. However, they do not require that these examples be effectively computable and that the learner be successful for any finite superset of these examples.

(Motoki, 1991) and (Baliga, Case and Jain, 1993) study language learning from positive data and some (finite) number of negative data. The negative data are not required to be computable and in addition to them the learning strategy is provided with all positive data.

The approach in (Goldman and Mathias, 1993) is essentially the same as ours. Furthermore, for some formal definition of "unfair coding trick", there called collusion, they formally prove that this approach avoids collusion.

We will use the following abbreviations:

GEX-FIN$_\psi = \{U | U$ is finitely learnable from good examples with respect to $\psi\}$,

GEX-FIN $= \bigcup_{\psi \in P^2}$ GEX-FIN$_\psi$.

For the proofs of the results of this section the reader is referred to (Freivalds, Kinber and Wiehagen, 1993).

Our first result shows that all enumerable classes of recursive functions are finitely learnable from good examples with respect to suitably chosen numberings. Therefore, let

$$\text{NUM} = \{R_\psi | \psi \in R^2\}$$

denote the family of all enumerable classes of recursive functions. It is well-known that NUM is not contained in FIN (more exactly, NUM and FIN are set-theoretically incomparable, cf. (Klette and Wiehagen, 1980)), whereas it follows from Theorem 7 that NUM is contained in GEX-FIN. In order to formulate Theorem 7, let $R_=^2$ denote the set of all numberings $\psi \in R^2$ such that $\{(i,j)|\psi_i = \psi_j\}$ is decidable.

**Theorem 7** For any $\psi \in R_=^2$, $R_\psi \in$ GEX-FIN$_\psi$.

Thus, we learn from Theorem 7 that good examples for finitely learning NUM-classes can be effectively computed with respect to arbitrary numberings from $R_=^2$. Moreover, the goodness of these examples consists in the strategy's ability to distinguish any function $\psi_i$ (without knowing a priori the index $i$, of course) from all the different previous ones in the numbering $\psi$, i.e. from any $\psi_j$, where $j < i$ and $\psi_j \neq \psi_i$. This leads naturally to learning strategies which work enumeratively. On the other hand, the question whether or not there is "another type" of good examples leading to strategies which construct the hypotheses "directly" from the good examples, i.e. without enumerative search through the space of hypotheses, will be answered affirmatively in Section 4.

Note that the decidability of $\{(i,j)|\psi_i = \psi_j\}$ is also necessary for $R_\psi \in$ GEX-FIN$_\psi$. Actually, $\psi_i = \psi_j$ iff $ex_i \subseteq \psi_j$ and $ex_j \subseteq \psi_i$.

Since it is well-known that for any class $U \in$ NUM, there is a numbering $\psi \in R_=^2$ such that $R_\psi = U$, cf. (Eršov, 1977), we get immediately the following corollary from Theorem 7.

**Corollary 8** NUM $\subseteq$ GEX-FIN

This already contrasts with the NUM $\not\subseteq$ FIN result for finite aex-inference.
However, our next result shows that finite gex-inference is even more powerful than finite aex-inference by "two orders of magnitude" corresponding to the inclusions FIN $\subset$ LIM $\subset$ BC from Theorem 4.

**Theorem 9** GEX-FIN = BC.

Thus, even using the "strongest" way to get the good examples, namely to compute them effectively, and the "strongest" way of inference, namely finite learning, it is possible to learn all the classes from the aex-type BC. In order to achieve this result the underlying numberings have to be chosen carefully. Our next results point out that this is necessary in some sense. Theorem 10 shows that the goal of Theorem 9 cannot be achieved if we confine ourselves to Gödel numberings.

**Theorem 10** For any $\varphi \in G$, GEX-FIN$_\varphi \subset$ GEX-FIN.

Hence for finite gex-inference nonstandard numberings can be more powerful than Gödel numberings. Moreover, this effect can be realized even on "easy" function classes, namely enumerable ones.

**Corollary 11** There is a class $U \in$ NUM such that
(1) for any $\varphi \in G$, $U \notin$ GEX-FIN$_\varphi$,
(2) for some $\psi \in P^2$, $U \in$ GEX-FIN$_\psi$.

Theorem 10 and Corollary 11 clearly contrast with Lemma 5 which characterizes the power of Gödel numberings for aex-inference. While the formal proof of Theorem 10 uses mutual recursion theorem, intuitively, the reason for the weakness of Gödel numberings for gex-inference may be explained as follows. In order to compute good examples with respect to a numbering $\psi$ for learning a class $U$ two properties for $\psi$ turn out to be very helpful: the tightness of $P_\psi$ compared with $U$ and the decidability of $\psi_i = \psi_j$ for any $i, j$. As to these properties a "positive extreme" are the numberings from $R^2_-$, since for them $P_\psi$ even coincides with $U$ and functional equality is decidable. On the other hand, a "negative extreme" are in a sense just Gödel numberings $\varphi$, since then $P_\varphi = P$ is a maximal superset of $U$. Furthermore, any function $f \in P_\varphi$ has even infinitely many $\varphi$-indices, and functional equality is clearly undecidable.

In our approach, for any function $\psi_i \in U$, the good examples for finitely learning $\psi_i$ can be computed effectively from $i$ (by $ex \in P^2$ and $z \in P$). The question naturally arises whether it is possible to enlarge the capabilities of finite gex-inference by weakening the way to get the good examples. It turns out that the answer to this question is negative. We have defined gex-inference where the good examples are only computable in the *limit*, or they do simply *exist* but nothing is required concerning the way to compute them. Then we were able to prove that these weaker versions of good examples do not increase the power of finite gex-inference defined above. For the exact definitions and the proofs the reader is referred to (Freivalds, Kinber and Wiehagen, 1989).

But there may be another way of possibly enlarging the capabilities of gex-inference, namely by allowing the learning strategy to process the finite set of examples in the limit. This leads to the following definition.

**Definition 12** Let $U \subseteq R$ and let $\psi$ be any numbering.
$U$ is called *limit learnable from good examples* with respect to $\psi$ iff
there is a numbering $ex \in P^2$, a strategy $S \in P^2$, and a function $z \in P$ such that $U \subseteq P_\psi$ and, for any $i \in N$ with $\psi_i \in U$,
(1) $ex_i$ is a finite subfunction of $\psi_i$, $z(i)$ is defined and $z(i) = \text{card}(ex_i)$,
(2) for any finite subfunction $\varepsilon$ of $\psi_i$, there is $j$ such that $\psi_j = \psi_i$ and,
    for almost all $n \in N$, $S(ex_i \cup \varepsilon, n) = j$.

Thus, for any function $\psi_i \in U$, on any finite function $\delta$ such that $ex_i \subseteq \delta \subseteq \psi_i$ the strategy $S$ produces an infinite sequence of hypotheses converging to a correct $\psi$-number of the function $\psi_i$.

Of course, the question arises whether this additional "degree of freedom", namely allowing the strategy of a finite number of mind changes, can really increase its power, since the information processed is always the same, namely $\delta = ex_i \cup \varepsilon$. We now will answer this question affirmatively. We set

GEX-LIM$_\psi = \{U \mid U$ is limit learnable from good examples with respect to $\psi\}$,
GEX-LIM $= \bigcup_{\psi \in P^2}$ GEX-LIM$_\psi$.

**Theorem 13** $R \in$ GEX-LIM.

Consequently, limit gex-inference is more powerful than finite gex-inference though in both cases the same kind of information will be processed.

Moreover, compared with LIM $\subset$ BC $\subset$ $pR$ from Theorem 4 limit gex-inference is also more powerful than limit aex-inference by "two orders of magnitude".

We like to mention that Martin Kummer, cf. (Kummer, 1993), has solved two open problems from (Freivald, Kinber and Wiehagen, 1993). Therefore let GEX-LIM$_m$ be defined as GEX-LIM but allowing the limit strategy no more than $m$ mind changes. Then, for any $m \in \mathbb{N}$, GEX-LIM$_m \subset$ GEX-LIM$_{m+1}$. Hence, for any $m \in \mathbb{N}$, $R \notin$ GEX-LIM$_m$. Furthermore, for any $\varphi \in G$, GEX-LIM$_\varphi \subset$ GEX-LIM can be proved by the same method as Theorem 10 above. Consequently, for any $\varphi \in G, R \notin$ GEX-LIM$_\varphi$.

# 4 Learning in polynomial time from good examples

Another problem left open in (Freivalds, Kinber and Wiehagen, 1993) follows from the observation that the main reason why good examples are good for learning recursive functions is because of the strategy's ability to distinguish a function to be learnt from all different previous ones in the underlying numbering. This leads naturally to inference strategies which work enumeratively. Thus, the question arises whether there are other such reasons for goodness and, if any, whether they can yield "constructive" learning strategies building their hypotheses without an enumerative search through the space of hypotheses. Is it, therefore, reasonable to deal with classes of objects to be learnt possessing more "structure" than recursive functions do? And using this structure, is it even possible to learn these objects in polynomial time from good examples?

In this section we will answer these question affirmatively for pattern languages and for finite automata. It turns out that in these cases the number of the good examples is not only finite but even polynomial in the size of the objects to be learnt (length of the pattern, number of states, respectively) and, moreover, the good examples are also computable in polynomial time.

We first will deal with learning of pattern languages, cf. (Angluin, 1980). Other papers concerning learning of pattern languages are (Shinohara, 1983), (Kearns and Pitt, 1989), (Ko, Marron and Tzeng, 1990).

Let $A$ be a finite, nonempty alphabet containing at least two elements. Let $X = \{x_i| i \in \mathbb{N}\}$ be a finite set of distinct variables such that $A \cap X = \emptyset$.

Then let $Pat = (A \cup X)^+$, the set of all nonempty words from $A \cup X$, denote the set of all *patterns*. We say that $w \in A^+$ is derivable from $p \in Pat$ iff $p$ can be transformed into $w$ by replacing any variable of $p$ with a word from $A^+$. Thus $aabb$ is derivable from $ax_1x_2b$, while $aabba$ is not.

Let $L(p)$ denote the set of all $w \in A^+$ derivable from $p \in Pat$. Then $L(p)$ is called the *pattern language generated by* $p$.

Let $PAT$ denote the set of all pattern languages.

**Definition 14** The class *PAT* of all pattern languages is said to be *finitely learnable in polynomial time from good examples* iff
there is a computable mapping $ex$ from *Pat* into the set $fin(A^+)$ of all finite subsets of $A^+$, a computable strategy $S$ from $fin(A^+)$ into *Pat* and a polynomial *pol* such that, for any $p \in Pat$,
(1) $ex(p) \subseteq L(p)$ and $card(ex(p)) \leq pol(length(p))$,
(2) for any finite $W$ with $ex(p) \subseteq W \subseteq L(p)$,
   $L(S(W)) = L(p)$ and time to compute $S(W) \leq pol(\Sigma_{w \in W} length(w))$.

Then in (Lange and Wiehagen, 1991) the following result is proved.

**Theorem 15** *PAT* is finitely learnable in polynomial time from good examples.

The "structure" of the pattern languages used in proving Theorem 15 consists in that the set $L_{min}$ of all shortest words of any pattern language $L$ contains enough information to learn $L$. Even a polynomially sized subset of $L_{min}$ will suffice, and such a subset can be computed in polynomial time from a pattern $p$ generating $L$.

Note that it is easy to see that *PAT* ist *not* finitely learnable from *all* examples provided the examples may be presented in any order as it is the usual approach in language learning from positive data, cf. (Gold, 1967).

A similar result can be proved for finite automata. Therefore let *DFA* denote the set of all deterministic finite automata over some input alphabet $X$ and output alphabet $Y$. Any automaton $A \in DFA$ is assumed to possess an initial state; hence $A$ computes some function $f_A$ from $X^*$ to $Y^*$. Let $Beh\text{-}DFA = \{f_A | A \in DFA\}$ denote the set of all "behaviors" of automata from *DFA*. Let $fin(Beh\text{-}DFA)$ denote the set of all finite subfunctions from the functions of $Beh\text{-}DFA$. Finally, for $A \in DFA$, let $Z_A$ denote the set of states of $A$.

**Definition 16** A set $\mathcal{A} \subseteq DFA$ is said to be *finitely learnable in polynomial time from good examples* iff
there is a computable mapping $ex$ from *DFA* into $fin(Beh\text{-}DFA)$, a computable strategy $S$ from $fin(Beh\text{-}DFA)$ into *DFA*, and a polynomial *pol* such that, for any $A \in \mathcal{A}$,
(1) $ex(A) \subseteq f_A$ and $card(ex(A)) \leq pol(card(Z_A))$,
(2) for any $g \in fin(Beh\text{-}DFA)$ sucht that $ex(A) \subseteq g \subseteq f_A$,
   $f_{S(g)} = f_A$ and time to compute $S(g) \leq pol$ *(length of description of $g$)*.

**Definition 17** A set $\mathcal{A} \subseteq DFA$ is called a *set of measure 1* iff $lim_{k \to \infty} card(\mathcal{A}_k) / card(DFA_k) = 1$ where for $\mathcal{A}' \subseteq DFA$ and $k \in \mathbb{N}$, $\mathcal{A}'_k = \{A | A \in \mathcal{A}' \& card(Z_A) = k\}$.

The following theorem is proved in (Wiehagen, 1993) essentially using results from (Trakhtenbrot and Barzdin, 1973).

**Theorem 18** There is $\mathcal{A} \subseteq DFA$ such that
(1) $\mathcal{A}$ is a set of measure 1,
(2) $\mathcal{A}$ is finitely learnable in polynomial time from good examples.

The "structure" of finite automata used in proving Theorem 18 consists in that, for any $A \in \mathcal{A}$, the knowledge of $f_A$ for all words up to length $O(log\ card(Z_A))$ is sufficient for learning $A$.

This result contrasts with a variety of difficulties in learning finite automata including hardness results contained in (Angluin, 1978), (Pitt, 1989) and (Pitt and Warmuth, 1989).

# 5 Conclusions

As experience shows, if one learns from examples then there are "important" examples as well as less important ones. Often it is not necessary to see as much examples as possible but it suffices to solve the learning problem if you see the "right" examples. We have formalized this scenario by introducing learning from good examples. Informally, good examples
– are considerably less examples than all examples, but they are "important",
– can be computed effectively from the objects to be learnt,
– are intended to be sufficient for learning rich classes of objects.

In inductive inference of recursive functions only *finitely many* examples are allowed as good examples. Hence, formally, an inference strategy working with good examples only, misses *almost all* examples in comparison with an inference strategy provided with *all* examples. Nevertheless, it turns out that from good examples considerably more classes of recursive functions can be learnt than from all examples.

First, we have proved NUM $\subseteq$ GEX-FIN which already yields some contrast to the result that the inference type FIN where potentially *all* examples are available, does *not* fully contain the family NUM of all recursively enumerable classes of recursive functions. The goodness of the examples used consists in the strategy's ability to distinguish any function to be learnt from all the different previous ones in the underlying numbering with respect to which both the good examples are computed and the correct indices have to be found.

We then have shown GEX-FIN = BC. Thus, even using the "strongest" way to get the good examples, namely to compute them effectively, and the "strongest" way of inference, namely finite ("one shot") learning, it is possible to learn all the classes from BC. This considerably enlarges the capabilities compared with inductive inference from all examples, since there we have FIN $\subset$ LIM $\subset$ BC.

Finally, it turned out that the capabilites of inductive inference from good examples can be enlarged further when allowing the strategy to process the set of good examples (being the *same* during the whole learning process!) in the limit. We got $R \in$ GEX-LIM in contrast to LIM $\subset$ BC $\subset pR$ for inductive inference from all examples.

Intuitively, the additional power of inductive inference from good examples comes from two sources. It comes from the knowledge of the function $f$ to be learnt (more exactly: from the knowledge of an index of $f$ within the underlying numbering $\psi$) when computing the good examples for that function. And, in a sense simultaneously, it results from the possibility to build the corresponding numbering $\psi$ in such a manner that any finite and consistent superset of the good examples allows to learn $f$ just with respect to that numbering $\psi$. We note that the additional power does *not* come from some "unfair tricks" of encoding an index of $f$ into the good examples, though we have no formal proof up to now that our approach definitely excludes all such tricks.

The necessity of choosing the underlying numberings carefully is supported by proving the relative weakness of Gödel numberings for inductive inference from good examples, GEX-FIN$_\varphi \subset$ GEX-FIN for any $\varphi \in G$. The same is true for learning in the limit from good examples, (Kummer, 1993). While the formal proof of these results uses mutual recursion theorem, intuitively, the reason for the weakness of Gödel number-ings may be explained as follows. In order to compute good examples with respect to a numbering $\psi$ for learning a class $U$ of recursive functions two properties of $\psi$ turn out to be helpful, namely $P_\psi$ being close to $U$ and $\psi_i = \psi_j$ being decidable for any $i, j$. As to these properties a "negative extreme" are in a sense just Gödel numberings $\varphi$, since $P_\varphi = P$ is a maximal superset of $U$. Moreover, any function $f \in P_\varphi$ has even infinitely many $\varphi$-indices and functional equality within $\varphi$ is undecidable.

In inductive inference of recursive functions from good examples the corresponding strategies are working enumeratively, in general. Thus, the question arises whether there are other objects to be learnt from good examples where the strategies can build their hypotheses without an enumerative search through the underlying space of hypotheses. We have presented an affirmative answer to this question for pattern languages and for finite automata.
The class of all pattern languages is finitely learnable from good examples.
A class of "almost all" finite automata is finitely learnable from good examples.
In order to achieve these results the "structure" of the objects to be learnt is used essentially. This even yields learning strategies which run in polynomial time. More-over, also the good examples are computable in polynomial time which implies that their number is not only finite but in fact polynomial in the size of the objects to be learnt (length of pattern, number of states, respectively). Note that we feel it quite reasonable or even necessary for a "sound" result on polynomial-time learning from good examples that the good examples be also computable in polynomial time.

Thus, we have seen that learning from good examples can lead to several positive effects such as
– decreasing the number of examples,
– enlarging the learning power considerably,
– strengthening the mode of convergence of the sequences of hypotheses,
– ensuring learnability in polynomial time.
There may be more such effects including the existence of learning problems solvable from all examples in polynomial time but solvable from good examples (much) faster. Anyway, learning from good examples seems to be an approach which may turn out to be remarkably useful when one has access to the choice of the information to be processed within the learning process.

On the other hand, good examples do not exist always. Therefore let $B_n$ denote the set of all Boolean functions of $n$ variables. Then, obviously, for any $f \in B_n$, the set of *all* examples contains $2^n$ elements. If we require from a set of *good* examples that its cardinality has to be bounded by a polynomial in $n$, then it is easy to see that good examples for learning the whole class $B_n$ cannot exist. Of course, this negative result does not exclude the possibility that for subclasses of $B_n$ good examples (of polynomial size) do exist.
Hence directions of further research may consist in
– finding criteria that, given some class of objects to be learnt, good examples do exist,
– if good examples exist, then clarifying why they may be good and to what kind of learning strategies this may lead.

# Acknowledgment

The research of the two first authors was supported by the grant No. 93.599 from the Latvian Science Council.

The third author was supported by the German Ministry for Research and Technology (BMFT) under Grant GOSLER 01 IW 101 B9 and E7.

# References

Angluin, D. (1978), On the complexity of minimum inference of regular sets. *Information and Control* 39, 337-350.

Angluin, D. (1980), Finding patterns common to a set of strings. *Journal of Computer and System Sciences* 21, 46-62.

Angluin, D. and Smith, C. H. (1983), Inductive inference: theory and methods. *Computing Surveys* 15, 237-269.

Baliga, G., Case, J. and Jain, S. (1993), Language learning with some negative information. In: Proceedings, 10th Annual Symposium on Theoretical Aspects of Computer Science, *Lecture Notes in Computer Science* 665, 672-681.

Barzdin, J. (1974), Two theorems on the limiting synthesis of functions. *Theory of Algorithms and Programs* 1, 82-88 (Russian).

Barzdin, J., ed. (1974, 1975, 1977), *Theory of Algorithms and Programs* 1, 2, 3, Latvian State University, Riga (Russian).

Blum, L. and Blum, M. (1975), Toward a mathematical theory of inductive inference. *Information and Control* 28, 122-155.

Case, J. and Smith, C. (1983), Comparison of identification criteria for machine inductive inference. *Theoretical Computer Science* 25, 193-220.

Daley, R., Pitt, L., Velauthapillai, M. and Will, T. (1992), Relations between probabilistic and team one-shot learners. In: Proceedings, Fourth Annual Workshop on Computational Learning Theory, pp. 228-239.

Eršov, Yu. L. (1977), *Theory of Numberings*, Nauka, Moscow (Russian).

Freivalds, R. (1979), Finite identification of general recursive functions by probabilistic strategies. In: Proceedings, Conference on Foundations of Computation Theory, pp. 138-145.

Freivalds, R., Kinber, E. B. and Wiehagen, R. (1982), Inductive inference and computable one-one numberings. *Zeitschrift für Mathematische Logik und Grundlagen der Mathematik* 28, 463-479.

Freivalds, R., Kinber, E. B. and Wiehagen, R. (1988), Probabilistic versus deterministic inductive inference in nonstandard numberings. *Zeitschrift für Mathematische Logik und Grundlagen der Mathematik* 34, 531-539.

Freivalds, R., Kinber, E. B. and Wiehagen, R. (1989), Inductive inference from good examples. In: Proceedings, International Workshop on Analogical and Inductive Inference, *Lecture Notes in Artificial Intelligence* 397, 1-17.

Freivalds, R., Kinber, E. B. and Wiehagen, R. (1993), On the power of inductive inference from good examples. *Theoretical Computer Science* 110, 131-144.

Gold, E. M. (1967), Language identification in the limit. *Information and Control* 10, 447-474.

Goldman, S. A. and Mathias, H. D. (1993), Teaching a smarter learner. In: Proceedings, Sixth Annual ACM Conference on Computational Learning Theory, pp. 67-76.

Jain, S. and Sharma, A. (1990), Finite learning by a team. In: Proceedings, Third Annual Workshop on Computational Learning Theory, pp. 163-177.

Kearns, M. and Pitt, L. (1989), A polynomial-time algorithm for learning $k$-variable pattern languages from examples. In: Proceedings, Second Annual Workshop on Computational Learning Theory, pp. 57-70.

Klette, R. and Wiehagen, R. (1980), Research in the theory of inductive inference by GDR mathematicians – a survey. *Information Sciences* 22, 149-169.

Ko, Ker-I, Marron, A. and Tzeng, W. G. (1990), Learning string patterns and tree patterns from examples. In: Proceedings, Seventh International Conference on Machine Learning, pp. 384-391.

Kummer, M. (1993), personal communication to E. B. Kinber and R. Wiehagen.

Lange, S. and Wiehagen, R. (1991), Polynomial-time inference of arbitrary pattern languages. *New Generation Computing* 8, 361-370.

Motoki, T. (1991), Inductive inference from all positive and some negative data. *Information Processing Letters* 39, 177-182.

Nessel, J. (1993), personal communication to R. Wiehagen.

Osherson, D. N., Stob, M. and Weinstein, S. (1986), *Systems that learn.* MIT Press, Cambridge.

Pitt, L. (1989), Inductive inference, DFAs, and computational complexity. In: Proceedings, International Workshop on Analogical and Inductive Inference, *Lecture Notes in Artificial Intelligence* 397, 18-44.

Pitt, L. and Warmuth, M. K. (1989), The minimum consistent DFA problem cannot be approximated within any polynomial. *Techn. Report UIUCDCS-R-89-1499,* University of Illinois at Urbana-Champaign.

Podnieks, K. (1974), Comparing various concepts of limiting synthesis and function prediction. *Theory of algorithms and programs* 1, 68-81 (Russian).

Rogers, H.Jr. (1967), *Theory of recursive functions and effective computability*, McGraw-Hill, New York.

Shinohara, A. and Miyano, S. (1991), Teachability in computational learning. *New Generation Computing* 8, 337-347.

Shinohara, T. (1983), Polynomial-time inference of extended regular pattern languages. In: Proceedings, RIMS Symposium on Software Science and Engineering, *Lecture Notes in Computer Science* 147, 115-127.

Trakhtenbrot, B. A. and Barzdin, J. (1973), *Finite automata: Behavior and synthesis*, North-Holland, Amsterdam.

Wiehagen, R. (1993), From inductive inference to algorithmic learning theory. In: Proceedings, Third Workshop on Algorithmic Learning Theory, 1992, *Lecture Notes in Artificial Intelligence* 743, 13-24 (to appear in *New Generation Computing*).

# Towards Reduction Arguments for FINite Learning

Robert Daley and Bala Kalyanasundaram

Department of Computer Science

University of Pittsburgh

Pittsburgh, PA 15260, USA

{daley, kalyan}@cs.pitt.edu

### Abstract

This paper deals with the ability of cooperating teams of learners to learn classes of total recursive functions. The main contribution of the research described here is the development of analytical tools which permit the determination of team learning capabilities. The basis of our analytical framework is a reduction technique. We extend the notion of finite learning in order to successfully apply the reduction technique.

## 1  Introduction

Cooperation is often essential for successful completion of a task when multiple agents are involved in the process. We are primarily interested in the task of learning total recursive functions from examples. In this context, we attempt to understand and answer the fundamental question of how teams of learners (i.e., learning algorithms) can work cooperatively to learn (from examples) classes of functions which individually they would be unable to learn.

Given a function $f$ from class of $\mathcal{F}$ of total recursive functions, we say that a learner $L$ successfully learns $f$, if after seeing examples of input/output behavior of $f$, $L$ produces a program that computes $f$ correctly. More precisely, the learner $L$ receives values $(0, f(0)), (1, f(1)), (2, f(2)), \ldots$ and after seeing a finite portion of the input, $L$ will issue only one hypothesis (i.e., program) $h$. We say that $L$ correctly learns the function $f$ with respect to $FIN$-type learning (denoted by $f \in \mathbf{FIN}[L]$) if the hypothesis of $L$ is a correct program for $f$. Intuitively, the learner $L$ is capable of differentiating one function from another in the class $\mathcal{F}$. We say that a class $\mathcal{F}$ of functions is $FIN$-learnable (denoted by $\mathcal{F} \in \mathbf{FIN}$) if there is a learner $L$ that can correctly learn every function $f$ in $\mathcal{F}$ with respect to $FIN$-type learning.

It is natural to consider the case of multiple learners *cooperatively* learning a target concept/function. As witnessed in the scientific community, it is the case that the learners form groups where different groups try different approaches with the hope that some group would succeed. This notion of *pluralistic* learning process [8] has been considered for $FIN$-type learning. Let $L = \{L_1, L_2, \ldots, L_s\}$ be the team of learners who co-operate to learn a class $\mathcal{F}$ of functions. Each member of the team is a *FIN*-type learner. The team $L$ learns a function $f$ in $\mathcal{F}$ with plurality $r/s$ if at least $r$ out of $s$ members output a final program which computes $f$ correctly. The team $L$ learns the class $\mathcal{F}$ with plurality $r/s$ if it learns every function $f$ in $\mathcal{F}$ with plurality $r/s$. We denote the collection of such classes $\mathcal{F}$ by $\mathbf{FIN}\langle\mathbf{T}:r/s\rangle$. Note that the modifier $\langle\mathbf{T}:r/s\rangle$ to *FIN* denotes that the learner consists of a **team** of $s$ learners with success ratio at least $r/s$.

If we replace the team of learners by a single probabilistic learner whose hypothesis is based not only on the input but also on the outcome of coin flips, then we get the notion of *probabilistic FIN*-type learning. We denote the collection of classes $\mathcal{F}$ learnable by probabilistic learners with success probability $p$ by $\mathbf{FIN}\langle\mathbf{P}:p\rangle$. Again, note that the modifier $\langle\mathbf{P}:p\rangle$ to *FIN* denotes that the learner is a probabilistic learner with **probability** of success is at least $p$.

## 2 Learning Capabilities

It is natural to ask how the learning capability of a team of learners with plurality $r/s$ compares to that of a single probabilistic learner whose success probability is at least $\frac{r}{s}$. Similarly, under what conditions can a team with plurality $r/s$ successfully simulate another team with plurality $a/b$.

Work on these kinds of questions was begun by Freivalds [6] who showed that the learning capabilities of probabilistic learners beginning with probability 1 and ending with probability $\frac{1}{2}$ form discrete intervals (whose endpoints are given by the sequence $\frac{n}{2n-1}$ for $n \geq 2$) such that any two probabilities in an interval yield equivalent learning power. This result was extended to teams of learners by Daley et. al in [5]. To illustrate the significance of these results, we consider the following example. Consider the interval $(\frac{2}{3}1]$ which is the first one defined by the sequence $\frac{n}{2n-1}$. Consider a team $M$ of 4 members out of which at least 3 must succeed in learning the target function. Since $\frac{2}{3} < \frac{3}{4} \leq 1$, we can prove that if 3 members can succeed then all 4 can succeed too. In other words, a single deterministic learner can successfully simulate $M$ and learn what $M$ can learn with plurality $3/4$.

Velauthapillai [10] first observed that a team of size 2 with plurality $1/2$ was less capable than a team of size 4 with plurality $2/4$. This showed that for the ratio $\frac{1}{2}$ the capabilities of probabilistic and team learners are different. Later, Jain and Sharma [7] showed that those two are the pluralistic capabilities at ratio $\frac{1}{2}$.

Progress on understanding team/probabilistic learning capabilities for success ratios below $\frac{1}{2}$ has been very slow. Initially, it had been conjectured [5] that the learning capability increases if we decrease the success ratio below $\frac{1}{2}$ by any tiny amount. We [3] disproved this conjecture by establishing the following capability intervals $(\frac{16}{33}, \frac{17}{35}], (\frac{17}{35}, \frac{18}{37}], (\frac{18}{37}, \frac{20}{41}], (\frac{20}{41}, \frac{24}{49}], (\frac{24}{49}, \frac{1}{2}]$. This result showed that the capability sequence for *FIN*-type learning is very complex for success ratios below $\frac{1}{2}$. In contrast, Pitt and Smith [9] showed that the capability sequence for *LIM*-type learning is $\{1/n : n \geq 1\}$.

# 3  Current Status

Even though several capability intervals have been established for success ratios below $\frac{1}{2}$, our understanding of *FIN*-type learning below $\frac{1}{2}$ is vague. The simulation and diagonalization constructions used to establish these intervals had to be *hand-crafted* and it appears that we could continue to establish additional intervals but only one at a time. Moreover, the ratios that define these intervals seem to appear rather mysteriously and the pattern seems to be quite complex.

Typically, the fact that a team $M_1$ with plurality $x/y$ can be more powerful than another team $M_2$ with plurality $r/s$ is established by constructing a set of total recursive functions $\mathcal{F}$ learnable by $M_1$ by not by $M_2$. Recall that for successful learning, the team must learn every function in $\mathcal{F}$. Unfortunately, input/output behaviors of these functions are somewhat complex. Due to this high complexity, many results in this area are not clearly understood. In our research experience and building on the notion that the ability to learn a function is the ability to discriminate it from alternative (perhaps closely related) functions, we have found that the class $\mathcal{F}$ of functions can be expressed as a tree (called a *function-tree*) that captures the relationships of the functions in $\mathcal{F}$. This enables us to suppress many technical details of the construction and present clearly why a given team learns (or otherwise) functions from this class. We strongly feel that this approach will make these results more accessible.

Consider the output of two total recursive functions $f_1$ and $f_2$ in some canonical order. Typically, outputs of these two functions may agree up to some input. Pictorially, the agreement of the two functions can be represented as a single path. At the point where the outputs of the two functions disagree for the first time, we create two branches where $f_1$ is assumed to follow one and $f_2$ the other. This can be generalized to any collection of functions. See Figure 1 for the representation of functions in the set $\mathcal{F} = \{f_0, f_1, f_2, f_1^1, f_1^2, f_2^1, f_2^2\}$.

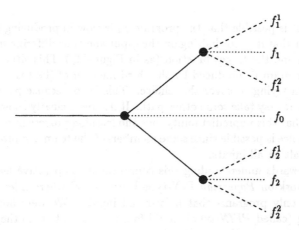

Figure 1: Function Tree for $\mathcal{F} = \{f_0, f_1, f_2, f_1^1, f_1^2, f_2^1, f_2^2\}$

In order to explain some of the complex behaviors of the team members in a learning process, we consider a simple example of a team with 4 members out of which at least 2 should learn a given function, which we refer to as the target function. After seeing some initial portion of the input, two members of the team produce programs $p_1$ and $p_2$ respectively. It is possible that these two programs compute the target function and therefore the third and fourth members need not produce a program at all. On the other hand, it is possible that these two programs compute two different functions and depending on which function is fed as the input, the third member will produce a program $p_3$ to join either $p_1$ or $p_2$ and successfully learn the target function. To make matters worse, neither $p_1$ nor $p_2$ may compute the target function correctly. Notice that any other team that can learn these functions must also cope with these choices and should have enough resources (team members) to cover all possible alternatives. Again, it is best to visualize these choices in terms of branches of a tree as in Figure 2. We use the notation $p$ or $\widehat{p}$ to denote the production of program $p$ at that point by the learner if the target function were to follow that branch.

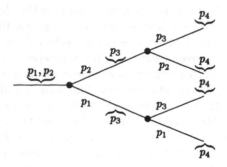

Figure 2: Simple Behaviour of Programs

Sometimes, it is possible that the program $p_2$ is slow in producing its output and so it may appear that it is not halting on the input and thus differing from both what $p_1$ is computing and the target function (as in Figure 2.) This situation, combined with the new program $p_3$ produced by the third member of the team, might confuse some other team trying to cover this choice. This is so because $p_2$ may eventually join this path or it may take some other path. It has been clearly shown (e.g., see [3] and Figure 3) that this unpredictability foils the learning process in many situations. This cunning choice is possible since some members of the team can produce programs that need not halt on all inputs.

As a step towards understanding this complicated co-operative learning process, we began our work on *Popperian FIN*-type learning [4] where a learner is permitted to produce only programs that halt on all inputs. We were hopeful that this type of learning (called *PFIN*-type) would focus our attention to the combinatorial complexity of the co-operative learning process.

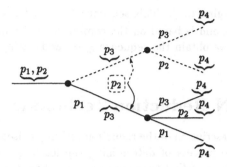

Figure 3: Complex Behaviour of Programs

# 4 Popperian type Learning

First, we [4] showed that the capability intervals for *PFIN*-type learning coincide with that for *FIN*-type learning for success ratio above $\frac{1}{2}$. It was then shown in [4] that the learning capabilities of *PFIN*-type learners in the interval $(\frac{4}{9}, \frac{1}{2}]$ are broken into subintervals whose end-points are given by the sequence $\frac{4n}{9n-2}$ for $n \geq 2$. For the first time, a reduction type argument was used to establish this result.

The process of determining the learning capability of a particular probabilistic or team *PFIN*-type learner involves showing that this learner (the pursuing learner) can simulate any probabilistic or team learner (the target learner) with a success ratio within its capability interval. The pursuing learner's simulation in turn involves the simulation of the programs produced by the target learner. As we described earlier, the programs of the target learner may split into groups and compute different functions of which only one is the (target) function to be learned. Thus, the task of the pursuer's hypothesized programs will be to cover all these different functions (i.e., different groups of programs) in such a way that the correct plurality is maintained along each path, where the correct plurality is roughly proportional to the size of the group following a particular function. This is the genesis of our reduction technique. This covering task is considerably simplified if the distribution of the target learner's programs on any given input is fully known to the pursuing learner. Since the programs produced by a *PFIN*-type learner always compute a total function, it is always possible to fully classify the programs of the target learner according to what they compute thus far and identify the distribution. On the other hand, this is not the case for *FIN*-type learning. The amount of simplification can be seen by comparing the strategy given for the *PFIN*-type learner with plurality 2/4 in [4] with that for the corresponding *FIN*-type learner given in [3].

Our reduction technique makes use of the previously determined capability sequence. This approach sheds considerable light on the origin of the sequences of intervals of learning capabilities. For example, the sequence $\frac{n}{2n-1}$ giving the capabilities above $\frac{1}{2}$ can be used in establishing the capability sequence $\frac{4n}{9n-2}$. In particular, the sequence $\frac{4n}{9n-2}$ is generated by the combination of reductions $R_2^1 + R_n^1$, where $R_i^1$ is the reduction to the learning capability of the ratio $\frac{i}{2i-1}$. Furthermore, using these techniques it is possible to construct an $\omega^2$ sequence of learning capabilities beginning at $\frac{1}{2}$ and converging to $\frac{2}{5}$. This sequence has the form $\frac{2mn}{(5m-1)n-m}$ for $m \geq 2$ and $n \geq m \cdot (m-1)$, and is based on the combination of reductions $R_m^1 + R_n^1$. For example, for $m = 2$ we obtain the sequence $\frac{4n}{9n-2}$, and letting $m = 3$ we obtain the next sequence $\frac{6n}{14n-3}$.

# 5  The PFIN Reduction Technique

Now we give a brief description of the reduction technique used in our work on *PFIN*. As stated before, the process of determining the learning capability of a particular probabilistic or team *PFIN*-type learner $L$ involves showing that this learner (the pursuing learner) can simulate any probabilistic or team learner $M$ (the target learner) with a success ratio within its capability interval, and the task of the programs produced by $L$ is to cover the different functions computed by groups of programs produced by $M$. Suppose $M$ is a **PFIN**$\langle$**P**: $p\rangle$-type learner, and let $L$ be a **PFIN**$\langle$**P**: $\frac{r}{s}\rangle$-type learner that successfully simulates $M$ and learns all that $M$ can learn. Even though $L$ is intended to be a probabilistic learner (with success ratio $\frac{r}{s}$), we will actually implement it as a team of learners (with plurality $kr/ks$, for an appropriate choice of $k$). Let $f \in$ **PFIN**$\langle$**P**: $p\rangle[M]$ be an arbitrary function learnable by $M$. We will refer to $M$ as the target learner and $f$ as the target function, and we will refer to $L$ as the pursuing team of learners. Initially, $L$ will wait until $M$ produces programs with weight at least $p$. At this point $kr$ of $L$'s members output programs $\{S_1, \ldots, S_{kr}\}$.

Let $g$ be one of the functions computed by $M$'s programs and let $q$ be the total weight of $M$'s programs which compute $g$ thus far. Since $L$ continues to see the input function, it knows whether $g$ agrees with the target function thus far or not. On the other hand, $L$'s original programs must decide on the number of programs that will follow $g$. They expect that if $g$ continues to agree with the target function, then $L$ will issue additional programs to compensate those that did not follow this path. $L$ will do so only after it sees additional programs with weight $p - q$ produced by $M$ to join this path so that the cumulative weight of programs along this point is at least $p$. This event on the part of $M$ is called a *breakaway* and it corresponds to a split in the *function-tree*. Since weight $p - q$ of $M$'s programs are wrong on $g$, the *reduced success ratio* of $M$ on $g$ is at most $\frac{p}{1-(p-q)}$. We call this the *reduced target ratio*. Since $M$'s programs compute total functions, $L$ and its initial programs will calculate this target ratio correctly by observing (through simulation) the input/output behavior of $M$'s initial program. So, $L$'s programs must respond in a proportionate manner by having $x$ of its programs compute $g$, where $x$ is chosen so that its reduced success ratio $\frac{kr}{k(s-r)+x}$ (called the *reduced pursuer ratio*) on $g$ is *equivalent* to the reduced target ratio. Since these reduced success ratios will be for less capable teams whose capabilities have already been established and known to form intervals, the weight $q$ is partitioned into a number of cases, depending on the capability of the resulting reduced target ratio. In order for the reduced target ratio to have the capability of a team with plurality in the interval $(\frac{i+1}{2i+1}, \frac{i}{2i-1}]$ (the $R_i^1$ *Reduction*), it must be the case that $\frac{(3i-1)p}{i} - 1 \leq q < \frac{3(i+1)-1)p}{i+1}$. Similarly, in order for the reduced pursuer ratio to be of equivalent capability $L$ must have $\frac{k((3i-1)r-is)}{n}$ of its programs compute $g$. If $q < Q_1 \equiv \frac{5p}{2} - 1$, then the function $g$ can be safely ignored by $L$'s programs since the reduced target ratio is equivalent to a deterministic learner, and $L$ can issue an additional $kr$ programs which will correctly compute $g$. If $q > T_1 \equiv p - Q_1 = 1 - \frac{3p}{2}$, then all other functions can be safely ignored, so that all of $L$'s $kr$ programs will correctly compute $g$.

For the reduction argument used in [4], which deals with the capability sequence $\frac{4n}{9n-2}$, the value $q$ is further decomposed into the five cases ($R_2^1, R_3^1, R_4^1, R_5^1$ and $R_{1,\infty}^1$), defined by the following subintervals of $[Q_1, T_1]$: $[Q_1, \frac{8p}{3} - 1)$, $[\frac{8p}{3} - 1, \frac{11p}{4} - 1)$, $[\frac{11p}{4} - 1, \frac{14p}{5} - 1)$, $[\frac{14p}{5} - 1, \frac{17p}{6} - 1)$, and $[\frac{17p}{6} - 1, T_1]$. The cases and the required number of $L$'s programs which must follow the weight $q$ programs of $M$ is given in Table 1.

Table 1: Cases and Pursuer Strategy for interval $(\frac{4}{9}, \frac{1}{2}]$

| Case | Target Team | Target Ratio | Pursuing Team | Pursuing Ratio |
|------|-------------|--------------|---------------|----------------|
| $R_1^1$ | $0 \leq q < Q_1$ | $> 2/3$ | $0$ | $4n/(5n-2)$ |
| $R_2^1$ | $Q_1 \leq q < \frac{8p}{3} - 1$ | $> 3/5$ | $k(n+2)$ | $2/3$ |
| $R_3^1$ | $\frac{8p}{3} - 1 \leq q < \frac{11p}{4} - 1$ | $> 4/7$ | $k(\frac{7n}{3} - 2)$ | $3/5$ |
| $R_4^1$ | $\frac{11p}{4} - 1 \leq q < \frac{14p}{5} - 1$ | $> 5/9$ | $k(2n+2)$ | $4/7$ |
| $R_5^1$ | $\frac{14p}{5} - 1 \leq q < \frac{17p}{6} - 1$ | $> 6/11$ | $k(\frac{11n}{5} + 2)$ | $5/9$ |
| $R_{6,\infty}^1$ | $\frac{17p}{6} - 1 \leq q \leq T_1$ | $\geq \frac{2p}{4-5p}$ | $k(3n-2)$ | $2/4$ |

It is possible for multiple breakaways to occur, and so we must demonstrate that $L$ has sufficient resources (i.e., programs) to handle all possibilities. For example, 2 Case $R_2^1$ breakaways (denoted $2R_2^1$) are possible, when $2Q_1 \leq p \equiv p \leq \frac{1}{2}$ or $n \geq 2$. Fortunately if $n \geq 2$, then (precisely) $2k(n+2) \leq k(4n)$, so that $L$ will have enough initial programs to send along both breakaways. Table 2 summarizes the *critical* multiple events.

Table 2: Multiple Events

| Combination | Case Possible | $L$ OK |
|-------------|---------------|--------|
| $2R_2^1$ | $n \geq 2$ | $n \geq 2$ |
| $R_2^1 + R_3^1$ | $n \geq 3$ | $n \geq 3$ |
| $R_2^1 + R_4^1$ | $n \geq 4$ | $n \geq 4$ |
| $R_2^1 + R_5^1$ | $n \geq 5$ | $n \geq 5$ |
| $R_2^1 + R_6^1$ | $n \geq 6$ | $n \geq 6$ |
| $3R_2^1$ | $n \geq 6$ | $n \geq 6$ |
| $2R_3^1$ | $n \geq 6$ | $n \geq 6$ |
| $R_3^1 + R_4^1$ | $n \geq 12$ | $n \geq 12$ |
| $2R_2^1 + R_3^1$ | $n \geq 18$ | $n \geq 18$ |
| $R_3^1 + R_5^1$ | $n \geq 30$ | $n \geq 30$ |
| $4R_2^1$ | $n \geq \infty$ | **NO** |
| $2R_4^1$ | $n \geq \infty$ | **NO** |
| $2R_2^1 + R_4^1$ | $n \geq \infty$ | **NO** |
| $R_2^1 + R_{6,\infty}^1$ | $n \geq \infty$ | **NO** |
| $R_2^1 + 2R_3^1$ | $n > \infty$ | **NO** |

We observe that the combination $R_2^1 + R_i^1$ is possible precisely when $\frac{5p}{2} - 1 + \frac{(3i-1)p}{i} - 1 \leq p$, and hence when $p \leq \frac{4i}{9i-2}$. Thus, this case combination accounts for the limitations on learning for ratios in the interval $(\frac{4}{9}, \frac{1}{2}]$, i.e., a team with ratio $\frac{4i}{9i-2}$ does *not* have sufficient team size to handle to combination $R_2^1 + R_{i+1}^1$. Moreover, the diagonalizing tree of functions for this case consists of a two-way branch at the root with two subtrees which are the diagonalizing subtrees for the ratios $\frac{2}{3}$ and $\frac{i+1}{2i+1}$, respectively.

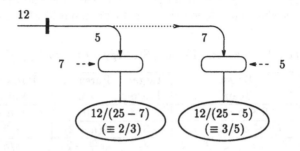

Figure 4: A Distribution of Programs for Team with Plurality 12/25.

It is important to note that the success of the simulating team also depends on the fact that $k$ is a sufficiently large integer (viz., 15) so that the fractions given in the table for the pursuing team are whole numbers.

We now turn our attention to *FIN*-type learning. The reduction technique described above fails since $L$ or its initial programs can not clearly identify the target ratio along a path. The main reason for the inability to identify the target ratio is that the programs of $M$ may not compute total functions. Consider a team with plurality $x$ *out of* $z$.

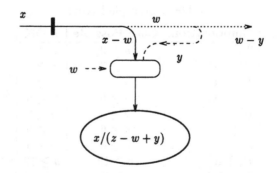

Figure 5: Changing Ratio Due to Extra $y$ Programs

Suppose $x - w$ programs of $M$ followed the *breakaway* path of a function $g$. $L$ or its programs cannot clearly conclude that $w$ initial programs of $M$ are wrong (see Figure 5). On the other hand, $L$ or its initial programs can not afford to simulate those $w$ programs until they produce an output since they need not halt on all inputs.

So, depending upon how those $w$ initial programs of $M$ behave, the reduced target ratio could be anywhere in the range $[\frac{x}{z-w}, \frac{x}{z}]$. In the worst case (where $y = w$) the reduced target ration could be $\frac{x}{z}$, which is the original target ratio. As a consequence, it appears that no reduction takes place (i.e., the argument becomes circular). Fortunately, a closer look at this situation reveals a way around this problem. In order to see this, consider two pluralistic learners $M_1$ and $M_2$ with plurality $x$ out of $z$. After seeing sufficient portion of the input, team $M_1$ produces exactly $x$ programs whereas team $M_2$ produces $x + y$ programs. Even though the success ratio is $x/z$ for both teams, the team $M_2$ may be weaker than $M_1$ if $y$ is sufficiently large. This disparity arises since $M_1$ can use those $y$ extra programs more effectively. This is possible since the programs produced by a learner no longer observe the input whereas the learner continues to see the input and produce additional programs to possibly correct its mistake.

At the beginning, the learner $M$ behaves like $M_1$ in producing exactly $x$ programs after a seeing sufficient portion of the input. But, along the *breakaway* path, even though the target ratio is $x/z$, the strategy employed by $M$ is similar to that of $M_2$ since the $y$ programs which later join the breakaway path are extra programs produced by $M$ initially. Since the strategy of $M_2$ is weaker than that of $M_1$ for sufficiently large $y$, it is possible to view this as some form of *reduction*. To facilitate this form of reduction, it is necessary to classify learners based on not only the success ratio ($x$ out of $z$) but also how many extra programs ($y$) they are required to produce.

# 6  A Generalization of FINite Learning

From now on, we concentrate only on *FIN*-type team learning. Any smart *FIN*-type team learner with plurality $x$ out of $z$ will produce exactly $x$ programs after seeing an *adequate* portion of the input. So for successful learning, this smart team need not produce any additional programs. We will use the notation $\mathbf{FIN}\langle\mathbf{T}\colon (x,0)/z\rangle$ to denote $\mathbf{FIN}\langle\mathbf{T}\colon x/z\rangle$ where zero indicates that the team does not produce any extra programs. We now generalize *FIN*-type learning by stipulating that any successful team of size $z$ must produce at least $x + y$ programs out of which at least $x$ programs compute the target function. We use the term "a team with plurality $\langle x, y, z\rangle$" (for short "$\langle x, y, z\rangle$-team") to denote this generalized success criterion. As before, we say a team learns a class $\mathcal{F}$ of functions with plurality $\langle x, y, z\rangle$, if it learns every function in the class with that plurality. We will denote such collection of classes $\mathcal{F}$ by $\mathbf{FIN}\langle\mathbf{T}\colon (x,y)/z\rangle$.

For arbitrary integers $x, y, z$ and $a, b, c$, our goal is to compare $\mathbf{FIN}\langle\mathbf{T}\colon (x,y)/z\rangle$ with $\mathbf{FIN}\langle\mathbf{T}\colon (a,b)/c\rangle$. Notice that it is very easy to establish the following:

1. $\mathbf{FIN}\langle\mathbf{T}\colon (x,y)/z\rangle \subseteq \mathbf{FIN}\langle\mathbf{T}\colon (x,y')/z\rangle$ if $y' \leq y$.

2. For $n > 0$, $\mathbf{FIN}\langle\mathbf{T}\colon (n,0)/2n - 1\rangle \subset \mathbf{FIN}\langle\mathbf{T}\colon (n+1,0)/2n+1\rangle$.

In fact, all of the results established for *FIN*-type learning can be restated in the new form where the second parameter (i.e., $y$) is zero.

# 7 Capability Trees

As explained earlier, the process of determining the learning capability of a particular team *FIN*-type learner involves showing that this learner (the pursuing learner) can simulate an other team learner (the target learner) with a success ratio within its capability interval. The end point of the capability interval gives the success ratio of a team that is capable of learning more than the pursuing team. This is often established through a diagonalization argument (involving the construction of function trees) which shows that the choices handled successfully by the target team is strictly more than that of the pursuing team. For details of such diagonalization arguments, we refer the readers to [3, 1, 4]. We [3, 1, 4] have used *capability trees* as a tool to analyze various choices a team learner can handle. We now illustrate this with an example. Consider a team with plurality *3 out of 5*.

In a typical learning scenario, after seeing a sufficient portion of the input, three members will each produce a program and these three programs behave in any one of the following ways.

The three programs split in three ways and any one of the three could be computing the target function. This is possible since, along the target path and after the split-up, the remaining two learners produce their programs and so exactly three programs are computing the target function. Using a tree with three branches, we depict this possibility (see Figure 6).

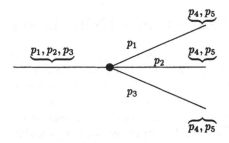

Figure 6: Three-way Split

Notice that after the first split, the programs can split further. If they do so then the team will not have sufficient programs to compute the target function. This is the case even if two programs followed one branch and the third followed a different one.

On the other hand, consider the case that two out of three original programs follow the same path. Suppose further that the third program is very slow in computing its function. For any outsider, it looks like a two-way split up where two follows one path (say the **A**-path) and the third program follows the second path (say the **B**-path). In order to make this convincing, the fourth member of the team produces a program that joins the **A**-path. Much later, the third program from the original group of three programs joins the **A**-path too. Notice that four programs are following the **A**-path. Now they can split into two groups and follow two different paths. Each one of these two paths can be the target function since the last member of the team can wait for this split-up and produce its program so that three programs are computing the target function correctly. See Figure 3 for this type of tree.

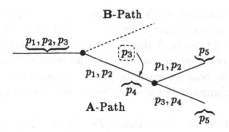

Figure 7: Two-way Split at the Second Level

Given a team with a specified success ratio, we must identify the set of trees that this team can *handle*. This essentially captures the potential learning power of the team. We say that a tree $T_1$ is more powerful than $T_2$ if there is a team $\langle x, y, z \rangle$ that survives $T_2$ but not $T_1$. So, understanding the *power* of trees will result in understanding the relative learning power of teams with differing plurality. This leads to the obvious question of comparing the power of two arbitrary trees $T_1$ and $T_2$. For example, it is not hard to prove that a team with plurality $\langle 4, 1, 7 \rangle$ survives the tree in Figure 7, but does not survive the tree in Figure 6.

A fundamental combinatorial question we are interested in addressing is the classification of *capability trees* based on their power. It is imperative that we at least identify the set of *capability trees* before attempting to classify them. For this reason, we restrict our focus to teams $\langle x, y, z \rangle$ where $2x > z$. This is not unreasonably restrictive since many of the reductions we have noticed in [3] fall into this category. Moreover, this could be a good starting point since the capabilities of teams $\langle x, 0, z \rangle$ where $2x > z$ have been well understood.

In the case of a team with plurality $\langle 3, 0, 5 \rangle$, we described two trees (see Figures 6 and 7) that the team *barely* survives. Of course, there are other *simpler* trees that this team can survive where in there is no branch along which the team has expended all of its resources (i.e., produced five programs). In an analogous manner, one can construct $n-1$ groups of trees, denoted by $\{Tree\langle n, 1 \rangle, Tree\langle n, 2 \rangle, \ldots, Tree\langle n, n-1 \rangle\}$ for a team with plurality $\langle n, 0, 2n - 1 \rangle$. For such construction, one can prove that a team of the form $\langle n, 0, 2n - 1 \rangle$ survives trees of the form $Tree\langle i, j \rangle$ where $n \geq i > j$. The group $Tree\langle i, j \rangle$ is a collection of equivalent *capability trees*. That is, if a $\langle x, y, z \rangle$-team satisfies a tree in $Tree\langle i, j \rangle$, then it satisfies every other tree in $Tree\langle i, j \rangle$.

The first interesting property we can show is that the set $Tree\langle i, j \rangle$ where $i > j \geq 1$ is not empty. Therefore, we can identify a representative tree for each class $Tree\langle i, j \rangle$ and the construction of such trees is by induction on $i$ and $j$. So, for the ease of presentation, we view the class $Tree\langle i, j \rangle$ as a single (representative) tree.

We now introduce the relation $\ll$ to compare the power of two trees. The notation $Tree\langle i, j \rangle \ll Tree\langle x, y \rangle$ denotes that the tree $Tree\langle x, y \rangle$ is strictly more powerful than the tree $Tree\langle i, j \rangle$. It is not hard to prove that the relation $\ll$ is transitive. We can show that the relation $\ll$ induces a proper partial order on $\mathcal{T} = \{Tree\langle i, j \rangle : i > j \geq 1\}$. In fact, the partial order induced by $\ll$ can be easily described. For arbitrary integers $i, j$ such that $i > j \geq 1$, $Tree\langle i, j-1 \rangle \ll Tree\langle i, j \rangle$, $Tree\langle i-1, j \rangle \ll Tree\langle i, j \rangle$ and $\ll$ is transitive. On the other hand, it is not hard to prove that two distinct trees

$Tree\langle i, j\rangle$ and $Tree\langle x, y\rangle$ are incomparable if they are not related by $\ll$.

Consider a team with plurality $\langle x, y, z\rangle$. Any such arbitrary team survives a set of trees $\Delta$ from $\mathcal{T}$. So, if we drop trees in $\Delta$ that are subsumed by other trees in $\Delta$, then we get a minimal set $\Delta'$ of trees that are satisfied by the team with plurality $\langle x, y, z\rangle$. So in order to understand the relative learning power of teams we must identify the sets of trees in $\mathcal{T}$ that are minimal sets for some team. We refer to such minimal sets as *atomic* sets.

For $n \geq 2$, our current results show that $\{Tree\langle n, n-1\rangle\}$, $\{Tree\langle n, n-2\rangle\}$ and $\{Tree\langle n, 1\rangle\}$ are *atomic* sets. Moreover, for any integer $n - 2 > i > 1$, the minimal set $\{Tree\langle n, i\rangle\}$ is not *atomic* since we can show that if an *atomic* set contains $Tree\langle n, i\rangle$ where $n - 1 > i > x \geq 1$, then it also contains either $Tree\langle n - x, i + x\rangle$ or $Tree\langle n + x, i - x\rangle$.

One research goal is to identify *atomic* sets. Our experimental results show that any arbitrary team with plurality $\langle x, y, z\rangle$ where $2x > z$ has an *atomic* set in the powerset of $\mathcal{T}$. We plan to identify *atomic* sets for arbitrary teams. It is then easy to see that the *atomic* set for a team reveals the relative learning power of the team.

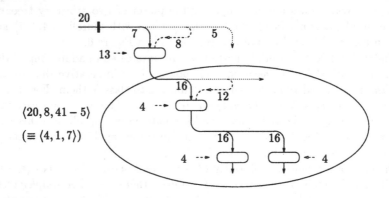

Figure 8: A Distribution of Programs of 20/41-Team

In closing, we note that several of the cases in the simulation construction (see [3]) of a team with plurality 20/41 simulating other teams with plurality in the range $(\frac{18}{37}, \frac{20}{41}]$, the reduced follower strategy is equivalent to that of a team with plurality $\langle 4, 1, 7\rangle$. Figure 8 illustrates one such case. Recall that (see Figures 7 and 6) the learning capability of team with plurality $\langle 4, 1, 7\rangle$ is strictly weaker than that of a team with plurality $\langle 3, 0, 5\rangle$.

# 8  Acknowledgements

Both authors are supported in part by NSF Grant CCR-9202158.

# References

[1]   R. Daley, and B. Kalyanasundaram, Capabilities of Probabilistic Learners with Bounded Mind Changes, In *Proceedings of the 1993 Workshop on Computational Learning Theory*, 1993.

[2]   R. Daley, and B. Kalyanasundaram, Use of Reduction Arguments in Determining Popperian FIN-type Learning Capabilities, In *Proceedings of the 1993 Workshop on Algorithmic Learning Theory*, 1993.

[3]   R. Daley, B. Kalyanasundaram, and M. Velauthapillai, Breaking the probability $\frac{1}{2}$ barrier in FIN-type learning, In *Proceedings of the 1992 Workshop on Computational Learning Theory*, 1992.

[4]   R. Daley, B. Kalyanasundaram, and M. Velauthapillai, The Power of Probabilism in Popperian FINite Learning, In *Proceedings of the 1992 Workshop on Analogical and Inductive Inference*, Lecture Notes in Computer Science **642**, 151-169.

[5]   R. Daley, L. Pitt, M. Velauthapillai, and T. Will, Relations between probabilistic and team one-shot learners, In *Proceedings of the 1991 Workshop on Computational Learning Theory*, pages 228-239, 1991.

[6]   R.V. Freivalds, Finite Identification of General Recursive Functions by Probabilistic Strategies, Akademie Verlag, Berlin, 1979.

[7]   S. Jain, and A. Sharma, Finite learning by a team, In *Proceedings of the 1990 Workshop on Computational Learning Theory*, pages 163-177, 1990.

[8]   D. Osherson, M. Stob, and S. Weinstein, *Systems that Learn, An Introduction to Learning Theory for Cognitive and Computer Scientists*, MIT Press, Cambridge, Mass., 1986.

[9]   L. Pitt, and C. Smith, Probability and plurality for aggregations of learning machines, *Information and Computation*, 77(1):77-92, 1988.

[10]  M. Velauthapillai, Inductive inference with a bounded number of mind changes, In *Proceedings of the 1989 Workshop on Computational Learning Theory*, pages 200-213, 1989.

# Not-So-Nearly-Minimal-Size Program Inference (Preliminary Report)

John Case and Mandayam Suraj

Department of Computer and Information Sciences

University of Delaware

Newark, DE 19716

USA

{case, suraj}@cis.udel.edu

Sanjay Jain

Institute of Systems Science

National University of Singapore

Singapore 0511

Republic of Singapore

sanjay@iss.nus.sg

## Abstract

Freivalds defined an acceptable programming system independent criterion for learning programs for functions in which the final programs were required to be both correct and "nearly" minimal size, i.e, within a computable function of being purely minimal size. Kinber showed that this parsimony requirement on final programs severely limits learning power. Nonetheless, in, for example, scientific inference, parsimony is considered highly desirable. A *lim-computable function* is (by definition) one computable by a procedure allowed to change its mind finitely many times about its output. Investigated is the possibility of assuaging somewhat the limitation on learning power resulting from requiring parsimonious final programs by use of criteria which require the final, correct programs to be "not-so-nearly" minimal size, e.g., to be within a lim-computable function of actual minimal size. It is interestingly shown that some parsimony in the final program is thereby retained, yet learning power strictly increases. Also considered are lim-computable functions as above but for which notations for constructive ordinals are used to bound the number of mind changes allowed regarding the output. This is a variant of an idea introduced by Freivalds and Smith. For this ordinal complexity bounded version of lim-computability, the power of the resultant learning criteria form strict infinite hierarchies intermediate between the computable and the lim-computable cases. Many open questions are also presented.

## 1 Introduction

Freivalds [Fre75] defined an acceptable programming system [Rog58, Rog67, MY78] independent criterion for learning programs for functions in which the final programs were required to be both correct and "nearly" minimal size, i.e, within a computable function of being purely minimal size. Kinber [Kin74] announced that this parsimony requirement on final programs severely limited learning power. Refinements for which final programs are allowed to be anomalous [BB75, CS83] appear in [Che81, Che82]. The language learning case is considered in [CJS89]. More stringent parsimony requirements on final programs have been studied too [Fre75, Kin74, FK77, Kin77b, Kin83] [Fre90, JS91], for example, in which the final programs are required to be strictly minimal size. These parsimony restrictions even further limit learning power in ways which are interestingly dependent on the underlying acceptable programming system.

In, for example, scientific inference, parsimony is considered highly desirable; however, the above mentioned results indicate that even weak parsimony restrictions limit learning or inferring power. To begin explaining the results of the present paper: a *lim-computable function* is (by definition) one computable by a procedure allowed to change its mind finitely many times about its output. Investigated in this paper is the possibility of assuaging somewhat the limitation on learning power resulting from requiring parsimonious final programs by use of criteria which require the final, correct programs to be "not-so-nearly" minimal size, i.e., to be within a lim-computable function of actual minimal size. It is interestingly shown (Theorem 4 below) that some parsimony in the final program is thereby retained, yet learning power strictly increases.

Proposition 2, implies that, adding another limit to the parsimony bounding functions results in no parsimony being preserved (and no loss of learning power).

In Section 6 we consider some refinements of our learning criteria. Especially interesting is a refinement in Section 6.2 in which, for the lim-computable functions, notations for constructive ordinals [Rog67] are used to bound the number of mind changes allowed regarding the output. This is a variant of an idea introduced by Freivalds and Smith [FS91]. For this ordinal complexity bounded version of lim-computability, the power of the resultant learning criteria form strict infinite hierarchies intermediate between the computable and the lim-computable cases. Interesting open questions are also presented regarding just how fine are the learning criteria hierarchies generated by these ordinal complexity bounds.

# 2 Notation

$N$ denotes the set of natural numbers, $\{0, 1, 2, 3, \ldots\}$. $i, j, k, m, n, p, q, s, t, w, x, y, z$ (with or without subscripts, superscripts, ...) range over $N$. '*' denotes a non-member of $N$ such that $(\forall n \in N)[n < * < \infty]$ ('*' represents 'unbounded but finite'). $a, b, c, d$, similarly, range over $N \cup \{*\}$. $x \dotminus y$ denotes $\max(\{0, x - y\})$.

$\emptyset$ denotes the empty set. $\in, \notin, \subseteq, \subset$ respectively denote 'is a member of', 'is not a member of', 'is a subset of' and 'is a proper subset of'. $\uparrow$ denotes 'is undefined'. $\downarrow$ denotes 'is defined'.

For $S$, a subset of $N$, card$(S)$ denotes the cardinality of $S$. So then, 'card$(S) \leq *$' means that card$(S)$ is finite. $\max(S)$ and $\min(S)$ denote, respectively, the maximum and minimum of the set $S$, where $\max(\emptyset) = 0$ and $\min(\emptyset) = \infty$. $f, g, h$ with or without decorations range over *total* functions with arguments and values from $N$. For $a \in (N \cup \{*\})$, if $\eta_1$ and $\eta_2$ are partial functions, then $\eta_1 =^a \eta_2$ means that card$(\{x \mid \eta_1(x) \neq \eta_2(x)\}) \leq a$. domain$(\eta)$ and range$(\eta)$ respectively denote the domain and range of the partial function $\eta$. The set of all total computable functions of one variable is denoted by $\mathcal{R}$. $\mathcal{C}$ and $\mathcal{S}$, with or without decorations, ranges over subsets of $\mathcal{R}$.

$\varphi$ denotes a fixed *acceptable* programming system for the partial computable functions: $N \rightarrow N$ [Rog58, Rog67, MY78, Ric80, Ric81, Roy87, Mar89]. $\varphi_p$ denotes the partial computable function computed by program $p$ in the $\varphi$-system; $W_p$ denotes the domain of $\varphi_p$. $\Phi$ denotes an arbitrary fixed Blum complexity measure for the $\varphi$-system [Blu67]. For a computable function $f$, MinProg$(f) \overset{\text{def}}{=} \min(\{p \mid \varphi_p = f\})$.

The quantifier '$\forall^\infty$' means 'for all but finitely many'; '$\exists^\infty$' means 'there exists infinitely many' and '∃!' means 'there exists a unique'. $\sigma$ ranges over finite initial segments of total functions. Any unexplained notation is from [Rog67].

# 3 Explanatory Function Identification

A *learning machine* [Gol67, BB75, CS83] is a computable mapping from the set of all finite initial segments of total functions: $N \to N$ into $N \cup \{?\}$. Natural number outputs are interpreted as programs in the $\varphi$-system. Initially, a learning machine is allowed to output ?'s to indicate that it has not decided on its first program output yet, but once it outputs some program, it is not allowed to output ?'s again. $f[n]$ denotes the finite initial segment $((0, f(0)), (1, f(1)), \ldots, (n-1, f(n-1)))$. We say that $M(f)$ *converges to* $p$ (written $M(f)\!\downarrow = p$) iff $(\exists p)(\forall^\infty n)[M(f[n]) = p]$; $M(f)$ is undefined if no such $p$ exists.

**Definition 1 ([Gol67, BB75, CS83])** Suppose $a, b \in N \cup \{*\}$.

(a) $\mathbf{M}$ $\mathbf{Ex}_b^a$*-identifies* $f$ (written: $f \in \mathbf{Ex}_b^a(\mathbf{M})$) $\overset{\text{def}}{\Leftrightarrow}$ $[(\exists i \mid \varphi_i =^a f)$
$(\forall^\infty n)[M(f[n]) = i] \ \wedge \ \text{card}(\{n \mid ? \neq M(f[n]) \neq M(f[n+1])\}) \leq b]$.

(b) $\mathbf{Ex}_b^a = \{ \mathcal{S} \mid (\exists \mathbf{M})[\mathcal{S} \subseteq \mathbf{Ex}_b^a(\mathbf{M})] \}$.

$\mathbf{Ex}_*^0$ is written sometimes as $\mathbf{Ex}$ and $\mathbf{Ex}_*^a$ is sometimes written as $\mathbf{Ex}^a$. Theorem 1 below gives some of the results about $\mathbf{Ex}_b^a$ criteria.

**Theorem 1 ([CS83])** For all $m, n$,

(a) $\mathbf{Ex}_0^{n+1} - \mathbf{Ex}^n \neq \emptyset$;

(b) $\mathbf{Ex}_{m+1}^0 - \mathbf{Ex}_m^* \neq \emptyset$;

(c) $\mathbf{Ex}_0^* - \bigcup_{n \in N} \mathbf{Ex}^n \neq \emptyset$;

(d) $\mathbf{Ex}_*^0 - \bigcup_{m \in N} \mathbf{Ex}_m^* \neq \emptyset$.

Blum and Blum [BB75] first showed that $\mathbf{Ex} \subset \mathbf{Ex}^*$.

# 4 Nearly-Minimal Identification

Freivalds considered the learning of minimal-size programs and showed that such learning is dependent on the acceptable programming system from which programs for functions are learned. He, however, considered a variant of such learning, where the conditions of parsimony on the size of the final programs are relaxed. The $a = 0, b = *$ case of the definition immediately below is essentially the way he relaxed the constraints on parsimony. The criteria of this definition are acceptable programming system independent.

**Definition 2 ([Fre75, Che82])**

(a) A learning machine $\mathbf{M}$ $\mathbf{Mex}_b^a$*-identifies* $\mathcal{S}$ (written: $\mathcal{S} \subseteq \mathbf{Mex}_b^a(\mathbf{M})$) $\overset{\text{def}}{\Leftrightarrow}$ there is a computable function $g$ such that, for all $f \in \mathcal{S}$, $\mathbf{M}$ $\mathbf{Ex}_b^a$-identifies $f$ and $M(f) \leq g(\text{MinProg}(f))$.

(b) $\mathbf{Mex}_b^a = \{ \mathcal{S} \mid (\exists \mathbf{M})[\mathcal{S} \subseteq \mathbf{Mex}_b^a(\mathbf{M})] \}$.

In the definition above, the $g$ represents a fudge factor by which the parsimony constraint is loosened. The final programs are, in a sense, *nearly-minimal-size*.

Theorem 2 below gives some of the results about the $\mathbf{Mex}_b^a$ criteria.

**Theorem 2 ([Che82])** For all $m, n, a, b$,

(a) $\mathbf{Mex}_b^a \subseteq \mathbf{Ex}_b^a$;

(b) $\mathbf{Ex} - \mathbf{Mex}^n \neq \emptyset$;

(c) $\mathbf{Mex}_0^{n+1} - \mathbf{Ex}_m^n \neq \emptyset$;

(d) $\mathbf{Mex}_{m+1}^0 - \mathbf{Ex}_m^* \neq \emptyset$;

(e) $\mathbf{Mex}^* = \mathbf{Ex}^*$;

(f) $\mathbf{Ex}_m^n \subset \mathbf{Mex}_*^n$.

**Corollary 1** For all $m, n, a, b$,

(a) $\mathbf{Mex}^n \subset \mathbf{Ex}^n$;

(b) $\mathbf{Mex}_m^a \subseteq \mathbf{Mex}_n^b \Leftrightarrow (a \leq b) \wedge (m \leq n)$.

Kinber [Fre75, Kin77a] announced that $\mathbf{Mex} \subset \mathbf{Ex}$. Jain has recently shown that $\mathbf{Mex}_0^{n+1} \not\subseteq \mathbf{Ex}^n$.

# 5   Not-So-Nearly-Minimal-Size Program Inference

Nearly minimal size program inference, as defined by $\mathbf{Mex}$, requires that the final program size be within a computable fudge factor of the actual minimum program. In the present paper, we wish to successively relax the computable fudge factor constraint and investigate whether the learning power is enhanced. The first means we choose to relax the constraint imposed by $\mathbf{Mex}$, is essentially to allow $lim_d$-*computable* fudge factors. $\text{Lim}_d$-computability is defined below (Definition 4).

**Definition 3**
$$\lim_{t \to \infty} h(x, t) \stackrel{\text{def}}{=} \begin{cases} y & \text{if } (\forall^\infty t)[h(x, t) = y]; \\ \uparrow & \text{otherwise} . \end{cases}$$

We write $h(x, \infty)$ for $\lim_{t \to \infty} h(x, t)$.

**Definition 4** $g : N \to N$ is $lim_d$-*computable* $\stackrel{\text{def}}{\Leftrightarrow}$ ($\exists$ computable $h : (N \times N) \to N)(\forall x)[g(x) = h(x, \infty)] \wedge (\forall x)[\text{card}(\{t \mid h(x, t) \neq h(x, t+1)\}) \leq d]$.

Intuitively, in Definition 4, $h(x, t)$ is the output at discrete time $t$ of a mind changing algorithm for $g$ (acting on input $x$). $(\forall x)[g(x) = h(x, \infty)]$, for $h$ computable, means, then, that, for all $x$, for all but finitely many times $t$, the output of the mind changing algorithm on input $x$ is $g(x)$. $d$ is just a bound on how many times the mind changing algorithm for $g$ is allowed to change its mind.

We write lim-computable for $lim_*$-computable. It is easy to show that there is a lim-computable function $g$ such that $(\forall \text{ computable } f)(\forall^\infty x)[g(x) > f(x)]$. Hence, the lim-computable functions go way beyond the computable ones; in fact, they have been known since Post [Sha71] to characterize the functions computable with an oracle for the halting problem.

It turns out that, for $d \notin \{0, *\}$, the class of $\lim_d$-computable functions *fail* to have some useful closure properties one easily (and correctly) takes for granted in the $d \in \{0, *\}$ cases: it is easy to show that, for $d \notin \{0, *\}$, there is a $\lim_1$-computable function $g$ so that for *no* $\lim_d$-computable, *monotone non-decreasing* function $g'$ do we have $g' \geq g$. Of course, intuitively, the fudge factors that make the most sense to use are monotone non-decreasing and many proofs ostensibly require them too. Hence, in our definition just below, we employ the device of considering *only* monotone non-decreasing fudge factors. This trick enables one, for example, to show the criteria so introduced are acceptable programming system independent.

**Definition 5**

(a) A learning machine **M** $\mathbf{Lim}_d\mathbf{Mex}_b^a$–*identifies* $\mathcal{S}$ (written: $\mathcal{S} \subseteq \mathbf{Lim}_d\mathbf{Mex}_b^a(\mathbf{M})$) $\overset{\text{def}}{\Leftrightarrow}$ there is a monotone non-decreasing $\lim_d$-computable function $g$ such that, for all $f \in \mathcal{S}$, **M** $\mathbf{Ex}_b^a$–identifies $f$ and $\mathbf{M}(f) \leq g(\mathrm{MinProg}(f))$.

(b) $\mathbf{Lim}_d\mathbf{Mex}_b^a = \{\mathcal{S} \mid (\exists \mathbf{M})[\mathcal{S} \subseteq \mathbf{Lim}_d\mathbf{Mex}_b^a(\mathbf{M})]\}$.

Hence, our definition requires that the machines converge to a program that is *not-so-nearly-minimal-size*. We mostly write $\mathbf{LimMex}_b^a$ instead of $\mathbf{Lim}_*\mathbf{Mex}_b^a$. The following proposition is obvious.

**Proposition 1** For all $m,a,b$,

(a) $\mathbf{Mex}_b^a \subseteq \mathbf{LimMex}_b^a \subseteq \mathbf{Ex}_b^a$;

(b) $\mathbf{Lim}_m\mathbf{Mex}_b^a \subseteq \mathbf{Lim}_{m+1}\mathbf{Mex}_b^a$;

(c) $\mathbf{Lim}_0\mathbf{Mex}_b^a = \mathbf{Mex}_b^a$.

The following theorem is essentially proved in Chen [Che82] using the class of functions of finite support (i.e., functions that have value 0 on all but finitely many inputs).

**Theorem 3 ([Che82])** For all $n$, $\mathbf{Ex} - \mathbf{LimMex}^n \neq \emptyset$.

Theorem 4 below shows that relaxing the parsimony constraint on final programs from being within a *computable* fudge factor of minimal size to being within a *lim-computable* fudge factor of minimal size *does* result in an increase in learning power. However, by Theorem 3 above, the requirement that final programs be within a lim-computable fudge factor of minimal size nonetheless retains *some* parsimony in the final programs.

**Theorem 4** For all $n$, $\mathbf{LimMex} - \mathbf{Mex}^n \neq \emptyset$.

Theorem 4 turns out to be a consequence of a result we prove later (Theorem 14 in Section 6), and, hence, we do not prove Theorem 4 here. Theorem 4 originally encouraged us to explore whether there was a fine hierarchy between **Mex** and **LimMex** based on $\lim_d$-computable fudge factors. We consider this next.

**Lemma 1** For each $n > 0$, every monotone non-decreasing $\lim_n$-computable function is dominated by a monotone non-decreasing *computable* function.

PROOF.

We do the $n = 1$ case only. The other cases are, then, a straightforward lift.

Suppose $g$ is a monotone non-decreasing $\lim_1$-computable function as witnessed by computable $h$.

Case 1: $(\forall^\infty x)(\forall t)[h(x, t) = h(x, 0)]$.

Clearly in this case, there exists a $g'$, computable and monotone non-decreasing, such that $g' \geq g$.

Case 2: $(\exists^\infty x)(\exists t)[h(x, t) \neq h(x, 0)]$.

In this case, we define $g'$ as follows. $g'(0) = g(0)$. For each $x > 0$, $g'(x)$ is defined as follows. Search for a $y \geq x$ and a $t > 0$ such that $h(y, 0) \neq h(y, t)$ and $h(y, t) \geq g'(x - 1)$; set $g'(x) = h(y, t)$, for the $y$ and $t$ so found. Clearly, $g'$ is computable, monotone non-decreasing, and dominates $g$ everywhere. ∎

Clearly by Lemma 1, we have the following

**Theorem 5** For each $n \in N$, $\mathbf{Lim}_n\mathbf{Mex}_b^a = \mathbf{Mex}_b^a$.

We had originally hoped the immediately previous theorem was not true, that there was a fine hierarchy between **Mex** and **LimMex** based on $\lim_d$-computable fudge factors. In the next section we successfully explore some different sources of restricted parsimony fine structure.

# 6 Further Generalizations

In Section 6.1 we briefly explore the effect of allowing even looser fudge factors and indicate many presently open questions.

We saw in Theorem 5 above that *natural number* bounds on convergence of limiting procedures for computing fudge factors do *not* provide a hierarchy of criteria between **Mex** and **LimMex**. In Section 6.2 we consider *constructive ordinal* [Rog67] bounds on such limiting procedures instead. This approach was nicely inspired by [FS91]. We present in Section 6.2 some interesting results providing a fine structure between **Mex** and **LimMex**. We also indicate many questions open as of the writing of this preliminary report.

## 6.1 Looser Fudge Factors

One more way that we can examine how programs inferred can be allowed to be not-so-nearly-minimal-size is by allowing even looser fudge factors. To this end, consider the following definitions.

**Definition 6** For $h : N^{n+1} \to N, x \in N, i < n$, $h(x, t_1, t_2, \ldots, t_i, \infty, \ldots, \infty) = \lim_{t_{i+1} \to \infty} h(x, t_1, t_2, \ldots, t_i, t_{i+1}, \infty, \ldots, \infty)$.

**Definition 7** $f : N \to N$ is $lim_{d_1, d_2, \ldots, d_n}^n$-computable$\overset{\text{def}}{\Leftrightarrow}$ ($\exists$ computable $h : N^{n+1} \to N$)$(\forall x)[f(x) = h(x, \infty, \ldots, \infty)]$ and $(\forall i \mid 1 \leq i \leq n)(\forall x, t_1, t_2, \ldots, t_i)[$
card($\{t \mid h(x, t_1, \ldots, t_{i-1}, t, \infty, \ldots, \infty) \neq h(x, t_1, \ldots, t_{i-1}, t + 1, \infty, \ldots, \infty)\}) \leq d_i]$.

We write $lim^n$-*computable* for $lim_{*, \ldots, *}^n$-computable. The above definitions could be also be generalized to finite but unbounded (i.e., $*$) iterations of limits. In the definition below, we use $lim_{d_1, d_2, \ldots, d_n}^n$-computable functions to measure allowed deviance of programs from being nearly-minimal-size.

**Definition 8**

(a) Suppose **M** is a learning machine. $\mathbf{M}\ \mathbf{Lim}^n_{d_1,\dots,d_n}\mathbf{Mex}^a_b$–*identifies* $\mathcal{S}$ (written: $\mathcal{S} \subseteq \mathbf{Lim}^n_{d_1,\dots,d_n}\mathbf{Mex}^a_b(\mathbf{M})$) $\overset{\text{def}}{\Leftrightarrow}$ there is a $\lim^n_{d_1,\dots,d_n}$-computable monotone non-decreasing function $g$ such that, for all $f \in \mathcal{S}$, $\mathbf{M}\ \mathbf{Ex}^a_b$–identifies $f$ and $\mathbf{M}(f) \leq g(\mathrm{MinProg}(f))$.

(b) $\mathbf{Lim}^n_{d_1,\dots,d_n}\mathbf{Mex}^a_b = \{\mathcal{S} \mid (\exists \mathbf{M})[\mathcal{S} \subseteq \mathbf{Lim}^n_{d_1,\dots,d_n}\mathbf{Mex}^a_b(\mathbf{M})]\}$.

We mostly write $\mathbf{Lim}^n\mathbf{Mex}^a_b$ instead of $\mathbf{Lim}^n_{*,\dots,*}\mathbf{Mex}^a_b$. The following proposition implies that, for fudge factors computed by two levels of unrestricted iterated limits, there is essentially no longer any parsimony retained in the resultant final programs.

**Proposition 2** $\mathbf{Lim}^2\mathbf{Mex}^a = \mathbf{Ex}^a$.

PROOF. ($\subseteq$) Trivial.
($\supseteq$) Suppose $\mathcal{S} \subseteq \mathbf{Ex}^a(\mathbf{M})$. Then, $\mathcal{S} \in \mathbf{Lim}^2\mathbf{Mex}^a$ as witnessed by **M** and $\lim^2$-computable monotone non-decreasing $g$, such that, for all $x$, $g(x) \overset{\text{def}}{=} h(x, \infty, \infty)$, where $h$ is defined below. We first define $h'$ as below. It is to be understood, that for values of $h'$, ?'s are changed to 0's.

$$h'(i, t_1, t_2) = \begin{cases} \mathbf{M}(\varphi_i[t_1]) & \text{if } (\forall x < t_1)[\Phi_i(x) \leq t_2] \wedge \\ & (\forall y \mid t_1 \leq y \leq t_2 \wedge (\forall x < y)[\Phi_i(x) \leq t_2]) \\ & [\mathbf{M}(\varphi_i[t_1]) = \mathbf{M}(\varphi_i[y])]]; \\ 0 & \text{otherwise.} \end{cases}$$

We then define $h$ as
$h(i, t_1, t_2) = \max(\{h'(x, t_1, t_2) \mid x \leq i\})$.
Clearly, $h$ is monotone non-decreasing and can be seen to dominate $h'$. ∎

**Corollary 2** $\mathbf{Mex}^n \subset \mathbf{LimMex}^n \subset \mathbf{Lim}^2\mathbf{Mex}^n = \mathbf{Lim}^3\mathbf{Mex}^n = \dots = \mathbf{Ex}^n$.

There are many mostly uninvestigated questions still open. What happens with the iterated limits when we consider criteria that don't necessarily require convergence to a single final program, such as $\mathbf{Bc}^a$ [Bar74, CS83]? Which $\mathbf{Lim}_d\mathbf{Mex}^a_b$ criteria have "limiting-standardizability" style characterizations similar to those first obtained for $\mathbf{Mex}$ in [Fre75]. Generally, except for the cases noted above and their trivial consequences, how do the learning classes $\mathbf{Lim}^n_{d_1,\dots,d_n}\mathbf{Mex}^a_b$ compare to one another?

## 6.2 Constructive Ordinal Bounds on Limits

We proceed very informally. Some familiarity with a treatment of constructive ordinals such as the ones in [Rog67, Sac90] may be useful to readers of this section. Readers may also find [FS91] useful in this regard.

Intuitively ordinals [Sie65] are representations of well-orderings. 0 represents the empty ordering, 1 represents the ordering of 0 by itself, 2 the ordering $0 < 1$, 3 the ordering $0 < 1 < 2$, ... . The ordinal $\omega$ represents the standard ordering of all of $N$. $\omega + 1$ represents the ordering of $N$ consisting of the positive integers in standard order *followed by* 0. $\omega + \omega$ represents the ordering of $N$ consisting of the even numbers in standard order followed by the odd numbers in standard order. The *constructive ordinals* are just those that have a program (called a *notation*) in some system which specifies how to build them (lay them out end to end so to speak). We will informally employ, as our system of notation, the variant of Kleene's system O presented in [Rog67]. In this system, $2^0$ is (by definition) the notation for 0. *Successor* ordinals are those with an immediate predecessor; for example, $1, 2, 3, \omega + 1, \dots$ are successor ordinals with respective immediate predecessors $0, 1, 2, \omega, \ldots$. If $u$ is a notation for the immediate predecessor of a successor ordinal, then a notation for that successor ordinal is (by definition) $2^u$. All other ordinals are *limit* ordinals; for example, $\omega$, $\omega + \omega$, $\ldots$ are limit ordinals. Kleene [Kle38, Rog67, Sac90] defined a natural partial ordering of notations, $<_o$, so that two notations so ordered represent respective ordinals with the second larger than the first. We omit details. Suppose $\varphi_p(0), \varphi_p(1), \varphi_p(2), \ldots$ are each notations in $<_o$ order. Suppose that the corresponding ordinals are longer and longer initial segments of some limit ordinal which is their sup. For example, some such $p$ generates the respective notations for $0, 1, 2, \ldots$ in $<_o$ order, and $\omega$ is the sup of this sequence. In general, then, $p$ essentially describes how to build the limit ordinal which is the sup of the ordinals with notations $\varphi_p(0), \varphi_p(1), \varphi_p(2), \ldots$. A notation for this limit ordinal is (by definition) $3 \cdot 5^p$. Clearly such limit ordinals have infinitely many such notations, different ones for different generating $p$'s. Nothing else is a notation. As in the literature on constructive ordinals, we use '$x \leq_o y$' for '$x <_o y \vee x = y$', '$x \geq_o y$' to mean '$y \leq_o x$ and '$x >_o y$' to mean '$y <_o x$'. We also recall the function $| \cdot |_o : O \to$ the set of ordinals, defined as follows [Kle55, Rog67, Sac90]

$$
\begin{aligned}
|1|_o &= 0 \\
|2^u|_o &= |u|_o + 1 \\
|3 \cdot 5^p|_o &= \lim_{n \to \infty} |\varphi_p(n)|_o
\end{aligned}
$$

The following properties of $<_o$ will be useful to recall [Kle55, Rog67, Sac90].

**Fact 1** For all $x, y \in N$,

(a) $x <_o y \Rightarrow (x \in O \wedge y \in O)$.

(b) $x \in O \Rightarrow 1 \leq_o x$.

(c) $x <_o y \Rightarrow y \neq 1$.

(d) $x <_o 2^y \Rightarrow x \leq_o y$.

(e) $x <_o 3 \cdot 5^p \Rightarrow (\exists n)[x <_o \varphi_p(n)]$.

(f) $(x \leq_o z \wedge y \leq_o z) \Rightarrow (x <_o y \vee x = y \vee x >_o y)$.

The following fact on notations [Rog67, Sac90] is also important to us.

**Fact 2** There exist computable functions $h_1$ and $h_2$ such that, for all $v \in O$,

(a) $W_{h_1(v)} = \{u \mid u <_o v\} \in O$;

(b) $W_{h_2(v)} = \{\langle u_1, u_2 \rangle \mid u_1 <_o u_2 <_o v\}$ is a well-ordering isomorphic to $|v|_o$.

Everyone knows how to use natural numbers as counters. [FS91] introduced the use of constructive ordinals as more general counters. In this subsection we use constructive ordinals to count the allowed mind changes of limiting procedures.

**Convention 1** If $n \in N$, then **n** is the unique notation of $n$ in the O notation system.

So, for example, $\mathbf{0} = 1$ and $|\mathbf{0}|_o = 0$; $\mathbf{2} = 2^{2^1} = 4$ and $|\mathbf{2}|_o = 2$.

In the definition of $lim_d$-*computable* (Definition 7) $d \in N$ played the role of a counter for allowed mind-changes in the limiting process. For each notation $u$ in O, we will define $lim_u$-*computable* (Definition 9), where, intuitively, $u$ serves as a *transfinite* counter of allowed mind changes in the limiting procedure. This definition will conflict slightly with Definition 7, and, hence, after Definition 9, we no longer use Definition 7. As we will see, though, for $d \in N$, $\lim_d$-computable from Definition 9 corresponds to $\lim_d$-computable from Definition 7.

Intuitively, $h$ in Definition 9 just below plays a similar role to $h$ in Definition 7, and the function *tfcounter* in Definition 9 serves as a transfinite counter. As before, $t$ can be thought of a discrete time paramenter. Further explanation is given just after Definition 9.

**Definition 9** Suppose $u \in O$. $g : N \to N$ is $\lim_u$-computable $\overset{\text{def}}{\Leftrightarrow}$ there exist computable functions $h : (N \times N) \to N$ and *tfcounter* : $(N \times N) \to N$ such that

(a) $(\forall y)[g(y) = h(y, \infty)]$,

(b) $(\forall y, t)[\text{tfcounter}(y, t) \in O]$,

(c) $(\forall y)[\text{tfcounter}(y, 0) = u]$,

(d) $(\forall y, t)[\text{tfcounter}(y, t + 1) \leq_o \text{tfcounter}(y, t)]$, and

(e) $(\forall y, t)[h(y, t + 1) \neq h(y, t) \Rightarrow \text{tfcounter}(y, t + 1) <_o \text{tfcounter}(y, t)]$.

Part (b) of Definition 9 restricts the transfinite counter values to be notations $\in O$. Part (c) of Definition 9 initializes the transfinite counter at $u$. By Fact 2, the notations $<_o u$ are well-ordered; hence, part (d) of Definition 9 implies the counter cannot not descend infinitely. Part (e) of Definition 9 guarantees that, when $h$ has a mind change, then the transfinite counter *must* decrement. This part does *not* restrict how much it decrements. It also allows the transfinite counter to decrement without an accompanying mind change in $h$. These latter two properties are combinatorially convenient. Note that parts (b) through (e) imply that $h(y, \infty)$ is defined and part (a) defines $g(y)$ to be the value $h(y, \infty)$.

For $u \in O$, we now (partly re-)define the learning criterion $\mathbf{Lim}_u\mathbf{Mex}_b^a$ to be just like $\mathbf{LimMex}_b^a$ except that the fudge factor $g$ is $\lim_u$-computable as defined in Definition 9. $\mathbf{Lim_*Mex}$ retains it original meaning. Clearly, for $d \in N$, $\mathbf{Lim}_d\mathbf{Mex}_b^a$ from this definition corresponds to $\mathbf{Lim}_d\mathbf{Mex}_b^a$ from Definition 5. It is easy to show $\mathbf{Lim}_u\mathbf{Mex}_b^a$ is acceptable programming system independent.

We are interested in comparing, for various $u \in O$, the classes $\mathbf{Lim}_u\mathbf{Mex}_b^a$. We should note that, unfortunately it is open and mostly uninvestigated[1] whether, for all $u, u' \in O$ such that $|u|_o = |u'|_o$, $\mathbf{Lim}_u\mathbf{Mex}_b^a = \mathbf{Lim}_{u'}\mathbf{Mex}_b^a$. Moreover, we do not know whether, for all $u, u' \in O$ such that $|u|_o = |u'|_o$, the class of $\lim_u$-computable functions = the class of $\lim_{u'}$-computable functions. We have also not investigated the possible connections between the $\lim_u$-computable characteristic functions and the hierarchies of [Ers68]. We have further not considered the possible dependencies of the $\lim_u$-computable functions or of the classes $\mathbf{Lim}_u\mathbf{Mex}_b^a$ on the choice of notation *system* [Kle38, Rog67].

Before we proceed to compare, for various $u \in O$, the classes $\mathbf{Lim}_u\mathbf{Mex}_b^a$, we state the following six theorems.

**Theorem 6 ([CK37, Kle55, Rog67, Sac90])** There exists a computable function $+_o$ such that, for all $x, y \in N$,

$$x +_o y = \begin{cases} x & \text{if } y = 1; \\ 2^{(x+_o m)} & \text{if } y = 2^m, m > 1; \\ 3 \cdot 5^q & \text{if } y = 3 \cdot 5^p, (\text{where } (\forall n)[\varphi_q(n) = x +_o \varphi_p(n)]); \\ 7 & \textbf{otherwise} . \end{cases}$$

Furthermore, $q$ is a computable, 1–1 function of $x$ and $p$.

---

[1]We know a few special cases.

The 1–1-ness of $+_o$ just mentioned is crucial for proving parts of Theorem 7, which in turn are necessary for proving many result that follow.

$+_o$ has the following useful properties.

**Theorem 7 ([CK37, Kle55, Sac90])** For all $x, y$ and $z \in N$,

(a) $x, y \in O \Leftrightarrow x +_o y \in O$.

(b) $x, y \in O \Rightarrow |x +_o y|_o = |x|_o + |y|_o$.

(c) $(x, y \in O \wedge y \neq 1) \Rightarrow x <_o x +_o y$.

(d) $(x \in O \wedge z <_o y) \Leftrightarrow (x +_o z) <_o (x +_o y)$.

(e) $(x \in O \wedge y = z \in O) \Leftrightarrow (x +_o y) = (x +_o z)$.

(f) $x \leq_o z <_o (x +_o y) \Rightarrow (\exists! z)[y' <_o y \wedge (x +_o y') = z]$.

Note that $+_o$ (on O) is non-commutative like $+$ for ordinals; $+_o$ is, however, also non-associative (on O) unlike $+$ for ordinals. We adopt the convention that $x +_o y +_o z$ means $(x +_o y) +_o z$. The non-associativity of $+_o$ leads to some subtleties that are otherwise absent when dealing with ordinals, as opposed to notations.

The next theorem is a slight modification of a theorem in [CK37]. The $y = 2$ case is treated differently from therein and ensures that all the parts of Theorem 9 hold.

**Theorem 8 ([CK37])** There is a computable function $\times_o$ such that, for all $x, y \in N$,

$$
x \times_o y = \begin{cases}
1 & \text{if } y = 1; \\
x & \text{if } y = 2; \\
(x \times_o m) +_o x & \text{if } y = 2^m, m > 1; \\
3 \cdot 5^q & \text{if } y = 3 \cdot 5^p, \text{ (where } (\forall n)[\varphi_q(n) = x \times_o \varphi_p(n)]); \\
7 & \text{otherwise.}
\end{cases}
$$

Furthermore, $q$ is a computable, 1–1 function of $x$ and $p$.

Like $+_o$, $\times_o$ is neither commutative nor associative (on O), and, as for $+_o$, in unparenthesized expressions involving $\times_o$, we associate to the left.

Analogous to Theorem 7, we have the following theorem for $\times_o$.

**Theorem 9** For all $x, y$ and $z \in N$.

(a) $(y \neq 1) \Rightarrow [x, y \in O \Leftrightarrow x \times_o y \in O]$.

(b) $x, y \in O \Rightarrow |x \times_o y|_o = |x|_o \times |y|_o$.

(c) $(x \neq 1 \wedge y \neq 1 \wedge y \neq 2) \Rightarrow [x, y \in O \Leftrightarrow x <_o x \times_o y]$.

(d) $(x \neq 1) \Rightarrow [(x \in O \wedge z <_o y) \Leftrightarrow x \times_o z <_o x \times_o y]$.

(e) $(x \neq 1) \Rightarrow [(x \in O \wedge y = z \in O) \Leftrightarrow x \times_o y = x \times_o z]$.

(f) $x' <_o x \Leftrightarrow (\forall y)[x \times_o y +_o x' <_o x \times_o (y +_o 1)]$.

(g) $x \leq_o z <_o (x \times_o y) \Rightarrow (\exists! y' <_o y, x' <_o x)[z = (x \times_o y') +_o x']$.

Another theorem from [CK37] is the following, except for a slight modification for the $y = 2$ case as in Theorem 9.

**Theorem 10 ([CK37])** There is a computable function $\exp_o$ such that, for all $x, y \in N$,

$$x \exp_o y = \begin{cases} 2 & \text{if } y = 1; \\ x & \text{if } y = 2; \\ (x \exp_o m) \times_o x & \text{if } y = 2^m, m > 1; \\ 3 \cdot 5^q & \text{if } y = 3 \cdot 5^p, \text{(where } (\forall n)[\varphi_q(n) = x \exp_o \varphi_p(n)]); \\ 7 & \text{otherwise.} \end{cases}$$

Furthermore, $q$ is a computable, 1–1 function of $x$ and $p$.

Again, similar comments about commutativity and associativity hold for $\exp_o$ as for $\times_o$ and $+_o$. The following are some of the properties of $\exp_o$ defined immediately above.

**Theorem 11** For all $x, y$ and $z \in N$.

(a) $(y \neq 1) \Rightarrow [x, y \in O \Leftrightarrow x \exp_o y \in O]$.

(b) $x, y \in O \Rightarrow |x \exp_o y|_o = |x|_o \exp_o |y|_o$.

(c) $(x \neq 1 \wedge x \neq 2 \wedge y \neq 1 \wedge y \neq 2) \Rightarrow [x, y \in O \Leftrightarrow x <_o x \exp_o y]$.

(d) $(x \neq 1 \wedge x \neq 2) \Rightarrow [(x \in O \wedge z <_o y) \Leftrightarrow x \exp_o z <_o x \exp_o y]$.

(e) $(x \neq 1 \wedge x \neq 2) \Rightarrow [(x \in O \wedge y = z \in O) \Leftrightarrow x \exp_o y = x \exp_o z]$.

(f) $(x \neq 1) \Rightarrow [x' <_o x \Leftrightarrow (\forall y)[(x \exp_o y) \times_o x' <_o x \exp_o (y +_o 1)]]$.

(g) $x \leq_o z <_o (x \exp_o y) \Rightarrow (\exists! y' <_o y, x' <_o x, z' <_o (x \exp_o y'))[z = ((x \exp_o y') \times_o x') +_o z']$.

We recall that $\omega = \lim_{n \to \infty} |n|_o$.

**Convention 2** $w$, with or without *subscripts*, ranges over notations for $\omega$.

Similar to Proposition 1, we have

**Proposition 3** *For all $u, v \in O$ such that $u \leq_o v$ and $a, b \in N \cup \{*\}$,*

(a) $\mathbf{Lim}_u \mathbf{Mex}_b^a \subseteq \mathbf{Lim}_v \mathbf{Mex}_b^a$,

(b) $\mathbf{Lim}_0 \mathbf{Mex}_b^a = \mathbf{Mex}_b^a$.

Again, similar to Lemma 1, we have

**Lemma 2** For all $u, v, w \in O$ such that $v <_o u \times_o w$, every monotone, non-decreasing $\lim_v$-computable function is dominated by a monotone, non-decreasing $\lim_u$-computable function.

PROOF. Let $u, y, w \in O$ be such that $y <_o u \times_o w$. Using Fact 1, there exists $k$ such that $y <_o u \times_o k$. So it suffices to prove the lemma for $y <_o u \times_o k$, for each $k$. The proof proceeds similarly to that of Lemma 1.

We will do only the $k = 2$ case. The other cases can be proved on similar lines.

Suppose $g$ is a monotone, non-decreasing $\lim_{u \times_o 2}$-computable function as witnessed by $h$ and *tfcounter*.

*Case 1:* $(\forall^\infty y)[tfcounter(y, \infty) >_o u]$.

Let $C = \{y \mid tfcounter(y, \infty) \leq_o u\}$. Since $C$ is finite, the set $C'$ defined as $C' = \{\langle y, n \rangle \mid y \in C \wedge h(y, \infty) = n\}$ is also finite and hence recursive.

For all $y \notin C$, $u +_o u \geq_o tfcounter(y, \infty) >_o u$. So, by Theorem 9, part (g), for all $v \notin C, t$, there exists a unique $u_t$ such that $0 <_o u_t \leq_o u$ and $u +_o u_t = tfcounter(v, t)$. We note that these $u_t$'s can be found effectively. Define computable functions $h'$ and $tfcounter'$ thus.

$$h'(v, t) = \begin{cases} n & \text{if } \langle v, n \rangle \in C'; \\ h(y, t) & \text{if } y \notin C. \end{cases}$$

$$tfcounter'(y, t) = \begin{cases} u & \text{if } y \in C; \\ u_t & \text{if } y \notin C \wedge tfcounter(y, t) = u +_o u_t. \end{cases}$$

Define $g'(y) = h'(y, \infty)$. Then, clearly, $g'$ is a monotone non-decreasing $\lim_u$-computable function as witnessed by $h'$ and $tfcounter'$ and $g'$ dominates $g$.

*Case 2: Not Case 1.*

So, $(\exists^\infty y)[tfcounter(y, \infty) \leq_o u]$. Let $C = \{y \mid tfcounter(y, \infty) \leq_o u\}$. Note that $C$ is an infinite, recursively enumerable set. Hence, there exists $C' \subseteq C$, such that $C'$ is recursive. Let $C' = \{y_0 < y_1 < \ldots\}$ be such an infinite recursively enumerable subset of $C$. Define computable functions $h'$ and $tfcounter'$ thus.

$$h'(z, t) = \begin{cases} 0 & \text{if } tfcounter(y_z, t) >_o u; \\ h(y_z, t) & \text{otherwise}. \end{cases}$$

$$tfcounter'(z, t) = \begin{cases} u & \text{if } tfcounter(y_z, t) >_o u; \\ tfcounter(y_z, t) & \text{otherwise}. \end{cases}$$

Define $g'(y) = h'(y, \infty)$. Then, clearly, $g'$ is a monotone non-decreasing $\lim_u$-computable function as witnessed by $h'$ and $tfcounter'$ and $g'$ dominates $g$. ∎

The above lemma immediately gives us

**Theorem 12** For all $a, b$, for all $u, v, w \in O$ such that $v <_o u \times_o w$, $\mathbf{Lim}_v\mathbf{Mex}_b^a = \mathbf{Lim}_u\mathbf{Mex}_b^a$.

The immediately above theorem shows that no gain in learning power results by using $\lim_v$-computable fudge factors instead of $\lim_u$-computable fudge factors, if $u$ and $v$ are related as above (i.e., there exists $w \in O$ such that $v <_o u \times_o w$). Our next theorem, Theorem 13, shows that, for suitable $u \in O$, when $|u|_o < \omega^\omega$, learning power strictly increases if we use $\lim_{u \times_o w}$-computable fudge factors instead of $\lim_u$-computable fudge factors. It is useful first to have the immediately following proposition, our inspiration for which came from Cantor's Normal Form Theorem for ordinals [Sie65, Page 323].

We recall, by Convention 2, that $w_1, w_2, \ldots$ (as well as $w$) are all notations for $\omega$.

**Proposition 4** For all $m$, for all $w_1, w_2, \ldots, w_{m+1}$, for all $x$, $x <_o (w_1 \times_o w_2 \times_o \ldots \times_o w_{m+1}) \Leftrightarrow (\exists! n_1, n_2, \ldots, n_{m+1})[x = (w_1 \times_o w_2 \times_o \ldots \times_o w_m \times_o \mathbf{n_1}) +_o (w_1 \times_o w_2 \times_o \ldots \times_o w_{m-1} \times_o \mathbf{n_2}) +_o \ldots +_o (w_1 \times_o \mathbf{n_m}) +_o \mathbf{n_{m+1}}]$.

Furthermore, for the left to right direction, the values for $n_1, n_2, \ldots, n_{m+1}$ can be algorithmically found.

The above proposition can be proved by induction on $m$.

**Convention 3** For every $u \in O, n \in N$, $u^n = u \exp_o \mathbf{n}$.

**Theorem 13** For all $w_1, w_2, \ldots, w_{m+1}$, $m$, $n$,
$\mathbf{Lim}_{w_1 \times_o w_2 \times_o \ldots \times_o w_{m+1}}\mathbf{Mex} - \mathbf{Lim}_{w_1 \times_o w_2 \times_o \ldots \times_o w_m}\mathbf{Mex}^n \neq \emptyset$.

PROOF.

For typographical convenience, we will prove the theorem for the case when $w_1 = w_2 = \ldots = w_{m+1} = w$. The other cases easily follow. Also, we do only the $n = 0$ case here. The $n \neq 0$ cases, then, can be proved easily by modifying steps 2.3 and 4 in the second half of this proof. We first introduce some definitions that will help us in turn to define classes to prove this theorem.

For all $f$, $p$, $n$, let

$$S(f,p,n) = \{f(\langle p,x \rangle)) \mid f(\langle p,x \rangle)) \neq 0 \wedge \mathrm{card}(\{y \leq x \mid f(p,y) \neq 0\}) \leq n\}.$$

Intuitively, $S(f,p,n)$ is the set of all non-zero values in the $p^{\mathrm{th}}$ cylinder of the computable function $f$, provided there are less than $n$ such values; otherwise, it is the first $n$ non-zero values in the $p^{\mathrm{th}}$ cylinder. Suppose without loss of generality that $\langle 0,0 \rangle = 0$.

For all $f$ and $k > 0$, let

$$L_1^f = \{f(\langle 0,0 \rangle)\}$$
$$L_{k+1}^f = \bigcup_{\langle p,n \rangle \in L_k^f} S(f,p,n)$$

Intuitively, if $L_1^f = \{\langle p,n \rangle\}$, then $L_2^f$ is just $S(f,p,n)$. For $k > 0$, $L_{k+1}^f$ is the union of sets of numbers, each of whose cardinality and content are determined by one or more elements of $L_k^f$. In the proof immediately below, we define and use a computable function $f$ for which, for $k > 0$, $L_{k+1}^f$ is a *disjoint* union of sets of numbers, each of whose cardinality and content are determined by a *distinct* element of $L_k^f$. Such an $f$ helps in clarity of presentation, though it is not necessary for proving this theorem.

For all $m$, let $\hat{S}_{w^m} = \{f \mid \lim_{t \to \infty} f(\langle 1,t \rangle) \downarrow = p \wedge \varphi_p = f \wedge p \leq \max(L_m^f)\}$.

We will now construct an inductive inference machine $\mathbf{M}$ and $\lim_{w^{m+1}}$computable $g$ such that $\hat{S}_{w^{m+1}} \in \mathbf{Lim}_{w^{m+1}}\mathbf{Mex}$ as witnessed by $\mathbf{M}$ and $g$. (We note that the same class can be used for different $w$'s that are notations for $\omega$.) For all $n$, define $\mathbf{M}(f[n])$ as follows. Let $i_n = \max(\{j \mid \langle 1,j \rangle < n\})$. Let $\mathbf{M}(f[n]) = f(\langle 1, i_n \rangle)$.

Firstly, we define total, computable functions $\varphi_j^t$ for each $j$ and $t$ as follows.

$$\varphi_j^t(x) = \begin{cases} \varphi_j(x) & \text{if } (\forall y \leq x)[\Phi_j(y) \leq t]; \\ 0 & \text{otherwise .} \end{cases}$$

Next, for all $j$, $t$, $p$, $n$, let

$$T(\langle j,t \rangle, p, n) = S(\varphi_j^t, p, n,).$$

For all $k > 0$, and $i$, $t$, let

$$P_1^{\langle \leq i,t \rangle} = \{\varphi_j(\langle 0,0 \rangle) \mid j \leq i \wedge \Phi_j(\langle 0,0 \rangle) \leq t\}$$
$$P_{k+1}^{\langle \leq i,t \rangle} = \bigcup_{j \leq i} \bigcup_{\langle p,n \rangle \in P_k^{\langle \leq i,t \rangle}} T(\langle j,t \rangle, p, n)$$

So, for all $k > 0$, $\lim_{t \to \infty} P_k^{\langle \leq i,t \rangle} \supseteq \bigcup_{j \leq i \wedge \varphi_j \in \mathcal{R}} L_k^{\varphi_j}$.

Also, let

$$\mathrm{card}_k^{\langle \leq i,t \rangle} = \mathrm{card}(P_k^{\langle \leq i,t \rangle}).$$
$$\mathrm{sum}_k^{\langle \leq i,t \rangle} = \sum_{\langle p,n \rangle \in P_k^{\langle \leq i,t \rangle}} n.$$

We now define $h$, *tfcounter* as follows. For all $i$, let $h(i,0) = 0$; *tfcounter*$(i,0) = w^{m+1}$;

For $t > 0$, we define $h(i,t)$ and *tfcounter*$(i,t)$ as follows.
$$h(i,t) = \max(P_{m+1}^{(\le i,t)});$$

Let $n_1 = i + 1 - \text{card}_1^{(\le i,t)}$. For $1 \le k \le m$ let $n_{k+1} = \text{sum}_k^{(\le i,t)} - \text{card}_{k+1}^{(\le i,t)}$.
*tfcounter*$(i,t) = w^m \times_o n_1 +_o w^{m-1} \times_o n_2 +_o \ldots +_o w \times_o n_m +_o n_{m+1}$.

Finally, we define $g$ as follows. For all $y$, $g(y) = h(y, \infty)$.

It can be verified that $g$ is $\lim_{w^{m+1}}$computable, as witnessed by $h$ and *tfcounter*, and that for every $\varphi_i \in \mathcal{S}_{\omega^{m+1}}$, $\mathbf{M}(\varphi_i) \le g(\text{MinProg}(\varphi_i))$.

We next show that $\mathcal{S}_{\omega^{m+1}} \notin \mathbf{Lim}_{\omega^m}\mathbf{Mex}$. We will show this only for $m > 0$ case. $m = 0$ case can be proved in a similar but much simpler manner.

Let $\wp_1, \wp_2, \ldots$ be the increasing sequence of prime numbers.
For all notations $v$ of the form $w^{m-1} \times_o n_1 +_o w^{m-2} \times_o n_2 +_o \ldots +_o w \times_o n_{m-1} +_o n_m$, for all $k$, such that $1 \le k \le m$, let
$$\text{num}_k^v = n_k.$$

For $k \le m$, let
$$\text{prod}_k^v = 1 + \prod_{i=1}^k \wp_i^{1+n_i}.$$

We note that, for all $v$, $\text{prod}_0^v = 2$. Suppose $v = w^{m-1} \times_o n_1 +_o w^{m-2} \times_o n_2 +_o \ldots +_o w \times_o n_{m-1} +_o n_m$ and $v' = w^{m-1} \times_o n_1' +_o w^{m-2} \times_o n_2' +_o \ldots +_o w \times_o n_{m-1}' +_o n_m'$. Then, $\text{prod}_k^v = \text{prod}_k^{v'}$ if and only if, for $1 \le i \le k$, $n_i = n_i'$.

Suppose by way of contradiction that $\mathcal{S}_{\omega^{m+1}} \in \mathbf{Lim}_{\omega^m}\mathbf{Mex}$ as witnessed by $\mathbf{M}$ and $\lim_{\omega^m}$-computable $g$. Let $h$, *tfcounter* witness that $g$ is $\lim_{\omega^m}$-computable. For $u$ such that $|u|_o \ne 0$, any $\lim_u$-computable function $g$ is dominated by some $\lim_u$-computable function $g'$ such that $g'$ makes at least one mind change on every input; this can be proved on the lines of Lemma 1.

By the Operator Recursion Theorem, there exists a recursive 1-1, increasing $e$ such that, for all $x$, the functions $\varphi_{e(x)}$ may be defined as follows.

Let $t$ be the least number such that $h(e(0), t) \ne h(e(0), 0)$.

Let curbnd $= h(e(0), t)$; curbot $=$ current $= 1$; curtop $=$ curbot $+$ curbnd $+ 1$.

Let $v = $ *tfcounter*$(e(0), t)$;

Let $\varphi_{e(0)}(\langle 0, 0 \rangle) = \langle \text{prod}_0^v, 1 + \text{num}_1^v \rangle$.

**for** $k = 0$ **to** $m - 2$ **do**

$\quad \varphi_{e(0)}(\langle \text{prod}_k^v, 0 \rangle) = \langle \text{prod}_{k+1}^v, 1 + \text{num}_{k+2}^v \rangle$;

**endfor**

Let $\varphi_{e(0)}(\langle \text{prod}_{m-1}^v, 0 \rangle) = e(\text{curtop})$.

For $x \le \max(\{\langle 0,0 \rangle, \langle \text{prod}_0^v, 0 \rangle, \ldots, \langle \text{prod}_{m-1}^v, 0 \rangle\})$, such that $\varphi_{e(0)}(x)$, has not been defined till now let $\varphi_{e(0)}(x) = 0$. Let $x_s$ denote the least $x$ such that $\varphi_{e(0)}(x)$ has not been defined before stage $s$.

Let Cancel $= \emptyset$.

Let lastmindch $= t$.

Go to stage 0.

**Begin Stage $s$**

1. For $x < x_s$, let $\varphi_{e(\text{current})}(x) = \varphi_{e(0)}(x)$.
2. Let $y = x_s$
   **repeat**
   2.1. If $y$ is of the form $\langle 1, z \rangle$, then let
        $$\varphi_{e(\text{current})}(y) = e(\text{current}).$$
        Otherwise let $\varphi_{e(\text{current})}(y) = 0$.
   2.2. If $h(e(0), \text{lastmindch}) \neq h(e(0), y + \text{lastmindch})$, then go to step 3.
   2.3. If there exists a $i \leq \text{curbnd}$, $i \notin \text{Cancel}$, and $x_s < \langle 0, x \rangle < y$, such that
        $\varphi_i(\langle 0, x \rangle)\downarrow$ in $\leq y$ steps, then go to step 4.
   2.4. If $\mathbf{M}(\varphi_{e(\text{current})}[y + 1]) > \text{curbnd}$, then go to step 5.
   2.5. Let $y = y + 1$.
   **forever**
3. Let $v = \textit{tfcounter}(e(0), \text{lastmindch})$;
   Let $\bar{v} = \textit{tfcounter}(e(0), \text{lastmindch} + y)$;
   Let $\text{curbnd} = h(e(0), \text{lastmindch} + y)$.
   Let $\text{curbot} = \text{curtop} + 1$.
   Let $\text{curtop} = \text{curtop} + 1 + \text{curbnd}$.
   Let $\text{lastmindch} = \text{lastmindch} + y$
   Let $i$ be the least value such that $\text{num}_i^v \neq \text{num}_i^{\bar{v}}$ (So, $\text{prod}_{i-1}^v = \text{prod}_{i-1}^{\bar{v}}$. Also, for $i \leq k \leq m-1$, $\varphi_{e(0)}(\langle \text{prod}_k^{\bar{v}}, . \rangle)$ has no non-zero values wherever it is defined till now.)
   Let $x$ be the least value such that $\varphi_{e(0)}(\langle \text{prod}_{i-1}^{\bar{v}}, x \rangle)$ has not been defined till now.
   Let $\varphi_{e(0)}(\langle \text{prod}_{i-1}^v, x \rangle) = \langle \text{prod}_i^{\bar{v}}, 1 + \text{num}_{i+1}^{\bar{v}} \rangle$.
   **for** $k = i$ **to** $m - 2$ **do**
       Let $x$ be the least value such that $\varphi_{e(0)}(\langle \text{prod}_k^{\bar{v}}, x \rangle)$ has not been defined till now.
       $\varphi_{e(0)}(\langle \text{prod}_k^{\bar{v}}, x \rangle) = \langle \text{prod}_{k+1}^{\bar{v}}, 1 + \text{num}_{k+2}^{\bar{v}} \rangle$;
   **endfor**
   Let $x$ be the least value such that $\varphi_{e(0)}(\langle \text{prod}_{m-1}^{\bar{v}}, x \rangle)$ has not been defined till now.
   Let $\varphi_{e(0)}(\langle \text{prod}_{m-1}^{\bar{v}}, x \rangle) = e(\text{curtop})$;
   For $x_s \leq z < \max(\{ \langle \text{prod}_{i-1}^{\bar{v}}, x \rangle, \langle \text{prod}_i^{\bar{v}} \rangle, \ldots, \langle \text{prod}_{m-1}^{\bar{v}} \rangle \})$ such that $\varphi_{e(0)}(z)$ has not been defined till now, let $\varphi_{e(0)}(z) = 0$.
   Go to stage $s + 1$.
4. Let current $=$ current $+ 1$. For $i, \langle 0, x \rangle$ as found in step 2.3, let $\varphi_{e(0)}(\langle 0, x \rangle) = \varphi_i(\langle 0, x \rangle) + 1$.
   For $x_s \leq y < \langle 0, x \rangle$, let $\varphi_{e(0)}(y) = 0$.
   Let $\text{Cancel} = \text{Cancel} \cup \{i\}$.
   Go to stage $s + 1$.
5. For $x_s \leq x \leq y$, let $\varphi_{e(0)}(x) = \varphi_{e(\text{current})}(x)$.
   Go to stage $s + 1$.

**End stage $s$**

*Case 1:* Each stage is entered and terminates.

Since $<_o$ is well–founded, step 2.2 can succeed only a finite number of times. The value of curbnd is changed only when step 2.2 succeeds. Since each time step 2.3 occurs, a new $i < \text{curbnd}$ is cancelled, step 2.3 can succeed only a finite number of times in between occurrences of step 2.2. Thus, all but finitely often, step 2.4 succeeds. Also, since the values of current and curtop are changed only when step 2.2 or step 2.3 succeeds, they eventually stabilize. Let $current_{fin}$ and $curtop_{fin}$ be the eventual values of these variables.

Furthermore, $\varphi_{e(0)} = \varphi_{e(current_{fin})}$, and is total. Let $f = \varphi_{e(0)}$. We now show that $f \in S_{\omega^m+1}$. Firstly, $\lim_{t\to\infty} f(\langle 1, t \rangle) = e(current_{fin})$. Next, $f(\langle 0, 0 \rangle) = \langle \text{prod}_0^v, 1 + \text{num}_v^1 \rangle$, where $v = tfcounter(e(0), t)$, for $t$ as found before stage 0. The only cause for $f(\langle \text{prod}_0^v, x \rangle)$ to take a non-zero value is either before stage 0 or when the step just before the **for** loop in step 3 occurs with $i = 1$. This can happen, in all, only $1 + \text{num}_1^v$ times, which is $\leq \pi_2(f(\langle 0, 0 \rangle))$. Similarly, it can be shown that for each $0 < k \leq m$, for each $\langle p, n \rangle \in L_k^f$, $\text{card}(\{x \mid f(\langle p, x \rangle) \neq 0\}) \leq n$. Also, current is always $\leq$ curtop since step 4 can occur at most $curbnd + 1$ times between occurrences of step 3. Finally, $e(\text{curtop}) \in L_{m+1}^f$ at all stages, and since $e$ is 1–1 increasing, $e(current_{fin}) \leq e(curtop_{fin})$. Hence, $f \in S_{\omega^m+1}$. However, $\mathbf{M}(f))\uparrow$ or $\mathbf{M}(f) \not\leq$ curbnd $= \lim_{t\to\infty} h(p(0), t)$.

So, $f \notin \mathbf{Lim}_{\omega^m}\mathbf{Mex}$ as witnessed by $\mathbf{M}$ and $g$.

*Case 2:* Some stage $s$ starts, but does not terminate.

Let $current_{fin}, curbnd_{fin}$ and $curtop_{fin}$ be the final values of current, curbnd and curtop (i.e., those before stage $s$ starts). Let $f = \varphi_{p(current_{fin})}$. It can be argued on lines similar to those in *Case 1* that $f \in S_{\omega^m+1}$. $\mathbf{M}$, on all but finitely many initial segments of $f$ outputs a program $\leq curbnd_{fin}$ (otherwise step 2.4. would succeed). However, for all $i \leq curbnd_{fin}$, either $i \in$ Cancel, and thus $\varphi_i \neq f$, or $\varphi_i$ diverges on infinitely many inputs (otherwise step 2.3. would succeed). It follows that $\mathbf{M}$ does not **Ex**-identify $f$.

From the above cases it follows that $S_{\omega^m+1} \notin \mathbf{Lim}_{\omega^m}\mathbf{Mex}$ as witnessed by $\mathbf{M}$ and $g$. ∎

The immediately previous theorem leaves unanswered the comparisons of $\mathbf{Lim}_u\mathbf{Mex}$ with $\mathbf{Lim}_v\mathbf{Mex}$, when $|u|_o \geq \omega^\omega$ and $u \times_o w \leq_o v$. The next theorem partly resolves some of these comparisons.

**Theorem 14** For all notations $u$, there exists a notation $v >_o u$ such that, for all $n$, $\mathbf{Lim}_v\mathbf{Mex} - \mathbf{Lim}_u\mathbf{Mex}^n \neq \emptyset$.

PROOF. We assume without loss of generality that $|u|_o \geq \omega$. Consider the following class of functions.

$$\mathcal{C} = \{f \mid$$
$$f(\langle 3, \infty \rangle)\downarrow = p \wedge \varphi_p = f \wedge$$
$$f(\langle 2, \infty \rangle)\downarrow \geq p \wedge$$
$$(\forall z)[f(\langle 2, z \rangle) \neq f(\langle 2, z+1 \rangle) \Rightarrow f(\langle 1, z \rangle) \neq f(\langle 1, z+1 \rangle)] \wedge$$
$$(\forall z)[f(\langle 1, z \rangle) \in O] \wedge$$
$$(\forall z)[f(\langle 1, z \rangle) \geq_o f(\langle 1, z+1 \rangle)] \wedge$$
$$f(\langle 1, 0 \rangle) = u$$
$$\}$$

It can be shown, using a variant of the proof of the negative part of Theorem 13, that $\mathcal{C} \notin \mathbf{Lim}_u\mathbf{Mex}^n$. We will show that there exists a $v >_o u$ such that $\mathcal{C} \in \mathbf{Lim}_v\mathbf{Mex}$.

Let $\mathbf{M}$ be such that, for every $n$, $\mathbf{M}(f[n])$ is defined as follows. Let $i_n = \max(\{j \mid \langle 3, j \rangle < n\})$. Let $\mathbf{M}(f[n]) = f(\langle 3, i_n \rangle)$. This machine clearly **Ex**-identifies any $f \in \mathcal{C}$. We will construct a $\mathbf{Lim}_v$ function, $g$, such that for every $f \in \mathcal{C}, g(\text{MinProg}(f)) \geq \mathbf{M}(f)$.

To this end let $\eta_1(j,t) = \varphi_j(\langle 2,t\rangle)$, and $\eta_2(j,t) = \varphi_j(\langle 1,t\rangle)$. Let $h'$ and *tfcounter'* be such that the following 6 conditions are satisfied. (Note that such a $h'$, *tfcounter'* can be easily constructed; we omit the details).

1. $h'$ and *tfcounter'* are total, computable functions.
2. $(\forall j, z)[h'(j,z) \neq h'(j,z+1) \Rightarrow \textit{tfcounter}'(j,z) \neq \textit{tfcounter}'(j,z+1)]$.
3. $(\forall j, z)[\textit{tfcounter}'(j,z) \in O]$.
4. $(\forall j, z)[\textit{tfcounter}'(j,z) \geq_o \textit{tfcounter}'(j,z+1)]$.
5. $(\forall j)[\textit{tfcounter}'(j,0) = u +_o \mathbf{1}]$.
6. **if** $\eta_1(j,.)$ and $\eta_2(j,.)$ are such that

$$[\,(\forall t)[\eta_1(j,t)\!\downarrow \,\wedge\, \eta_2(j,t)\!\downarrow]\wedge$$
$$(\forall z)[\eta_1(j,z) \neq \eta_1(j,z+1) \Rightarrow \eta_2(j,z) \neq \eta_2(j,z+1)]\wedge$$
$$(\forall z)[\eta_2(j,z) \in O]\wedge$$
$$(\forall z)[\eta_2(j,z) \geq_o \eta_2(j,z+1)]\wedge$$
$$[\eta_2(j,0) = u]\,]$$

   **then** $\lim_{t\to\infty}[\eta_1(j,t)] = h'(j,\infty)]$.

Let $g'(y) = h(y,\infty)$, for every $y$. Clearly, $g'$ is a lim-computable function. Also, $g'(\text{MinProg}(f)) \geq \mathbf{M}(f)$, for $f \in C$.

We will next show that there exists a $v$ such that some $\lim_v$-computable function dominates $g'$.

Let $v = \mathbf{2}\exp_o(u \times_o w)$;
Define $h$ and *tfcounter* as follows.
For all $j,t$, $h(j,t) = \max(\{h'(i,t) \mid i \leq j\})$.
For all $j$, $\textit{tfcounter}(j,t) = v$, if $t = 0$.
$\textit{tfcounter}(j,t) = \text{match}(\textit{tfcounter}'(j,t), \ldots, \textit{tfcounter}'(0,t))$, for $t > 0$, where match is as defined below.
(To avoid unnecessary complexity, we allow match to take a variable number of arguments.)

Let $\mathbf{2i}$ be the notation for $2i$. We now define match.

Begin $\text{match}(u_j, u_{j-1}, \ldots, u_0)$

   For $1 \leq i \leq j$, let $u_i' = (u \times_o \mathbf{2i}) +_o u_i$ and $v_i = \mathbf{2}\exp_o u_i'$.
   Let $\text{sum}_0 = v_0$; for $i < j$, let $\text{sum}_{i+1} = v_{i+1} +_o \text{sum}_i$.

   (Note that $\text{sum}_j$ is just the summation of $v_i$'s in a *right associative* manner.)

   Let $\text{match}(u_j, u_{j-1}, \ldots, u_0) = \text{sum}_j$.

End match

We now define $g$ as follows. For all $y$, $g(y) = h(y,\infty)$. Clearly $g$ dominates $g'$. We will next show that $g$ is indeed $\lim_v$-computable as witnessed by $h$ and *tfcounter*.

Note that (in the definition of match), since for all $i$, $1 \leq i \leq j$, $u_i$ is $\leq_o u +_o \mathbf{1}$, we have that $u_i' <_o u_{i+1}'$, for $0 \leq i < j$. The following claim is helpful.

**Claim 1** Suppose $j \in N$, and $u_0, \ldots, u_j \in O$, for $i \leq j$, are given. Assume further that $u_i \leq u +_o \mathbf{1}$, for $i \leq j$. For $i \leq j$, let $\text{sum}_i$, $u_i'$ and $v_i$ be as defined in the procedure for $\text{match}(u_j, \ldots, u_0)$. Then, for $k < j$, $v_{k+1} >_o \text{sum}_k$.

PROOF. By induction on $k$.
*Base Case:* $k = 1$.
Since $u_0' <_o u_1'$, $\text{sum}_0 = \mathbf{2}\exp_o u_0' <_o \mathbf{2}\exp_o u_1' = v_1$ (using properties of $+_o$ and $\exp_o$ from Theorems 7 and 11). Hence, $v_1 >_o \text{sum}_0$.
*Inductive Case:* Suppose the claim is true for $k = r - 1$, where $r < j - 1$. We will show that it holds for $k = r$. $\text{sum}_r = v_r +_o \text{sum}_{r-1} <_o v_r +_o v_r$ (by the inductive hypothesis) $= (\mathbf{2}\exp_o u_r') +_o (\mathbf{2}\exp_o u_r') = \mathbf{2}\exp_o(u_r' +_o \mathbf{1}) \leq_o \mathbf{2}\exp_o u_{r+1}' = v_{r+1}$.

This proves the inductive hypothesis. □

We continue with the proof of Theorem 14.

Let $j$ be an arbitrary, fixed value. We note that $h(j,t) \neq h(j,t+1)$ implies that for some $i \leq j$, $tfcounter'(i,t) \neq tfcounter'(i,t+1)$. To show that $g$ is $\lim_v$-computable, it is then sufficient to show that, given, for $i \leq j$, $u_i \leq_o u +_o 1$ and $\bar{u}_k <_o u_k$, for some $k \leq j$, $[\mathrm{match}(u_j,\ldots,u_k,\ldots,u_0) <_o \mathrm{match}(u_j,\ldots,\bar{u}_k,\ldots,u_0)]$.

Now, in the definition of match, for $0 \leq i \leq j$, let $\mathrm{sum}_i, u_i'$ and $v_i$ be as defined in the procedure for $\mathrm{match}(u_j,\ldots,u_0)$; also, let $\overline{\mathrm{sum}}_i, \overline{u}_i'$ and $\overline{v}_i$, be the values of $\mathrm{sum}_i, u_i', v_i$ respectively, as defined in the procedure for $\mathrm{match}(u_j,\ldots,u_{k+1},\overline{u}_k,u_{k-1},\ldots,u_0)$. Thus, to show that $\mathrm{sum}_j >_o \overline{\mathrm{sum}}_j$, it suffices to show that $v_k >_o \overline{\mathrm{sum}}_k$. But by Claim 1, we have $\overline{v}_k >_o \overline{\mathrm{sum}}_{k-1}$ and thus, $\overline{\mathrm{sum}}_k <_o \overline{v}_k \times_o 2 = 2\exp_o(\overline{u}_k' +_o 1) \leq_o 2\exp_o u_k' = v_k$. Hence $\mathrm{sum}_j >_o \overline{\mathrm{sum}}_j$. ∎

As a corollary to Theorem 14, we have

**Corollary 3** For all $u \in O$, $\mathbf{LimMex} - \mathbf{Lim}_u\mathbf{Mex}^n \neq \emptyset$.

Theorem 4 of Section 5 is a consequence of the immediately above result.

We conjecture that, for all constructive ordinals $\alpha$, for suitable $u \in O$ such that $|u|_o = \alpha$, Theorem 13 can be extended to: $\mathbf{Lim}_{u\times_o w}\mathbf{Mex} - \mathbf{Lim}_u\mathbf{Mex}_n \neq \emptyset$. We are a bit more confident of this conjecture for $\alpha <$ small constructive epsilon numbers [Sie65, CK37].

Just as we iterated limits in Section 6.1, we can do the same with our new definition of $\mathbf{Lim}_u\mathbf{Mex}_b^a$ and study the learning classes $\mathbf{Lim}_{u_1,\ldots,u_n}^n\mathbf{Mex}_b^a$. Generally, except for the cases noted above and their trivial consequences, we do not know how the learning classes $\mathbf{Lim}_{u_1,\ldots,u_n}^n\mathbf{Mex}_b^a$ compare to one another.

# References

[Bar74]   J. M. Barzdin. Two theorems on the limiting synthesis of functions. *Theory of Algorithms and Programs, Latvian State University, Riga*, 88:82–88, 1974.

[BB75]   L. Blum and M. Blum. Toward a mathematical theory of inductive inference. *Information and Control*, 28:125–155, 1975.

[Blu67]   M. Blum. A machine independent theory of the complexity of recursive functions. *Journal of the ACM*, 14:322–336, 1967.

[Che81]   K. Chen. *Tradeoffs in Machine Inductive Inference*. PhD thesis, Computer Science Department, SUNY at Buffalo, 1981.

[Che82]   K. Chen. Tradeoffs in inductive inference of nearly minimal sized programs. *Information and Control*, 52:68–86, 1982.

[CJS89]   J. Case, S. Jain, and A. Sharma. Convergence to nearly minimal size grammars by vacillating learning machines. In R. Rivest, D. Haussler, and M.K. Warmuth, editors, *Proceedings of the Second Annual Workshop on Computational Learning Theory, Santa Cruz, California*, pages 189–199. Morgan Kaufmann Publishers, Inc., August 1989. Journal version in press for *Journal of Computer and System Sciences*.

[CK37]   A Church and S. C. Kleene. Formal definitions in the theory of ordinal numbers. *Fundamenta Mathematicae*, 28:11–21, 1937.

[CS83]   J. Case and C. Smith. Comparison of identification criteria for machine inductive inference. *Theoretical Computer Science*, 25:193–220, 1983.

[Ers68]  Y.L. Ershov. A hierarchy of sets II. *Algebra and Logic*, 7:212–232, 1968.

[FK77]  R. Freivalds and E. B. Kinber. Limit identification of minimal Gödel numbers. *Theory of Algorithms and Programs 3;Riga 1977*, pages 3–34, 1977.

[Fre75]  R. Freivalds. Minimal Gödel numbers and their identification in the limit. *Lecture Notes in Computer Science*, 32:219–225, 1975.

[Fre90]  R. Freivalds. Inductive inference of minimal programs. In M. Fulk and J. Case, editors, *Proceedings of the Third Annual Workshop on Computational Learni ng Theory*, pages 3–20. Morgan Kaufmann Publishers, Inc., August 1990.

[FS91]  R Freivalds and C. H. Smith. On the role of procrastination for machine learning. Technical Report TR-91-27, UMIACS, 1991. To appear in *Information and Computation*.

[Gol67]  E. M. Gold. Language identification in the limit. *Information and Control*, 10:447–474, 1967.

[JS91]  S. Jain and A. Sharma. Program size restrictions in inductive learning. In *AAAI Symposium Series, Symposium: Machine Learning of Natural Language and Ontology*, March 1991. Journal version accepted by *Theoretical Computer Science*.

[Kin74]  E. B. Kinber. On the synthesis in the limit of almost minimal Gödel numbers. *Theory Of Algorithms and Programs, LSU, Riga*, 1:221–223, 1974.

[Kin77a]  E. B. Kinber. On a theory of inductive inference. *Lecture Notes in Computer Science*, 56:435–440, 1977.

[Kin77b]  E. B. Kinber. On limit identification of minimal Gödel numbers for functions from enumerable classes. *Theory of Algorithms and Programs 3;Riga 1977*, pages 35–56, 1977.

[Kin83]  E. B. Kinber. A note on limit identification of c-minimal indices. *Electronische Informationverarbeitung und Kybernetik*, 19:459–463, 1983.

[Kle38]  S. C. Kleene. Notations for ordinal numbers. *Journal of Symbolic Logic*, 3:150–155, 1938.

[Kle55]  S. C. Kleene. On the forms of predicates in the theory of constructive ordinals, II. *American Journal of Mathematics*, 77:405–428, 1955.

[Mar89]  Y. Marcoux. Composition is almost as good as s-1-1. In *Proceedings, Structure in Complexity Theory–Fourth Annual Conference*. IEEE Computer Society Press, 1989.

[MY78]  M. Machtey and P. Young. *An Introduction to the General Theory of Algorithms*. North Holland, New York, 1978.

[Ric80]  G. Riccardi. *The Independence of Control Structures in Abstract Programming Systems*. PhD thesis, SUNY Buffalo, 1980.

[Ric81]  G. Riccardi. The independence of control structures in abstract programming systems. *Journal of Computer and System Sciences*, 22:107–143, 1981.

[Rog58]  H. Rogers. Gödel numberings of partial recursive functions. *Journal of Symbolic Logic*, 23:331–341, 1958.

[Rog67]  H. Rogers. *Theory of Recursive Functions and Effective Computability*. Mc-Graw Hill, New York, 1967. Reprinted, MIT Press, 1987.

[Roy87]  J. Royer. *A Connotational Theory of Program Structure*. Lecture Notes in Computer Science 273. Springer Verlag, 1987.

[Sac90]  G. E. Sacks. *Higher Recursion Theory*. Springer-Verlag, 1990.

[Sha71]  N. Shapiro. Review of "Limiting recursion" by E.M. Gold and "Trial and error predicates and the solution to a problem of Mostowski" by H. Putnam. *Journal of Symbolic Logic*, 36:342, 1971.

[Sie65]  W. Sierpinski. *Cardinal and ordinal numbers*. PWN –Polish Scientific Publishers, 1965. Second revised edition.

# Optimization Problem in Inductive Inference[*]

Andris Ambainis

Institute of Mathematics and Computer Science

University of Latvia

Raina bulv. 29, Riga, Latvia

ambainis@mii.lu.lv

## Abstract

Algorithms recognizing to which of $n$ classes some total function belongs are constructed ($n > 2$). In this construction strategies determining to which of two classes the function belongs are used as subroutines. Upper and lower bounds for number of necessary strategies are obtained in several models: $FIN-$ and $EX-$ identification and $EX-$ identification with limited number of mindchanges. It is proved that in $EX-$ identification it is necessary to use $\frac{n(n-1)}{2}$ strategies. In $FIN-$ identification $\lceil \frac{3n}{2} - 2 \rceil$ strategies are necessary and sufficient, in $EX-$ identification with one mindchange- $n \log_2 n + o(n \log_2 n)$ strategies.

## 1  Introduction

The following problem is considered:

We have several classes of objects and have to write an algorithm deciding to which class some given object belongs. If the number of classes is large, such algorithm can be complicated and difficult to write. If at the beginning some smaller algorithms solving some parts of this problem are written, this task becomes easier. Then algorithm deciding to which class the object belongs can be constructed from these smaller algorithms used as subroutines. To make the algorithm more efficient, we are interested to use as small number of these subroutines as possible.

In this paper it is assumed that object is total function and smaller algorithms decide to which of two classes the function belongs. In this case the problem is as follows:

$n$ disjoint classes of total functions mapping $N$ into $N$ are given. These classes are denoted as $U_1, U_2, \ldots, U_n$. There is a black box computing some function $f(x)$ belonging to one of these classes and giving $f(0), f(1), \ldots$ as an output. For each pair of classes $U_i$ and $U_j$ we have algorithm called strategy which from output given by black box recognizes to which of the classes $U_i$ and $U_j$ the function computed by black box belongs. This strategy is denoted as $A_{ij}$. In case if function belongs neither to $U_i$ nor to $U_j$, strategy $A_{ij}$ is allowed to give any possible result or even give no result at all.

[*]This research was supported by Latvian Science Council Grant No.93.599

Our aim is to construct from these strategies an algorithm recognizing to which of $U_1, U_2, \ldots, U_n$ the function computed by black box belongs. We should use as small number of strategies as possible.

We assume that it is known that for each two classes there exists algorithm recognizing to which of classes the function belongs and this algorithm can be used as strategy. The question of existence of such algorithms is discussed in [1]. Some other problems of inductive inference are surveyed in [2].

In section 2, this problem will be considered in cases if strategies are FIN-strategies or EX-strategies.

In section 3, this problem for strategies making no more than one mindchange will be considered. It will be proved that $n \log_2 n + o(n \log_2 n)$ strategies are necessary and sufficient in this case.

In section 4, case if strategies are making no more than const mindchanges will be considered (const > 1). Several upper and lower bounds for number of necessary strategies will be proved.

In section 5, it will be considered at which number of mindchanges $M(n)$ recognition with no more than $M(n)$ mindchanges is not better than recognition with unlimited number of mindchanges. (Each algorithm constructed from strategies with no more than $M(n)$ mindchanges has to use all strategies $A_{ij}$ on some function). It will be proved that $M(n) \leq 2\sqrt{n} + o(\sqrt{n})$.

# 2 EX- and FIN- strategies

There are two different ways how to construct algorithm from strategies:

First possibility is that before the algorithm begins its work it has to name all strategies it needs. In this case it can be proved that it is necessary to use all $\frac{n(n-1)}{2}$ possible strategies.

Another possibility is that at the beginning of its work, algorithm asks for some strategies, then after some time when it will have some results from strategies it can ask for more strategies and so on. Further only this case will be considered.

Strategies could be of different types, too.

Strategy $A_{ij}$ recognizing whether the function belongs to $U_i$ or to $U_j$ is called FIN-strategy if, being applied to black box, it analyses black box's output and after some time gives correct answer to which of the classes the function belongs. It is not allowed for strategy to change its answer later. In case if function belongs to none of two classes, strategy is allowed to give any possible answer or even to give no answer at all.

**Theorem 1** *There exists algorithm which for arbitrary classes $U_i (i = 1, \ldots, n)$ and strategies $A_{ij} (i = 1, \ldots, n, j = 1, \ldots, n)$ recognizes to which class the function belongs and uses not more than $\lceil \frac{3n}{2} - 2 \rceil$ strategies.*

**Proof.**

**1st step.** We divide classes into pairs. If n is even, then pairs will be $(U_1, U_2)$, $(U_3, U_4)$, ..., $(U_{n-1}, U_n)$. If n is odd then they will be $(U_1, U_2)$, $(U_3, U_4)$, ..., $(U_{n-2}, U_{n-1})$, $(U_{n-1}, U_n)$. For each of these pairs $(U_i, U_j)$ we take strategy $A_{ij}$.

So far we have used $\lceil \frac{n}{2} \rceil$ strategies. We have obtained situation when for each class we have 1 or 2 strategies deciding whether the function belongs to this class or to some other.

Now we wait until one of used strategies gives answer. If function belongs to $U_i$ where $i \in \{1, \ldots, n\}$, it will happen, because we have at least one strategy deciding if the function belongs to $U_i$ and this strategy must give the correct answer.

**2nd step.** We assume that strategy $A_{ij}$ has given answer $U_i$. Then we can conclude that the function does not belong to $U_j$. We consider two cases:

**Case 1.** Our algorithm uses two strategies which decide whether the function belongs to $U_j$ : $A_{ij}$ and $A_{kj}$. In this case, we take strategy $A_{ik}$ instead of strategies $A_{ij}$ and $A_{kj}$. **Case 2.** Algorithm uses only one strategy: $A_{ij}$. Then we find some class $U_k$ such that only one strategy deciding if the function belongs to $U_k$ is used by algorithm. (It can be proved that if we follow this algorithm such class always will exist.) We take strategy $A_{ik}$ instead of $A_{ij}$.

In result the number of classes to which the function can belong will diminish by 1. For each of remaining classes we have 1 or 2 strategies deciding if the function computed by black box belongs to this class. Now, once again we wait until some strategy will give answer, then we repeat 2nd step and so on, until one class only will remain. Evidently, the function belongs to this class.

This algorithm uses $\lceil \frac{n}{2} \rceil$ strategies during 1st step and 1 additional strategy each time when 2nd step is repeated. Each time when we repeat 2nd step, number of classes to which the function can belong becomes less. So it can be repeated not more than $n - 1$ times. So, our algorithm will use not more than $\lceil \frac{n}{2} \rceil + (n - 2)$ strategies. $\square$

It appears that this upper bound on number of necessary strategies is precise. There exist such classes $U_i$ and strategies $A_{ij}$ that for each algorithm there exists function from one of $U_i$ such that algorithm uses at least $\lceil \frac{3n}{2} - 2 \rceil$ strategies if it receives this function as output of black box.

There exists another type of strategies:

Strategy EX-identifies to which of the classes $U_i$ and $U_j$ function belongs if, being applied to black box, it gives some answer, after some time it is allowed to change its answer. Voluntary number of such changes called mindchanges is allowed, but after some time strategy should give the correct answer and make no more mindchanges. In case if function belongs to none of two classes, strategy is allowed to give any possible answer or even to give no answer at all(in case if the strategy makes infinite number of mindchanges).

**Theorem 2** *There exist classes $U_i$ and strategies $A_{ij}$ EX-identifying to which of the classes $U_i$ and $U_j$ the function belongs such that each algorithm identifying to which of $U_i (i = 1, \ldots, n)$ a function belongs, uses $\frac{n(n-1)}{2}$ strategies while working on some function $f \in U_i$.*

So, for each algorithm there are bad cases when it has to use all $\frac{n(n-1)}{2}$ possible strategies.

From Theorem 2 we can see that behaviour of EX- strategies can be so complicated that it is even impossible to construct algorithm which does not use all strategies. In sections 3 and 4 we shall consider particular case of EX- strategies:EX- strategies with limited number of mindchanges. This type is simpler than general EX-strategies and for this type it is possible to construct algorithms using relatively small number of strategies.

# 3   Strategies making no more than 1 mindchange

The object of main concern in this paper will be the case if strategies $A_{ij}$ are EX-strategies making no more then $c$ mindchanges where $c$ is some constant.

**Theorem 3** *If strategies are making no more than 1 mindchange then $n \cdot \log_2 n + o(n \cdot \log_2 n)$ strategies are necessary and sufficient for the construction of algorithm.*

**Proof. Sufficiency.**

**1st step.** We divide classes $U_1, U_2, \ldots, U_n$ into $\lfloor \frac{n}{2} \rfloor$ pairs: $U_1$ and $U_2$, $U_3$ and $U_4$,etc. and use strategies $A_{12}, A_{34}$,etc.. If n is odd, one class will have no pair.

**2nd step.** Let us take $\lceil \frac{n}{2} \rceil$ classes: the class to which the function according to $A_{12}$ belongs, the class to which according to $A_{34}$ the function belongs,etc.. If n is odd,we take class,which had no pair in 1st step,too. We divide these classes into pairs and take for each class the strategy which decides to which of two classes from this pair the function belongs.

We continue similarly until one class only will remain. Then we give this class as the correct answer. This construction uses $n - 1$ strategies. If no mindchange will occur, its answer will be correct and no more strategies will be used. The result of this construction could be visualised in following tree:

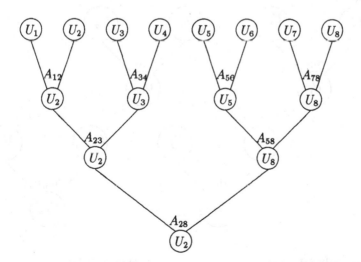

If $n = 2^m$ then after 1st step only $\frac{n}{2} = 2^{m-1}$ classes will remain, after 2nd step $\frac{n}{4} = 2^{m-2}$ classes will remain, ..., after $m$th step 1 class will remain. So, in this case described construction consists of $m$ steps. Evidently, if $2^{m-1} < n < 2^m$ this construction consists of not more steps thean in case if $n = 2^m$. So, this construction consists of $\lceil \log_2 n \rceil$ steps. Hence, the depth of constructed tree will be $\lceil \log_2 n \rceil$.

Now we assume that some strategy has made a mindchange. Let us assume it is strategy which decides whether the function belongs to $U_i$ or to $U_j$, it has changed its answer from $U_i$ to $U_j$ and it is used in $k$th step of our construction.

We denote by $U_{i_1}$ such class that strategy $A_{ii_1}$ was used in 1st step, ..., by $U_{ii_{k-1}}$ such class that $A_{ii_{k-1}}$ was used in $(k-1)$-th step. $U_{j_1}$ denotes such class that strategy $A_{ij_1}$ was used in $(k+1)$-th step will be denoted, $U_{j_2}$ denotes such class that strategy deciding whether the function belongs to $U_{l_1}$ or to $U_{j_2}$ was used during $(k+2)$-th step, where $U_{l_1}$ is the class to which according to $A_{ij_1}$ the function belongs. Notations $U_{j_3}, \ldots$ are introduced similarly.

As one mindchange only is allowed for strategies, $A_{ij}$ can make no more mind-changes and, hence $U_i$ is not the class to which the function belongs. So, we can throw $U_i$ out of our construction.

After mindchange we rebuild the tree in following way:

Instead of strategies $A_{ii_1}$ and $A_{ii_2}$ we use strategy $A_{i_1i_2}$. Let us denote the class to which according to this strategy the function belongs by $U_{k_2}$. Then instead of $A_{ii_3}$ we use $A_{k_2i_3}, \ldots$, instead of $A_{ij}$ we use $A_{k_{m-1}j}$.

Let us denote with $U_{k_m}$ the class to which according to $A_{k_{m-1}j}$ the function belongs. We take strategy $A_{k_mj_1}$, denote the class to which according to this strategy the function belongs, with $U_{k_{m+1}}$. If necessary, we take strategy $A_{k_{m+1}j_2}$. We continue so as long as necessary.

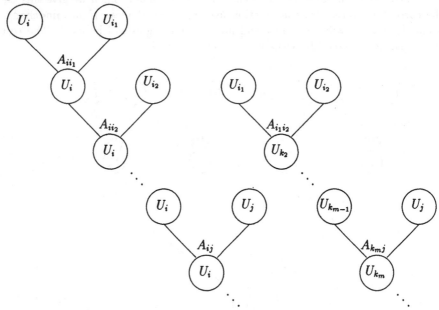

**Before mindchange.**         **After mindchange.**

As the depth of our tree is $\lceil \log_2 n \rceil$, we need not more than $\lceil \log_2 n \rceil$ strategies during each rebuilding. After each rebuilding the number of classes to which the function can belong diminishes by 1. So, not more than $n-1$ rebuildings are possible and not more than $(n-1)\lceil \log_2 n \rceil$ strategies are used during rebuildings. So, together with $n-1$ strategies used at the beginning of algorithm, we have used $(n-1)(\lceil \log_2 n \rceil +$

1) $= n \log_2 n + o(n \log_2 n)$ strategies in this algorithm.

**Necessity.**

We assume we have some algorithm which decides to which class the function belongs. It will be proved that this algorithm uses at least $n \cdot \log_2 n - o(n \cdot \log_2 n)$ strategies or there exist such classes $U_1, \ldots, U_n$, strategies $A_{12}, \ldots, A_{n-1,n}$ and function $f(x)$ belonging to one of classes that this algorithm does not work correctly on this function.

We take all $n!$ permutations of $U_1, U_2, \ldots, U_n$ and code them by numbers from 1 to $n!$. The code number for the permutation $(U_{i_1}, U_{i_2}, \ldots, U_{i_n})$ will be denoted as $C(U_{i_1}, U_{i_2}, \ldots, U_{i_n})$.

Now the way how strategies work is described:

Strategy $A_{ij}$ gets current value of the function computed by black box and considers it as the code number of some permutation. It searches in this permutation for $U_i$ and $U_j$ and if $U_i$ is before $U_j$ in this permutation then $U_i$ strategy gives as its hypothesis. Otherwise $U_j$ is its hypothesis.

Class $U_1$ consists of all such total functions that all strategies $A_{12}, \ldots, A_{1n}$ make no more than one mindchange and give $U_1$ as final answer. Classes $U_2, \ldots, U_n$ are defined similarly.

Now we take the function $f(x) = C$ where $C = C(U_{i_1}, \ldots, U_{i_n})$. This function evidently belongs to $U_{i_1}$. Let us look how considered algorithm works if black box computes this function. As it works correctly on each function belonging to $U_{i_1}$, after some time it should give $U_{i_1}$ as its hypothesis and make no more mindchanges. As it uses only finite number of strategies, there is such moment that no new strategies are required by algoritm after this moment. Denote by $m_1$ such moment that, for each permutation $C(U_{i_1}, \ldots, U_{i_n})$, after $m_1$ values of $f(x) = C(U_{i_1}, \ldots, U_{i_n})$ are given by black box, no additional strategies are required by considered algorithm and its hypothesis has stabilysed on $U_{i_1}$.

At this moment for each $k \in \{2, 3, \ldots, n\}$ considered algorithm must have strategy $A_{i_k i_l}$ where $l \in \{1, 2, \ldots, k-1\}$. (If for some k it is not so, then we can take

$$g(x) = C(U_{i_k}, U_{i_1}, U_{i_2}, \ldots U_{i_{k-1}}, U_{i_{k+1}}, \ldots, U_{i_n}).$$

All strategies but $A_{i_1 i_k}, A_{i_2 i_k}, \ldots, A_{i_{k-1} i_k}$ work similarly on $f(x)$ and $g(x)$. So, while considered algorithm works on $g(x)$ it works similarly as on $f(x)$ and gives the same result. But $g(x) \in U_{i_k}$ and hence algorithm does not work correctly on $g(x)$ in this case.)

Now we consider the function

$$f_1(x) = \begin{cases} C(U_{i_1}, \ldots, U_{i_n}) & x \le m_1 \\ C(U_{i_2}, \ldots, U_{i_n}, U_{i_1}) & x > m_1 \end{cases}$$

This function belongs to $U_{i_2}$. Similarly as for $f(x)$ the existence of $m_1$ was proved it can be proved that there exists number $m_2$ such that, after $m_2$ values of $f_1(x)$ will be computed by black box, algorithm will not require new strategies and stabilyse its hypothesis on $U_{i_2}$. Also, in this moment for each $k \in \{3, \ldots, n\}$ algorithm should have strategy $A_{i_k l_k}$ such that it gives $U_{l_k}$ as its answer.

Then we consider a function

$$f_2(x) = \begin{cases} C(U_{i_1}, \ldots, U_{i_n}) & x \le m_1 \\ C(U_{i_2}, \ldots, U_{i_n}, U_{i_1}) & m_1 < x \le m_2 \\ C(U_{i_3}, \ldots, U_{i_n}, U_{i_2}, U_{i_1}) & m_2 < x \end{cases}$$

We continue similarly until we get

$$
f_{n-1}(x) = \begin{cases}
C(U_{i_1}, \ldots, U_{i_n}) & x \leq m_1 \\
C(U_{i_2}, \ldots, U_{i_n}, U_{i_1}) & m_1 < x \leq m_2 \\
\ldots & \ldots \\
C(U_{i_n}, U_{i_{n-1}}, \ldots, U_{i_1}) & m_{n-1} < x
\end{cases}
$$

Now we consider such functions $f_{n-1}(x)$ for each of $n!$ possible initial permutations $C(U_{i_1}, \ldots, U_{i_n})$. While algorithm works on $f_{n-1}(x)$ it gives following hypotheses: $U_{i_1}$ when $m_1$ values of $f_{n-1}(x)$ are computed by black box, $U_{i_2}$ when $m_2$ values of $f_{n-1}(x)$ are computed by black box, $\ldots$, $U_{i_n}$ at the end.

If we consider two functions $f_{n-1}(x)$ for two different initial permutations $C(U_{i_1}, \ldots, U_{i_n})$ and $\dot{C}(U_{j_1}, \ldots, U_{j_n})$ there exists such $k \in \{1, \ldots, n\}$ that $i_k \neq j_k$. At the moment when $m_k$ values of function are computed by black box algorithm should give $U_{i_k}$ as hypothesis if black box computes first function and $U_{j_k}$ if it computes second. Hence on these two functions algorithm works differently. But, algorithm could work differently only if it receives different information from strategies in these two cases.

We assume that on each of functions $f_{n-1}(x)$ algorithm uses not more than $m$ strategies.

One strategy $A_{ij}$ can give 2 possible answers: $U_i$ and $U_j$. So $m$ strategies can give at most $2^m$ possible combinations of answers.

We considered only initial answers given by strategies. A question may appear:
· At the beginning there are two answers strategy can give, but later it can make a mindchange. Does this mindchange give additional information? If it gives, one strategy can behave in more than 2 different ways and algorithm can receive more information from strategy, not only its initial answer.

However, we prove that mindchanges do not give additional information, Mindchanges happen only when $m_1, \ldots, m_{n-1}$ values of function $f_{n-1}(x)$ are computed by black box. In these moments from information available from strategies algorithm already uses it can be concluded which class is first in permutation code number of which was outputted by black box before mindchange. (For each other class $U_j$ algorithm has used some strategy $A_{jk}$ which says that the function belongs to another class $U_j$, not to $U_k$ and hence it can be concluded that $U_j$ is not first.) But mindchanges occurs only with these strategies which recognize whether the function belongs to first class or some other class. So before each mindchange from hypotheses of strategies algorithm already has it could be predicted which strategies exactly will make mindchange and mindchanges do not give additional information.

On each two of $n!$ functions $f_{n-1}(x)$ algorithm should work in different ways and there are at most $2^m$ possible different combinations of information obtained from strategies. Hence, $2^m \geq n!$. From Stirling's formula

$$
n! \approx \sqrt{2\pi n} \left(\frac{n}{e}\right)^n
$$

it follows that

$$
2^m \geq \sqrt{2\pi n} \left(\frac{n}{e}\right)^n
$$

Taking a logarithm from both sides we get that

$$
m \geq n \log_2 n - o(n \log_2 n)
$$

□

# 4 Strategies making more than 1 mindchange

The following result can be proved. Proof is rather complicated and will be omitted.

**Theorem 4** *If strategies make no more than $2d + 1$ mindchanges,*

$$const \cdot n \cdot \log_2 n \cdot \left( \frac{\log_2 n}{\log_2 \log_2 n} \right)^d$$

*strategies are necessary for construction of algorithm recognizing to which class the function belongs.*

In classes constructed in proof of Theorem 3 each 3 strategies $A_{ij}, A_{ik}, A_{jk}$ had following property:if at some moment $A_{ij}$ preferred $U_i$ to $U_j$(gave $U_i$ as hypothesis) and $A_{jk}$ preferred $U_j$ to $U_k$ then at this moment $A_{ik}$ preferred $U_i$ to $U_k$. If for any 3 different $i, j, k \in \{1, 2, \ldots, n\}$ this property holds, set of strategies $A_{ij}$ is called transitive.

Set of strategies used in proof of Theorem 4 is non-transitive and this property is used in proof. No upper bounds for number of necessary strategies are proved in case if strategies are allowed to be non-transitive. For transitive strategies there are some more results:

**Theorem 5** *If two mindchanges are allowed for strategies and it is known that set of strategies is transitive , $2n \lceil \log_2 n \rceil$ strategies are sufficient for construction of algorithm.*

**Proof.** The algorithm will be almost the same as in the proof of Theorem 3. The only difference is that if some strategy $A_{ij}$ changes hypothesis from $U_i$ to $U_j$ then class $U_i$ is not thrown out of tree, but only in places after $A_{ij}$ where some strategies were used to determine whether the function belongs to $U_i$ or to some other class, $U_j$ is substituted instead of $U_i$ and new strategies are used if necessary.

Now let us take some vertice of tree. We denote it with $B$. While our algorithm works different strategies appear in this vertice.We assume that subtree left from this vertice contains $m_1$ classes and subtree right from this vertice — $m_2$ classes.

Let us take root of subtree left from $B$. We write out sequence of classes which are standing at this vertice. If some class remains here for some time, it is written only once. It can be written next time only after some other classes are written.

**Lemma 1** *This sequence contains no subsequence of type $U_i \ldots U_j \ldots U_i \ldots U_j$ where by $\ldots$ any possible sequence of classes is denoted.*

**Proof.** From contrary. If such subsequence exists then from the transitiveness of strategies it follows that, if $U_k$ is some class from left subtree and at some moment $U_i$ is the class standing at the root of subtree then $A_{ik}$ prefers $U_i$ to $U_k$ at that moment. Hence at the moment when $U_i$ is the class at the root of subtree $A_{ij}$ gives $U_i$ as hypothesis and when $U_j$ is at the root of subtree it gives $U_j$. But in this case $A_{ij}$ makes at least 3 mindchanges. It is in contradiction with assumption of theorem that strategies make no more than 2 mindchanges and so lemma is proved. □

**Lemma 2** *If the sequence constructed from $m_1$ different elements contains no subsequence of type $U_i \ldots U_j \ldots U_i \ldots U_j$, it contains no more than $2m_1 - 1$ elements.*

**Proof.** By induction. If $m_1 = 1$ then only possible sequence is sequence consisting of one element which has length $2m_1 - 1 = 1$.

Let us assume that lemma holds for all $m_1 < m$. We take some sequence of $m$ elements and denote first its element as $C$. Let us assume that sequence contains $k$ $C$'s. Then sequence will look so: $CS_1CS_2C \ldots CS_k$, where $S_1, \ldots, S_k$ are some subsequences which does not contain $C$.

If there is some element $D$ in sequence which belongs to two of $S_1, \ldots, S_k$, sequence contains fragment in form $C \ldots D \ldots C \ldots D$, but we have assumed there is no such fragment.

We denote the number of different elements in subsequence $S_i$ by $k_i$. As every two of these subsequences have no common elements, $k_1 + k_2 + \ldots + k_k = n - 1$.

¿From inductive assumption length of $S_i$ is less or equal than $2k_i - 1$. Hence the length of all sequence is less or equal than

$$(2k_1 - 1) + \ldots + (2k_k - 1) + k = 2(k_1 + \ldots + k_k) - k + k = 2n - 2$$

The last subsequence $S_k$ could be empty. In this case the length of sequence does not exceed

$$(2k_1 - 1) + \ldots + (2k_{k-1} - 1) + k = 2n - 1$$

So lemma is proved. □

A new strategy in vertice $B$ can be necessary in two cases: if the class in the vertice to the left from it has changed or if the same thing has happened in the vertice to the right from it. As the sequence of classes in vertice to the left from it contains at most $2m_1 - 1$ classes, class in this vertice changes not more than $2m_1 - 2$ times. Similarly, class in vertice to the right from B changes at most $2m_2 - 2$ times. Hence at most $2m_1 - 2 + 2m_2 - 2 + 1 < 2(m_1 + m_2)$ strategies are necessary in vertice $B$.

Now let us take all vertices of tree formed in one step. Each other vertice can be upper than only one of these vertices. Hence, taking the sum of strategies possibly necessary at each of vertices, we get that at all the vertices formed at one step less than $2n$ strategies are necessary. As tree was formed in $\lceil \log_2 n \rceil$ steps, less than $2n \lceil \log_2 n \rceil$ strategies will be necessary during all the algorithm. □

Similarly to theorem 5 a following theorem could be proved

**Theorem 6** *If it is known than strategies make no more than 3 mindchanges and set of strategies is transitive, algorithm using at most $const \cdot n \cdot (\log_2 n)^2$ strategies can be constructed.*

Proof of this theorem is omitted. It uses the following analogue of Lemma 2

**Lemma 3** *Sequence of $n$ elements $U_1, \ldots, U_n$ containing no fragments of kind $U_i \ldots U_j \ldots U_i \ldots U_j \ldots U_i$ have not more than $n \lceil \log_2 n + 3 \rceil$ elements.*

For transitive strategies there is a following lower bound on number of necessary strategies

**Theorem 7** *If it is known that strategies are transitive and make no more than $d$ mindchanges, $const \cdot n \log_2 n + o(n \log_2 n)$ strategies are necessary for construction of algorithm , where $const = 2^{\frac{d-1}{6}}$.*

# 5 Minimal number of mindchanges

**Definition 1** *Minimal number of mindchanges for n classes is such number M that there exist classes $U_1, \ldots, U_n$ and strategies $A_{12}, \ldots, A_{n-1,n}$ making not more than M mindchanges such that for each algorithm constructed from strategies there exists such function belonging to one of classes $U_i$ that algorithm correctly does not recognize to which class it belongs or while working on this function uses all $\frac{n(n-1)}{2}$ possible strategies. This number of mindchanges will be denoted with $M(n)$.*

The main result of this section is

**Theorem 8** $M(n) \le 2\sqrt{n} + o(\sqrt{n})$

**Proof.** The classes $U_1, \ldots, U_n$ and strategies $A_{ij}$ will be same as in proof of Theorem 3. The only difference is that the function will belong to some class $U_i$ in case if no strategy makes more than M mindchanges on it.

At the beginning the simpler result will be proved

**Lemma 4** $M(n) \le 2n$

**Proof.** We consider the function $f_2^{(1)}(x) = C(U_1, U_2 \ldots, U_n)$

While working on this function, algorithm should use strategy $A_{12}$, otherwise it will work in same way on the function $g(x) = C(U_2, U_1, U_3, \ldots, U_n)$. But this function belongs to another class and, hence, if algorithm works correctly on each function, it should give different results on these two functions. So, algorithm uses $A_{12}$.

Now, let us take some moment when this strategy is already used and denote the number of values of $f_2^{(1)}(x)$ computed by black box at this moment as $m_{12}$. We consider the function

$$f_3^{(1)}(x) = \begin{cases} C(U_1, U_2, \ldots, U_n) & \text{if } x < m_{12} \\ C(U_1, U_3, \ldots, U_n, U_2) & \text{if } x \ge m_{12} \end{cases}$$

If $f_3^{(1)}(x)$ is computed by black box algorithm has to use strategy $A_{13}$. It can be proved similarly as it was proved that, if $f_2^{(1)}(x)$ is computed by black box algorithm has to use $A_{12}$. Algorithm has to use $A_{12}$ on $f_3^{(1)}(x)$ too, because before the moment then algorithm began to use $A_{12}$ on $f_2^{(1)}(x)$ all values of $f_2^{(1)}(x)$ were the same as corresponding values of $f_3^{(1)}(x)$.

Now let us take the moment when algorithm has begun to use $A_{13}$ on $f_3^{(1)}(x)$ and denote the number of values of $f_3^{(1)}(x)$ computed at this moment as $m_{13}$. We consider the function

$$f_4^{(1)}(x) = \begin{cases} C(U_1, U_2, \ldots, U_n) & \text{if } x < m_{12} \\ C(U_1, U_3, \ldots, U_n, U_2) & \text{if } m_{12} \le x < m_{13} \\ C(U_1, U_4, \ldots, U_n, U_3, U_2) & \text{if } m_{13} \le x \end{cases}$$

We continue similarly until we get

$$f_n^{(1)}(x) = \begin{cases} C(U_1, U_2, \ldots, U_n) & \text{if } x < m_{12} \\ \ldots & \ldots \\ C(U_1, U_n, \ldots, U_2) & \text{if } m_{1n-1} < x \end{cases}$$

On this function algorithm has to use all strategies $A_{12}, \ldots, A_{1n}$. Note that each strategy makes at most one mindchange on $f_n^{(1)}(x)$.

We denote the number of values of $f_n^{(1)}(x)$ computed by black box at the moment when algorithm has used all strategies $A_{12}, \ldots, A_{1n}$ on this function as $m_{1n}$ and consider the function

$$f_3^{(2)}(x) = \begin{cases} f_n^{(1)}(x) & \text{if } x < m_{1n} \\ C(U_2, U_3, \ldots, U_n, U_1) & \text{if } m_{1n} \le x \end{cases}$$

As we previously constructed $f_2^{(1)}(x)$, ..., $f_n^{(1)}(x)$ we can now construct $f_3^{(2)}(x)$, ..., $f_n^{(2)}(x)$ so that algorithm has to use all strategies $A_{23}$, ..., $A_{2n}$ while working on $f_{n-1}^{(2)}(x)$ and each strategy makes at most 3 mindchanges on $f_n^{(2)}(x)$.

Then we can similarly construct $f_4^{(3)}(x), \ldots, f_n^{(3)}(x)$ and so on. At the end we shall get such $f_n^{(n-1)}(x)$ that all strategies from $A_{12}(x)$ to $A_{n-1,n}(x)$ should be used by algorithm while working on $f_n^{(n-1)}$ and no strategy makes more than $2n$ mindchanges on it. $\square$

**Lemma 5** *If $p$ is a prime then $M(p^2) \le 4p$*

**Proof.** We use following result from [3].

**Lemma 6** *If $p$ is a prime then there exist $p + 1$ way how to divide $p^2$ classes in $p$ groups so that there are exactly $p$ classes in each group and each two classes are in one group exactly in one division.*

This construction is known as finite affine plane of order $p$ [3].

Now let us denote the i-th class in j-th group of k-th division as $U_{ji}^k$. ¿From Lemma 4 it follows that it is possible to construct some function on which an algorithm will have to use all strategies which recognize to which of two classes selected from some $p$ classes the function belongs so each strategy will make no more than $2 \cdot p$ mindchanges.

Now we construct the function so that its value at the beginning will be $C(U_{11}^1, \ldots, U_{1n}^1, \ldots, U_{nn}^1)$ then we construct it further so that algorithm will be forced to take all strategies which work on two classes from $U_{11}^1, \ldots, U_{1n}^1$ and no strategy makes more than $2 \cdot p$ mindchanges. (During this construction the order of $U_{21}, \ldots, U_{nn}$ should not be changed. It will guarantee that each strategy working on two classes at least one of which does not belong to 1st group will make no mindchanges at all.)

At some moment, when all strategies working on 2 classes from 1st part will be already used, the value of function will be

$$C(U_{1i_1}^1, \ldots, U_{1i_n}^1, U_{21}^1, \ldots, U_{nn}^1).$$

From this moment the value of function will become

$$C(U_{21}^1, \ldots, U_{nn}^1, U_{1i_1}^1, \ldots, U_{1i_n}^1).$$

Then we construct function further so that algorithm will have to take every strategy working on two classes from 2nd group and no more than $2 \cdot p$ mindchanges will happen with each of these mindchanges and no mindchanges at all with other strategies. After it we set the value of function to

$$C(U_{31}^1, \ldots, U_{nn}^1, U_{2j_1}^1, \ldots, U_{2j_n}^1, U_{1i_1}^1, \ldots)$$

and do the same thing with 3rd group and so on.

At the end of this process algorithm will be using each strategy working on 2 classes from the same group. During this time each strategy working on 2 classes from the same group has made at most $2 \cdot p$ mindchanges, each other - at most 1.

Then we set function's value from this moment to

$$C(U_{11}^2, U_{12}^2, \ldots, U_{nn}^2).$$

In result of it one more mindchange could occur with some strategies. Then similarly as with 1st partition we force the algorithm to take each strategy working on 2 classes from the same group in 2nd partition. Then we do the same thing for 3rd, ..., $(p+1)$-st partition.

In this process for each strategy $A_{ij}$ makes at most $2 \cdot p$ mindchanges while working with partition in which $U_i$ and $U_j$ belong to the same class, 1 while working on each other partition and at most 1 while going from one partition to another. So, in total there are at most $2 \cdot p + 2 \cdot p = 4 \cdot p$ mindchanges. $\square$

**Lemma 7** $M(n) \leq 4\sqrt{n} + o(\sqrt{n})$.

This lemma can be deduced from Lemma 5 so: let us take as $p_1$ the smallest prime such that $p_1^2 \geq n$, then

$$M(n) \leq M(p_1^2) \leq 4p_1$$

**Lemma 8 ([4], p.164)** *For any $\epsilon > 0$ there exists such $N$ that for all $n > N$ there is at least one prime between $n$ and $(1 + \epsilon)n$.*

Let us take some $\epsilon > 0$. If n is large enough, we have

$$p_1 \leq (1 + \epsilon)\sqrt{n}$$
$$M(n) \leq 4(1 + \epsilon)\sqrt{n}$$

As this inequality holds for all positive $\epsilon$,

$$M(n) \leq 4\sqrt{n} + o(\sqrt{n})$$

$\square$

Now we can repeat proof of Lemma 7 , using in it Lemma 7 instead of Lemma 4. It will give us the Theorem 8. $\square$

**Acknowledgements.**

I am grateful to Rusins Freivalds and Kalvis Apsitis for help during this research and preparation of this paper.

# References

[1] M.Velauthapillai, W.I.Gasarch and M.G.Pleszkoch, *Classification Using Information*. This book.

[2] R.Freivalds, *Inductive Inference of Recursive Functions:Qualitative Theory*. Baltic Computer Science. Lecture Notes in Computer Science, Vol. 502 (1991) , pp. 77-110.

[3] M.Hall, *Combinatorial Theory*. Blaisdell Publishing Company,1967.

[4] W.Sierpinski, *Elementary Theory of Numbers*. North-Holland,1988.

# On Identification by Teams and Probabilistic Machines

Sanjay Jain

Institute of Systems Science

National University of Singapore

Singapore 0511, Republic of Singapore

sanjay@iss.nus.sg

Arun Sharma

School of Computer Science and Engineering

The University of New South Wales

Sydney, NSW 2052, Australia

arun@cse.unsw.edu.au

## 1 Introduction

Inductive inference in the scientific domain is seldom an individual enterprise. Many a scientific breakthrough are result of the efforts of several scientists investigating a problem; scientific success is achieved if any one or more of members of the scientific community are successful. This observation about the practice of science can be partially incorporated in a model of computational learning that employs a 'team' of algorithmic machines instead of a single algorithmic machine. The team is said to be successful just in case one or more members in the team are successful.

Another variation on the notion of an algorithmic learning machine is obtained by considering devices that in addition to being algorithmic are also capable of basing their actions on the outcomes of random events. Such learning agents can be modeled using probabilistic Turing machines.

The present paper surveys the work on both team and probabilistic learning. The notion of team learning in the context of identification in the limit of functions was first investigated by Smith [36]. The study of probabilistic learning machines was initiated by Freivalds [15] and Pitt [32]. Freivalds' study is in the context of finite identification of functions and Pitt's study is for identification in the limit of functions.

Like most investigations in Learning Theory, the work on team and probabilistic learning can be classified under two dimensions:

- *Concepts being learned:* computable functions and recursively enumerable languages.

- *Criteria of Success:* learning in the limit, learning with bounded number of mind changes and finite learning, vacillatory learning, and behaviorally correct learning.

Most progress has been reported on team and probabilistic learning in the limit of computable functions. Partial results have been reported on identification in the limit of r.e. languages by teams and probabilistic machines and on finite identification of computable functions by teams and probabilistic machines. Only preliminary results are known for other cases. Given this state of affairs, we begin with a extensive treatment of identification in the limit by teams and identification in the limit by probabilistic machines of computable functions. After showing that these two notions turn out to be equivalent, we turn our attention to language identification in the limit by both teams and probabilistic machines. This is followed by a discussion of results about team finite identification.[1] Finally, we present pointers to other investigations about team and probabilistic learners.

In what follows, Section 2 introduces the preliminaries, Section 3 describes team identification of functions, Section 4 introduces probabilistic identification of functions, Section 5 is devoted to both team and probabilistic identification of languages, Section 6 discusses results about finite identification of functions by teams, and finally in Section 7 we present pointers to the literature for additional results.

# 2 Preliminaries

In this section, we introduce our notation and describe the fundamental learning paradigms.

## 2.1 Notation

Any unexplained recursion theoretic notation is from [35]. The symbol $N$ denotes the set of natural numbers, $\{0, 1, 2, 3, \ldots\}$. The symbol $N^+$ denotes the set of positive natural numbers, $\{1, 2, 3, \ldots\}$. Unless otherwise specified, $i$, $j$, $k$, $l$, $m$, $n$, $q$, $r$, $s$, $t$, $x$, $y$, with or without decorations[2], range over $N$. Symbols $\emptyset$, $\subseteq$, $\subset$, $\supseteq$, and $\supset$ denote empty set, subset, proper subset, superset, and proper superset, respectively. Symbols $A$ and $S$, with or without decorations, range over sets. $P$, $Q$, and $X$, with or without decorations, range over finite sets. $D_0, D_1, \ldots$, denotes a canonical (recursive) indexing of finite sets [35]. Cardinality of a set $S$ is denoted by $\text{card}(S)$. We say that $\text{card}(A) \leq *$ to mean that $\text{card}(A)$ is finite. Intuitively, the symbol, $*$, denotes 'finite without any prespecified bound.' The letters $a$ and $b$, with or without decorations, range over

---

[1]This subject is addressed in detail by Daley and Kalyanasundaram elsewhere in this volume.
[2]Decorations are subscripts, superscripts and the like.

$N \cup \{*\}$. The maximum and minimum of a set are denoted by $\max(\cdot), \min(\cdot)$, respectively, where $\max(\emptyset) = 0$ and $\min(\emptyset) = \uparrow$. We also order pairs in the following manner. We say that a pair $(i, j)$ is $< (k, l)$ just in case $[(i < k) \lor (i = k \land j < l)]$.

Letters $f$, $g$, $h$ and $G$, with or without decorations, range over *total* functions with arguments and values from $N$. Symbol $\mathcal{R}$ denotes the set of all total computable functions. $\mathcal{C}$ and $\mathcal{S}$, with or without decorations, range over subsets of $\mathcal{R}$.

We let $\psi$, with or without decorations, range over partial functions. For $a \in (N \cup \{*\})$, $\psi_1 =^a \psi_2$ means that $\operatorname{card}(\{x \mid \psi_1(x) \neq \psi_2(x)\}) \leq a$.

A pair $\langle i, j \rangle$ stands for an arbitrary, computable, one-to-one encoding of all pairs of natural numbers onto $N$ [35]. $\pi_1(\langle x, y \rangle) = x$ and $\pi_2(\langle x, y \rangle) = y$. Similarly, we can define $\langle \cdot, \ldots, \cdot \rangle$ for encoding multiple tuples of natural numbers onto $N$.

By $\varphi$ we denote a fixed *acceptable* programming system for the partial computable functions: $N \rightarrow N$ [34, 35, 27]. By $\varphi_i$ we denote the partial computable function computed by program $i$ in the $\varphi$-system. The letter, $p$, in some contexts, with or without decorations, ranges over programs; in other contexts $p$ ranges over total functions with its range being construed as programs. By $\Phi$ we denote an arbitrary fixed Blum complexity measure [2, 19] for the $\varphi$-system. By $W_i$ we denote domain$(\varphi_i)$. $W_i$ is, then, the r.e. set/language $(\subseteq N)$ accepted (or equivalently, generated) by the $\varphi$-program $i$. Symbol $\mathcal{E}$ will denote the set of all r.e. languages. Symbol $L$, with or without decorations, ranges over $\mathcal{E}$. Symbol $\mathcal{L}$, with or without decorations, ranges over subsets of $\mathcal{E}$. We denote by $W_{i,s}$ the set $\{x \leq s \mid \Phi_i(x) < s\}$. $L_1 \triangle L_2$ denotes $(L_1 - L_2) \cup (L_2 - L_1)$, the symmetric difference of $L_1$ and $L_2$. For $a \in (N \cup \{*\})$, $L_1 =^a L_2$ means that $\operatorname{card}(L_1 \triangle L_2) \leq a$.

$[i \mathrel{..} j]$ denotes the set of real numbers $\geq i$ and $\leq j$.

## 2.2 Learning Machines

We first describe function learning machines.

We assume, without loss of generality, that the graph of a function is fed to a machine in canonical order. For $f \in \mathcal{R}$ and $n \in N$, we let $f[n]$ denote the finite initial segment $\{(x, f(x)) \mid x < n\}$. Clearly, $f[0]$ denotes the empty segment. SEG denotes the set of all finite initial segments, $\{f[n] \mid f \in \mathcal{R} \land n \in N\}$.

**Definition 1** [18] A *function learning machine* is an algorithmic device which computes a mapping from SEG into $N$.

We now consider language learning machines. A *sequence* $\sigma$ is a mapping from an initial segment of $N$ into $(N \cup \{\#\})$. The *content* of a sequence $\sigma$, denoted content$(\sigma)$, is the set of natural numbers in the range of $\sigma$. The *length* of $\sigma$, denoted $|\sigma|$, is the number of elements in $\sigma$. For $n \leq |\sigma|$, the initial sequence of $\sigma$ of length $n$ is denoted $\sigma[n]$. Intuitively, #'s represent pauses in the presentation of data. We let

$\sigma$, $\tau$, and $\gamma$, with or without decorations, range over finite sequences. SEQ denotes the set of all finite sequences. We let $\sigma \diamond x$ denote the concatenation of $x$ at the end of $\sigma$. Thus $\tau = \sigma \diamond x$ may be defined as follows:

$$\tau(z) = \begin{cases} \sigma(z), & z < |\sigma|; \\ x, & z = |\sigma|; \\ \uparrow, & \text{otherwise.} \end{cases}$$

A text $T$ is a mapping from $N$ into $(N \cup \{\#\})$. The content of a text $T$, denoted by content$(T)$, is the set of natural numbers in the range of $T$. A text $T$ is for $L$ iff content$(T) = L$. $T[n]$ denotes the initial segment of $T$ with length $n$.

**Definition 2** A *language learning machine* is an algorithmic device which computes a mapping from SEQ into $N$.

The set of all finite initial segments, SEG, can be coded onto $N$. Also, the set of all finite sequences of natural numbers and #'s, SEQ, can be coded onto $N$. Thus, in both Definitions 1 and 2, we can view these machines as taking natural numbers as input and emitting natural numbers as output. Henceforth, we will refer to both function-learning machines and language-learning machines as just learning machines, or simply as machines. We let **M**, with or without decorations, range over learning machines.

It should be noted that for all the identification criteria surveyed in this paper, we are assuming, without loss of generality, that the learning machines are total.

## 2.3 Function Identification in the Limit

The next definition describes identification in the limit of functions. We also consider the case in which the final program is allowed to have anomalies.

**Definition 3** [18, 1, 5] Let $a \in N \cup \{*\}$. **M** **Ex**$^a$-*identifies* $f$ (read: $f \in$ **Ex(M)**) $\iff$ $(\exists i \mid \varphi_i =^a f) (\overset{\infty}{\forall} n)[\mathbf{M}(f[n]) = i]$. We define the class **Ex**$^a$ = $\{\mathcal{S} \subseteq \mathcal{R} \mid (\exists \mathbf{M})[\mathcal{S} \subseteq \mathbf{Ex}^a(\mathbf{M})]\}$.

The relationship between the above criteria is summarized in the following theorem.

**Theorem 1** [5, 1] **Ex** = **Ex**$^0 \subset$ **Ex**$^1 \subset$ **Ex**$^2 \subset \cdots \subset$ **Ex**$^*$.

A variant on the above criterion, described next, was introduced by Case and Smith [5] and is useful in the proof of some of the results in the present chapter.

**Definition 4** [5] Let $a \in N \cup \{*\}$. **M Oex$^a$-identifies** $f$ (written: $f \in$ **Oex$^a$(M)**) just in case there exists a nonempty finite set $D$ such that the following hold:

1. $(\exists i \in D)[\varphi_i =^a f])$;

2. $(\overset{\infty}{\forall} n)[\mathbf{M}(f[n]) \in D]$;

3. $(\forall i \in D)(\overset{\infty}{\exists} n)[\mathbf{M}(f[n]) = i]]$.

We define the class **Oex$^a$** $= \{S \mid (\exists \mathbf{M})[S \subseteq \mathbf{Oex}^a(\mathbf{M})]\}$.

Thus, **M Oex$^a$** identifies a function $f$ just in case **M**, fed the graph of $f$, vacillates among a nonempty finite set $D$ of indexes such that there is at least one $a$-error index for $f$ in the set $D$ and each index in $D$ is conjectured infinitely often by **M**.

The following formulation of **Oex$^a$** is equivalent to the above definition. We often employ the following variant in our applications of **Oex$^a$**.

**Definition 5** [5] Let $a \in N \cup \{*\}$. **M Oex$^a$-identifies** $f$ (written: $f \in$ **Oex$^a$(M)**) just in case there exists an $i$ such that

1. $(\exists j \in D_i)[\varphi_j =^a f]$;

2. $(\overset{\infty}{\forall} n)[\mathbf{M}(f[n]) = i]$;

The following is true about **Oex$^a$** criteria.

**Theorem 2** [5]

1. *For $m \in N$, **Oex$^m$** = **Ex$^m$**.*

2. ***Oex$^*$** − **Ex$^*$** $\neq \emptyset$.*

## 2.4 Language Identification in the Limit

We now introduce language identification in the limit.

**Definition 6** [18, 4, 30] Let $a \in N \cup \{*\}$. **M TxtEx$^a$-identifies** $L$ (read: $L \in$ **TxtEx(M)**) $\iff$ ($\forall$ texts $T$ for $L$) $(\exists i \mid W_i =^a L)$ $(\overset{\infty}{\forall} n)[\mathbf{M}(T[n]) = i]$. We define the class **TxtEx$^a$** $= \{\mathcal{L} \subseteq \mathcal{E} \mid (\exists \mathbf{M})[\mathcal{L} \subseteq \mathbf{TxtEx}^a(\mathbf{M})]\}$.

The relationship between the above criteria are summarized in the following theorem.

**Theorem 3** [4, 30] **TxtEx** = **TxtEx$^0$** $\subset$ **TxtEx$^1$** $\subset$ **TxtEx$^2$** $\subset \cdots \subset$ **TxtEx$^*$**.

# 3 Limiting Identification of Functions by Teams

Consider the following well known result from Learning Theory.

**Theorem 4** [1] *Let*

$$S_1 = \{f \in \mathcal{R} \mid \varphi_{f(0)} = f\} \text{ and}$$

$$S_2 = \{f \in \mathcal{R} \mid (\overset{\infty}{\forall} n)[f(n) = 0]\}.$$

*Then, $S_1 \in \mathbf{Ex}$, $S_2 \in \mathbf{Ex}$, but $S_1 \cup S_2 \notin \mathbf{Ex}$.*

The above result, popularly referred to as 'non-union theorem,' says that the class **Ex** is not closed under union. In other words, there are collections of functions which are identifiable, but the union of these collections is not identifiable. This result may be viewed as a fundamental limitation on building a general purpose device for machine learning, and, to an extent, justifies the use of heuristic methods in Artificial Intelligence. However, this result also suggests a more general criterion of identification in which a team of scientists is employed and success of the team is the success of any member in the team. We illustrate this idea next.

Consider the collections of functions $S_1$ and $S_2$ in Theorem 4. Let $\mathbf{M_1}$ **Ex**-identify $S_1$ and $\mathbf{M_2}$ **Ex**-identify $S_2$. Now, if we employed a team of $\mathbf{M_1}$ and $\mathbf{M_2}$ to identify $S_1 \cup S_2$ and weakened the criterion of success to the requirement that success is achieved just in case any one member in the team is successful, then the collection $S_1 \cup S_2$ becomes identifiable by the team consisting of $\mathbf{M_1}$ and $\mathbf{M_2}$ under this new criterion of success. This idea can be extended to teams of $n$ machines out of which at least $m$ ($m \leq n$) are required to be successful. The formal definitions for team function identification and team language identification are presented next. J. Case first suggested the notion of team function identification based on the non-union theorem of the Blums, and it was extensively investigated by C. Smith. The general case of $m$ out of $n$ teams is due to Osherson, Stob, and Wienstein [28].

We now formally define team identification for functions.

A team of learning machines is a multiset of learning machines.

**Definition 7** [36, 28] Let $a \in N \cup \{*\}$ and let $m, n \in N^+$.

(a) Let $f \in \mathcal{R}$. A team of $n$ machines $\mathbf{M_1}, \mathbf{M_2}, \ldots, \mathbf{M_n}$ is said to **Team$_n^m$Ex$^a$**-*identify* $f$ (written: $f \in \mathbf{Team}_n^m\mathbf{Ex}^a(\mathbf{M_1}, \mathbf{M_2}, \ldots, \mathbf{M_n})$) just in case there exist $m$ distinct numbers $i_1, i_2, \ldots, i_m$, $1 \leq i_1 < i_2 < \cdots < i_m \leq n$, such that each of $\mathbf{M}_{i_1}, \mathbf{M}_{i_2}, \ldots, \mathbf{M}_{i_m}$ **Ex$^a$**-identifies $f$.

(b) **Team$_n^m$Ex$^a$** is defined to be the class of sets $S$ of computable functions such that some team of $n$ machines **Team$_n^m$Ex$^a$**-identifies each function in $S$.

For the criterion $\textbf{Team}_n^m\textbf{Ex}^a$-identification, we refer to the fraction $\frac{m}{n}$ as the *success ratio* of the criterion.

We now turn our attention to results. We first describe results about team function criteria in which success of the team requires only one member in the team to be successful, namely, $\textbf{Team}_n^1\textbf{Ex}$-identification. Section 4 describes identification by probabilistic machines. These results illustrate an intimate relationship between $\textbf{Team}_n^1\textbf{Ex}$-identification and identification by probabilistic machines. This relationship is then used to obtain results about the general team function criteria, $\textbf{Team}_n^m\textbf{Ex}$-identification.

All the results to follow in the present section are due to Smith [36].

The following result says that there are collections of functions for which a correct program can be synthesized by a team of $n + 1$ machines, at least one of which is successful, but for which even a finite variant program cannot be synthesized by a team of $n$ machines with the requirement that at least one of them be successful.

**Theorem 5** [36] $(\forall n \geq 1)[\textbf{Team}_{n+1}^1\textbf{Ex} - \textbf{Team}_n^1\textbf{Ex}^* \neq \emptyset]$.

PROOF. For $n \in N^+$, let $\mathcal{C}_n = \{f \in \mathcal{R} \mid (\exists x \leq n)[\text{card}(W_{f(x)}) < \infty \wedge \varphi_{\max(W_{f(x)})} = f]\}$.

It is easy to verify that $\mathcal{C}_n \in \textbf{Team}_{n+1}^1\textbf{Ex}$. Below, we show using a diagonalization argument that $\mathcal{C}_2 \notin \textbf{Team}_2^1\textbf{Ex}^*$. The following argument can easily be generalized to show that $\mathcal{C}_n \notin \textbf{Team}_n^1\textbf{Ex}^*$.

Suppose by way of contradiction, there exist machines $\textbf{M}_0$ and $\textbf{M}_1$ such that $\mathcal{C}_2 \subseteq \textbf{Team}_2^1(\textbf{M}_0, \textbf{M}_1)$. Then, by the implicit use of the operator recursion theorem, there exists a one to one, monotone increasing, recursive function $p$ such that $\varphi_{p(\cdot)}$ $(W_{p(\cdot)})$ can be described in stages below.

We initialize $\varphi_{p(3)}(0) = p(0)$, $\varphi_{p(3)}(1) = p(1)$, and $\varphi_{p(3)}(2) = p(2)$. Enumerate $p(3)$ in to $W_{p(0)}$.

Let avail $= 3$. Intuitively, avail denotes the least number such that, for all $i >$ avail, $p(i)$ has not been used in the diagonalization before. Let $x_s$ denote the least $x$ such that $\varphi_{p(3)}(x)$ has not been defined before stage $s$. Go to stage 0.

Begin {stage $s$}
1. Let avail = avail + 1.
   Let cur = avail.
   Enumerate $p(\text{cur})$ into $W_{p(1)}$.
   For $x < x_s$, let $\varphi_{p(\text{cur})}(x) = \varphi_{p(3)}(x)$.
   Let $r = s \mod 2$.
2. Dovetail steps 3 and 4 until, if ever, step 3 succeeds. If and when step 3 succeeds go to step 5.

(∗ *Intuitively, if step 3 succeeds in each stage, then $\varphi_{p(3)} \in C_2$ and both $\mathbf{M}_0$ and $\mathbf{M}_1$ do not $\mathbf{Ex}^*$-identify $\varphi_{p(3)}$.* ∗)

3. Search for an extension $\sigma \in$ SEQ of $\varphi_{p(3)}[x_s]$ such that $\varphi_{\mathbf{M}_r(\sigma)}(|\sigma|)\downarrow$.

4. Let $x_{s,s'}$ denote the least $x$ such that $\varphi_{p(\mathrm{cur})}(x)$ has not been defined before sub-stage $s'$ of stage $s$.

   Go to substage 0.

   Begin {substage $s'$}

   4.1. Let avail = avail + 1.

   4.2. Enumerate $p(\mathrm{avail})$ into $W_{p(2)}$.

   4.3. For $x < x_{s,s'}$, let $\varphi_{p(\mathrm{avail})}(x) = \varphi_{p(\mathrm{cur})}(x)$.

   4.4. Dovetail steps 4.5 and 4.6 until, if ever, step 4.5 succeeds. If and when step 4.5 succeeds, go to step 4.7.

   4.5. Search for an extension $\tau \in$ SEQ of $\varphi_{p(\mathrm{cur})}[x_{s,s'}]$ such that $\varphi_{\mathbf{M}_{1-r}(\tau)}(|\tau|)\downarrow$.

   4.6. Let $x = x_{s,s'}$.

   **repeat**

       Let $\varphi_{p(\mathrm{avail})}(x) = 0$.

       Let $x = x + 1$.

   **forever**

   4.7. Let $\tau$ be as found in step 4.5.

   For $x < |\tau|$, let $\varphi_{p(\mathrm{cur})}(x) = y$ such that $(x, y) \in$ content$(\tau)$.

   Let $\varphi_{p(\mathrm{cur})}(|\tau|) = \varphi_{\mathbf{M}_{1-r}(\tau)}(|\tau|) + 1$.

   4.8 Go to substage $s' + 1$.

   End {substage $s'$}

5. Let $\sigma$ be as found in step 3.

   5.1. For $x < |\sigma|$, let $\varphi_{p(3)}(x) = y$ such that $(x, y) \in$ content$(\sigma)$.

   5.2. Let $\varphi_{p(3)}(|\sigma|) = \varphi_{\mathbf{M}_r(\sigma)}(|\sigma| + 1)$.

6. Go to stage $s + 1$.

End {stage $s$}

Now, consider the following cases.

*Case 1:* Each stage terminates.

    Let $f = \varphi_{p(3)}$. Clearly, $f$ is computable and a member of $C_2$ (since $f(0) = p(0)$, and $W_{p(0)} = \{p(3)\}$). Also, because of the success of step 3 and the diagonalization at step 5.2 in each even (odd) stage, $\mathbf{M}_0$ ($\mathbf{M}_1$) either diverges on $f$ or the last program output by $\mathbf{M}_0$ ($\mathbf{M}_1$) on $f$ commits infinitely many convergent errors.

*Case 2:* Some stage $s$ starts but does not terminate.

    Let $r$ and cur be as defined in step 1 of stage $s$. Since step 3 does not succeed, $\mathbf{M}_r$ does not $\mathbf{Ex}^*$-identify any extension of $\varphi_{p(3)}$, and thus it does not $\mathbf{Ex}^*$-identify any extension of $\varphi_{p(\mathrm{cur})}$.

Case 2.1: Each substage in stage $s$ terminates.

Let $f = \varphi_{p(\text{cur})}$. Clearly, $f$ is computable and a member of $C_2$, since $f(1) = p(1)$ and $\max(W_{p(1)}) = p(\text{cur})$. Also, by the success of step 4.5 and the diagonalization at step 4.7 in each substage, $M_{1-r}$ either diverges on $f$, or the last program output by $M_{1-r}$ on $f$ commits infinitely many convergent errors.

Case 2.2: Some substage $s'$ in stage $s$ starts but does not terminate.

In this case let avail be as at step 4.2 in substage $s'$ of stage $s$. Let $f = \varphi_{p(\text{avail})}$. Clearly, $f$ is recursive and an extension of $\varphi_{p(\text{cur})}$. Also, $f$ is a member of $C_2$, since $f(2) = p(2)$ and $\max(W_{p(2)}) = p(\text{avail})$. However, since step 4.5 does not succeed, $M_{1-r}$, does not $\mathbf{Ex}^*$-identify any extension of $\varphi_{p(\text{cur})}$ and thus does not $\mathbf{Ex}^*$-identify $f$.

From the above cases it follows that $C_2 \notin \mathbf{Team}_2^1(M_0, M_1)$. ∎

The following corollary to the above theorem says that increasing the size of team renders larger collections of functions identifiable.

**Corollary 1** [36] *Let* $a \in N \cup \{*\}$. *Then,*
$$\mathbf{Ex}^a = \mathbf{Team}_1^1\mathbf{Ex}^a \subset \mathbf{Team}_2^1\mathbf{Ex}^a \subset \mathbf{Team}_3^1\mathbf{Ex}^a \subset \cdots.$$

Now, if $m, n \in N^+$ such that $m \leq n$, then we would like to know for which values of $i, j \in N$, $\mathbf{Team}_m^1\mathbf{Ex}^i \subseteq \mathbf{Team}_n^1\mathbf{Ex}^j$. From the above corollary, it is clear that the $\subseteq$ relationship holds if $i \leq j$, but we wish to determine for a given $n$, by how much can the value of $j$ be reduced so that the $\subseteq$ relationship still holds. In other words, we would like to know how anomalies in the final program can be traded for extra team members. This is the subject of next result; we omit the proof.

**Theorem 6** [36] *For all* $i, j \in N$ *and* $m \in N^+$, $\mathbf{Team}_m^1\mathbf{Ex}^i \subseteq \mathbf{Team}_n^1\mathbf{Ex}^j$, *where* $n = m(1 + \lfloor \frac{i}{j+1} \rfloor)$.

The next two results show that above Theorem 6 is optimal. For Theorems 7 and 8 below, define $C_{r,l}$, for $r, l \geq 1$, to be the collection of functions $\{f \in \mathcal{R} \mid \varphi_{f(0)} =^{r \cdot l} f \wedge (\exists i \leq r)[\text{card}(\{x \mid \varphi_{f(0)}(x) \neq f(x)\}) = i \cdot l]\}$.

**Theorem 7** [36] *For all* $k$, $C_{r,l} \in \mathbf{Team}_m^1\mathbf{Ex}^{k \cdot l}$, *where* $m = 1 + \lfloor \frac{r}{k+1} \rfloor$.

**Theorem 8** [36] $C_{r,l} \notin \mathbf{Team}_r^1\mathbf{Ex}^{l-1}$.

PROOF. The proof of the above theorem involves a complicated priority construction. Fix $r, l \geq 1$. Suppose by way of contradiction there exist machines $M_1, M_2, \ldots, M_r$ such that $C_{r,l} \in \mathbf{Team}_r^1\mathbf{Ex}^{l-1}(M_1, M_1, \ldots, M_r)$. Then, by implicit use of Kleene's recursion theorem, there exists an $e$ such that the (partial) function $\varphi_e$ may be described as follows.

$\varphi_e$ employs $r$ moving anomaly markers, each marking $l$ consecutive numbers, which we are temporarily trying to keep out of the domain of $\varphi_e$. We name the $r$ markers $\alpha_0, \ldots, \alpha_{r-1}$. At any time, we let the set variable $A_i$ denote the set of numbers marked by $\alpha_i$ at that time. $A_i$'s will be pairwise disjoint at all times. $A_i^s$ denotes the value of $A_i$ at the beginning of stage $s$.

In the construction, we will assign tasks, numbered 0 to $\infty$, to the markers. Priority of a task numbered $t$ is $t$. Lower number means higher priority. The tasks may get "done" at some stage. However, a higher priority task may undo a lower priority task which was completed earlier. Priority of a marker, at any time, is the priority of the highest priority task assigned to it which has not been done.

We now proceed to give an informal description of $\varphi_e$. Let $\varphi_e(0) = e$. For $i < r$, let $A_i^0 = \{l \cdot i + 1 + x \mid x < l\}$. Let $\varphi_e^s$ denote the part of $\varphi_e$ defined before stage $s$. We let $x_s$ denote the least element not in $\text{domain}(\varphi_e^s) \cup \bigcup_{i<r} A_i^s$. It will be the case that $\text{domain}(\varphi_e^s) \cup \bigcup_{i<r} A_i^s$ is an initial segment of $N$. Let $\tau^s$ denote the sequence such that $\text{content}(\tau^s) = \varphi_i^s \cup \{(x, 0) \mid x \in \bigcup_{i<r} A_i^s\}$. Let $\sigma_i^s$ denote the initial segment of $\tau^s$ with length $\min(A_i^s)$.

Initially assign task $i$ to $\alpha_i$. Let nexttask denote, at any time, the least task number which has not been assigned to any marker till that time. Thus, initially nexttask $= r$. Go to stage 0.

Begin {stage $s$}

1. We say that $\alpha_i$ requires attention at this stage just in case
$$(\exists \tau' \mid \sigma_i^s \subseteq \tau' \subseteq \tau^s)[\mathbf{M}_i(\sigma_i^s) \neq \mathbf{M}_i(\tau')] \text{ or}$$
there exists an $x \in A_i^s$ such that $\Phi_{\mathbf{M}_i(\sigma_i^s)} \leq s$.

2. **if** no $\alpha_i$ requires attention, then let $\varphi_e(x_s) = 0$ and go to stage $s + 1$.
**endif**

3. (* *Some $\alpha_i$ requires attention.* *)
Let $\alpha_i$ be the highest priority marker which requires attention.
Let $t$ be the priority of highest priority marker which requires attention.

4. "undo" all tasks with lower priority than $t$.

5. (* *In steps 5 and 6 task $t$ gets "done".* *)
Let $y = x_s$.
**for** $j = 0$ **to** $r - 1$ **do**
    **if** priority of $\alpha_j$ is lower than that of $\alpha_i$,
    **then**
        For $x \in A_j^s$, let $\varphi_e(x) = 0$.
        Let $A_j = \{y + x \mid x < l\}$.
        Let $y = y + l$.
        (* *Note that in this step $A_j$ changes. Thus, the marker $\alpha_j$ moves.* *)
    **endif**
**endfor**

6. **if** there exists an $x \in A_i^s$ such that $\Phi_{\mathbf{M}_i(\sigma_i^s)} \leq s$

**then**

> Let $x' \in A_i^s$ be such that $\Phi_{M_i(\sigma_i^s)}(x') \leq s$.
> Let $\varphi_e(x') = \varphi_{M_i(\sigma_i^s)}(x') + 1$.
> For $x \in A_i^s - \{x'\}$, let $\varphi_e(x) = 0$.
> Let $A_i^s = \{y + x \mid x < l\}$.
> Let $y = y + l$.

**else**

> For $x \in A_i^s$, let $\varphi_e(x) = 0$.
> Let $A_i = \{y + x \mid x < l\}$.
> Let $y = y + l$.

**endif**

(∗ *Note that in this step $A_i$ changes. Thus, the marker $\alpha_i$ "moves".* ∗)

Mark task $t$ as "done".

7. Assign task nexttask to marker $\alpha_i$.

   Let nexttask = nexttask + 1.

8. Go to stage $s + 1$.

End {stage $s$}

It is easy to see that every stage terminates.

**Claim 1** *Each task gets "done" or "undone" only finitely often.*

PROOF. A proof by induction suffices. Suppose all tasks numbered $< t$, get done or undone only finitely often. Let $s$ be a stage such that no task numbered $< t$, gets done or undone beyond stage $s$. Then beyond stage $s$ task $t$ can never get undone, and thus it can get done at most once more beyond stage $s$. $\square$

**Claim 2** *A marker can move due to step 5 at most finitely many times before it moves (afresh) due to step 6.*

PROOF. A marker can move due to step 5 in some stage $s$, only if it has lower priority than some marker which requires attention and gets done at stage $s$. It is now easy to prove this claim using Claim 1. We leave the details to the reader. $\square$

**Claim 3** *If a marker requires attention only finitely often, then*

   *(a) the set of numbers assigned to it stabilizes in the limit, and*

   *(b) only finitely many tasks are assigned to it.*

PROOF. A marker can move at stage $s$ only if the highest priority task assigned to it, which is not done at the beginning of stage $s$, gets done at stage $s$, or a higher priority task gets done at stage $s$. Part (a) now follows using Claims 1 and 2.

Part (b) is immediate because a task can be assigned to a marker at stage $s$ only if it requires attention at stage $s$. □

We say that a task is completed (at stage $s$), if it gets done at some stage $s$ and never gets undone thereafter.

**Claim 4** *If a marker requires attention infinitely often, then each task assigned to it gets completed, and thus*

*(a) it moves infinitely often, and*

*(b) infinitely many tasks are assigned to it.*

PROOF. Let $t$ be the least numbered task such that $t$ never gets completed, and the marker to which $t$ is assigned gets attention infinitely often. Let $s$ be a stage such that all tasks with priority higher than $t$ which ever get completed are completed before stage $s$ and no marker, which requires attention only finitely often, requires attention beyond stage $s$. Let $s' > s$ be such that the marker to which $t$ is assigned gets attention at stage $s'$. Then, task $t$ gets done at stage $s'$ and never gets undone after stage $s'$—a contradiction. □

Let $f$ be the zero extension of $\varphi_e$. Clearly, $\varphi_e(x)\uparrow$ iff there exists an $i < r$ such that $\lim_s A_i^s$ exists and $x \in \lim_s A_i^s$. Thus, $f \in \mathcal{C}_{r,l}$.

Now for each machine $\mathbf{M}_i$, $i < r$, we show that $\mathbf{M}_i$ does not $\mathbf{Ex}^{l-1}$-identify $f$.

Let lastfin be such that (a) no marker, which requires attention only finitely often, requires attention beyond stage lastfin, and (b) no marker which moves only finitely often, moves after stage lastfin.

For each $i < r$, consider the following cases.

Case 1: $\alpha_i$ requires attention finitely often.

In this case, $A_i^{\text{lastfin}} = \lim_s A_i^s$ and $\mathbf{M}_i(f) = \mathbf{M}(\sigma_i^{\text{lastfin}})$ and $A_i^{\text{lastfin}} \cap \text{domain}(\varphi_{\mathbf{M}(f)}) = \emptyset$ (otherwise, $\alpha_i$ would require attention beyond stage lastfin). Thus, $\mathbf{M}_i$ does not $\mathbf{Ex}^{l-1}$-identify $f$.

Case 2: $\alpha_i$ requires attention infinitely often.

By Claim 4, infinitely many tasks are assigned to $\alpha_i$. Note that if a task assigned to $\alpha_i$ gets completed at stage $s > \text{lastfin}$, then $\sigma_i^s \subseteq f$ and either $\mathbf{M}_i$ is forced to change its mind on $f$ after $\sigma_i^s$, or $\varphi_{\mathbf{M}_i(f)}$ commits an error in $A_i^s$. Thus, either $\mathbf{M}_i$ changes mind infinitely often on $f$, or $\mathbf{M}(f)$ commits infinitely many convergent errors. ∎

**Theorem 9** [36] $\mathbf{Team}_m^1\mathbf{Ex}^a \subseteq \mathbf{Team}_n^1\mathbf{Ex}^b$ *iff*

*(a) $m \leq n$, and*

*(b) $b = *$ or $n \geq m \cdot (1 + \lfloor a/(b+1) \rfloor)$.*

PROOF. If part follows from Theorem 6.

For the only if part, observe that by Theorem 5, $n$ must be $\geq m$. Suppose $b \neq *$. Now, let $l = b+1$, and $r = m \cdot (1 + \lfloor a/(b+1) \rfloor) - 1$. Let $C_{r,l}$ be as defined just before Theorem 7. Now, by Theorem 7, $C_{r,l} \in \mathbf{Team}_m^1\mathbf{Ex}^{(b+1)\cdot\lfloor a/(b+1)\rfloor} \subseteq \mathbf{Team}_m^1\mathbf{Ex}^a$. Also, by Theorem 8, $C_{r,l} \notin \mathbf{Team}_r^1\mathbf{Ex}^b$. ∎

# 4 Limiting Identification of Functions by Probabilistic Machines

The present section considers machines whose actions may be determined by the outcome of random events. These devices, referred to as probabilistic machines, behave very much like algorithmic machines except that every now and then they have the ability to base their actions on the outcome of a random event like a coin flip.

More precisely, let $t$ be a positive integer greater that 1. Then, a probabilistic machine **P** may be construed as a algorithmic machine that is equipped with a $t$-sided coin. The response of **P** to an evidential situation $\sigma$ not only depends upon $\sigma$ but also on the outcomes of coin flips performed by **P** till that point. It is useful to make the notion of sequence of outcomes of a $t$-ary coin precise.

**Definition 8** *Let $t > 1$.*

*(a) $N_t$ denotes the set $\{0, 1, 2, \ldots, t-1\}$.*

*(b) An oracle for a $t$-sided coin, also referred to as a $t$-ary oracle is an infinite sequence of integers $i_1, i_2, i_3, \ldots$ such that for each $j$, $i_j \in N_t$. (A typical variable for oracles is $O$).*

Clearly, $N_t^\infty$, the infinite cartesian product of $N_t$ with itself, denotes the collection of all $t$-sided coin oracles. Observe that a $t$-ary oracle is somewhat like a text for the finite language $N_t$, and notations for texts carry over to oracles; the next definition records these conventions.

**Definition 9** *Let $t > 1$.*

*(a) Let $O$ be a $t$-ary oracle. Then, the $n^{th}$ member of $O$ is denoted $O_n$. The initial finite sequence of $O$ of length $n$ is denoted $O[n]$.*

*(b) The set $\{O[n] \mid O$ is a t-ary oracle and $n \in N\}$ is the collection of all finite t-ary sequences. (A typical variable for finite t-ary sequences is $\rho$).*

*(c) Let $\rho$ be a finite t-ary sequence. The length of $\rho$ is denoted by $|\rho|$. For $n < |\rho|$, the $n^{th}$ member of $\rho$ is denoted by $\rho_n$, and the initial sequence of length $n$ in $\rho$ is denoted by $\rho[n]$.*

Let $\rho$ be a finite $t$-ary sequence and $\mathbf{P}$ be a probabilistic machine equipped with a $t$-sided coin. Let $\sigma \in \text{SEG}$. Then, $\mathbf{P}^\rho(\sigma)$ denotes the output of $\mathbf{P}$ on $\sigma$ such that the result of any coin flip performed by $\mathbf{P}$ are 'read' from $\rho$, that is, the outcome of the first coin flip is $\rho_0$, the outcome of the second coin flip is $\rho_1$, and so on and so forth. If $\mathbf{P}$ performs more coin flips than $|\rho|$ in responding to the evidential state $\sigma$, then $\mathbf{P}^\rho(\sigma)$ is undefined.

Similarly, we can describe the behavior of $\mathbf{P}$ for a given $t$-ary oracle $O$. $\mathbf{P}^O$ behaves like $\mathbf{P}$ except whenever $\mathbf{P}$ flips its coin, $\mathbf{P}^O$ reads the result of the coin flip from the oracle $O$, that is, the result of the first coin flip is $O_0$, the result of the second coin flip is $O_1$, and so on and so forth. Now, if the sequence of hypotheses issued by $\mathbf{P}^O$ on the graph of a computable function $f$ corresponds to an **Ex**-identification of $f$, then $\mathbf{P}^O$ is said to **Ex**-identify $f$.

Our first task is to define the probability of a probabilistic machine $\mathbf{P}$ **Ex**-identifying $f$. The subject of identification by probabilistic machine was first investigated by R. Freivalds [16] and L. Pitt [31, 32]. Our presentation closely follows that of Pitt. We first review some necessary probability theory.

## 4.1   Background Probability Theory

Let the outcomes of an experiment be elements of some universal set $\Omega$. A probability measure may then be thought of as a function that assigns real values between 0 and 1 to outcomes of an experiment. In practice it is useful to define a probability measure on subsets of $\Omega$. However, defining a probability measure on the power set of $\Omega$ poses technical difficulties, and hence it is defined only on those collections of subsets of $\Omega$ that satisfy certain properties stated in the following definition.

**Definition 10** $\mathcal{B} \subseteq 2^\Omega$ is a Borel field *just in case the following conditions hold:*

*(a) $\Omega \in \mathcal{B}$,*

*(b) $A \in \mathcal{B} \Rightarrow \Omega - A \in \mathcal{B}$,*

*(c) $\mathcal{B}$ is closed under countable unions and intersections, i.e., if $\{A_i\}_{i \in I}$ is a finite or countable collection of elements of $\mathcal{B}$, then $\bigcup_{i \in I} A_i \in \mathcal{B}$ and $\bigcap_{i \in I} A_i \in \mathcal{B}$.*

Given any collection $\mathcal{C}$ of subsets of $\Omega$, there is a unique smallest (with respect to containment) Borel field containing $\mathcal{C}$. The next definition introduces the notion of a probability measure on a Borel field $\mathcal{B}$ on subsets of $\Omega$.

**Definition 11** *A probability measure pr on a Borel field $\mathcal{B}$ of subsets of $\Omega$ is a function $pr: \mathcal{B} \rightarrow [0 .. 1]$ such that*

*(a) $pr(\Omega) = 1$,*

*(b) $(\forall A)[A \in \mathcal{B} \Rightarrow pr(A) \geq 0]$,*

*(3) If $\{A_i\}$ is a finite or countable collection of mutually disjoint elements of $\mathcal{B}$, then $pr(\bigcup_i A_i) = \sum_i pr(A_i)$.*

Elements of $\mathcal{B}$ are called *measurable* sets. We note some properties of measurable sets.

If $\{A_i\}$ is a countable collection of sets, then $\lim_{k \to \infty} \sup A_k = \bigcap_{k=0}^{\infty} \bigcup_{i=k}^{\infty} A_i$ and $\lim_{k \to \infty} \inf A_k = \bigcup_{k=0}^{\infty} \bigcap_{i=k}^{\infty} A_i$. If the limit supremum and limit infimum of a sequence of sets $\{A_i\}$ are equal, then this is the limit of the sequence. A sequence of sets $\{A_i\}$ is *monotone* if either $(\forall k)[A_k \subseteq A_{k+1}]$ or $(\forall k)[A_{k+1} \subseteq A_k]$. Every monotone sequence of sets has a limit, and every Borel field is closed under lim inf and lim sup. If $\{A_i\}$ is a sequence of measurable sets for which the limit is defined, then $pr(\lim_{k \to \infty} A_k) = \lim_{k \to \infty} pr(A_k)$.

**Definition 12** *A probability space is a triple $(\Omega, \mathcal{B}, pr)$ of a sample space $\Omega$, a Borel field $\mathcal{B}$ on subsets of $\Omega$, and a probability measure pr on $\mathcal{B}$.*

Given a probability space $(\Omega, \mathcal{B}, pr)$ and a set $A \subseteq \Omega$, $A$ can be shown to be measurable by expressing $A$ in terms of countable intersections, unions, and complements of known measurable sets. Similarly, $pr(A)$ can be computed by using properties of probability measures on the values of these known measurable sets.

The aim of all this machinery is to eventually define a probability space on oracle sequences which in turn is used to calculate the probability of a machine to Ex-identify a function. To this end, we first introduce a probability measure on a single coin flip. For a $t$-sided coin, let $(N_t, \mathcal{B}_t, pr_t)$ be a probability space on the sample space $N_t$, where $\mathcal{B}_t = \{S \mid S \subseteq N_t\}$ and $pr_t = card(S)/t$. Intuitively, this measure simply says that the probability of the outcome of flipping a $t$-sided coin belonging to a set $S \subseteq N_t$ is $card(S)/t$. We use this measure next to describe a probability measure on $t$-ary oracles.

Now, identification by a probabilistic machine may be viewed as an ongoing process in which a machine receives data, flips coin, and issues hypotheses. During identification, each of these activities may occur infinitely often. We would like to introduce a reasonable probability measure on an infinite sequence of coin flips. As already mentioned, the act of recording the outcomes of an infinite sequence of coin flips can be viewed as reading values off an infinite $t$-ary oracle. Thus, the sample space of events for oracles of a $t$-sided coin is $N_t^\infty$—the set of all infinite sequences of numbers less than $t$. Let $\mathcal{B}_t^\infty$ be the smallest Borel field of subsets of $N_t^\infty$ containing all the sets $N_t^{j-1} \times A_j \times N_t^\infty$, where for each $j$, $A_j \in \mathcal{B}_t$. Then, let $(N_t^\infty, \mathcal{B}_t^\infty, pr_t^\infty)$ be a probability space where $pr_t^\infty$ is defined as follows:

Given a nonempty set of $n$ integers, $i_1, i_2, i_3, \ldots, i_n$, such that $0 < i_1 < i_2 < i_3 < \cdots < i_n$, let $A_{i_1, i_2, i_3, \ldots, i_n}$ denote the set $N_t^{i_1-1} \times A_{i_1} \times N_t^{i_2-i_1-1} \times A_{i_2} \times N_t^{i_3-i_2-1} \times A_{i_3} \times \cdots \times A_{i_n} \times N_t^\infty$, where each $A_{i_j} \in \mathcal{B}_t$. Then, $\mathrm{pr}_t^\infty$ is defined on $\mathcal{B}_t^\infty$ such that $\mathrm{pr}_t^\infty(A_{i_1, i_2, \ldots, i_n}) = \prod_{j=1}^n \mathrm{pr}_t(A_{i_j})$, for each choice of $n$ integers $i_1, i_2, \ldots, i_n$.

Clearly, sets $A_{i_1, i_2, i_3, \ldots, i_n}$ are measurable. Let us now look at some examples of measurable sets of oracles.

Consider a $t$-sided coin and $j$ such that $0 \leq j \leq t-1$. Then the set $\{O \mid O_n = j\}$ consists of all such $t$-ary oracles that have $j$ as their $n$th value. As an immediate consequence of the forgoing discussion, $\{O \mid O_n = j\}$ is measurable, and $\mathrm{pr}_t^\infty(\{O \mid O_n = j\}) = 1/t$.

As another example consider a finite $t$-ary sequence $\rho$ of length $k$. Then, a $t$-ary oracle $O$ *extends* $\rho$ just in case $O[k] = \rho$. Again, as an immediate consequence of the forgoing discussion, the set of oracles $\{O \mid O \text{ extends } \rho\}$ is measurable, and $\mathrm{pr}_t^\infty(\{O \mid O \text{ extends } \rho\}) = 1/t^k$. This fact is used below in showing that the set of oracles that correspond to a successful identification of a function is measurable.

## 4.2 Probability of Function Identification

Let $\mathbf{P}$ be a probabilistic machine equipped with a $t$-sided coin and let $f \in \mathcal{R}$. Then, the probability of $\mathbf{P}$ Ex-identifying $f$ is taken to be $\mathrm{pr}_t^\infty(\{O \mid \mathbf{P}^O \text{Ex-identifies } f\})$. However, to be able to compute such a probability, it needs to be established that the set $\{O \mid \mathbf{P}^O \text{Ex-identifies } f\}$ is measurable. This is the subject of next lemma.

**Lemma 1** [31, 32] *Let* $\mathbf{P}$ *be a probabilistic machine and let* $f \in \mathcal{R}$. *Then* $\{O \mid \mathbf{P}^O$ Ex-*identifies* $f\}$ *is measurable.*

PROOF. Let plausible$(\mathbf{P}, f, j, \varrho)$ be a boolean predicate, where $\mathbf{P}$ ranges over probabilistic machines equipped with a $t$-ary oracle, $f$ ranges over $\mathcal{R}$, $j$ ranges over $N^+$, and $\varrho$ ranges over $N_t^\infty \cup \bigcup_{k=j}^\infty N_t^k$ (i.e., $\varrho$ can be any $t$-ary sequence of length $\geq j$). Then, plausible$(\mathbf{P}, f, j, \varrho) \iff \mathbf{P}^\varrho(f[j]) = \mathbf{P}^\varrho(f[j-1]) \wedge \varphi_{\mathbf{P}^\varrho(f[j])} = f]$. Then,

$\{O \mid \mathbf{P}^O \text{Ex-identifies } f\}$

$= \{O \mid (\exists k)(\forall j \geq k)[\text{plausible}(\mathbf{P}, f, j, O)]\}$

$= \bigcup_{k=1}^\infty \{O \mid (\forall j \geq k)[\text{plausible}(\mathbf{P}, f, j, O)]\}$

$= \bigcup_{k=1}^\infty \bigcap_{j=k}^\infty \{O \mid \text{plausible}(\mathbf{P}, f, j, O)\}$

$= \bigcup_{k=1}^\infty \bigcap_{j=k}^\infty \bigcup_{\rho \in N_t^j \wedge \text{plausible}(\mathbf{P}, f, j, \rho)} \{O \mid O \text{ extends } \rho\}$.

But, it has already been shown that the set of oracles $\{O \mid O \text{ extends } \rho\}$ is measurable. Thus, $\{O \mid \mathbf{P}^O \text{Ex-identifies } f\}$ is measurable because it can be expressed as countable unions and intersections of measurable sets. ∎

The following definition is motivated by the above lemma.

**Definition 13** [31, 32] Let $f \in \mathcal{R}$ and $\mathbf{P}$ be a probabilistic machine equipped with a $t$-sided coin ($t \geq 2$). Then, $\mathrm{pr}_t^\infty(\mathbf{P}$ Ex-identifies $f) = \mathrm{pr}_t^\infty(\{O \mid \mathbf{P}^O$ Ex-identifies $f\})$.

The next lemma says that we do not sacrifice any learning power by restricting our attention to the investigation of identification by probabilistic machines equipped with only a two-sided coin. The proof of the lemma follows from a result in probability theory and we omit the details (the reader is directed to Pitt [32]) for a proof).

**Lemma 2** [31, 32] *Let $t > 2$. Let $\mathbf{P}$ be a probabilistic machine with a $t$-sided coin. Then, there exists a probabilistic machines $\mathbf{P}'$ with a two-sided coin such that for each $f \in \mathcal{R}$, $\mathrm{pr}_2^\infty(\mathbf{P}'$ Ex-identifies $f) = \mathrm{pr}_t^\infty(\mathbf{P}$ Ex-identifies $f)$.*

We now present identification by probabilistic machines as a paradigm. The above lemma frees us from specifying the number of sides of the coin, thereby allowing us to talk about probability function $\mathrm{pr}_t^\infty$ without specifying $t$. For this reason, we will refer to $\mathrm{pr}_t^\infty$ as simply pr in the sequel. Also, we are at liberty to use whatever value of the number of sides of a coin that is convenient for the presentation at hand.

**Definition 14** [31, 32] Let $p \in [0 .. 1]$.

(a) $\mathbf{P}$ $\mathbf{Prob}^p\mathbf{Ex}$-*identifies* $f$ (written: $f \in \mathbf{Prob}^p\mathbf{Ex}(\mathbf{P})$) just in case $\mathrm{pr}(\mathbf{P}$ Ex-identifies $f) \geq p$.

(b) $\mathbf{Prob}^p\mathbf{Ex} = \{\mathcal{S} \subseteq \mathcal{R} \mid (\exists \mathbf{P})[\mathcal{S} \subseteq \mathbf{Prob}^p\mathbf{Ex}(\mathbf{P})]\}$.

An immediate result is the following theorem which links identification by probabilistic machines and team identification. The result shows that any collection of functions which can be identified by a team of $n$ machines, at least one of which is required to be successful, can be identified by a probabilistic machine with probability $\geq 1/n$.

**Theorem 10** [31, 32] $(\forall n \geq 1)[\mathbf{Team}_n^1\mathbf{Ex} \subseteq \mathbf{Prob}^{\frac{1}{n}}\mathbf{Ex}]$.

PROOF. Let $\mathcal{S} \in \mathbf{Team}_n^1\mathbf{Ex}$. Then, there exists a team of $n$ machines $\mathbf{M}_1, \mathbf{M}_2, \ldots, \mathbf{M}_n$ that $\mathbf{Team}_n^1\mathbf{Ex}$-identifies each $f \in \mathcal{S}$. Let $\mathbf{P}$ be a probabilistic machine equipped with an $n$-sided coin. The behavior of $\mathbf{P}$ is described thus. $\mathbf{P}$ flips its coin once and obtains with probability $1/n$ a number $i \in N_n$. $\mathbf{P}$ then simulates machine $\mathbf{M}_{i+1}$. Clearly, for each $f \in \mathcal{S}$, $\mathrm{pr}(\mathbf{P}$ Ex-identifies $f) \geq 1/n$. ∎

Pitt [31, 32] also established the converse of the above result, $(\forall n \geq 1)[\mathbf{Prob}^{\frac{1}{n}}\mathbf{Ex} \subseteq \mathbf{Team}_n^1\mathbf{Ex}]$, thereby showing that probabilistic identification and team identification are successful on essentially the same collections on functions. This result will be an immediate corollary of the main result of this section (Theorem 11). In order to prove this main result, Pitt used a technique of calculating probabilities on "infinite computation tress," which we describe next. To facilitate the description, it is expedient to place some "harmless" restrictions on our probabilistic machines. The next definition describes these restrictions.

**Definition 15** [31, 32] A probabilistic machine **P** is *nice* just in case **P** is equipped with a two-sided coin and the performance of **P** on a function $f$ follows the following sequence in an infinite loop:

(a) receive an element of the graph of $f$;

(b) issue a hypothesis;

(c) flip its coin.

The following lemma allows us to restrict our attention to only nice probabilistic machines; its proof is left to the reader.

**Lemma 3** [31, 32] *Let* **P** *be a probabilistic machine. Then there exists a nice* **P'** *such that* $(\forall f \in \mathcal{R})[pr(\mathbf{P}$ *Ex-identifies* $f) \leq pr(\mathbf{P'}$ *Ex-identifies* $f)]$.

## 4.3   Infinite Computation Trees

Let **P** be a nice probabilistic machine and $f \in \mathcal{R}$. An infinite computation tree for **P** on $f$, denoted $\mathcal{T}_{\mathbf{P},f}$, is simply a description of **P**'s behavior on all possible 2-ary oracles when **P** is fed the graph of $f$ in canonical order. $\mathcal{T}_{\mathbf{P},f}$ is an infinite complete binary tree whose nodes represent the state just after **P** has performed the following two actions:

(1) received an element of the graph (in canonical order) of $f$;

(2) issued an hypothesis.

Since **P** is nice, the next action of **P** is a coin flip. The two edges emanating from a node correspond to the two possible directions that the computation of **P** can take as determined by the result of the coin flip.

The nodes of $\mathcal{T}_{\mathbf{P},f}$ are numbered in breadth first search order starting with the root node which is numbered '1'. Observe that the root node represents the state of **P** just after it has received $(0, f(0))$ and issued its first hypothesis. At this stage, **P**, being nice, flips its coin and if the outcome is '0' the computation follows the left child and if the outcome is '1' the computation follows the right child. Thus, node 2 represents the state just after the following events have taken place in sequence:

(1) **P** flips its coin for the first time;

(2) the outcome of the coin flip in (1) is '0';

(3) **P** receives $(1, f(1))$; and

(4) **P** issues its second hypothesis.

The depth of a node in $T_{\mathbf{P},f}$ is denoted by depth($n$), where depth($n$) = $\lfloor \log_2(n) \rfloor$. Note that the depth of the root node is 0. To summarize, a node $n$ of depth $d$ in $T_{\mathbf{P},f}$ corresponds to the state of **P** reached if **P** has received $d+1$ data points, issued $d+1$ hypotheses, and the outcomes of the sequence of $d$ coin flips performed by **P** were exactly the sequence of 0's and 1's that lead to the node $n$ in the tree $T_{\mathbf{P},f}$.

We now define two useful functions on nodes of the tree $T_{\mathbf{P},f}$. First, for any node $n$, the parent of $n$, denoted parent($n$), is the immediate ancestor of node $n$ in $T_{\mathbf{P},f}$; parent(1) is undefined. Second, guess($n$) denotes the hypothesis that **P** has just issued when it is in the state corresponding to node $n$. A *path* $P$ in $T_{\mathbf{P},f}$ is an infinite sequence of nodes $P_0, P_1, P_2, P_3, \ldots$, such that $P_0 = 1$ (the root node) and for each $i$, $P_i = \text{parent}(P_{i+1})$. Observe that for each $i$, the $i$th node $P_i$ in $P$ occurs at depth $i$ of $T_{\mathbf{P},f}$. Also observe that each path in $T_{\mathbf{P},f}$ corresponds to a unique 2-ary oracle and for each 2-ary oracle there is a unique path in $T_{\mathbf{P},f}$. This isomorphism between the set of coin oracles and the set of paths allows us to extend the function pr to sets of paths in $T_{\mathbf{P},f}$ as follows:

Let $C$ denote a collection of paths in $T_{\mathbf{P},f}$. Then $\text{pr}(C) = \text{pr}(\{O \mid O \text{ corresponds to a path } P \in C\})$. An especially useful collection of paths is introduced in the following definition.

**Definition 16** *For each node $n$ in $T_{\mathbf{P},f}$, $P\langle n \rangle = \{P \mid P \text{ is a path in } T_{\mathbf{P},f} \text{ and } P \text{ contains node } n\}$.*

It is easy to verify that $\text{pr}(P\langle n \rangle) = 2^{-\text{depth}(n)}$, since $P\langle n \rangle$ corresponds to $\{O \mid O \text{ extends } \rho\}$, where $\rho$ corresponds to the finite path segment starting from the root and leading to node $n$. The measurable sets $P\langle n \rangle$ will be used in computing probabilities of more interesting collections of paths. But, first we develop some more machinery about paths in $T_{\mathbf{P},f}$. The next definition describes what it means for paths in $T_{\mathbf{P},f}$ to converge.

**Definition 17** *Let $P = P_0, P_1, P_2, \ldots$ be a path in $T_{\mathbf{P},f}$.*

*(a) $P$ converges to $j$ just in case $(\overset{\infty}{\forall} k)[guess(P_k) = j]$.*

*(b) $P$ converges at node $n$ just in case the following hold:*

*(i) $P$ passes through node $n$ (that is, $P_{depth(n)} = n$);*
*(ii) $(\forall k \geq depth(n))[guess(P_k) = guess(P_n)]$;*
*(iii) $\neg(\exists k < depth(n))(\forall m \geq k)[guess(P_m) = guess(P_n)]$.*

**Definition 18** $C(A) = \{P \mid P$ *is a path in* $T_{P,f}$ *and there exists an* $a \in A$ *such that* $P$ *converges to* $a\}$.

$C(A)$ is the collection of all such paths in $T_{P,f}$ that converge to some index in the set $A$. Let $good_f$ denote the collection of all $\varphi$-indices for $f$, i.e., $good_f = \{i \mid \varphi_i = f\}$. Then, $C(good_f)$ is the collection of all such paths (oracles) which result in successful **Ex**-identification of $f$ by **P**. Hence, we write $pr(\mathbf{P}$ **Ex**-identifies $f) = pr(C(good_f))$.

One of the aims of developing this machinery is to be able to compute $pr(C(A))$. To this end, the next definition introduces further refinements on the collection of paths $C(A)$.

**Definition 19** *(a)* $C_j = \{P \mid P$ *is a path in* $T_{P,f}$ *and* $P$ *converges at node* $j\}$.

*(b) A path* $P = P_0, P_1, P_2, \ldots$ *k-agrees with* $C_j$ *just in case the following hold:*

(i) $P_{depth(j)} = j$;

(ii) $(\forall i \mid depth(j) \le i \le k)[guess(P_i) = guess(P_j)]$;

(iii) $[j$ *is the root*$] \vee [guess(P_{depth(j)-1}) \ne guess(j)]$.

*(c)* $C_{j,k} = \{P \mid P$ *is a path in* $T_{P,f} \wedge P$ *k-agrees with* $C_j\}$.

Observe that $C_j$ is the collection of paths that converge at node $j$ (to $guess(j)$), and $C_{j,k}$ is the collection of paths that appear to converge to $guess(j)$ up to level $k$ in $T_{P,f}$. Also, observe that $C_{j,k}$ provides a better estimate of $C_j$ with increasing $k$, and $C_j = \bigcap_{k=depth(j)}^{\infty} C_{j,k}$. These and some other properties of these collections of paths are summarized in the next lemma, a proof of which is left to the reader.

**Lemma 4** [31, 32] *(a)* $(\forall k \ge depth(j))[C_{j,k} \supseteq C_{j,k+1}]$.

*(b)* $(\forall k \ge depth(j))[pr(C_{j,k}) \ge pr(C_j)]$.

*(c)* $pr(C_j) = \lim_{k \to \infty} pr(C_{j,k})$.

Now, observe that $C(A) = \bigcup_{guess(j) \in A} C_j$, where the $C_j$'s are mutually disjoint because any path converges at a single node and $j_1 \ne j_2$ implies $C_{j_1} \cap C_{j_2} = \emptyset$. Thus, if we can show that $C_{j,k}$'s are measurable, then so will be $C_j$ and $C(A)$. This is the subject of the next lemma. But, first a technical definition.

**Definition 20** *Let* $j \in N$ *and let* $k \ge depth(j)$. *Then,* $N_{j,k} = \{n \mid depth(n) = k \wedge (\exists P \in C_{j,k})[P_k = n]\}$.

**Lemma 5** [31, 32] *For each $j$, for each $k \geq depth(j)$, the following hold:*

*(a) $C_{j,k}$ is measurable;*

*(b) $pr(C_{j,k}) = card(N_{j,k})/2^k$;*

*(c) $pr(C_{j,k})$ can be computed by looking at only the first $k$ levels of $T_{P,f}$.*

PROOF. (a) Recall that $P\langle x \rangle$, the collection of paths in $T_{P,f}$ passing through node $x$, is measurable. $C_{j,k}$ is shown to be measurable by expressing it as union of mutually disjoint $P\langle x \rangle$'s.

Observe that for each $y_1, y_2 \in N_{j,k}$, $y_1 \neq y_2 \Rightarrow P\langle y_1 \rangle \cap P\langle y_2 \rangle = \emptyset$. This is because $depth(y_1) = depth(y_2) = k$, and every path must pass through exactly one node at each level.

It is now claimed that $C_{j,k} = \cup_{x \in N_{j,k}} P\langle x \rangle$.

To see that $C_{j,k} \subseteq \cup_{x \in N_{j,k}} P\langle x \rangle$, let $P \in C_{j,k}$. Then $P$ passes through some node $y$ at level $k$, and $y \in N_{j,k}$. Therefore, $P \in P\langle y \rangle$ and $P\langle y \rangle \subseteq \cup_{x \in N_{j,k}} P\langle x \rangle$.

Similarly, to see that $\cup_{x \in N_{j,k}} P\langle x \rangle \subseteq C_{j,k}$, let $P \in \cup_{x \in N_{j,k}} P\langle x \rangle$, and let $y$ be the node at depth $k$ on $P$. Now, since the definition of $N_{j,k}$ doesn't depend on nodes deeper than level $k$, all paths passing through $y$ must be in $C_{j,k}$.

Thus, $C_{j,k}$ is measurable.

(b) The proof of part (a) implies that
$$pr(C_{j,k}) = \sum_{x \in N_{j,k}} pr(P\langle x \rangle) = \sum_{x \in N_{j,k}} 2^{-depth(x)} = \sum_{x \in N_{j,k}} 2^{-k} = card(N_{j,k})/2^k.$$

(c) It is easy to see that $N_{j,k}$ can be computed by observing only the first $k$ levels of $T_{P,f}$. Thus, $pr(C_{j,k})$ can be computed from the first $k$ levels of $T_{P,f}$. ∎

We now present a lemma that is crucial to the proof of the main result of this section.

**Lemma 6** [31, 32] *For all $A \subseteq N$ and for all $p \in [0 .. 1]$, if $pr(C(A)) > p$, then there exist nodes $\{n_1, n_2, \ldots, n_k\}$ such that for each $i$, $1 \leq i \leq k$, $guess(n_i) \in A$ and $pr(\cup_{j=1}^k C_{n_j}) > p$.*

PROOF. Observe that for $j_1$ and $j_2$, $j_1 \neq j_2 \Rightarrow C_{j_1} \cap C_{j_2} = \emptyset$. Thus,

$$pr(C(A)) = \sum_{j \in \{m | guess(m) \in A\}} pr(C_j) > p.$$

But, since a path can converge at at most one node, there is a finite collection of nodes $\{n_1, n_2, \ldots, n_k\}$ such that $pr(\cup_{j=1}^k C_{n_j}) = \sum_{j=1}^k pr(C_{n_j}) > p$. ∎

**Theorem 11** [31, 32] $(\forall n \geq 1)(\forall p)[1/(n+1) < p \leq 1 \Rightarrow \mathbf{Prob}^p\mathbf{Ex} \subseteq \mathbf{Team}_n^1\mathbf{Ex}]$.

Theorem 11 immediately follows from the following theorem and the fact that **Oex** = **Ex** (see Theorem 2).

**Theorem 12** [31, 32] *Let* $p > 1/(n+1)$. *Let* $\mathcal{S} \in \mathbf{Prob}^p\mathbf{Ex}$. *Then,* $(\exists \mathbf{M}_1, \mathbf{M}_2, \ldots, \mathbf{M}_n)$ *such that* $(\forall f \in \mathcal{S})(\exists i \mid 1 \leq i \leq n)[\mathbf{M}_i\mathbf{Oex}\text{-}identifies\ f]$.

PROOF. Let $\mathbf{P}$ be a probabilistic machine such that $\mathcal{S} \subseteq \mathbf{Prob}^p\mathbf{Ex}(\mathbf{P})$. Using the description of $\mathbf{P}$, a team of $n$ deterministic machines, $\mathbf{M}_1, \mathbf{M}_2, \ldots, \mathbf{M}_n$, is described such that for each $f \in \mathcal{S}$, some member of the team **Oex**-identifies $f$. This is achieved by constructing the machines in such a way that each machine guesses a different range of converging paths in $\mathcal{T}_{\mathbf{P},f}$ and for each $f$, one of the machines has the correct guess. This will also be the machine which **Oex**-identifies $f$. The machines are described below.

Begin $\{\mathbf{M}_i(f[k])\}$

1. Construct $\mathcal{T}_k$, the first $k$ levels of $\mathcal{T}_{\mathbf{P},f}$, by simulating $\mathbf{P}$ with input $f[k]$ and all 2-ary sequences of length $k$.

2. For each node $j$ in $\mathcal{T}_k$, compute $\mathrm{pr}(C_{j,k})$.

3. Let $c_k$ be the least numbered node in $\mathcal{T}_k$ such that $\sum_{j=1}^{c_k} \mathrm{pr}(C_{j,k}) > i/(n+1)$.

4. **if** $c_k$ found in Step 3,

   **then** output $q$ such that $D_q = \{\mathrm{guess}(i) \mid 1 \leq i \leq c_k\}$

   **else** output 0

   **endif**

End $\{\mathbf{M}_i(f[k])\}$

Now, $f \in \mathbf{Prob}^p\mathbf{Ex}(\mathbf{P})$ implies that $\mathrm{pr}(C(\mathrm{good}_f)) \geq p$. Recall that $C(\mathrm{good}_f)$ is the collection of paths that converge to a $\varphi$-index of $f$ and $C(N)$ is the collection of all converging paths in $\mathcal{T}_{\mathbf{P},f}$. Hence, $C(\mathrm{good}_f) \subseteq C(N)$ and $\mathrm{pr}(C(N)) \geq \mathrm{pr}(C(\mathrm{good}_f)) > 1/(n+1)$. Since $1/(n+1) < \mathrm{pr}(C(N)) \leq 1$, there exists an $m$, $1 \leq m \leq n$, such that $m = \max(\{i \mid i/(n+1) < \mathrm{pr}(C(N))\})$.

It will be shown that the machine $\mathbf{M}_m$ **Oex**-identifies $f$. Let us focus on the behavior of $\mathbf{M}_m$ on $f[k]$. $\mathbf{M}_m$ correctly assumes that the probability of converging paths in $\mathcal{T}_{\mathbf{P},f}$ is greater that $m/(n+1)$ and attempts to find, in the limit, a finite collection of nodes where most paths converge. To this end, $\mathbf{M}_m$ first finds the smallest number $c_k$ such that $\sum_{j=1}^{c_k} \mathrm{pr}(C_{j,k}) > m/(n+1)$, and then outputs the canonical index for the finite set $\{\mathrm{guess}(x) \mid 1 \leq x \leq c_k\}$.

Now, by Lemma 6, there exists a finite collection of nodes $\{n_1, n_2, \ldots, n_v\}$ in $\mathcal{T}_{\mathbf{P},f}$ such that $\sum_{i=1}^{v} \mathrm{pr}(C_{n_i}) > m/(n+1)$. This implies that there exists a smallest numbered node $s$, such that $\sum_{j=1}^{s} \mathrm{pr}(C_j) > m/(n+1)$. (Choosing any $s \geq \max(\{n_1, n_2, \ldots, n_v\})$ satisfies the inequality.)

Now the theorem follows from the following claim.

**Claim 5** *(a)* $(\overset{\infty}{\forall} k)[c_k = s]$.

*(b)* $\{guess(x) \mid 1 \le x \le s\}$ *contains a $\varphi$-index for $f$.*

It is easy to see that the theorem follows from the above claim. Since $\mathbf{M}_m$, fed $f[k]$, outputs the canonical index for the finite set $\{guess(x) \mid 1 \le x \le c_k\}$, (a) implies that $\mathbf{M}_m$ converges to the canonical index for $\{guess(x) \mid 1 \le x \le s\}$. And, according to (b) $\{guess(x) \mid 1 \le x \le c_k\}$ contains a $\varphi$-index for $f$, thereby implying that $\mathbf{M}_m$ **Oex**-identifies $f$. We now prove the claim.

(a) Observe that the choice of $s$ implies that for each $k \ge \text{depth}(s)$, nodes $1, 2, \ldots, s$ will be in the partial tree $\mathcal{T}_k$ constructed in Step 1 of $\mathbf{M}_m(f[k])$. Moreover, Lemma 4 implies that $\sum_{j=1}^{s} \text{pr}(C_{j,k}) \ge \sum_{j=1}^{s} \text{pr}(C_j) > m/(n+1)$. Hence, $(\overset{\infty}{\forall} k)[c_k \le s]$.

Again, Lemma 4 implies that, for all $j$, and, for all $k \ge \text{depth}(j)$, $\text{pr}(C_{j,k}) \ge \text{pr}(C_{j,k+1})$. Thus, for all but finitely many $k$, the sequence $\{c_k\}$ is a nondecreasing one, as $c_k$ is chosen as the smallest value satisfying the inequality $\sum_{j=1}^{c_k} \text{pr}(C_{j,k}) > m/(n + 1)$. Now, since $\{c_k\}$ is a nondecreasing sequence bounded above by $s$, it converges. If $\{c_k\}$ converges to $s$, we are done. Therefore, let $\{c_k\}$ converge to $s' < s$. Then, for all but finitely many $k$, $\sum_{j=1}^{s'} \text{pr}(C_{j,k}) > m/(n + 1)$. But, then $\sum_{j=1}^{s'} \text{pr}(C_j) > m/(n + 1)$ because $\sum_{j=1}^{s'} \text{pr}(C_j)$ is $\lim_{k \to \infty} \sum_{j=1}^{s'} \text{pr}(C_{j,k})$. This is a contradiction because $s$ is the least integer such that $\sum_{j=1}^{s} \text{pr}(C_j) > m/(n + 1)$. Therefore, $\{c_k\}$ converges to $s$.

(b) Since $\text{good}_f$ is the set of all $\varphi$-indexes for $f$, $N - \text{good}_f$ is the collection of all such $\varphi$-indexes that are not for $f$. Now, observe that since $C(\text{good}_f)$ and $C(N - \text{good}_f)$ are mutually disjoint, $\text{pr}(C(N)) = \text{pr}(C(\text{good}_f)) + \text{pr}(C(N - \text{good}_f))$. We also know by the hypothesis of the theorem and the choice of $m$ that $\text{pr}(C(N)) \le (m+1)/(n+1)$ and $\text{pr}(C(\text{good}_f)) > 1/(n + 1)$. Thus, $\text{pr}(C(N - \text{good}_f)) < m/(n + 1)$.

Let $I$ denote the set $\{guess(x) \mid 1 \le x \le s\}$. Observe that $\text{pr}(C(I)) \ge m/(n+1)$. Therefore, at least one element in $I$ must be a correct $\varphi$-index for $f$, because otherwise $I \subseteq N - \text{good}_f$, $C(I) \subseteq C(N - \text{good}_f)$, and $\text{pr}(C(N - \text{good}_f)) \ge m/(n + 1)$ — a contradiction. Hence, $I$ contains a $\varphi$-index for $f$.

This completes the proof of the theorem. ∎

As an immediate corollary to Theorems 10 and 11, we have the following:

**Corollary 2** [31, 32] $(\forall n \ge 1)[\mathbf{Prob}^{\frac{1}{n}}\mathbf{Ex} = \mathbf{Team}^1_n\mathbf{Ex}]$.

The above corollary, together with Corollary 1 implies the following:

**Corollary 3** [31, 32] $(\forall n \ge 1)[\mathbf{Prob}^{\frac{1}{n}}\mathbf{Ex} \subset \mathbf{Prob}^{\frac{1}{n+1}}\mathbf{Ex}]$.

Thus, the team hierarchy is contained in the probabilistic hierarchy. However, it turns out that the probabilistic hierarchy is no finer than the team hierarchy. To see this, let $1/(n+1) < p \leq 1/n$. Clearly, $\mathbf{Prob}^{\frac{1}{n}}\mathbf{Ex} \subseteq \mathbf{Prob}^p\mathbf{Ex}$. Now, by Theorem 11, $\mathbf{Prob}^p\mathbf{Ex} \subseteq \mathbf{Team}_n^1\mathbf{Ex}$. But, Corollary 2 implies that $\mathbf{Team}_n^1\mathbf{Ex} = \mathbf{Prob}^{\frac{1}{n}}\mathbf{Ex}$. Thus, $\mathbf{Prob}^{\frac{1}{n}}\mathbf{Ex} = \mathbf{Prob}^p\mathbf{Ex}$. We have essentially shown the following corollary which says that the probabilistic hierarchy is exactly the same as the team hierarchy.

**Corollary 4** [31, 32] $(\forall n \geq 1)(\forall p)[1/(n+1) < p \leq 1/n \Rightarrow \mathbf{Prob}^p\mathbf{Ex} = \mathbf{Team}_n^1\mathbf{Ex}]$.

We would like to note that counterpart of Corollary 4 is also true when anomalies are allowed in the final program; we direct the reader to Pitt [32] for details.

Corollary 4 can be used to characterize generalized team identification paradigms in which more than one member of the team is required to be successful. In Section 3, results about $\mathbf{Team}_n^1\mathbf{Ex}$-identification were presented; the rest of the present section is devoted to results about $\mathbf{Team}_n^m\mathbf{Ex}$-identification.

We start by stating the following notion of interval.

**Definition 21** *Let $p \in (0 .. 1]$. Then $\mathrm{IN}(p)$ is defined to be $1/n$, where $n$ is such that $1/(n+1) < p \leq 1/n$.*

It is easy to verify that for $p \in (0 .. 1]$, $\mathrm{IN}(p) = 1/\lfloor\frac{1}{p}\rfloor$. The next result is simply a restatement of Corollary 4 using this notion of interval.

**Corollary 5** [33] $(\forall p \in (0 .. 1])[\mathbf{Prob}^p\mathbf{Ex} = \mathbf{Team}_{\frac{1}{\mathrm{IN}(p)}}^1\mathbf{Ex}]$.

The following result says that all such collections of functions that can be identified by a team of $n$ machines with the requirement that at least $m$ out of $n$ are correct can also be identified by a single probabilistic machine with probability $\frac{m}{n}$.

**Theorem 13** [33] $(\forall m, n \in N^+ \mid m \leq n)(\forall p \in (0 .. 1])[\mathbf{Team}_n^m\mathbf{Ex} \subseteq \mathbf{Prob}^{\frac{m}{n}}\mathbf{Ex}]$.

PROOF. Let $\mathcal{S} \subseteq \mathcal{R}$. Let $\mathbf{M}_1, \mathbf{M}_2, \ldots, \mathbf{M}_n$ be (deterministic) machines witnessing $\mathcal{S} \in \mathbf{Team}_n^m\mathbf{Ex}$. Let $\mathbf{P}$ be a probabilistic machine equipped with an $n$-sided coin. The behavior of $\mathbf{P}$ can be described thus: $\mathbf{P}$, before receiving any input, flips its $n$-sided coin and obtains a number $i \in N_n$. $\mathbf{P}$ then simulates the deterministic machine $\mathbf{M}_{i+1}$. Clearly, for each $f \in \mathcal{S}$, $\mathrm{pr}(\mathbf{P} \ \mathbf{Ex}\text{-identifies} f) \geq m/n$. Hence, $\mathcal{S} \in \mathbf{Prob}^{\frac{m}{n}}\mathbf{Ex}$. ∎

The next result completely characterizes $\mathbf{Team}_n^m\mathbf{Ex}$-identification in terms of probabilistic identification.

**Theorem 14** [33] $(\forall m, n \in N^+ \mid m \leq n)$
$[\mathbf{Team}_n^m\mathbf{Ex} = \mathbf{Team}_{\lfloor\frac{n}{m}\rfloor}^1\mathbf{Ex} = \mathbf{Prob}^{\mathrm{IN}(\frac{m}{n})}\mathbf{Ex}]$.

PROOF. We first show that $\mathbf{Team}^1_{\lfloor\frac{n}{m}\rfloor}\mathbf{Ex} = \mathbf{Prob}^{\text{IN}(\frac{m}{n})}\mathbf{Ex}]$. The definition of IN implies that for all $p \in (0 .. 1]$, $\text{IN}(\text{IN}(p)) = \text{IN}(p)$. Now, by Corollary 5, we have $\mathbf{Prob}^{\text{IN}(\frac{m}{n})}\mathbf{Ex} = \mathbf{Team}^1_{\frac{1}{\text{IN}(\text{IN}(\frac{m}{n}))}}\mathbf{Ex} = \mathbf{Team}^1_{\frac{1}{\text{IN}(\frac{m}{n})}}\mathbf{Ex} = \mathbf{Team}^1_{\frac{1}{1/\lfloor\frac{n}{m}\rfloor}}\mathbf{Ex} = \mathbf{Team}^1_{\lfloor\frac{n}{m}\rfloor}\mathbf{Ex}$.

We now show that $\mathbf{Team}^m_n\mathbf{Ex} = \mathbf{Team}^1_{\lfloor\frac{n}{m}\rfloor}\mathbf{Ex}$. Since $m \leq n$, Theorem 13 implies that $\mathbf{Team}^m_n\mathbf{Ex} \subseteq \mathbf{Prob}^{\frac{m}{n}}\mathbf{Ex}$. Now, observe that $1/(\lfloor\frac{n}{m}\rfloor + 1) < \frac{m}{n} \leq 1/\lfloor\frac{n}{m}\rfloor$. Thus, by Corollary 4, we have $\mathbf{Prob}^{\frac{m}{n}}\mathbf{Ex} = \mathbf{Team}^1_{\lfloor\frac{n}{m}\rfloor}\mathbf{Ex}$. Hence, $\mathbf{Team}^m_n\mathbf{Ex} \subseteq \mathbf{Team}^1_{\lfloor\frac{n}{m}\rfloor}\mathbf{Ex}$. Now, we only need show that $\mathbf{Team}^1_{\lfloor\frac{n}{m}\rfloor}\mathbf{Ex} \subseteq \mathbf{Team}^m_n\mathbf{Ex}$. Now observe that for any $c \in N^+$, $\mathbf{Team}^1_k\mathbf{Ex} \subseteq \mathbf{Team}^c_{c\cdot k}\mathbf{Ex}$. Thus, $\mathbf{Team}^1_{\lfloor\frac{n}{m}\rfloor}\mathbf{Ex} \subseteq \mathbf{Team}^m_{m\cdot\lfloor\frac{n}{m}\rfloor}\mathbf{Ex}$. Now, since $m \cdot \lfloor n/m \rfloor \leq n$, we have $\mathbf{Team}^m_{m\cdot\lfloor\frac{n}{m}\rfloor}\mathbf{Ex} \subseteq \mathbf{Team}^m_n\mathbf{Ex}$. Therefore, $\mathbf{Team}^1_{\lfloor\frac{n}{m}\rfloor}\mathbf{Ex} \subseteq \mathbf{Team}^m_n\mathbf{Ex}$. ∎

# 5 Team and Probabilistic Identification of Languages

Consider the following result about language identification in the limit.

**Theorem 15** [18] *Let*

$$\mathcal{L}_1 = \{L \in \mathcal{E} \mid \text{card}(L) < \infty\} \text{ and}$$

$$\mathcal{L}_2 = \{N\}.$$

*Then, $\mathcal{L}_1 \in \mathbf{TxtEx}$, $\mathcal{L}_2 \in \mathbf{TxtEx}$, but $\mathcal{L}_1 \cup \mathcal{L}_2 \notin \mathbf{TxtEx}$.*

Clearly, the above non-union theorem for **TxtEx** motivates the notion of teams for language identification. We introduce team identification and probabilistic identification for languages next.

## 5.1 Team Identification of Languages

We define team identification of languages.

**Definition 22** Let $m, n \in N^+$ and $a \in N \cup \{*\}$.

(a) Let $L \in \mathcal{E}$. A team of $n$ machines $\mathbf{M}_1, \mathbf{M}_2, \ldots, \mathbf{M}_n$ is said to $\mathbf{Team}^m_n\mathbf{TxtEx}^a$-*identify* $L$ (written: $L \in \mathbf{Team}^m_n\mathbf{TxtEx}^a(\mathbf{M}_1, \mathbf{M}_2, \ldots, \mathbf{M}_n)$) just in case there exist $m$ distinct numbers $i_1, i_2, \ldots, i_m$, $1 \leq i_1 < i_2 < \cdots < i_m \leq n$, such that each of $\mathbf{M}_{i_1}, \mathbf{M}_{i_2}, \ldots, \mathbf{M}_{i_m}$ $\mathbf{TxtEx}^a$-identifies $L$.

(b) $\mathbf{Team}^m_n\mathbf{TxtEx}^a$ is defined to be the class of sets $\mathcal{L}$ of recursively enumerable languages such that some team of $n$ machines $\mathbf{Team}^m_n\mathbf{TxtEx}^a$-identifies each language in $\mathcal{L}$.

For the criterion **Team$_n^m$TxtEx$^a$**-identification, we refer to the fraction $\frac{m}{n}$ as the *success ratio* of the criterion.

## 5.1.1 Probabilistic Language Identification

Let **P** be a probabilistic machine equipped with a $t$-sided coin and let $T$ be a text for some language $L \in \mathcal{E}$. Then, the probability of **P TxtEx$^a$**-identifying $T$ is taken to be $\mathrm{pr}_t^\infty(\{O \mid \mathbf{P}^O\mathbf{TxtEx}^a\text{-identifies } T\})$. The next lemma establishes that the set $\{O \mid \mathbf{P}^O\mathbf{TxtEx}^a\text{-identifies } T\}$ is measurable.

**Lemma 7** [31] *Let* **P** *be a probabilistic machine and let* $T$ *be a text. Then* $\{O \mid \mathbf{P}^O \mathbf{TxtEx}^a\text{-identifies } T\}$ *is measurable.*

The following definition, motivated by the above lemma, introduces probability of identification of a text.

**Definition 23** [31] Let $T$ be a text and **P** be a probabilistic machine equipped with a $t$-sided coin ($t \geq 2$). Then, $\mathrm{pr}_t^\infty(\mathbf{P}\ \mathbf{TxtEx}^a\text{-identifies } T) = \mathrm{pr}_t^\infty(\{O \mid \mathbf{P}^O\ \mathbf{TxtEx}^a$ -identifies $T\})$.

As in the case of function identification, there is no loss of generality in assuming a two sided coin.

**Lemma 8** (Adopted from [31, 32]) *Let* $t, t' > 2$. *Let* **P** *be a probabilistic machine with a* $t$-*sided coin. Then, there exists a probabilistic machine* **P$'$** *with a* $t'$-*sided coin such that for each text* $T$, $\mathrm{pr}_{t'}^\infty(\mathbf{P}'\ \mathbf{TxtEx}^a\text{-identifies } T) = \mathrm{pr}_t^\infty(\mathbf{P}\ \mathbf{TxtEx}^a\text{-identifies } T)$.

The next definition describes language identification by probabilistic machines. As in the function case, the above lemma frees us from specifying the number of sides of the coin, thereby allowing us to talk about probability function $\mathrm{pr}_t^\infty$ without specifying $t$. For this reason, we will refer to $\mathrm{pr}_t^\infty$ as simply pr in the sequel.

**Definition 24** [31] Let $0 \leq p \leq 1$.

(a) **P Prob$^p$TxtEx$^a$**-*identifies* $L$ (written: $L \in \mathbf{Prob}^p\mathbf{TxtEx}^a(\mathbf{P})$) just in case for each text $T$ for $L$ $\mathrm{pr}(\mathbf{P}\ \mathbf{TxtEx}^a\text{-identifies } T) \geq p$.

(b) **Prob$^p$TxtEx$^a$** $= \{\mathcal{L} \subseteq \mathcal{E} \mid (\exists \mathbf{P})[\mathcal{L} \subseteq \mathbf{Prob}^p\mathbf{TxtEx}^a(\mathbf{P})]\}$.

## 5.2 Results

In the context of functions, the reader can verify that as a simple consequence of the equivalence of team and probabilistic identification if the success ratio of a team is greater that $\frac{1}{2}$, then the team can be simulated by a single leraning machine without any loss in learning power. Such a cut-off ratio is referred to as the *aggregation ratio* of the learning criterion. It is also clear that the only success ratios of interest are of the form $\frac{1}{k}$, $k > 1$. However, the story is completely different for language identification in the limit. First, the aggregation ratio for language identification in the limit turns out to be $\frac{2}{3}$. Second, the notion of team and probabilistic identification are different for languages. In fact, probabilistic identification turns out to be strictly more powerful than team identification. Finally, the results for languages are more difficult to obtain. In what follows, we first present results (with proofs) for team identification of languages with success ratios $\geq \frac{2}{3}$. This is followed by presentation of results for success ratios of the form $\frac{1}{k}$, $k > 2$.

### 5.2.1 Team Language Identification with Success Ratio $\geq \frac{2}{3}$

We first consider the problem of when can a team of learning machines be simulated by a single learning machine.

As noted above, in the context of function identification, Osherson, Stob, and Weinstein [28] and Pitt and Smith [33] have shown that the collections of functions that can be identified by teams with success ratio *greater than one-half* (that is, a majority of members in the team are required to be successful) are the same as those collections of functions that can be identified by a single machine.

**Theorem 16** [28, 33] $(\forall j, k \mid \frac{i}{k} > \frac{1}{2})(\forall a)[\mathbf{Team}_k^j \mathbf{Ex}^a = \mathbf{Ex}^a]$.

Surprisingly, an analog of Theorem 16 for language identification holds for success ratio 2/3 as opposed to success ratio 1/2 for function identification. Corollary 6 to Theorem 17 below says that the collections of languages that can be identified by teams with success ratio greater than 2/3 (that is, more than two-thirds of the members in the team are required to be successful) are the same as those collections of languages which can be identifies by a single machine.[3] Corollary 7 is a similar result about $\mathbf{TxtEx}^*$-identification.

**Theorem 17** $(\forall j, k \mid \frac{i}{k} > \frac{2}{3})(\forall a)[\mathbf{Team}_k^j \mathbf{TxtEx}^a \subseteq \mathbf{TxtEx}^{\lceil (j+1)/2 \rceil \cdot a}]$.

**Corollary 6** $(\forall j, k \mid \frac{i}{k} > \frac{2}{3})[\mathbf{Team}_k^j \mathbf{TxtEx} = \mathbf{TxtEx}]$.

**Corollary 7** $(\forall j, k \mid \frac{i}{k} > \frac{2}{3})[\mathbf{Team}_k^j \mathbf{TxtEx}^* = \mathbf{TxtEx}^*]$.

---

[3]Corollary 6 also appears in Osherson, Stob, and Weinstein [28], and may also be shown using an argument from Pitt [31] about probabilistic language learning.

To facilitate the proof of Theorem 17 and other simulation results, we define the following technical notion:

Let $A^m$ be a *nonempty finite* multiset of grammars. We define grammar majority $(A^m)$ as follows:
$$W_{\text{majority}(A^m)} = \{x \mid \text{for majority of } g \in A^m, x \in W_g\}.$$

Clearly, majority$(A^m)$ can be defined using the *s-m-n* theorem [35]. Intuitively, majority$(A^m)$ is a grammar for a language that consists of all such elements that are enumerated by a majority of grammars in $A^m$. Below, whenever we use a set as an argument to majority we assume the argument to be a multiset.

PROOF OF THEOREM 17. Let $j, k$, and $a$ be as given in the hypothesis of the theorem. Let $\mathcal{L}$ be $\text{Team}_k^j\text{TxtEx}^a$-identified by the team of machines $\{\mathbf{M}_1, \mathbf{M}_2, \ldots, \mathbf{M}_k\}$. We define a machine $\mathbf{M}$ that $\text{TxtEx}^{\lceil (j+1)/2 \rceil \cdot a}$-identifies $\mathcal{L}$.

Let $\text{conv}(\mathbf{M}', \sigma) = \max(\{|\tau| \mid \tau \subseteq \sigma \wedge \mathbf{M}'(\tau) \neq \mathbf{M}'(\sigma)\})$. Let $m_1^\sigma, m_2^\sigma, \ldots, m_k^\sigma$ be a permutation of $1, 2, \ldots, k$, such that, for $1 \leq r < k$, $[(\text{conv}(\mathbf{M}_{m_r^\sigma}, \sigma), m_r^\sigma) < (\text{conv}(\mathbf{M}_{m_{r+1}^\sigma}, \sigma), m_{r+1}^\sigma)]$.

Let $\mathbf{M}(\sigma) = \text{majority}(\{\mathbf{M}_{m_1^\sigma}(\sigma), \mathbf{M}_{m_2^\sigma}(\sigma), \ldots, \mathbf{M}_{m_j^\sigma}(\sigma)\})$.

It is easy to verify that if $\{\mathbf{M}_1, \mathbf{M}_2, \ldots, \mathbf{M}_k\}$ $\text{Team}_k^j\text{TxtEx}^a$-identify $L \in \mathcal{L}$, then $\mathbf{M}$ $\text{TxtEx}^{\lceil (j+1)/2 \rceil \cdot a}$-identifies $L$. ∎

The reader is directed to [22] for a better analysis of the errors in the above simulation.

Corollary 8 to Theorem 18 below says that the collections of languages that can be identified by a team with success ratio 2/3 (that is, at least two-thirds of the members in the team are required to be successful) are the same as those collections of languages that can be identified by a team of three machines at least two of which are required to be successful. Corollary 9 is a similar result about $\text{TxtEx}^*$-identification with success ratio exactly 2/3.

**Theorem 18** $(\forall j > 0)(\forall a)[\text{Team}_{3j}^{2j}\text{TxtEx}^a \subseteq \text{Team}_3^2\text{TxtEx}^{(j+1)\cdot a}]$.

**Corollary 8** $(\forall j > 0)[\text{Team}_{3j}^{2j}\text{TxtEx} = \text{Team}_3^2\text{TxtEx}]$.

**Corollary 9** $(\forall j > 0)[\text{Team}_{3j}^{2j}\text{TxtEx}^* = \text{Team}_3^2\text{TxtEx}^*]$.

PROOF OF THEOREM 18. Let $j$ and $a$ be as given in the hypothesis of the theorem. Suppose $\{\mathbf{M}_1, \ldots, \mathbf{M}_{3j}\}$ $\text{Team}_{3j}^{2j}\text{TxtEx}^k$-identify $\mathcal{L}$. We describe machines $\mathbf{M}'_1, \mathbf{M}'_2$, and $\mathbf{M}'_3$ such that $\mathcal{L} \subseteq \text{Team}_3^2\text{TxtEx}^{(j+1)\cdot a}(\{\mathbf{M}'_1, \mathbf{M}'_2, \mathbf{M}'_3\})$.

Let conv be as defined in the proof of Theorem 17. Let $m_1^\sigma, m_2^\sigma, \ldots, m_{3j}^\sigma$ be a permutation of $1, 2, \ldots, 3j$, such that, for $1 \leq r < 3j$, $[(\text{conv}(\mathbf{M}_{m_r^\sigma}, \sigma), m_r^\sigma) < (\text{conv}(\mathbf{M}_{m_{r+1}^\sigma}, \sigma), m_{r+1}^\sigma)]$.

$$\mathbf{M}'_1(\sigma) = \mathbf{M}_{m_1^\sigma}(\sigma).$$

$$\mathbf{M}'_2(\sigma) = \text{majority}(\{\mathbf{M}_{m_2^\sigma}(\sigma), \mathbf{M}_{m_3^\sigma}(\sigma), \ldots, \mathbf{M}_{m_{2j}^\sigma}(\sigma)\}).$$

$$\mathbf{M}'_3(\sigma) = \text{majority}(\{\mathbf{M}_{m_1^\sigma}(\sigma), \mathbf{M}_{m_2^\sigma}(\sigma), \ldots, \mathbf{M}_{m_{2j+1}^\sigma}(\sigma)\}).$$

Now suppose $T$ is a text for $L \in \mathcal{L}$. Consider the following two cases.

*Case 1:* At least $2j + 1$ of the machines in $\{\mathbf{M}_1, \mathbf{M}_2, \ldots, \mathbf{M}_{3j}\}$ converge on $T$.

In this case clearly, $\mathbf{M}'_3$ $\mathbf{TxtEx}^{(j+1)\cdot a}$-identifies $T$. Moreover, $\mathbf{M}'_1$ ($\mathbf{M}'_2$) $\mathbf{TxtEx}^{(j+1)\cdot a}$-identifies $T$ if $\mathbf{M}_{\lim_{s\to\infty} m_1^{T[s]}}$ $\mathbf{TxtEx}^a$-identifies $T$ (does not $\mathbf{TxtEx}^a$-identifies $T$).

*Case 2:* Not case 1.

In this case clearly, $\mathbf{M}'_1$ and $\mathbf{M}'_2$ $\mathbf{TxtEx}^{(j+1)\cdot a}$ identify $T$. ∎

Above proof can be modified to show the following result which says that probabilistic identification of languages with probability of success at least 2/3 is the same as team identification of languages with success ratio 2/3.

**Theorem 19 $\mathbf{Prob}^{2/3}\mathbf{TxtEx} = \mathbf{Team}_3^2\mathbf{TxtEx}$.**

Theorem 20 below establishes that 2/3 is indeed the cut-off point at which team identification of languages becomes more powerful than identification by a single machine.

**Theorem 20 $\mathbf{Team}_3^2\mathbf{TxtEx} - \mathbf{TxtEx}^* \neq \emptyset$.**

PROOF OF THEOREM 20.

Let $\mathcal{L} = \{L \mid (\exists \text{ distinct } x_1, x_2 \in \{0, 1, 2\})(\text{for } i = 1, 2)[\{y \mid \langle x_i, y\rangle \in L\} \text{ is non-empty and finite and } W_{\max(\{y\mid\langle x_i,y\rangle\in L\})} = L]\}$.

Clearly, $\mathcal{L} \in \mathbf{Team}_3^2\mathbf{TxtEx}$. Suppose by way of contradiction some machine $\mathbf{M}$ $\mathbf{TxtEx}^*$-identifies $\mathcal{L}$. Without loss of generality, assume that $\mathbf{M}$ is order independent [1]. Then, by the operator recursion theorem [3], there exists a 1-1 increasing, nowhere 0, recursive function $p$ such that $W_{p(i)}$'s can be described as follows.

Enumerate $\langle 0, p(0)\rangle$ and $\langle 1, p(1)\rangle$ in both $W_{p(0)}$ and $W_{p(1)}$. Let $\sigma_0$ be such that content$(\sigma_0) = \{\langle 0, p(0)\rangle, \langle 1, p(1)\rangle\}$. Let $W_i^s$ denote $W_i$ enumerated before stage $s$. Go to stage 1.

Begin {stage $s$}

1. Enumerate $W^s_{p(0)} \bigcup W^s_{p(1)}$ in $W_{p(0)}, W_{p(1)}, W_{p(2s)}$, and $W_{p(2s+1)}$.

   Enumerate $\langle 2, p(2s) \rangle$ in $W_{p(0)}, W_{p(2s)}$.

   Enumerate $\langle 2, p(2s+1) \rangle$ in $W_{p(1)}, W_{p(2s+1)}$.

   Let $\tau_0$ be an extension of $\sigma_s$ such that content$(\tau_0) = W_{p(0)}$ enumerated till now.

   Let $\tau_1$ be an extension of $\sigma_s$ such that content$(\tau_1) = W_{p(1)}$ enumerated till now.

2. Let $x = 0$. Dovetail steps 2a and 2b until, if ever, step 2b succeeds. If and when step 2b succeeds, go to step 3.

   2a. Go to substage 0.

   Begin {substage $s'$}

   Enumerate $\langle 4, x \rangle$ in $W_{p(0)}, W_{p(2s)}$.

   Enumerate $\langle 5, x \rangle$ in $W_{p(1)}, W_{p(2s+1)}$.

   Let $x = x + 1$.

   Go to substage $s' + 1$.

   End {substage $s'$}

   2b. Search for $i \in \{0, 1\}$ and $n \in N$ such that $\mathbf{M}(\tau_i \diamond \langle 4 + i, 0 \rangle \diamond \langle 4 + i, 1 \rangle, \ldots, \langle 4 + i, n \rangle) \neq \mathbf{M}(\sigma_s)$.

3. If and when 2b succeeds, let $i, n$ be as found in step 2b.

   Let $S =$

   $W_{p(0)}$ enumerated till now

   $\bigcup W_{p(1)}$ enumerated till now

   $\bigcup \{\langle 4 + i, 0 \rangle, \langle 4 + i, 1 \rangle, \ldots, \langle 4 + i, n \rangle\}$.

4. Let $\sigma_{s+1} =$ an extension of $\tau_i \diamond \langle 4 + i, 0 \rangle \diamond \langle 4 + i, 1 \rangle \diamond \ldots \diamond \langle 4 + i, n \rangle$ such that content$(\sigma_{s+1}) = S$.

   Enumerate $S$ in $W_{p(0)}$.

   Go to stage $s + 1$.

End {stage $s$}

Consider the following cases:

*Case 1*: All stages terminate.

In this case, let $L = W_{p(0)} = W_{p(1)} \in \mathcal{L}$. Let $T = \bigcup_s \sigma_s$. Clearly, $T$ is a text for $L$. But, $\mathbf{M}$ on $T$ makes infinitely many mind changes (since the only way in which infinitely many stages can be completed is by the success of step 2b infinitely often). Thus, $\mathbf{M}$ does not $\mathbf{TxtEx^*}$-identify $\mathcal{L}$.

*Case 2*: Some stage $s$ starts but does not terminate.

In this case, let $L_1 = W_{p(0)} = W_{p(2s)} \in \mathcal{L}$ and $L_2 = W_{p(1)} = W_{p(2s+1)} \in \mathcal{L}$. Also, $L_1, L_2$ are infinitely different from each other. Let $T_i = \tau_i \diamond \langle 4 + i, 0 \rangle \diamond \langle 4 + i, 1 \rangle \diamond \ldots \diamond \langle 4 + i, n \rangle$, where $i \in \{0, 1\}$ and $\tau_i$ is as defined in stage $s$. Now, $\mathbf{M}$ converges to $\mathbf{M}(\sigma_s)$ for both $T_1$ and $T_2$. Since $L_1, L_2$ are infinitely different from each other, $W_{\mathbf{M}(\sigma_s)}$ is infinitely different from at least one of $L_1$ and $L_2$. Hence, $\mathbf{M}$ does not $\mathbf{TxtEx^*}$-identify at least one of $L_1$ and $L_2$.

From the above cases we have that **M** does not **TxtEx**\*-identify $\mathcal{L}$. ∎

## 5.2.2 Team Language Identification for Success Ratios $\frac{1}{k}$

We first present results for success ratio $\frac{1}{2}$. In the context of functions, the following result immediately follows from Theorem 14.

**Theorem 21** [31, 33] $(\forall j > 0)[\textbf{Team}_{2j}^j\textbf{Ex} = \textbf{Team}_2^1\textbf{Ex}]$.

This result says that the collections of functions that can be identified by a team with success ratio $1/2$ are the same as those collections of functions that can be identified by a team employing 2 machines and requiring at least 1 to be successful. Consequently, $\textbf{Team}_2^1\textbf{Ex} = \textbf{Team}_4^2\textbf{Ex} = \textbf{Team}_6^3\textbf{Ex} = \cdots$, etc.

Surprisingly, in the context of language identification, Theorem 22 below implies that there are collections of languages that can be identified by a team employing 4 machines and requiring at least 2 to be successful, but cannot be identified by any team employing 2 machines and requiring at least 1 to be successful. As a consequence of this result, a direct analog of Pitt's connection for function inference does *not* lift to language learning. A proof of this result can be obtained by a complicated adaptation of the proof of Theorem 20; we direct the reader to [21, 22] for the details.

**Theorem 22** $\textbf{Team}_4^2\textbf{TxtEx} - \textbf{Team}_2^1\textbf{TxtEx}^* \neq \emptyset$.

Even more surprising is Corollary 10 to Theorem 23 below which implies that the collections of languages that can be identified by teams employing 6 machines and requiring at least 3 to be successful are exactly the same as those collections of languages that can be identified by teams employing 2 machines and requiring at least 1 to be successful!

**Theorem 23** $(\forall j)(\forall i)[\textbf{Team}_{4j+2}^{2j+1}\textbf{TxtEx}^i \subseteq \textbf{Team}_2^1\textbf{TxtEx}^{i\cdot(j+1)}]$.

**Corollary 10** $(\forall j)[\textbf{Team}_{4j+2}^{2j+1}\textbf{TxtEx} = \textbf{Team}_2^1\textbf{TxtEx}]$.

PROOF OF THEOREM 23. Suppose $\textbf{M}_1, \textbf{M}_2, \dots, \textbf{M}_{4j+2}$ $\textbf{Team}_{4j+2}^{2j+1}\textbf{TxtEx}^i$-identify $\mathcal{L}$. Let $\textbf{M}_1'$ and $\textbf{M}_2'$ be defined as follows.

Let conv be as defined in the proof of Theorem 17. Let $m_1^\sigma, m_2^\sigma, \dots, m_{4j+2}^\sigma$ be a permutation of $1, 2, \dots, 4j+2$, such that, for $1 \leq r < 4j+2$, $[(\text{conv}(\textbf{M}_{m_r^\sigma}, \sigma), m_r^\sigma) < (\text{conv}(\textbf{M}_{m_{r+1}^\sigma}, \sigma), m_{r+1}^\sigma)]$.

Let $\text{match}(r, \sigma) = \max(\{n \leq |\sigma| \mid \text{card}((\text{content}(\sigma[n]) - W_{r,|\sigma|}) \cup (W_{r,n} - \text{content}(\sigma))) \leq i\})$.

Let $S_\sigma \subseteq [1 \mathinner{.\,.} 2j+1]$ be the (lexicographically least) set of cardinality $j$ such that, for $1 \leq r, k \leq 2j+1$, $[r \in S_\sigma \wedge k \notin S_\sigma] \Rightarrow [\mathrm{match}(\mathbf{M}_{m_r^\sigma}(\sigma), \sigma) \geq \mathrm{match}(\mathbf{M}_{m_k^\sigma}(\sigma), \sigma)]$.

$$\mathbf{M}_1'(\sigma) = \mathrm{majority}(\{\mathbf{M}_{m_1^\sigma}(\sigma), \mathbf{M}_{m_2^\sigma}(\sigma), \ldots, \mathbf{M}_{m_{2j+1}^\sigma}(\sigma)\}).$$

$$\mathbf{M}_2'(\sigma) = \mathrm{majority}(\{\mathbf{M}_{m_{2j+2}^\sigma}(\sigma), \mathbf{M}_{m_{2j+3}^\sigma}(\sigma), \ldots, \mathbf{M}_{m_{3j+2}^\sigma}(\sigma)\} \cup \{\mathbf{M}_{m_r^\sigma}(\sigma) \mid r \in S_\sigma\}).$$

It is easy to see that the team $\{\mathbf{M}_1', \mathbf{M}_2'\}$ witness that $\mathcal{L} \in \mathbf{Team}_2^1\mathbf{TxtEx}^{i \cdot (j+1)}$. ∎

The scenario for team success ratio $1/2$ is completely settled by Theorems 24 below. A proof of this result turns out to be very complicated and the reader is directed to [22] for the details.

**Theorem 24** $(\forall n, m \in N^+ \mid 2n \text{ does not divide } m)$
$[\mathbf{Team}_{4n}^{2n}\mathbf{TxtEx} - \mathbf{Team}_{2m}^m\mathbf{TxtEx} \neq \emptyset]$.

The following corollary of the above theorem is evident.

**Corollary 11** $(\forall m, n \in N^+)$
$[\mathbf{Team}_{2m}^m\mathbf{TxtEx} \subseteq \mathbf{Team}_{2n}^n\mathbf{TxtEx} \Leftrightarrow [m \text{ divides } n \bigvee m \text{ is odd}]]$.

Theorem 24 can also be used to show the following result which establishes that probabilistic identification of languages with probability of success at least $1/2$ is strictly more powerful than team identification of languages with success ratio $1/2$ (see [24]).

**Theorem 25** $\mathbf{Prob}^{1/2}\mathbf{TxtEx} - \bigcup_m \mathbf{Team}_{2m}^m\mathbf{TxtEx} \neq \emptyset$.

A similar result can be shown for the ratio $1/k, k > 2$ as noted in the following three results. Again we direct the reader to [22] for the details

**Theorem 26** $(\forall k \geq 2)(\forall \text{ even } j > 1)(\forall i \mid j \text{ does not divide } i)[\mathbf{Team}_{j \cdot k}^j\mathbf{TxtEx} - \mathbf{Team}_{i \cdot k}^i\mathbf{TxtEx} \neq \emptyset]$.

**Corollary 12** $(\forall a \in N)(\forall k \geq 2)(\forall \text{ even } j > 1)(\forall i \mid j \text{ does not divide } i)$
$[\mathbf{Team}_{j \cdot k}^j\mathbf{TxtEx} - \mathbf{Team}_{i \cdot k}^i\mathbf{TxtEx}^a \neq \emptyset]$.

**Theorem 27** $(\forall k \geq 2)[\mathbf{Prob}^{1/k}\mathbf{TxtEx} - \bigcup_j \mathbf{Team}_{j \cdot k}^j\mathbf{TxtEx} \neq \emptyset]$.

# 6 Finite Identification of Functions by Teams

The results considered so far have been about identification in the limit criterion. A more practical learning criterion than learning in the limit is *finite identification* in which a machine, fed the graph of a recursive function $f$, outputs a program for $f$ as its first conjecture and never abandons this conjecture. Finite identification by a probabilistic machine was first studied by Freivalds [16]. A lot of research activity has taken place in the last few years on finite team identification of functions. For example, Pitt's equivalence between team and probabilistic machines for function identification in the limit does not hold for finite function identification. In the present section, we survey a few preliminary results and refer the reader to a more comprehensive survey by Daley and Kalyanasundaram in the current volume.

We first formally introduce finite identification of functions.

## 6.1 Finite Function Identification

It is useful to extend the definition of a function learning machine as follows.

**Definition 25** [18] A *learning machine* is an algorithmic device that computes a mapping from SEG into $N \cup \{\perp\}$. We further assume that for all $\sigma \subseteq \tau$, if $\mathbf{M}(\sigma) \neq \perp$, then $\mathbf{M}(\tau) \neq \perp$.

Intuitively, $\perp$ is a nonnumeric element that a machine issues to say that it does not wish to conjecture a hypothesis, that is, $\mathbf{M}(\sigma) = \perp$ denotes that $\mathbf{M}$ on $\sigma$ does not output a conjecture.

We now describe what it means for a learning machine to finite identify a function.

**Definition 26** A learning machine $\mathbf{M}$ is said to **Fin**-*identify* a function $f$ just in case there exists $n_0$ such that the following hold:

1. for all $n < n_0$, $\mathbf{M}(f[n]) = \perp$;

2. $\varphi_{\mathbf{M}(f[n_0])} = f$; and

3. for all $n \geq n_0$, $\mathbf{M}(f[n]) = \mathbf{M}(f[n_0])$.

If $\mathbf{M}$ **Fin**-identifies $f$, then we write $f \in \mathbf{Fin}(\mathbf{M})$.

**Definition 27** **Fin** denotes the class of all sets $S$ of recursive functions such that some learning machine **Fin**-identifies each function in $S$.

## 6.2  Finite Function Identification by Teams

Based on the definitions in Smith [36], Pitt and Smith [33], and Freivalds, Smith, and Velauthapillai [17], we have the following definition of finite identification of functions by teams.

**Definition 28** Let $m, n \in N^+$, $m \leq n$. A team of machines $M_1, M_2, M_3, \ldots, M_n$ $\text{Team}_n^m \text{Fin-identifies}$ $f$ (written: $f \in \text{Team}_n^m \text{Fin}(M_1, M_2, M_3, \ldots, M_n)) \Leftrightarrow$ $\text{card}(\{l \mid 1 \leq l \leq n \wedge f \in \text{Fin}(M_l)\}) \geq m$.

$\text{Team}_n^m \text{Fin} = \{\mathcal{S} \mid (\exists M_1, M_2, \ldots, M_n)[\mathcal{S} \subseteq \text{Team}_n^m \text{Fin}(M_1, M_2, \ldots, M_n)]\}$.

## 6.3  Results

The results presented in the sequel can be divided into two groups. We refer the reader to Daley and Kalyanasundaram paper in the current volume for additional results. The first group of results is about success ratios greater than $\frac{1}{2}$ and the second group is about success ratio equal to $\frac{1}{2}$.

The following theorem shows that for success ratios greater than two-thirds, there is no advantage in using a team over a single machine. This result, together with the next theorem, implies that the aggregation ratio for finite function identification is $\frac{2}{3}$. This ratio is the same as the aggregation ratio for language identification in the limit and in fact the following two results can be established using techniques similar to those used to prove the corresponding language identification results.

**Theorem 28** *For all $j, k \in N$ such that $j > 2k/3$, $\text{Team}_k^j \text{Fin} = \text{Fin}$.*

**Theorem 29** $\text{Team}_3^2 \text{Fin} - \text{Fin} \neq \emptyset$.

The above result can be generalized to the following; we direct the reader to [26] for details of the proof.

**Theorem 30** $(\forall n \in N)[\text{Team}_{2n+3}^{n+2} \text{Fin} - \text{Team}_{2n+1}^{n+1} \text{Fin} \neq \emptyset]$.

Daley, Pitt, Velauthapillai, and Will [13] used techniques from Freivalds [16] to prove the following result which shows that Theorem 30 is tight.

**Theorem 31** *[13] For all $r, s$ such that $\frac{n+2}{2n+3} < \frac{r}{s} \leq \frac{n+1}{2n+1}$,* $\text{Team}_s^r \text{Fin} = \text{Team}_{2n+1}^{n+1} \text{Fin}$.

We refer the reader to [16, 13] for related results about probabilistic and team finite identification of functions. We now turn our attention to the success ratio $\frac{1}{2}$. Velauthapillai [37] showed that the Pitt's equivalence between probabilistic and team identification in the limit does not hold for finite identification of functions.

**Theorem 32** [37] $\mathbf{Team}_4^2\mathbf{Fin} - \mathbf{Team}_2^1\mathbf{Fin} \neq \emptyset$.

We refer the reader to [37, 26] for a proof. The scenario at success ratio $\frac{1}{2}$ is settled by the following two results; the details can be found in [20, 26].

**Theorem 33** $\mathbf{Team}_{4j+2}^{2j+1}\mathbf{Fin} \subseteq \mathbf{Team}_2^1\mathbf{Fin}$.

**Theorem 34** $\mathbf{Team}_{4j}^{2j}\mathbf{Fin} \subseteq \mathbf{Team}_4^2\mathbf{Fin}$.

Many additional results have been obtained for finite function identification by teams. We direct the reader to Daley, Pitt, Velauthapillai, and Will [13], and Daley, Kalyanasundaram, and Velauthapillai [10].

The problem of teams for Popperian finite identification of functions is addressed by Daley, Kalyanasundaram, and Velauthapillai [11] and Daley and Kalyanasundaram [9].

Allowing teams of finite learners to make up to a finite number of errors in the hypothesis conjectured has been addressed by Daley, Kalyanasundaram, and Velauthapillai [12].

# 7 Team and Probabilistic Identification for Other Criteria

The problem of teams and probabilistic machines for identification in the limit with bounded number of mind changes has been addressed by Wiehagen, Freivalds, and Kinber [38] and Daley and Kalyanasundaram [8].

Behaviorally correct function identification has been studied by Daley [6, 7, 14].

In the context of language identification, work has hardly begun on other criteria. We direct the reader to [23, 25] for results on finite, vacillatory, and behaviorally correct identification of languages by teams.

# References

[1] L. Blum and M. Blum. Toward a mathematical theory of inductive inference. *Information and Control*, 28:125–155, 1975.

[2] M. Blum. A machine independent theory of the complexity of recursive functions. *Journal of the ACM*, 14:322–336, 1967.

[3] J. Case. Periodicity in generations of automata. *Mathematical Systems Theory*, 8:15–32, 1974.

[4] J. Case and C. Lynes. Machine inductive inference and language identification. In M. Nielsen and E. M. Schmidt, editors, *Proceedings of the 9th International Colloquium on Automata, Languages and Programming*, volume 140, pages 107–115. Springer-Verlag, Berlin, 1982.

[5] J. Case and C. Smith. Comparison of identification criteria for machine inductive inference. *Theoretical Computer Science*, 25:193–220, 1983.

[6] R. Daley. On the error correcting power of pluralism in BC-type inductive inference. *Theoretical Computer Science*, 24:95–104, 1983.

[7] R. P. Daley. Inductive inference hierarchies: Probabilistic vs pluralistic. *Lecture Notes in Computer Science*, 215:73–82, 1986.

[8] R. P. Daley and B. Kalyanasundaram. Capabilities of probabilistic learners with bounded mind changes. In *Proceedings of the Sixth Annual Conference on Computational Learning Theory, Santa Cruz, California*, pages 182–191. A. C. M. Press, 1993.

[9] R. P. Daley and B. Kalyanasundaram. Use of reduction arguments in determining popperian fin-type learning capabilities. In K.P. Jantke, S. Kobayashi, E. Tomita, and T. Yokomori, editors, *Proceedings of the Fourth International Workshop on Algorithmi Learning Theory, Tokyo, Japan, Lecture Notes in Artificial Intelligence, No. 744*, pages 173–186. Springer-Verlag, November 1993.

[10] R. P. Daley, B. Kalyanasundaram, and M. Velauthapillai. Breaking the probability 1/2 barrier in fin-type learning. In *Proceedings of the Fifth Annual Workshop on Computational Learning Theory, Pittsburgh, Pennsylvania*, pages 203–217. A. C. M. Press, 1992.

[11] R. P. Daley, B. Kalyanasundaram, and M. Velauthapillai. The power of probabilism in popperian finite learning. In *Proceedings of the Third International Workshop on Analogical and Inductive Inference, Dagstuhl Castle, Germany*, pages 151–169, October 1992.

[12] R. P. Daley, B. Kalyanasundaram, and M. Velauthapillai. Capabilities of fallible finite learning. In *Proceedings of the Sixth Annual Conference on Computational Learning Theory, Santa Cruz, California*, pages 199–208. A. C. M. Press, 1993.

[13] R. P. Daley, L. Pitt, M. Velauthapillai, and T. Will. Relations between probabilistic and team one-shot learners. In L. Valiant and M. Warmuth, editors, *Proceedings of the Workshop on Computational Learning Theory*, pages 228–239. Morgan Kaufmann Publishers, Inc., 1991.

[14] R.P. Daley. Transformation of probabilistic learning strategies into deterministic learning strategies. In D. Haussler and L. Pitt, editors, *Proceedings of the Workshop on Computational Learning Theory*, pages 157–163. Morgan Kaufmann Publishers, Inc., 1988.

[15] R. Freivalds. Functions computable in the limit by probabilistic machines. *Mathematical Foundations of Computer Science*, 1975.

[16] R. Freivalds. Finite identification of general recursive functions by probabilistic strategies. In *Proceedings of the Conference on Algebraic, Arithmetic and Categorical Methods in Computation Theory*, pages 138–145. Akedemie-Verlag, Berlin, 1979.

[17] R Freivalds, C. H. Smith, and M. Velauthapillai. Trade-off among parameters affecting inductive inference. *Information and Computation*, 82:323–349, 1989.

[18] E. M. Gold. Language identification in the limit. *Information and Control*, 10:447–474, 1967.

[19] J. Hopcroft and J. Ullman. *Introduction to Automata Theory Languages and Computation*. Addison-Wesley Publishing Company, 1979.

[20] S. Jain and A. Sharma. Finite learning by a team. In M. Fulk and J. Case, editors, *Proceedings of the Third Annual Workshop on Computational Learning Theory, Rochester, New York*, pages 163–177. Morgan Kaufmann Publishers, Inc., August 1990.

[21] S. Jain and A. Sharma. Language learning by a team. In M. S. Paterson, editor, *Proceedings of the 17th International Colloquium on Automata, Languages and Programming*, pages 153–166. Springer-Verlag, July 1990.

[22] S. Jain and A. Sharma. Computational limits on team identification of languages. Technical Report 9301, School of Computer Science and Engineering; University of New South Wales, 1993.

[23] S. Jain and A. Sharma. On aggregating teams of learning machines. In K.P. Jantke, S. Kobayashi, E. Tomita, and T. Yokomori, editors, *Proceedings of the Fourth International Workshop on Algorithmi Learning Theory, Tokyo, Japan, Lecture Notes in Artificial Intelligence, No. 744*, pages 150–163. Springer-Verlag, November 1993.

[24] S. Jain and A. Sharma. Probability is more powerful than team for language identification. In *Proceedings of the Sixth Annual Conference on Computational Learning Theory, Santa Cruz, California*, pages 192–198. ACM Press, July 1993.

[25] S. Jain and A. Sharma. On aggregating teams of learning machines. Technical Report 9405, School of Computer Science and Engineering; University of New South Wales, 1994.

[26] S. Jain, A. Sharma, and M. Velauthapillai. Finite identification of function by teams with success ration 1/2 and above. In preparation, 1994.

[27] M. Machtey and P. Young. *An Introduction to the General Theory of Algorithms.* North Holland, New York, 1978.

[28] D. Osherson, M. Stob, and S. Weinstein. Aggregating inductive expertise. *Information and Control*, 70:69–95, 1986.

[29] D. Osherson, M. Stob, and S. Weinstein. *Systems that Learn, An Introduction to Learning Theory for Cognitive and Computer Scientists.* MIT Press, Cambridge, Mass., 1986.

[30] D. Osherson and S. Weinstein. Criteria of language learning. *Information and Control*, 52:123–138, 1982.

[31] L. Pitt. *A characterization of probabilistic inference.* PhD thesis, Yale University, 1984.

[32] L. Pitt. Probabilistic inductive inference. *Journal of the ACM*, 36:383–433, 1989.

[33] L. Pitt and C. Smith. Probability and plurality for aggregations of learning machines. *Information and Computation*, 77:77–92, 1988.

[34] H. Rogers. Gödel numberings of partial recursive functions. *Journal of Symbolic Logic*, 23:331–341, 1958.

[35] H. Rogers. *Theory of Recursive Functions and Effective Computability.* McGraw Hill, New York, 1967. Reprinted, MIT Press 1987.

[36] C. Smith. The power of pluralism for automatic program synthesis. *Journal of the ACM*, 29:1144–1165, 1982.

[37] M. Velauthapillai. Inductive inference with bounded number of mind changes. In *Proceedings of the Workshop on Computational Learning Theory*, pages 200–213, 1989.

[38] R. Wiehagen, R. Freivalds, and E. B. Kinber. On the power of probabilistic strategies in inductive inference. *Theoretical Computer Science*, 28:111–133, 1984.

# Topological Considerations in Composing Teams of Learning Machines

Kalvis Apsītis

Institute of Mathematics and Informatics

University of Latvia

Raina bulv. 29, Riga, Latvia

apsitis@mii.lu.lv

### Abstract

Classes of total recursive functions may be identifiable by a team of strategies, but not by a single strategy, in accordance with a certain identification type ($EX$, $FIN$, etc.). Qualitative aspects in composing teams are considered. For each $W \notin EX$ all recursive strategies can be split into several families so that any team identifying $W$ contains strategies from all the families. For $W \notin FIN$ the possibility of such splitting depends upon $W$. The relation between these phenomena and "voting" properties for types $EX$, $FIN$, etc. is revealed.

## 1  Introduction

General learning problem can be represented by the following scheme: Learning mashine $F$ (called also the strategy) receives sequence of input/output values:

$$f(0), f(1), \ldots$$

of a total recursive function $f$ and outputs conjectures about the function $f$:

$$h_0, \ h_1, \ldots.$$

The sequence of conjectures should satisfy some conditions, for example:

- converge to a correct Goedel number of the function $f$ (identification type $EX$),

- converge to a correct Goedel number with no more than $n$ mindchanges (identification type $EX_n$),

- particular case $EX_0$ is named also $FIN$, i. e. after receiving some values of $f$ strategy outputs a correct number and never changes this conjecture.

In the theory of inductive inference we are interested in statements like "Given strategy identifies given function in accordance with some type". This relation can be characterized also by the system of classes of total recursive functions, each class being identifiable by a single strategy. So, for each identification type we obtain a system of subsets in the space of total recursive functions. We can investigate properties of this system.

There are two contrasting results, which show properties of the identification type $EX$. There exist two classes $U_1$ and $U_2$ which are both identifiable by a single strategy in the sense of $EX$, but their union is not [1]. If unions of all pairs of three classes are in $EX$, then the union of all three classes is also in $EX$ [4].

There are two possibilities to ilustrate this phenomenon. One was proposed by C. Smith [3]. The stress is put upon the functional aspect of identification — the teams of strategies. The power of pluralism (as well as it can be observed in the scientific community) allows to eliminate incorrect hypotheses, provided a certain number of correctly working strategies (as formal analogues of scientists).

On the contrary in [4] stress is put upon set theoretical aspect, i. e. the possibility to obtain one covering with certain density from the other. Coverings by subsets of one universal space (in this case — all total recursive functions) are investigated in the general topology. It was quite natural that topology could be used in this situation. Namely, it turned out that for any class $W$, not $EX$ identifiable by a single strategy, all $EX$ identifiable classes can be split into two disjoint families, such that any finite collection of these classes covering $W$ should contain classes from both families. In the terms of strategies — a team should contain strategies admitting different kinds of errors rather than strategies admitting the same errors.

In the Section 2 basic identification types are discussed. We formulate "voting" properties of these types. They are the theorems stating something about the possibility of obtaining one correct strategy from a given team of strategies provided a certain number of strategies output correct answers. It is the necessary background from the inductive inference and all the rest of this article is devoted to drawing conclusions from these theorems.

In the Section 3 the method is exposed which allows to obtain specific splittings of all recursive strategies. Section 4 shows the irregularities which appear when we replace $EX$ with identification with a bound to the number of mindchanges. Using splitting results in another branches of the theory of recursive functions is discussed in the Section 5.

# 2   Teams of $EX$ strategies

An arbitrary identification type $T$ (e. g. $EX, FIN, BC$) will be considered to have two meanings:

1. As a predicate in expressions like: machine (or strategy) $M$ identifies $f \in \Re$ in the sense of a type $T$.

2. As a collection of all classes of total recursive functions identifiable by some recursive strategy.

In the following the class of all total recursive functions will be denoted by $\Re$.

**Definition 1** *We shall say that a class $U \in \Re$ is* identifiable by a team *of $n$ strategies in the sense of a type $T(k : n)$ (denotation $U \in T(k : n)$) if there exist strategies $M_1, \ldots, M_n$ that any $f \in U$ is identified in the sense $T$ by at least $k$ of these strategies.*

Accordingly $T(k : n)$ can be considered as a complex identification type involving $n$ strategies as well as an aggregation of classes:

$$\left\{ \bigcup_{|I|=k, I \subset [1,n]} \bigcap_{i \in I} U_i \;\middle|\; U_i \in T, \, i \in [1, n] \right\}$$

where $T \subset 2^{\aleph}$ — some identification type.

**Theorem 1 ([1])** *Identification types $EX$ and $EX(1 : 2)$ are different. (In set notation — there exist classes $U_1, U_2 \in EX$ such that $U_1 \cup U_2 \notin EX$.)*

This result was generalized:

**Theorem 2 ([3])** *1. $\forall m \geq 1 : EX(1 : m + 1) \neq EX(1 : m)$*

*2. $\frac{k}{n} \in \left( \frac{1}{m+1}, \frac{1}{m} \right] \Rightarrow EX(k : n) = EX(1 : m)$*

(Briefly: all $EX(1 : m)$ are different and all the other types derived from $EX$ by team inference are reducible to them.)

Let us denote $W_j := \bigcup\limits_{i=1, i \neq j}^{n+2} U_i$ and $W := \bigcup\limits_{i=1}^{n+2} U_i$. The following result holds:

**Lemma 1** *Let $U_1, \ldots, U_{n+2}$ be classes of total recursive functions. If all $W_j \in EX(1 : n)$ then also $W \in EX(1 : n)$.*

**Proof.** Each $W_j$ is identified by a team of $n$ strategies $M_{j1}, \ldots, M_{jn}$. Arbitrary $f \in W$ belongs to all $W_j$ excepting at most one. Therefore $W \in EX(n + 1 : n(n + 2))$ and by Theorem 2 we conclude $W \in EX(1 : n)$.$\square$
Particular case ([4]), where n=1:

$$U_1 \cup U_2, U_1 \cup U_3, U_2 \cup U_3 \in EX \Rightarrow U_1 \cup U_2 \cup U_3 \in EX$$

**Lemma 2** *Let $U_1, \ldots U_k$ $(k \geq n + 2)$ be classes of total recursive functions. If all unions of $n+1$ of these classes belong to $EX(1 : n)$, then also $U_1 \cup \ldots \cup U_k \in EX(1 : n)$.*

**Proof.** We denote

$$U_1' := U_1,$$

$$\ldots$$

$$U_{n+1}' := U_{n+1},$$

$$U_{n+2}' := U_{n+2} \cup \ldots \cup U_k$$

and use Lemma 1. $\square$

**Lemma 3** *Let $W \notin EX(1 : n)$ and $W = V_1 \cup \ldots \cup V_m$, where $V_1, \ldots, V_m \in EX$. Then there exist $n + 1$ functions $f_1, \ldots, f_{n+1} \in W$ such that any $V_i$ contains no more than one of these fuctions.*

**Proof.** From the contrary. Let us consider nonempty classes of equivalence among functions in $W$, where two functions are equivalent iff they belong to the same $V_i$'s. We denote these classes $U_1, \ldots, U_k$ and select one representative from each class: $f_1 \in U_1, \ldots, f_k \in U_k$ ( $k \leq 2^m - 1$, so there are only finite number of such classes). For every set of functions $f_{j_1}, \ldots, f_{j_{n+1}}$ there exists $V_i$ which contains at least two of these functions (or else Lemma would hold). Assume that $f_{j_n} \in V_i$ and $f_{j_{n+1}} \in V_i$. Then $U_{j_n} \cup U_{j_{n+1}} \subset V_i$ and hence $U_{j_n} \cup U_{j_{n+1}} \in EX$. Moreover $U_j \in EX$ for every $j \in [1, k]$, because every $U_j$ is included in some $V_i$. We have obtained that $U_{j_1} \cup \ldots \cup U_{j_{n-1}} \cup U_{j_n} \cup U_{j_{n+1}} \subset U_{j_1} \cup \ldots \cup U_{j_{n-1}} \cup V_i \in EX(1:n)$ for arbitrary indices $j_1, \ldots, j_{n+1}$. Using Lemma 2 we obtain $W = U_1 \cup \ldots \cup U_k \in EX(1:n)$. Contradiction. $\square$

**Lemma 4** *Let $W \notin EX(1:n)$ and $\mathcal{M} = \{M_1, \ldots, M_m\}$ — finite set strategies. We can split them into $n+1$ disjoint families $\mathcal{M}_1, \ldots, \mathcal{M}_{n+1}$ ($\mathcal{M}_1 \cup \ldots \cup \mathcal{M}_{n+1} = \mathcal{M}$) so that $W$ cannot be identified by a team $\mathcal{M}' \subset \mathcal{M}$ not containing strategies from all $n+1$ families.*

**Proof.** Statement becomes trivial when $W$ cannot be identified (in the sense $EX(1:m)$) by the whole team $\{M_1, \ldots, M_m\}$. So, let us assume $W \subset U_1 \cup \ldots \cup U_m$, where $U_i$ is the maximal $\mathfrak{R}$ class identifiable by the strategy $M_i$. We denote $V_i := W \cap U_i$. Now $W = V_1 \cup \ldots \cup V_m$ and $V_i \in EX$ because $V_i \subset U_i$. By Lemma 3 we obtain list of functions $f_1, \ldots, f_{n+1} \in W$ such that any $V_i$ (and any $U_i$) contains no more than one function from the list. Now

$$\mathcal{M}_1 := \{M_i \mid f_1 \in U_i\},$$

$$\ldots$$

$$\mathcal{M}_n := \{M_i \mid f_n \in U_i\},$$

$$\mathcal{M}_{n+1} := \{M_i \mid f_{n+1} \in U_i \text{ or } U_i \text{ contains none of the functions } f_j\}.$$

Clearly, families $\mathcal{M}_j$ are disjoint and all of them are required to build a team identifying $W$. $\square$

## 3 Main theorem

We need to introduce some mathematics here. The set of all paths is compact in a tree where each node has a finite number of child nodes. More precisely:

**Lemma 5 (König)** *In any infinite directed tree in which each node has only a finite number of direct successors, there is an infinite path leading from the root.*

**Proof.** Start at the root with node $x_0$. Since there are only a finite number of direct successors to $x_0$, but the total number of nodes in the tree is infinite, at least one of the direct successors of $x_0$ must be the root of an infinite subtree. (If all the subtrees of direct successors of $x_0$ were finite, then the whole tree would be finite.) Pick a node $x_1$ which is a direct successor of $x_0$ with an infinite subtree. Now one of its direct successors is also the root of an infinite subtree; pick $x_2$ to be such a direct successor. Continuing in this manner, we produce the infinite path $x_0 x_1 x_2 \ldots$ in the tree. $\square$

$M_1$

$M_2$

$M_3$

$M_4$

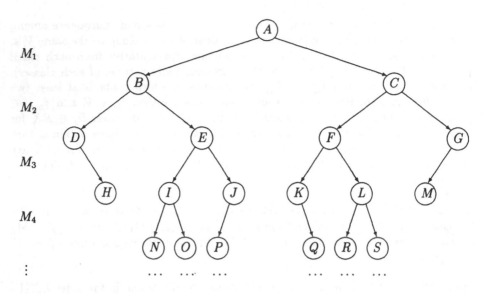

Figure 1: Tree of splittings.

**Theorem 3** *Let $W \notin EX$ be a class of total recursive functions. Then all recursive strategies can be split into two families such that $W$ cannot be identified by a finite team taken from one family.*

This result can be generalized:

**Theorem 4** *Let $W \notin EX(1 : n)$ be a class of total recursive functions. Then all recursive strategies can be split into $n + 1$ families $\mathcal{M}_1, \ldots, \mathcal{M}_{n+1}$ ($\mathcal{M}_i \cap \mathcal{M}_j = \emptyset$ when $i \neq j$, $\bigcup \mathcal{M}_i$ — the set of all strategies) so that $W$ cannot be identified by a (finite) team not representing all $n + 1$ families.*

**Remark.** If $W \in EX(1 : n)$, then evidently splitting as stated in Theorem 4 does not exist. On the other hand, the Theorem becomes trivial, when $W \notin EX(1 : k)$ for all $k > n$.

**Proof.** Let us consider particular $W \notin EX(1 : n)$. All recursive strategies can be enumerated in some way. Let $\{M_1, M_2, \ldots\}$ be a complete list of $EX$ strategies. The splittings of initial segments $\{M_1, M_2, \ldots, M_m\}$ of this list satisfying Lemma 4 we shall represent by nodes in a directed $n + 1$-ary tree (i. e. each node has at most $n + 1$ direct successors). Figure 1 shows an example of such a tree where $n = 1$.

Root of the tree corresponds to the "empty splitting": $A = \langle \emptyset, \emptyset \rangle$. Downward arcs in the level $M_i$ correspond to the possible ways how to add $M_i$ to one of $n + 1$ families of the splitting that corresponds to the departure node of the arc. (For example, node $R$ corresponds to the splitting $\langle \{M_2, M_4\}, \{M_1, M_3\} \rangle$. The presence of the node $R$ in the tree means that neither the team $\{M_2, M_4\}$ nor $\{M_1, M_3\}$ identifies the class $W$ in sense $EX$. The node $D$ does not have the left successor, because the corresponding splitting $\langle \{M_1, M_2, M_3\}, \emptyset \rangle$ is not good — the team $\{M_1, M_2, M_3\}$ identifies $W$.)

By Lemma 4 the $n + 1$-ary tree is infinite. By Lemma 5 there is an infinite path in that tree. The splitting of all strategies $M_1, M_2, \ldots$, obtained by following this path is the needed one. $\square$

Two simple results characterize the absence of uniqueness and universality for splittings satisfying Teorem 4.

**Theorem 5** *For a fixed $W \notin EX(1 : n)$ there are uncountably many (continuum) splittings which satisfy Theorem 4.*

**Proof.** Infinitely many strategies which identify no one function can be put in any family. $\square$

**Theorem 6** *There exist two (disjoint) classes $W_1, W_2 \notin EX$ such that no splitting into two families will satisfy Theorem 4 for both $W_1$ and $W_2$.*

**Proof.** By Theorem 1 there are two classes $U_1, U_2 \in EX$ such that $U_1 \cup U_2 \notin EX$. We can construct from here two pairs of counterexamples $U_1^1, U_2^1$ and $U_1^2, U_2^2$ so that $U_1^1, U_2^1, U_1^2, U_2^2 \in EX$ but $W_1 = U_1^1 \cup U_2^1 \notin EX$ and $W_2 = U_1^2 \cup U_2^2 \notin EX$. Moreover, we can require the classes $W_1$ and $W_2$ to be disjoint (for example, redefining the all the functions in classes $W_1$ and $W_2$ for the argument 0). There exist strategies $M_1, M_2, M_3, M_4$ identifying the unions $U_1^1 \cup U_2^1, U_1^1 \cup U_2^2, U_2^1 \cup U_1^2, U_1^1 \cup U_2^2$ respectively. We can easily check that for any splitting of strategies $M_1, M_2, M_3, M_4$ into two subfamilies at least one of them will identify $W_1$ or $W_2$. $\square$

# 4   The properties of $FIN$ and $EX_n$

**Theorem 7**   1. There is a class $W'$ ($W' \notin FIN$ and $W' \in FIN(1 : 2)$) such that for any splitting of all $FIN$ strategies into two subfamilies one family will provide a finite team identifying $W'$.

2. There is a class $W''$ ($W'' \notin FIN$ and $W'' \in FIN(1 : 2)$) for which exists a splitting of all $FIN$ strategies into two subfamilies such that any team identifying $W''$ contains strategies from both families.

**Proof.**

1. As shown in [4] there exist classes $U_1, U_2, U_3$ such that $U_1 \cup U_2, U_1 \cup U_3, U_2 \cup U_3 \in FIN$ but $U_1 \cup U_2 \cup U_3 \notin FIN$. We take $M_1, M_2, M_3$ — strategies which identify unions of pairs and $W' := U_1 \cup U_2 \cup U_3$. For any splitting two of the strategies will appear in the same part and this part will provide a team identifying $W'$.

2. We choose
$$W'' := \{f \in \Re \mid f \equiv 0 \text{ or } \exists! x : f(x) \neq 0\}$$

In the family $\mathcal{M}_1$ we put all strategies identifying $f \equiv 0$ and in $\mathcal{M}_2$ — all the other strategies. Any team must contain strategies from both these families, because any strategy from $\mathcal{M}_1$ identifies only finite number of nonzero functions.

$\square$

**Remark.** The reason for these contrasting examles is the following. Any class of functions $\mathbf{N} \to \mathbf{N}$ can be considered as a point of the Cartesian power $\mathbf{N}^{\aleph_0}$ of the discrete topological space of natural numbers $\mathbf{N}$. Then all functions in $W'$ are isolated, but $W''$ has one accumulation point, namely the zero function. (The definitions of

Cartesian product of spaces as well as accumulation point can be found in [2], but here they can be considered more intuitively.)

For an arbitrary $W \notin FIN$ we can state something only about splittings into three families. As in the case of the type $EX$ splitting result follows from the following "voting" theorem:

**Theorem 8 ([4])** *For arbitrary classes $U_1, U_2, U_3, U_4 \in \Re$ if all unions of three classes are in $FIN$ then also $U_1 \cup U_2 \cup U_3 \cup U_4 \in FIN$.*

**Lemma 6** *Let $W \notin FIN$ and $W = V_1 \cup \ldots \cup V_m$, where $V_1, \ldots, V_m \in FIN$. Then there exist $f_1, f_2, f_3 \in W$ such that any $V_i$ contains no more than two of these fuctions.*

**Lemma 7** *Let $W \notin FIN$ and $M_1, \ldots, M_m$ — some strategies. We can split them into 3 disjoint families $\mathcal{M}_1, \mathcal{M}_2, \mathcal{M}_3$ ($\mathcal{M}_1 \cup \mathcal{M}_2 \cup \mathcal{M}_3 = \{M_1, \ldots M_m\}$) such that $W$ cannot be identified by a team which includes strategies from one family only.*

**Theorem 9** *Let $W \notin FIN$ be a class of total recursive functions. Then all recursive strategies can be split into 3 families $\mathcal{M}_1, \mathcal{M}_2, \mathcal{M}_3$ ($\mathcal{M}_i \cap \mathcal{M}_j = \emptyset$ when $i \neq j$, $\bigcup \mathcal{M}_i$ — the set of all strategies) so that $W$ cannot be identified by a (finite) team consisting of strategies from one team only.*

For the identification type $EX_n$ (identification with no more than $n$ mindchanges) when $n > 0$ the situation is opposite to the case of $EX$ (compare with the Theorem 3):

**Lemma 8** *For every $W \in EX_k$ ($k \geq 1$) there exist classes $U_1, \ldots, U_k$ such that $U_1 \cup \ldots \cup U_k = W$ and all unions of pairs $U_i \cup U_j$ are in $EX_1$.*

**Proof.** Suppose that $M$ is a strategy identifying $W$ in the sense $EX_k$. We put in $U_i$ all those functions $f \in W$ for which $M$ outputs a correct Goedel number as the $i$-th hypothesis and perfoms no more minchanges. To identify $U_i \cup U_j$ in the sense $EX_1$ we simulate $M$ and output only its hypotheses with numbers $i$ and $j$. $\square$

**Theorem 10** *For every $W$ (such that $W \notin EX_n$ but $W \in EX_n(1 : m)$ for some finite $m$) and every splitting of all recursive strategies into two families, at least one of these families contains a finite team identifying $W$.*

**Proof.** ¿From $W \in EX_n(1 : m)$ we conclude $W \in EX_k$ for some finite $k$ (in fact $k \leq 2m(n + 1) - 1$). We obtain classes $U_1, \ldots, U_k$ in accordance with the Lemma 8. Let $\mathcal{M}_1, \mathcal{M}_2$ be an arbitrary splitting of all $EX_n$ strategies. Strategies $M_{ij}$ identifying all pairs $U_i \cup U_j$ are somehow distributed between $\mathcal{M}_1$ and $\mathcal{M}_2$. Suppose that $\mathcal{M}_1$ does not provide a finite team identifying $W$. Then $\mathcal{M}_1$ must not contain any $M_{i_0 j}$ for some index $i_0$, or else we can make a team identifying all $U_{i_0}$'s, i. e. the whole $W$. Consequently, they should be in $\mathcal{M}_2$. But $\{M_{i_0 1}, \ldots M_{i_0 k}\}$ is a team identifying $W$. $\square$

# 5 Conclusion

Let us consider two classes of total recursive functions — selfdescribing functions and those of finite support:
$$SD := \{f \in \Re \mid f \equiv \phi_{f(0)}\},$$
$$FS := \{f \in \Re \mid \forall^\infty x : f(x) = 0\}.$$

Both $SD$ and $FS$ are $EX$ identifiable, but their union is not (classical example for the Theorem 3). Applying the Theorem 3 we get two families of strategies. Then strategies identifying $SD$ and $FS$ respectively should be in different families. These strategies show the contrast between "deduction" and "induction" in machine learning. Using the Theorem 3 for $W = SD \cup FS$ we obtain the following corollary:

**Theorem 11** *Let us denote*

$$R := \{n \mid \phi_n \text{ is total function}\}.$$

*Then $\Sigma_1 \cup \Pi_1$ (the family of all recursively enumerable sets and their complements) can be split into two disjoint subfamilies $\mathcal{A}_1$ and $\mathcal{A}_2$ such that*

1. *For every finite subfamily $\mathcal{A}_1' \subset \mathcal{A}_1$ the set difference $R \setminus \bigcup \mathcal{A}_1' \neq \emptyset$.*

2. *For every finite subfamily $\mathcal{A}_2' \subset \mathcal{A}_2$ the set difference $\bigcap \mathcal{A}_2' \setminus R \neq \emptyset$.*

**Proof.** Let us introduce two strateteqies (designed to identify classes $SD$ and $FS$ respectively) and their combinations.

Strategy $M'$: receives $f(0)$ and outputs it as the only hypothesis.

Strategy $M''$: at every step outputs the hypothesis, which for initial segment of arguments assigns the values from the received graph of $f$ till the last nonzero value, for all the following arguments assigns zero value.

For the fixed set $A \in \Sigma_1 \cup \Pi_1$ we consider the following strategy $M_A$:

- receive the value $f(0)$,

- if $A$ is recursively enumerable ($A \in \Sigma_1$)

  - ask whether $f(0) \in A$ and wait for confirmation, at the same time simulating $M''$,

  - when the confirmation arrives, simulate $M'$,

- if $A$ is co-recursively enumerable ($A \in \Pi_1$)

  - ask whether $f(0) \in A$ and wait for rejection, at the same time simulating $M'$,

  - when the rejection arrives, simulate $M''$,

We split all these strategies into two families $\mathcal{M}_1, \mathcal{M}_2$ in accordance to the Theorem 3. This splitting induces splitting $\mathcal{A}_1, \mathcal{A}_2$ in the family of sets from $\Sigma_1 \cup \Pi_2$ ($A \in \mathcal{A}_i \iff M_A \in \mathcal{M}_i$). We choose notations so that $\emptyset \in \mathcal{A}_1$. $\square$

Inductive inference serves as a mathematical model for methodology of scientific research. Inductive inference gives an example where qualitative aspects in organizing researcher's teams are as important as quantitative. All kinds of methods need to be put together to solve difficult problems.

# References

[1] Barzdin J., Two Theorems on the Limiting Synthesis of Functions. *Theory of Algorithms and Programs*, Vol. 1, Latvian State University, 1974. (Russian).

[2] Engelking R., General Topology. Warsaw, Polish Scientific Publishers, 1977.

[3] Pitt L., Smith C., Probability and plurality for aggregations of learning machines. *Information and Computation*, Vol. 77 (1988), pp. 77–92.

[4] Apsītis K., Freivalds R., Kriķis M., Simanovskis R. a. o., Unions of Identifiable Classes of Total Recursive Functions. *"Analogical and Inductive Inference"*, International Workshop, Dagstuhl Castle, Germany. Berlin, Springer-Verlag, 1992, pp. 99–107.

# Probabilistic versus Deterministic Memory Limited Learning

Rūsiņš Freivalds and Efim B. Kinber*
Institute of Mathematics and Computer Science
University of Latvia
Raiņa bulvāris 29
LV-1459, Riga, Latvia

Carl H. Smith†
Department of Computer Science
University of Maryland
College Park, MD 20912
USA

## 1   Introduction

A new, complexity theoretic, model of space utilization during a dynamic learning process has been recently introduced [2, 4]. In this paper, we give precise upper and lower bounds logarithmic bounds for a class of functions that can be learned probabilistically in constant space with probability 1. Hence, a space complexity advantage can be gained using probabilistic techniques that sacriface no certainty. We begin with defintions and notation.

For the purposes of a mathematical treatment of learning, it suffices to consider only the learning of functions from natural numbers to natural numbers. The result of the learning will be a program that computes the function that the machine is trying to learn. A variety of models for learning recursive functions have been considered, each representing some different aspect of learning. Historically, these models are motivated by various aspects of human learning [5] and perspectives on the scientific method [11].

We say that learning has taken place because the machines we consider must produce the resultant program after having ascertained only finitely much information about the behavior of the function. The models we use are all based on the model of Gold [5] that was cast recursion theoretically in [1]. First, we briefly review the basics of the Gold model and then proceed to define the memory limited version of the basic model that will be investigated in this paper.

Gold, in a seminal paper [5], defined the notion called *identification in the limit*. This definition concerned learning by algorithmic devices now called *inductive inference machines* (IIMs). An IIM inputs the range of a recursive function, an ordered pair at a time, and, while doing so, outputs computer programs. Since we will only discuss the inference of (total) recursive functions, we may assume, without loss of generality, that the input is received by an IIM in its natural domain increasing order,

---

*Currently at the Department of Computer Science, University of Delaware, Newark, DE 19716, USA.

†Supported in part by NSF Grant 9020079.

$f(0)$, $f(1)$, $\cdots$. An IIM, on input from a function $f$ will output a potentially infinite sequence of programs $p_0$, $p_1$, $\cdots$. The IIM *converges* if either the sequence is finite, say of length $n + 1$, or there is program $p$ such that for all but finitely many $i$, $p_i = p$. In the former case we say the IIM converges to $p_n$, and in the latter case, to $p$. In general, there is no effective way to tell when, and if, an IIM has converged.

Following Gold, we say that an IIM $M$ *identifies* a function $f$ (written: $f \in EX(M)$), if, when $M$ is given the range of $f$ as input, it converges to a program $p$ that computes $f$. If an IIM identifies some function $f$, then some form of learning must have taken place, since, by the properties of convergence, only finitely much of the range of $f$ was known by the IIM at the (unknown) point of convergence. The terms *infer* and *learn* will be used as synonyms for identify. Each IIM will learn some set of recursive functions. The collection of all such sets, over the universe of effective algorithms viewed as IIMs, serves as a characterization of the learning power inherent in the Gold model. This collection is symbolically denoted by $EX$ (for explanation) and is defined rigorously by $EX = \{U \mid \exists M(U \subseteq EX(M))\}$. Mathematically, this collection is set-theoretically compared with the collections that arise from the other models we discuss below. Many intuitions about machine learning have been gained by working with Gold's model and its derivatives. In the next section, we describe the variants of Gold's model that we examine in this paper.

## 2 Limited Memory Learning

We now describe the model investigated in this paper. To insure an accurate accounting of the memory used by an IIM, we will henceforth assume that each IIM receives its input in such a way that it is impossible to back up and reread some input after another has been read. All of the previously mentioned models of learning languages or functions measured memory used in the number of data items or hypotheses that could be remembered. Since it is possible to encode an arbitrary finite set within any single hypothesis, coding techniques played a major role in the proofs of some of the above mentioned results. Computers, and humans, use storage proportional to the size of what is being remembered. To circumvent the use of coding techniques, the memory used will be measured in trits, as opposed to integers. Each data entry will appear as a bit string with a designated delimeter separating the entries. The delimiter will be viewed as a "special bit" and we will henceforth count the memory utilization in bits.

Each of the machines we consider will have two types of memory. In the *long term memory* the IIM will remember portions of the input it has seen, prior conjectures, state information pertaining to the underlying finite state device and perhaps other information as well. In addition, each machine will have a potentially unlimited *short term memory* that will be annihilated every time the IIM either outputs a new conjecture or begins reading the bits corresponding to another point in the graph of the mystery function providing the input to the IIM. The short term memory clear operation is done automatically and takes one time step. The short term memory is necessary to insure an accurate accounting of the real long term memory utilization of a learning process. It might be, as indicated by our results in the section on trade offs between long and short term memory, that some very space consuming computation must be performed in order to decide which few bits of information to retain and which to discard. Without a short term memory, such a temporary use of space would artificially inflate the long term memory need by a learning algorithm.

Under the above conventions, we proceed to define our limited memory model. We say that $U \subseteq LEX : g(M)$ if $g$ is a recursive function such that for any $f \in U$, $f \in EX(M)$ and $M$ uses no more than $g(n)$ bits of memory, where $n$ is the number of bits of the range of $f$, from the natural domain increasing order enumeration, that $M$ has observed. The collection of all sets of functions inferrible with memory bound given by $g$ is denoted by $LEX : g$, where $LEX : g = \{U \mid \exists M(U \subseteq LEX : g(M)\}$. In the special case where $g$ is a constant function, we will write $LEX : c$.

A few more technical definitions are needed. Natural numbers ($\mathbb{N}$) will serve as names for programs. The function computed by program $i$ will be denoted by $\varphi_i$. It is assumed that $\varphi_0, \varphi_1, \cdots$ forms an acceptable programming system [8, 12]. Sometimes, it will be convenient to represent a function by a sequence of values from its range. Such a representation is called a *string* representation. So, for example, the sequence $01^2 0^4 3^\infty$ represents the (total) function:

$$f(x) = \begin{cases} 0 & \text{if } x = 0 \text{ or } 3 \leq x \leq 6, \\ 1 & \text{if } 1 \leq x \leq 2 \\ 3 & \text{otherwise.} \end{cases}$$

This example function has two *blocks* of consecutive 0's, one of length 1 and the other of length 4. The string representation of a finite function is called a *fragment*. The length of any string $\alpha$, in characters, is denoted by $|\alpha|$.

# 3 Probabilistic Limited Memory Machines

Probabilistic inductive inference machines were introduced in [9] and studied further in [10]. A *probabilistic* inductive inference machine is an IIM that makes use of a fair coin in it deliberations. We say that $f \in EX(M)\langle p \rangle$ if $M$ learns $f$ with probability $p$, $0 \leq p \leq 1$. The collection $EX\langle p \rangle$ is defined to be $\{U \mid \exists M(U \subseteq EX(M)\langle p \rangle\}$. Pitt showed that for $p > \frac{1}{2}$, $EX\langle p \rangle = EX$ [9]. Limiting the memory available to a probabilistic IIM, according to the conventions of this paper, gives rise to the class $LEX : c\langle p \rangle$.

In this section we define a class of recursive functions, called $\bar{U}$, and prove two theorems about it. It was shown in [4] that $\bar{U}$ can be probabilistically learned (with probability 1) by an algorithm that uses only a constant amount of long term memory. We show that both the upper and lower bounds for learning $\bar{U}$ determiniistically are logarithmic. We proceed with the definition of $\bar{U}$.

Every function in $\bar{U}$ will take on only four values, 0, 1 and two self referential indices. Members of $\bar{U}$ will be constructed via suitable recursion theorems. Every function $f \in \bar{U}$ will have several (perhaps infinitely many) blocks of 0's. Let $\tau_1, \tau_2,$ ... denote the length of the first block of 0's, the second block, etc. Similarly, $\sigma_1, \sigma_2,$ ... denotes the lengths of the blocks of 1's, in their order of appearance in the range. For a function $f$ to be in $\bar{U}$, one of the following two conditions must be met:

$$\sum_{n=1}^{\infty} \frac{1}{2^{\tau_n}} \text{ converges and } \sum_{n=1}^{\infty} \frac{1}{2^{\sigma_n}} \text{ diverges, or} \tag{1}$$

$$\sum_{n=1}^{\infty} \frac{1}{2^{\tau_n}} \text{ diverges and } \sum_{n=1}^{\infty} \frac{1}{2^{\sigma_n}} \text{ converges.} \qquad (2)$$

Furthermore, in case (1) occurs, $f \in \bar{U}$ iff the sequence of values $f(x_1)$, $f(x_2)$, ..., for points $x_i$ immediately following a block of 0's or 1's, converges to a program for $f$. Similarly, for (2) to qualify a function $f$ for membership in $\bar{U}$, the sequence of values $f(y_1)$, $f(y_2)$, ... converges to a program for $f$, where $y_i = x_i + 1$, e.g. the $y_i$'s are points immediately following a point that immediately follows a block of 0's or 1's.

**Theorem 1** [3] $\bar{U} \in LEX : c\langle 1 \rangle$.

**Theorem 2** *Suppose that $g = o(\log n)$ For all IIMs $M$, $\bar{U} \notin LEX : g(M)$.*

Proof: Suppose $g = o(\log n)$. Suppose by way of contradiction that $M$ is a IIM such that $\bar{U} \subseteq LEX : g(M)$. Define $a_n = n$. Let $LCM(n)$ denote the least common multiple of $\{1, \cdots, n\}$. We would like to define $b_n \geq a_n + LCM(n)$. To do so, we must develope an upper bound for $LCM(n)$. From elementary number theory, see for example [6], the number of primes less than or equal to $n$ is $O(n/\ln n)$. The largest possible factor of any prime in $LCM(n)$ is $n$. Consequently, an upper bound for $LCM(n)$ is

$$O(n^{\frac{n}{\ln n}}).$$

Thus, we can choose $b_n = c \cdot n^{n/\ln n}$ for some constant $c$. Notice that for our choice of $b_n$, we have that $a_n = O(\log b_n)$. Let $t_n$ be the length of the initial segment of the string representation of some $f \in \bar{U}$ ending with exactly $a_n$ zeros. Hence, $b_n = O(t_n)$ and $a_n = O(\log t_n)$. Consequently,

$$\sum_{n=1}^{\infty} \frac{1}{2^{a_n}} \text{ diverges and } \sum_{n=1}^{\infty} \frac{1}{2^{b_n}} \text{ converges.}$$

The sequences of $a_i$'s and $b_i$'s will be used to determine the sizes of the blocks of consecutive 0's and 1's in the functions that we will construct below. Before defining the function from $\bar{U}$ that $M$ will fail to identify, we must first describe a transformation on programs. Recall that functions in $\bar{U}$ have string representations that look like:

$$0^{a_1} x \, y 1^{b_1} x \, y 0^{a_2} x \, y 1^{b_2} x \, y \cdots.$$

If $\varphi_i$ has a string representation that conforms to the above schema, then $\varphi_{g(i)}$ will appear as:

$$0^{a_1} x \, y 1^{b_1} x \, y \cdots x \, y 0^{a_c} x \, y 1^{b_c} x \, y 0^{b_c+1} x \, y 1^{a_c+1} x \, y 0^{b_c+2} x \, y 1^{a_c+2} x \, y \cdots.$$

The transformation $g$ is specified by the construction of $\varphi_{g(i)}$, uniformly in $i$ in effective stages of finite extension below. Consequently, $g$ will be a total recursive function, even if some of the programs in its range compute functions with finite (or empty) domains. $\varphi_{g(i)}^s$ denotes the finite amount of $\varphi_{g(i)}$ determined prior to stage $s$. $\varphi_{g(i)}^0 = \emptyset$. $x^s$ denotes the least number not in the domain of $\varphi_{g(i)}^s$. Consequently, $x^0 = 0$.

*Begin stage* 0. Look for the least $z$ such that $\varphi_i(z) = 0$ and there are $2 \cdot c$ numbers $y < z$ such that $\varphi_i(y)$ is defined to some number other than 0 or 1. Set $\varphi^1_{g(i)} = \{(x, \varphi_i(x) \mid x < z\}$ and go to stage 1.
*End stage* 0.

*Begin stage* $s > 0$. Look for the least $z \geq x^s$ such that $\varphi_i(z)$ is defined and $\varphi_i(z) \neq 0$. If $\varphi_i(z)$ is undefined for some value, then $\varphi_{g(i)}$ has finite domain. Look for the least $w > z + 1$ such that $\varphi_i(w)$ is defined and $\varphi_i(w) \neq 1$. Again, if $\varphi_i$ is undefined for some value involved in the search, then $\varphi_{g(i)}$ has finite domain. Define:

$$\varphi^{s+1}_{g(i)}(x) = \begin{cases} \varphi^s_{g(i)}(x) & \text{if } x < x^s \\ 0 & \text{if } x^s \leq x < x^s + w - (z + 2) \\ \varphi_i(z) & \text{if } x = x^s + w - (z + 2) \\ \varphi_i(z + 1) & \text{if } x = x^s + w - (z + 2) + 1 \\ 1 & \text{if } x^s + w - (z + 2) + 1 < x < w \\ \varphi_i(w) & \text{if } x = w \\ \varphi_i(w + 1) & \text{if } x = w + 1 \end{cases}$$

Go to stage $s + 1$.
*End stage* $s$.

We are now ready to define the function $f \in \bar{U}$ that cannot be identified by $M$. By implicit use of the recursion theorem, define a function $\varphi_e$ with string representation:

$$0^{a_1} e\, g(e) 1^{b_1} e\, g(e) 0^{a_2} e\, g(e) 1^{b_2} e\, g(e) \dots.$$

Clearly, $\varphi_e$ is a total function. By the choice of the $a_i$'s and $b_i$'s, $\varphi_e \in \bar{U}$. Let $n_{i+1}$ denote the length of the string

$$0^{a_1} e\, g(e) 1^{b_1} e\, g(e) \cdots 0^{a_i} e\, g(e) 1^{b_i} e\, g(e).$$

Let $f = \varphi_e$. To complete the proof, we define a recursive function $f'$ that is different from $f$ but that $M$ cannot distinguish from $f$. The argument is similar to a pumping lemma argument. Notice that $a_i = c \cdot \log n_i$. Each block of 0's (length $a_i$) and block of 1's (length $b_i$) is longer than $h(n_i)$ in length. Choose an $i$ such that $h(x) \leq c \cdot \log(x)$ for all $x \geq n_i$. So, for large enough $i$ there is a block of $d_i \leq h(n_i)$ 0's such that $M$'s memory (and internal state) are in the same configuration when those 0's are just about to be read, and just after they have all been read. Similarly, there is a block of $j_i \leq h(n_i)$ 1's. Redrawing the string representation of $f$, given the above observation yields:

$$\cdots \underbrace{000 \cdots 0000^{d_i} 00 \cdots 000}_{a_i} e\, g(e) \underbrace{111 \cdots 1111^{j_i} 111 \cdots 1111}_{b_i} \cdots$$

Since $b_i - a_i = LCM(i)$, both $d_i$ and $j_i$ divide $b_i - a_i$, for large enough $i$. Consequently, for such $i$'s, it is possible to expand the $i^{\text{th}}$ block of 0's by a multiple of $d_i$ to make the block have exactly $b_i$ 0's. Similarly, it is possible to remove a multiple of $j_i$ 1's from the $i^{\text{th}}$ block of 1's, leaving the block with exactly $a_i$ 1's. Performing this transformation on all but finitely many blocks of 0's and 1's results in a function that we will call $f'$. Notice that the second value following each block of 0's or 1's ($g(e)$) is an index for $f'$, hence $f' \in \bar{U}$. $M$, on input from $f'$ will be in the same state when it leaves the $n^{\text{th}}$ block of 0's (or 1's) as it will be when using $f$ as input. Consequently, $M$ will produce the same outputs on input from $f$ and $f'$. Hence, $M$ cannot infer both $f$ and $f'$, a contradiction to the assumption that $\bar{U} \subseteq LEX : h(M)$. $\boxtimes$

**Theorem 3** *Let* $g = \lambda x[2 \cdot \log x]$. *Then* $\bar{U} \in LEX : g$.

Proof: Let $\bar{U}$ and $g$ be as in the hypothesis. The key to inferring some $f \in \bar{U}$ is to decide which of the two series:

$$\sum_{n=1}^{\infty} \frac{1}{2^{\tau_n}} \tag{3}$$

$$\sum_{n=1}^{\infty} \frac{1}{2^{\sigma_n}} \tag{4}$$

converges.

We will estimate the values is the series (3) and (4). This estimate will be kept in long term memory. The series with the smaller estimate will assumed to be the one that is converging. Suppose that we have an estimate of the sum of the first $t - 1$ values of both series. The value of $1/2^{\tau_t}$ can be obtained by reading $\tau_t$ zeros into short term memory. If $\tau_t > \log t + 2 \log \log t$ (e.g. $1/2^{\tau_t} < 2^{-\log t - 2 \log \log t}$) then this value is ignored, hence at most a logarithmic amount of long term memory will be used for this purpose. Otherwise, the value of $1/2^{\tau_t}$ is added to the estimate of (4) in long term memory. The value of (3) is updated similarly. Since only small values are added to the sums, $\log n$ is sufficient space to maintain estimates for the series (4). The same is true for the series (3).

The proof is completed by showing that the terms that are ignored do not have any effect on the convergence or divergence of the series. Since the series

$$\sum_{n=1}^{\infty} \frac{1}{n(\log n)^2}$$

converges, there is no need to consider terms smaller than $1/t(\log t)^2$. This happens precisely when $\tau_t > \log t + 2 \log \log t$. $\boxtimes$

161

# References

[1] L. Blum and M. Blum. Toward a mathematical theory of inductive inference. *Information and Control*, 28:125–155, 1975.

[2] R. Freivalds, E. Kinber, and C. Smith. On the impact of forgetting on learning machines. In L. Pitt, editor, *Proceedings of the Sixth Annual Workshop on Computational Learning Theory*, pages 165–174. ACM Press, 1993.

[3] R. Freivalds and C. Smith. On the power of procrastination for machine learning. *Information and Computation*, 1993. To appear.

[4] R. Freivlalds and C. Smith. Memory limited inductive inference machines. In *Proceedings of the Third Scandinavian Workshop on Algorithms Theory*, pages 19–29. Springer-Verlag, 1992. Lecture Notes in Computer Science Vol. 621.

[5] E. M. Gold. Language identification in the limit. *Information and Control*, 10:447–474, 1967.

[6] H. Griffin. *Elementary Theory of Numbers*. McGraw Hill, New York, 1954.

[7] D. Levine. *Introduction to Neural and Cognitive Modeling*. Lawrence Earlbaum Associates, 1991.

[8] M. Machtey and P. Young. *An Introduction to the General Theory of Algorithms*. North-Holland, New York, 1978.

[9] L. Pitt. Probabilistic inductive inference. *Journal of the ACM*, 36(2):383–433, 1989.

[10] L. Pitt and C. Smith. Probability and plurality for aggregations of learning machines. *Information and Computation*, 77:77–92, 1988.

[11] K. Popper. *The Logic of Scientific Discovery*. Harper Torch Books, N.Y., 1968.

[12] H. Rogers, Jr. *Theory of Recursive Functions and Effective Computability*. McGraw Hill, New York, 1967.

[13] P. Rosenbloom, J. Laird, A. Newell, and R. McCarl. A preliminary analysis of the soar architecture as a basis for general intelligence. *Artificial Intelligence*, 47:289–325, 1991.

[14] E. Servan-Schreiber. *The Competitive Chunking Theory: Models of Perception, Learning, and Memory*. PhD thesis, Carnegie Mellon University, 1991. Ph.D. thesis, Department of Psychology.

# Classification Using Information

William I. Gasarch *

Department of Computer Science and

Institute for Advanced Computer Studies

The University of Maryland

College Park, MD 20742

gasarch@cs.umd.edu

Mark G. Pleszkoch

IBM Corporation

Gaithersburg, MD 20879

markp@vnet.ibm.com

Mahendran Velauthapillai

Department of Computer Science

Georgetown University

Washington, D.C. 20057

mahe@cs.georgetown.edu

### Abstract

Smith and Wiehagen [9] introduced a model of classification that is similar to the Gold model of learning [2]. In this model the learner is limited in *both* computing power and access to information. samples. In particular the learner is limited to Turing computability and initial segments of the function to be classified. When a function cannot be classified with respect to some desired property, it may be for either computational or information-theoretic reasons.

We would like to separate the computational limitations from the information-theoretic ones. To this end we study a model of learning originally due to Kelly that has *no* computational limits; however, the objects that we will be concerned with are rather complex. Fix a set $\mathcal{A} \subseteq \{0,1\}^\omega$ We will examine if a classifier (without computational limits) can classify a string $x \in \{0,1\}^\omega$ with respect to $\mathcal{A}$.

We will be varying the amount of information the learner can access. To increase the models ability to access information, we will give it the ability to ask more powerful questions. To decrease the models ability to access information, we will bound the number of mindchanges it may make.

## 1 Introduction

Smith and Wiehagen [9] introduced a model of classification that is similar to the Gold model of learning [2]. In this model the learner is limited in *both* computing power and access to information. samples. In particular the learner is limited to

---

*Supported by NSF grants CCR-880-3641 and CCR 9020079

Turing computability and initial segments of the function to be classified. When a function cannot be classified with respect to some desired property, it may be for either computational or information-theoretic reasons.

When a function cannot be classified it may be for either computational or information-theoretic reasons. For ease of presentation we will give examples from learning functions of when these two parameters are relevant. The set of all recursive function $(REC)$ cannot be learned in the $EX$ model; however, this is because $EX$ lacks the needed computing power. Additional computing power helps: if an oracle for the halting problem is allowed then $REC$ can be $EX$-learned. The set of functions that are almost always zero ($FS$ for finite support) cannot be learned by $EX_0$; however, this is because $EX_0$ has to make a guess before having enough information. More computing power would not help: for all oracles $X$ $REC \notin EX_0^X$.

We would like to separate the computational limitations from the information-theoretic ones. To this end we study a model of learning originally due to Kelly that has *no* computational limits; however, the objects that we will be concerned with are rather complex. Fix a set $A \subseteq \{0,1\}^\omega$ We will examine if a classifier (without computational limits) can classify a string $x \in \{0,1\}^\omega$ with respect to $A$.

We will be varying the amount of information the learner can access. To increase the models ability to access information, we will give it the ability to ask more powerful questions. To decrease the models ability to access information, we will bound the number of mindchanges it may make.

## 2   Definitions and Notations

In this section we formalize our notions. Throughout this section $A$ denotes a subset of $N^\omega$ and $\overline{A}$ denotes its complement. All these definitions make sense for $A \subseteq \{0,1\}^\omega$ as well.

A *classifiction function* (denoted c.f.) is a function $F$ from $N^*$ to $\{YES, NO, DK\}$ (DK stands for DON"T KNOW). Our intention is that $F$ is fed initial segments of some $f$ and eventually decides if it is in $A$ or not. Let $f$ be a function from $N$ to $N$. $F$ *classifies $f$ with respect to $A$* if (1) when $F$ is given initial segments of $f$ as input, the resultant sequence of anwers converges (after some point there are no more mind changes) (2) if $f \in A$ then the sequence converges to YES, and (3) if $f \notin A$ then the sequence coverges to NO.

$F$ *classifies $A$* if, for every function $f$, $F$ classifies $f$ with respect to $A$. The class $DE$ is the collection of all sets $A$ such that there exists a c.f. ($DE$ stands for DEscion) $F$ that classifies $A$. We denote this by saying "$A \in DE$ via $F$."

The class $DE_c$ is the collection of all sets in $DE$ that have classification functions that change there mind about each $f$ at most $c$ times. The initial change from DK to either YES or NO is not counted as a mind change.

A *query inference machine* (QIM), defined by Gasarch and Smith [4] is an algorithmic device that asks a teacher questions about some unknown function, and while doing so, outputs programs. For more details and technical results about QIM's see [1,3,4,5].

We want to define an analog of that notion in our context. The c.f. F will no longer be seeing initial segments of the function. Instead it will be asking questions about the function. The questions are formulated in some query language $L$. The nature of the language and the questions will be given after the formal definition.

A *query classification function* (denoted q.c.f.) is a function $F$, which takes as input a string of bits $\vec{b}$ (the empty string is allowed), corresponding to the answers to previous queries about $f$, and outputs an ordered pair whose first component is one of $\{YES, NO, DK\}$ and whose second component is question $\psi$ in the language $L$. Our intention is that $F$ is conjencturing whether $f$ is in $\mathcal{A}$ or not and also genereateing the next question to ask about $f$. The definition of when $F$ *classifies $f$ with respect to $\mathcal{A}$* is straightforward but tedious (it is analogous to the definition in [4].

Every language $L$ allows the use of $\wedge$, $\neg$, $=$, symbols for the natural numbers (members of $N$ ), variables that range over $N$, and a single unary function symbol $f$ which to representing the function being classified. (If we are classifying a set of 0-1 valued functions then we will have a single unary set symbol $X$ representing the set being classified. Inclusion of these symbols in every language will be implicit. The *base* language contains only these symbols. If $L$ has auxiliary symbols, then $L$ is denoted just by these symbols. For example, the language that has auxiliary symbols for plus and less than is denoted by $[+, <]$. The language that has auxiliary symbols for plus and times is denoted by $[+, \times]$. The language with extra symbols for successor and less than is denoted by $[S, <]$, where $S$ indicates the symbol for the successor operation. The symbol "$\star$" will be used to denote an arbitrary language that includes all the symbols common to all the languages we consider and some (possibly empty) subset of operational symbols denoting operations. e.g. $+$, $<$, $\times$ and $S$. These operations need not be computable.

By convention, all questions are assumed to be sentences in prenex normal form (quantifiers followed by a quantifier-free formula, called the matrix of the formula) and questions containing quantifiers are assumed to begin with an existential quantifier. This convention entails no loss of generality.

Let $L$ be a language. The class $QDE[L]$ is the collection of all sets $\mathcal{A}$ such that there exists a q.c.f. $F$ that classifies $\mathcal{A}$ and only asks queries that use the symbols in $L$. We denote this by saying "$\mathcal{A} \in QDE[L]$ via $F$." The class $QDE_c[L]$ is the collection of all sets in $QDE[L]$ that have classification functions that change there mind about each $f$ at most $c$ times. The initial change from DK to either YES or NO is not counted as a mind change.

All the query languages that we will consider allow the use of quantifiers. Restricting the applications of quantifiers is a technique that we will use to regulate the expressive power of a language. Of concern to us is the alternations between blocks of existential and universal quantifiers. Suppose that $f \in QDE[L](F)$ for some $F$ and $L$. If $F$ only asks quantifier-free questions, then we will say that $f \in Q_0DE[L](F)$. If $F$ only asks questions with existential quantifiers, then we will say that $f \in Q_1DE[L](F)$ In general, if $F$'s questions begin with an existential quantifier and involve $a > 0$ alternations between blocks of universal and existential quantifiers, then we say that $f \in Q_{a+1}DE[L](F)$. The classes $Q_aDE[L]$ and $Q_aDE_c[L]$ are defined analogously. By convention, if a QDE restricted to $c$ mind changes actually achieves that bound, then it will ask no further questions.

# 3 Decisions with Queries

## 3.1 Existential queries but no mind changes

We show that $Q_1DE_0[\star]$ is not very powerful.

THEOREM 1. $Q_1DE_0[\star] \subseteq DE_\star$

PROOF: Let $F$ be any q.c.f. that shows some $\mathcal{A} \in Q_1DE_0[\star]$. We can construct a $DE_\star$ function $F'$ such that $F'$ simulates $F$. Since $F$ is allowed only $\exists$ questions we first answer NO to a query until later evidence is found otherwise. The number of questions asked by the q.c.f. is finite since it is allowed only one guess. Hence $F'$ can answer those questions by waiting and seeing the inputs from the function. ☒

Using the same proof technique Theorem 1 can be extended to show $Q_{a+1}DE_0[\star] \subseteq Q_aDE_\star[\star]$ where $a \in N$.

COROLLARY 2. $a \in N$, $Q_{a+1}DE_0[\star] \subseteq Q_aDE_\star[\star]$

We now show that Theorem 1 is optimal in terms of (1) mindchanges for $DE$ (2) mindchanges for $QDE$, and (3) quantifiers for $QDE$.

THEOREM 3. $(\forall n \geq 0)[Q_1DE_0[\star] - DE_n \neq \emptyset]$.

PROOF: The set used in the proof of this theorem consists of all possible step functions which tail off with an even number that is $\leq 2n$. Formally
$$\mathcal{A} = \bigcup_{i=0}^n \{0^\star 1^\star 2^\star \cdots (2i-1)^\star (2i)^\omega\}$$

We show $\mathcal{A} \in Q_1DE_0[\star]$. Let $F$ be the q.c.f. that operates as follows.

0) Set $i = n$.

1) $F$ asks $(\exists x)\ [f(x) = 2i]$. If the answer is yes goto step (3), if the answer is no goto step (2).

2) If $(i = 0)$ then $F$ outputs NO and QUITS, else set $i = i - 1$ and goto step (1).

3) $F$ waits until it sees $2i$ and $x_0$ such that $f(x_0) = 2i$. It also makes sure that the initial segment of the function it has seen so far is from one of the functions in $\mathcal{A}$. If it is not the case $F$ outputs NO, else $F$ asks $(\forall x)\ [x \neq 0,\ x \neq 1,\ \cdots,\ x \neq x_0\ f(x) = 2i]$. If the answer is no then $F$ outputs NO else outputs YES.

We will show that $\mathcal{A} \notin DE_n$. Assume, by way of contradiction, that $F$ is a c.f. for $\mathcal{A} \in DE_n$. We construct a function $f$ that leads to contradiction.

0) Let $t = 0$, $\sigma = \emptyset$.

1) ($t$ is even and $t \leq 2n$) Extend $\sigma$ with more and more values of $t$ until $F$ produces a YES. Set $t = t + 1$.

2) ($t$ is odd) Extend $\sigma$ with more and more values of $t$ until $F$ produces NO. Set $t = t + 1$. If $t \leq 2n$ then and goto step (1) else exit the construction.

The construction produces a finite initial segment that forces $F$ to change its mind $2n$ times. Let $f$ be any extension of that segment. Since $F$ changes its mind $2n$ times while classifying $f$, and it was supposed to only change its mind $n$ times, we have a contradiction. ⊠

THEOREM 4. $Q_1DE_1[\star] - DE_\star \neq \emptyset$

PROOF: Let $\mathcal{A} = \{f \mid f =^* 0\}$.

We will exhibit a q.c.f. $F$ such that $\mathcal{A} \in Q_1DE_1[\star]$ via $F$. Given any $f$, $F$ execute the following steps. Let $i$ be a variable.

0) Set $i = 0$ and $A = \emptyset$.

1) $F$ asks $(\exists x)[x \notin A \wedge f(x) \neq 0]$. If the answer is no then $F$ outputs YES forever more. If the answer is yes then (1) by observing $f$ find an $a$ such that $a \notin A$ and $f(a) \neq 0$, (2) let $A$ be $A \cup \{a\}$, (3) output NO, and (4) repeat this step.

It is easy to see that this q.c.f. will classify $\mathcal{A}$.

We show $\mathcal{A} \notin DE_\star$. Assume, by way of contradiction, that $\mathcal{A} \in DE_\star$ via c.f. $F$. We will construct an $f$ that leads to a contradiction.

0) Let $\sigma = \emptyset$.

1) Extend $\sigma$ with more and more values of zeros until $F$ produces a YES. Goto step 2.

2) Extend $\sigma$ with more and more values of 1 until $F$ produces a NO. Goto step 1.

Let $f$ be the limit of the $\sigma$'s. Clearly $F$ does not converge while trying to classify $f$. Hence $F$ does not classify $\mathcal{A}$. ⊠

We would like to proof that Theorem 1 is optimal in terms of number of quantifiers. We do not have this for general langauges but we do have it for any language that contains $<$. It is an open question to obtain this result for the empty language.

THEOREM 5. $Q_2DE_0[<] - DE_\star \neq \emptyset$

PROOF: Let $\mathcal{A} = \{f \mid f =^* 0\}$ We show $\mathcal{A} \in Q_2DE_0[<] - DE_\star$

$\mathcal{A} \in Q_2DE_0[<]$ via a $F$: The q.c.f $F$ operates as follows. Given any $f$ $F$ asks $(\exists y)(\forall x > y)[f(x) = 0]$. If the answer is Yes then $F$ conjectures YES, else NO. Clearly $F$ classifies $\mathcal{A}$.

We show $\mathcal{A} \notin DE_\star$. Assume, by way of contradiction, that $\mathcal{A} \in DE_\star$ via c.f. $F$. We will construct an $f$ that leads to a contradiction.

0) Let $\sigma = \emptyset$.

1) Extend $\sigma$ with more and more values of zeros until $F$ produces a YES. Goto step 2.

2) Extend $\sigma$ with more and more values of 1 until $F$ produces a NO. Goto step 1.

Let $f$ be the limit of the $\sigma$'s. Clearly $F$ does not converge while trying to classify $f$. Hence $F$ does not classify $\mathcal{A}$. ⊠

COROLLARY 6. $Q_1DE_*[\star] - DE_* \neq \emptyset$

PROOF: Using Corollary 2 and Theorem 5 the result follows.    ☒

## 3.2  Existential queries and $n \geq 1$ mindchanges

THEOREM 7. Let $n \geq 1$. a) $DE_n \subset Q_1DE_n[\star]$. b) $DE_* \subset Q_1DE_*[\star]$.

PROOF: The inclusions are obvious. The inclusions are proper by Theorem 4.    ☒

We show that Theorem 7 is optimal. We need some of the machinery from [3].

DEFINITION 8. A finite function is a cycle if it is of the form

$$\{(a+i, a+i+1)|0 \leq i < k\} \cup \{(a+k, a)\},$$

where $a, k \in N$ and $k \geq 1$. The cycle above has *starting point* $a$ and *length* $k$. It is denoted by $C(a, k)$.

LEMMA 9. Let $\Theta$ be an existential query, $\sigma$ a finite initial segment such that $\sigma(0) = 0$. Assume that for all functions $h$ such that $h$ extends $\sigma$ and $(h - \sigma)$ is cycle-free, $h$ does not make $\Theta$ true. Then there exists $k \geq 1$ with the following property: if $g$ extends $\sigma$ and the only cycles in $(g - \sigma)$ are of length $\geq k$, then $g$ does not make $\Theta$ true.

PROOF: Similar to Lemma 14 of [3].    ☒

THEOREM 10. $(\forall n > 0)$  $DE_n - Q_1DE_{n-1}[\star] \neq \emptyset$.

PROOF: We prove this theorem for $n$ even. The proof for $n$ odd is similar.

Let $\mathcal{A} = \{f | f$ has 1 or 3 $\cdots$ or $n - 1$ cycles $\}$

We construct a c.f $F$ such that $\mathcal{A} \in DE_n$ via $F$. Given any $f$, $F$ executes the following steps.

0) Let $i = 0$. ($i$ will keep track of the number of cycles seen.)

1) (We have seen $i \leq n$ cycles and $i$ is even.) While looking at the function output NO. Look for an $i + 1$st cycle in $f$. If such is observed then (1) set $i = i + 1$ and (2) if $i < n$ then goto step else output NO continiously.

2) (We have seen $i \leq n$ cycles and $i$ is odd.) While looking at the function output YES. Look for an $i + 1$st cycle in $f$. If such is observed then let $i = i + 1$ and goto step (1).

It is easy to see that the function $F$ classifies $\mathcal{A}$

We show that $\mathcal{A} \notin Q_1DE_{n-1}[\star]$. Assume, by way of contradiction, that $\mathcal{A} \in Q_1DE_{n-1}[\star]$ via $F$. We will construct an $f$ that causes a contradiction.

0) Let $\sigma = \emptyset$, let $i = 0$. ($i$ will count the number of cycles in $f$.) Let $\Theta$ be the statement $(\exists x)[f(x) = x + 1 \land f(x + 1) = x]$. (The only important property of $\Theta$ is no finite cycle free extension of $\sigma$ can make it true. $\Theta$ and $\sigma$ will have this property throughout the construction.)

1) $(i \leq n)$ Let $q$ be the current query produced by $F$. If a cycle free finite extension for $\sigma$ exists such that $q$ is true, then extend $\sigma$ using that extension, answer the query $q$ as true. If not answer $q$ as false and set $\Theta = \Theta \wedge q$. (The queries we answered yes will remain true nomatter how $\sigma$ is extended. The queries we answered no form $\Theta$ which can be made into an existential question. No finite cycle free extention can makes $\Theta$ true.) If $i$ is even then repeat this step until $F$ produces a YES. If $i$ is odd then repeat this step until $F$ produces a NO. (This must happen since $F$ classifies $\mathcal{A}$.) Goto step (2).

2) By Lemma 9 there exists an extension of $\sigma$ that has a new cycle and is consistent with the answers to all the queries. Extend $\sigma$ using this extension and set $i = i + 1$. If $i \leq n$ then goto step (1) else exit.

At the end of the construction we have a finite initial segment $\sigma$. Let $f$ be a cycle-free extension of $\sigma$. If $F$ tries to classify $f$ then $n$ mindchanges will be encountered. This contradicts the nature of $F$. ⊠

## 3.3 Unbounded quantification

We have seen that minchanges impose a restriction and queries enhance with power. The question arises as to whether the restriction of queries can overcome the limitation of mindchanges. The next theorem shows that mindchanges can be so severe a restriction that even unbounded queries do not help.

THEOREM 11. $DE_1 - Q_* DE_0[\star] \neq \emptyset$

PROOF: Let the language have symbols $S_1, S_2, \ldots$. Let $\mathbf{s}_i$ be the Turing degree of $S_i$. Let $B$ be a set of Turing degree $\bigoplus_{i=1}^{\infty} \mathbf{s}_i$. Let $A = B'$. Finally, let $\mathcal{A} = \{A\}$. (That is, $\mathcal{A}$ is the singleton set that contains one 0-1 valued function which is the characteristic function of $A$.) We show $\mathcal{A} \in DE_1 - Q_* DE_0[\star]$.

$\mathcal{A} \in DE_1$: Initially the classifier guesses YES. If ever the function being observed differs from $\chi_A$ guess NO forever more.

$\mathcal{A} \notin Q_* DE_0[\star]$. Assume, by way of contradiction, that $\mathcal{A} \in Q_* DE_0[\star]$ via q.c.f $F$. Since $\mathcal{A}$ contains just 0-1 valued functions we can assume the queries have a set symbol $X$ instead of a function symbol. Simluate $F$ by answering questions as though $A$ is the set being classified. After a finite number of questions $F$ will produce a YES. Let $q(X)$ be the conjunction of all queries asked about $A$ that were true and the negations of those that were false. Note that if $C$ is any set such that $q(C)$ is true then $F$ will classify $C \in \mathcal{A}$.

We claim

$$(\forall x)[x \in A \rightarrow q(X) \vdash x \in X];$$

$$(\forall x)[x \notin A \rightarrow q(X) \vdash x \notin X];$$

We proof the first one, the second is similar. Assume, by way of contradiction, that $(\exists x_0)[x_0 \in A \wedge q(X) \not\vdash x_0 \in X]$. Then the set of sentences $\{q(X), x_0 \in X\}$ is a consistent set of sentences. By the completeness theorem this set has a model. This model is a set $C$ such that $q(C)$ is true but $x_0 \notin C$. Since $x_0 \notin C$ we know $C \neq A$; but since $q(C)$ is true $F$ will classify $C \in \mathcal{A}$ so $C = A$. This is a contradiction.

We can use there two facts to obtain a reduction $A \leq_T B$: on input $x$ enumerate all proofs that can use $q(X)$ as an axiom (you need the set $B$ to be able to use $q(X)$ intelligently) until either $x \in X$ or $x \notin X$ is derived. Whichever one is derived is true for $A$. Since $A = B'$ we have $B' \leq_T B$ which is a contradiction. ☒

It is an open question to extend Theorem 11.

**Conjecture** $DE_n - Q_*DE_{n-1}[\star] \neq \emptyset$. However, if we specify the language to $[S, <]$ we can obtain the result.

**DEFINITION 12.** A string is *dull* if it is of the form $\sigma(\tau)^{|\sigma|}$ where $3 \leq |\tau| \leq |\sigma|$.

**THEOREM 13.** $DE_{n+1} - QDE_n[S, <] \neq \emptyset$.

**PROOF:** We prove this for $n$ odd. The proof for $n$ even is similar.

Let $\mathcal{A} = \{A \mid A$ has either $1, 3, \ldots,$ or $n$ dull prefixes$\}$. We show that $\mathcal{A} \in DE_{n+1} - QDE_n[S, <]$.

$\mathcal{A} \in DE_{n+1}$: Initially conjecture NO. If an $i$th dull prefix is seen where $i$ is odd and $i \leq n$ then say YES. If an $i$th dull prefix is seen where $i$ is even or $i \geq n + 1$ then say NO.

$\mathcal{A} \notin QDE_n[S, <]$: Assume, by way of contradiction, that $\mathcal{A} \in QDE_n[S, <]$ via q.f.l $F$. We construct a set $A$ that $F$ does not classify correctly.

CONSTRUCTION

1) Set $A$ to a set that has no dull prefixes. Set $MC$ and $ND$ to 0. ($MC$ is the number of mindchanges seen so far; $ND$ is the number of dull prefixes seens so far.)

2) ($MC$ and $ND$ are even and $\leq n + 1$.) Simulate $F$. Answer questions about it as if the set is $A$. Stop when the conjecture is NO. (This must happen.) If $ND = n + 1$ then stop. Else set $MC$ to $MC + 1$.

3) Let $N$ be the $\omega$-automata that accepts all languages that satisfy the query answers supplied in the simulation. Not that $N$ accepts $A$. Therefore we can find $\sigma, \tau \in \{0, 1\}^*$, $\gamma \in \{0, 1\}^\omega$, and $i < |\sigma|$ such that $A = \sigma(\tau)^i \gamma$, $\sigma(\tau)^{i+1} \not\preceq A$, and $N$ accepts $\sigma(\tau)^j \gamma$ for any $j \geq i$. Note that the set $\sigma(\tau)^{|\sigma|}\gamma$ has *exactly* one more dull prefix then $A$. Set $A$ to $\sigma(\tau)^{|\sigma|}\gamma$ and $ND$ to $ND + 1$. Note that the answers supplied by the simulation are also correct for the new $A$.

4) ($MC$ and $ND$ are odd and $\leq n$.) Simulate $F$. Answer questions about it as if the set is $A$. Stop when the conjecture is YES. (This must happen.) Set $MC$ to $MC + 1$ and goto step

5) Identical to step 3 except that when its over we goto step 2.

END OF CONSTRUCTION

The set $A$ we obtain at the end forces $F$ to change its mind $n + 1$ times, which is a contradiction. ☒

# 4 Classification with Mind Changes and Anomalies

In this section we establish exactly when $DE_a^b \subseteq DE_c^d$.

**DEFINITION 14.** Let $\mathcal{A}$ be any set, $|\mathcal{A}|$ will denote the cardinality of $\mathcal{A}$.

DEFINITION 15. Let $f$ and $g$ be functions, if $|\{x | g(x) \neq f(x)\}| \leq a$, then we say that $g$ is an *a variant of f* .

DEFINITION 16. Let $\mathcal{A}$ be a set of functions, $F$ a classification function, $a \in N$ and $f$ be any function. We say $f \in DE^a(F)$ if $F(f) \downarrow$ to YES, then $f \in \mathcal{A}$ and no $a$ variant of $f$ is in the complement of $\mathcal{A}$ or if $F(f) \downarrow$ to NO, then $f \notin \mathcal{A}$ and no $a$ variant of $f$ is in $\mathcal{A}$. Note that for functions that are in $\mathcal{A}$ but have a-variants in $\overline{\mathcal{A}}$ there are no constraints on what $F$ will do.

THEOREM 17. $(\forall a > 0)$ and $(\forall n \geq 0)$ $DE_a - DE_{a-1}^n \neq \emptyset$

PROOF: Let $a > 0$ and $n \geq 0$ be given.

**Case 1.** $a$ even, let $b = a/2$.

Let $\mathcal{A} = \{f |$ range $f$ has exactly $2(n+1)$ 1's or $4(n+1)$ 1's or $\cdots$ or $2b(n+1)$ 1's $\}$.

We show $\mathcal{A} \in DE_a$. Let $F$ be a classification function such that given any $f$ it initially conjectures NO, then waits until it sees $2(n+1)$ ones and then says YES. If $F$ sees a one, it changes its conjecture to NO. Waits for a total of $4(n+1)$ ones and changes its conjeucture to YES. It can repeat this process until it sees $2b(n+1)$ ones and says YES. Up to now $M$ has made $2b$ conjectures. If $F$ sees an additional one it will say NO. Clearly $F$ has made at most $2b+1$ conjeuctures and $F$ is correct. Since $2b = a$, $\mathcal{A} \subseteq DE_a(F)$.

We show $\mathcal{A} \notin DE_{a-1}^n$. Assume, by way of contraction, that $\mathcal{A} \in DE_{a-1}^n$ via $F$. We will construct an $f$ that causes a contradiction.

0) Let $\sigma = \emptyset$.

1) Extend $\sigma$ with $(n+1)$ ones and then with more and more zeros until $F$ produces NO. (This must happen since the resulting function is in $\overline{\mathcal{A}}$ and no $n$-variant is in $\mathcal{A}$.) Goto step (2).

2) Extend $\sigma$ with $(n+1)$ ones. Then extend $\sigma$ with zeros, until $F$ changes its produces YES. (This must happen since the resulting function is in $\mathcal{A}$ and no $n$-variant is in $\overline{\mathcal{A}}$.) Goto step (1).

Clearly, $F$ has to make $2b+1$ conjectures to be correct on a function with $(2b+1)(n+1)$ ones, or it has converged to a wrong conjecture. Hence $\mathcal{A} \notin DE_{a-1}^n$ for the case $a$ even.

**Case 2.** $a$ odd, let $b = (a+1)/2$.

Let $\mathcal{A} = \{f |$ range $f$ has exactly $2(n+1)$ 1's or $4(n+1)$ 1's $\cdots$ or $\geq 2b(n+1)$ 1's $\}$.

The rest of the proof is similar to the proof in case (1). ⊠

DEFINITION 18. Let $f$ and $g$ be functions, if $|\{x | g(x) \neq f(x)\}|$ is finite then we say $g$ is a *finite variant of f*.

DEFINITION 19. Let $\mathcal{A}$ be a set of functions, $F$ a classification function and $f$ be any function. We say $f \in DE^*(F)$ if $F(f) \downarrow$ to YES, then $f \in \mathcal{A}$ and no finite variant of $f$ is in the complement of $\mathcal{A}$, or $F(f) \downarrow$ to NO, then $f$ in the complement of $\mathcal{A}$ and no finite variant of $f$ is in $\mathcal{A}$.

THEOREM 20. $(\forall n \geq 0)$ $DE_0^{n+1} - DE_*^n \neq \emptyset$

PROOF: Let

$\mathcal{A} = \{f |$ number of 1's in the range of $f$ is a multiple of $2(n+1)$ or is infinite$\}$.

Let $f$ be any function. If $f$ has an infinite number of 1's then $f \in \mathcal{A}$. If $f$ has a finite number of 1's then that number is at most $n+1$ away from a multiple of $2(n+1)$. Hence $f$ is an $n$-variant of some function in $\mathcal{A}$. This is true for *any* $f$. Hence the c.f. that always answers YES shows that $\mathcal{A} \in DE_0^{n+1}$.

We show that $\mathcal{A} \notin DE_*^n$. Assume, by way of contradiction, that $\mathcal{A} \in DE_*^n$ via $F$. We will construct an $f$ that leads to a constradiction.

0) Let $\sigma = \emptyset$,

1) (the number of 1's seen so far is an even multiple of $n+1$) Extend $\sigma$ with more and more zeros until $F$ says YES. (This must happen since the resulting function is in $\mathcal{A}$ and no $n$-variant of it is in $\overline{\mathcal{A}}$.) Add $n+1$ 1's and goto to step (2).

2) (the number of 1's seen so far is an odd multiple of $n+1$) Extend $\sigma$ with more and more zeros until $F$ says NO. (This must happen since the resulting function is in $\overline{\mathcal{A}}$ and no $n$-variant of it is in $\mathcal{A}$.)

Let $f$ be the limit of the $\sigma$'s. Clearly $F$ does not converge on $f$. This contradicts the nature of $F$.                                                   ☒

THEOREM 21. $DE_1 \subset DE_0^*$

PROOF: By Theorem 20 $DE_0^* - DE_1 \neq \emptyset$. Now we will show the inclusion. Let $\mathcal{A} \in DE_1$ via $F$. Now we will construct an $F'$ such that $\mathcal{A} \in DE_0^*$ via $F'$

Let $f$ be any function, now $F$ on some initial segment $\sigma$ of $f$ will conjecture G (either YES or NO). Now $F'$ simulates $F$, by feeding all possible extensions of $\sigma$ and checks for a mind change. If no mind change is found then $F'$ output $F$'s initial conjecture G, else output the new conjecture output by $F$.

Clearly if $F$ does not change its mind, then $F'$'s conjecture G (which was $F$'s only conjecture) is correct. If $F$ changes its mind, then the new conjecture was output by $F$ after seeing $\sigma\tau$ for some segment $\tau$.

Case 1 $\sigma\tau$ is initial segment of $f$.

   $F$'s new conjecture must be correct, hence $F'$'s new conjecture is correct.

Case 2 $\sigma\tau$ is initial segment of some function $g \in \mathcal{A}$.

   If $f \in \mathcal{A}$, since $g \in \mathcal{A}$ $F$'s conjecture would be YES hence, $F'$'s new conjecture would be correct. If $f \notin \mathcal{A}$, since $g$ is a finite variant of $f$ and $g \in \mathcal{A}$, by definition of $DE^*$ $F'$ can conjecture any thing, hence it is correct.

Case 3 $\sigma\tau$ is initial segment of some function $g \notin \mathcal{A}$.

   If $f \notin \mathcal{A}$ then $F'$'s new conjecture is correct. If $f \in \mathcal{A}$, since $g$ is a finite variant of $f$ by the definition of $DE^*$ $F'$'s conjecture is correct.

                                                   ☒

THEOREM 22. $(\forall a, b, n, m \in N)$ $DE_n^a \subseteq DE_m^b$ if and only if $(a \leq b)$ and $(n \leq m)$.

PROOF: $\Rightarrow$ Let $a, b, n, m \in N$ be given. Suppose $DE_n^a \subseteq DE_m^b$ and $a > b$. Then by Theorem 20 $DE_n^a - DE_m^b \neq \emptyset$. Hence $a \leq b$. suppose $DE_n^a \subseteq DE_m^b$ and $n > m$. Then by Theorem 17 $DE_n^a - DE_m^b \neq \emptyset$. Hence $n \leq m$.

$\Leftarrow$ Let $a, b, n, m \in N$ be given. if $(a \leq b)$ and $(n \leq m)$ the result is obvious. ⊠

Note the above Theorem 22 will not hold if $b = *$ since it will contradict Theorem 21

# 5 Decisions with Teams

Team inference was introduced by Smith [7]. Next we define team classification similar to team inference defined by Smith.

DEFINITION 23. For $n, m \in N$ such that $n \leq m$, $a \in N$ and for any $f$, $[n, m]DE_a$ denotes a team of $m$ classifiers out of which at least $n$ of them correctly classify $f$ after at most $a$ mind changes.

THEOREM 24. Let $\mathcal{A}$ be any set of functions then $\mathcal{A} \in [1, 2]DE_0$.

PROOF: Let $F_1$ and $F_2$, be two classification functions which do the following: on input from any function $f$, $F_1$ will always conjecture YES and $F_2$ will always conjecture NO. ⊠

THEOREM 25. $(\forall n > 0)$ $[n + 1, 2n + 1]DE_0 = DE_0$

PROOF: Let $\mathcal{A} \in [n + 1, 2n + 1]DE_0$, this implies that there exists classifications functions $F_1, F_2, \cdots, F_{2n+1}$ such that on any $f$ $n + 1$ of these classifiers can correctly classify $f$ with respect to $\mathcal{A}$. We will construct a classification function $F$ such that $\mathcal{A} \subseteq DE_0(F)$. $F$ simulates the the team by waiting for at least $n + 1$ of the team members to agree (either YES or NO). Then $F$ outputs that answer. This implies that $[n + 1, 2n + 1]DE_0 \subseteq DE_0$. Clearly $DE_0 \subseteq [n + 1, 2n + 1]DE_0$. ⊠

# References

1) L. Fortnow, S. Jain, W. Gasarch, E. Kinbar, M. Kummer, S. Kurtz, M. Pleszkoch, T. Slaman, F. Stephan and R. Solovay, *Extremes in the Degrees of Inferability*, Annals of pure and applied logic (to appear).

2) E. M. Gold, *Learning Identification in the Limit*, Information and Control, vol 10, 1967, pp. 447-474.

3) William Gasarch, Mark Pleszkoch and Robert Solovay, *Learning via Queries to* [+, <]", Journal of Symbolic Logic; vol 57, March 1992, pp. 53-81.

4) William Gasarch and Carl H. Smith, *Learning via Queries*, Journal of the Association for Computing Machinery, vol 39, July 1992, pp. 649-675.

5) William Gasarch, Efim Kinber, Mark Pleszkoch, Carl Smith, and Thomas Zeugmann, *Learning via Queries with Teams and Anomalies*, Fundamenta Informaticae (to appear).

# Classifying Recursive Predicates and Languages*

## Rolf Wiehagen[†]

Universität Kaiserslautern
Fachbereich Informatik
P.O. Box 3049
67653 Kaiserslautern, Germany
wiehagen@informatik.uni-kl.de

## Carl H. Smith[‡]

Department of Computer Science
University of Maryland
College Park,
MD 20742 USA
smith@cs.umd.edu

## Thomas Zeugmann[§]

TH Darmstadt
Institut für Theoretische Informatik
Alexanderstr. 10
64283 Darmstadt, Germany
zeugmann@iti.informatik.th-darmstadt.de

### Abstract

Our goal is to arrive at a deeper understanding of the classification problem. We study a particular collection of classification problems, the classification of recursive predicates and languages. In particular, we compare the classification of predicates and languages with the classification of arbitrary recursive functions and with learning. Moreover, we refine our investigations by introducing classification within a resource bound and establish a new hierarchy. Furthermore, we introduce a formalization of *multi-classification* and characterize it. Finally, we study the classification of families of languages that have attracted a lot of attention in learning theory.

---

*A preliminary version of this paper appeared at the first European Workshop on Computational Learning Theory

[†]The first author was supported by the German Ministry for Research and Technology (BMFT) under grant no. 01 IW 101 E7.

[‡]The second author was supported in part by NSF Grants 9020079 and 9301339.

[§]The current address of the third author is: Research Institute of Fundamental Information Science,Kyushu University 33, Fukuoka, 812 Japan, thomas@rifis.sci.kyushu-u.ac.jp

6) Kelly, Kevin T., 1994, *The Logic of Reliable Inquiry* Oxford: Oxford University Press, forthcoming.

7) C. H. Smith, *The Power of Pluralism for Automatic Program Synthesis*, Journal of the Association for Computing Machinery, vol 29, 1982, pp. 1144-1165.

8) L. G. Valiant, *A theory of Learnable*, Communications of the ACM, vol 27, 1987, pp.1134-1142.

9) R. Wiehagen and C.H. Smith, *Classification versus Generalization*, in Proceedings 5th Annual ACM Workshop on Computational Learning Theory, Pittsburgh (1992), pp. 224-230, ACM Press, New York.

10) R. Wiehagen, C.H. Smith and T. Zeugmann *Classifying Recursive Predicates and Languages*, Gossler Report 21/93, December 93.

# 1. Introduction

*Learning* and *classification* have attracted considerable attention by computer scientists, both in theory and practice. *Inductive inference* is an important aspect of learning that has been widely studied (cf. Angluin and Smith (1983, 1987)). The inductive inference problem is to take finite samples of some target concept and to *generalize* an algorithm that can produce all other samples of the same concept. Hence, inductive inference may be regarded as the most general framework to study the *generalization problem* (cf. Michalski et al. (1983)). The *classification problem* may be described as follows: Given a number of, usually finite, choices, one takes finite samples of a target concept and has to find out algorithmically to which of the possible choices the concept belongs (cf. Duda and Hart (1973)).

Recently, the problem of classification has been compared with the inductive inference problem in a recursion theoretic setting (cf. Wiehagen and Smith (1994)). In that paper a new formalization of classification was introduced. The algorithms studied there classified arbitrary functions. Herein, we consider the classification of $\{0, 1\}$ valued functions. These functions are often called *predicates* as they represent binary decisions on the input. By utilizing the isomorphism between strings of symbols and the natural numbers, the predicates over the natural numbers also represent *formal languages*. Hence, we simultaneously study the classification of predicates and languages. Previous studies of learning have revealed some subtle and not so subtle differences between the learning of functions versus the learning of languages. We are interested in learning the differences and similarities between the classification of predicates and arbitrary recursive functions.

Our interest in such a restricted class of functions stems from consideration of some practical classification problems where the input is similarly restricted. Many such classification problems exist. We give two examples. Consider the problem of medical diagnosis. Every patient can be abstractly modeled as a mapping from symptoms to an indication of their presence or absence. The goal is to classify the collection of symptoms as to which malady is manifesting them. While there are clearly only finitely many possible symptoms, an a priori restriction on their number would place a technological bound on the applicability of our results. Our orientation is theoretical and we are hoping for results with longevity in the midst of a rapidly changing technological base.

As another example of when classification input can be restricted to examples of predicates considered the problem of battlefield arena classification. The presence or absence of various types of weaponry and terrain features may be sufficient to produce a useful classification. In this example, we formally consider the classification of functions that map the myriad of weapons and landscape parameters to single bits, representing their inclusion in the scene.

In both of the above examples, it appears that they would still be within the scope of classification results that applied only to predicates. The hope is that by pushing the study of classification of predicates far enough, a difference with the unrestricted classification will be reveled that suggests an enhancement that can be made in proposed solutions to problems such as the ones described above.

Aside from having their input restricted to predicates, there is another feature shared by the two examples above. For a given set of characteristics, there may be several simultaneously appropriate classifications. In the case of medical diagnosis, it is crucial to know all of the potential diseases that may be manifesting the observed symptoms. We call this variant of the classification problem called *multi-classification* where the object is to identify all the appropriate classifications. The multi-classification problem is known to be very difficult (cf. Bylander et al. (1991) and Cho and Reggia (1993)). We prove that every multi-classification problem is equivalent to a classification problem, but the cardinality of the potential choices increases exponentially.

The technical approach of the present paper has five parts. First, we apply the previously developed formalism to investigate the classification of $\{0,1\}$ valued recursive functions. Secondly, we consider the case were the classification algorithm is to produce *all* of the correct classifications (cf. Definition 3). Thirdly, we compare the power of classification algorithms that are allowed to produce only a single guess (finite classification, cf. Definition 2, the $c = 0$ case) with those that may change their mind a predetermined fixed number of times (cf. Definition 2, the $c \in \mathbb{N}$ case). Fourthly, we introduce the notion of *consistent* classification (cf. Definition 4) and compare it with general classification. The goal of these studies is to find some other reasonable restrictions that may make a profound difference on the classifyability of certain sets of functions. Finally, we study classification of families of languages that have received considerable attention in learning theory and elsewhere in computer science.

## 2. Technical Preliminaries

By $\mathbb{N} = \{0,1,2,...\}$ we denote the set of all natural numbers. Members of $\mathbb{N}$ will serve as names for programs. The function computed by program $i$ will be denoted by $\varphi_i$. Most reasonable ways of assigning names to programs results in a list $\varphi_0$, $\varphi_1$, ... called an *acceptable programming system* (cf. Machtey and Young (1978)). By $\mathcal{R}$ we denote the class of all recursive functions. The class of $\{0,1\}$ valued recursive functions, our model of both predicates and languages, is denoted by $\mathcal{R}_{0,1}$. A set is *recursively enumerable* (r.e.) iff it is the domain of some $\varphi_i$. A more intuitive, equivalent characterization of the r.e. sets is to call a set r.e. if it is either the range of a recursive function or it is empty. In this way it is easy to see that the r.e. sets are the ones for which we can write a procedure that prints out, eventually, all and only members of the set in question. The $i^{\text{th}}$ r.e. set, corresponding to the domain of $\varphi_i$, is denoted by $W_i$. A collection $C$ of recursive functions is an *r.e. set of recursive functions* iff there is a recursive function $f$ such that $C = \{\varphi_{f(i)} | i \in \mathbb{N}\}$. By NUM we denote the collection of all subsets of r.e. sets of recursive functions. Subset is denoted by $\subseteq$ and $\subset$ denotes *proper* subset. The quantifier $\forall^\infty$ is interpreted as "all but finitely many." For a function $f \in \mathcal{R}$ and $n \in \mathbb{N}$, let $f^n = \text{cod}(f(0), f(1), ..., f(n))$, where cod denotes a computable and bijective mapping from the set $\mathbb{N}^*$ of all finite sequences of natural numbers onto $\mathbb{N}$. Sometimes, for the sake of simplicity of notation, we identify $\alpha \in \mathbb{N}^*$ with $\text{cod}(\alpha)$, for $\alpha$ a finite function.

Whenever appropriate we shall represent a recursive function by the *sequence of its values.* For example, the sequence $0^2 1^3 2^\infty$ denotes the function

$$f(x) = \begin{cases} 0, & \text{if} \quad x < 2 \\ 1, & \text{if} \quad 2 \leq x < 5 \\ 2, & \text{otherwise} \end{cases}$$

Next, we formalize the models of identification and classification mentioned in the introduction. As in Gold (1967) we define an *inductive inference machine* (abbr. IIM) to be an algorithmic device which works as follows: The IIM takes as its input larger and larger initial segments of the graph of a function and it either requests the next function value, or it first outputs a hypothesis, i.e., a name of a program, and then it requests the next function value.

A classification machine (abbr. CM) takes as input the graph of a function (as IIMs do) and it either requests the next function value, or it first outputs an integer chosen from a finite set, and then it requests the next function value.

Let $M$ be an IIM or a CM. Furthermore, let $i$ and $j$ be two consecutive hypotheses produced by $M$. We say that $M$ changes its mind, or synonymously, $M$ performs a mind change, iff $i \neq j$. When dealing with mind changes, it is technically much more convenient to require the IIMs to behave as follows. Let $f$ be a recursive function. If $M$ on $f(0), ..., f(n)$ outputs its first guess, then it has to output a hypothesis at any subsequent step. It is easy to see that any IIM $M$ may be straightforwardly converted into an IIM $\hat{M}$ behaving as required such that both machines produce the same sequence of mind changes.

We start with the formalization of learning. The following definition is due to Gold (1967) (the $c = *$ case).

**Definition 1.** *Let $U \subseteq \mathcal{R}$ and let $c \in \mathbb{N} \cup \{*\}$. The class $U$ is said to be learnable with at most $c$ mind changes iff there is an IIM $M$ such that for all $f \in U$*

(1) *there is a $j$ such that $\varphi_j = f$ and $M(f^n) = j$ for almost all $n \in \mathbb{N}$,*

(2) *$M$, when successively fed $f(0)$, $f(1)$, ... performs at most $c$ ($c = *$ means at most finitely many) mind changes, i.e., $card(\{n \mid M(f^n) \neq M(f^{n+1})\}) \leq c$.*

If $U$ can be learned by an IIM $M$ with at most $c$ mind changes, then we write $U \in EX_c(M)$. The class of all sets of recursive functions that are learnable with at most $c$ mind changes is denoted by $EX_c$, an abbreviation for *explains* as a program for $f$ can be regarded as an explanation of the set of examples constituting the graph of $f$ (cf. Case and Smith (1983)). If $U$ can be learned with 0 mind changes, then we also say that $U$ is *finitely* learnable. Moreover, we set $FIN =_{df} EX_0$. If $c = *$, then we usually omit the lower index and simply say $U$ can be learned.

Next, we formalize classification of finitely many sets.

**Definition 2.** *Let $S_0, ..., S_{k-1} \subseteq \mathcal{R}$ and let $S = S_0 \cup ... \cup S_{k-1}$. Furthermore, let $c \in \mathbb{N} \cup \{*\}$. Then $(S_0, ..., S_{k-1})$ is said to be classifiable with at most $c$ mind changes iff there is a CM $M$ such that for all $f \in S$*

(1) *for all $n \in \mathbb{N}$, whenever $M$, on input $f^n$, outputs a hypothesis $j$, then $j \in \{0, ..., k-1\}$,*

(2) *there is a $j$ such that $f \in S_j$ and $M(f^n) = j$ for almost all $n \in \mathbb{N}$,*

(3) *$M$, when successively fed $f(0)$, $f(1)$, ... performs at most $c$ ($c = *$ means at most finitely many) mind changes, i.e., $card(\{n \mid M(f^n) \neq M(f^{n+1})\}) \leq c$.*

If $(S_0, ..., S_{k-1})$ is classified by a CM with at most $c$ mind changes, then we write $(S_0, ..., S_{k-1}) \in CL_k^c(M)$. By $CL_k^c$ we denote the collection of all $k$–tuples of sets that are classifiable with at most $c$ mind changes, i.e.,

$$CL_k^c = \{(S_0, ..., S_{k-1}) \mid \exists \text{CM } M \, [(S_0, ..., S_{k-1}) \in CL_k^c(M)]\}.$$

Moreover, we set $CL^c =_{df} \bigcup_{k \geq 2} CL_k^c$. If $c = *$, then we usually omit the upper index, and say simply that $(S_0, ..., S_{k-1})$ is classifiable. Furthermore, if $c = 0$, then we also say that $(S_0, ..., S_{k-1})$ is *finitely classifiable*, and set $FCL_k =_{df} CL_k^0$. In other words, a $k$–tuple $(S_0, ..., S_{k-1})$ is finitely classifiable if $M$'s first guess is always a correct one. Finally, we set $FCL =_{df} \bigcup_{k \geq 2} FCL_k$.

In the definition above requirement (1) specifies the set of allowed hypotheses. Clearly, any guess not contained in $\{0, ..., k-1\}$ cannot be correct. Hence, it is only natural to restrict the hypothesis space to the set $\{0, ..., k-1\}$. Nevertheless, this requirement does not restrict the capabilities of CMs. This can be seen as follows. Suppose we are given a CM $M$ classifying some $k$–tuple $(S_0, ..., S_{k-1})$ of sets that uses the set $\mathbb{N}$ as its hypothesis space. Then $M$ may be converted into a CM $\hat{M}$ satisfying requirement (1) such that $(S_0, ..., S_{k-1}) \in CL_k(\hat{M})$. On any input, the CM $\hat{M}$ simply simulates $M$. If $M$ outputs a guess from $\{0, ..., k-1\}$ then $\hat{M}$ behaves thus. Otherwise, $\hat{M}$ suppresses M's output and requests the next input. It is easy to prove that $CL_k^c(M) = CL_k^c(\hat{M})$. Consequently, when dealing with classification, class preserveness (cf. Jantke and Beick (1981)) can be realized without loss of generality. On the other hand, looking at IIMs the situation changes considerably. The analog of requirement (1) reads as "for all $f \in U$, all $n \in \mathbb{N}$, whenever $M$ on input $f^n$ outputs a hypothesis $j$, then $\varphi_j \in U$." However, the demand to work class preservingly does seriously restrict the learning power of IIMs (cf. Jantke and Beick (1981)).

In the next definition we explicitly consider the situation where the sets $S_0, ..., S_{k-1}$ are not necessarily disjoint. Looking at potential applications, it might be highly desirable not to obtain only *one* index of a set the target function $f$ belongs to, but the indices of *all* those that contain $f$. For example, consider the case of automated medical diagnosis. In this case, we would certainly desire to be aware of *all* the diseases that manifest the observed symptoms. In our formalism, each disease is represented by a set $S_i$ and the functions to be classified map symptoms to *present* or *not present*.

**Definition 3.** *Let $S_0, ..., S_{k-1} \subseteq \mathcal{R}$, and let $S = S_0 \cup ... \cup S_{k-1}$. Furthermore, let $ALL = \{0, ..., k-1\}$. Then $(S_0, ..., S_{k-1})$ is said to be multi–classifiable iff there is a CM $M$ such that for all $f \in S$*

(1) *for all $n \in \mathbb{N}$, whenever $M$, on input $f^n$, outputs a hypothesis HYP, then HYP $\subseteq$ ALL,*

(2) there is a non-empty set $SUB \subseteq ALL$ such that

    (a) $M(f^n) = SUB$ for almost all $n$,

    (b) $f \in S_j$ for all $j \in SUB$,

    (c) $f \notin S_m$ for all $m \in ALL \backslash SUB$.

If $(S_0, ..., S_{k-1})$ is multi–classified by a CM, then we write $(S_0, ..., S_{k-1}) \in Multi\text{-}CL_k(M)$. By $Multi\text{-}CL_k$ we denote the collection of all $k$–tuples of sets that are multi–classifiable. Furthermore, we set $Multi\text{-}CL = \bigcup_{k \geq 2} Multi\text{-}CL_k$.

Finally, we introduce *consistent* classification. The main intention is as follows. Since potential users of a CM $M$ never know whether $M$ has successfully finished its classification task, they might want to be sure that the actual hypotheses they receive correctly reflect the information the CM has received.

**Definition 4.** *Let* $S_0, ..., S_{k-1} \subseteq \mathcal{R}$ *and let* $S = S_0 \cup ... \cup S_{k-1}$. *Then* $(S_0, ..., S_{k-1})$ *is said to be consistently classifiable iff there is a CM $M$ such that*

(1) $(S_0, ..., S_{k-1}) \in CL_k(M)$,

(2) *for all* $f \in S$, *and for all* $n, i \in \mathbb{N}$, *if* $M(f^n) = i$, *then there must be a function* $g \in S_i$ *such that* $f$ *and* $g$ *coincide up to* $n$.

If $(S_0, ..., S_{k-1})$ is consistently classifiable by a CM $M$ then we write $(S_0, ..., S_{k-1}) \in Cons\text{-}CL_k(M)$. By $Cons\text{-}CL_k$ we denote the collection of all $k$–tuples of sets that are consistently classifiable. Finally, we set $Cons\text{-}CL =_{df} \bigcup_{k \geq 2} Cons\text{-}CL_k$.

## 3. Classification of Predicates versus Classification of Arbitrary Functions

In this section we compare the classification of $\{0, 1\}$ valued functions with the classification of functions in general. Looking at learning there are several results establishing major differences between the learnability of classes of predicates and the inferability of arbitrary classes of recursive functions (cf. Blum and Blum (1975), Zeugmann (1983, 1988), Osherson, Stob and Weinstein (1986)). Moreover, Freivalds, Kinber and Wiehagen (1992) discovered that consistent learning of predicates differs considerably from consistent identification of arbitrary recursive functions. Hence, it is only natural to ask whether there are differences between the classification of predicates and arbitrary recursive functions.

Clearly, if a collection of sets of $\{0, 1\}$ valued functions is classifiable, then it is classifiable as a collection of sets of arbitrary recursive functions. To consider the converse direction, we need the following notation. Let $S \subseteq \mathcal{R}$; then we use $\rho(S)$ to denote the restriction of $S$ to predicates, i.e., $\rho(S) = S \cap \mathcal{R}_{0,1}$.

**Theorem 1.** *There is a collection of pairwise disjoint sets* $S_0, S_1, S_2$ *such that*

(1) $\mathcal{R} = S_0 \cup S_1 \cup S_2$,

(2) $(S_0, S_1, S_2) \notin CL$,

(3) $(\rho(S_0), \rho(S_1), \rho(S_2)) \in CL_3^2$.

The theorem has the following corollary.

**Corollary 2.** *For any $n \geq 3$ there is a collection of pairwise disjoint sets exhausting $\mathcal{R}$ that is not in $CL_n$, but the collection of their restrictions to predicates is in $CL_n$.*

The latter results show that there might be interesting differences between the classification of predicates and arbitrary functions. Later on, we shall point out some more differences. In the next section we study the power of classification algorithms with respect to the number of mind changes allowed.

## 4. Finite Classification versus Classification and Learnability

Our next theorem states that even the classification of two sets might be too complex to be done by a finitely working CM. Furthermore, the anticipted distinction between classification and finite classification is manifested.

**Theorem 3.** *There are pairwise disjoint sets $S_0, S_1$ such that*

(1) $S_0 \cup S_1 = \mathcal{R}_{0,1}$,

(2) $(S_0, S_1) \in CL \setminus FCL$.

*Proof.* Let $S_0$ be the class containing only the function $0^\infty$. To immediately satisfy (1) and (2) above, let $S_1 = \mathcal{R}_{0,1} \setminus S_0$. A CM $M$ that classifies $(S_0, S_1)$ initially outputs "0" and then waits for a non zero input. When, and if, this input arrives, $M$ changes its mind to "1." Clearly, $(S_0, S_1) \in CL(M)$.

Suppose by way of contradiction that $\hat{M}$ is a CM such that $(S_0, S_1) \in FCL(\hat{M})$. Then there must be an $n$ such that $\hat{M}$, on input $0^n$, outputs "0" as its conjectured classification. If not, then $\hat{M}$ fails to classify $0^\infty$ as a member of $S_0$, a contradiction. On the other hand, $\hat{M}$ outputs, when successively fed $0^n 1^\infty$, the hypothesis "0" as its first guess. Therefore, $\hat{M}$ cannot finitely distinguish $0^\infty$ from $0^n 1^\infty$. Consequently, $\hat{M}$ fails to properly classify at least one of those functions. $\boxtimes$

The above theorem has an easy extension to the following:

**Theorem 4.** *For any $k > 1$ there are pairwise disjoint sets $S_0, \cdots, S_{k-1}$ such that*

(1) $S_0 \cup S_1 \cup \cdots \cup S_{k-1} = \mathcal{R}_{0,1}$,

(2) $(S_0, S_1, \cdots, S_{k-1}) \in CL \setminus FCL$.

*Proof.* Let $k > 1$ be arbitrarily fixed. For $0 \leq i < k - 1$, $S_i$ is the subset of $\mathcal{R}_{0,1}$ that contains only functions $f$ such that the cardinality of the set $\{x \mid f(x) \neq 0\}$ is exactly $i$. Moreover, we set $S_{k-1} = \mathcal{R}_{0,1} \setminus (S_0 \cup \cdots \cup S_{k-2})$. Clearly, (1) aboveis satisfied. A CM $M$ that classifies $S_0, S_1, \cdots, S_{k-1}$ initially outputs "0" and then reads input, counting the number of nonzero inputs. After a nonzero input is observed, resulting in a total of $j$ nonzero inputs, $M$ outputs the minimum of $\{j, k-1\}$. Clearly, $(S_0, S_1, \cdots, S_{k-1}) \in CL_k(M)$.

Suppose by way of contradiction that $M'$ is a CM such that $(S_0, S_1, \cdots, S_{k-1}) \in FCL_k(M')$. As in Theorem 3, there must be an $n$ such that $M'$, on input $0^n$ produces a conjecture "0." Then $M'$ will improperly classify at least one of $0^\infty$ or $0^n 10^\infty$. ⊠

In contrast to Theorem 4, it is possible to split $\mathcal{R}_{0,1}$ into disjoint, finitely classifiable sets.

**Theorem 5.** *For any $k > 1$ there are pairwise disjoint sets $S_0, \cdots, S_{k-1}$ such that*

(1) $S_0 \cup \cdots \cup S_{k-1} = \mathcal{R}_{0,1}$,

(2) $(S_0, \cdots, S_{k-1}) \in FCL$.

Next we compare finite classification and learnability. If a classification machine outputs a hypothesis $i$, then we know almost *all* about the corresponding set $S_i$, since there are only finitely many sets $S_0, ..., S_{k-1}$. On the other hand, if an IIM outputs a hypothesis $i$, then we know almost *nothing* about the corresponding function $\varphi_i$. Hence, at first glance it seems much easier to disprove a CM than to fool an IIM. However, the situation is much more subtle, as the following theorems show.

**Theorem 6.** *For any $S_0 \subset \mathcal{R}_{0,1}$ such that $S_0 \in FIN$, there is a $S_1$ such that*

(1) $S_1 \subset \mathcal{R}_{0,1}$,

(2) $S_1 \in FIN$,

(3) $S_0 \cap S_1 = \emptyset$,

(4) $(S_0, S_1) \in FCL$.

The latter theorem allows the following interpretation. Any "easily" learnable class can be completed to an "easily" classifiable pair. Thus, sometimes learning and classification are *not* very distinct. On the other hand, we have the following:

**Theorem 7.** *For any $S_0 \subset \mathcal{R}_{0,1}$ such that $S_0 \in FIN$, there is a $S_1$ such that*

(1) $S_1 \subset \mathcal{R}_{0,1}$,

(2) $S_1 \notin EX$,

(3) $S_0 \cap S_1 = \emptyset$,

(4) $(S_0, S_1) \in FCL$.

## 5. Bounding the Number of Mind Changes

For finite classification ($FCL$) a CM is not allowed to change its conjecture at all. For standard classification ($CL$) a CM is allowed to change its conjecture an arbitrary finite number of times. The precise number of mind changes has not to be determined in advance. In the study of inductive inference, a mind change hierarchy was discovered by fixing in advance a particular number of mind changes that an IIM was allowed to make (cf. Case and Smith (1983)). In the sequel we present a hierarchy for classification based on a fixed number of allowed mind changes.

**Theorem 8.** *For any $k$ there are sets $S_0, S_1, \cdots, S_{k+1}$ such that*

(1) $S_0 \cup S_1 \cup \cdots \cup S_{k+1} = \mathcal{R}_{0,1}$,

(2) $(S_0, \cdots, S_{k+1}) \in CL^{k+1} \setminus CL^k$.

Moreover, it is also possible to prove a hierarchy in the number of mind changes that is not related to the number of sets to be classified.

**Theorem 9.** *For any $c \in \mathbb{N}$ there exist pairwise disjoint sets $S_0, S_1 \subseteq \mathcal{R}_{0,1}$ such that $(S_0, S_1) \in CL_2^{c+1} \setminus CL_2^c$.*

## 6. Classification versus Multi–Classification and Consistent Classification

In this section we compare the power of classification, multi–classification and consistent classification. In particular, we are interested in learning whether or not multi–classification or consistent classification is harder to achieve than ordinary classification. Since neither multi–classification nor consistent classification has been studied in the framework presented here, our goal is twofold. First we are interested in general results concerning the classification power of these models. Second, we ask whether or not the results obtained extend to the classification of predicates.

Our next theorem compares multi–classification and ordinary classification in the finite case. There is a simple argument that separates finite multi–classifcation from finite classification. Start with two sets $S_0$ and $S_1$ such that $(S_0, S_1) \notin FCL_2$. Then $(S_0, S_0 \cup S_1) \in FCL_2$ as witnessed by a classification machine that always selects $S_0 \cup S_1$. However, if $(S_0, S_0 \cup S_1)$ were in $Multi\text{-}FCL_2$ then it would be possible to finitely classify $(S_0, S_1)$. The more complicated argument below uses a reduction to the halting problem. This more complicated argument yields some complexity theoretic corollaries not obtainable from the simpler argument outlined above.

**Theorem 10.** *Multi-$FCL_2 \subset FCL_2$*

Applying a simple coding technique, the proof of Theorem 10 directly yields the following corollary.

**Corollary 11.** *There are sets $S_0, S_1 \subseteq \mathcal{R}_{0,1}$ such that $(S_0, S_1) \in FCL_2 \setminus Multi\text{-}FCL_2$.*

**Corollary 12.** *The complexity of the finite multi–classification problem is bounded below by the halting problem.*

In contrast to the above Corollary, we note that the complexity of the inference problem has been found to be strictly less than the complexity of the halting problem (cf. Adleman and Blum (1991)). Hence, in a complexity theoretic sense, classification is more difficult than learning.

Corollary 11 gives an example of sets of sets from $\mathcal{R}_{0,1}$ that are classifiable but not multiclassifiable. Using similar proof techniques, it is possible to give another such example where the sets are chosen from NUM. All the sets in NUM are known to be easy to learn.

**Theorem 13.** *There are sets* $S_0, S_1 \subseteq NUM$ *such that* $(S_0, S_1) \in FCL_2 \backslash$ *Multi–FCL$_2$.*

In the proof of Theorem 13 we used, instead of $K$, some set that was limit r.e. but not limiting recursive (Gold 1965), the sets $S_0$ and $S_1$ would still be in NUM. Furthermore, they would not be in *Multi–CL$_2$*.

Next we aim to characterize multi–classification in terms of standard classification. For that purpose, we introduce the notion of a *mosaic*. Let $S_0, ..., S_{k-1} \subseteq \mathcal{R}$ and $S = S_0 \cup ... \cup S_{k-1}$. Let $ALL = \{0, ..., k-1\}$ and $SUB \subseteq ALL$. Then let $S_{SUB} = \bigcap_{j \in SUB} S_j \backslash \bigcup_{i \in ALL \backslash SUB} S_i$. $S_{SUB}$ is the set of all $f \in S$ that belong to all of the classes $S_j$, $j \in SUB$, and to none of the classes $S_i$, $i \in ALL \backslash SUB$. Finally, let $mosaic(S_0, ..., S_{k-1})$ be the tuple of all sets $S_{SUB}$, where $SUB \subseteq ALL$.

Obviously, $mosaic(S_0, ..., S_{k-1})$ is a $2^k$–tuple of pairwise disjoint sets the union of which is $S$ (cf. Figure 1 for the $k = 3$ case). Note that some components of $mosaic(S_0, ...S_{k-1})$ may be empty.

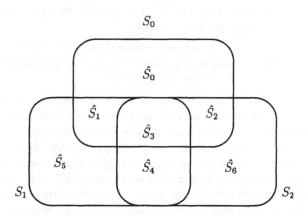

$$S_0$$

Figure 1: The mosaic $\hat{S}_0, ..., \hat{S}_6, \hat{S}_7$ of the sets $S_0, S_1, S_2$, where $\hat{S}_7 = \emptyset$.

Finally, let $mosaic(S_0, ..., S_{k-1}) = (T_0, ..., T_{2^k-1})$. Moreover, without loss of generality we assume that the $T_j$'s, $0 \leq j \leq 2^k - 1$, are ordered in such a way that from the index $j$ the corresponding set $SUB$ can be computed such that $S_{SUB} = T_j$ and vice versa. Formally, this can be realized by a one-to-one mapping $m$ from the set of all subsets $SUB$ of $ALL$ onto the set $\{0, ...2^k - 1\}$ such that for any $SUB \subseteq ALL$, $S_{SUB} = T_{m(SUB)}$. We have obtained the following characterization.

**Theorem 14.** *For all $k \geq 2$ and all sets $S_0, ..., S_{k-1} \subseteq \mathcal{R}$ we have:* $(S_0, ..., S_{k-1}) \in$ *Multi–CL if and only if* $mosaic(S_0, ..., S_{k-1}) \in CL$.

Notice that Theorem 14 equates a multi-classification problem with a classifcation problem with exponentially many more possible classifications. To the extent that the number of possible classifications is regarded as complexity measure, Theorem 14 highlights the relative difficulty of classification and multi-classification. Finally in this section we relate consistent classification to ordinary classification.

**Theorem 15.** $Cons\text{-}CL \subset CL$

**Corollary 16.** *There are sets $S_0$, $S_1 \subseteq \mathcal{R}_{0,1}$ such that $(S_0, S_1) \in CL \setminus Cons\text{-}CL$.*

# 7. Classification of Famous Languages

In this section first we examine the classification of the regular languages (cf. Lewis and Papadimitriou (1981)). The regular languages can be modeled as predicates as well. This is done by fixing an isomorphism between strings over the alphabet of the regular language and the natural numbers. Then a (regular) language represented by a $\{0, 1\}$ valued function $f$ is the set of strings that correspond to the natural numbers in the set $\{x \mid f(x) = 1\}$. The details of this encoding will be suppressed as much as possible without sacrificing clarity. By a *positive example* we mean a string that corresponds to a value $x$ such that $f(x) = 1$. Similarly, by a *negative example* we mean a string that corresponds to a value $x$ such that $f(x) = 0$.

**Theorem 17.** *It is impossible to classify an arbitrary language from positive and negative examples as being either regular or not regular.*

By way of contrast with Theorem 17, it is possible to separate arbitrarily large subsets of the regular languages from the rest.

**Theorem 18.** *Let $n$ be an arbitrary natural number. Let $S_0$ be the set of all regular languages that are recognized by some $k$-state finite automaton, $k \leq n$. Let $S_1$ be all the languages not in $S_0$. Then $(S_0, S_1) \in CL$.*

Next we ask whether or not Theorem 18 may be generalized. Disregarding the obvious direction to handle more complex cases of finite sets of languages we consider the problem under what circumstances infinite sets of languages are separable from the rest. As we have already seen, this is not always the case. Moreover, Theorem 17 allows a conclusion that is interesting in its own right. On the one hand, the set of all regular languages is even reliably learnable on the set of all total functions (cf. Blum and Blum (1975)). On the other hand, no algorithm that learns the set of all regular languages can be converted into a classification machine as Theorem 17 shows. Hence, it isinteresting to ask for an explanation of that phenomenon.

Analyzing the regular languages from an algorithmic point of view indicates that they possess several favorable properties. First, the set of all regular languages is recursively enumerable. Second, membership in the regular languages is uniformly decidable. Finally, the regular languages possess several structural properties that may be tested algorithmically. Nevertheless, they are not separable, even in the limit, from the rest of all languages. Thissuggests that their unclassifiability might be caused not by their algorithmic but their topological properties. Namely, from a topological point of view the set of all regular languages is dense, i.e., it consists only of accumulation points. As a consequence, there is no learning algorithm inferring the regular languages that does not exceed any a priorily fixed number of allowed mind changes. On the other hand, for any fixed $n$, the set of all regular languages acceptable by some $n$-state finite automaton may be obviously inferred within an a priori fixed number of mind changes.

Therefore, we will try to generalize Theorem 18 by considering learning algorithms not exceeding a number of mind changes fixed in advance and trying to convert them into classification machines. For that purpose we need some notation. Let $\Sigma$ be any fixed alphabet. A recursively enumerable set $\mathcal{L} = (L_j)_{j \in \mathbb{N}}$ of languages over $\Sigma$ is said to be an indexed family if all languages $L_j$ are non–empty and there is an algorithm that uniformly decides membership in $L_j$ for all $j \in \mathbb{N}$ and all strings $s \in \Sigma^*$ (cf. Angluin (1980)). That means $\mathcal{L} = (L_j)_{j \in \mathbb{N}}$ is an indexed family iff there is a recursive function $f$ such that for all numbers $j$ and all strings $s \in \Sigma^*$ we have

$$f(j, s) = \begin{cases} 1, & \text{if } s \in L_j, \\ 0, & \text{otherwise.} \end{cases}$$

Assuming $\Sigma^*$ to be lexicographically ordered, we may describe $\mathcal{L}$ by a sequence $\mathcal{F} = (f_j)_{j \in \mathbb{N}}$ of uniformly recursive predicates, where $f_j(s) = f(j, s)$ for all $j \in \mathbb{N}$ and all $s \in \Sigma^*$. Moreover, in the sequel we identify $2^{\Sigma^*}$ with the set of all $\{0, 1\}$ valued total functions.

The inferability of indexed families has attracted a lot of attention in learning theory (cf. Lange and Zeugmann (1992a), (1993) and the references therein). As it turned out, when dealing with the inferability of indexed families the choice of the hypothesis space is of importance. It may effect both the learnability as well as the efficiency (cf. Lange and Zeugmann (1992a), (1993)). In particular, not requiring an IIM to learn within the given enumeration $\mathcal{F} = (f_j)_{j \in \mathbb{N}}$ may reduce the number of necessary mind changes. Therefore, in all what follows we consider *class preserving* learning, i.e., when inferring an indexed family $\mathcal{F} = (f_j)_{j \in \mathbb{N}}$ we allow any suitable chosen hypothesis space $\mathcal{G} = (g_j)_{j \in \mathbb{N}}$ of uniformly recursive predicates such that any predicate in $\mathcal{F}$ possesses a description in $\mathcal{G}$ and any hypothesis $g_j$ describes a language from $\mathcal{F}$, i.e., $range(\mathcal{G}) = range(\mathcal{F})$. Now we are ready to present the next theorem.

**Theorem 19.** *Let $m \in \mathbb{N}$, $m \geq 1$, and let $\mathcal{F}$ be any indexed family over some fixed alphabet $\Sigma$ that can be learned from positive and negative data with at most $m$ mind changes. Then there exists a partition of $2^{\Sigma^*}$ into $m + 2$ pairwise disjoint classes $\mathcal{F}_0, ..., \mathcal{F}_{m+1}$ such that*

(1) $\mathcal{F}_0 \cup ... \cup \mathcal{F}_m = \mathcal{F}$,

(2) $(\mathcal{F}_0, ..., \mathcal{F}_{m+1}) \in CL$.

The latter theorem directly allows the following corollary.

**Corollary 20.** *Let $m \geq 1$, and let $\mathcal{F}$ be any indexed family over some fixed alphabet $\Sigma$ that can be learned from positive and negative data with at most $m$ mind changes. Then it is possible to classify an arbitrary language from positive and negative data as belonging to $\mathcal{F}$ or not.*

Looking at all the results obtained above we see that we have always dealt with complete information concerning the objects to be learned or classified. However, a huge part of language learning theory is devoted to learning from positive data only. Hence, it is only natural to consider classification of languages from positive data. We now briefly examine this issue.

Considering learning or classification from positive data requires some carefulness. First of all, we have to deal with the order of information presentation. Clearly, we cannot assume to receive the data in lexicographical order, since this would implicitly deliver much more information than allowed. Consequently, one demands a CM or IIM to learn on *all* sequences of positive data that eventually contain every string from the language under consideration. More precisely, let $L$ be a language and $t = s_0, s_1, s_2, \ldots$ an infinite sequence of strings from $\Sigma^*$ such that $range(t) = \{s_k \mid k \in \mathbb{N}\} = L$. Then $t$ is said to be a *positive presentation* for $L$ or, synonymously, a *text*. We define $Text(L)$ to be the set of all texts for $L$. Moreover, let $t$ be a text and let $x \in \mathbb{N}$: then $t_x$ denotes the initial segment of $t$ of length $x + 1$. Note that we do not require a text to be computable. Now we ask whether or not we may extend Theorem 19 to the case of learning from positive data. The answer is twofold. It is still possible to transform a learning algorithm that works with a number of mind changes fixed a priori into a classification machine. Nevertheless, we conjecture that it is no longer possible to partition $2^{\Sigma^*}$. However, we still get a partition of the indexed family. For the sake of readability we present the next theorem in terms of languages.

**Theorem 21.** *Let $m \in \mathbb{N}$ and let $\mathcal{L}$ be any indexed family over some fixed alphabet that can be learned from positive data with at most $m$ mind changes. Then there exist pairwise disjoint classes $\mathcal{L}_0, \ldots, \mathcal{L}_m$ such that*

(1) $\mathcal{L}_0 \cup \ldots \cup \mathcal{L}_m = \mathcal{L}$,

(2) $(\mathcal{L}_0, \ldots, \mathcal{L}_m) \in CL$.

# 8. Conclusions and Open Problems

We have studied the classification of $\{0, 1\}$ valued recursive functions, and simultaneously the classification of languages from positive and negative data. Moreover, extending previous work by Wiehagen and Smith (1992) we introduced new models of classification, i.e., classification with a bounded number of mind changes, multi-classification and consistent classification. We related all these classification types to each other, thereby showing what they have in common and where the differences are. However, there are several question that deserve further study.

First, it would be desirable to gain a deeper understanding under what circumstances the restriction of arbitrary recursive function classes to predicates is classifiable, provided the original function classes are not. Second, the impact of consistent classification should be investigated in some more detail. Looking at potential applications there are several scenarios where consistent classification is preferable. Nevertheless, as we have seen, this requirement might prevent one from successfully designing a classification machine. Hence, it seems to be highly desirable to elaborate sufficient and necessary conditions for consistent classification. Third, we would like to find characterizations of all the classification types introduced. Characterizations play an important role in learning theory (cf. e.g. Blum and Blum (1975), Angluin (1980), Zeugmann (1983), Wiehagen (1991), Lange and Zeugmann (1992b)). As it turned out, most of the characterizations obtained lead to a better understanding into the problem how algorithms performing the learning process may be designed. Hence, characterizing classification might yield a deeper insight into the nature of classification. Moreover, this might help to gain a better understanding of the complex relation between classification and learning.

Finally, we have mainly dealt with the classification of languages from positive and negative data. Nevertheless, from the point of view of potential applications classification from positive data deserves attention as well. We regard Theorem 21 as a starting point for further research in that direction. In this context, Fulk's (1990) results suggest interesting problems. In particular, Fulk (1990) studied the impact of several demands on the learning power of IIMs, e.g.; prudence, rearrangement independence or set–driveness. Since these requirements reflect postulates of naturalness, it is interesting to consider their influence on the power of CMs.

## Acknowledgement

The third author heartly acknowledges enlightening discussions with Rüdiger Reischuk. The second author would like to acknowledge similar conversations with James Reggia.

## 9. References

ADLEMAN, L., AND BLUM, M. (1991), Inductive inference and unsolvability, *Journal of Symbolic Logic* **56**, 891 - 900.

ANGLUIN, D. (1980), Inductive inference of formal languages from positive data, *Information and Control* **45**, 117 - 135.

ANGLUIN, D., AND SMITH, C.H. (1983), Inductive inference: theory and methods, *Computing Surveys* **15**, 237 - 269.

ANGLUIN, D., AND SMITH, C.H. (1987), Formal inductive inference, *in* "Encyclopedia of Artificial Intelligence" (St.C. Shapiro, Ed.), Vol. 1, pp. 409 - 418, Wiley-Interscience Publication, New York.

BARZDIN. J. (1971), Complexity and frequency solution of some algorithmically unsolvable problems, Doct. Diss., Novosibirsk, State University, (in Russian).

BYLANDER, T., ALLEMANG, D., AND TANNER, M. (1991), The computational complexity of diagnosis, *Artificial Intelligence* **49**, 25 - 60.

BLUM, L., AND BLUM, M. (1975), Toward a mathematical theory of inductive inference, *Information and Control* **28**, 122 - 155.

CASE, J., AND SMITH, C.H. (1983), Comparison of identification criteria for machine inductive inference, *Theoretical Computer Science* **25**, 193 - 220.

CHO, S., AND REGGIA, J. (1993) Multiple disorder diagnosis with adaptive competitive neural networks, *Artificial Intelligence in Medicine* **5**, 469 - 487.

DUDA, R., AND HART, P. (1973), "Pattern Classification and Scene Analysis," Wiley-Interscience Publication, New York.

FREIVALDS, R., KINBER, E.B., AND WIEHAGEN, R. (1992), Convergently versus divergently incorrect hypotheses in inductive inference, GOSLER Report 05/92, January 1992, Fachbereich Mathematik und Informatik, TH Leipzig.

FULK, M. (1990), Prudence and other restrictions in formal language learning, *Information and Computation* **85**, 1 - 11.

FREIVALDS, R.V., AND WIEHAGEN, R. (1979), Inductive inference with additional information, *Journal of Information Processing and Cybernetics (EIK)* **15**, 179 - 184.

GOLD, M.E. (1965), Limiting recursion, *Journal of Symbolic Logic* **30**, 28 - 48.

GOLD, M.E. (1967), Language identification in the limit, *Information and Control* **10**, 447 - 474.

JANTKE, K.P., AND BEICK, H.R. (1981). Combining postulates of naturalness in inductive inference, *Journal of Information Processing and Cybernetics (EIK)* **17**, 465 - 484.

LANGE, S., AND ZEUGMANN, T. (1992a), Learning recursive languages with bounded mind changes, GOSLER–Report 16/92, FB Mathematik und Informatik, TH Leipzig, September 1992.

LANGE, S., AND ZEUGMANN, T. (1992b), Types of monotonic language learning and their characterization, *in* "Proceedings 5th Annual ACM Workshop on Computational Learning Theory," Pittsburgh, pp. 377 - 390, ACM Press.

LANGE, S., AND ZEUGMANN, T. (1993), Language learning in dependence on the space of hypotheses, *in* "Proceedings 6th Annual ACM Conference on Computational Learning Theory," Santa Cruz, pp. 127 - 136, ACM Press.

LEWIS, H., AND PAPADIMITRIOU, C. (1981), "Elements of the Theory of Computation," Prentice-Hall, Inc., Englewood Cliffs, New Jersey.

MACHTEY, M., AND YOUNG, P. (1978), "An Introduction to the General Theory of Algorithms," North-Holland, New York.

MICHALSKI, R.S., CARBONELL, J.G., AND MITCHELL, T.M. (1983), "Machine Learning," Tioga Publishing Co., Palo Alto, CA.

OSHERSON, D., STOB, M., AND WEINSTEIN, S. (1986), "Systems that Learn, An Introduction to Learning Theory for Cognitive and Computer Scientists," MIT-Press, Cambridge, Massachusetts.

WIEHAGEN, R. (1991), A thesis in inductive inference, *in* "Proceedings First International Workshop on Nonmonotonic and Inductive Logic," Karlsruhe, December 1990, J.Dix, K.P. Jantke and P.H. Schmitt (Eds.), Lecture Notes in Artificial Intelligence 543, pp. 184 - 207, Springer-Verlag.

WIEHAGEN, R., AND SMITH, C. (1994), Classification versus generalization, *Journal of Experimental and Theoretical Artificial Intelligence*, to appear.

ZEUGMANN, T. (1983), A-posteriori characterizations in inductive inference of recursive functions, *Journal of Information Processing and Cybernetics (EIK)* **19**, 559 - 594.

ZEUGMANN, T. (1988), On the power of recursive optimizers, *Theoretical Computer Science* **62**, 289 - 310.

# A Guided Tour Across the Boundaries of Learning Recursive Languages

Thomas Zeugmann

Research Institute of

Fundamental Information Science

Kyushu University 33

Fukuoka 812, Japan

thomas@rifis.kyushu-u.ac.jp

Steffen Lange

HTWK Leipzig

FB Mathematik und Informatik

PF 66

04251 Leipzig

steffen@informatik.th-leipzig.de

## Abstract

The present paper deals with the learnability of indexed families of uniformly recursive languages *from positive data* as well as from both, *positive and negative data*. We consider the influence of various monotonicity constraints to the learning process, and provide a thorough study concerning the influence of several parameters. In particular, we present examples pointing to typical problems and solutions in the field. Then we provide a *unifying* framework for learning. Furthermore, we survey results concerning learnability in dependence on the hypothesis space, and concerning order independence. Moreover, new results dealing with the efficiency of learning are provided. First, we investigate the power of *iterative* learning algorithms. The second measure of efficiency studied is the number of *mind changes* a learning algorithm is allowed to perform. In this setting we consider the problem whether or not the monotonicity constraints introduced do influence the efficiency of learning algorithms.

The paper mainly emphasis to provide a comprehensive summary of results recently obtained, and of *proof techniques* developed. Finally, throughout our guided tour we discuss the question of what a natural language learning algorithm might look like.

## 1. Introduction

Humans have the ability to learn and to adapt. During the long evolution of mankind humans have developed the particular ability to acquire their maternal language as well as other languages. Since these abilities have always been considered the hallmark of intelligence, the challenge to design an "intelligent" computer has led to considerable interest in learning in the computer science community. Hence, it would be very nice if we could start our guided tour with a satisfying definition of what learning really is. But our understanding of learning is still too limited. Hence, answering the question what learning is has to be considered to be one of the major goals of algorithmic learning theory (cf. Angluin (1992)). On the other hand, there is a broad consensus that *induction* constitutes an important feature of learning. The corresponding theory is called *inductive inference*. Inductive inference of formal languages may be characterized as the study of systems that map evidence on a language into hypotheses about it. Of special interest is the investigation of scenarios in which the sequence of hypotheses *stabilizes* to an *accurate* and *finite* description (a grammar) of the target language. If evidence is understood as reasonable information, then all these scenarios model at least a certain aspect of learning. This can be seen as follows. Up to the unknown point of stabilization only finitely many data concerning the target language have been provided. Nevertheless, more information about the language to be learned does not lead to a new, and different hypothesis. Hence, some form of *generalization* must have taken place, i.e., of a grammar that accurately generates the target language. The precise definitions of the concepts "evidence," "stabilization," and "accuracy" go back to Gold (1965, 1967) who introduced the model of learning in the limit. Gold-style formal language learning has been intensively studied (cf., e.g., Angluin and Smith (1983, 1987), Osherson, Stob and Weinstein (1986) and the references therein). For more information concerning recent developments in inductive inference, the reader is referred to the annual Workshops on Computational Learning Theory, COLT (cf., e.g., Rivest, Haussler and Warmuth (1989), Fulk and Case (1990), Haussler (1992)), the International Workshops on Algorithmic Learning Theory, ALT (cf., e.g., Arikawa et al. (1990, 1991)) and the workshops on Analogical and Inductive Inference, AII (cf., e.g., Jantke (1989, 1992)).

Most of the work done in the field has been aimed at two goals: the characterization of those collections of languages that can be learned, and to study the impact of several postulates on the behavior of learners to their learning power. Moreover, a considerable amount of interest has been devoted to the learnability of recursively enumerable languages. In this particular setting many interesting and sometimes surprising results have been obtained (cf., e.g., Wiehagen (1978), Case and Lynes (1982), Schäfer-Richter (1984), Case (1988), Jain and Sharma (1989) and Fulk (1990)).

The present paper surveys results that deal with the learnability of *recursive languages*. Looking at potential applications, Angluin (1980a, 1980b) started the systematic study of learning enumerable families of uniformly recursive languages, henceforth called *indexed families*. A sequence $L_0, L_1, L_2, \ldots$ is said to be an *indexed family* provided all languages $L_j$ are non-empty and membership in $L_j$ is uniformly decidable for all numbers $j$. Note that the definition of an indexed families includes both, a description for every language $L_j$, and a particular enumeration of all the languages. Well-known examples of indexed families are the set of all context sensitive languages in canonical enumeration (cf. Hopcroft and Ullman (1969)) or the set of all pattern languages in canonical enumeration (cf. Angluin (1980a)).

Next we specify the information from which the target languages have to be learned.

A *text* of a language $L$ is an infinite sequence of strings that eventually contains all strings of $L$. Alternatively, we consider learning from *informant*. An informant of a language $L$ is an infinite sequence of all strings over the underlying alphabet that are classified with respect to their containment in $L$.

An algorithmic learner, henceforth called *inductive inference machine* (abbr. IIM), takes as input initial segments of a text (an informant), and outputs, from time to time, a hypothesis about the target language. The set $\mathcal{G}$ of all admissible hypotheses is called *hypothesis space*. Furthermore, the sequence of hypotheses has to converge to a hypothesis correctly describing the language to be learned, i.e., after some point, the IIM stabilizes to an accurate hypothesis. If there is an IIM that learns a language $L$ from all texts (informants) for it, then $L$ is said to be *learnable from text (learnable from informant) in the limit* with respect to the hypothesis space $\mathcal{G}$ (cf. Definition 1).

Having reached that point of precision a question naturally arising is how a "natural" learning algorithm may be designed. A thorough answer to this question, if ever possible, requires a systematic study of the various aspects that might influence the learnability. Our guided tour aims to summarize results obtained in this regard. We continue with some notations that are needed to motivate and to discuss these investigations. The starting point of our studies goes back to different learning strategies that have been discussed controversially in the machine learning community. Clearly, whenever one learns inductively from examples one has to perform a generalization. On the other hand, it is by no means obvious whether one should generalize only as little as necessary or as much as possible. In the first case, the learning algorithm might achieve the learning goal by producing a sequence of better and better generalizations. The second approach might lead to an algorithm that initially outputs a most general hypothesis. Afterwards, the learning algorithm might specialize its actual hypotheses until it eventually reaches a correct guess. Finally, it is plausible to combine the two strategies, i.e., to learn by a suitable interplay between generalization and specialization. There has been an extensive debate in the machine learning community for and against each of these learning modes (cf., e.g., Michalski, Carbonell and Mitchell (1984, 1986) or Kodratoff and Michalski (1990)). Inspired by recent results in non-monotonic reasoning Jantke (1991a, 1991b) proposed several sound formalizations of "generalization." Moreover, he studied the problem to what extend non-monotonic reasoning has to be incorporated into the learning process. Subsequently, Wiehagen (1991) refined Jantke's (1991a) approach, and Kapur (1992) introduced the dual versions of it. This led to the following learning models:

Interpreting generalization and specialization in their strongest sense means that we are forced to produce an augmenting (descending) chain of languages, i.e., $L_i \subseteq L_j$ ($L_i \supseteq L_j$) in case $L_j$ is hypothesized later than $L_i$ (cf. Definitions 5 and 7, Part (A)). The resulting learning types are called *strong-monotonic* and *dual strong-monotonic* learning, respectively.

Subsequently, Wiehagen (1991) refined this definition by restricting "better generalization" to the language $L$ that has to be learned, and required $L_i \cap L \subseteq L_j \cap L$ provided $L_j$ appears later in the sequence of guesses than $L_i$ does (cf. Definition 5 (B)). This means that a new hypothesis is never allowed to reject some string that a previously generated guess already *correctly includes*.

The dual version of the latter requirement directly yields the demand that the learner is never allowed to hypothesize a grammar that can generate a string that a previously guessed hypothesis *correctly excluded* (cf. Definition 7 (B)). Learning devices behaving thus are called *monotonic* and *dual monotonic*, respectively.

Weakening the (dual) strong-monotonicity constraint in the same way as the monotonicity principle of classical logic is generalized to cumulativity (cf., e.g., Brewka (1991)) directly yields *(dual) weak-monotonic* learning, i.e., now the learner is required to behave (dual) strong-monotonic as long as it does not receive data contradicting its actual hypothesis (cf. Definitions 5 and 7, Part (C)).

Another serious problem one has to deal with when learning from text, is to avoid or to detect *overgeneralizations* (also called the *subset problem*), i.e., hypotheses that describe proper *supersets* of the target language. Several authors proposed the so-called *subset principle* to handle the subset problem (cf., e.g., Berwick (1985), Wexler (1992)). Informally, the subset principle requires the learner to guess the "least" language from the hypothesis space with respect to set inclusion that fits with the data the learner has seen so far. Clearly, each of the monotonicity constraints described above can be regarded as a sound formalization of "least," and therefore, as a realization of the subset principle. But there is another important aspect that we have not touched yet, i.e., the choice of the hypothesis space. Obviously, the hypothesis space must contain at least one description for each target language. Hence, we might be tempted to take the indexed family itself as hypothesis space. And indeed, most authors did (cf. eg. Angluin (1980a, 1980b), Shinohara (1982), Jantke (1991b), Mukouchi (1992)). Moreover, looking at potential applications of a learning system, users of such a system might even be highly interested in getting as hypotheses just the descriptions they proposed. That means they might formulate their learning problems just by specifying a particular indexed family. If an indexed family $\mathcal{L}$ can be learned with respect to $\mathcal{L}$ itself, then we call it *exactly* learnable.

On the other hand, it is only natural to ask whether the requirement to learn exactly may lead to a decrease of the learning power. Results obtained in the setting of PAC-learning impressively show that at least the *efficiency* of learning can be heavily affected if one insists to learn with respect to a particular hypothesis space (cf., e.g., Pitt and Valiant (1988), Blum and Singh (1990)). Similar effects have been observed in Gold-style language learning, too (cf. Lange and Zeugmann (1993b)). Therefore, we also consider the following options to choose a suitable hypothesis space. An indexed family $\mathcal{L}$ is said to be *class preservingly* inferable, if there is a hypothesis space $\mathcal{G} = G_0, G_1, G_2, \ldots$ such that every grammar $G_j$ generates a language contained in $\mathcal{L}$, and the learning algorithm infers $\mathcal{L}$ with respect to $\mathcal{G}$. Note that this in particular means that $range(\mathcal{L})$ and $\{L(G_j) \mid j \in \mathbb{N}\}$ have to coincide ($\mathbb{N}$ is the set of all natural numbers). That means, when dealing with class preserving language learning we are free to choose a possibly *different enumeration* of $\mathcal{L}$ and possibly *different descriptions* for the target languages $L \in \mathcal{L}$. Or in other words, class preserving learning just means that there is at least one suitable hypothesis space having the same range as $\mathcal{L}$ with respect to which $\mathcal{L}$ is inferable.

Finally, we consider *class comprising* learning. In this setting a learning algorithm is allowed to use any hypothesis space $\mathcal{G} = G_0, G_1, \ldots$ such that every $L \in \mathcal{L}$ possesses a description $G_j$ but $\mathcal{G}$ may additionally contain elements $G_k$ not describing any language from $\mathcal{L}$. Although we might be tempted to exclude class comprising hypothesis spaces, since any grammar not generating a language from $\mathcal{L}$ cannot be correct, this learning model has its peculiarities as we shall see.

Moreover, we study the question what all the described learning models have in *common* and what their *differences* are. As we shall see, *characterizations* are a very useful tool to answer this question (cf. Section 4). In particular, we outline a *unifying framework for learning* from *informant* as well as from *text*.

Next we describe some further requirements that correspond to desirable properties a "natural" learning algorithm should have. For example, can we require an IIM to be *semantically finite*? An IIM is called *semantically finite* if the hypothesis it converges to is the first correct one in the sequence of all its guesses. Again, this seems to be a very reasonable demand. As we have already mentioned, inductive learning has its peculiarities. There has been a long debate in the philosophy of science for and against induction as a legitimate form of reasoning. As far as learning is concerned, Poper's (1968) *falsification theory*, and his *refutation principle* are of special interest. While finite sequences of data can never prove a hypothesis to be correct, single data can falsify it. Therefore, Popper (1968) considered induction as a legitimate form of drawing conclusions as long as they are built up in such a way that their refutation is possible as long as they are wrong. Adapting that approach to learning we directly arrive at semantical finite learners, since any wrong hypothesis is rejected sometimes, and the sequence of all generated guesses stabilizes to the first correct one. Note that other authors have interpreted Poper's (1968) refutation principle in a different, and much more restrictive way (cf., e.g., Case and Smith (1983), Gasarch and Velauthapillai (1992)).

Furthermore, we deal with the question whether or not the *order* of information presentation does really influence the capabilities of inductive inference machines. Since an IIM is required to learn the target languages from *all* texts (informants), one might conjecture that they just extract the strings provided. While this is true for learning from informant, the situation with respect to text is completely different. This phenomenon has been first observed by Schäfer-Richter (1984), and later independently by Fulk (1990). However, they proved their results in a setting allowing self-referential arguments. Since self-referential arguments are mainly applicable in settings where the membership problem for languages is algorithmically undecidable, it worth to study the problem of order independence in our more realistic setting.

Finally, we consider different aspects dealing with the efficiency of learning. Looking at the definition of learning in the limit, we see that in any learning step an IIM has access to the whole initial segment of a text (informant) it has been fed. Clearly, such a learning mode requires a huge amount of storage. Therefore, we consider *iterative* learning introduced by Wiehagen (1976). An iteratively learning IIM *exclusively* uses its last hypothesis and the next input string to compute its actual guess (cf. Definition 8). Hence that model of learning takes into account the limitation of space in all realistic computations.

The second measure of efficiency we deal with is the number of mind changes an IIM $M$ is allowed to perform. We say that $M$ *changes its mind*, or synonymously, $M$ performs a *mind change* iff two consecutively hypotheses output by $M$ are different (cf. Definition 3). This measure of efficiency has been introduced by Barzdin and Freivalds (1972). Subsequently, various authors used the number of mind changes to characterize the complexity of learning (cf., e.g., Barzdin and Freivalds (1974), Barzdin, Kinber and Podnieks (1974), Case and Smith (1983), Wiehagen, Freivalds and Kinber (1984), Mukouchi (1992, 1994)). Gasarch and Velauthapillai (1992) studied *active learning* in dependence on the number of mind changes.

The paper is organized as follows. Section 2 presents preliminaries, i.e., notations and definitions. In Section 3 we exemplify several basic concepts and ideas of language learning. We continue with characterizations of the learning models introduced (cf. Section 4). Then, we survey results showing that the learnability of indexed families is sensitive with respect to an appropriate choice of the relevant hypothesis space (cf. Section 5). Fundamental results concerning iterative learning are outlined in Section 6. Subsequently, we present results dealing with the efficiency of learning measured in the number of allowed mind changes (cf. Section 7). A comprehensive summary of recently obtained results dealing with different degrees of order independence is provided in Section 8. Finally, we discuss problems that remain open and outline further questions that might lead to interesting results (cf. Section 9). All references are given in Section 10.

## 2. Preliminaries

Let $\mathbb{N} = \{0, 1, 2, ...\}$ be the set of all natural numbers. We set $\mathbb{N}^+ = \mathbb{N} \setminus \{0\}$. Let $\varphi_0, \varphi_1, \varphi_2, ...$ denote any fixed **programming system** of all (and only all) partial recursive functions over $\mathbb{N}$, and let $\Phi_0, \Phi_1, \Phi_2, ...$ be any associated **complexity measure** (cf. Machtey and Young (1978)). Then $\varphi_k$ is the partial recursive function computed by program $k$ in the programming system. Furthermore, let $k, x \in \mathbb{N}$. If $\varphi_k(x)$ is defined (abbr. $\varphi_k(x) \downarrow$) then we also say that $\varphi_k(x)$ converges; otherwise, $\varphi_k(x)$ diverges (abbr. $\varphi_k(x) \uparrow$). By $\langle \cdot, \cdot \rangle \colon \mathbb{N} \times \mathbb{N} \to \mathbb{N}$ we denote **Cantor's pairing function**, i.e., $\langle x, y \rangle = ((x+y)^2 + 3x + y)/2$ for all $x, y \in \mathbb{N}$. In the sequel we assume familiarity with formal language theory (cf., e.g., Hopcroft and Ullman (1969)). By $\Sigma$ we denote any fixed finite alphabet of symbols. Let $\Sigma^*$ be the free monoid over $\Sigma$, and let $\Sigma^+ = \Sigma^* \setminus \{\varepsilon\}$, where $\varepsilon$ denotes the empty string. The length of a string $s \in \Sigma^*$ is denoted by $|s|$. Any subset $L \subseteq \Sigma^*$ is called a language. By $co-L$ we denote the complement of $L$, i.e., $co-L = \Sigma^* \setminus L$. Let $L$ be a language and $t = s_0, s_1, s_2, ...$ an infinite sequence of strings from $\Sigma^*$ such that $range(t) = \{s_k \mid k \in \mathbb{N}\} = L$. Then $t$ is said to be a **text** for $L$ or, synonymously, a **positive presentation**. Let $L$ be a language. By $text(L)$ we denote the set of all positive presentations of $L$. Furthermore, let $i = (s_0, b_0), (s_1, b_1), ...$ be an infinite sequence of elements of $\Sigma^* \times \{+, -\}$ such that $range(i) = \{s_k \mid k \in \mathbb{N}\} = \Sigma^*$, $i^+ = \{s_k \mid (s_k, b_k) = (s_k, +), k \in \mathbb{N}\} = L$ and $i^- = \{s_k \mid (s_k, b_k) = (s_k, -), k \in \mathbb{N}\} = co-L$. Then we refer to $i$ as an **informant**. If $L$ is classified via an informant then we also say that $L$ is represented by **positive and negative data**. Let $L$ be a language. By $info(L)$ we denote the set of all informants for $L$. Moreover, let $t, i$ be a text and an informant, respectively, and let $x$ be a number. Then $t_x, i_x$ denote the initial segment of $t$ and $i$ of length $x + 1$, respectively, e.g., $i_2 = (s_0, b_0), (s_1, b_1), (s_2, b_2)$. Let $t$ be a text and let $x \in \mathbb{N}$. Then we define $t_x^+ = \{s_k \mid k \leq x\}$. Furthermore, by $i_x^+$ and $i_x^-$ we denote the sets $\{s_k \mid (s_k, +) \in i, k \leq x\}$ and $\{s_k \mid (s_k, -) \in i, k \leq x\}$, respectively. Finally, we write $t_x \sqsubseteq t_y$ $(t_x \sqsubset t_y)$, iff $t_x$ is a (proper) prefix of $t_y$.

Next we introduce the notion of the **canonical text** that will be very helpful in proving several theorems. Let $L$ be any non-empty recursive language, and let $s_0, s_1, ...$ be the lexicographically ordered text of $\Sigma^*$. Test sequentially whether $s_z \in L$, for $z = 0, 1, 2, ...$, until the first $z$ is found such that $s_z \in L$. Since $L \neq \emptyset$, there must be at least one $z$ fulfilling the test. Set $t_0 = s_z$. We proceed inductively, $x \geq 0$,

$$t_{x+1} = \begin{cases} t_x \cdot s_{z+x+1}, & \text{if } s_{z+x+1} \in L, \\ t_x \cdot s, & \text{otherwise, where } s \text{ is the last string in } t_x. \end{cases}$$

Following Angluin (1980b), we restrict ourselves to deal exclusively with indexed families of uniformly recursive languages defined as follows: A sequence $L_0, L_1, L_2, \ldots$ is said to be an **indexed family** $\mathcal{L}$ of uniformly recursive languages provided all $L_j$ are non-empty and there is a recursive function $f$ such that for all numbers $j$ and all strings $s \in \Sigma^*$ we have

$$f(j,s) = \begin{cases} 1, & \text{if } s \in L_j, \\ 0, & \text{otherwise.} \end{cases}$$

In the following we refer to indexed families of uniformly recursive languages as indexed families for short. Moreover, we sometimes denote an indexed family and its range by the same symbol $\mathcal{L}$. The meaning will be clear from the context.

As in Gold (1967), we define an **inductive inference machine** (abbr. IIM) to be an algorithmic device which works as follows: The IIM takes as its input larger and larger initial segments of a text $t$ (or an informant $i$) and it either requests the next input, or it first outputs a hypothesis, i.e., a number encoding a certain computer program, and then it requests the next input (cf., e.g., Angluin (1980b)).

At this point we have to clarify what space of hypotheses we should choose, thereby also specifying the goal of the learning process. Gold (1967) and Wiehagen (1977) pointed out that there is a difference in what can be inferred depending on whether we want to synthesize in the limit grammars (i.e., procedures generating languages) or decision procedures, i.e., programs of characteristic functions. Case and Lynes (1982) investigated this phenomenon in detail. As it turns out, IIMs synthesizing grammars can be more powerful than those ones which are requested to output decision procedures. However, in the context of identification of indexed families, both concepts are of equal power. Nevertheless, we decided to require the IIMs to output grammars. This decision has been caused by the fact that there is a big difference between the possible monotonicity requirements. A straightforward adaptation of the approaches made in inductive inference of recursive functions directly yields analogous requirements with respect to the corresponding characteristic functions of the languages to be inferred. On the other hand, it is only natural to interpret monotonicity with respect to the language to be learned, i.e., to require containment of languages as described in the introduction. It turns out that the latter approach considerably increases the power of all types of monotonic and dual monotonic language learning. Furthermore, since we exclusively deal with the learnability of indexed families $\mathcal{L} = (L_j)_{j \in \mathbb{N}}$ we always take as hypothesis space an enumerable family of grammars $\mathcal{G} = G_0, G_1, G_2, \ldots$ over the terminal alphabet $\Sigma$ satisfying $\mathcal{L} \subseteq \{L(G_j) | j \in \mathbb{N}\}$. Moreover, we require that membership in $L(G_j)$ is uniformly decidable for all $j \in \mathbb{N}$ and all strings $s \in \Sigma^*$. As it turns out, it is sometimes very important to choose the space of hypotheses appropriately in order to achieve the desired learning goal (cf., e.g., Section 5 and 8). When an IIM outputs a number $j$, we interpret it to mean that the machine is hypothesizing the grammar $G_j$. Furthermore, let $\mathcal{G} = (G_j)_{j \in \mathbb{N}}$ be any hypothesis space. Then we set $\mathcal{L}(\mathcal{G}) = \{L(G_j) | j \in \mathbb{N}\}$. Note that $\mathcal{L}(\mathcal{G})$ constitutes itself an indexed family for all hypothesis spaces $\mathcal{G} = (G_j)_{j \in \mathbb{N}}$ .

Let $\sigma$ be a text or informant, respectively, and $x \in \mathbb{N}$. Then we use $M(\sigma_x)$ to denote the last hypothesis produced by $M$ when successively fed $\sigma_x$. The sequence $(M(\sigma_x))_{x \in \mathbb{N}}$ is said to **converge in the limit** to the number $j$ if and only if either $(M(\sigma_x))_{x \in \mathbb{N}}$ is infinite and all but finitely many terms of it are equal to $j$, or $(M(\sigma_x))_{x \in \mathbb{N}}$ is non-empty and finite, and its last term is $j$. Now we are ready to define learning in the limit.

**Definition 1. (Gold, 1967)** *Let $\mathcal{L}$ be an indexed family, let $L$ be a language, and let $\mathcal{G} = (G_j)_{j \in \mathbb{N}}$ be a hypothesis space. An IIM M CLIM-TXT [CLIM-INF]–identifies L from text [ informant ] with respect to $\mathcal{G}$ iff for every text $t$ [informant $i$ ] for $L$, there exists a $j \in \mathbb{N}$ such that the sequence $(M(t_x))_{x \in \mathbb{N}}$ $[(M(i_x))_{x \in \mathbb{N}}]$ converges in the limit to $j$ and $L = L(G_j)$.*

*Furthermore, $M$ CLIM$-$TXT [CLIM$-$INF]–identifies $\mathcal{L}$ with respect to $\mathcal{G}$ iff, for each $L \in \mathcal{L}$, $M$ CLIM$-$TXT [CLIM$-$INF]–identifies $L$ with respect to $\mathcal{G}$.*

*Finally, let CLIM$-$TXT [CLIM$-$INF] denote the collection of all indexed families $\mathcal{L}$ for which there are an IIM $M$ and a hypothesis space $\mathcal{G}$ such that $M$ CLIM$-$TXT [CLIM$-$INF]–identifies $\mathcal{L}$ with respect to $\mathcal{G}$.*

Since, by the definition of convergence, only finitely many data of $L$ were seen by the IIM upto the (unknown) point of convergence, whenever an IIM identifies the language $L$, some form of learning must have taken place. For this reason, hereinafter the terms *infer*, *learn*, and *identify* are used interchangeably.

In the above Definition $LIM$ stands for "limit." Furthermore, the prefix $C$ is used to indicate **class comprising** learning, i.e., the fact that $\mathcal{L}$ may be learned with respect to some hypothesis space comprising $range(\mathcal{L})$. The restriction of $CLIM$ to **class preserving** inference is denoted by $LIM$. That means $LIM$ is the collection of all indexed families $\mathcal{L}$ that can be learned in the limit with respect to a hypothesis space $\mathcal{G} = (G_j)_{j \in \mathbb{N}}$ such that $range(\mathcal{L}) = \{L(G_j) | \ j \in \mathbb{N}\}$. Moreover, if a target indexed family $\mathcal{L}$ has to be inferred with respect to the hypothesis space $\mathcal{L}$ itself, then we replace the prefix $C$ by $E$, i.e., $ELIM$ is the collection of indexed families that can be **exactly** learned in the limit. Finally, we adopt this convention in defining all the learning types below.

Note that, in general, it is not decidable whether or not $M$ has already inferred $L$. With the next definition, we consider a special case where it has to be decidable whether or not an IIM has successfully finished the learning task.

**Definition 2. (Gold, 1967; Trakhtenbrot and Barzdin, 1970)** *Let $\mathcal{L}$ be an indexed family, let $L$ be a language, and let $\mathcal{G} = (G_j)_{j \in \mathbb{N}}$ be a hypothesis space. An IIM M CFIN-TXT [CFIN-INF]–identifies L from text [informant ] with respect to $\mathcal{G}$ iff for every text $t$ [informant $i$ ] for $L$, there exists a $j \in \mathbb{N}$ such that $M$, when successively fed $t$ [ $i$ ], outputs the single hypothesis $j$, $L = L(G_j)$, and stops thereafter.*

*Furthermore, $M$ CFIN$-$TXT [ CFIN$-$INF]–identifies $\mathcal{L}$ with respect to $\mathcal{G}$ iff, for each $L \in \mathcal{L}$, $M$ CFIN$-$TXT [ CFIN$-$INF]–identifies $L$ with respect to $\mathcal{G}$.*

The resulting learning type is denoted by $CFIN-TXT$ $[CFIN-INF]$.

The next definition shows a natural way of weakening the requirement of finite identification. Here, the number of mind changes which an IIM $M$ may perform when inferring a target language is bounded by a number *a priori* fixed. When dealing with mind changes it is technically much more convenient to require the IIMs to behave as follows. Let $t$ be any text ($i$ be any informant), and $x \in \mathbb{N}$. If $M$ on $t_x$ ($i_x$) outputs for the first time a guess, then it has to output at any subsequent step a hypothesis. It is easy to see that any IIM $M$ may be straightforwardly converted into an IIM $\hat{M}$ behaving as required such that both machines produce the same sequence of mind changes.

**Definition 3.** **(Barzdin and Freivalds, 1974)** *Let $\mathcal{L}$ be an indexed family, let $L$ be a language, and let $\mathcal{G} = (G_j)_{j \in \mathbb{N}}$ be a hypothesis space, $k \in \mathbb{N} \cup \{*\}$. An IIM $CLIM_k\text{-}TXT$ $[CLIM_k\text{-}INF]$–identifies $L$ from text [informant] with respect to $\mathcal{G}$ iff*

(1) *$M$ $CLIM - TXT$ $[CLIM - INF]$–identifies $L$ from text [informant] with respect to $\mathcal{G}$,*

(2) *for every text $t$ [informant $i$] for $L$ the IIM $M$ performs, when fed $t$ [$i$], at most $k$ ($k = *$ means at most finitely many) mind changes, i.e., $card(\{x \mid M(t_x) \neq M(t_{x+1})\}) \leq k$ [$card(\{x \mid M(i_x) \neq M(i_{x+1})\}) \leq k$].*

*Moreover, $M$ $CLIM_k\text{-}TXT$ [ $CLIM_k\text{-}INF$ ]–identifies $\mathcal{L}$ with respect to $\mathcal{G}$ iff, for each $L \in \mathcal{L}$, $M$ $CLIM_k\text{-}TXT$ [ $CLIM_k\text{-}INF$ ]–identifies $L$ with respect to $\mathcal{G}$.*

$CLIM_k - TXT$ and $CLIM_k - INF$ are defined in the same way as above.

Obviously, $\lambda FIN - TXT = \lambda LIM_0 - TXT$ and $\lambda FIN - INF = \lambda LIM_0 - INF$ for all $\lambda \in \{E, \varepsilon, C\}$. Moreover, it is easy to see that $\lambda LIM_* - TXT = \lambda LIM - TXT$ as well as $\lambda LIM_* - INF = \lambda LIM - INF$ for all $\lambda \in \{E, \varepsilon, C\}$.

Next, we want to formally define strong-monotonic, monotonic and weak-monotonic inference. But before doing this, we first define *consistent* identification. Consistent learning devices have been introduced by Barzdin (1974). Intuitively, consistency means that the IIM has to correctly reflect the information it has already been fed.

**Definition 4. (Barzdin, 1974)** *Let $\mathcal{L}$ be an indexed family, let $L$ be a language, and let $\mathcal{G} = (G_j)_{j \in \mathbb{N}}$ be a hypothesis space. An IIM $M$ $CCONS\text{-}TXT$ $[CCONS\text{-}INF]$–identifies $L$ from text [informant] with respect to $\mathcal{G}$ iff*

(1) *$M$ $CLIM - TXT$ $[CLIM - INF]$–identifies $L$ from text [informant] with respect to $\mathcal{G}$,*

(2) *for every text $t$ [informant $i$] for $L$ the following condition is satisfied: whenever $M$ on $t_x$ [on $i_x$] produces a hypothesis $j_x$, then $t_x^+ \subseteq L(G_{j_x})$ [$i_x^+ \subseteq L(G_{j_x})$ and $i_x^- \subseteq co - L(G_{j_x})$].*

*Moreover, $M$ $CCONS - TXT$ $[CCONS - INF]$–identifies $\mathcal{L}$ with respect to $\mathcal{G}$ iff, for each $L \in \mathcal{L}$, $M$ $CCONS - TXT$ $[CCONS - INF]$–identifies $L$ with respect to $\mathcal{G}$.*

$CCONS - TXT$ and $CCONS - INF$ are analogously defined as above.

Now we are ready to formally define the three types of monotonic language learning introduced in Section 1.

**Definition 5. (Jantke, 1991a; Wiehagen, 1991)** *Let $L$ be a language, and let $\mathcal{G} = (G_j)_{j \in \mathbb{N}}$ be a hypothesis space. An IIM $M$ is said to identify the language $L$ from text [informant] with respect to $\mathcal{G}$*

(A) **strong-monotonically**

(B) **monotonically**

(C) **weak-monotonically**

*iff*

$M$ $CLIM-TXT$ $[CLIM-INF]$–*identifies* $L$ *with respect to* $\mathcal{G}$ *and for every text* $t$ *[informant* $i$*] of* $L$ *as well as for any two consecutive hypotheses* $j_x, j_{x+k}$ *which* $M$ *has produced when fed* $t_x$ *and* $t_{x+k}$ *[$i_x$ and $i_{x+k}$], where* $k \geq 1, k \in \mathbb{N}$, *the following conditions are satisfied:*

(A) $L(G_{j_x}) \subseteq L(G_{j_{x+k}})$

(B) $L(G_{j_x}) \cap L \subseteq L(G_{j_{x+k}}) \cap L$

(C) *if* $t_{x+k}^+ \subseteq L(G_{j_x})$, *then* $L(G_{j_x}) \subseteq L(G_{j_{x+k}})$ *[if* $i_{x+k}^+ \subseteq L(G_{j_x})$ *and* $i_{x+k}^- \subseteq co - L(G_{j_x})$, *then* $L(G_{j_x}) \subseteq L(G_{j_{x+k}})]$.

In particular, requirement (C) means that $M$ behaves strong-monotonically as long as its guess $j_x$ is consistent with *all* the data fed to $M$ both before and after $M$ has output $j_x$.

We denote by $CSMON-TXT$, $CSMON-INF$, $CMON-TXT$, $CMON-INF$, $CWMON-TXT$, $CWMON-INF$ the collection of all those indexed families $\mathcal{L}$ for which there are a hypothesis space $\mathcal{G}$ and an IIM inferring them strong-monotonically, monotonically, and weak-monotonically from text or informant with respect to $\mathcal{G}$, respectively.

With the following figure we summarize the known results concerning monotonic language learning (cf. Lange and Zeugmann (1992, 1993a)). We restrict ourselves to the class preserving case, since this case already reflects the characteristic relations between the monotonic learning models defined above. Each learning type is represented as a vertex in a directed graph. A directed edge from vertex $A$ to vertex $B$ indicates that $A$ is a proper subset of $B$, a bidirectional edge represents $A = B$, and no edge between vertices not connected by a directed path implies that $A$ and $B$ are incomparable.

### Monotonic Learning from Text versus Monotonic Learning from Informant

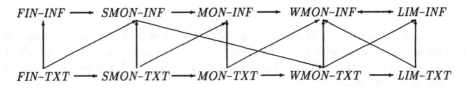

**Figure 1**

Next, we define *conservative* IIMs. Intuitively speaking, conservative IIMs maintain their actual hypothesis at least as long as they have not seen data contradicting it. Hence, whenever a conservative IIM performs a mind change it is because it has perceived clear inconsistency between its guess and the input.

**Definition 6. (Angluin, 1980b)** *Let $\mathcal{L}$ be an indexed family, let $L$ be a language, and let $\mathcal{G} = (G_j)_{j \in \mathbb{N}}$ be a hypothesis space.* **An IIM M CCONSERVATIVE-TXT [CCONSERVATIVE-INF]-identifies $L$ from text [informant] with respect to $\mathcal{G}$ iff**

(1) *$M$ $CLIM-TXT$ $[CLIM-INF]$-identifies $L$ with respect to $\mathcal{G}$,*

(2) *for every text $t$ [informant $i$] for $L$ the following condition is satisfied: whenever $M$ on input $t_x$ [on $i_x$] makes the guess $j_x$ and then makes the guess $j_{x+k} \neq j_x$ at some subsequent step, then $L(G_{j_x})$ must fail to contain some string from $t_{x+k}^+$ [$L(G_{j_x})$ must either fail to contain some string $s \in i_{x+k}^+$ or it generates some string $s \in i_{x+k}^-$].*

*Finally, $M$ $CCONSERVATIVE$-$TXT$ $[CCONSERVATIVE$-$INF]$-identifies $\mathcal{L}$ with respect to $\mathcal{G}$ if and only if, for each $L \in \mathcal{L}$, $M$ $CCONSERVATIVE$-$TXT$ $[CCONSERVATIVE$-$INF]$-identifies $L$ with respect to $\mathcal{G}$.*

The collection of sets $CCONSERVATIVE$-$TXT$ and $CCONSERVATIVE$-$INF$ are defined in a manner analogous to that above.

Note that $\lambda WMON-TXT = \lambda CONSERVATIVE$-$TXT$ as well as $\lambda WMON-INF = \lambda CONSERVATIVE$-$INF$ for all $\lambda \in \{C, \varepsilon, E\}$ (cf. Lange and Zeugmann (1993a)). Hence, looking at Figure 1 we may conclude that conservative IIMs are less powerful than unrestricted IIMs, in case one deals with the inferability of indexed families. Note that the latter assertion is not true if one deals with the learnability of arbitrary *recursively enumerable* languages (cf. Osherson, Stob and Weinstein (1986), pp. 75).

We continue in formally defining the three types of dual monotonic language learning introduced in Section 1.

**Definition 7. (Kapur, 1992)** *Let $L$ be a language, and let $\mathcal{G} = (G_j)_{j \in \mathbb{N}}$ be a hypothesis space.* **An IIM M is said to identify a language $L$ from text [informant] with respect to $\mathcal{G}$**

(A) **dual strong-monotonically**

(B) **dual monotonically**

(C) **dual weak-monotonically**

*iff*

*$M$ $CLIM-TXT$ $[CLIM-INF]$-identifies $L$ with respect to $\mathcal{G}$ and for any text $t$ [informant $i$] of $L$ as well as for any two consecutive hypotheses $j_x$, $j_{x+k}$ which $M$ has produced when fed $t_x$ and $t_{x+k}$ [$i_x$ and $i_{x+k}$], for some $k \geq 1, k \in \mathbb{N}$, the following conditions are satisfied:*

(A) $co-L(G_{j_x}) \subseteq co-L(G_{j_{x+k}})$

(B) $co-L(G_{j_x}) \cap co-L \subseteq co-L(G_{j_{x+k}}) \cap co-L$

(C) if $t_{x+k}^+ \subseteq L(G_{j_x})$, then $co-L(G_{j_x}) \subseteq co-L(G_{j_{x+k}})$ [if $i_{x+k}^+ \subseteq L(G_{j_x})$ and $i_{x+k}^- \subseteq co-L(G_{j_x})$, then $co-L(G_{j_x}) \subseteq co-L(G_{j_{x+k}})$].

By $CSMON^d$–$TXT, CSMON^d$–$INF, CMON^d$–$TXT, CMON^d$–$INF, CWMON^d$–$TXT$, and $CWMON^d-INF$ we denote the collections of all those indexed families $\mathcal{L}$ for which there are a hypothesis space $\mathcal{G}$ and an IIM identifying them dual strong-monotonically, dual monotonically and dual weak-monotonically from text and informant with respect to $\mathcal{G}$, respectively.

The next figure shows the relations between the defined modes of class preserving dual monotonic inference (cf. Lange, Zeugmann and Kapur (1992), and Lange and Zeugmann (1994)). The semantics of Figure 2 is analogous to that of Figure 1. On comparing with Figure 1, the similarities as well as the differences between the various types of monotonic and dual monotonic inference are clearly illustrated.

**Dual Monotonic Learning from Text versus Dual Monotonic Inference from Informant**

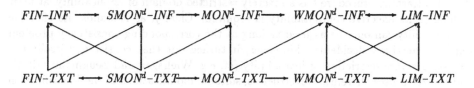

**Figure 2**

Note that the notions of monotonicity and of dual monotonicity are truly duals of *each other*.

Finally, we define iterative IIMs. An iterative IIM is only allowed to use its last guess and the next string of the text and informant, respectively, of the language it is supposed to learn. Conceptionally, an iterative IIM $M$ defines a sequence $(M_n)_{n \in N}$ of machines each of which takes as its input the output of its predecessor. Hence, the IIM $M$ has always to produce a hypothesis.

**Definition 8. (Wiehagen, 1976)** *Let $\mathcal{L}$ be an indexed family, let $L$ be a language, and let $\mathcal{G} = (G_j)_{j \in \mathbb{N}}$ be a hypothesis space. **An IIM $M$ CIT–TXT [CIT–INF ]-identifies $L$ from text [informant ] with respect to $\mathcal{G}$ iff** for every text $t = (s_j)_{j \in \mathbb{N}}$ [informant $i = ((w_j, b_j))_{j \in \mathbb{N}}$] the following conditions are satisfied:*

(1) *for all $n \in \mathbb{N}$, $M_n(t)$ $[M_n(i)$ ] is defined, where $M_0(t) =_{df} M(s_0)$ $[M_0(i) =_{df} M((w_0, b_0))$ ] and for all $n \geq 0$: $M_{n+1}(t) =_{df} M(M_n(t), s_{n+1})$ $[M_{n+1}(i) =_{df} M(M_n(i), (w_{n+1}, b_{n+1}))$ ],*

(2) *the sequence $(M_n(t))_{n \in \mathbb{N}}$ $[(M_n(i))_{n \in \mathbb{N}}]$ converges in the limit to a number $j$ such that $L = L(G_j)$.*

*Finally, $M$ CIT–TXT [CIT–INF ]-identifies $\mathcal{L}$ with respect to $\mathcal{G}$ iff, for each $L \in \mathcal{L}$, $M$ CIT–TXT [CIT–INF ]-identifies $L$ with respect to $\mathcal{G}$.*

The resulting identification types $CIT-TXT$ and $CIT-INF$ are analogously defined as above.

The combination of iterative and monotonic inference is denoted by $\lambda MON-IT-TXT$ ($\lambda MON-IT-INF$), where $\lambda \in \{S, W, \varepsilon\}$.

The next section starts our guided tour across the boundaries of learning recursive languages. We begin with several examples pointing to typical problems, ideas, and solutions in the field.

# 3. Examples

One of the first discovered learning algorithms has been *identification by enumeration* (cf. Solomonoff (1964), Gold (1965)). Nowadays, this learning algorithm is usually referred to as Gold's *identification by enumeration principle*. The main idea behind this algorithm is as follows. Choose a suitable enumeration of all the objects to be learned. Then, after having seen the data $d_0, ..., d_x$, search for the first enumerated object that is consistent with the data read so far. However, at first glance it seemed that this learning procedure has a severely restricted domain of applicability, at least as long as its effective computability is required. Clearly, as it stands, its effective computability can only be assured as long as the corresponding consistency problem remains effectively decidable. Moreover, it turned out that consistency itself constitutes a severe restriction of learnability (cf. e.g. Wiehagen and Zeugmann (1994), and the references therein). Nevertheless, suitable modifications of the identification by enumeration principle have been discovered that turned out to be very powerful. Nowadays, for the setting of inductive inference of recursive functions the following thesis is widely accepted (cf. Wiehagen (1991), pp. 184):

*"Any class of recursive functions which is identifiable at all can always be identified by an **enumeratively working** learning device. Moreover, the identification can always be realized with respect to a suitable non-standard (i.e., non-Gödel) numbering of the target class of functions."*

Thus, the question arises whether or not enumeratively working IIMs are of the same importance in language learning, too.

We start our guided tour with a series of examples pointing to major problems in answering the latter question. Furthermore, we exemplify fundamental ideas that have been developed to handle the arising difficulties. Thereby we restrict ourselves to the learnability of indexed families. Let us start with the easiest case, i.e., with the learnability of indexed families from positive and negative data. Inference from informant may be understood, at least conceptually, as inductive inference of enumerable classes of recursive predicates. Therefore, it is easy to see that Gold's (1967) *identification by enumeration principle* serves as a universal learning method. Moreover, we may even use any hypothesis space comprising all the target languages. In particular, successful inference can be always achieved, if we choose the target indexed family itself as the underlying hypothesis space. For the sake of completeness, let us continue with the definition of an IIM that realizes the identification by enumeration principle.

Let $\mathcal{L}$ be any indexed family, $L \in \mathcal{L}$, let $i \in info(L)$, and $x \in \mathbb{N}$. The wanted IIM $M$ works as follows. When fed $i_x$ it searches for the least index $j$ satisfying $i_x^+ \subseteq L_j$

and $i_x^- \cap L_j = \emptyset$, i.e., the first enumerated language that is consistent with all data read so far. Then, $M$ outputs the hypothesis $j$.

Some remarks are mandatory. Since membership is uniformly decidable for all languages enumerated in $\mathcal{L}$, the consistency test can be effectively performed. Moreover, since $i \in \mathit{info}(L)$ and $L \in \mathcal{L}$, the described search has to terminate. Hence, $M$ is indeed an IIM. Furthermore, $M$ converges to the least number $j$ satisfying $L = L_j$, and performs at most $j$ mind changes. But still, this is not the whole story. The described IIM $M$ possesses some further advantages that we are going to describe. First, any mind change performed by $M$ is justified by a "provable misclassification" of its previous guess. Therefore, $M$ will never reject a guess that is correct for the language to be learned. Hence, $M$ is *semantical finite*. Second, $M$ is *set-driven*, too, i.e., its output exclusively depends on the range of its input. Next, identification by enumeration is the most efficient learning method with respect to learning time, i.e., the first time such that $M$ outputs a correct guess that will be repeated in every subsequent learning step (cf. Gold (1967)). More precisely, Gold proved that there is no IIM $\hat{M}$ inferring $\mathcal{L}$ which is *uniformly faster* than the IIM $M$ described above with respect to learning time. Hence, in the setting of learning indexed families identification by enumeration is particularly tailored for learning from informant.

However, the situation remarkably changes when learning from positive data is concerned. There are several reasons for that phenomenon. The first one is a topological one, and has been discovered by Gold (1967). In particular, he proved the following theorem.

**Proposition 1. (Gold, 1967)** *Let $\mathcal{L}$ be any class of languages containing all finite languages and at least one infinite language. Then $\mathcal{L} \notin CLIM-TXT$.*

Note that Proposition 1 remains true, even in case one restricts itself to learning from *recursive* text (cf. Gold (1967)). Moreover, a closer look to Gold's proof directly implies that even quite simple indexed families are not identifiable from text as our first example shows.

### Example 1. Nonlearnability of simple indexed families

Consider the following indexed family $\mathcal{L} = (L_j)_{j \in \mathbb{N}}$ where $L_0 = \{a\}^+$ and $L_j = \{a^m \mid 1 \le m \le j\}$ for all $j \in \mathbb{N}^+$. We show that $\mathcal{L}$ is not learnable in the limit from positive data. Suppose the converse, i.e., there is an IIM $M$ which witnesses $\mathcal{L} \in ELIM-TXT$. Then, $M$ in particular has to identify the language $L_1$ on its uniquely defined text $t$. Hence, there exists an $x \in \mathbb{N}$ such that $M(t_x) = 1$. Obviously, it is possible to extend $t_x$ in order to obtain a text for the infinite language $L_0$. Namely, we may choose the text $t_x \cdot \hat{t}$ where $\hat{t}$ is the lexicographically ordered text of $L_0$. Since $M$ has to infer $L_0$ from this text, too, $M$ is forced to change its mind to the hypothesis 0. Therefore, there is a $y \in \mathbb{N}^+$ such that $M(t_x \cdot \hat{t}_y) = 0$. But now we may conclude that $t_x \cdot \hat{t}_y$ is an initial segment of a text $\tilde{t}$ for the finite language $L_y$. Consequently, $M$ has to perform one more mind change when successively fed $\tilde{t}$. By iterating this idea one may effectively construct a text for the infinite language $L_0$ on which $M$ has to change its mind infinitely often, a contradiction. Hence $\mathcal{L} \notin ELIM-TXT$. As we shall see later (cf. Section 5, Theorem 11), this result implies that $\mathcal{L}$ is not learnable at all in the limit, i.e., $\mathcal{L} \notin CLIM-TXT$. $\diamond$

This negative result is mainly caused by the problem that both finite and infinite languages have to be simultaneously handled. Moreover, Proposition 1 as well as our example do not only point to a weakness of identification by enumeration but to a serious weakness of learning from text. Hence, it is still imaginable that identification by enumeration remains a universal learning method provided the target indexed family is learnable in the limit from positive data. Our next example shows that the situation is much more subtle than one might expect.

### Example 2. The weakness of identification by enumeration

Consider the following indexed family $\mathcal{L} = (L_j)_{j \in \mathbb{N}}$ where $L_0 = \{a\}^+$ and $L_j = \{a^j\}$ for all $j \in \mathbb{N}^+$. An IIM $\hat{M}$ which conservatively infers $\mathcal{L}$ may be designed as follows. As long as a text for a singleton language, say $L_j$, is presented, $\hat{M}$ outputs just the guess $j$. If at least two different strings appear, $\hat{M}$ changes its mind to its final guess 0. Thus, on the one hand, $\mathcal{L} \in ELIM-TXT$.

But on the other hand, any IIM $M$ realizing the identification by enumeration principle cannot infer $\mathcal{L}$ from positive data. To see this, suppose the converse, i.e., there is such an IIM $M$ inferring $\mathcal{L}$ with respect to any class comprising hypothesis space $\mathcal{G}$. Hence, there is a least index $z \in \mathbb{N}$ such that $L_0 = L(G_z)$. Therefore, there has to be a singleton language $L$ satisfying $L(G_k) \neq L$ for all $k \leq z$. Since $L \subseteq L(G_z)$, $M$ will never output a hypothesis $j > z$ when fed a text for $L$. Thus, $M$ fails to infer the singleton language $L$. $\diamond$

The indexed family $\mathcal{L}$ from the above example contains a language $L$ as well as infinitely many proper sublanguages of $L$. A constellation like this always implies that identification by enumeration fails to learn the corresponding target indexed family from text. As mentioned above, when learning from informant is considered identification by enumeration is insensible to the choice of the hypothesis space as long as learnability at all is concerned. Our next example shows that this is no longer the case when learning from positive data is considered.

### Example 3. Sensibility of identification by enumeration with respect to the hypothesis space

Consider the indexed family $\mathcal{L} = (L_j)_{j \in \mathbb{N}}$ where $L_0 = \{a\}^+$ and $L_j = \{a\}$ for all $j \in \mathbb{N}^+$. Again, identification by enumeration fails when $\mathcal{L}$ is selected as hypothesis space. On the other hand, identification by enumeration yields successful inference, if a hypothesis space $\mathcal{G} = (G_j)_{j \in \mathbb{N}}$ is chosen such that $L(G_0) = \{a\}$ and $L(G_j) = \{a\}^+$ for all $j \in \mathbb{N}^+$. $\diamond$

Taking the above examples into consideration, the question arises whether or not identification by enumeration may be suitably modified for language learning from positive data. The crucial point is how overgeneralization may be avoided or, in case overgeneralization is inevitable, how the resulting problems may be handled. Furthermore, it would be interesting to know if all, or at least some, of the useful properties of identification by enumeration can be maintained. After Gold's (1967) pioneering paper these problems faced more than a decade of decline. Proposition 1 had been misinterpreted. Namely, many authors concluded that there is no interesting class of languages at all that can be learned from positive data, and hence, there is no need to study the question mentioned above. The breakthrough has been provided by Angluin (1980a) who showed that there are very interesting languages that can be inferred from text, for example the class of all pattern languages. Subsequently, the learnability of pattern languages has been intensively studied within different learning models (cf. e.g. Shinohara (1982), Kearns and Pitt (1989), Lange and Wiehagen (1991)). Besides that, pattern languages form the basis of applications in different fields, e.g. in the "intelligent" text processing system EBE (cf. Nix (1983)) or in a classification system for transmembrane proteins (cf. Arikawa et. al (1992)). So let us have a closer look to them.

### Example 4. The pattern languages

Let $\Sigma = \{a, b, ..\}$ be any non-empty finite alphabet containing at least two letters. Furthermore, let $X = \{x_0, x_1, x_2, ...\}$ be an infinite set of variables such that $\Sigma \cap X = \emptyset$. *Patterns* are non-empty strings from $\Sigma \cup X$, e.g., $ab$, $ax_1ccc$, $bx_1x_1cx_2x_2$ are patterns. If $p$ is a pattern, then $L(p)$, the language generated by pattern $p$, is the set of strings which can be obtained by substituting non-null strings $s_i \in \Sigma^*$ for each occurrence of the variable $x_i$ in the pattern $p$. Thus $aabbb$ is generable from pattern $ax_1x_2b$, while $aabba$ is not. From a practical point of view it is highly desirable to choose the hypothesis space as small as possible. For that purpose we use the canonical form of patterns (cf. Angluin (1980a)). A pattern $p$ is in *canonical form* provided that if $k$ is the number of variables in $p$, then the variables occurring in $p$ are precisely $x_0, ..., x_{k-1}$. Moreover, for every $j$ with $0 \leq j < k - 1$, the leftmost occurrence of $x_j$ in $p$ is to the left of the leftmost occurrence of $x_{j+1}$ in $p$. If a pattern $p$ is in canonical form then we refer to $p$ as a canonical pattern. Let *Patc* denote the set of all canonical patterns. Clearly, for every pattern $p$ there exists a unique $q \in Patc$ such that $L(p) = L(q)$. Finally, choose any repetition free effective enumeration $p_0, p_1, ...$ of *Patc* and define $PAT = (L(p_j))_{j \in \mathbb{N}}$. Then $PAT$ establishes an indexed family (cf. Angluin (1980a)).

In the sequel, we discuss the learnability of the family $PAT$ from different perspectives. Thereby, we are mainly interested in principal solutions. Technicalities are suppressed as much as possible.

First, we summarize some characteristic features of pattern languages. From the above definition it immediately follows that given any two patterns $p$ and $q$ it is decidable whether or not $L(p) = L(q)$. Furthermore, let $T_p = \{w \mid w \in L(p), |w| = |p|\}$ for every pattern $p \in Patc$. Then, every pattern language $L(p)$ is uniquely characterized by its finite subset $T_p$ as the following proposition shows.

**Proposition 2. (Angluin, 1980a)** *Let $p, q$ be any patterns. Then we have:*

(1) $L(p) = L(q)$ iff $T_p \subseteq L(q)$ and $T_q \subseteq L(p)$,

(2) $T_p \subseteq L(q)$ implies $\neg L(q) \subset L(p)$.

Let $S$ denote any finite set of strings. A pattern $p$ is said to be **descriptive for $S$** provided that $S \subseteq L(p)$ and there does not exists any pattern $q$ satisfying $S \subseteq L(q) \subset L(p)$. Therefore, any IIM $M$ which exclusively outputs descriptive patterns as hypotheses realizes the subset principle, i.e., it never generates an overgeneralized hypothesis. The sets $T_p$, henceforth called *tell-tale sets*, can be effectively computed, if $p$ is given. Hence, tell-tale sets may guide a learning device to avoid the problem of overgeneralization.

Based on this idea, the following IIM conservatively infers $PAT$ with respect to the hypothesis space $PAT$. Assume that any initial segment $t_x$ of any text $t$ for any pattern language $L(q)$ is presented. Initially, $M$ searches for all indices $j \leq x$ such that $t_x^+ \subseteq L(p_j)$. Among these candidate hypotheses, $M$ chooses the least $j$ satisfying $T_{p_j} \subseteq t_x^+$, if such an index exists. Because of Assertion (2), $p_j$ is descriptive for the set $T_{p_j}$. Since $T_{p_j} \subseteq t_x^+ \subseteq L(p_j)$, $p_j$ is descriptive for the set $t_x^+$, too. Thus, $M$ has seen enough evidence to output just the hypothesis $j$. $M$ does not change the hypothesis $j$ as long as it is consistent. If $j$ turns out to be inconsistent then $M$ again starts the same search as explained above. Now, taking Proposition 2 into account, it is easy to see that $M$ converges on $t$. Moreover, since $M$ never outputs an overgeneralized hypothesis, $M$ learns $L(q)$ from text. Thus, we have the following theorem.

**Theorem 1.** *PAT* $\in$ *ECONSERVATIVE* $-$ *TXT*.

The IIM $M$ explained above works enumeratively, too. But, $M$'s search within the hypothesis space does not only aim to find any consistent hypothesis. Instead, $M$ does not output any hypothesis until it has collected enough evidence. It measures the evidence obtained with respect to the relevant tell-tale sets. If at least one tell-tale set is completely contained in the range of its input $M$ creates a suitable subspace of candidate hypotheses, i.e., the set of all those patterns $p$ satisfying $T_p \subseteq t_x^+$. Then it searches the first consistent hypothesis, say $p$, and outputs it. If $p$ is not a correct guess, Assertion (2) of Proposition 2 guarantees that data contradicting it have to appear.

As we have seen, there is some hope to suitably modify identification by enumeration for learning from positive data. Moreover, for the particular case of pattern languages the tell-tale sets are the main ingredient to solve the subset problem. Consequently, it is only natural to ask whether or not the approach outlined above may be generalized. This is indeed the case as we shall see below. But before dealing with possible generalizations we provide some more information concerning the learnability of pattern languages. First, we ask whether Theorem 1 may be strengthened, for example to *PAT* $\in$ *SMON* $-TXT$. Recently, it has been shown that the inclusion problem for pattern languages is undecidable. This implies the following result (cf. Zeugmann, Lange and Kapur (199?) for a detailed discussion).

**Theorem 2.** *PAT* $\notin$ *MON* $-$ *TXT*.

Hence, Theorem 1 cannot be improved with respect to class preserving learning. On the other hand, the pattern languages possess another favorable property, namely they are iteratively learnable (cf. Lange and Wiehagen (1991)).

**Theorem 3.** *PAT* $\in$ *EIT* $-$ *TXT*.

The basic idea may be described as follows. Ignore for a moment that the desired IIM has to be iterative. As we have already seen, every pattern language is uniquely characterized by the set of all its minimal strings. This observation is the main ingredient to the following IIM $M$. At each learning step, $M$ first determines the set $S$ of all minimal strings it has been fed so far. All other strings will be simply ignored. Then, $M$ generates a pattern $p_j$ that is descriptive for $S$. Thus, $M$ outputs in every step a hypothesis $j$ which is consistent with all the shortest strings seen so far. Now, another property of $p_j$ comes into the play. Namely, $M$ can effectively reproduce all information it has used to compute $p_j$ from $p_j$. Therefore, when fed its last guess as well as the next input string, it can effectively decide whether or not it has to perform a mind change. This is the gist underlying the construction in Lange and Wiehagen (1991). We omit the details.

Furthermore, their result has some special features. They have shown that the IIM they actually use runs in time polynomial in the length of the input, since it totally avoids to test membership. The price paid is that it sometimes outputs inconsistent hypotheses. For a more detailed discussion concerning the consistent versus inconsistent learnability of the pattern languages the reader is referred to Wiehagen and Zeugmann (1994). ◇

Reviewing the results discussed so far the questions arises whether or not any indexed family learnable from text can be inferred by a conservative IIM or even by an iterative one. In each case, the answer is negative (cf. Lange and Zeugmann (1992), (1993c)).

**Theorem 4.**

(1) $CCONSERVATIVE - TXT \subset ELIM - TXT$

(2) $CIT - TXT \subset ELIM - TXT$

Assertion (1) proves that overgeneralization is inevitable, in general, if one considers language learning from positive examples. In order to show a particular way to solve the subset problem, we discuss the relation between conservative learners and learning in the limit in some more detail. In Angluin's pioneering paper (cf. Angluin (1980b)) the following characterization of those indexed families for which learning in the limit from positive data is possible has been shown.

**Proposition 3. (Angluin, 1980b)** *Let $\mathcal{L}$ be an indexed family of recursive languages. Then: $\mathcal{L} \in ELIM - TXT$ if and only if there is an effective procedure which on every input $j \in \mathbb{N}$ enumerates a tell-tale set $T_j$ of strings such that*

(1) *for all $j \in \mathbb{N}$, $T_j$ is finite,*

(2) *for all $j \in \mathbb{N}$, $T_j \subseteq L_j$,*

(3) *for all $j, z \in \mathbb{N}$, if $T_j \subseteq L_z$, then $L_z \not\subset L_j$.*

From the characterization above one may deduce how the identification by enumeration principle has to be modified in order to obtain a suitable learning method for learning from positive data. In particular, this method provides insight into the problem of how to deal with overgeneralization.

**Example 5. A universal IIM for learning from text**

Let $\mathcal{L} \in ELIM - TXT$. Moreover, assume a corresponding procedure which on every input $j \in \mathbb{N}$ enumerates a tell-tale set $T_j$ of strings satisfying the above requirements. Let $T_j^{(x)}$ denotes the finite subset of $T_j$ which may be enumerated within $x$ steps. The following IIM $M$ $ELIM - TXT$–identifies $\mathcal{L}$. When fed an initial segment $t_x$ of any text $t$ for a language $L \in \mathcal{L}$, $M$ searches for the least index $j \le x$ satisfying $T_j^{(x)} \subseteq t_x^+ \subseteq L_j$. In case an index $j$ is found, then $M$ outputs the guess $j$. Otherwise, $M$ requests the next input. ◇

Again, the tell-tale sets are used to control the search within the hypothesis space in order to find a suitable consistent hypothesis. If the tell-tale set $T_j$ is not completely enumerated within $x$ steps, $M$ may be forced to produce an overgeneralized hypothesis when fed a text $t$ for $L$. Namely, after processing $t_x$ it may happen that $M$ outputs a hypothesis $j$ with $L \subset L_j$. But, then there has to be a $y > x$ such that $T_j^{(y)}$ contains a string $s$ not belonging to $L$ (cf. Proposition 3, Condition (3)). Hence, $s$ never appears in the text $t$ for $L$ and $M$ will reject its former guess $j$. Furthermore, $M$ will never output the guess $j$ in any subsequent step.

Thus, we already know one way to design suitable enumeratively working IIMs that can solve every learning task from positive data as long as indexed families are concerned. However, a straightforward analysis shows that $M$ is neither set-driven nor semantically finite. Hence, some desirable properties are still missing. We postpone the problem of order independence for a while and refer the reader to Section 8 for a detailed discussion. The remaining part of this section is devoted to the problem whether or not semantical finiteness can always be achieved. Clearly, any conservative IIM is semantically finite, too. Therefore, let us have a closer look to conservative learning. We start with the following characterization of class comprising conservative inference.

**Theorem 5. (Lange and Zeugmann, 1993d)** *Let $\mathcal{L}$ be an indexed family. Then: $\mathcal{L} \in CCONSERVATIVE - TXT$ if and only if there are a hypothesis space $\mathcal{G} = (G_j)_{j \in \mathbb{N}}$ and a uniformly recursively generable family $(T_j)_{j \in \mathbb{N}}$ of finite non-empty sets such that*

(1) *$range(\mathcal{L}) \subseteq \mathcal{L}(\mathcal{G})$,*

(2) *for all $j \in \mathbb{N}$, $T_j \subseteq L(G_j)$,*

(3) *for all $j$, $z \in N$, if $T_j \subseteq L(G_z)$, then $L(G_z) \not\subseteq L(G_j)$.*

A family of finite sets $(T_j)_{j \in \mathbb{N}}$ is said to be **uniformly recursively generable** iff there is a total effective procedure $g$ which, on every input $j$, generates all elements of $T_j$ and stops.

Hence, the main difference between conservative learning and learning in the limit is characterized by the different degree of recursiveness of the corresponding tell-tale families. In case of conservative learning they are recursively generable, and in the general case of learning in the limit they are recursively enumerable. And indeed, recursive generability cannot always be achieved as our next example shows.

### Example 6. The weakness of conservative learners

In order to verify $ELIM - TXT \setminus CCONSERVATIVE - TXT \neq \emptyset$ we define the following indexed family $\mathcal{L} = (L_{\langle j,k \rangle})_{k,j \in \mathbb{N}}$. For all $k \in \mathbb{N}$, let $L_{\langle k,0 \rangle} = \{a^k b^n \mid n \in \mathbb{N}^+\}$. For all $k \in \mathbb{N}$ and all $j \in \mathbb{N}^+$, we distinguish the following cases:

*Case 1.* $\neg\, \Phi_k(k) \leq j$

Then we set $L_{\langle k,j \rangle} = L_{\langle k,0 \rangle}$.

*Case 2.* $\Phi_k(k) \leq j$

Let $d = 2 \cdot \Phi_k(k) - j$. Now, we set:

$$L_{\langle k,j \rangle} = \begin{cases} \{a^k b^m \mid 1 \leq m \leq d\}, & \text{if } d \geq 1, \\ \{a^k b\}, & \text{otherwise.} \end{cases}$$

$\mathcal{L} = (L_{\langle k,j \rangle})_{j,k \in \mathbb{N}}$ is an indexed family of recursive languages, since the predicate "$\Phi_i(y) \leq z$" is uniformly decidable in $i$, $y$, and $z$. It is easy to see how a recursively enumerable tell-tale family has to be defined, and hence $\mathcal{L} \in ELIM - TXT$. Thus, it remains to ask whether or not $\mathcal{L}$ can be class comprisingly, and conservatively identified. An affirmative answer would imply that a finite tell-tale set for the infinite language $L_{(k,0)}$ can be recursively generalized. But any procedure which recursively generates a corresponding tell-tale set may be used to solve simultaneously the halting problem, a contradiction. ◇

Note that the same family may be used to witness the weakness of iterative IIMs, too. However, the reasons for $\mathcal{L} \notin CCONSERVATIVE - TXT$ and $\mathcal{L} \notin CIT - TXT$ are *different*. Conservative learners cannot handle overgeneralization at all, but iterative learners sometimes *can* (cf. Section 6, Theorem 18). The main reason for $\mathcal{L} \notin CIT - TXT$ is the topological structure of the finite languages in $\mathcal{L}$. Every IIM learning $\mathcal{L}$ has to output an overgeneralized hypothesis. Taking this into account, it is intuitively clear that every iterative IIM fails to memorize the maximal element (with respect to lexicographical order) of some finite language a text of which it is fed. A comprehensive discussion concerning the power and limitations of iterative IIMs is provided in Section 6.

Up to now, we have discussed learning from text and learning from informant independently. Finally, let us mention an interesting aspect related to the interplay between information presentation and learnability constraints. In Lange and Zeugmann (1993a) it was shown that the family *PAT* is finitely identifiable from positive and negative examples. On the other hand, *PAT* is even learnable from text. Surprisingly enough, this observation can be generalized as follows.

**Theorem 6.** $SMON - INF \subseteq CONSERVATIVE - TXT$

Finally, we present a proof of the theorem above which is conceptually completely different from the one published in Lange and Zeugmann (1993a). It is mainly based on characterizations recently obtained (cf. Lange and Zeugmann (1992), (1994)).

*Proof.* The main ingredient is the following characterization of strong-monotonic inference from positive and negative data (cf. Lange and Zeugmann (1994)).

**Theorem 7.** *Let $\mathcal{L}$ be an indexed family of recursive languages. Then: $\mathcal{L} \in SMON - INF$ if and only if there are a hypothesis space $\mathcal{G} = (G_j)_{j \in \mathbb{N}}$ and uniformly recursively generable families $(P_j)_{j \in \mathbb{N}}$ and $(N_j)_{j \in \mathbb{N}}$ of finite sets such that*

(1) $range(\mathcal{L}) = \mathcal{L}(\mathcal{G})$,

(2) *for all $j \in \mathbb{N}$, $\emptyset \neq P_j \subseteq L(G_j)$ and $N_j \subseteq co - L(G_j)$,*

(3) *for all $j$, $z \in \mathbb{N}$, if $P_j \subseteq L(G_z)$ as well as $N_j \subseteq co - L(G_z)$, then $L(G_j) \subseteq L(G_z)$.*

Let $\mathcal{G}$ be the hypothesis space from the characterization above. We show that the family $(P_j)_{j \in \mathbb{N}}$ serves as a family of finite tell-tale sets satisfying the requirements in Theorem 5. In doing so, it suffices to show that $P_j \subseteq L(G_z)$ implies $L(G_z) \not\subseteq L(G_j)$ for all $j, z \in \mathbb{N}$. Suppose the converse, i.e., $P_j \subseteq L(G_z)$ as well as $L(G_z) \subset L(G_j)$ for any $j, z \in \mathbb{N}$.

*Case 1.* $N_j \cap L(G_z) = \emptyset$.

Thus, $P_j \subseteq L(G_z)$ as well as $N_j \subseteq co - L(G_z)$ implies $L(G_j) \subseteq L(G_z)$ by Theorem 7, Property (3). This contradicts $L(G_z) \subset L(G_j)$.

*Case 2.* $N_j \cap L(G_z) \neq \emptyset$.

Now, there has to be a string $s \in L(G_z)$ such that $s \in N_j \subseteq co - L(G_j)$. Therefore, $s \in L(G_z) \setminus L(G_j)$. This contradicts $L(G_z) \subset L(G_j)$.

The tell-tale family $(P_j)_{j\in\mathbb{N}}$ satisfies Conditions (2) and (3) in Theorem 5, if we select the class preserving hypothesis space $\mathcal{G} = (G_j)_{j\in\mathbb{N}}$. From the proof of Theorem 5 (cf. Lange and Zeugmann (1993c)) it follows that $\mathcal{L}$ can be conservatively inferred with respect to the hypothesis space $\mathcal{G}$. Hence, $\mathcal{L} \in CONSERVATIVE - TXT$. q.e.d.

As we have seen, the learnability of indexed families provides several interesting problems that are worth to be studied in some more detail. The following sections survey recently obtained results in a systematic way.

# 4. Characterizations

As we have already seen, characterizations provide a useful tool to answer the question how learning algorithms may be designed (cf. Example 5). Moreover, they may help to gain a better understanding of what different learning types have in *common* and where the *differences* are (cf. Proposition 3 and Theorem 5). Furthermore, characterizations may be applied to solve particular learning problems and to solve deeper theoretical questions (cf. Example 4 and Theorem 6). Therefore, it is justified to deal with characterizations in some more detail. We continue our guided tour with a survey of representative results and proof techniques. For that purpose it suffices to deal with class preserving learning. We start with learning from positive and negative data.

## 4.1. Learning from Informant

Remembering our discussion in Section 3, we already know that Gold's (1967) *identification by enumeration principle* serves as a universal inference algorithm for learning in the limit. Moreover, every IIM realizing the identification by enumeration principle fulfills the weak-monotonic and dual weak-monotonic constraint. Hence, there is no need to characterize these learning models. On the other hand, neither $MON - INF$, $MON^d - INF$, $SMON - INF$ nor $SMON^d - INF$ is as powerful as learning in the limit. Hence, learning under these monotonicity constraints cannot be realized by a straightforward implementation of Gold's identification by enumeration principle. Therefore, we are interested in answering the question whether or not there is a universal inference method for these learning types. The affirmative answer is given by our next theorem that characterizes $MON - INF$ in terms of recursively generable finite tell-tale sets. Note that the same proof technique applies *mutatis mutandis* to all remaining learning types (cf. Lange and Zeugmann (1994)).

**Theorem 8.** *Let $\mathcal{L}$ be an indexed family of recursive languages. Then: $\mathcal{L} \in MON - INF$ if and only if there are a hypothesis space $\mathcal{G} = (G_j)_{j\in\mathbb{N}}$ and recursively generable families $(P_j)_{j\in\mathbb{N}}$ and $(N_j)_{j\in\mathbb{N}}$ of finite sets such that*

(1) $range(\mathcal{L}) = \mathcal{L}(\mathcal{G})$,

(2) *for all $j \in \mathbb{N}$, $\emptyset \neq P_j \subseteq L(G_j)$ and $N_j \subseteq co - L(G_j)$,*

(3) *for all $k, j \in \mathbb{N}$, and for all $L \in \mathcal{L}$, if $P_k \cup P_j \subseteq L(G_j) \cap L$ as well as $N_k \cup N_j \subseteq$*

$co - L(G_j) \cap co - L$, then $L(G_k) \cap L \subseteq L(G_j) \cap L$.

*Proof.* Necessity: Let $\mathcal{L} \in MON\text{--}INF$. Then there are an IIM $M$ and a hypothesis space $(\hat{G}_j)_{j\in\mathbb{N}}$ such that $M$ infers every $L \in \mathcal{L}$ monotonically from any informant with respect to $(\hat{G}_j)_{j\in\mathbb{N}}$. Without loss of generality, we can assume that $M$ is conservative, too, (cf. Lange and Zeugmann (1993a)). We proceed in showing how to construct $(\hat{G}_j)_{j\in\mathbb{N}}$. This is done in two steps. First, we define a hypothesis space $(\tilde{G}_j)_{j\in\mathbb{N}}$ as well as corresponding recursively generable families $(\tilde{P}_j)_{j\in\mathbb{N}}$ and $(\tilde{N}_j)_{j\in\mathbb{N}}$ of finite sets, where $\tilde{P}_j$ may be empty for some $j \in \mathbb{N}$. Afterwards, we define a procedure which enumerates a certain subset of $\mathcal{G}$.

First step: For all $k, x \in \mathbb{N}$ we set $\tilde{G}_{\langle k,x\rangle} = \hat{G}_k$. By construction, $range(\mathcal{L}) = \mathcal{L}(\tilde{\mathcal{G}})$ is obvious. Let $i^k$ be the lexicographically ordered informant for $L(\hat{G}_k)$, and let $x \in \mathbb{N}$. We define:

$$\tilde{P}_{\langle k,x\rangle} = \begin{cases} i_y^{k,+}, & \text{if } y = min\{z \mid z \leq x,\ M(i_z^k) = k,\ i_z^{k,+} \neq \emptyset\}, \\ \emptyset, & \text{otherwise.} \end{cases}$$

If $\tilde{P}_{\langle k,x\rangle} = i_y^{k,+} \neq \emptyset$, then we set $\tilde{N}_{\langle k,x\rangle} = i_y^{k,-}$. Otherwise, we define $\tilde{N}_{\langle k,x\rangle} = \emptyset$.

The intuitive idea behind the definition of the families $(\tilde{P}_j)_{j\in\mathbb{N}}$ and $(\tilde{N}_j)_{j\in\mathbb{N}}$ is as follows. If an IIM $M$ is fed initial segments of an informant then there is almost no hope to determine from the appearing outputs what the IIM $M$ has learned from its input. However, in the particular case that we have an index $k$ of the language $L$, the lexicographically ordered informant $i^k$ of which is successively fed $M$, there is a syntactical criterion that can be effectively tested. Namely, if $M(i_z^k) = k$, then we know for sure that $M$ has done a pretty good job on input $i_z^k$. Clearly, it has output a correct guess for the language it should learn. Therefore, it seems very reasonable to suitably collect all the information contained in these initial segments in the corresponding families $(\tilde{P}_j)_{j\in\mathbb{N}}$ and $(\tilde{N}_j)_{j\in\mathbb{N}}$. And indeed, it even suffices to collect the positive data in $\tilde{P}_j$, and the negative data in $\tilde{N}_j$.

Second step: The hypothesis space $(G_j)_{j\in\mathbb{N}}$ will be defined by simply striking off all grammars $\tilde{G}_{\langle k,x\rangle}$ with $\tilde{P}_{\langle k,x\rangle} = \emptyset$. In order to save readability, we omit the corresponding mapping yielding the enumeration $(G_j)_{j\in\mathbb{N}}$ from $(\tilde{G}_j)_{j\in\mathbb{N}}$. If $G_j$ is referring to $\tilde{G}_{\langle k,x\rangle}$, we set $P_j = \tilde{P}_{\langle k,x\rangle}$ and $N_j = \tilde{N}_{\langle k,x\rangle}$.

We have to show that $(G_j)_{j\in\mathbb{N}}$, $(N_j)_{j\in\mathbb{N}}$, and $(P_j)_{j\in\mathbb{N}}$ do fulfill the announced properties. (1) and (2) follow immediately, since $M$ has, in particular, to infer every $L \in \mathcal{L}$ from its lexicographically ordered informant. It remains to show (3). Suppose $L \in \mathcal{L}$ and $k, j \in \mathbb{N}$ such that $P_k \cup P_j \subseteq L(G_j) \cap L$ as well as $N_k \cup N_j \subseteq co - L(G_j) \cap co - L$. We have to show $L(G_k) \cap L \subseteq L(G_j) \cap L$. Due to our construction, we can make the following observations. There is a uniquely defined initial segment of the lexicographically ordered informant $i^k$ for $L(G_k)$, say $i_x^k$, such that $range(i_x^k) = P_k \cup N_k$. Moreover, $M(i_x^k) = m$ with $L(G_k) = L(\hat{G}_m)$. By $i_y^j$ we denote the uniquely defined initial segment of the lexicographically ordered informant $i^j$ for $L(G_j)$ with $range(i_y^j) = P_j \cup N_j$. Furthermore, $M(i_y^j) = n$ and $L(G_j) = L(\hat{G}_n)$. From $P_k \subseteq L(G_j)$ and $N_k \subseteq co - L(G_j)$, it follows $i_x^k \sqsubseteq i^j$. Since $P_j \subseteq L$ and $N_j \subseteq co - L$, we conclude that $i_y^j$ is an initial segment of the lexicographically ordered informant $i^L$ for $L$.

We have to distinguish the following three cases.

*Case 1.* $x = y$

Hence, $m = n$ and therefore $L(G_k) = L(G_j)$. This implies $L(G_k) \cap L \subseteq L(G_j) \cap L$.

*Case 2.* $x < y$

Now, we have $i_x^k \sqsubseteq i_y^j \sqsubseteq i^L$. Moreover, $M$ monotonically infers L from informant $i^L$. By the transitivity of "$\subseteq$" we immediately obtain $L(G_k) \cap L \subseteq L(G_j) \cap L$.

*Case 3.* $y < x$

Hence, $i_y^j \sqsubseteq i_x^k \sqsubseteq i^j$. Since $M$ is conservative, too, it follows $m = n$. Therefore, $L(G_k) = L(G_j)$. This implies $L(G_k) \cap L \subseteq L(G_j) \cap L$.

Hence, $(G_j)_{j \in \mathbb{N}}$, $(P_j)_{j \in \mathbb{N}}$ as well as $(N_j)_{j \in \mathbb{N}}$ have indeed the announced properties.

Sufficiency: It suffices to prove that there is an IIM $M$ inferring any $L \in \mathcal{L}$ monotonically from any informant with respect to $\mathcal{G}$. Interestingly enough, an easy modification of the universal IIM described in Example 5 is all we need. So let $L \in \mathcal{L}$, let $i$ be any informant for $L$, and $x \in \mathbb{N}$.

$M(t_x) = $ "Generate $P_j$ and $N_j$ for $j = 0, ..., x$ and test whether

$$P_j \subseteq i_x^+ \subseteq L(G_j) \text{ and } N_j \subseteq i_x^- \subseteq co - L(G_j).$$

In case there is at least a $j$ fulfilling the test, output the minimal one and request the next input. Otherwise, output nothing and request the next input."

Since all of the $P_j$ and $N_j$ are uniformly recursively generable and finite, we see that $M$ is an IIM. We have to show that it infers $L$. Let $z$ be the least $k$ such that $L = L(G_k)$. We claim that $M$ converges to $z$. Consider $P_0, ..., P_z$ as well as $N_0, ..., N_z$. Then there must be an $x$ such that $P_z \subseteq i_x^+ \subseteq L(G_z)$ and $N_z \subseteq i_x^- \subseteq co - L(G_z)$. That means, at least after having fed $i_x$ to $M$, the machine $M$ outputs a hypothesis. Moreover, since $P_z \subseteq i_{x+r}^+ \subseteq L(G_z)$ as well as $N_z \subseteq i_{x+r}^- \subseteq co - L(G_z)$ for all $r \in \mathbb{N}$, the IIM $M$ never produces a guess $j > z$ on $i_{x+r}$.

Suppose, $M$ converges to $j < z$. Then we have: $P_j \subseteq i_{x+r}^+ \subseteq L(G_j) \neq L(G_z)$ and $N_j \subseteq i_{x+r}^- \subseteq co - L(G_j)$ for all $r \in \mathbb{N}$.

*Case 1.* $L(G_z) \setminus L(G_j) \neq \emptyset$

Consequently, there is at least one string $s \in L(G_z) \setminus L(G_j)$ such that $(s, +)$ has to appear sometime in $i$, say in $i_{x+r}$ for some $r$. Thus, we have $i_{x+r}^+ \not\subseteq L(G_j)$, a contradiction.

*Case 2.* $L(G_j) \setminus L(G_z) \neq \emptyset$

Then we may restrict ourselves to the case $L(G_z) \subset L(G_j)$, since otherwise we are again in Case 1. Consequently, there is at least one string $s \in L(G_j) \setminus L(G_z)$ such that $(s, -)$ has to appear sometime in $i$, say in $i_{x+r}$ for some $r$. Thus, $i_{x+r}^- \not\subseteq co - L(G_j)$, a contradiction.

Consequently, $M$ converges to $z$ on informant $i$. To complete the proof we show that $M$ monotonically learns $L$. Suppose $M$ outputs $k$ and changes its mind to $j$ in some subsequent step. Consequently, $M(i_x) = k$ and $M(i_{x+r}) = j$ , for some $x, r \in \mathbb{N}$.

*Case* 1. $L(G_j) = L$

Hence, $L(G_k) \cap L \subseteq L(G_j) \cap L = L$ is obviously fulfilled.

*Case* 2. $L(G_j) \neq L$

Due to the definition of $M$, it holds $P_k \subseteq i_x^+ \subseteq i_{x+r}^+ \subseteq L(G_j)$. Hence, $P_k \subseteq L \cap L(G_j)$. Furthermore, we have $N_k \subseteq i_x^- \subseteq i_{x+r}^- \subseteq co - L(G_j)$. This implies $N_k \subseteq co - L(G_j) \cap co - L$. Since $M(i_{x+r}) = j$, it holds that $P_j \subseteq L$ and $N_j \subseteq co - L$. This yields $P_k \cup P_j \subseteq L(G_j) \cap L$ as well as $N_k \cup N_j \subseteq co - L(G_j) \cap co - L$. From (3), we obtain $L(G_k) \cap L \subseteq L(G_j) \cap L$.

Hence, $M$ $MON-INF$–identifies $\mathcal{L}$.                                q.e.d.

As a matter of fact, the machine defined above uses the tell-tale sets to control its search within the hypothesis space. Therefore, the desired modification of the identification by enumeration principles has been obtained using the same ideas that we have exemplified in the proof of Theorem 1 in Section 3.

Exploiting the same proof method similar characterizations for $MON^d - INF$, $SMON - INF$, and $SMON^d - INF$ have been obtained (cf. Lange and Zeugmann (1994)). Hence, the different monotonicity constraints are completely characterized by the specific properties of the relevant recursively generable tell-tale families. Note that the resulting characterization for $SMON - INF$ is stated in Section 3, Theorem 7. Finally, the characterization of $LIM_k - INF$ required some new ingredients (cf. Lange and Zeugmann (1993a)). However, the difficulties one has to overcome when characterizing $LIM_k - INF$ are closely related to the problems one has to handle in characterizing $LIM_k - TXT$. Therefore, we refer the reader to Theorem 10 below.

## 4.2. Learning from Text

When investigating monotonic language learning from text, the situation is much more subtle. As we shall see later, the IIM $M$ defined in the proof of Theorem 8 does not longer serve as a universal learning device. Consequently, a relaxation of the basic approach underlying $M's$ definition is necessary. We shall come back to this point.

Although Angluin (1980b) established some sufficient conditions that guarantee exact conservative learning from positive data, it remained open whether the class of those indexed families for which exact conservative learning from positive data is possible may be characterized in terms of finite non-empty tell-tale sets. Next, we present a preliminary solution to this long standing open problem. In doing so, we characterize $WMON - TXT$ in terms of recursively generable finite tell-tales. The underlying proof method is powerful enough to successfully attack the original problem, too, (cf. Section 8, Theorem 42).

**Theorem 9.** *Let $\mathcal{L}$ be an indexed family. Then: $\mathcal{L} \in WMON-TXT$ if and only if there are a hypothesis space $\mathcal{G} = (G_j)_{j \in \mathbb{N}}$ and a recursively generable family $(T_j)_{j \in \mathbb{N}}$ of finite and non-empty sets such that*

(1) *$range(\mathcal{L}) = \mathcal{L}(\mathcal{G})$,*

(2) *for all $j \in \mathbb{N}$, $T_j \subseteq L(G_j)$,*

(3) *for all* $j$, $z \in \mathbb{N}$, *if* $T_j \subseteq L(G_z)$, *then* $L(G_z) \not\subseteq L(G_j)$.

*Proof.* Necessity: Let $\mathcal{L} \in WMON{-}TXT = CONSERVATIVE{-}TXT$. Then there are an IIM $M$ and a hypothesis space $\hat{\mathcal{G}} = (\hat{G}_j)_{j\in\mathbb{N}}$ such that $M$ conservatively infers every $L \in \mathcal{L}$ with respect to $\hat{\mathcal{G}}$. The desired hypothesis space $\mathcal{G} = (G_j)_{j\in\mathbb{N}}$ and the corresponding tell-tale family $(T_j)_{j\in\mathbb{N}}$ can be defined in a similar way as in the demonstration of Theorem 8. Therefore, we point to the differences, only. First, we construct a hypothesis space $\tilde{\mathcal{G}} = (\tilde{G}_j)_{j\in\mathbb{N}}$ as well as a recursively generable family $(\tilde{T}_j)_{j\in\mathbb{N}}$ of finite but possibly empty sets. For all $k$, $x \in \mathbb{N}$, we set $\tilde{G}_{\langle k,x\rangle} = \hat{G}_k$. Furthermore, for any language $L(\hat{G}_k)$, let $t^k$ be the canonically ordered text of $L(\hat{G}_k)$.

We define:

$$
\tilde{T}_{\langle k,x\rangle} = \begin{cases} range(t_y^k), & \text{if } y = min\{z \mid z \leq x,\ M(t_z^k) = k\}, \\ \emptyset, & \text{otherwise.} \end{cases}
$$

Obviously, $(\tilde{T}_j)_{j\in\mathbb{N}}$ is a uniformly recursively generable family of finite sets.

Conceptually, we use the same idea as in the proof of Theorem 8. The main new ingredient is the introduction of the *canonical* text. Clearly, if $L(\hat{G}_k)$ is finite, then the sequence of its lexicographically ordered strings is finite, too. Thus, it does not constitute a text for $L(\hat{G}_k)$. The tempting idea to repeat the lexicographically largest string infinitely often fails, since the resulting text becomes non-recursive. As a consequence, the tell-tales were no longer uniformly recursively generable. Using the canonical text, all these difficulties vanish.

The desired hypothesis space $\mathcal{G}$ is obtained from $\tilde{\mathcal{G}}$ by simply striking off all grammars $\tilde{G}_{\langle k,x\rangle}$ for which $\tilde{T}_{\langle k,x\rangle} = \emptyset$. Analogously, $(T_j)_{j\in\mathbb{N}}$ is obtained from $(\tilde{T}_j)_{j\in\mathbb{N}}$. Obviously, $(T_j)_{j\in\mathbb{N}}$ is a recursively generable family of finite and non-empty sets. In order to save notational convenience, we refer to $T_j$ as to $T_{\langle k,x\rangle}$, i.e., we omit the corresponding mapping yielding the enumeration of the sets $T_j$ from $\tilde{T}_z$. It remains to show that $\mathcal{G} = (G_j)_{j\in\mathbb{N}}$ and $(T_j)_{j\in\mathbb{N}}$ do fulfill the announced properties. Due to our construction, (2) holds obviously. In order to prove (1), let $L \in \mathcal{L}$. We have to show that there is at least a $j \in \mathbb{N}$ such that for $j = \langle k,x\rangle$ we have $L = L(G_{\langle k,x\rangle})$. For this purpose, due to our construction, it suffices to show that $\tilde{T}_{\langle k,x\rangle} \neq \emptyset$. Let $t$ be $L$'s canonically ordered text. Since $M$ has to infer $L$ from $t$, there are $k$, $y \in \mathbb{N}$ such that for all $z < y$, $M(t_z) \neq k$, $M(t_y) = k$ and $L = L(\hat{G}_k)$. Consequently, $\tilde{T}_{\langle k,y\rangle} = t_y^+$. Hence, by the convention made above, we get that $T_{\langle k,y\rangle} = t_y^+$. Moreover, it immediately follows that $L = L(G_{\langle k,x\rangle})$ for any $x \geq y$. This proves Property (1).

Finally, we have to show (3). It results from the requirement that any conservative IIM is never allowed to output an overgeneralized hypothesis. To see this, suppose the converse, i.e., there are $j$, $z \in \mathbb{N}$ such that $T_j \subseteq L(G_z)$ and $L(G_z) \subset L(G_j)$. By definition, there are uniquely determined $k, x \in \mathbb{N}$ such that $j = \langle k,x\rangle$. Let $s_0, ..., s_y$ be the sequence of strings of $T_j$ in canonical order with respect to $L(G_{\langle k,x\rangle})$ such that $M(s_0, ..., s_y) = k$. Now we conclude that $s_0, ..., s_y$ is an initial segment of the canonically ordered text for $L(G_z)$, since $T_j \subseteq L(G_z) \subset L(G_j) = L(G_{\langle k,x\rangle})$. Finally, $M$ has to infer $L(G_z)$ from its canonically ordered text. Thus, it has to perform a mind change in some subsequent step which cannot be caused by an inconsistency. This contradiction yields (3).

Sufficiency: It suffices to prove that there is a conservative IIM $M$ inferring every $L \in \mathcal{L}$ from text with respect to $\mathcal{G}$. First, we slightly modify the corresponding tell-tale family. For all $j \in \mathbb{N}$, we set $\hat{T}_j = \bigcup_{n \leq j} T_n \cap L(G_j)$. Note that the new tell-tale family fulfills Properties (1) through (3). Let $L \in \mathcal{L}$, $t \in text(L)$, and $x \in \mathbb{N}$.

$M(t_x) = $ "For $j = 0, ..., x$, generate $\hat{T}_j$ and test whether $\hat{T}_j \subseteq t_x^+ \subseteq L(G_j)$.

In case there is one $j$ fulfilling the test, output the minimal one and request the next input. Otherwise, output nothing and request the next input."

Since all of the $\hat{T}_j$ are uniformly recursively generable and finite, we see that $M$ is an IIM. Now it suffices to show that $M$ conservatively infers $L$ from $t$.

*Claim 1.* $M$ is conservative.

Let $k$ and $j$ be two hypotheses produced by $M$ on input $t_x$ and $t_{x+r}$, respectively. We have to show that $t_{x+r}^+ \not\subseteq L(G_k)$. For that purpose we distinguish the following cases.

*Case 1.* $k < j$

Due to $M$'s definition we immediately obtain $t_{x+r}^+ \not\subseteq L(G_k)$.

*Case 2.* $j < k$

Suppose, $t_{x+r}^+ \subseteq L(G_k)$. In accordance with its definition, $M$ has verified that $\hat{T}_j \subseteq t_{x+r}^+ \subseteq L(G_j)$. Moreover, the definition of the tell-tale family directly yields $\hat{T}_j \subseteq \hat{T}_k$, since $j < k$ and $\hat{T}_j \subseteq t_{x+r}^+ \subseteq L(G_k)$. Taking into account that $\hat{T}_k \subseteq t_x^+$, this implies $\hat{T}_j \subseteq t_x^+ \subseteq L(G_j)$. Finally, since $j < k$ we conclude $M(t_x) = j$, a contradiction. Hence, the claim is proved.

*Claim 2.* $M$ infers $L$ from $t$.

Let $z$ be the least $k$ such that $L(G_k) = L$. Therefore, $L(G_j) \neq L$ for all $j \leq z$. By Property (3) we obtain that $L \setminus L(G_j) \neq \emptyset$ for all $j < z$ provided $\hat{T}_j \subseteq L$. Consequently, every candidate hypothesis $j < z$ is sometimes rejected by $M$, and $M$ converges to $z$. Hence, the claim follows.

This proves the theorem. q.e.d.

Looking at the definition of the IIM $M$ it is easy to see that this machine is conceptually the same as that one used in the demonstration of Theorem 8. Since $M$ is conservative, $M$ it is semantically finite, too. Moreover, $M$'s output exclusively depends on the length as well as on the range of its input. IIMs satisfying the latter requirement are called *rearrangement-independent* (cf. Definition 12, Section 8).

The proof method explained above applies *mutatis mutandis* to characterize strong-monotonic as well as dual strong-monotonic inference from positive data. All these characterizations express the different monotonicity constraints the relevant learner has to fulfill by a specific modification of Property (3) from the latter theorem (cf. Lange and Zeugmann (1992)). Hence, we again arrived at a *unifying framework*. As a consequence, class preserving strong-monotonic as well as dual strong-monotonic inference can always be realized by a semantically finite and rearrangement-independent IIM.

Looking at monotonic language learning from text, the situation considerably changes (cf. Section 8, Theorem 41). Thus, the IIM $M$ defined in the demonstration of Theorem 9 does not serve as universal learning algorithm for monotonic and dual monotonic inference from text. The same difficulties arise when dealing with learning within an *a priori* fixed number of mind changes. Therefore, we continue with a characterization of $LIM_k-TXT$, and explain the new proof technique. Note that the following theorem establishes a new method how to handle overgeneralization. This solution to the subset problem considerably improves Angluin's method (cf. Example 5). Finally, the main idea used in the following proof is powerful enough to establish characterizations for monotonic and dual monotonic learning, respectively (cf. Zeugmann, Lange and Kapur (199?)).

In order to characterize $LIM_k-TXT$ in terms of recursively generable finite tell-tale sets we have been forced to define an easily computable relation $\prec \subseteq \mathbb{N} \times \mathbb{N}$ that can be used to distinguish appropriate chains of tell-tales with the help of which an IIM $M$ may compute its hypotheses. Now we are ready to present the desired characterization.

**Theorem 10.** *Let $\mathcal{L}$ be an indexed family, and $k \in \mathbb{N}^+$. Then: $\mathcal{L} \in LIM_k-TXT$ if and only if there are a hypothesis space $\mathcal{G} = (G_j)_{j\in\mathbb{N}}$, a computable relation $\prec$ over $\mathbb{N}$, and a recursively generable family $(T_j)_{j\in\mathbb{N}}$ of finite and non-empty sets such that*

(1) *$range(\mathcal{L}) = \mathcal{L}(\mathcal{G})$,*

(2) *for all $L \in \mathcal{L}$ and all $z \in \mathbb{N}$, $T_z \subseteq L(G_z)$,*

(3) *for all $L \in \mathcal{L}$ and every $z \in \mathbb{N}$, and all finite $A \subseteq L$, if $T_z \subseteq L$, $L(G_z) \neq L$, then there is a $j$ such that $z \prec j$, and $A \subseteq T_j \subseteq L(G_j) = L$,*

(4) *for all $L \in \mathcal{L}$, there is no sequence $(z_j)_{j=0,\ldots,k+1}$ such that for all $j \leq k$, $z_j \prec z_{j+1}$ as well as all $T_{z_j} \subseteq T_{z_{j+1}} \subseteq L$*

*Proof.* Necessity: Without loss of generality, let $M$ be an IIM consistently inferring $\mathcal{L}$ with respect to some hypothesis space $\hat{\mathcal{G}} = (\hat{G}_j)_{j\in\mathbb{N}}$ (cf. Lange and Zeugmann (1993b)). Then, for every $L \in \mathcal{L}$ and every $t \in text(L)$ the IIM $M$ performs at most $k$ mind changes when successively fed $t$. First, we construct a hypothesis space $\tilde{\mathcal{G}} = (\tilde{G}_j)_{j\in\mathbb{N}}$ as well as a recursively generable family $(\tilde{T}_j)_{j\in\mathbb{N}}$ of finite but possibly empty sets. Then, we describe a procedure enumerating a certain subset of $\tilde{\mathcal{G}}$ which we call $\mathcal{G}$. Finally, we define the desired relation $\prec$.

Let $\sigma_0, \sigma_1, \sigma_2, \ldots$ be an effective enumeration of all finite, non-null sequences of strings from $\Sigma^*$ such that $\sigma_x \sqsubset \sigma_y$ implies $x < y$ for all $x, y \in \mathbb{N}$. Furthermore, for all $n, x \in \mathbb{N}$ we set $\tilde{G}_{\langle n,x\rangle} = \hat{G}_n$. The family $(\tilde{T}_{\langle n,x\rangle})_{n,x\in\mathbb{N}}$ is defined as follows.

$$\tilde{T}_{\langle n,x\rangle} = \begin{cases} \sigma_x^+, & \text{if } M(\sigma_x) = n, \\ \emptyset, & \text{otherwise.} \end{cases}$$

Obviously, $(\tilde{T}_{\langle n,x\rangle})_{n,x\in\mathbb{N}}$ is a uniformly recursively generable family of finite sets. Furthermore, by construction we have $\mathcal{L}(\tilde{\mathcal{G}}) = range(\mathcal{L})$.

*Claim 1.* For all $L \in \mathcal{L}$ there exists an index $\langle n, x\rangle$ such that $\tilde{T}_{\langle n,x\rangle} \neq \emptyset$ and $L(\tilde{G}_{\langle n,x\rangle}) = L$.

Let $t$ be the canonical text of $L$. Since $M$ learns $L$, there exist $n, y \in \mathbb{N}$ such that $M(t_y) = n$ and $L = L(\hat{G}_n)$. Moreover, $t_y$ is a finite, non-null sequence. Hence, there has to be an $x$ such that $\sigma_x = t_y$. Consequently, $\tilde{T}_{\langle n,x \rangle} \neq \emptyset$, and $L(\tilde{G}_{\langle n,x \rangle}) = L$. This proves the claim.

We proceed with the definition of the desired hypothesis space $\mathcal{G}$ and the relation $\prec$. For that purpose we define a recursive function $f$ as follows. Let $f(0)$ be the least $j$ with $\tilde{T}_j \neq \emptyset$, and for all $j \geq 1$ let

$$f(j) = \begin{cases} j, & \text{if } \tilde{T}_j \neq \emptyset, \\ f(j-1), & \text{otherwise.} \end{cases}$$

Furthermore, we define $G_j = \tilde{G}_{f(j)}$ and $T_j = \tilde{T}_{f(j)}$ for all $j \in \mathbb{N}$. Finally, let $z, j \in \mathbb{N}$, and let $m, n, x, y$ be the uniquely determined numbers such that $f(z) = \langle m, y \rangle$ and $f(j) = \langle n, x \rangle$. Then we define $z \prec j$ if and only if $m \neq n$ and $\sigma_y \sqsubseteq \sigma_x$.

Clearly, $(T_j)_{j \in \mathbb{N}}$ is a uniformly recursively generable family of finite and non-empty sets and the relation $\prec$ is computable. It remains to show that Properties(1) through (4) are satisfied. Property (1) is an immediate consequence of Claim 1 and the definition of $\mathcal{G}$. In order to prove (2) it suffices to show that $n = M(\sigma_x)$ implies $\sigma_x^+ \subseteq L(\hat{G}_n)$. But this is obvious, since $M$ is a consistent IIM.

We continue in proving Property (3). Let $L \in \mathcal{L}$, let $A \subseteq L$ be any finite set, and let $z \in \mathbb{N}$ be any index such that $T_z \subseteq L$ and $L(G_z) \neq L$. We have to show that there is a $j$ with $z \prec j$ and $A \subseteq T_j \subseteq L(G_j) = L$. In accordance with our construction we have $T_z = \tilde{T}_{f(z)}$ and $G_z = \tilde{G}_{f(z)}$. Let $m, y$ be the uniquely determined numbers with $f(z) = \langle m, y \rangle$. Then we know that $M(\sigma_y) = m$ and $L \neq L(\hat{G}_m)$, since $L(\hat{G}_m) = L(\tilde{G}_{\langle m,y \rangle}) = L(G_z) \neq L$. Moreover, $T_z = \sigma_y^+ \subseteq L$. Hence, $\sigma_y$ is an initial segment of a text for $L$. Since $L \neq L(G_z)$, we additionally know that $M$, on input $\sigma_y$, has not yet converged to a correct hypothesis for $L$. Now, let $t$ be the canonical text of $L$. Since $A \subseteq L$, there exists an $a \in \mathbb{N}$ such that $A \subseteq t_a^+$. Moreover, $M$ has to learn $L$ from every text for it. Consequently, there has to be an $r \in \mathbb{N}$ such that for $n = M(\sigma_y t_{a+r})$ the condition $L(\hat{G}_n) = L$ is satisfied. Furthermore, since $\sigma_y t_{a+r}$ is a finite sequence, there exits an index $x$ with $\sigma_x = \sigma_y t_{a+r}$. By construction we get $\emptyset \neq \tilde{T}_{\langle n,x \rangle} \subseteq L(\tilde{G}_{\langle n,x \rangle}) = L$. Thus, there is a number $j$ such that $f(j) = \langle n, x \rangle$, and for every $j$ with $f(j) = \langle n, x \rangle$ we get $\sigma_y \sqsubseteq \sigma_x$ and $m \neq n$. Therefore, $z \prec j$, and (3) is proved.

We proceed with the demonstration of (4). Looking at the definition of the relation $\prec$ we immediately realize that $z \prec j$ implies $T_z \subseteq T_j$. Suppose there is a finite sequence $(z_j)_{j=0,\ldots,k+1}$ such that for all $j \leq k$, $z_j \prec z_{j+1}$ and $T_{z_j} \subseteq T_{z_{j+1}} \subseteq L$. Since $z_j \prec z_{j+1}$ and $T_{z_j} \subseteq T_{z_{j+1}} \subseteq L$, we get an initial segment of a text $t$ of $L$ on which $M$ changes its mind $k + 1$ times, a contradiction. Hence, (4) is proved.

Sufficiency: Again, it suffices to describe an IIM $M$ that infers $\mathcal{L}$ in the limit with at most $k$ mind changes from text with respect to $\mathcal{G}$. Let $L \in \mathcal{L}$, let $t$ be any text for $L$, and let $x \in \mathbb{N}$. We define the desired IIM $M$ as follows:

$M(t_x) = $ "If $x = 0$ or $x > 0$ and $M$ when successively fed $t_{x-1}$ does not produce any guess, then goto (A). Else goto (B).

(A) Search for the least $j \leq x$ such that $T_j \subseteq t_x^+$. In case it is found, set

$y_j = x$, output $j$ and request the next input. Otherwise, output nothing and request the next input.

(B) Let $j = M(t_{x-1})$. Test whether there exists a $z \leq x$ such that $j \prec z$ and $t_{y_j}^+ \subseteq T_z \subseteq t_x^+$. In case one $z$ is found, set $y_z = x$ , output $z$ and request the next input. Otherwise, output $j$ and request the next input."

Since all of the $T_j$ are uniformly recursively generable and finite and since $\prec$ is computable, we directly obtain that $M$ is an IIM. We proceed in showing that $M$ identifies $L$ from $t$ with at most $k$ mind changes.

*Claim 1.* $M$ converges and $card(\{x| \ M(t_x) \neq M(t_{x+1})\}) \leq k$.

Because of (1) and (2), $M$ generates at least one hypothesis when fed the text $t$. Furthermore, assume for a moment that $M$ performs more than $k$ mind changes when inferring $L$ from $t$. It is easy to recognize that this assumption would imply the existence of a sequence $(T_{z_j})_{j=0,...,m}$ with $m > k$ such that for all $j < m$, $z_j \prec z_{j+1}$, and $T_{z_j} \subseteq T_{z_{j+1}} \subseteq L$. This would contradict (4). Thus, the number of possible mind changes $M$ may perform when fed $t$ is bounded by $k$. Moreover, $M$ outputs after a certain period always a hypothesis. Hence, we may conclude that $M$ converges.

*Claim 2.* If $M$ converges, then the hypothesis $M$ converges to is correct.

Assume that $M$ converges to a hypothesis $z$ with $L(G_z) \neq L$. Let $x$ be the least index such that $M(t_x) = z$. Note that $T_z \subseteq t_x^+$ by $M$'s definition. By Property (3), there has to be a $j$ such that $z \prec j$, $t_x^+ \subseteq L(G_j)$, and $L(G_j) = L$. Hence, $M$ performs an additional mind change when fed a sufficiently large initial segment $t_x$ of $t$ satisfying $T_j \subseteq t_x^+$, a contradiction.

By Claim 1 and 2, $M$ infers any $L \in \mathcal{L}$ with at most $k$ mind changes. Thus, the theorem is proved. $\hspace{2cm}$ q.e.d.

Note that the IIM defined in the proof of Theorem 10 uses a new technique to detect whether or not it has to perform a mind change. Clearly, no IIM can prove that its actual guess is correct, except in case it finitely learns. Hence, the machine has to collect evidence allowing it to decide whether it should prefer a new guess instead of maintaining its actual one. The machine defined in the proof above achieves this goal by using *a priori* knowledge concerning the hypothesis space as well as concerning the family of tell-tale sets. This *a priori* knowledge is provided by the computable relation. We believe that this approach considerably refines Angluin's (1980b) method how to detect overgeneralization. Finally, it should be mentioned that a conceptually similar, but technically different approach has been successfully applied to limit learning of recursive functions (cf. Wiehagen (1991)).

# 5. Learnability in Dependence on the Hypothesis Space

Historically, most authors have investigated exact learnability. Moreover, many investigations in other domains of algorithmic learning theory deal with exact learning too (cf. e.g. Natarajan (1991)). And indeed, as long as one considers learning in the limit without any additional demand, every indexed family that is class comprisingly learnable may be exactly inferred, too (cf. Lange and Zeugmann (1993b)). However, when dealing with characterizations it turned out to be very helpful to construct class preserving hypothesis spaces (cf. Kapur and Bilardi (1992), Lange and Zeugmann (1992)). Consequently, it is only natural to ask whether or not class preserving learning algorithms are more powerful than exact ones. Dealing with a measure of efficiency we found that an appropriate choice of a class preserving hypothesis space may eventually increase the learning power (cf. Lange and Zeugmann (1993b)). Recently, these results have been considerably improved and similar effects concerning the relation between class preserving and class comprising inference have been elaborated (cf. Lange (1994)). Furthermore, studying the capabilities of learning algorithms in dependence on the hypothesis space has yield very interesting results concerning probabilistic learning models (cf., e.g., Anthony and Biggs (1992), Freivalds, Kinber and Wiehagen (1988)). Therefore, it is worth to study this phenomenon in some more detail.

First, we present results demonstrating the superiority of class comprising to class preserving monotonic learning algorithms that are themselves superior to exact ones. These separations have been obtained by developing a *new powerful proof technique*. Establishing the announced separations using standard proof techniques would require to diagonalize against all hypothesis spaces and all IIMs. Instead, we have elaborated an *almost always effective reduction* of the halting problem to monotonic learning problems. This approach yields easy to describe indexed families witnessing the desired separations. Next, we present results comparing class comprising and exact inference procedures. These results strongly recommend the designer of learning algorithms to carefully choose the enumeration as well as the description of the target languages to get exact learning procedures of maximal power (cf. Theorem 15).

Finally, we ask why, for example, class preserving inference is sometimes more powerful than exact learning. Obviously, as long as there is an effective compiler from the space $\mathcal{G}$ of hypotheses into the indexed family $\mathcal{L}$, both models of inference are of equal power. Looking at learning in the limit, Gold (1967) proved that even limiting recursive compilers do suffice. What we present is a characterization result stating that exact learning is of the same power as class preserving inference if and only if there is a limiting recursive compiler satisfying an appropriate monotonicity requirement (cf. Theorem 17). Hence, our separations prove the non-existence of such compilers.

## 5.1. Separations

In this subsection we compare the learning capabilities of most of the introduced models of monotonic and dual-monotonic inference in dependence on the hypothesis space. The underlying selection aims to illustrate different effects which occur. The following theorem provides a summary of results obtained that relate the power of exact identification, class preserving inference, and class comprising learning under various monotonicity constraints to one another (cf. Lange, Zeugmann and Kapur (1992), Lange and Zeugmann (1993c, 1993d)).

**Theorem 11.**

$$
\begin{array}{ccccc}
ELIM-TXT & = & LIM-TXT & = & CLIM-TXT \\
\cup & & \cup & & \| \\
EWMON^d-TXT & \subset & WMON^d-TXT & \subset & CWMON^d-TXT \\
\cup & & \cup & & \cup \\
EWMON-TXT & \subset & WMON-TXT & \subset & CWMON-TXT \\
\cup & & \cup & & \cup \\
ESMON-TXT & \subset & SMON-TXT & \subset & CSMON-TXT \\
\cup & & \cup & & \cup \\
EFIN-TXT & = & FIN-TXT & = & CFIN-TXT \\
\| & & \| & & \cap \\
ESMON^d-TXT & = & SMON^d-TXT & \subset & CSMON^d-TXT
\end{array}
$$

For instance, it turns out that dual weak-monotonic learning is exactly as powerful as learning in the limit, if class comprising hypothesis spaces are admissible. In particular, a dual weak-monotonic learner may realize a suitable interplay between generalization and specialization (cf. Theorem 15). In comparison to $CWMON-TXT \subset CLIM-TXT$, having the freedom to combine both, generalization and specialization is essential in order to achieve maximal learning power. We consider this as a particular answer to the long-standing debate in the machine learning community for and against learning by generalization and learning by specialization, respectively.

Furthermore, the following incomparabilities have been shown (cf. Lange and Zeugmann (1993c, 1993d)).

**Theorem 12.**

(1) $WMON-TXT \ \# \ CSMON-TXT$

(2) $EWMON-TXT \ \# \ CSMON-TXT$

(3) $EWMON-TXT \ \# \ SMON-TXT$

(4) $CSMON^d-TXT \ \# \ CSMON-TXT$

Detailed proofs of both theorems can be found in Lange and Zeugmann (1993d). Because of the lack of space, we demonstrate one separation, only. On the one hand, this should illustrate the underlying proof technique. On the other hand, the corresponding result has some special features distinguishing it from most of the other ones (cf. Theorem 14).

**Theorem 13.** $SMON^d-TXT \subset CSMON^d-TXT$

*Proof.* Obviously, by definition $SMON^d-TXT \subseteq CSMON^d-TXT$. It suffices to show that $CSMON^d-TXT \setminus SMON^d-TXT \neq \emptyset$. The desired indexed family $\mathcal{L}_{csd} = (L_{\langle k,j \rangle})_{k,j \in \mathbb{N}}$ is defined as follows. For all $k \in \mathbb{N}$ we set $L_{\langle k,0 \rangle} = \{a^{k+1}\} \cup \{b^n \mid n \in \mathbb{N}^+\}$. For all $k \in \mathbb{N}$ and all $j \geq 1$, we distinguish the following cases:

*Case 1.* $\neg \ \Phi_k(k) \leq j$

We set $L_{\langle k,j \rangle} = L_{\langle k,0 \rangle}$.

*Case 2.* $\Phi_k(k) = x \leq j$

Then, we set $L_{\langle k,j \rangle} = \{a^{k+1}\} \cup \{b^m \mid 1 \leq m \leq x\} \cup \{c^j\}$.

**Lemma 1.** $\mathcal{L}_{csd} \notin SMON^d - TXT$

Since $EFIN - TXT = SMON^d - TXT$ (cf. Theorem 11), it remains to show that there is no IIM $M$ which finitely infers $\mathcal{L}_{csd}$ with respect to $\mathcal{L}_{csd}$. Thereby, we effectively reduce the halting problem to $\mathcal{L}_{csd} \in EFIN - TXT$.

*Claim.* If there exists an IIM $M$ witnessing $\mathcal{L}_{csd} \in EFIN - TXT$, then one can effectively construct an algorithm deciding for all $k \in \mathbb{N}$ whether or not $\varphi_k(k)$ converges.

Let $M$ be any IIM witnessing $\mathcal{L}_{csd} \in EFIN - TXT$. First of all, we define an algorithm $\mathcal{A}$ solving the halting problem. On input $k \in \mathbb{N}$ the algorithm $\mathcal{A}$ executes the following instructions:

(A1) For $z = 0, 1, 2, \ldots$ generate successively the lexicographically ordered text $t$ of $L_{\langle k,0 \rangle}$ until $M$ on input $t_z$ outputs for the first time a hypothesis of the form $\langle k, j \rangle$, i.e., $M(t_z) = \langle k, j \rangle$.

(A2) Test whether $\Phi_k(k) \leq max\{j, z\}$. In case it is, output "$\varphi_k(k)$ converges." Otherwise output "$\varphi_k(k)$ diverges."

Due to our assumption, $M$ in particular finitely infers $L_{\langle k,0 \rangle}$ from its lexicographically ordered text. Taking $\mathcal{L}_{csd}$'s definition into account one can easily deduce that $M$ has to output a hypothesis of the form $\langle k, j \rangle$, since any other hypotheses describe a language which is definitely different from $L_{\langle k,0 \rangle}$. Thus, Instruction (A1) has to terminate. Due to the definition of a complexity measure Instruction (A2) can be effectively accomplished. Therefore, algorithm $\mathcal{A}$ eventually terminates for every number $k$.

It remains to show that $\varphi_k(k)$ is undefined, if $\neg\, \Phi_k(k) \leq max\{j, z\}$. Suppose the converse, i.e., $\varphi_k(k)$ is defined. Then, $\Phi_k(k) = x$ for some $x > max\{z, j\}$. Taking again $\mathcal{L}_{csd}$ definition into account it follows $L_{\langle k,j \rangle} = L_{\langle k,0 \rangle}$, since $x > j$. Now, let $m$ be the maximal index such that $b^m \in t_z^+$. Obviously, $m < x$, since $t$ is the lexicographically ordered text of $L_{\langle k,0 \rangle}$. Thus, $t_z$ is an initial segment of a text for the finite language $L_{\langle k,x \rangle}$. Note that $L_{\langle k,x \rangle} \neq L_{\langle k,0 \rangle}$. Thus, $M$ fails to finitely infer $L_{\langle k,x \rangle}$ from every text having the initial segment $t_z$. This contradiction completes the proof of the above claim. Hence, Lemma 1 follows.

**Lemma 2.** $\mathcal{L}_{csd} \in CSMON^d - TXT$

We have to show that there are an appropriate hypothesis space $\mathcal{G}_{csd}$ comprising $\mathcal{L}_{csd}$ and an IIM $M$ inferring $\mathcal{L}$ dual strong-monotonically with respect to $\mathcal{G}_{csd}$.

We define the wanted hypothesis space $\mathcal{G}_{csd} = (G_{\langle k,j \rangle})_{k,j \in \mathbb{N}}$ as follows. For all $k, j \in \mathbb{N}$, we set $L(G_{\langle k,0 \rangle}) = \bigcup_{j \in \mathbb{N}} L_{\langle k,j \rangle}$ and $L(G_{\langle k,j+1 \rangle}) = L_{\langle k,j \rangle}$. Taking the definition of $\mathcal{L}_{csd}$ into account, it is easy to verify that membership is uniformly decidable for $\mathcal{G}_{csd}$.

Now, let $k \in \mathbb{N}$. If $\varphi_k(k)$ is undefined, we have $L(G_{\langle k,0 \rangle}) = L_{\langle k,j \rangle} = L_{\langle k,0 \rangle}$ for all $j \in \mathbb{N}$. Otherwise, i.e., if $\varphi_k(k)$ is defined, we have $L(G_{\langle k,0 \rangle}) \supset L_{\langle k,j \rangle}$ for all $j \in \mathbb{N}$. Thus, a dual strong-monotonic learner $M$ may simply output the hypothesis $\langle k, 0 \rangle$ after the corresponding identifier $a^{k+1}$ has been presented. No matter whether or not $\varphi_k(k)$ is defined, $\langle k, 0 \rangle$ is a suitable hypothesis. If $\varphi_k(k)$ is undefined, $\langle k, 0 \rangle$ is already the desired final guess. Otherwise, one string has to appear which tells $M$ in which way the language $L(G_{(k,0)})$ has to be specialized. Consequently, $M$ $CSMON^d-TXT-$ identifies $\mathcal{L}_{csd}$ with respect to the class comprising hypothesis space $\mathcal{G}_{csd}$. q.e.d.

The *new proof technique* demonstrated above applies to obtain most of the stated separations. In particular, we can almost always effectively reduce the halting problem to several monotonic learning problems. These reductions imply that the considered learning problems are at least as hard as the halting problem. This insight deserves some attention. Gold (1967) showed that no IIM can learn the class $\mathcal{R}$ of all recursive functions in the limit. On the other hand, the degree of the algorithmic unsolvability of $\mathcal{R} \in LIM$ is strictly less than the degree of the halting problem (cf., Adleman and Blum (1991)). This puts the constraint to learn monotonically with respect to a particular hypothesis space into a new perspective. An algorithmically solvable learning problem (e.g. $\mathcal{L}_{csd} \in CSMON^d-TXT$) may become algorithmically unsolvable, if an at first glance natural demand is added (e.g. to learn class preservingly). Moreover, the degree of unsolvability may be at least as high as that of the halting problem, and is, therefore, strictly higher than that of learning all recursive functions. As far as we know, there is only one paper stating an analogous result in the setting of inductive inference of recursive functions, namely Freivalds, Kinber and Wiehagen (1992).

## 5.2. Class Comprising and Exact Learning

When dealing with monotonic inference, class comprising learning is almost always more powerful than class preserving inference which itself is superior to exact learning. In particular, the results obtained give strong evidence that exclusively changing the descriptions for the objects to be learned as well as their enumeration does not suffice to get learning algorithms of maximal power. Therefore, we are interested in knowing what kind of languages has to be supplemented to hypothesis spaces in order to design superior inference procedures. Moreover, we ask whether or not these added languages may be learned themselves as well. As the following theorems show, the answer to these questions strongly depends on the type of monotonicity requirement involved.

First, we investigate dual-strong monotonic learning. Applying the same idea used in the demonstration of $\mathcal{L}_{csd} \notin EFIN-TXT$ (cf. Theorem 13, Lemma 1) one can easily show that $\mathcal{L}(\mathcal{G}_{csd}) \notin SMON^d-TXT$. Hence, in order to learn the family $\mathcal{L}_{csd}$ strong-monotonically one is required to add grammars to the hypothesis space that describe languages being *not learnable themselves*. It turns out that this property is characteristic for dual strong-monotonic inference as the following theorem shows.

**Theorem 14.** Let $\mathcal{L}$ be any indexed family satisfying $\mathcal{L} \in CSMON-TXT^d \setminus SMON^d-TXT$. Then there is no hypothesis space $\mathcal{G} = (G_j)_{j\in\mathbb{N}}$ such that $\mathcal{L} \subset \mathcal{L}(\mathcal{G})$, and $\mathcal{L}(\mathcal{G}) \in SMON^d-TXT$.

*Proof.* Suppose the converse, i.e., there is a hypothesis space $\mathcal{G} = (G_j)_{j\in\mathbb{N}}$ such that $\mathcal{L}(\mathcal{G}) \in SMON^d-TXT$. By assumption, $\mathcal{L} \in CSMON^d-TXT \setminus SMON^d-TXT$, and hence, $\mathcal{L} \subset \mathcal{L}(\mathcal{G})$. Moreover, due to Theorem 11 we know that $FIN-TXT = SMON^d-TXT$. Therefore, $\mathcal{L}(\mathcal{G}) \in SMON^d-TXT$ implies $\mathcal{L}(\mathcal{G}) \in FIN-TXT$. Consequently, there is an IIM $M$ that finitely infers $\mathcal{L}(\mathcal{G})$. On the other hand, $\mathcal{L} \subset \mathcal{L}(\mathcal{G})$. Hence, $M$ finitely infers $\mathcal{L}$, too. Applying Theorem 11 once again yields $\mathcal{L} \in EFIN-TXT$. Thus, we conclude $\mathcal{L} \in SMON^d-TXT$ which contradicts our assumption. q.e.d.

The situation completely changes, if weak-monotonic learning and its dual counterpart are investigated.

**Theorem 15.** *For all indexed families $\mathcal{L}$ we have:*

*If $\mathcal{L} \in CWMON^d-TXT$, then there is a hypothesis space $\mathcal{G} = (G_j)_{j\in\mathbb{N}}$ comprising $\mathcal{L}$ such that $\mathcal{L}(\mathcal{G}) \in EWMON^d-TXT$.*

*Proof.* Let $\mathcal{L} \in CWMON^d-TXT$. Since $CWMON^d-TXT = ELIM-TXT$ (cf. Theorem 11), there is an IIM $M$ which $ELIM-TXT$–infers $\mathcal{L}$ with respect to the hypothesis space $\mathcal{L}$.

Let $\hat{\mathcal{L}} = (\hat{L}_j)_{j\in\mathbb{N}}$ denote any canonical enumeration of all singleton languages over the underlying alphabet and all languages in $\mathcal{L}$. Obviously, $M$ can be easily converted into an IIM $\hat{M}$ which $ELIM-TXT$ identifies $\hat{\mathcal{L}}$. Without loss of generality we may assume that $\hat{M}$ is consistent, too (cf. Lange and Zeugmann (1993a)). Furthermore, assume that $\hat{M}$ outputs a canonical number of a singleton language as long as the initial segment presented to $\hat{M}$ does not contain two different strings.

It remains to define an IIM $\tilde{M}$ which dual weak-monotonically infers $\hat{\mathcal{L}}$ with respect to $\hat{\mathcal{L}}$. This proves the above theorem, if we choose $\mathcal{G} = (G_j)_{j\in\mathbb{N}}$ such that $(L(G_j))_{j\in\mathbb{N}} = (\hat{L}_j)_{j\in\mathbb{N}}$.

Let $\hat{L}$ be any language in $\hat{\mathcal{L}}$, $t \in text(\hat{L})$, and $x \in \mathbb{N}$. Furthermore, let $j_0, j_1, j_2, \ldots$ denote the sequence of hypotheses generated by $\hat{M}$ when successively fed $t$. Instead of this sequence, $\tilde{M}$ produces the following sequence of hypotheses $j_0, k_0, j_1, k_1, j_2, k_2, \ldots$ when fed $t$, too. Thereby, the indices $k_0, k_1, k_2, \ldots$ generated by $\tilde{M}$ as intermediate hypotheses are defined as follows. Let $z \in \mathbb{N}$. If $j_z = j_{z+1}$, then let $k_z = j_z$. Otherwise, i.e., $j_z \neq j_{z+1}$, let $k_z$ denote the number of the singleton language containing the first string in $t$.

Obviously, $\tilde{M}$ converges to a correct number of $\hat{L}$, since $\hat{M}$ infers $\hat{L}$ when fed $t$. It remains to show that $\tilde{M}$ works dual weak-monotonically. It suffices to discuss the case $j_z \neq j_{z+1}$. Since $\hat{M}$ exclusively produces consistent hypotheses, it follows $L_{j_z} \supseteq L_{k_z}$ because of the choice of the hypothesis $k_z$. Hence, $\tilde{M}$ has specialized its former guess $L_{j_z}$. On the other hand, $j_z \neq j_{z+1}$ implies that at least two different strings occur in the initial segment $\hat{M}$ is fed. Consequently, $L_{k_z}$ is an inconsistent hypothesis and, therefore, the mind change from $k_z$ to $j_{z+1}$ is a justified one. Thereby, $\tilde{M}$ has generalized its former hypothesis $k_z$, since $j_{z+1}$ is consistent. Thus, we may conclude that $\tilde{M}$ satisfies the dual weak-monotonicity constraint. q.e.d.

In fact, the IIM $\tilde{M}$ defined above realizes a suitable interplay between learning by generalization and learning by specialization. Thereby, $\tilde{M}$ doubles the number of mind changes which $\hat{M}$ performs when processing the same text.

An analogous result can be shown for weak-monotonic learning, too (cf. Section 8, Corollary 40).

**Theorem 16.** *For all indexed families $\mathcal{L}$ we have:*

*If $\mathcal{L} \in CWMON-TXT$, then there is a hypothesis space $\mathcal{G} = (G_j)_{j\in\mathbb{N}}$ comprising $\mathcal{L}$ such that $\mathcal{L}(\mathcal{G}) \in EWMON-TXT$.*

## 5.3. Limiting Recursive Compilers

This subsection is devoted to the problem why an indexed family $\mathcal{L}$ that can be learned with respect to some hypothesis space $\mathcal{G} = (G_j)_{j\in\mathbb{N}}$ might become non-inferable with respect to other hypothesis spaces $\hat{\mathcal{G}} = (\hat{G}_j)_{j\in\mathbb{N}}$ satisfying $\mathcal{L} \subseteq \mathcal{L}(\hat{\mathcal{G}})$. A first hint how to answer this question has already been given by Gold (1967). Namely, he proved that, whenever there is a limiting recursive compiler (cf. Definition 9 below) from $\mathcal{G}$ into $\hat{\mathcal{G}}$, then any IIM inferring a class $\mathcal{L}$ of languages with respect to $\mathcal{G}$ can easily be converted into one that learns $\mathcal{L}$ with respect to $\hat{\mathcal{G}}$. Considering indexed families being learnable with respect to some space $\mathcal{G}$ of hypotheses, we could prove that there is always a limiting recursive compiler from $\mathcal{G}$ into $\mathcal{L}$. The same is, *mutatis mutandis*, true for finite learning, i.e., there is always a recursive compiler from $\mathcal{G}$ into $\mathcal{L}$. However, if some monotonicity requirement is involved, then the situation considerably changes. The reason for that phenomenon is as follows. A limiting recursive compiler in general does not preserve any of the introduced monotonicity demands. But even if it does, it is a highly non-trivial task to convert an IIM that, for example, class preservingly learns an indexed family $\mathcal{L}$ with respect to some appropriate chosen hypothesis space $\mathcal{G}$ into an IIM exactly learning $\mathcal{L}$. The latter difficulty is caused by the fact that one has to combine two limiting processes into one.

For the sake of presentation we give only one of the theorems obtained, since it does already suffice to convey the spirit of the insight achievable. We start with the formal definition of limiting recursive compilers.

**Definition 9.** *Let* $\mathcal{G} = (G_j)_{j\in\mathbb{N}}$ *and* $\hat{\mathcal{G}} = (\hat{G}_j)_{j\in\mathbb{N}}$ *be two spaces of hypotheses such that* $L(\mathcal{G}) = \mathcal{L}(\hat{\mathcal{G}})$. *A recursive function* $f: \mathbb{N} \times \mathbb{N} \to \mathbb{N}$ *is said to be a* ***limiting recursive compiler from*** $\mathcal{G}$ ***into*** $\hat{\mathcal{G}}$ *iff* $k := \lim_{x\to\infty} f(j,x)$ *exists and satisfies* $L(G_j) = L(\hat{G}_k)$ *for all* $j \in \mathbb{N}$.

Next we introduce limiting recursive compilers fulfilling a certain monotonicity demand.

**Definition 10.** *Let* $\mathcal{G} = (G_j)_{j\in\mathbb{N}}$ *and* $\hat{\mathcal{G}} = (\hat{G}_j)_{j\in\mathbb{N}}$ *be two hypothesis spaces such that* $\mathcal{L}(\mathcal{G}) = \mathcal{L}(\hat{\mathcal{G}})$. *A limiting recursive compiler* **f** *from* $\mathcal{G}$ *into* $\hat{\mathcal{G}}$ *is said to be* ***strong-monotonic*** *iff* $L(\hat{G}_{f(j,x)}) \subseteq L(\hat{G}_{f(j,x+1)})$ *for all* $j, x \in \mathbb{N}$

Now we are ready to present the announced characterization comparing the power of exact and class preserving learning algorithms under the constraint to learn strong-monotonically. Note that the proof presented below is a considerably improved version of that one in Lange and Zeugmann (1993c).

**Theorem 17.** *Let* $\mathcal{L}$ *be an indexed family and let* $\mathcal{G} = (G_j)_{j\in\mathbb{N}}$ *be a hypothesis space such that* $\mathcal{L} \in SMON - TXT$ *with respect to* $\mathcal{G}$. *Then we have:*

$\mathcal{L} \in ESMON - TXT$ *if and only if there is a strong-monotonic limiting recursive compiler from* $\mathcal{G}$ *into* $\mathcal{L}$.

*Proof.* Necessity. Let $\mathcal{L} \in ESMON - TXT$. Then there is an IIM $M$ strong-monotonically inferring $\mathcal{L}$ with respect to $\mathcal{L}$. We define the desired limiting recursive compiler from $\mathcal{G} = (G_j)_{j\in\mathbb{N}}$ into $\mathcal{L}$ as follows. Let $j, x \in \mathbb{N}$ and let $t^j$ be the canonical text of $L(G_j)$. We set:

$f(j,x) = $ "Compute the sequence $(M(t^j_z))_{z\in\mathbb{N}}$ up to length $x$. Let $j_y$ be the last element of this sequence. Set $f(j,x) = j_y$."

It is straightforward to verify that $f$ is a strong-monotonic limiting recursive compiler from $\mathcal{G}$ into $\mathcal{L}$.

Sufficiency. Let $\mathcal{L} \in SMON-TXT$ with respect to $\mathcal{G}$ be witnessed by $\hat{M}$, and let $f$ be a strong-monotonic limiting recursive compiler from $\mathcal{G}$ into $\mathcal{L}$. Without loss of generality we may assume that $\hat{M}$ exclusively outputs consistent hypotheses (cf. Lange and Zeugmann (1993a)). We have to define an IIM $M$ that $ESMON-TXT-$ infers $\mathcal{L}$. The main difficulty we have to deal with is the combination of two limiting recursive processes into one yielding an IIM strong-monotonically inferring $\mathcal{L}$ with respect to $\mathcal{L}$.

Let $L \in \mathcal{L}$, $t \in text(L)$, and $x \in \mathbb{N}$. Then, we define:

$M(t_x) = $ "Simulate $\hat{M}$ when fed $t_x$. If $\hat{M}$ does not output any hypothesis, then output nothing and request the next input. Otherwise, execute Instruction (A).

    (A) Let $\hat{M}(t_x) = j$. Determine the least $y \in \mathbb{N}$ such that $t_x^+ \subseteq L_{f(j,y)}$. Output $f(j,y)$ and request the next input."

Recall that $\hat{M}$ is consistent. Consequently, $\hat{M}(t_x) = j$ implies $t_x^+ \subseteq L(G_j)$. Since $f$ defines a limiting recursive compiler from $\mathcal{G}$ into $\mathcal{L}$, there exists a $y \in \mathbb{N}$ such that $L_{f(j,y)} = L(G_j)$. Furthermore, since $\mathcal{L}$ is an indexed family, $M$ always effectively finds an index $y \in \mathbb{N}$ satisfying $t_x^+ \subseteq L_{f(j,y)}$. Thus, Instruction (A) terminates and $M$ is indeed an IIM.

Next, we show that $M$ infers $L$ when fed $t$. Since $\hat{M}$ witnesses $\mathcal{L} \in SMON-TXT$, there is a $z \in \mathbb{N}$ such that $\hat{M}(t_{z+r}) = j$ with $L(G_j) = L$ for all $r \in \mathbb{N}$. Since $f$ defines a strong monotonic limiting recursive compiler from $\mathcal{G}$ into $\mathcal{L}$, there is a least $y \in \mathbb{N}$ such that $L_{f(j,y)} = L(G_j)$. Furthermore, $L_{f(j,n)} \subset L_{f(j,y)}$ for all $n < y$. By definition, $M$ converges to the correct guess $L_{f(j,y)}$ when fed $t$.

Finally, it remains to show that $M$ behaves strong-monotonically when processing the text $t$ for $L$. First, we prove the following claim.

*Claim.* $\hat{M}(t_x) = j$ implies $L(G_j) \subseteq \hat{L}$ for all $\hat{L} \in \mathcal{L}$ satisfying $t_x^+ \subseteq \hat{L}$.

Let $\hat{L} \in \mathcal{L}$ such that $t_x^+ \subseteq \hat{L}$. Obviously, $t_x^+ \subseteq \hat{L}$ implies that there is a text $\hat{t}$ for $\hat{L}$ having the initial segment $t_x$. Since $\hat{M}$, in particular, strong-monotonically infers $\hat{L}$ on $\hat{t}$, $\hat{M}(t_x) = \hat{M}(\hat{t}_x) = j$ implies $L(G_j) \subseteq \hat{L}$. This proves the claim.

Now, let $f(j,y)$ and $f(k,z)$ denote any two different hypotheses subsequently generated by $M$ when fed $t$, i.e., $M(t_x) = f(j,y)$ and $M(t_{x+r}) = f(k,z)$ for any $x \in \mathbb{N}$ and $r \in \mathbb{N}^+$. It remains to show $L_{f(j,y)} \subseteq L_{f(k,z)}$.

*Case 1.* $j = k$

By the definition of $M$, $y < z$. Since $f$ defines a strong-monotonic limiting recursive compiler from $\mathcal{G}$ into $\mathcal{L}$, $y < z$ directly implies $L_{f(j,y)} \subseteq L_{f(j,z)}$.

*Case 2.* $j \neq k$

By definition of a strong-monotonic limiting recursive compiler $L_{f(j,y)} \subseteq L(G_j)$. Taking $M$'s definition into consideration we obtain $t_{x+r}^+ \subseteq L_{f(k,z)}$. Therefore, $t_x^+ \subseteq$

$L_{f(k,x)}$, too. On the other hand $\hat{M}(t_x) = j$ by the definition of $M$. Thus, by applying the claim above we obtain $L(G_j) \subseteq L_{f(k,x)}$. Consequently, $L_{f(j,y)} \subseteq L(G_j) \subseteq L_{f(k,x)}$ and, therefore, $L_{f(j,y)} \subseteq L_{f(k,x)}$.

This proves the theorem.                                                    q.e.d.

Let us finish our survey on the learnability in dependence on the hypothesis space with the remark that this filed is large and the discourse here is brief. Further information concerning this subject is in part provided in the subsequent sections. Finally, the most intriguing open problems are outlined in Section 9.

# 6.  Iterative IIMs

Within the standard definition of inductive inference machines the limitation of space in realistic computations is not considered. Weakening the requirement that a learner has always access to the whole initial segment of a text (an informant) it has been fed results in the concept of iterative learning. An iterative IIM is only allowed to use its last guess and the next string of a text and an informant, respectively, in order to produce its next guess. From the viewpoint of potential applications this approach seems to be well-suited. As discussed in Section 3, the class of all pattern languages can be identified by an iterative IIM from text. On the other hand, the question naturally arises whether this restriction seriously affects the learning capabilities. In answering this question, we are mainly interested in estimating the power of iterative learners which are required to fulfill simultaneously certain monotonicity constraints.

## 6.1.  On the Strength of Iterative IIMs

Conceptually, it seems to be appropriate to think about an iterative IIM $M$ as follows: When fed a text (an informant) of a language $M$ is supposed to learn, $M$ defines a sequence $(M_n)_{n\in\mathbb{N}}$ of learning devices each of which takes as its input the output of its predecessor. Furthermore, since iterative learners are always required to produce an output (cf. Definition 8), it seems to be reasonable to consider exclusively iterative IIMs which are allowed to work with respect to a class comprising hypothesis space. On the other hand, we have seen that the learning capabilities of monotonic IIMs essentially depend on the selection of the underlying hypothesis space (cf. Section 5). Consequently, it is interesting to know whether or not iterative learners are also sensitive to the the choice of the underlying space of hypotheses.

**Theorem 18.** $EIT-TXT \subset IT-TXT$

*Proof.* By definition it suffices to show $IT-TXT \setminus EIT-TXT \neq \emptyset$. Again, we reduce the halting problem to a suitably chosen learning task. The desired indexed family $\mathcal{L}_{eit} = (L_{\langle k,j \rangle})_{k,j\in\mathbb{N}}$ is defined as follows. For all $k \in \mathbb{N}$, we set $L_{\langle k,0 \rangle} = \{a^{k+1}\} \cup \{b^n \mid n \in \mathbb{N}^+\}$. For all $j \geq 1$, we distinguish the following cases.

*Case 1.* $\neg \, \Phi_k(k) \leq j$

We set $L_{\langle k,j \rangle} = \{a^{k+1}\}$.

*Case 2.* $\Phi_k(k) = x \leq j$

Then, we set $L_{\langle k,j \rangle} = \{a^{k+1}\} \cup \{b^m \mid 1 \leq m \leq x\}$.

Obviously, $\mathcal{L}_{eit}$ is an indexed family. The non-learnability of $\mathcal{L}_{eit}$ in the sense of $EIT-TXT$ is due to the following facts. For every $k \in \mathbb{N}$, there is exactly one index for the infinite language $L_{\langle k,0\rangle}$. Moreover, no IIM weak-monotonically infers $\mathcal{L}_{eit}$ with respect to $\mathcal{L}_{eit}$. Hence, every IIM learning $\mathcal{L}_{eit}$ has to produce at least once an overgeneralized hypothesis. Therefore, it has sometimes to shrink its guess to a finite language. But afterwards, it might receive data forcing it to output the corresponding number of the relevant infinite language. Now, every iterative IIM exactly learning $\mathcal{L}_{eit}$ is in serious trouble, since the only available hypothesis does not suffice to memorize the fact that the shrunk guess has been provably rejected. We continue with the formal proof.

*Claim 1.* $\mathcal{L}_{eit} \notin EIT-TXT$

Suppose that there exists any IIM $M$ which $EIT-TXT$-identifies $\mathcal{L}_{eit}$. Let us consider $M$'s behavior when fed the text $t = a^{k+1}, b, b^2, \ldots$ for the language $L_{\langle k,0\rangle}$. Since $\mathcal{L}_{eit} \notin EWMON-TXT$ (cf. Lange and Zeugmann (1993b)), there have to be indices $k, x \in \mathbb{N}$ such that $\varphi_k(k) \downarrow$ with $\Phi_k(k) > x$ and $M$ outputs the hypothesis $\langle k,0\rangle$ after processing $t_x$. Obviously, $t_x$ serves as an initial segment of a text for $L_{\langle k,\Phi_k(k)\rangle}$, too. Thus, there has to be a string $s \in L_{\langle k,\Phi_k(k)\rangle}$ such that $M(\langle k,0\rangle, s) = \langle k,y\rangle$ for some $y \geq \Phi_k(k)$. (Note that $L_{\langle k,y\rangle} = L_{\langle k,\Phi_k(k)\rangle}$, if $y \geq \Phi_k(k)$.) On the other hand, $M$ has, in particular, to infer the infinite language $L_{\langle k,0\rangle}$ from its text $\hat{t} = t_x, s, b, s, b^2, \ldots$ Since the string $s$ appears infinitely many times, $M$ outputs infinitely many times the wrong hypothesis $\langle k,y\rangle$. Thus, $M$ fails to converge to a correct guess on $\hat{t}$, a contradiction.

*Claim 2.* $\mathcal{L}_{eit} \in IT-TXT$

We sketch the underlying idea, only. Now, assume any class preserving hypothesis space $\mathcal{G}$ which contains for every $k \in \mathbb{N}$ at least two different indices, say $j_k$ and $\hat{j}_k$, for the infinite language $L_{\langle k,0\rangle}$. Applying this *a priori* knowledge about the underlying hypothesis space, an iterative IIM $M$ is able to handle overgeneralization. Thereby, $M$ may use each of both semantically equivalent hypotheses to represent different stages. Clearly, as long as $M$ is exclusively fed $a^{k+1}$, it outputs a canonical number of that singleton language. Now we describe how $M$ uses the semantical equivalent hypotheses. The index $j_k$ may be used to encode that $M$'s last guess $L_{\langle k,0\rangle}$ is a possibly overgeneralized hypothesis which may be changed in some subsequent step. $M$ outputs this hypothesis as long as it has no knowledge whether or not $\Phi_k(k) \downarrow$, i.e., as long as it has exclusively seen strings $b^z$ such that $\neg\Phi_k(k) \leq z$. On the other hand, if $M$ has been fed a string $b^z$ satisfying $\Phi_k(k) \leq z$ then it knows for sure that $\Phi_k(k) \downarrow$. After having gained this knowledge, it never outputs $j_k$. Instead, it either output an index for the corresponding finite language or, in case enough evidence has been presented, the index $\hat{j}_k$ for $L_{\langle k,0\rangle}$. We omit the details.                   q.e.d.

As the latter proof shows iterative IIMs may successfully handle overgeneralization. Moreover, their ability to solve the subset problem seriously depends on the choice of the relevant hypothesis space. However, it remained open whether or not the power of iterative IIMs increases, if class comprising hypothesis spaces are admissible. But it is known that $CIT-TXT \subset ELIM-TXT$ (cf. Lange and Zeugmann (1992)). Hence, iterative learning does not achieve the whole power of learning in the limit. Nevertheless, the proof technique presented above is powerful enough to compare exact iterative learning and all types of weak-monotonic inference. Moreover, the following theorems additionally relate the power of $CMON-TXT$ and of $CSMON-TXT$ to the capabilities of iterative IIMs.

**Theorem 19.**

(1) $EIT-TXT \setminus CSMON-TXT \neq \emptyset$

(2) $EIT-TXT \setminus CMON-TXT \neq \emptyset$

(3) $EIT-TXT \setminus CWMON-TXT \neq \emptyset$

*Proof.* First, we proof Assertion (2). We define an indexed family $\mathcal{L}$ over the alphabet $\Sigma = \{a, b\}$ as follows. Let $L_0 = \{a\}^+$ and $L_{k,n} = \{a^j \mid 1 \leq j \leq k\} \cup \{b^k, a^n, b^n\}$. $\mathcal{L} \in EIT-TXT$ can be easily verified. On the other hand, $\mathcal{L} \notin CMON-TXT$ results from the following observations. Suppose that there is an IIM $M$ which monotonically infers $\mathcal{L}$ with respect to a class preserving hypothesis space $\mathcal{G}$. Since $M$ has to infer $L_0$ on its lexicographically ordered text $t$, there is an $x \in \mathbb{N}$ such that $M(t_x) = j$ with $L(G_j) = L_0$. Now, $t_x$ may be extended to become a text $\hat{t}$ for the language $L_{x,x}$ on which $M$ sometimes has to output a correct hypothesis $z$, say after processing $\hat{t}_{x+r}$. Obviously, $\hat{t}_{x+r}$ forms an initial segment of a text for the language $L_{x,x+1}$. When fed $\hat{t}_{x+r}$, $M$'s first guess $j$ correctly contains the string $a^{x+1} \in L_{x,x+1}$, but $a^{x+1}$ is incorrectly excluded by its subsequent guess $z$. Thus, $M$ violates the monotonicity constraint when inferring $L_{x,x+1}$ on a text having the initial segment $\hat{t}_{x+r}$.

Since $CSMON-TXT \subset CMON-TXT$ Assertion (1) follows immediately. Note that we do not know whether or not $CMON-TXT \subseteq CWMON-TXT$. Thus, proving Assertion (3) requires a different approach.

Subsequently, we use the following shorthands. For all $n, m \in \mathbb{N}$, let $\hat{L}_{\langle n,0\rangle} = \{b^n c^j \mid 1 \leq j\}$ and $\hat{L}_{\langle n,m\rangle} = \{b^n c^j \mid 1 \leq j \leq m\}$. The desired indexed family $\mathcal{L} = (L_{\langle k,j\rangle})_{k,j\in\mathbb{N}}$ will be defined as follows. Let $k \in \mathbb{N}$. We distinguish the following cases.

*Case 1.* $j \leq 1$

Then, we set $L_{\langle k,j\rangle} = \{a^{k+1}\} \cup (\bigcup_{n\in\mathbb{N}} \hat{L}_{\langle n,0\rangle})$.

*Case 2.* $j \geq 2$

We distinguish the following subcases:

*Subcase 2.1.* $\neg\, \Phi_k(k) \leq j - 1$

Then, let $L_{\langle k,j\rangle} = L_{\langle k,0\rangle}$.

*Subcase 2.2.* $\Phi_k(k) \leq j - 1 \leq 2\Phi_k(k)$

Let $d = (j-1) - \Phi_k(k)$. Then, we set $L_{\langle k,j\rangle} = \{a^{k+1}\} \cup (\bigcup_{n\leq d} \hat{L}_{\langle n,0\rangle}) \cup (\bigcup_{n>d} \hat{L}_{\langle n,\Phi_k(k)\rangle})$.

*Subcase 2.3.* $j - 1 > 2\Phi_k(k)$

Then, we set $L_{\langle k,j\rangle} = \{a^{k+1}\} \cup \hat{L}_{\langle 0,0\rangle} \cup (\bigcup_{n>0} \hat{L}_{\langle n,\Phi_k(k)\rangle})$.

$\mathcal{L} \notin CWMON-TXT$ follows by applying our standard proof idea, namely by reducing the halting problem to $\mathcal{L} \in CWMON-TXT$ (cf. Lange and Zeugmann (1993c)). Next, we define an iterative IIM $M$ which infers $\mathcal{L}$ with respect to the hypothesis space $\mathcal{L}$. Let $L \in \mathcal{L}$ and let $t = s_0, s_1, s_2, \ldots$ be any text for $L$. Without loss of generality, we may assume that $s_0 = a^{k+1}$ for some $k \in \mathbb{N}$. (If $s_0 \neq a^{k+1}$, $M$ simply ignores all strings presented until a string $a^{k+1}$ appears for the first time.) The IIM $M$ is defined in stages, where Stage $x$ conceptually describes $M_x$.

Stage 0: Let $s_0 = a^{k+1}$ for some $k \in \mathbb{N}$. Set $j_0 = \langle k, 0 \rangle$. Output $\langle k, 0 \rangle$, and goto Stage 1.

Stage $x$: $M$ receives as input $j_{x-1}$ and the $x + 1$st element $s_x$ of $t$. If $s_x = a^{k+1}$ for some $k \in \mathbb{N}$, then set $j_x = j_{x-1}$. Output $j_x$, and goto Stage $x + 1$. Otherwise, $s_x = b^n c^m$ for some $n, m \in \mathbb{N}$.

Case 1. $j_{x-1} = \langle k, 0 \rangle$ for some $k \in \mathbb{N}$

Test whether or not $\Phi_k(k) \leq m$. In case it is, set $j_x = \langle k, \Phi_k(k) + 1 \rangle$, output $j_x$, and goto Stage $x + 1$. Otherwise, set $j_x = j_{x-1}$, output $j_x$, and goto Stage $x + 1$.

Case 2. $j_{x-1} = \langle k, 1 \rangle$ for some $k \in \mathbb{N}$

Set $j_x = j_{x-1}$, output $j_x$, and goto Stage $x + 1$.

Case 3. $j_{x-1} = \langle k, z \rangle$ for some $k \in \mathbb{N}$ and some $z \geq 1$

Test whether or not $s_x = b^n c^m \in L_{\langle k, z \rangle}$. In case it is, set $j_x = j_{x-1}$, output $j_x$, and goto Stage $x + 1$. Otherwise, execute Instruction (A).

(A) Test whether or not $n \leq \Phi_k(k)$. In case it is, set $j_x = \langle k, \Phi_k(k) + n + 1 \rangle$, output $j_x$, and goto Stage $x + 1$. Otherwise, set $j_x = \langle k, 1 \rangle$, output $j_x$, and goto Stage $x + 1$.

It remains to show that $M$ infers $\mathcal{L}$. Let $k, z \in \mathbb{N}$. Assume that a text $t$ for the target language $L = L_{\langle k, z \rangle}$ is presented. If $\varphi_k(k)$ is undefined, then $M$ outputs in every step the guess $\langle k, 0 \rangle$. Since $L_{\langle k, 0 \rangle} = L_{\langle k, z \rangle}$ for all $z \in \mathbb{N}$, $M$ infers $L$ from text $t$. It remains to discuss the case that $\varphi_k(k)$ is defined.

Because of the definition of $\mathcal{L}$, there has to be an $x \in \mathbb{N}$ such that $s_x = c^m$ with $m \geq \Phi_k(k)$. Hence, $M$ eventually rejects its current guess $\langle k, 0 \rangle$ and changes its mind to the guess $\langle k, \Phi_k(k) + 1 \rangle$. Afterwards, $M$ realizes the subset principle. In particular, $M$ avoids overgeneralization in every subsequent step. Since $M$ has to distinguish between finitely many possible hypotheses, only, $M$ converges to a correct hypotheses. Note that every language is uniquely characterized by infinitely many strings of the form $b^n c^m$ satisfying $m > \Phi_k(k)$ whereas the maximal index $n$ is referring to a correct number of the target language $\mathcal{L}$.

Thus, $M$ behaves as required. This finishes the proof of Assertion (3). q.e.d.

If language learning from informant is investigated, the situation slightly changes. The difference is caused by the fact that the weak-monotonicity constraint does not further restrict learning power. A detailed proof of the theorem below may be found in Lange and Zeugmann (1992).

**Theorem 20.**

(1) $EIT-INF \setminus CSMON-INF \neq \emptyset$

(2) $EIT-INF \setminus CMON-INF \neq \emptyset$

(3) $CIT-INF \subset EWMON-INF$

## 6.2. Monotonic Inference by Iterative Machines

In this subsection we aim to give some more insight concerning the trade-offs between information presentation and monotonicity constraints. Our treatment is based on the following perspective. Obviously, an iterative learner has only a limited access to the history of the learning process. Contrary to that, a monotonic learner can inspect the whole initial segment it has been fed. Thus, it may recompute the whole sequence of hypotheses created so far, and may incorporate this knowledge into the production of its actual guess. On the other hand, learning under monotonicity constraints provides additional *a priory* knowledge concerning the relation of subsequently produced hypotheses. Hence, it is only natural to ask whether or not this knowledge suffices to learn iteratively, too. As we will see, the answer to this question heavily depends on the monotonicity constraint involved as well as on the class of admissible hypothesis spaces.

**Theorem 21.** $EMON-TXT \setminus CIT-TXT \neq \emptyset$

*Proof.* Let $L_1 = \{a\}^*$ and $L_{k,n} = \{a^z \mid z \leq k\} \cup \{a^z \mid z \geq n\} \cup \{b^k, b^n\} \cup \{c\}$ for all $k, n \in \mathbb{N}$, $k, n > 1$ and $k + 2 < n$. Finally, we set $L_{k,n,m} = L_{k,n} \setminus \{c\} \cup \{a^m\}$ for all $k, n \in N$ as above and $k < m < n$. Then define $\mathcal{L}$ to be the collection of all $L_1$, $L_{k,n}$ and $L_{k,n,m}$. It is not hard to prove that $\mathcal{L} \in EMON-TXT$. The following weakness of iterative learners will be exploited to prove $\mathcal{L} \notin CIT-TXT$. Suppose to the contrary that an iterative IIM $M$ yields successful inference. Let $t$ be any text for $L_1$. Since $M$ has to infer $L_1$, it has to reach a point of stabilization, i.e., after this point $M$ has to repeat its last guess, no matter which string $s \in L_1$ is actually presented. Let $a^k$ be the longest string $M$ has fed before reaching the point of stabilization. Later on, $M$ has no chance to deduce from its last hypothesis whether or not a particular string $s \in L_1$ has been fed to it. But this is necessary to distinguish, for instance, between the languages $L_{k,k+3,k+1}$ and $L_{k,k+3,k+2}$ . Hence, $M$ is fooled.                q.e.d.

The latter theorem directly yields the following consequence. Monotonic as well as weak-monotonic inference with iterative IIMs is less powerful than with ordinary machines.

**Corollary 22.** *Let* $\lambda \in \{E, \varepsilon, C\}$. *Then we have:*

(1) $\lambda MON-IT-TXT \subset \lambda MON-TXT$

(2) $\lambda WMON-IT-TXT \subset \lambda WMON-TXT$

Next, we study strong-monotonic inference performed by iterative IIMs. As our next theorem shows, there is a peculiarity. Namely, class *comprising strong-monotonic* inference from positive data is precisely as powerful as *class comprising strong-monotonic and iterative* learning. Moreover, class comprising hypothesis spaces are inevitable to achieve this equality.

**Theorem 23.**

(1) $ESMON-IT-TXT \subset ESMON-TXT$

(2) $SMON-IT-TXT \subset SMON-TXT$

(3) $CSMON-IT-TXT = CSMON-TXT$

*Proof.* First, we show (1) and (2). It suffices to present an indexed family $\mathcal{L} = (L_j)_{j \in \mathbb{N}}$ witnessing $ESMON-TXT \setminus SMON-IT-TXT \neq \emptyset$. Let $\mathcal{L}$ denote any canonical enumeration of all finite languages over $\Sigma = \{a\}$ which does not contain the singleton languages $\{a\}$ and $\{aa\}$.

Obviously, $\mathcal{L} \in ESMON-TXT$. The main reason for $\mathcal{L} \notin SMON-IT-TXT$ can be described as follows. Suppose, $M$ is initially fed the string $a$. Then, $M$ may either remain in its initial stage or it may guess a language $L$ from $\mathcal{L}$. However, the latter cannot be done without violating the strong-monotonicity constraint, since $L \neq \{a\}$ for all $L \in \mathcal{L}$. The same argument applies when $M$ is initially fed the string $aa$. Hence, in both cases $M$ is forced to maintain its initial stage. But this implies that $M$ guesses the same sequence of hypotheses when successively fed $t = a, a^3, a^3, \ldots$ and $\hat{t} = aa, a^3, a^3, \ldots$, respectively. Consequently, $M$ fails to infer at least one of the corresponding finite languages $L = \{a, a^3\}$ and $\hat{L} = \{aa, a^3\}$ in the sense of $SMON-IT-TXT$, respectively.

Next, we prove Assertion (3). Let $M$ strong-monotonically infer $\mathcal{L}$ with respect to a class preserving space of hypotheses $\mathcal{G}$. Without loss of generality, we may assume that $M$ outputs in every step a consistent hypothesis (cf. Lange and Zeugmann (1993a)). First, we define another strong-monotonic IIM $\hat{M}$ which infers $\mathcal{L}$. In doing so, we choose the hypothesis space $\hat{\mathcal{G}}$ which is obtained from $\mathcal{G}$ by enumerating its closure with respect to finite unions. Now, let $L \in \mathcal{L}$ and $t = s_0, s_1, \ldots$ be any text for $L$.

$\hat{M}(t_x) = $ "If $x = 0$, compute $M(t_0) = j$. Output, the canonical index $\hat{j}_0$ of $L(G_j)$ in $\hat{\mathcal{G}}$. Otherwise, execute Instruction (A).

(A) Let $\hat{j}_k = \hat{M}(t_x)$. If $s_x \subseteq L(\hat{G}_{\hat{j}_k})$, repeat the hypothesis $\hat{j}_k$. Otherwise, goto (B).

(B) Compute the initial segment $\hat{t}_z$ of the lexicographically ordered text of $L(\hat{G}_{\hat{j}_k})$ which contains all strings being smaller than $s_x$ with respect to the underlying lexicographical ordering. Compute $j = M(\hat{t}_z, s_x)$. Output the canonical index of the language $L(\hat{G}_{\hat{j}_k}) \cup L(G_j)$ in $\hat{\mathcal{G}}$."

By definition, $L(\hat{G}_{\hat{j}_k}) \subseteq L(\hat{G}_{\hat{j}_{k+1}})$ for every $k \in \mathbb{N}$. Thus, $\hat{M}$ works strong-monotonically, too. Moreover, $\hat{M}$ exclusively produces consistent hypotheses, because $M$ is a consistent IIM. When fed *any* initial segment $t_x$ of *any* text for $L$, $M$ always outputs a guess $j$ such that $L(G_j) \subseteq L$. Obviously, the same statement is true, if $t_x$ is an initial segment of a text for *any* of $L$'s sublanguages. Now, taking $\hat{M}$'s definition into account it can be easily verified that $\hat{M}$ never outputs an overgeneralized hypothesis.

It remains to show that $\hat{M}$ infers $L$ from text $t$. Since $\hat{M}$ exclusively performs justified mind changes, it suffices to show that $\hat{M}$ outputs once a correct hypothesis. This happens trivially, if $L$ is a finite language, since $\hat{M}$ is a consistent IIM. Otherwise, let $L$ be infinite. In order to verify that $\hat{M}$ succesfully handles this case, too, one has to take into consideration that $M$, in particular, strong-monotonically infers $L$ from its lexicographically ordered text $t^L$. (Note that this assumes that $L$ is infinite.) Thus, $M(t_x^L) = j$ with $L(G_j) = L$ for some $x \in \mathbb{N}$. On the other hand, $t$ is a text for $L$. Hence, there is a least $y \in \mathbb{N}$ such that $range(t_x^L) \subseteq t_y^+$. Moreover, $\hat{M}(t_y) = \hat{j}_y$ with $range(t_x^L) \subseteq L(\hat{G}_{\hat{j}_y})$. If $L = L(\hat{G}_{\hat{j}_y})$, we are done. Otherwise, $L(\hat{G}_{\hat{j}_y}) \subset L$. Then, there exists a least $r \in \mathbb{N}$ such that $s_{y+r} \notin range(t_x^L)$. Since $range(t_x^L) \subseteq L(\hat{G}_{\hat{j}_y}) \subset L$, the string $s_{y+r}$ forces $\hat{M}$ to compute an extension of $L$'s lexicographically ordered text having the initial segment $t_x^L$. Taking again $\hat{M}$'s definition into account it follows that $\hat{M}(t_{y+r}) = \hat{j}_{y+r}$ with $L(G_j) \subseteq L(\hat{G}_{\hat{j}_{y+r}})$. Since $\hat{M}$ avoids overgeneralization, we are done.

Finally, a closer look to the definition of $\hat{M}$ shows that, when fed $t_x$, $\hat{M}$'s output depends only on its last guess $\hat{j}_{x-1}$ and the actual string $s_x$. Consequently, $\hat{M}$ witnesses $\mathcal{L} \in CSMON-IT-TXT$. q.e.d.

Finally, we summarize the corresponding results concerning monotonic inference from positive and negative examples (cf. Lange and Zeugmann (1992)).

**Theorem 24.** *Let* $\lambda \in \{E, \varepsilon, C\}$. *Then we have:*

(1) $\lambda MON-IT-INF \subset \lambda MON-INF$

(2) $\lambda WMON-IT-INF \subset \lambda WMON-INF$

Furthermore, concerning strong-monotonic learning the following theorem can be proved. Thereby, the same idea already used in the demonstration of Theorem 23 applies *mutatis mutandis*.

**Theorem 25.**

(1) $ESMON-IT-INF \subset ESMON-INF$

(2) $SMON-IT-INF \subset SMON-INF$

Up to now, it remains open whether class comprising strong-monotonic inference from informant can be performed by iterative IIMs without limiting learning power.

# 7. Trading Monotonicity Constraints Versus Efficiency

This section deals with the efficiency of learning. The measure of efficiency we use is the number of mind changes an IIM is allowed to perform. Starting with the pioneering paper by Barzdin and Freivalds (1972) this measure of efficiency has been intensively studied (cf., e.g., Barzdin, Kinber and Podnieks (1974), Barzdin and Freivalds (1974), Case and Smith (1983), Wiehagen, Freivalds and Kinber (1984)). However, all the mentioned papers considered the learnability of recursive functions. Hence, it is only natural to ask whether or not this measure of efficiency is of equal importance in the setting of language learning. This is indeed the case as recently obtained results show. Therefore, we continue with a short survey that comprises relevant results concerning the inferability of indexed families. Mukouchi (1992) considered exact learning from both, text and informant, and established the following hierarchies:

$$ELIM_0-TXT \subset ELIM_1-TXT \subset \ldots \subset \bigcup_{n\in\mathbb{N}} ELIM_n-TXT \subset ELIM_*-TXT$$

$$ELIM_0-INF \subset ELIM_1-INF \subset \ldots \subset \bigcup_{n\in\mathbb{N}} ELIM_n-INF \subset ELIM_*-INF$$

Subsequently, in Lange and Zeugmann (1993b) we extended the latter result to the class preserving case. Moreover, we considered the problem whether or not information presentation can always be traded versus efficiency, and obtained $ELIM_{n+1}-TXT \setminus LIM_n-INF \neq \emptyset$ for all $n \in \mathbb{N}$ as well as $ELIM_1-INF \setminus LIM-TXT \neq \emptyset$. Furthermore, we studied the influence of an appropriate choice of the hypothesis space on the efficiency of learning. As it turned out, at least one mind change can be saved provided the right hypothesis space is used. Recently, Lange (1994) sharpened the latter result in the strongest possible way for learning from text as well as from informant, thereby, handling class comprising learning, too. Finally, we additionally succeeded to characterize $LIM_n-TXT$ and $LIM_n-INF$ in terms of uniformly generable recursive finite tell-tales (cf. Lange and Zeugmann (1993b) as well as Theorem 3) and M. Sato extended this result to exact learning (cf. Mukouchi (1994)).

Discussing some of the results outlined above, Kinber (1992) proposed the following interesting problem.

*Does any of the monotonicity constraints defined in Section 2 influence the efficiency of learning?*

Clearly, this question is directly related to the problem how a natural learning algorithm might look like. In particular, it is well imaginable that one may succeed in designing a learning algorithm that fulfills a desirable monotonicity demand. However, it seems to be interesting to know what price one might have to pay concerning the resulting efficiency. Therefore, we study the influence of different monotonicity constraints to the number of mind changes an IIM has to perform when inferring a target indexed family. Then, the right question to ask is whether a weakening of the monotonicity requirement may yield a speed-up. A partial answer to this problem can already be found in Lange, Zeugmann and Kapur (1992). There it has been shown that $CWMON^d-TXT = CLIM-TXT$. However, the construction presented uniformly transforms any IIM that learns a target indexed family in the limit into one that fulfills the dual weak-monotonicity constraint. But the price paid is high. The dual weak-monotonic learner may be forced to change its mind twice as often than the original IIM (cf. Section 5, Theorem 15). It is open whether or not this bound is tight. Furthermore, Lange, Zeugmann and Kapur (1992) presents results showing that indexed families learnable with an *a priori* fixed number of mind changes under some monotonicity constraint can become non-inferable at all if the monotonicity demand is strengthened.

Our approach below deals with a problem of higher granularity. We always start with a target indexed family inferable under some monotonicity constraint with an *a priori* fixed number of mind changes. Then we ask whether or not the least or some possible relaxation of the corresponding monotonicity requirement might help to uniformly reduce the number of mind changes. As we shall see, there is no unique answer to this problem. Finally, in the following we restrict ourselves to consider learning from positive data and incorporate the number of mind changes into the definition of all types of monotonic learning in the same way as it has been done in

Definition 3. The resulting learning types are denoted by $\lambda SMON_n-TXT$, $\lambda MON_n-TXT$ and $\lambda WMON_n-TXT$, where $n \in \mathbb{N} \cup \{*\}$, and $\lambda \in \{C, \varepsilon, E\}$.

## 7.1. Strong-Monotonic Inference

We start our investigations with the strongest possible monotonicity constraint, i.e., with $SMON-TXT$ and its variations. Note that it does not make sense to consider $ESMON^d-TXT$ or $SMON^d-TXT$, since $SMON^d-TXT = EFIN-TXT$, and hence, there is nothing to speed-up. Moreover, in the following we exclusively consider the case where at least one mind change is mandatory, since otherwise finite learning is compared with some type of monotonic learning.

**Theorem 26.** *Let $\mathcal{L}$ be an indexed family. Then, for every $n \in \mathbb{N}^+$ we have:*

(1) $\mathcal{L} \in ESMON_{n+1}-TXT \setminus ESMON_n-TXT$ *implies* $\mathcal{L} \notin CLIM_n-TXT$,

(2) $\mathcal{L} \in SMON_{n+1}-TXT \setminus SMON_n-TXT$ *implies* $\mathcal{L} \notin CLIM_n-TXT$.

*Proof.* The proof is based on the following observations.

(A) Any strong-monotonically working IIM $\hat{M}$ can be simulated by a consistent, conservative, and strong-monotonic IIM $M$ that performs at most as many mind changes than $\hat{M}$ does (cf. Lange and Zeugmann (1993a)).

(B) Let $\mathcal{L}$ be any indexed family with $\mathcal{L} \in ESMON_{n+1}-TXT \setminus ESMON_n-TXT$. Furthermore, let $\mathcal{L} \in ESMON_{n+1}-TXT$ be witnessed by $M$, where $M$ is chosen in accordance with (A). Since $\mathcal{L} \notin ESMON_n-TXT$, there has to be an $L \in \mathcal{L}$ and a text $t$ for $L$ such that $M$ changes its mind exactly $n + 1$ times when fed $t$. Let $j_0, \ldots, j_{n+1}$ denote the finite sequence of $M$'s mind changes produced on $t$. Since $M$ is strong-monotonic and conservative, we directly obtain that $L_{j_0} \subset \cdots \subset L_{j_{n+1}} = L$.

Now, $\mathcal{L} \notin CLIM_n-TXT$ is a direct consequence of Proposition 3.7 by Mukouchi (1994). Applying the same arguments, one easily proves Assertion (2). q.e.d.

The latter theorem allows the following interpretation. Relaxing the requirement to learn exactly (class preservingly) strong-monotonically as much as possible does not increase the efficiency. This is even true, if we are allowed to choose an arbitrary class comprising hypothesis space provided that the target indexed family is inferable in the sense of $ESMON_{n+1}-TXT$ ($SMON_{n+1}-TXT$), but cannot be class preservingly and strong-monotonically learned with at most $n$ mind changes for some $n \in \mathbb{N}$.

Next we consider the class comprising case. Interestingly enough, now the topological argument used above does not apply any more. The following theorem shows that a suitable choice of the hypothesis space may increase the efficiency of learning, even under the strong-monotonicity constraint.

**Theorem 27.** *For every $n \in \mathbb{N}^+$ there exists an indexed family $\mathcal{L}$ such that*

(1) $\mathcal{L} \in CSMON_{n+1}-TXT \setminus CSMON_n-TXT$,

(2) $\mathcal{L} \in ELIM_n-TXT$.

*Proof.* First we prove the $n = 1$ case. Moreover, we use this case to fully explain the basic *proof technique* developed. The first idea is to incorporate a non-recursive but recursively enumerable problem in the definition of the target indexed family. Note that this incorporation has to be done in a way such that membership in the enumerated languages remains uniformly decidable. For that purpose, we used the halting problem. Without loss of generality, we may assume that $\Phi_j(j) \geq 1$ for all $j \in \mathbb{N}$.

The desired indexed family is defined as follows. Let $k, j \in \mathbb{N}$. We set $L_{3\langle k,j \rangle} = \{a^k b^z \mid z \in \mathbb{N}^+\}$. The remaining languages will be defined as follows.

*Case 1.* $\neg \Phi_k(k) \leq j$

Then we set $L_{3\langle k,j \rangle+1} = L_{3\langle k,j \rangle+2} = L_{3\langle k,0 \rangle}$.

*Case 2.* $\Phi_k(k) \leq j$

Let $m = \Phi_k(k)$. Now we set $L_{3\langle k,j \rangle+1} = \{a^k b^z \mid 1 \leq z \leq m\} \cup \{a^k c^m\}$, and $L_{3\langle k,j \rangle+2} = L_{3\langle k,0 \rangle} \cup \{a^k d^m\}$.

Since the predicate "$\Phi_i(x) = y$" is uniformly decidable for all $i, x, y \in \mathbb{N}$, it is easy to see that $\mathcal{L} = (L_z)_{z \in \mathbb{N}}$ is an indexed family. Whenever $\Phi_k(k) \downarrow$, the main problem for any strong-monotonic IIM consists in learning the finite language $L_{3\langle k,\Phi_k(k) \rangle+1}$ with at most one mind change. Hence, for proving $\mathcal{L} \in CSMON_2-TXT$, another ingredient is required, i.e., a suitable choice of a hypothesis space (cf. Claim A). The harder part is to show that $\mathcal{L} \notin CSMON_1-TXT$. As long as only class preserving hypothesis spaces are allowed, it is intuitively obvious that any IIM $M$ strong-monotonically learning $\mathcal{L}$ has to solve the halting problem. However, we have additionally to show that no choice of the hypothesis space may prevent $M$ to recursively handle the halting problem. This part of the proof exploits to a larger extend the assumption that membership is uniformly decidable (cf. Claim C).

We continue with the formal proof.

*Claim A.* $\mathcal{L} \in CSMON_2-TXT$.

First of all we define a suitable hypothesis space $\tilde{\mathcal{L}} = (\tilde{L}_i)_{i \in \mathbb{N}}$. For all $k, j \in \mathbb{N}$ and $z \in \{0, 1, 2\}$, we set:

$$\tilde{L}_{3\langle k,j \rangle+z} = \begin{cases} \bigcap_{j \in \mathbb{N}} L_{3\langle k,j \rangle+1}, & \text{if } j = 0, \\ L_{3\langle k,j-1 \rangle+z}, & \text{otherwise.} \end{cases}$$

It is not hard to see that $\tilde{\mathcal{L}}$ is indeed an indexed family. Now we define an IIM $M$ which strong-monotonically identifies $\mathcal{L}$ with respect to $\tilde{\mathcal{L}}$.

Let $L \in \mathcal{L}$, let $t$ be any text for $L$, and let $x \in \mathbb{N}$.

$M(t_x) = $ "Determine the unique $k$ such that $a^k b^z \in t_x^+$ for some $z \in \mathbb{N}$. Test whether or not $t_x^+ \subseteq \tilde{L}_{3\langle k,0 \rangle}$. In case it is, output $3\langle k, 0 \rangle$. Otherwise, goto (A).

    (A) Compute $m = max\{z \mid a^k b^z \in \tilde{L}_{3\langle k,0 \rangle}\}$. In case that $a^k c^m \in t_x^+$, output $3\langle k, m \rangle + 1$. Otherwise, goto (B).

    (B) If $a^k d^m \in t_x^+$, then output $3\langle k, m \rangle + 2$. Else, output $3\langle k, 1 \rangle$."

Now, one straightforwardly verifies that $M\ CSMON_2-TXT$–learns $\mathcal{L}$. This proves Claim A.

Before showing the second part of Assertion(1), we prove Assertion(2).

*Claim* B. $\mathcal{L} \in ELIM_1-TXT$.

The desired IIM is defined as follows. Let $L \in \mathcal{L}$, let $t$ be any text for $L$, and let $x \in \mathbb{N}$. We define:

$M(t_x) = $ "Determine the unique $k$ such that $a^k b^z \in t_x^+$ for some $z \in \mathbb{N}$. Test whether or not $t_x^+ \subseteq L_{\langle k,0\rangle}$. In case it is, output $3\langle k,0\rangle$. Otherwise, goto (A).

   (A) Compute $m = \Phi_k(k)$. In case that $a^k c^m \in t_x^+$, output $3\langle k,m\rangle + 1$. Otherwise, output $3\langle k,m\rangle + 2$."

It remains to show that $M$ infers $\mathcal{L}$ in the sense of $ELIM_1-TXT$. By construction, if $M$ performs a mind change, then it has detected an inconsistency. But in accordance with the definitions of $\mathcal{L}$ and $M$, $t_x^+ \not\subseteq L_{3\langle k,0\rangle}$ can happen if and only if $\Phi_k(k)$ is defined. Hence, the IIM may compute $m = \Phi_k(k)$. By construction, only two cases are possible, i.e., either $L$ contains $a^k c^m$ or it comprises $a^k d^m$. Looking at the definitions of $M$ and $\mathcal{L}$ it directly follows that $M$'s second guess is correct. Hence, $M$ $ELIM_1-TXT$-infers $\mathcal{L}$. This proves Claim B.

*Claim* C. $\mathcal{L} \notin CSMON_1-TXT$.

Suppose, there are a class comprising hypothesis space $\mathcal{G}$ for $\mathcal{L}$, and an IIM $M$ witnessing $\mathcal{L} \in CSMON_1-TXT$ with respect to $\mathcal{G}$. Then $M$ may be used to design an effective procedure solving the halting problem for the programming system $\varphi_0, \varphi_1, \ldots$. This can be seen as follows.

**Procedure HALT**

"Let $k \in \mathbb{N}$, and let $t$ be the canonical text for $L_{3\langle k,0\rangle}$. For $x = 0,1,\ldots$, compute $M(t_x)$ until the minimal index $z$ is found such that $M$, on successive input $t_z$ outputs its first guess, say $j$. Test whether or not $\Phi_k(k) \leq z+1$. In case it is, output $\varphi_k(k) \downarrow$. Otherwise, output $\varphi_k(k) \uparrow$."

First, we show that **HALT** is an effective procedure. In particular, $M$ has to infer $L_{3\langle k,0\rangle}$ from $t$. Hence, there is a $z$ such that $M$ on input $t_z$ computes a hypothesis $j$. Hence, **HALT** is recursive and terminates for all $k \in \mathbb{N}$.

It remains to show that **HALT** correctly works. Obviously, if the output is $\varphi_k(k) \downarrow$, then $\varphi_k(k)$ is indeed defined. Suppose, **HALT** outputs $\varphi_k(k) \uparrow$ but $\varphi_k(k)$ is defined. Hence, $\Phi_k(k)$ is defined, too. Let $m = \Phi_k(k)$. By construction, $m > z+1$. Since $M$ is a strong-monotonic IIM, one easily verifies that $L(G_j) \notin \mathcal{L}$. Furthermore, $M$ has to infer $L_{3\langle k,0\rangle}$ from its canonical text. Hence, there has to be an $y > z$ such that $M(t_y) = r$ and $L(G_r) = L_{3\langle k,0\rangle}$. Therefore, $M$ performs at least one mind change when seeing $t_y$. Finally, due to our construction, there is a language $L' \in \mathcal{L}$ such that $t_y^+ \subseteq L'$ and $L' \neq L_{3\langle k,0\rangle}$, namely $L' = L_{3\langle k,0\rangle} \cup \{a^k d^m\}$. Consequently, $t_y$ may be extended to a text for $L'$ on which $M$ has to perform an additional mind change, a contradiction.

The cases $n > 1$ may be proved using the same "lifting" technique as in Lange and Zeugmann (1993b) (cf. proof of Theorem 11).                    q.e.d.

At this point it is only natural to ask whether the latter theorem generalizes to all indexed families from $CSMON_{n+1}-TXT \setminus CSMON_n-TXT$ not belonging to

$SMON-TXT$. As we show, removing the requirement to learn strong-monotonically does not necessarily lead to a speed-up with respect to the number of mind changes.

**Theorem 28.** *For all $n \in \mathbb{N}$, there exists an indexed family $\mathcal{L}$ such that*

(1) $\mathcal{L} \in CSMON_{n+1}-TXT \setminus CSMON_n-TXT$,

(2) $\mathcal{L} \notin SMON-TXT$,

(3) $\mathcal{L} \notin ELIM_n-TXT$.

*Proof.* We consider the following indexed family $\mathcal{L} = (L_k)_{k \in \mathbb{N}}$. For all $k \in \mathbb{N}$ we define $L_{2k} = \{a^k b^j \mid j \in \mathbb{N}^+\}$ and $L_{2k+1} = \{a^k b^j \mid 1 \leq j \leq \Phi_k(k)\} \cup \{c^{\Phi_k(k)}\}$. Note that the set $\{c^{\Phi_k(k)}\}$ is defined to be empty, if $\Phi_k(k)$ diverges. Then it is easy to show that $\mathcal{L} \in CSMON_1-TXT \setminus SMON-TXT$. On the other hand, one straightforwardly verifies that $\mathcal{L}$ cannot be finitely inferred. Again, an easy application of the same "lifting" technique as in Lange and Zeugmann (1993b) directly yields the Theorem for all $n \in \mathbb{N}$.                                          q.e.d.

Theorem 28 directly yields the problem whether or not Theorem 27 can be strengthened, i.e., whether or not the number of mind changes that can be traded versus the strong-monotonicity constraint is bounded by one. The answer is provided by our next theorem.

**Theorem 29.** *For every $n \in \mathbb{N}^+$ there exists an indexed family $\mathcal{L}$ such that*

(1) $\mathcal{L} \in CSMON_{n+1}-TXT \setminus CSMON_n-TXT$,

(2) $\mathcal{L} \in EMON_1-TXT$.

*Proof.* We restrict ourselves to present the case $n = 2$, since it suffices to explain the *proof technique* developed. The main idea is to suitably iterate the proof technique presented in the demonstration of Theorem 27. Therefore, we incorporate one more halting problem into the definition of the indexed family $\mathcal{L}$ witnessing $\mathcal{L} \in CSMON_3-TXT \setminus CSMON_2-TXT$, and $\mathcal{L} \in ELIM_1-TXT$. This is done as follows. Without loss of generality, we may assume that $\Phi_j(j) \geq 1$ for all $j \in \mathbb{N}$. We define:

$L_{4\langle k_1,k_2,j \rangle} = \{a^{\langle k_1,k_2 \rangle} b^z \mid z \in \mathbb{N}^+\}$ for all $k_1, k_2, j \in \mathbb{N}$. In order to define the remaining languages of $\mathcal{L}$ we distinguish the following cases.

*Case 1.* $\neg \Phi_{k_1}(k_1) \leq j$

Then we set $L_{4\langle k_1,k_2,j \rangle+1} = L_{4\langle k_1,k_2,j \rangle+2} = L_{4\langle k_1,k_2,j \rangle+3} = L_{4\langle k_1,k_2,0 \rangle}$.

*Case 2.* $\Phi_{k_1}(k_1) \leq j$

Then, let $\ell = \Phi_{k_1}(k_1)$, and set $L_{4\langle k_1,k_2,j \rangle+1} = \{a^{\langle k_1,k_2 \rangle} b^z \mid 1 \leq z \leq \ell\} \cup \{a^{\langle k_1,k_2 \rangle} c^\ell\}$.

Furthermore, we distinguish the following subcases.

*Subcase 2.1.* $\neg \Phi_{k_2}(k_2) \leq j$

Then let $L_{4\langle k_1,k_2,j \rangle+2} = L_{4\langle k_1,k_2,j \rangle+3} = L_{4\langle k_1,k_2,0 \rangle}$.

*Subcase 2.2.* $\Phi_{k_2}(k_2) \leq j$

Let $\ell = \Phi_{k_1}(k_1)$, and $m = \Phi_{k_2}(k_2)$.

We set $L_{4\langle k_1,k_2,j\rangle+2} = \{a^{\langle k_1,k_2\rangle}b^z \mid 1 \le z \le \ell + m\} \cup \{a^{\langle k_1,k_2\rangle}d^{\ell+m}\}$, and $L_{4\langle k_1,k_2,j\rangle+3} = L_{4\langle k_1,k_2,0\rangle} \cup \{a^{\langle k_1,k_2\rangle}e^{\ell+m}\}$.

Now, it is easy to see that $\mathcal{L} = (L_z)_{z\in\mathbb{N}}$ constitutes an indexed family. It remains to show that $\mathcal{L}$ fulfills the stated requirements. This is done by the following lemmata.

**Lemma 1.** $\mathcal{L} \in EMON_1-TXT$.

An IIM $M$ witnessing $\mathcal{L} \in ELIM_1-TXT$ can be easily defined. Initially, it outputs $4\langle k_1,k_2,0\rangle$. As long as this guess is consistent, it is repeated. Otherwise, $M$ reads one of the following strings $a^{\langle k_1,k_2\rangle}c^\ell$, $a^{\langle k_1,k_2\rangle}d^{\ell+m}$ or $a^{\langle k_1,k_2\rangle}e^{\ell+m}$. These strings serve as a label as the definition of $\mathcal{L}$ shows. Therefore, $M$ can change its mind to a correct hypothesis which it repeats subsequently. Moreover, it is easy to see that the possible mind change satisfies the monotonicity requirement. This proves the lemma.

**Lemma 2.** $\mathcal{L} \in CSMON_3-TXT$.

The wanted hypothesis space $\mathcal{G} = (G_j)_{j\in\mathbb{N}}$ is defined to be a canonical enumeration of all languages of $\mathcal{L}$ and all languages $\hat{L}_{4\langle k_1,k_2\rangle+1} = \bigcap_{j\in\mathbb{N}} L_{4\langle k_1,k_2,j\rangle+1}$ as well as $\hat{L}_{4\langle k_1,k_2\rangle+2} = \bigcap_{j\in\mathbb{N}} L_{4\langle k_1,k_2,j\rangle+2}$ for all $k_1, k_2 \in \mathbb{N}$. We suppress the technicalities and refer to hypotheses in $\mathcal{G}$ as to canonical numbers of the corresponding languages.

The desired IIM $M$ is defined as follows. Let $L \in \mathcal{L}$, $t \in text(L)$, and $x \in \mathbb{N}$. We define:

$M(t_x) =$ "If $a^{\langle k_1,k_2\rangle}c^\ell \subseteq t_x^+$ output the canonical number of $L_{4\langle k_1,k_2,\ell\rangle+1}$.

If $a^{\langle k_1,k_2\rangle}d^{\ell+m} \subseteq t_x^+$ output the canonical number of $L_{4\langle k_1,k_2,\ell+m\rangle+2}$.

If $a^{\langle k_1,k_2\rangle}e^{\ell+m} \subseteq t_x^+$ output the canonical number of $L_{4\langle k_1,k_2,\ell+m\rangle+3}$.

Otherwise, i.e., if $t_x^+ \subseteq \{a^{\langle k_1,k_2\rangle}b^z \mid z \in \mathbb{N}^+\}$, test successively whether or not the canonical number for $\hat{L}_{4\langle k_1,k_2\rangle+1}$, or $\hat{L}_{4\langle k_1,k_2\rangle+2}$ or $L_{4\langle k_1,k_2,0\rangle}$ is consistent. Output the first consistent hypothesis."

The definitions of $\mathcal{L}$ and $\mathcal{G}$ directly imply that $M$ satisfies the strong-monotonicity constraint. Moreover, it is easy to see that $M$ learns $\mathcal{L}$ with respect to $\mathcal{G}$. Hence, it remains to show that three mind changes are sufficient. Obviously, the worst case occurs when $M$ is forced to output successively the canonical numbers for $\hat{L}_{4\langle k_1,k_2\rangle+1}$, $\hat{L}_{4\langle k_1,k_2\rangle+2}$ and $L_{4\langle k_1,k_2,0\rangle}$ before seeing $a^{\langle k_1,k_2\rangle}e^{\ell+m}$. However, even in this case $M$ performs precisely three mind changes. This proves the lemma.

The remaining part, i.e., $\mathcal{L} \notin CSMON_2-TXT$, is much harder to prove. The critical part is to show that any IIM which strong-monotonically infers $\mathcal{L}$ has to be at least as careful, when fed a text for $L_{4\langle k_1,k_2,0\rangle}$, as the IIM $M$ provided in Lemma 2. For that purpose we need some additional insight into the behavior of every IIM that strong-monotonically learns $\mathcal{L}$. In particular, we are mainly interested in knowing how every IIM inferring $\mathcal{L}$ strong-monotonically behaves when successively fed the lexicographically ordered text for $L_{4\langle k_1,k_2,0\rangle}$. The desired information is provided by the following lemma.

**Lemma 3.** *Let $\mathcal{G} = (G_j)_{j\in\mathbb{N}}$ be any class comprising hypothesis space for $\mathcal{L}$ and let $M$ be any IIM witnessing $\mathcal{L} \in CSMON-TXT$ with respect to $\mathcal{G}$. Then we have: For all $k_2$ there are numbers $k_1, x, j \in \mathbb{N}$ such that*

(1) $M(t_x) = j$,

(2) $\Phi_{k_1}(k_1) > x + 1$ *and* $\varphi_{k_1}(k_1) \downarrow$,

*where $t$ is the lexicographically ordered text of $L_{4\langle k_1, k_2, 0\rangle}$.*

Suppose the converse. Then there is a $k_2$ such that for all $k_1, x, j$ we have: $M(t_x) = j$ implies $\Phi_{k_1}(k_1) \leq x + 1$ or $\Phi_{k_1}(k_1) \uparrow$.

Assuming the latter statement we have the following claim.

*Claim.* Provided the latter statement is true, any program for $M$ may be used to obtain *non-effectively* an algorithm deciding "$\varphi_{k_1}(k_1) \downarrow$."

By assumption, there is a $k_2$ such that for all $k_1, x, j$: If (1) is fulfilled, then either $\Phi_{k_1}(k_1) \leq x + 1$ or $\Phi_{k_1}(k_1) \uparrow$. Using this $k_2$ we can define the following algorithm $\mathcal{A}$.

**Algorithm $\mathcal{A}$:** "On input $k_1$ execute (A1) and (A2).

(A1) Generate successively the lexicographically ordered text $t$ of $L_{4\langle k_1, k_2, 0\rangle}$ and simulate $M$ until the first hypothesis $j$ is produced.
Let $x_0$ be the least $x$ such that $M(t_x) = j$.

(A2) Test whether $\Phi_{k_1}(k_1) \leq x_0 + 1$.
In case it is, output "$\varphi_{k_1}(k_1) \downarrow$."
Otherwise, output "$\varphi_{k_1}(k_1) \uparrow$" and stop."

First we observe that $M$ has to infer $L_{4\langle k_1, k_2, 0\rangle}$ from its lexicographically ordered text $t$. Hence, $M$ should eventually output a hypothesis $j$ when fed $t$. Furthermore, Instruction (A2) can be effectively accomplished, too. Hence, $\mathcal{A}$ is an algorithm and the execution of (A1) and (A2) must eventually terminate. Finally, by assumption we immediately obtain the correctness of $\mathcal{A}$'s output. This proves the claim. Since the halting problem is algorithmically undecidable, the lemma follows.

**Lemma 4.** $\mathcal{L} \notin CSMON_2 - TXT$.

Suppose the converse, i.e., there exist a hypothesis space $\mathcal{G} = (G_j)_{j \in \mathbb{N}}$ and an IIM $M$ that $CSMON_2 - TXT$–learns $\mathcal{L}$ with respect to $\mathcal{G}$. Then we can prove the following lemma.

**Lemma A.** *Given any hypothesis space $\mathcal{G} = (G_j)_{j \in \mathbb{N}}$ and any program for $M$ witnessing $\mathcal{L} \in CSMON_2 - TXT$, one can effectively construct an algorithm deciding whether or not "$\varphi_{k_2}(k_2) \downarrow$."*

Let $K = \{k | \varphi_k(k) \downarrow\}$ and let $j_0, j_1, j_2, \ldots$ be any fixed effective enumeration of $K$. We define an algorithm $\mathcal{A}$ as follows.

**Algorithm $\mathcal{A}$:** "On input $k_2$ execute (A1) and (A2).

(A1) For $z = 0, 1, 2, \ldots$ successively compute the lexicographically ordered texts $t^{j_0}, t^{j_1}, t^{j_2}, \ldots$ for $L_{4\langle j_0, k_2, 0\rangle}, L_{4\langle j_1, k_2, 0\rangle}, \ldots, L_{4\langle j_z, k_2, 0\rangle}$ of length $z + 1$, respectively. Then, dovetail the simulation of $M$ on successive input of each of these initial segments until the first initial segment $t_x^{j_r}$ $(r, x \leq z)$ and the first hypothesis $j$ are found such that

($\alpha$1)  $M(t_x^{j_r}) = j$,

($\alpha$2)  $\Phi_{j_r}(j_r) > x + 1$.

(* By Lemma 3, the execution of (A1) has to terminate *)

(A2) Let $f =_{df} \langle j_r, k_2 \rangle$ and $\ell = \Phi_{j_r}(j_r)$. Furthermore, we define $\hat{t}_{\ell+y}$ as follows:
$$\hat{t}_{\ell+y} = \underbrace{a^f b, \ ..., \ a^f b^{x+1}, \ ..., \ a^f b^{\ell}}_{=t_{\ell-1}^{j_r}}, \ a^f b^{\ell}, \ \underbrace{a^f b^{\ell+1}, \ ..., \ a^f b^{\ell+y}}_{y-\text{strings}}$$

For $y = 0$, 1, 2, ... execute in parallel ($\beta$1) and ($\beta$2) until ($\beta$3) or ($\beta$4) happens.

($\beta$1)  Test whether $\Phi_{k_2}(k_2) \leq \ell + y$.

($\beta$2)  Compute $j_{\ell+y} = M(\hat{t}_{\ell+y})$.

($\beta$3)  $\Phi_{k_2}(k_2) \leq \ell + y$ is verified. Then output "$\varphi_{k_2}(k_2) \downarrow$."

($\beta$4)  In ($\beta$2) a hypothesis $j_{\ell+y} = M(\hat{t}_{\ell+y})$ is computed such that $a^f b^{\ell+1} \in L(G_{j_{\ell+y}})$. Then output "$\varphi_{k_2}(k_2) \uparrow$" and stop."

It remains to show that $\mathcal{A}$ terminates on every input, and behaves correctly.

*Claim 1.* On every input $k_2$, the algorithm $\mathcal{A}$ terminates.

As we have already mentioned, by Lemma 3 we know that the execution of (A1) has to terminate. Hence, it suffices to show that either ($\beta$3) or ($\beta$4) happens. Suppose, ($\beta$3) does not happen. Then, for all $y \in \mathbb{N}$ we have $\neg \Phi_{k_2}(k_2) \leq \ell + y$. Consequently, $\Phi_{k_2}(k_2) \uparrow$. Therefore, when $y$ tends to infinite, then $\hat{t}_{\ell+y}$ converges to a text for $L_{4\langle j_n, k_2, 0\rangle}$, and hence, $M$ eventually has to output a hypothesis $j_{\ell+y}$ such that $a^f b^{\ell+1} \in L(G_{j_{\ell+y}})$. Thus, ($\beta$4) must happen. This proves the claim.

*Claim 2.* Algorithm $\mathcal{A}$ works correctly.

Obviously, if ($\beta$3) happens then $\varphi_{k_2}(k_2)$ is indeed defined. Suppose, ($\beta$4) happens. We have to show that $\varphi_{k_2}(k_2) \uparrow$. Suppose the converse, i.e., $\varphi_{k_2}(k_2) \downarrow$. Thus, $\Phi_{k_2}(k_2)$ converges, too. We distinguish the following cases.

*Case 1.* The hypothesis $j_{\ell+y}$ satisfies $L(G_{j_{\ell+y}}) = L_{4\langle j_r, k_2, 0\rangle}$.

Then $M$ fails to infer $L_{4\langle j_r, k_2, \Phi_{j_r}(j_r)+\Phi_{k_2}(k_2)\rangle+2}$ strong-monotonically. This can be seen as follows. Since ($\beta$3) did not happen, we have $\Phi_{k_2}(k_2) > \ell + y$. Hence, $\hat{t}_{\ell+y}$ is an initial segment of a text for $L_{4\langle j_r, k_2, 0\rangle}$ and of a text $\tilde{t}$ for $L_{4\langle j_r, k_2, \Phi_{j_r}(j_r)+\Phi_{k_2}(k_2)\rangle+2}$. On the other hand, when successively fed $\tilde{t}$, the IIM $M$ sometimes outputs $j_{\ell+y}$, and $L(G_{j_{\ell+y}}) = L_{4\langle j_r, k_2, 0\rangle}$. Since $L_{4\langle j_r, k_2, 0\rangle} \not\subseteq L_{4\langle j_r, k_2, \Phi_{j_r}(j_r)+\Phi_{k_2}(k_2)\rangle+2}$, we directly see that $M$ violates the strong-monotonicity constraint.

*Case 2.* The hypothesis $j_{\ell+y}$ does not satisfy $L(G_{j_{\ell+y}}) = L_{4\langle j_r, k_2, 0\rangle}$.

Then, $M$ fails to learn $\mathcal{L}$ with at most two mind changes. Recall that $M$ has already generated the guesses $j$ and $j_{\ell+y}$ when successively fed $\hat{t}_{\ell+y}$. First, we show that $j \neq j_{\ell+y}$. Suppose to the contrary that $j = j_{\ell+y}$. Remember that $\ell = \Phi_{j_r}(j_r)$. Then $M$ fails to infer $L_{4\langle j_r, k_2, \ell\rangle+1}$ strong-monotonically. This can be seen as follows. By construction, $a^f b^{\ell+1} \in L(G_{j_{\ell+y}})$, and hence, $a^f b^{\ell+1} \in L(G_j)$. But $j = M(t_x^{j_r})$, and $x < \ell$. Therefore, $t_x^{j_r}$ is an initial segment of some text for $L_{4\langle j_r, k_2, \ell\rangle+1}$, too. On the other hand, $a^f b^{\ell+1} \notin L_{4\langle j_r, k_2, \ell\rangle+1}$. Consequently, $L(G_j) \not\subseteq L_{4\langle j_r, k_2, \ell\rangle+1}$, a contradiction.

Finally, since $j \neq j_{\ell+y}$, $M$ has already performed at least one mind change when successively fed $\hat{t}_{\ell+y}$. Hence, $\hat{t}_{\ell+y}$ is an initial segment of a text for $L_{4\langle j_r, k_2, 0\rangle}$ as well as for $L_{4(j_r,k_2,\ell+\Phi_{k_2}(k_2))+3}$. In accordance with $\mathcal{L}$'s definition we additionally have $L_{4(j_r,k_2,0)} \subset L_{4(j_r,k_2,\ell+\Phi_{k_2}(k_2))+3}$. Thus, we may extend $\hat{\imath}_{\ell+y}$ with $a^f b^{\ell+y+1}$, $a^f b^{\ell+y+2}$, ... until $M$ learns $L_{4(j_r,k_2,0)}$. This forces $M$ to change its mind again. Afterwards, we present $a^f e^{\ell+\Phi_{k_2}(k_2)}$, and hence, one more mind change has to occur. Thus, $\mathcal{L} \notin CSMON_2-TXT$. This contradiction proves Claim 3. Thus, Lemma 4 is shown, and the theorem follows. q.e.d.

Note that the proof of the latter theorem directly allows the following corollary.

**Corollary 30.** $EMON_1-TXT \setminus SMON-TXT \neq \emptyset$.

*Proof.* The indexed family $\mathcal{L}$ defined above belongs to $ELIM_1-TXT$. Hence, we have to argue that $\mathcal{L} \notin SMON-TXT$. This is a direct consequence of Lemma 3 in the above proof. q.e.d.

In the next subsection we study monotonic inference.

## 7.2. Monotonic Inference

This subsection deals with monotonic inference, and possible relaxations of the monotonicity requirement. But there is a peculiarity which we point out with the following theorem.

**Theorem 31.** $\lambda LIM_1-TXT = \lambda MON_1-TXT$ for all $\lambda \in \{E,\varepsilon,C\}$,

*Proof.* Let $\mathcal{L}$ be any indexed family such that $\mathcal{L} \in \lambda LIM_1-TXT$, where $\lambda \in \{E,\varepsilon,C\}$. Hence, there are a hypothesis space $\mathcal{G} = (G_j)_{j\in\mathbb{N}}$ and an IIM $M$ that $\lambda LIM_1-TXT$–infers $\mathcal{L}$ with respect to $\mathcal{G}$. Consequently, when fed any text of any language $L \in \mathcal{L}$ the IIM $M$ performs at most one mind change. Suppose, first $M$ outputs $k$, and then it changes its mind to $j$. Hence, $j$ has to be a correct guess for $L$, i.e., we have $L = L(G_j)$. Therefore, we directly obtain $L(G_k) \cap L \subseteq L(G_j) \cap L = L$. Hence, $M$ monotonically infers $\mathcal{L}$. q.e.d.

Next we show that the monotonicity constraint can be traded versus efficiency. This is even true, if the relaxation is as weak as possible, i.e., if the requirement to learn monotonically is relaxed to weak-monotonic inference.

**Theorem 32.** For every $n \in \mathbb{N}$, $n \geq 2$, there exists an indexed family such that

(1) $\mathcal{L} \in MON_{n+1}-TXT \setminus MON_n-TXT$,

(2) $\mathcal{L} \in EWMON_n-TXT$.

*Proof.* For the sake of presentation, we consider the case $n = 2$. The extension to all $n \geq 3$ may be easily obtained by applying the lifting technique of Lange and Zeugmann (1993b). The desired indexed family is defined as follows. For all $k \in \mathbb{N}$, we set $L_{4k} = \{a^k b^z \mid z \in \mathbb{N}^+\}$ and $L_{4k+1} = L_{4k} \cup \{b^k a\}$. In order to define the remaining languages we distinguish the following cases:

*Case 1.* $\Phi_k(k) \uparrow$

Then we set $L_{4k+2} = L_{4k+3} = L_{4k+1}$.

*Case 2.* $\Phi_k(k) \downarrow$

Then, let $m = \Phi_k(k)$, and let $\hat{L}_k = \{a^k b^z | 1 \leq z \leq m\} \cup \{b^k a\}$. We set $L_{4k+2} = \hat{L}_k \cup \{a^k c^m\}$, and $L_{4k+3} = \hat{L}_k \cup \{a^k c^m, a^k d^m\}$.

Obviously, $\mathcal{L} = (L_z)_{z \in \mathbb{N}}$ is an indexed family of recursive languages. To see this take into consideration that, for instance, $a^k b^z \in L_{4k+2}$ iff $\Phi_k(k) \geq z$. But $\Phi_k(k) \geq z$ is uniformly decidable for any $z$, $k \in \mathbb{N}$.

*Claim A.* $\mathcal{L} \in EMON_3 - TXT$.

We define the desired IIM $M$ as follows. Let $L \in \mathcal{L}$, let $t$ be any text for $L$, and let $x \in \mathbb{N}$.

$M(t_x) = $ "Determine the unique $k$ such that $a^k b^z \in t_x^+$ for some $m \in \mathbb{N}$. If $b^k a \notin t_x^+$ output $4k$. Otherwise, goto (A).

(A) If $a^k d^m \in t_x^+$ and $t_x^+ \subseteq L_{4k+3}$, then output $4k + 3$.
If $a^k c^m \in t_x^+$ and $t_x^+ \subseteq L_{4k+2}$, then output $4k + 2$.
Otherwise, output $4k + 1$."

Obviously, $M$ monotonically infers $\mathcal{L}$. In the worst case, $M$ changes its mind three times, namely it outputs successively the hypotheses $4k$, $4k+1$, $4k+2$, and $4k+3$. It is easy to verify that each of these mind changes satisfies the monotonicity requirement.

*Claim B.* $\mathcal{L} \in EWMON_2 - TXT$.

The desired IIM is defined as follows. Let $L \in \mathcal{L}$, let $t \in text(L)$, and let $x \in \mathbb{N}$.

$M(t_x) = $ "Determine the unique $k$ such that $a^k b^z \in t_x^+$ for some $z \in \mathbb{N}^+$. If $b^k a \notin t_x^+$ output $4k$. Otherwise, goto (A).

(A) If $t_x^+ \subseteq L_{4k+2}$ output $4k + 2$.
If $a^k d^m \in t_x^+$ output $4k + 3$.
Otherwise, i.e., a string $a^k b^z \notin L_{4k+2}$ occurred, output $4k + 1$."

Obviously, $M$ weak-monotonically infers $\mathcal{L}$. Thereby, $M$ changes its mind at most twice. This proves Claim B.

Note that the IIM $M$ defined in the latter proof may subsequently output the hypotheses $4k$, $4k + 2$, and $4k + 1$ when fed a text for $L_{4k+1}$. It is easy to verify that the latter mind change violates the monotonicity requirement. Moreover, it is easy to argue that $\mathcal{L} \notin EMON_2 - TXT$. But again, we show a slightly stronger result.

*Claim C.* $\mathcal{L} \notin MON_2 - TXT$.

Claim C follows by contraposition of Lemma 1.

**Lemma 1.** *Given any class preserving hypothesis space* $\mathcal{G}$ *and any program for an IIM* $M$ *witnessing* $\mathcal{L} \in MON_2 - TXT$ *with respect to* $\mathcal{G}$, *one can effectively define a total-recursive predicate* $\psi$ *solving the halting problem.*

*Proof.* Let $k \in \mathbb{N}$; the desired predicate $\psi$ is defined as follows.

$\psi(k) = $ "Let $t$ be the lexicographically ordered text for $L_{4k}$. For $x = 0$, $1$, ..., compute $M(t_x)$ until the first index $z$ is found such that $j = M(t_z)$ satisfies $a^k b \in L(G_j)$, and $b^k a \notin L(G_j)$.

(A)  For $r = 1, 2, \ldots$ simulate $M$, when fed the text $\hat{t} = t_z$, $b^k a$, $a^k b$, ..., $a^k b^r$ for $L_{4k+1}$, until the first index $y$ is found such that $j_{z+1+y} = M(\hat{t}_{z+1+y})$ satisfies $b^k a \in L(G_{j_{z+1+y}})$.

(B)  Test whether or not $\Phi_k(k) \leq z + 1 + y$. In case it is, output 1. Otherwise, output 0."

Since $M$ has to infer the languages $L_{4k}$ as well as $L_{4k+1}$, it is easy to verify that the procedure defined above terminates for every $k \in \mathbb{N}$. Hence, $\psi$ is total-recursive.

It remains to show that $\varphi_k(k)$ is undefined, if $\psi(k) = 0$. Suppose the converse, i.e., $\psi(k) = 0$ as well as $\varphi_k(k)$ is defined. Therefore, $\Phi_k(k) = m > z + 1 + y$.

Recall that $M$ has already performed at least one mind change when fed $\hat{t}_{z+1+y}$, namely from $j$ to $j_{z+1+y}$. Due to the definition of $\mathcal{L}$, $b^k a \notin L(G_j)$ together with $a^k b \in L(G_j)$ implies $L(G_j) = L_{4k}$. Since $M$ monotonically infers $L_{4k+1}$ from $\hat{t}$ and $b^k a \in L(G_{j_{z+1+y}})$, we obtain $L(G_{j_{z+1+y}}) = L_{4k+1}$. Otherwise, $M$ violates the monotonicity constraint when inferring $L_{4k+1}$ on its text $\hat{t}$. Now, taking $\mathcal{L}$'s definition into account, it follows that $\hat{t}_{z+1+y}$ may also serve as an initial segment of a text for the language $L_{4k+2}$ because $\Phi_k(k) = m > z + 1 + y$. Finally, since $L_{4k+2} \subset L_{4k+3}$, it is easy to verify that $\hat{t}_{z+1+y}$ can be extended to a text for $L_{4k+3}$ such that $M$ has to perform at least two additional mind changes in order to infer $L_{4k+3}$ from this text. This contradicts our assumption that $M$ monotonically infers $\mathcal{L}$ with at most two mind changes. Therefore, $\varphi_k(k)$ is undefined, if $\psi(k) = 0$. Hence, the predicate $\psi$ solves the halting problem for the $\varphi$-system. q.e.d.

Refining *mutatis mutandis* the latter proof analogously as the demonstration of Theorem 27 has been extended to show Theorem 29, one obtains the following result.

**Theorem 33.** *For every $n \geq 2$ there exists an indexed family such that*

(1)  $\mathcal{L} \in MON_{n+1} - TXT \setminus MON_n - TXT$,

(2)  $\mathcal{L} \in EWMON_2 - TXT$.

The latter theorems allow the following interpretation. Removing the constraint to learn monotonically may considerably increase the efficiency of the learning process.

## 7.3.  Weak-Monotonic Learning

Finally, we consider weak-monotonic learning. Possible relaxations include dual weak-monotonic learning as well as learning in the limit. However, much less is known. First, Theorem 31 directly implies $LIM_1 - TXT = WMON_1 - TXT$ as well as $ELIM_1 - TXT = EWMON_1 - TXT$, since $\lambda MON - TXT \subset \lambda WMON - TXT$ for $\lambda \in \{E, \varepsilon\}$. On the other hand, it is even open whether or not $CMON_1 - TXT \subseteq CWMON_1 - TXT$. Hence, showing $CLIM_1 - TXT = CWMON_1 - TXT$ requires a separate proof that is still missing. Nevertheless, we succeeded to obtain results that shed considerable light on the power of learning with at most one mind change.

**Theorem 34.**

(1)  $MON_1 - TXT \setminus EWMON - TXT \neq \emptyset$

(2)  $ELIM_2 - TXT \setminus WMON - TXT \neq \emptyset$

(3) $CMON_1 - TXT \setminus WMON - TXT \neq \emptyset$

*Proof.* Lange and Zeugmann (1993b) proved $LIM_1 - TXT \setminus EWMON - TXT \neq \emptyset$, and recently Lange (1994) shows $CLIM_1 - TXT \setminus WMON - TXT \neq \emptyset$. Combining these results with Theorem 31 we directly get Assertion (1) and (3). Finally, for a proof of Assertion (2) we refer the reader to Lange (1994).                    q.e.d.

Consequently, relaxing the weak-monotonicity constraint may considerably increase the inference capabilities.

We conclude this section with further problems that remain open. First of all, it would be very interesting to answer the following question. Does there exist a $k \in \mathbb{N}$ such that $CLIM_k \setminus CWMON \neq \emptyset$? Of course, one should ask similar questions for dual monotonic and especially for dual weak-monotonic learning.

Furthermore, our results show that a relaxation of the corresponding monotonicity demands sometimes yields a significant speed-up of the learning process. Hence, it seems highly desirable to investigate necessary and sufficient conditions $\mathcal{C}_{csmon}$, $\mathcal{C}_{mon}$, and $\mathcal{C}_{wmon}$ allowing assertions of the following type.

Let $LT$ as well as $LT'$ be any learning type, and let $\mathcal{L} \in LT$. Then one may learn $\mathcal{L}$ more efficiently in the sense of LT' if and only if $\mathcal{C}_{lt'}$ is satisfied but $\mathcal{C}_{lt}$ is not.

Moreover, it would be very interesting to relate possible relaxations of our monotonicity requirements to problems studied in complexity theory. Recently, such an approach has been undertaken concerning consistent and inconsistent learning resulting in a proof for the superiority of an inconsistent learning algorithm (cf. Wiehagen and Zeugmann, 1994)). We will see what the future brings concerning these problems.

# 8. Degrees of Order Independence

In this section we study the question whether or not the *order* of information presentation does really influence the capabilities of IIMs. Since an IIM is required to learn the target language from every text (informant) for it, one may conjecture that an IIM mainly extracts the range of the information fed to it, thereby neglecting the length and order of the data sequence it reads. While this is true for learning from informant, the situation considerably changes for inference from positive data. A first explanation for this phenomenon can be derived from the fact that, when fed an informant, an IIM can *decide* whether or not is has already seen a *complete* initial segment. Then it ignores all the other data fed to it, and behaves like an IIM learning from the *lexicographically* ordered informant. Clearly, when exclusively learning from positive data, an IIM never knows whether it possesses a complete initial segment. But this is only part of the story as we shall see. Next we define two modes of order independence.

**Definition 11.** (Wexler and Culicover, 1980, Sec. 2.2) *Let $\mathcal{L}$ be an indexed family.* ***An IIM is said to be set-driven*** *with respect to $\mathcal{L}$ iff its output depends only on the range of its input; that is, iff $M(t_x) = M(\hat{t}_y)$ for all $x, y \in \mathbb{N}$, all texts $t$, $\hat{t} \in \bigcup_{L \in range(\mathcal{L})} text(L)$ provided $t_x^+ = \hat{t}_y^+$.*

Schäfer-Richter (1984) as well as Fulk (1990), later, and independently proved that set-driven IIMs are less powerful than unrestricted ones. Fulk (1990) interpreted the weakening in the learning power of set-driven IIMs by the need of IIMs for time to "reflect" on the input. However, this time cannot be bounded by any *a priori* fixed computable function depending exclusively on the size of the range of the input, since otherwise set-drivenness would not restrict the learning power. Indeed, Osherson, Stob and Weinstein (1986) proved that any *non-recursive* IIM $M$ may be replaced by a *non-recursive* set-driven IIM $\hat{M}$ learning at least as much as $M$ does. On the other hand, the weakness of set-driven inference has been proved in a domain that allows self-referential arguments. Since this proof technique does not apply in the setting of indexed families, the problem whether or not set-drivenness constitutes a severe restriction in this domain remained open. But before starting our survey of results we consider a natural weakening of Definition 11.

**Definition 12. (Schäfer-Richter, 1984; Osherson et al., 1986))** *Let $\mathcal{L}$ be an indexed family.* ***An IIM is said to be rearrangement-independent*** *iff its output depends only on the range and on the length of its input; that is, iff $M(t_x) = M(\hat{t}_x)$ for all $x \in \mathbb{N}$, all texts $t$, $\hat{t} \in \bigcup_{L \in range(\mathcal{L})} text(L)$ provided $t_x^+ = \hat{t}_x^+$.*

We make the following convention. For all the learning models in this paper we use the prefix $s-$, and $r-$ to denote the learning model restricted to set-driven and rearrangement-independent IIMs, respectively. For example, $s-LIM$ denotes the collection of all indexed families that are $LIM$–inferable by some set-driven IIM.

Fulk (1990) proved that rearrangement-independence can be always achieved when learning in the limit is concerned. However, Fulk's proof technique does not preserve any of the monotonicity constraints defined in Section 2. On the other hand, the first result concerning order-independence with respect to the inferability of indexed families goes back to Angluin (1980a). As already mentioned in Section 3 she characterized learning in the limit using families of *recursively enumerable* finite and non-empty tell-tales. In particular, the IIM defined in the sufficiency part of her characterization theorem establishes that rearrangement-independence does not constitute a restriction for $ELIM$ (cf. Section 3, Example 5). In Lange and Zeugmann (1993b) we proved that $ELIM = LIM = CLIM$. Hence, learning in the limit can be always achieved by rearrangement-independent IIMs. Inspired by Angluin's (1980b) work we characterized conservative, monotonic, strong-monotonic, and finite learning in terms of *recursive* finite and non-empty tell-tales (cf. Lange and Zeugmann (1992)). These results directly yield that $r-EFIN = FIN$, and $r-SMON = SMON$. However, all remaining questions required special attention. In the following subsection we survey results concerning set-drivenness.

## 8.1. Learning with Set-driven IIMs

We start with finite learning. The next theorem in particular states that finite learning is invariant with respect to the specific choice of the hypothesis space. Moreover, for every hypothesis space comprising the target indexed family $\mathcal{L}$ there is a *set-driven* IIM that finitely learns $\mathcal{L}$.

**Theorem 35.** $EFIN = FIN = CFIN = s-EFIN$

*Proof.* $EFIN = FIN = CFIN$ is due to Lange and Zeugmann (1993c).

The main ingredient for the proof of $EFIN = s-EFIN$ is the following characterization of finite learning (cf. Lange and Zeugmann (1992)).

**Theorem 36.** *Let $\mathcal{L}$ be an indexed family. Then: $\mathcal{L} \in FIN-TXT$ if and only if there is a recursively generable family $(T_j)_{j\in\mathbb{N}}$ of finite non-empty sets such that*

(1) *for all $j \in \mathbb{N}$, $T_j \subseteq L_j$,*

(2) *for all $k, j \in \mathbb{N}$, if $T_k \subseteq L_j$, then $L_j = L_k$.*

Using this recursively generable family $(T_j)_{j\in\mathbb{N}}$ we define a IIM $M$ witnessing $\mathcal{L} \in s-EFIN-TXT$. Let $L \in \mathcal{L}$, $t \in text(L)$, and $x \in \mathbb{N}$.

$M(t_x) = $ " If $x = 0$ or $x > 0$ and $M$ when, fed successively $t_{x-1}$, does not stop, then execute stage $x$.

> *Stage $x$*: Search for the least $j$ such that $t_x^+ \subseteq L_j$. Test whether or not $T_j \subseteq t_x^+$. In case it is, output $j$ and stop.
> Otherwise, request the next input and output nothing."

We sketch only the idea behind the proof. The IIM defined above searches for the first language that comprises $t_x^+$. Since $t$ is a text of some language from $\mathcal{L}$, this *unbounded* search terminates. Then $M$ tests whether or not the relevant tell-tale belongs to the range of the initial text segment it has been fed. Hence, intuitively it is clear that $M$ is set-driven. It remains to show that $M$ has to stop sometimes. This part of the proof mainly exploits Property (2) of the tell-tale family. $M$ might fail to stop provided the first index $j$ that is found by $M$ is proper superset of the target language $L$ and $T_j \not\subseteq L$. But this is impossible, since then $T_L \subseteq L_j$, where $T_L$ is any tell-tale for the target language $L$. By Property (2) we conclude $L = L_j$, a contradiction.

For a formal proof of $M$ $s-EFIN-TXT$–learns $\mathcal{L}$ the reader is referred to Lange and Zeugmann (1993e). q.e.d.

The proof sketch given above makes its clear why set-drivenness may constitute a severe restriction. The main problem is just a suitable restriction of the actual search space an IIM may use to compute its actual guess. If the topological structure of $\mathcal{L}$ is more complicated than in case of finite learning, then the method presented above fails. The next theorem shows that any other method fails as well.

**Theorem 37.** $s-CLIM-TXT \subset ELIM-TXT = LIM-TXT = CLIM-TXT$

*Proof.* The part $ELIM-TXT = LIM-TXT = CLIM-TXT$ is due to Lange and Zeugmann (1993c). Again, the part $s-CLIM-TXT \subset ELIM-TXT$ is only sketched.

As a matter of fact, the proof technique introduced in Section 5 is powerful enough to show the desired result. The desired separation can be obtained by using the indexed family $\mathcal{L}$ of Example 6. Thus, $\mathcal{L}$ is defined as follows. For all $k \in \mathbb{N}$ we set $L_{\langle k,0\rangle} = \{a^k b^n \mid n \in \mathbb{N}^+\}$. For all $k \in \mathbb{N}$ and all $j \in \mathbb{N}^+$ we distinguish the following cases:

*Case 1.* $\neg\Phi_k(k) \leq j$

Then we set $L_{\langle k,j\rangle} = L_{\langle k,0\rangle}$.

*Case 2.* $\Phi_k(k) \leq j$

Let $d = 2 \cdot \Phi_k(k) - j$. Now, we set:

$$L_{\langle k,j \rangle} = \begin{cases} \{a^k b^m \mid 1 \leq m \leq d\}, & \text{if } d \geq 1, \\ \{a^k b\}, & \text{otherwise.} \end{cases}$$

$\mathcal{L} = (L_{\langle k,j \rangle})_{j,k \in \mathbb{N}}$ is an indexed family of recursive languages, since the predicate "$\Phi_i(y) \leq z$" is uniformly decidable in $i$, $y$, and $z$.

Any set-driven IIM that might learn $\mathcal{L}$ has to overcome two difficulties. First, it has to find a hypothesis, and second, it has to detect whether or not its actual guess is *overgeneralized*. Intuitively, detecting overgeneralization forces $M$ to handle the halting problem. Hence, it may try to avoid overgeneralized hypothesises. But again, this forces $M$ to search the *least* language with respect to set inclusion comprising $t_x^+$. Since the halting problem is algorithmically unsolvable, $M$ cannot decide whether or not to continue its search for a number of a least language. But if it gives up, it might overgeneralize, and we are back to Case 1. This can be well formalized, and indeed one can show that any set-driven IIM learning $\mathcal{L}$ directly yields an algorithm solving the halting problem (cf. Lange and Zeugmann (1993e)).

On the other hand, it is not hard to prove that $\mathcal{L}$ can be inferred in the limit with respect to the hypothesis space $\mathcal{L}$. The main idea can be described as follows. The desired IIM $M$ uses the *length* of its actual input to test whether $\Phi_k(k)$ might be defined. As long as $\Phi_k(k)$ does not turn out to be defined, $M$ simply outputs the corresponding index $\langle k, 0 \rangle$, where $k$ can be easily computed from $t_0$. In case $\Phi_k(k)$ happens to be defined, $M$ can *effectively* search for the least language in $\mathcal{L}$ that comprises $t_x$. $\qquad$ q.e.d.

As the latter theorem shows, sometimes there is no way to design a set-driven IIM. However, with the following theorems we mainly intend to show that the careful choice of the hypothesis space deserves special attention whenever set-drivenness is desired.

**Theorem 38.** *There is an indexed family $\mathcal{L}$ such that*

(1) $\mathcal{L} \in r-ESMON-TXT$,

(2) *no set-driven IIM $M$ $LIM-TXT$-infers $\mathcal{L}$,*

(3) *there are a hypothesis space $\mathcal{G}$ and an IIM $M$ witnessing $\mathcal{L} \in s-CSMON-TXT$ with respect to $\mathcal{G}$.*

As we have seen, set-drivenness constitutes a severe restriction. While this is true in general as long as exact and class preserving learning is considered, the situation looks differently in the class comprising case. On the one hand, learning in the limit cannot always be achieved by set-driven IIMs (cf. Theorem 37). On the other hand, conservative learners may always be designed to be set-driven, if the hypothesis space is appropriately chosen.

**Theorem 39.** $\quad s-CCONSERVATIVE-TXT = CCONSERVATIVE-TXT$

Again, we only sketch the main ideas of the proof, and refer the interested reader to Lange and Zeugmann (1993e) for any detail. The proof is partitioned into two parts. The first part establishes the equality of class comprising conservative and class comprising, rearrangement-independent conservative learning. The main ingredients into this proof are the characterization of *CCONSERVATIVE–TXT* (cf. Section 3, Theorem 5) as well as a technically simple, but powerful modification of the corresponding tell-tale family (cf. Section 4, Theorem 9). For the sake of readability, we recall these results.

Let $\mathcal{L} \in CCONSERVATIVE - TXT$. Then there exist a space $\mathcal{G} = (G_j)_{j \in \mathbb{N}}$ of hypotheses and a recursively generable tell-tale family $(T_j)_{j \in \mathbb{N}}$ of finite and non-empty sets such that

(1) $range(\mathcal{L}) \subseteq \mathcal{L}(\mathcal{G})$,

(2) for all $j \in N$, $T_j \subseteq L(G_j)$,

(3) for all $j, k \in \mathbb{N}$, if $T_j \subseteq L(G_k)$, then $L(G_k) \not\subseteq L(G_j)$.

Using this tell-tale family, we define a new recursively generable family $(\hat{T}_j)_{j \in \mathbb{N}}$ of finite and non-empty sets that allows the design of a rearrangement-independent IIM inferring $\mathcal{L}$ conservatively with respect to $\mathcal{G}$. But surprisingly enough, we can even do better, namely, we can define an IIM witnessing $\mathcal{L}(\mathcal{G}) \in r-ECONSERVATIVE - TXT$. For all $j \in \mathbb{N}$ we set $\hat{T}_j = \bigcup_{n \leq j} T_n \cap L(G_j)$. Note that the new tell-tale family fulfills Properties (1) through (3) above.

Now, the wanted IIM can be defined as follows: Let $L \in \mathcal{L}(\mathcal{G})$, $t \in text(L)$, and $x \in N$.

$M(t_x) = $ "Generate $\hat{T}_k$ for all $k \leq x$ and test whether $\hat{T}_k \subseteq t_x^+ \subseteq L(G_k)$. In case there is one $k$ fulfilling the test, output the minimal one, and request the next input. Otherwise, output nothing and request the next input."

Obviously, $M$ is rearrangement-independent. We omit the proof that $M$ *ECONSERVATIVE–TXT*–learns $\mathcal{L}(\mathcal{G})$.

The second part of the proof establishes set-drivenness. For that purpose, we define a new hypothesis space $\tilde{\mathcal{G}} = (\tilde{G}_j)_{j \in \mathbb{N}}$ as well as a new IIM $\tilde{M}$. The basis for these definitions are the hypothesis space $\mathcal{G} = (G_j)_{j \in \mathbb{N}}$ , and the IIM $M$ described above. The hypothesis space $\tilde{\mathcal{G}}$ is the canonical enumeration of all grammars from $\mathcal{G}$ and all finite languages over the underlying alphabet $\Sigma$. Before defining the IIM $\tilde{M}$, we introduce the notion of *repetition free* text $rf(t)$. Let $t = s_0, s_1, \ldots$ be any text. We set $rf(t_0) = s_0$ and proceed inductively as follows: For all $x \geq 1$, $rf(t_{x+1}) = rf(t_x)$, if $s_{x+1} \in rf(t_x)^+$, and $rf(t_{x+1}) = rf(t_x), s_{x+1}$ otherwise. Obviously, given any initial segment $t_x$ of a text $t$ one can effectively compute $rf(t_x)$. Now we are ready to present the definition of $\tilde{M}$. Let $L \in \mathcal{L}(\mathcal{G})$, $t \in text(L)$, and $x \in \mathbb{N}$.

$\tilde{M}(t_x) = $ "Compute $rf(t_x)$. If $M$ on input $rf(t_x)$ outputs a hypothesis, say $j$, then output the canonical index of $j$ in $\tilde{\mathcal{G}}$ and request the next input. Otherwise, output the canonical index of $t_x^+$ in $\tilde{\mathcal{G}}$ and request the next input."

Intuitively, it is clear that $\tilde{M}$ is set-driven. We omit the proof that $\tilde{M}$ *CCONSERVATIVE–TXT*–learns $\mathcal{L}$ with respect to $\tilde{\mathcal{G}}$. q.e.d.

The latter theorem allows a nice corollary that we present next. In particular, this corollary shows that the IIM $\tilde{M}$ defined above can be transformed into an IIM $M$ that learns much more than one might expect.

**Corollary 40.** *Let $\mathcal{L} \in CCONSERVATIVE - TXT$. Then, there exists a hypothesis space $\hat{\mathcal{G}} = (\hat{G}_j)_{j \in \mathbb{N}}$ comprising $\mathcal{L}$ such that $\mathcal{L}(\hat{\mathcal{G}}) \in s-ECONSERVATIVE - TXT$.*

*Proof.* Let $\mathcal{L} \in CCONSERVATIVE - TXT$. Furthermore, by the latter theorem, there are an IIM $\tilde{M}$ and a hypothesis space $\tilde{\mathcal{G}}$ such that $\tilde{M}$ $s - CCONSERVATIVE- TXT$–infers $\mathcal{L}$ with respect to $\tilde{\mathcal{G}}$.

Recall that $\tilde{\mathcal{G}}$ is a canonical enumeration of $\mathcal{G} = (G_j)_{j \in \mathbb{N}}$ satisfying $\mathcal{L} \subseteq \mathcal{L}(\mathcal{G})$ and of all finite languages over the underlying alphabet. Without loss of generality we may assume that $\tilde{\mathcal{G}}$ fulfills the following property. If $j$ is even, then $L(\tilde{G}_j) \in \mathcal{L}(\mathcal{G})$. Hence, $\tilde{M}$ $s - CCONSERVATIVE - TXT$–learns $L(\tilde{G}_j)$ with respect to $\tilde{\mathcal{G}}$. Otherwise, $L(\tilde{G}_j)$ is a finite language.

We start with the definition of the desired hypothesis space $\hat{\mathcal{G}} = (\hat{G}_j)_{j \in \mathbb{N}}$ If $j$ is even, then we set $\hat{G}_j = \tilde{G}_j$. Otherwise, we distinguish the following cases. If $M$ when fed the lexicographically ordered enumeration of all strings in $L(\tilde{G}_j)$ outputs the hypothesis $j$, then we set $\hat{G}_j = \tilde{G}_j$. In case it does not, we set $\hat{G}_j = \tilde{G}_{j-1}$.

Now we are ready to define the desired IIM $M$ witnessing $\mathcal{L}(\hat{\mathcal{G}}) \in s-ECONSERVA-TIVE–TXT$. Let $L \in \mathcal{L}(\hat{\mathcal{G}})$, $t \in text(L)$, and $x \in \mathbb{N}$.

$M(t_x) = $ "Simulate $\tilde{M}$ on input $t_x$. If $\tilde{M}$ does not output any hypothesis, then output nothing and request the next input.

Otherwise, let $\tilde{M}(t_x) = j$. Output $j$ and request the next input."

Since $\tilde{M}$ is a conservative and set-driven IIM, $M$ behaves thus. It remains to show that $M$ learns $L$. Obviously, if $L = L(\hat{G}_{2k})$ for some $k \in \mathbb{N}$, then $\tilde{M}$ infers $L$, since $\tilde{M}$ $s - CCONSERVATIVE - TXT$–infers $L$. Therefore, since $M$ simulates $\tilde{M}$, we are done.

Now, let us suppose, $L \neq L(\hat{G}_{2k})$ for some $k \in \mathbb{N}$. By definition of $\hat{\mathcal{G}}$, we know that $L$ is finite. Moreover, since $t$ is a text for $L$, there exists an $x$ such that $t_y^+ = L$ for all $y \geq x$. Recalling the definition of $\hat{\mathcal{G}}$, and by assumption, we obtain the following. There is a number $j$ such that $\tilde{M}(t_x) = j$, $L = t_x^+ = L(\tilde{G}_j) = L(\hat{G}_j)$. Hence, $M(t_x) = j$, too. Finally, since $M$ is set-driven, we directly get $M(t_y) = j$ for all $y \geq x$. Consequently, $M$ learns $L$.                    q.e.d.

## 8.2. Learning with Rearrangement-Independent IIMs

In this section we study the impact of rearrangement-independence on the learning power of IIMs. Recall that $r - ELIM - TXT = CLIM - TXT$ as well as $r - SMON - TXT = SMON - TXT$. So what about $ESMON - TXT$? By answering this question another proof technique comes into the play. The key idea consists in applying Theorem 17. Hence, we may use a rearrangement-independent IIM $\hat{M}$ as well as a class preserving hypothesis space $\mathcal{G}$ such that $\mathcal{L} \in r - SMON$ with respect to $\mathcal{G}$ is witnessed by $M$. Due to that Theorem there exists a strong-monotonic limiting recursive compiler $f$ from $\mathcal{G}$ into $\mathcal{L}$. Therefore, all we have to do is to combine the IIM $\hat{M}$ and the strong-monotonic limiting recursive compiler $f$. And indeed, this idea goes through. Thus, $ESMON - TXT = r - ESMON - TXT$.

Moreover, the latter result cannot be improved as the next theorem states. Furthermore, the sketched proof technique does not apply to monotonic language learning, and so does any other proof technique. As a matter of fact, monotonic inference is *very* sensitive with respect to the order in which the input data are presented.

**Theorem 41.**

(1) $s-EMON-TXT \subset r-EMON-TXT \subset EMON-TXT$,

(2) $s-MON-TXT \subset r-MON-TXT \subset MON-TXT$.

Finally, we consider rearrangement-independence in the context of exact and class preserving conservative learning. Since conservative learning is exactly as powerful as weak-monotonic one, by the latter theorem one might expect that rearrangement-independence is a severe restriction under the weak-monotonic constraint, too. On the other hand, looking at Theorem 39 we see that conservative learning has its peculiarities. And indeed, exact and class preserving learning can always be performed by rearrangement-independent IIMs. In order to prove this, we first characterize *ECONSERVATIVE* in terms of finite tell-tales. We present this theorem separately, since it is interesting in its own right.

**Theorem 42.** *Let $\mathcal{L}$ be an indexed family. Then, $\mathcal{L} \in ECONSERVATIVE - TXT$ if and only if there exists a recursively generable family $(T_j^y)_{j,y \in \mathbb{N}}$ of finite sets such that*

(1) *for all $L \in \mathcal{L}$ there exists a $j$ with $L_j = L$ and $T_j^y \neq \emptyset$ for almost all $y \in \mathbb{N}$,*

(2) *for all $j, y \in \mathbb{N}$, $T_j^y \neq \emptyset$ implies $T_j^y \subseteq L_j$ and $T_j^y = T_j^{y+1}$,*

(3) *for all $j$, $y$, $z \in \mathbb{N}$, $\emptyset \neq T_j^y \subseteq L_z$ implies $L_z \not\subseteq L_j$.*

For a proof, the reader is referred to Lange and Zeugmann (1993e).

Finally, applying the same technique as described in the proof of Theorem 39 one may modify *mutatis mutandis* the tell-tale family $(T_j^y)_{j,y \in \mathbb{N}}$ appropriately. Then, the new family as well as a suitable modification of the IIM defined in the proof of Theorem 39 directly yield the rearrangement-independence of exact conservative learning. Moreover, the same ideas are powerful enought to show the analogous result for class preserving conservative inference (cf. Section 4, Theorem 9). Hence, we have the following theorem.

**Theorem 43.**

(1) $r-ECONSERVATIVE - TXT = ECONSERVATIVE - TXT$,

(2) $r-CONSERVATIVE - TXT = CONSERVATIVE - TXT$.

With the following figure we summarize the results surveyed in this section and point to questions that remain open. We shall discuss them and some less obvious ones in Section 9.

For every model of learning $LT$ mentioned "*rearrangement-independence* +" indicates $r - LT = LT$ as well as $s - LT \subset LT$. "*Rearrangement-independence* −" implies $s - LT \subset r - LT \subset LT$ whereas "*set-drivenness* +" should be interpreted as $s - LT = LT$ and, therefore, $r - LT = LT$, too.

|  | exact learning | | class preserving learning | | class comprising learning | |
|---|---|---|---|---|---|---|
| FIN | set drivenness | + | set drivenness | + | set drivenness | + |
| SMON | rearrangement independence | + | rearrangement independence | + | ? | |
| MON | rearrangement independence | − | rearrangement independence | − | ? | |
| WMON | rearrangement independence | + | rearrangement independence | + | set drivenness | + |
| LIM | rearrangement independence | + | rearrangement independence | + | rearrangement independence | + |

# 9. Outlook

We started our guided tour with several question that are closely related to the design of "natural" learning algorithms. Therefore, we continue with a short discussion of our results in this regard. Mathematically sound formalizations of learning by generalization and specialization have been introduced. Furthermore, the models of weak-monotonic learning and of dual weak-monotonic inference formalized the problem to what extend non-monotonic reasoning has to be incorporated into the learning process. As we have seen, superior learning algorithms can be designed if and only if most of the monotonicity demands are dropped (cf. e.g. Section 5, Theorem 11 as well as Figure 1 and 2). Consequently, our results provide considerable evidence that learning has to be performed, at least to some extend, incorporating non-monotonic reasoning.

Furthermore, the characterizations obtained provide a unifying framework to all types of monotonic learning. Hence, we achieved considerable insight into the problem what is more appropriate, learning by specialization or learning by generalization. All the differences between these two global learning strategies can be expressed in terms of properties the hypothesis space and the corresponding finite tell-tale sets must satisfy. These results strongly recommend to study particular properties of indexed families that can be expressed by suitable descriptions of the objects to be learned and by finite tell-tale sets (cf. e.g. Example 4). As we have seen, it is mainly the interplay between the properties of the relevant hypothesis space and the relevant tell-tale sets that makes or does not make a learning problem solvable. The latter assertion even remains true, if additional postulates of naturalness are involved. Our theorem stating $s - CCONSERVATIVE - TXT = CCONSERVATIVE\text{-}TXT$ may serve as an illustrative example (cf. Section 8, Theorem 39).

However, some intriguing questions concerning order independence remain open. Two of them are presented in the figure above. Additionally, it would be highly desirable to elaborate characteristic conditions under what circumstances set-drivenness does not restrict the learning power. We expect that such characterizations might allow much more insight into the problem how to handle simultaneously both, finite and infinite languages in the learning process. Next, as we have seen, an algorithmically solvable learning problem might become infeasible, if one tries to solve it with set-driven IIMs. On the other hand, when dealing with particular learning problems it might often be possible to design a set-driven learning algorithm solving it. But what about the complexity of learning in such circumstances? More precisely, we are interested in knowing whether the "high-level" theorem separating set-driven learning from unrestricted one, has an analogue in terms of complexity theory. For example, it is well conceivable that an indexed family $\mathcal{L}$ may be learned in polynomial time but no set-driven algorithm can efficiently infer $\mathcal{L}$ provided $\mathcal{P} \neq \mathcal{NP}$.

Moreover, our results suggest some further avenues of research. All learning models described in this paper dealt with *passive* inference, i.e., the IIM itself has no influence to the data it is fed. Hence, it seems to be very promising to study *active* learning, too (cf. Angluin (1992) and the references therein). The most common types of queries are *equivalence* and *membership* queries. Clearly, each indexed family can be learned by equivalence queries alone. However, this approach may lead to non-efficient solutions. On the other hand, there are some results showing that particular indexed families are learnable in polynomial time using membership and equivalence queries (cf. e.g. Ishizaka (1989)). Obviously, the crucial point is to determine what membership queries the learner should ask. We conjecture that tell-tales might be very helpful to solve the latter problem.

Finally, it seems very promising to study the learnability of indexed families within probabilistic models of inductive inference. In the setting of inductive inference of recursive functions Freivalds, Kinber and Wiehagen (1988) proved the following interesting result. There are hypothesis spaces $\mathcal{H}$ such that non-exactly learnable function classes might become inferable with probability 1 with respect to $\mathcal{H}$. It would be interesting to know whether or not similar effects might occur in the setting of learning recursive languages. Furthermore, Wiehagen, Freivalds and Kinber (1984) proved the superiority of probabilistic inference algorithms with respect to the number of allowed mind changes. Again, we are interested in learning whether or not these results extend to our setting.

# 10. References

ADLEMAN, L.M., AND BLUM, M. (1991), Inductive inference and unsolvability, *Journal of Symbolic Logic* **56**, 891 – 900.

ANGLUIN, D. (1980a), Finding patterns common to a set of strings, *Journal of Computer and System Sciences*, **21**, 46 – 62.

ANGLUIN, D. (1980b), Inductive inference of formal languages from positive data, *Information and Control*, **45** (1980), 117 – 135.

ANGLUIN, D. (1992), Computational learning theory: Survey and selected bibliography, *in* "Proceedings 24th Annual ACM Workshop on Theory of Computing," pp. 351 – 369, ACM Press.

ANGLUIN, D., AND SMITH, C.H. (1983), Inductive inference: theory and methods, *Computing Surveys* **15**, 237 – 269.

ANGLUIN, D., AND SMITH, C.H. (1987), Formal inductive inference, *in* "Encyclopedia of Artificial Intelligence" (St.C. Shapiro, Ed.), Vol. 1, pp. 409 – 418, Wiley-Interscience Publication, New York.

ANTHONY, M. AND BIGGS, N. (1992), "Computational Learning Theory," Cambridge University Press, Cambridge.

ARIKAWA, S., GOTO, S., OHSUGA, S., AND YOKOMORI, T. (Eds.) (1990) "Proceedings 1st International Workshop on Algorithmic Learning Theory," October 1990, Tokyo, Japanese Society for Artificial Intelligence.

ARIKAWA, S., MARUOKA, A., AND SATO, T. (Eds.) (1991) "Proceedings 2nd International Workshop on Algorithmic Learning Theory," October 1991, Tokyo, Japanese Society for Artificial Intelligence.

ARIKAWA, S., KUHARA, S., MIYANO, S., MUKOUCHI, Y., SHINOHARA, A. AND SHINOHARA, T. (1992), A machine discovery from amino acid sequences by decision trees over regular patterns, *in* Proceedings International Conference on Fifth Generation Computer Systems, Vol. 2, pp. 618 – 625, Institute for New Generation Computer Technology (ICOT), Tokyo, Japan.

BARZDIN, YA.M. (1974), Inductive inference of automata, functions and programs, *in* "Proceedings International Congress of Math.," Vancouver, pp. 455 – 460.

BARZDIN, YA.M., AND FREIVALDS, R.V. (1972), On the prediction of general recursive functions, *Sov. Math. Dokl.* **13**, 1224 – 1228.

BARZDIN, YA.M., AND FREIVALDS, R.V. (1974), Прогнозирование и предельный синтез еффективно перечислимых классов функций, *in* "Теория Алгоритмов и Программ," Vol. 1 (Ya. M. Barzdin, ed.) Latvian State University, Riga, pp. 101 – 111.

BARZDIN, YA.M., KINBER, E.B., AND PODNIEKS, K.M. (1974), Об ускорении синтеза и прогнозирования функций, *in* "Теория Алгоритмов и Программ," Vol. 1 (Ya.M. Barzdin, Ed.) Latvian State University, Riga, pp. 117 – 128.

BERWICK, R. (1985), "The Acquisition of Syntatic Knowledge," MIT Press, Cambridge, Massachusetts.

BLUM, A., AND SINGH, M. (1990), Learning functions of *k* terms, *in* "Proceedings 3rd Workshop on Computational Learning Theory, July 1990, Rochester," (M. Fulk and J. Case, Eds.), pp. 144 – 153, Morgan Kaufmann Publishers Inc., San Mateo.

BREWKA, G. (1991), "Nonmonotonic Reasoning: Logical Foundations of Commonsense," Cambridge University Press, Cambridge.

CASE, J. (1988), The power of vacillation, *in* "Proceedings 1st Workshop on Computational Learning Theory, August 1988, Boston," (D. Haussler and L. Pitt, Eds.), pp. 196 – 205, Morgan Kaufmann Publishers Inc., San Mateo.

CASE, J., AND LYNES, C. (1982), Machine inductive inference and language identification, *in* "Proceedings Automata, Languages and Programming, Ninth Colloquium, Aarhus, Denmark," (M. Nielsen and E.M. Schmidt, Eds.), Lecture Notes in Computer Science Vol. 140, pp. 107 – 115, Springer-Verlag, Berlin.

CASE, J., AND SMITH, C.H. (1983), Comparison of identification criteria for machine inductive inference, *Theoretical Computer Science* **25**, 193 - 220.

FREIVALDS, R., KINBER, E.B. AND WIEHAGEN, R. (1988), Probabilistic versus deterministic inductive inference in nonstandard numberings, *Zeitschrift für Mathematische Logik und Grundlagen der Mathematik*, **34** (1988), 531 – 539.

FREIVALDS, R., KINBER, E.B. AND WIEHAGEN, R. (1992), Convergently versus divergently incorrect hypotheses in inductive inference, GOSLER–Report 02/92, January 1992, FB Mathematik und Informatik, TH Leipzig.

FULK, M. (1990), Prudence and other restrictions in formal language learning, *Information and Computation*, **85** 1 – 11.

FULK, M., AND CASE, J. (Eds.) (1990), Proceedings of the 3rd Annual Workshop on Computational Learning Theory, July 1990, Rochester, Morgan Kaufmann Publishers Inc., San Mateo.

GASARCH, W.I., AND VELAUTHAPILLAI, M. (1992), Asking questions versus verifiability, *in* "Proceedings 3rd International Workshop on Analogical and Inductive Inference," October 1992, Dagstuhl, (K.P. Jantke, ed.) Lecture Notes in Artificial Intelligence Vol. 642, pp. 197 – 213, Springer-Verlag, Berlin.

GOLD, M.E. (1965), Limiting recursion, *Journal of Symbolic Logic*, **30** 28 – 48.

GOLD, M.E. (1967), Language identification in the limit, *Information and Control* **10**, 447 – 474.

HAUSSLER, D. (Ed.) (1992), Proceedings of the 5th Annual Workshop on Computational Learning Theory, July 1992, Pittsburgh, ACM Press, New York.

HOPCROFT, J.E., AND ULLMAN, J.D. (1969), "Formal Languages and their Relation to Automata," Addison-Wesley, Reading, Massachusetts.

ISHIZAKA, H. (1989), Learning simple deterministic languages. *in* "Proceedings of the 2nd Annual Workshop on Computational Learning Theory, Santa Cruz, August 1989, (R. Rivest, D. Haussler and M.K. Warmuth, Eds.), pp. 162–174, Morgan Kaufmann Publishers Inc., San Mateo.

JAIN, S., AND SHARMA, A. (1989), Recursion theoretic characterizations of language learning, The University of Rochester, Dept. of Computer Science, TR 281.

JANTKE, K.P. (Ed.) (1989), "Proceedings 2nd International Workshop on Analogical and Inductive Inference, October 1989, Reinhardsbrunn Castle," Lecture Notes in Artificial Intelligence Vol. 397.

JANTKE, K.P. (1991a), Monotonic and non-monotonic inductive inference, *New Generation Computing* **8**, 349 – 360.

JANTKE, K.P. (1991b), Monotonic and non-monotonic inductive inference of functions and patterns, *in* "Proceedings 1st International Workshop on Nonmonotonic and Inductive Logics, December 1990, Karlsruhe," (J. Dix , K.P. Jantke and P.H. Schmitt, Eds.), Lecture Notes in Artificial Intelligence Vol. 543, pp. 161 – 177, Springer-Verlag, Berlin.

JANTKE, K.P. (Ed.) (1992), "Proceedings 3rd International Workshop on Analogical and Inductive Inference, October 1992, Dagstuhl Castle," Lecture Notes in Artificial Intelligence Vol. 642.

KAPUR, S. (1992), Monotonic language learning, *in* "Proceedings 3rd Workshop on Algorithmic Learning Theory," October 1992, Tokyo, (S. Doshita, K. Furukawa, K.P. Jantke and T. Nishida, Eds.), Lecture Notes in Artificial Intelligence Vol. 743, pp. 147 – 158, Springer-Verlag, Berlin.

KAPUR, S., AND BILARDI, G. (1992), Language learning without overgeneralization, *in* "Proceedings 9th Annual Symposium on Theoretical Aspects of Computer Science, Cachan, France, February 13 - 15," (A. Finkel and M. Jantzen, Eds.), Lecture Notes in Computer Science Vol. 577, pp. 245 – 256, Springer-Verlag, Berlin.

KEARNS, M., AND PITT, L. (1989), A polynomial-time algorithm for learning $k-$variable pattern languages from examples, *in* "Proceedings 1st Annual Workshop on Computational Learning Theory, August 1988, Boston," (D. Haussler and L. Pitt, Eds.), pp. 196 –205, Morgan Kaufmann Publishers Inc., San Mateo.

KINBER, E.B. (1992), personal communication.

KODRATOFF, Y., AND MICHALSKI, R.S. (1990), "Machine Learning, An Artificial Intelligence Approach," Vol. 3, Morgan Kaufmann Publishers Inc., San Mateo.

LANGE, S. (1994), The representation of recursive languages and its impact on the efficiency of learning, *in* "Proceedings 7th Annual ACM Conference on Computational Learning Theory, New Brunswick, July 1994," (M. Warmuth, Ed.), pp. 256 – 267, ACM Press, New York.

LANGE, S., AND WIEHAGEN, R. (1991), Polynomial-time inference of arbitrary pattern languages, *New Generation Computing* **8**, 361 – 370.

LANGE, S., AND ZEUGMANN, T. (1992), Types of monotonic language learning and their characterization, *in* "Proceedings 5th Annual ACM Workshop on Computational Learning Theory, Pittsburgh, July 1992," (D. Haussler, Ed.), pp. 377 – 390, ACM Press, New York.

LANGE, S., AND ZEUGMANN, T. (1993a), Monotonic versus non-monotonic language learning, *in* "Proceedings 2nd International Workshop on Nonmonotonic and Inductive Logic, December 1991, Reinhardsbrunn," (G. Brewka, K.P. Jantke and P.H. Schmitt, Eds.), Lecture Notes in Artificial Intelligence Vol. 659, pp. 254 – 269, Springer-Verlag, Berlin.

LANGE, S., AND ZEUGMANN, T. (1993b), Learning recursive languages with bounded mind changes, *International Journal of Foundations of Computer Science* **4**, 157 – 178.

LANGE, S., AND ZEUGMANN, T. (1993c), Language learning in dependence on the space of hypotheses, *in* "Proceedings 6th Annual ACM Conference on Computational Learning Theory," Santa Cruz, July 1993, pp. 127 – 136, ACM Press, New York.

LANGE, S., AND ZEUGMANN, T. (1993d), The learnability of recursive languages in dependence on the space of hypotheses, GOSLER–Report 20/93, July 1993, Fachbereich Mathematik und Informatik, TH Leipzig.

LANGE, S., AND ZEUGMANN, T. (1993e), On the impact of order independence to the learnability of recursive languages, Research Report ISIS-RR-93-17E, Institute for Social Information Science, FUJITSU Laboratories Ltd, Numazu.

LANGE, S., AND ZEUGMANN, T. (1994), Characterization of language learning on informant under various monotonicity constraints, *Journal of Experimental and Theoretical Artificial Intelligence* **6**, 73 – 94.

LANGE, S., ZEUGMANN, T., AND KAPUR, S (1992), Class preserving monotonic language learning, submitted to *Theoretical Computer Science*, and GOSLER–Report 14/92, FB Mathematik und Informatik, TH Leipzig.

MACHTEY, M., AND YOUNG, P. (1978), "An Introduction to the General Theory of Algorithms," North-Holland, New York.

MICHALSKI, R.S., CARBONELL, J.G., AND MITCHELL, T.M. (1984), "Machine Learning, An Artificial Intelligence Approach," Vol. 1, Springer-Verlag, Berlin.

MICHALSKI, R.S., CARBONELL, J.G., AND MITCHELL, T.M. (1986), "Machine Learning, An Artificial Intelligence Approach," Vol. 2, Morgan Kaufmann Publishers Inc., San Mateo.

MUKOUCHI, Y. (1992), Inductive inference with bounded mind changes, *in* "Proceedings 3rd Workshop on Algorithmic Learning Theory," October 1992, Tokyo, (S. Doshita, K. Furukawa, K.P. Jantke and T. Nishida, Eds.), Lecture Notes in Artificial Intelligence Vol. 743, pp. 125 – 134, Springer-Verlag, Berlin.

MUKOUCHI, Y. (1994), Inductive inference of recursive concepts, Ph.D. Thesis, RIFIS, Kyushu University 33, RIFIS-TR-CS-82, March 25th.

NATARAJAN, B.K. (1991), "Machine Learning, A Theoretical Approach," Morgan Kaufmann Publishers, Inc., San Mateo.

NIX, R.P. (1983), Editing by examples, Yale University, Dept. Computer Science, Technical Report 280.

OSHERSON, D., STOB, M., AND WEINSTEIN, S. (1986), "Systems that Learn, An Introduction to Learning Theory for Cognitive and Computer Scientists," MIT-Press, Cambridge, Massachusetts.

PITT, L., AND VALIANT, L.G. (1988), Computational limitations on learning from examples, *Journal of the ACM* **35**, 965 - 984.

POPPER, K. (1968), "The Logic of Scientific Discovery," Harper Torch Books.

RIVEST, R., HAUSSLER, D., AND WARMUTH, M.K. (Eds.) (1989), Proceedings of the 2nd Annual Workshop on Computational Learning Theory, August 1989, Santa Cruz, Morgan Kaufmann Publishers Inc., San Mateo.

SCHÄFER-RICHTER, G. (1984), Über Eingabeabhängigkeit und Komplexität von Inferenzstrategien, Rheinisch Westfälische Technische Hochschule Aachen, Dissertation.

SHINOHARA, T. (1982), Polynomial time inference of extended regular pattern languages, *in* "Proceedings RIMS Symposia on Software Science and Engineering," Kyoto, Lecture Notes in Computer Science 147, pp. 115 - 127, Springer-Verlag, Berlin.

SOLOMONOFF, R. (1964), A formal theory of inductive inference, *Information and Control* **7**, 1 - 22, 234 - 254.

TRAKHTENBROT, B.A., AND BARZDIN, YA.M. (1970) "Конечные Автоматы (Поведение и Синтез)," Наука, Москва,
English translation: "Finite Automata–Behavior and Synthesis, Fundamental Studies in Computer Science 1," North-Holland, Amsterdam, 1973.

WEXLER, K. (1992), The subset principle is an intensional principle, *in* "Knowledge and Language: Issues in Representation and Acquisition," ((E. Reuland and W. Abraham, Eds.), Kluwer Academic Publishers.

WEXLER, K., AND CULICOVER, P. (1980), "Formal Principles of Language Acquisition," MIT Press, Cambridge, Massachusetts.

WIEHAGEN, R. (1976), Limes–Erkennung rekursiver Funktionen durch spezielle Strategien, *Journal of Information Processing and Cybernetics (EIK)*, **12**, 93 - 99.

WIEHAGEN, R. (1977), Identification of formal languages, *in* "Proceedings Mathematical Foundations of Computer Science, Tatranska Lomnica," (J. Gruska, Ed.), Lecture Notes in Computer Science 53, pp. 571 - 579, Springer-Verlag, Berlin.

WIEHAGEN, R. (1978), Characterization problems in the theory of inductive inference, *in* "Proceedings 5th Colloquium on Automata, Languages and Programming," (G. Ausiello and C. Böhm, Eds.), Lecture Notes in Computer Science 62, pp. 494 - 508, Springer-Verlag, Berlin.

WIEHAGEN, R. (1991), A thesis in inductive inference, *in* "Proceedings First International Workshop on Nonmonotonic and Inductive Logic," (J. Dix, K.P. Jantke and P.H. Schmitt, Eds.), Lecture Notes in Artificial Intelligence 543, pp. 184 – 207, Springer-Verlag, Berlin.

WIEHAGEN, R., FREIVALDS, R., AND KINBER, E.B. (1984), On the power of probabilistic strategies in inductive inference, *Theoretical Computer Science* **28**, 111 – 133.

WIEHAGEN, R., AND ZEUGMANN, T. (1994), Learning and Consistency, this volume.

ZEUGMANN, T., LANGE, S., AND KAPUR, S. (199x), Characterizations of monotonic and dual monotonic language learning, *Information and Computation*, to appear.

# Pattern Inference

## Takeshi Shinohara

Department of Artificial Intelligence

Kyushu Institute of Technology

Iizuka 820, Japan

shino@ai.kyutech.ac.jp

## Setsuo Arikawa

Research Institute of Fundamental Information Science

Kyushu University 33

Fukuoka 812, Japan

arikawa@rifis.kyushu-u.ac.jp

### Abstract

A pattern is a string consisting of constant symbols and variables. The language of a pattern is the set of constant strings that are obtained by substituting nonempty constant strings for variables in the pattern. Pattern inference is a task of identifying a pattern from given examples of its language. This paper presents a survey of pattern inference from viewpoints of inductive inference from positive data and probably approximately correct (PAC) learning with typical applications.

## 1  Introduction

A pattern is a string consisting of constant symbols from a finite alphabet $\Sigma$ and variables from a countable alphabet $X$. The language $L(\pi)$ of a pattern $\pi$ is the set of constant strings obtained by substituting nonempty constant strings for variables in $\pi$. A regular pattern is a pattern containing at most one occurrence of each variable. For example, when $\Sigma = \{a, b\}$ and $X = \{x, y, \ldots\}$, $\pi = axby$ is a regular pattern but $\tau = axbx$ is not a regular pattern, and their languages are $L(\pi) = \{aubu \mid u \in \Sigma^+\}$ and $L(\tau) = \{aubv \mid u, v \in \Sigma^+\}$, respectively.

Pattern inference is a task of identifying a pattern from its examples. Pattern inference can be dealt with in several formal settings of learning. As such settings, in this paper, we are mainly concerned with "inductive inference (or identification in the limit)" due to Gold [14] and "probably approximately correct (PAC) learning" due to Valiant [45].

Inductive inference is formalized as an infinite process of guessing hypothesis based on successively given examples from the target language. When a sequence of hypotheses produced by an inference process eventually converges to a correct representation of given examples, the process is said to identify the language in the limit. Since for any language $L$ there exists at least one obvious inference process that identifies $L$, the most important question is whether inference process curried out by a fixed program can identify any member of a class of languages. Inductive inference from positive data is an inductive inference when examples are taken from the inside of the target language. Gold [14] showed that inductive inference from positive data is strictly less powerful than that from both positive and negative data. However, Angluin [2] pointed out that there remains not a small possibility in inductive inference from positive data by showing that the class of pattern languages is inferable from positive data.

When we consider applications of pattern inference, the efficiency of inference algorithms is also very important. Restricting the total computation time of inference process contradicts a natural observation that inductive inference is inherently an infinite process. Therefore, we consider the computation time required to produce a hypothesis from examples. Unfortunately polynomial time bound on computation time seems to be very hard to be overcome because even the membership problem to decide whether a given string belongs to the language of a pattern is NP-complete [2]. In Section 4 we consider polynomial time inference from positive data of several subclasses of pattern languages.

Pattern languages are not directly used for some applications because of their simplicity. The class of pattern languages is not closed under union. Therefore, the class of their unions is richer than the class of pattern languages. The class of unions of two pattern languages is shown to be inferable from positive data [42]. This result is extended to the classes of unions of arbitrarily fixed number of pattern languages by Wright [47]. Arimura et. al showed the polynomial time inferability of unions of regular pattern languages [9]. These results are summarized in Section 5.

PAC (probably approximately correct) learning introduced by Valiant [45] is formalized as a task to find an approximation of the unknown target from random sampling. PAC-learning has attracted much attention even from practical viewpoint. We also discuss the PAC-learnability of pattern languages in Section 6.

In Section 7, we give a brief sketch of some related works on pattern languages. Finally, in Section 8, we explain some applications of pattern inference to practical problems.

# 2    Patterns and Their Languages

In this section, we present basic definitions and properties of pattern languages, according to Angluin [2].

Let $\Sigma$ be a finite alphabet and $X = \{x_1, x_2, \ldots\}$ be a countable alphabet disjoint from $\Sigma$. Elements in $\Sigma$ are called *constants* and elements in $X$ are called *variables*. A *word* over an alphabet $\Delta$ is a finite string of symbols taken from $\Delta$. $\Delta^*$, $\Delta^+$, and $\Delta^{[n]}$ denote the sets of all the words, all the nonempty words, and all the words of length $n$ or less, respectively. A subset of $\Delta^*$ is called a *language* or *concept* over $\Delta$. For a set $S$, $\#S$ denotes the number of elements in $S$.

A *pattern* is a nonempty word over $\Sigma \cup X$. The set of variables appearing in a pattern $\pi$ is denoted by $val(\pi)$. The number of occurrences of a variable $x$ in a pattern $\pi$ is denoted by $occ(x, \pi)$. A pattern $\pi$ is called *one-variable* if $\#val(\pi) \leq 1$. A pattern

$\pi$ is called regular if $occ(x, \pi) = 1$ for each $x \in val(\pi)$. For instance, $ax_1bx_2a$ is regular but not one-variable, and $ax_1bx_1a$ is one-variable but not regular, where $\{a, b\} \subseteq \Sigma$. The length of a word $w$ is denoted by $|w|$.

A *substitution* is a homomorphism from patterns to patterns that maps every constant to itself. A substitution which maps some variables to the empty word is called an $\varepsilon$-*substitution*. For a pattern $\pi$ and a substitution $\theta$, we denote by $\pi\theta$ the image of $\pi$ by $\theta$. A *renaming of variables* is a substitution $\theta$ such that $x\theta \in X$, and $x \neq y$ implies $x\theta \neq y\theta$, for any $x, y \in X$. We use a set of replacements $\{x_1 := \pi_1, \ldots, x_k := \pi_k\}$ to represent a substitution which maps each variable $x_i$ to a pattern $\pi_i (i = 1, \ldots, k)$ and every other symbol to itself.

An equivalence relation $\equiv$ and a partial ordering $\preceq$ on patterns are defined as follows:

(1) $\pi \equiv \tau \iff \pi = \tau\theta$ for some renaming of variables $\theta$,

(2) $\pi \preceq \tau \iff \pi = \tau\theta$ for some substitution $\theta$.

Note that $\pi \equiv \tau \iff \pi \preceq \tau$ and $\tau \preceq \pi$. Precisely, $\preceq$ is not a partial ordering. When we identify equivalent patterns from each other, however, we can think $\preceq$ as a partial ordering. We write $\pi \prec \tau$ if $\pi \preceq \tau$ but $\pi \not\equiv \tau$.

The *language of a pattern* $\pi$, denoted by $L(\pi)$, is the set $\{w \in \Sigma^+ \mid w \preceq \pi\}$. We denote the sets of all the patterns, all the one-variable patterns, and all the regular patterns by $\mathcal{P}$, $\mathcal{P}_1$, and $\mathcal{RP}$, respectively. The class of pattern languages is $\mathcal{PL} = \{L \mid L = L(\pi), \text{ for some pattern } \pi\}$. $\mathcal{PL}_1$ and $\mathcal{RPL}$ are defined similarly.

If $\varepsilon$-substitutions are allowed, pattern languages are called *extended languages* [41]. $L_e(\pi)$ denotes the extended language of a pattern $\pi$ and $\mathcal{PL}_e$ denotes the class of extended pattern languages.

**Property 2.1.** (Angluin [2]) For any patterns $\pi$ and $\tau$,

(1) $\pi \preceq \tau \Longrightarrow L(\pi) \subseteq L(\tau)$, but the converse does not hold in general,

(2) if $|\pi| = |\tau|$ then $\pi \preceq \tau \iff L(\pi) \subseteq L(\tau)$, and

(3) $\pi \equiv \tau \iff L(\pi) = L(\tau)$.

A pattern $\pi$ is said to be *canonical* if $\pi$ contains exactly $n$ variables $x_1, \ldots, x_n$ and the leftmost occurrence of $x_i$ is to the left of the leftmost occurrence of $x_{i+1}$ for all $i = 1, \ldots, n - 1$. It is easily shown that, for any pattern $\pi$, we can uniquely compute a unique canonical pattern $\hat{\pi}$ with $\pi \equiv \hat{\pi}$ in linear time. For example, $\pi = x_2x_1x_2$ is not canonical and $\hat{\pi} = x_1x_2x_1 \equiv \pi$ is canonical. Thus, given patterns $\pi$ and $\tau$ we can determine whether $L(\pi) = L(\tau)$ in linear time. However, the inclusion problem to decide whether $L(\pi) \subseteq L(\tau)$ is unsolvable [22]. The *membership* problem is a decision problem to decide whether $w \in L(\pi)$ given a word $w$ and a pattern $\pi$. The membership problem for all the pattern languages is NP-complete [2]. For one-variable patterns and regular patterns, the membership problem is computable in linear time, that is, in $O(|w| + |\pi|)$ time [2, 40]. The following table summarizes the decision problems on pattern languages, where $O(n)$, $NP$, $U$, and ? mean "computable in linear time," "NP-complete," "undecidable," and "open," respectively.

| Class | Equivalence | Inclusion | Membership |
|-------|-------------|-----------|------------|
| $\mathcal{PL}$ | $O(n)$ | $U^{\ddagger}$ | $NP$ |
| $\mathcal{PL}_1$ | $O(n)$ | $O(n)$ | $O(n)$ |
| $\mathcal{RPL}$ | $O(n)$ | $O(n)^{\dagger}$ | $O(n)^{\dagger}$ |
| $\mathcal{PL}_{\varepsilon}$ | ? | $U^{\ddagger}$ | $NP$ |
| $\mathcal{RPL}_{\varepsilon}$ | $O(n)^{\dagger}$ | $O(n)^{\dagger}$ | $O(n)^{\dagger}$ |

**Table 2.1.** Decision Problems on Pattern Languages
(†: Shinohara [40, 41], ‡: Jiang et. al [22], others: Angluin [2])

# 3    Inductive Inference from Positive Data

One of the main objectives of the theoretical study on learning is to propose efficient mechanisms of learning for practical problems. First in this section, we give one of the most important and essential mathematical models of learning from examples, called "inductive inference" or "identification in the limit," and show some basic results on inductive inference of pattern languages.

In many practical inductive inference problems, inferences are naturally based on positive data rather than both positive and negative data. It is well-known that inference from positive data has strictly weaker power than that from positive and negative data. Gold [14] showed that any class of languages containing all the finite languages and at least one infinite language is not inferable from positive data. Since the class of regular languages contains all the finite languages and many infinite languages, it is not inferable from positive data. Although Gold's result might sound negative for approaches to practical applications of inductive inference, we know another important result proved by Angluin [3]. She showed a theorem characterizing classes inferable from positive data and presented non-trivial and interesting classes. The class of pattern languages is one of her classes [2].

Let $\Sigma$ be a finite alphabet of symbols to draw languages and $I = \{1, 2, \ldots\}$ be the set of indexes. A class of languages $\mathcal{L} = L_1, L_2, \ldots$ is said to be an *indexed family of recursive languages* if there exists a computable function $f : \Sigma^* \times I \rightarrow \{0, 1\}$ such that $f(w, i) = 1$ if $w \in L_i$ and $f(w, i) = 0$ otherwise. The index $i$ of a language $L_i$ can be considered as a description like a pattern or grammar which defines $L_i$. From here on, a class of languages is assumed to be an indexed family of recursive languages.

A *complete presentation* of a language $L$ is an infinite sequence $(w_1, t_1)$, $(w_2, t_2)$, ... such that $t_i$ is 0 or 1, $\{w \mid w = w_i \text{ and } t_i = 1 \text{ for some } i = 1, 2, \ldots\} = L$, and $\{w \mid w = w_i \text{ and } t_i = 0 \text{ for some } i = 1, 2, \ldots\} = \Sigma^* - L$. A *positive presentation* of a nonempty language $L$ is an infinite sequence of $w_1, w_2, \ldots$ such that $\{w \mid w = w_i \text{ for some } i = 1, 2, \ldots\} = L$.

An *inference machine* is an effective procedure that requests input from time to time and produces output from time to time. An output produced by an inference machine is called a *hypothesis*. Let $\sigma = w_1, w_2, \ldots$ be an infinite sequence, and $h_1$, $h_2, \ldots$ be the sequence of hypotheses produced by an inference machine $IM$ when elements of $\sigma$ are successively given to $IM$. Then we say that $IM$ on input $\sigma$ *converges* to $h$, if the sequence $h_1, h_2, \ldots$ of hypotheses is finite and ended by $h$, or there exists a positive integer $k_0$ such that $h_k = h$ for all $k \geq k_0$.

A class of languages $\mathcal{L} = L_1, L_2, \ldots$ is said to be *inferable from positive* (or *complete*) *data* if there exists an inference machine $IM$ such that $IM$ on input $\sigma$ converges to $h$ with $L_h = L_i$ for any index $i$ and any positive (or complete) presentation $\sigma$ of $L_i$.

Gold [14] showed that any indexed family of recursive languages is inferable from complete data. A class of languages is said to be *super-finite* if it contains all the finite languages and at least one infinite language. Gold also proved that any super-finite class is not inferable from positive data. Therefore, we know that inference from positive data is strictly less powerful than that from complete data.

Angluin characterized classes inferable from positive data by giving a necessary and sufficient condition and several sufficient conditions. Here we give one of the sufficient conditions for inferability from positive data.

A class $\mathcal{L}$ has *finite thickness* if $\#\{L \in \mathcal{L} \mid w \in L\}$ is finite for any word $w$. Finite thickness is established in [2, 3] and named by Wright [47].

**Theorem 3.1.** (Angluin [2, 3]) If a class has finite thickness then it is inferable from positive data.

By using the above theorem, we can easily show the inferability of pattern languages from positive data.

**Theorem 3.2.** (Angluin [2, 3]) The class $\mathcal{PL}$ of pattern languages is inferable from positive data.

**Proof.** Let $w$ be any word and $\pi$ be any pattern such that $w \in L(\pi)$. Then $|w| \geq |\pi|$ because $w = \pi\theta$ for some substitution $\theta$ and $\theta$ is not an $\varepsilon$-substitution. From Proposition 2.1, for any pattern $\pi$, there uniquely exists a canonical pattern $\hat{\pi}$ such that $L(\pi) = L(\hat{\pi})$. Clearly there exists only finitely many canonical patterns whose length is less than or equal to $|w|$. Therefore,

$$\#\{L \in \mathcal{PL} \mid w \in L\} \leq \#\{\hat{\pi} \mid \hat{\pi} \text{ is a canonical pattern and } |w| \geq |\hat{\pi}|\} < \infty.$$

This shows the finite thickness of $\mathcal{PL}$. By Theorem 3.1, $\mathcal{PL}$ is inferable from positive data. $\square$

# 4 Polynomial Time Inference

The computational complexity, as well as the inferability from positive data, is important when we consider applications of inductive inference to practical problems. Inductive inference machine should be naturally required to respond rapidly. We will define polynomial time inference from positive data whose inference machine responds in polynomial time with respect to the length of the input.

In this section, after giving definitions of polynomial time inference, we show that three subclasses of Angluin's pattern languages [2], which will be called one-variable pattern languages, regular pattern languages and non-cross pattern languages [40], respectively, are polynomial time inferable. One of the most important subprocedures in polynomial time inference is MINL calculation, that finds a minimal pattern language containing given a set of words. We also give a general method for MINL calculation using refinement operators [9]. We also show that the class of extended regular pattern languages [41] is polynomial time inferable.

## 4.1 Polynomial Time Inference

Polynomial time inference is defined as the inference that has two important features for practical applications; one is the limitation on data presentations and the other is the bound on the computing time of inference machines. Moreover we require polynomial time inference to be responsive, consistent and conservative. A *responsive* inference machine should produce a hypothesis after receiving every example. A *consistent* inference machine always produces a hypothesis that is consistent with the examples received so far. An inference machine is said to be *conservative* if once it produces a hypothesis, say $h$, it never produces the other output than $h$ while $h$ is consistent with the examples. These three properties are natural and valuable in inference problems.

A class $\mathcal{L}$ is said to be *polynomial time inferable from positive data* if there exists an inference machine that infers $\mathcal{L}$ responsively, consistently and conservatively from positive data, and computes the hypothesis in polynomial time with respect to the length of the input.

Angluin [3] showed a sufficient but not necessary condition for responsive, consistent and conservative inference from positive data. MINL calculation, which finds a minimal language containing a given nonempty finite set of words, plays an important role in consistent and conservative inference from positive data. MINL calculation for a class $\mathcal{L} = L_1, L_2, \ldots$ is defined as follows:

$$\mathrm{MINL}(S) = \text{ “Given nonempty finite set } S \text{ of words, find an index } i, \text{ if exists,}$$
$$\text{such that } S \subseteq L_i \text{ and for no index } j, \ S \subseteq L_j \subsetneqq L_i.”$$

**Theorem 4.1.** (Angluin [3]) If a class $\mathcal{L} = L_1, L_2, \ldots$ has finite thickness and MINL for $\mathcal{L}$ is computable, then the following procedure *INFER_BY_MINL* infers $\mathcal{L}$ responsively, consistently and conservatively from positive data.

**Theorem 4.2.** (Angluin [3]) If a class $\mathcal{L}$ has finite thickness and the membership and MINL for $\mathcal{L}$ are computable in polynomial time, then $\mathcal{L}$ is polynomial time inferable from positive data.

To realize polynomial time inference by using Theorem 4.2, we need polynomial time algorithms for the membership problem and MINL calculation. Unfortunately, the membership problem for pattern languages is NP-complete, and a special version of MINL for pattern languages is NP-hard. Therefore, in what follows, we will consider restricted pattern languages.

```
procedure INFER_BY_MINL;
input:    an infinite sequence w₁, w₂, ... of words;
output:   an infinite sequence h₁, h₂, ... of indexes;
method:
  begin
    h₀ := "none"; S := ∅;
    for i := 1 to ∞ do
      begin
        S := S ∪ {wᵢ};
        if wᵢ ∉ Lₕᵢ₋₁ bf then
          hᵢ := MINL(S)
        else
          hᵢ := hᵢ₋₁;
        output hᵢ
      end
  end
```

## 4.2  One-Variable Pattern Languages

Clearly the membership problem to decide whether $w \in L(\pi)$ is computable in $|w|^{O(k)}$ time, where $k = \#val(\pi)$. Therefore, if we restrict the number of variables in patterns at most $k$, then the membership problem for such a restricted pattern languages becomes polynomial time computable. Angluin presented an algorithm for computing MINL for one-variable pattern languages and showed that the class of one-variable pattern languages is polynomial time inferable from positive data.

**Theorem 4.3.** (Angluin[3]) The class $\mathcal{PL}_1$ of one-variable pattern languages is polynomial time inferable from positive data.

In Angluin's algorithm, the set of all the consistent one-variable patterns with a given set of words, which may contain exponentially many patterns, is computed using a special kind of finite automata in polynomial time, called pattern automata. From any pattern automaton, we can easily extract one of the longest patterns accepted by the pattern automaton. Any of the longest one-variable patterns consistent with a set of words represents a minimal language within $\mathcal{PL}_1$.

Angluin pointed out that we can construct an algorithm for $k$-variable patterns in case $k \geq 2$, and made a comment that there are several difficulties in guaranteeing the correctness and the time bound.

## 4.3  Regular Pattern Languages

To show polynomial time inferability of regular pattern languages, we should show that the membership problem and the MINL calculation are computable in polynomial time. It is almost obvious that the membership problem for regular pattern languages is computable in polynomial time. More precisely, by using the idea of pattern matching machines, for example, see Aho et. al [1], we can show the following lemma.

**Lemma 4.4.** [40] For any regular pattern $\pi$ and any word $w$, whether $w$ is in $L(\pi)$ or not is decidable in $O(|\pi| + |w|)$ time.

Consider the following procedure *MINL_RPL*:

**procedure** *MINL_RPL*;
**input:**   a nonempty set $S$ of nonempty words;
**output:** a regular pattern that represents a minimal regular pattern
          language containing $S$;
**method:**
  **begin**
    let $a_1 a_2 \cdots a_k (a_i \in \Sigma)$ be one of the shortest words in $S$;
    $\pi_1 := x_1 x_2 \cdots x_k$;
    **for** $i := 1$ **to** $k$ **do**
      **begin**
      $\tau := \pi_i \{ x_i := a_i \}$;
      **if** $S \subseteq L(\tau)$ **then**
         $\pi_{i+1} := \tau$
      **else**
         $\pi_{i+1} := \pi_i$
    **end**
    **output** $\pi_{k+1}$
  **end**

*MINL_RPL* starts from the longest and most general regular pattern $\pi_1 = x_1 x_2 \cdots x_k$ which is always consistent with $S$. Note that $k$ is the maximum possible length of regular patterns consistent with $S$. Then, for each $i = 1, \ldots, k$, it tries to substitute $a_i$ for $x_i$ as long as obtained pattern is consistent with $S$. Therefore, $\pi_{k+1}$ is a correct answer of MINL($S$) for regular pattern languages. The time complexity of *MINL_RPL* is clearly bounded by a polynomial in the maximum length of words in $S$ and the number of words in $S$.

**Lemma 4.5.** [40] MINL($S$) for the class of regular pattern languages is computable in $O(m^2 n)$ time, where $m = \max_{w \in S} |w|$ and $n = \#S$.

**Theorem 4.6.** [40] The class of regular pattern languages is polynomial time inferable from positive data.

## 4.4 Non-Cross Pattern Languages

A pattern $\pi$ is said to be *non-cross* if there are no occurrences of other variables than $x$'s between the leftmost occurrence and the rightmost occurrence of $x$ for each variable $x$ in $\pi$. For example, a pattern $\pi = x_1 x_1 a b x_2 x_2$ is non-cross and $\tau = x_1 x_2 a b x_1 x_2$ is not non-cross. Clearly from definitions, regular patterns and one-variable patterns are non-cross. Thus non-cross patterns are the extension of both one-variable patterns and regular patterns.

To show that the membership for non-cross pattern languages is decidable in polynomial time, we may use a two-way nondeterministic finite automaton with four heads. The definition and related concepts of two-way multihead non-deterministic finite automaton are found elsewhere (for example, see Ibarra [19]).

**Lemma 4.7.** [40] For any non-cross pattern $\pi$ and any word $w$, whether $w \in L(\pi)$ or not is decidable in polynomial time with respect to $|\pi|$ and $|w|$.

A polynomial time algorithm of MINL calculation for non-cross pattern languages is realized by a similar method to that for regular pattern languages. The initial patterns are the same. The MINL algorithms for regular patterns tries and checks only one substitution of constant symbol for each variable. On the other hand, for non-cross patterns, the MINL algorithm also tries and checks a substitution of the neighbor variable for each variable.

**Lemma 4.8.** [40] MINL($S$) for the class of non-cross pattern languages is computable in polynomial time.

**Theorem 4.9.** [40] The class of non-cross pattern languages is polynomial time inferable from positive data.

## 4.5 MINL Calculation based on Refinement Operators

In this section, we introduce a general method for computing MINL. Angluin's algorithm of MINL for one-variable pattern languages uses pattern automata to maintain all the patterns consistent with given set of words. On the other hand, *MINL_RPL* starts with the most general and longest pattern $x_1 x_2 \cdots x_k$ and tries to substitute a constant for some variable as long as obtained pattern is consistent with given set of words. Let $\pi$ be any regular pattern and $\tau = \pi\{x := a\}$, where $x$ is a variable in $\pi$ and $a$ is any constant. Then, we can easily show that $\tau \prec \pi$ but there is no regular pattern $\tau'$ such that $\tau \prec \tau' \prec \pi$. This is one of the most important observations to prove the correctness of the MINL algorithm for regular pattern languages. The reason why *MINL_RPL* starts with the longest possible pattern is just to guarantee that syntactically minimal pattern represents a minimal language, because $L(\tau) \subseteq L(\pi)$ does not always imply $\tau \preceq \pi$. Mukouchi [33] showed that for any regular pattern $\tau$ and $\pi$, $L(\tau) \subseteq L(\pi)$ implies $\tau \preceq \pi$ when $\#\Sigma \geq 3$. Under the condition that the syntactic relation "$\preceq$" coincides with the inclusion relation "$\subseteq$", we may start with the most general pattern "$x_1$" for MINL calculation.

We define the size of a pattern $\pi$ as $size(\pi) = 2 \times |\pi| - \#val(\pi)$. Clearly, $size(\pi) \geq 0$, and $\tau \prec \pi \implies size(\tau) > size(\pi)$. A binary relation $\rho$ is called a *refinement operator* if $\tau\rho\pi$ implies $\tau \prec \pi$. We denote by $\rho^+$ the transitive closure of $\rho$. A refinement operator $\rho$ is *complete* if $\rho^+ = \prec$. We denote the set $\{\tau \mid \tau\rho\pi\}$ by $\rho(\pi)$. A refinement operator $\rho$ is *polynomial time computable* if $\rho(\pi)$ is polynomial time computable. For regular patterns, we can define a complete and polynomial time computable refinement operator. A substitution $\theta$ is *basic* for regular pattern $\pi$ if $\theta$ satisfies one of the following:

(1) $\theta = \{x := a\}$ for some $x \in val(\pi)$ and some $a \in \Sigma$.

(2) $\theta = \{x := yz\}$ for some $x \in val(\pi)$ and some variables $y, z \notin val(\pi)$.

Let define $\rho(\pi) = \{\tau \mid \tau = \pi\theta, \theta \text{ is basic for } \pi\}$. Then $\rho$ is a complete and polynomial time computable refinement operator for regular patterns. If we add substitutions that unifies two different variables, then we have a complete refinement operator for all the patterns.

Using the notion of refinement operators, we can explain the computation by *MINL_RPL*. Let a nonempty set $S$ of nonempty words be given. First, we start with the most general pattern "$x_1$", and then apply a substitution of type (2) as long as obtained pattern is consistent with $S$. At this point we have the pattern equivalent to "$x_1 x_2 \cdots x_k$", where $k$ is the length of the shortest words in $S$. Then, we apply substitutions of type (1).

When the syntactic relation "$\preceq$" coincides with the inclusion relation "$\subseteq$" and a complete and polynomial time computable refinement operator $\rho$ is available, we can compute MINL($S$) by the following procedure.

**procedure** *MINL_BY_REFINEMENT*;
**input:** a nonempty set $S$ of nonempty words;
**output:** a pattern which represents a minimal pattern language
          containing $S$;
**method:**
  **begin**
    $\pi := $ "$x_1$";   { the most general pattern }
    **while** there exists a pattern $\tau \in \rho(\pi)$ such that $S \subseteq L(\tau)$ **do**
      $\pi := \tau$;
    **output** $\pi$
  **end**

The number of iterations by the while loop in *MINL_BY_REFINEMENT* is bounded by the size of shortest words, because $size(w) \geq size(\pi)$ for any $w \in L(\pi)$. Therefore, if the membership for the class is computable in polynomial time, then the procedure *MINL_BY_REFINEMENT* computes MINL($S$) in polynomial time.

## 4.6 Extended Regular Pattern Languages

The extended language $L_e(\pi)$ of a pattern $\pi$ is the set of words obtained by substituting possibly empty words for variables in $\pi$. In this section some substitutions are allowed to erase some variables. The class $\mathcal{PL}_e$ of extended pattern languages has many different properties from the class $\mathcal{PL}$. For example, $\mathcal{PL}_e$ does not have finite thickness, which is a sufficient for inferability from positive data. The equivalence problem is open for $\mathcal{PL}_e$, while it is decidable in linear time for $\mathcal{PL}$. Furthermore, the inferability of $\mathcal{PL}_e$ from positive data is still open.

We use the same definition of partial ordering $\preceq$, but slightly modify the definition of equivalence relation $\equiv$ by $\tau \equiv \pi \iff \tau \preceq \pi$ and $\pi \preceq \tau$. Note that $\tau \preceq \pi$ does not always mean $|\tau| \geq |\pi|$. We also need to modify the notion of canonical patterns. We say that a pattern $\pi$ is *canonical* if $\pi \equiv \tau$ implies $|\pi| \leq |\tau|$ for any pattern $\tau$, and $\pi$ contains exactly $k$ variables $x_1, x_2, \ldots, x_k$ for some integer $k$ and the leftmost occurrence of $x_i$ is to the left of the leftmost occurrence of $x_{i+1}$ for each $i = 1, 2, \ldots, k - 1$.

Here, we consider only regular patterns and the class $\mathcal{RPL}_e$ of their extended languages. First we show that $\mathcal{RPL}_e$ has finite thickness.

Clearly there exists a unique canonical pattern $\hat{\pi}$ such that $\hat{\pi} \equiv \pi$ for any regular pattern $\pi$, because any consecutive occurrences of variables can be replaced with a single variable. By $c(\pi)$ we denote a word obtained by erasing all the variables in a pattern $\pi$. Clearly $|\hat{\pi}| \leq 2|c(\hat{\pi})| + 1$ for any canonical regular pattern $\hat{\pi}$. If a word $w$ is contained in $L_e(\hat{\pi})$ for some canonical regular pattern $\hat{\pi}$, then $|c(\hat{\pi})| \leq |w|$, and therefore $|\hat{\pi}| \leq 2|w| + 1$. Thus, we have shown the following.

**Lemma 4.10.** [40] $\mathcal{RPL}_e$ has finite thickness.

Similarly as for regular pattern languages, we can show that the membership problem for extended regular pattern languages is polynomial time decidable.

**Lemma 4.11.** [40] For any regular pattern $\pi$ and any word $w$, whether $w$ is in the extended language $L_e(\pi)$ is decidable in $O(|\pi| + |w|)$ time.

For extended regular pattern languages, $\tau \preceq \pi \iff L_e(\tau) \subseteq L_e(\pi)$ under condition that $\Sigma$ contains three or more constants. Here we should note that the longest common subsequence problem [46], which is found in many practical problems, is closely related to the inductive inference problem of extended regular pattern languages. If we have one of the longest common subsequences of a set $S$, then we can easily compute MINL($S$). Unfortunately, the longest common subsequence problem is NP-complete [29]. However, we can efficiently find one of the maximally common subsequences when we do not require the longest one.

**Lemma 4.12.** [40] If $\#\Sigma \geq 3$, then $L_e(\tau) \subseteq L\varepsilon(\pi) \iff \tau \preceq \pi$ for any regular patterns $\pi$ and $\tau$.

Now we define a complete and polynomial time computable refinement operator $\rho_e$ for extended regular pattern languages. Let $\pi$ be any extended regular pattern of canonical form. We define $size(\pi) = 2c(\pi) - \#val(\pi) + 2$, where $c(\pi)$ is the total length of constant words appearing in $\pi$. A substitution $\theta$ is *extended-basic for* regular pattern $\pi$ if $\theta$ satisfies one of the following:

(1) $\theta = \{x := xay\}$, where $x \in val(\pi)$, $a \in \Sigma$, and $y \notin val(\pi)$.

(2) $\theta = \{x := \varepsilon\}$ for some $x \in val(\pi)$.

Let define $\rho_\varepsilon(\pi) = \{\tau \mid \tau = \pi\theta, \theta \text{ is extended basic for } \pi\}$. Then $\rho_\varepsilon$ is a complete and polynomial time computable refinement operator for extended regular patterns. Therefore we can use procedure *MINL_BY_REFINEMENT* to compute MINL(S) for $\mathcal{RPL}_\varepsilon$.

**Theorem 4.13.** [40] The class of extended regular pattern languages is polynomial time inferable from positive data.

# 5 Inductive Inference of Unions

Inductive inference of unions from positive data, we are concerning with in this section, is an inference of languages when given examples are not taken from one language but from two or more languages, and is found in the following problems.

(1) Bilingual learning of children whose parents are internationally married.

(2) Error detection when correct data and wrong data are shuffled. Normally, correct data should be based on a language. When the learning process infers that given data should be from two languages, one of them represents the correct data and the other is based on the wrong data.

In this section, we show that inductive inference from positive data is possible for the class of unions of at most $k$ pattern languages. Shinohara [42] proved a special case $k = 2$. Wright [47] extended the result to the general cases. We show a polynomial time inference algorithm for unions of regular pattern languages according to [9].

## 5.1 Class of Unions and Finite Elasticity

Let $\mathcal{L} = L_1, L_2, \ldots$ be an indexed family of recursive languages and $I = \{1, 2, \ldots\}$ be the set of indexes. For each $k \geq 1$, we define $I^k = \{S \mid S \in I \text{ and } 1 \leq \#S \leq k\}$, $L_S = \cup_{i \in S} L_i$, and the class of unions $\mathcal{L}^k = \{L_S \mid S \in I^k\}$. It is natural to ask whether $\mathcal{L}^k$ is inferable from positive data whenever $\mathcal{L}$ is so. It is not hard to see that the answer to this question is "not in general." Wright introduced a notion of finite elasticity [47, 31], which is an extension of finite thickness and sufficient for inferability from positive data. He showed that the property of finite elasticity is closed under union.

A class $\mathcal{L}$ has *infinite elasticity* if there exist two infinite sequences

$$w_0, w_1, w_2, \ldots \text{ and } L_1, L_2, L_3, \ldots,$$

where $w_i \in \Sigma^*$, $L_i \in \mathcal{L}(i = 1, 2, \ldots)$, such that

$$\{w_0, w_1, \ldots, w_{i-1}\} \subseteq L_i \text{ but } w_i \notin L_i$$

for any $i \geq 1$. $\mathcal{L}$ has *finite elasticity* if $\mathcal{L}$ does not have infinite elasticity. Note that words $w_0, w_1, w_2, \ldots$ and languages $L_1, L_2, L_3, \ldots$ in the definition should be mutually distinct. Then, it is easy to see that any class with finite thickness always has finite elasticity.

**Theorem 5.1.** (Wright [47]) If $\mathcal{L}$ has finite elasticity then $\mathcal{L}^k$ also has finite elasticity for any $k \geq 1$.

**Theorem 5.2.** (Wright [47]) If $\mathcal{L}$ has finite elasticity then $\mathcal{L}$ is inferable from positive data.

We have already seen that the class $\mathcal{PL}$ of pattern languages has finite thickness. From this fact and the above two theorems we have the following.

**Corollary 5.3.** (Wright [47]) The class $\mathcal{PL}^k$ of unions of at most $k$ pattern languages is inferable from positive data for any $k \geq 1$.

Here we should note that the class $\mathcal{L}^*$ of unions of unbounded number of languages is out of the scope of Wright's results.

## 5.2 Polynomial Time Inference of Unions of Regular Pattern Languages

In Section 4, we have established polynomial time inference from positive data by an inference machine that works responsively, consistently and conservatively and produces a hypothesis within polynomial time. We have also shown that procedure *INFER_BY_MINL* can correctly infer any class $\mathcal{L}$ with finite thickness whenever MINL for $\mathcal{L}$ is computable. In general, the class $\mathcal{L}^k$ of unions does not have finite thickness even if $\mathcal{L}$ has finite thickness. First, we show that *INFER_BY_MINL* also works for classes with finite elasticity.

Let $\mathcal{L}$ be any class with finite elasticity, for which MINL is computable. Assume *INFER_BY_MINL* fails to infer a language $L \in \mathcal{L}$, that is, it produces infinitely many different hypotheses $h_1, h_2, \dots$ when a positive presentation of $L$ is given. For any $i = 1, 2, \dots$, let $w_{i-1}$ be the last example before producing $h_i$. Since *INFER_BY_MINL* works consistently and conservatively, we have $\{w_0, \dots, w_{i-1}\} \subseteq L_i$ and $w_i \notin L_i$. Therefore, $\mathcal{L}$ has infinite elasticity, which contradicts our assumption. Thus we can extend the scope of Theorem 4.1 and Theorem 4.2 to classes with finite elasticity.

**Theorem 5.4.** [9] If a class $\mathcal{L}$ has finite elasticity and MINL for $\mathcal{L}$ is computable, then the procedure *INFER_BY_MINL* infers $\mathcal{L}$ consistently and conservatively from positive data.

**Theorem 5.5.** [9] If a class $\mathcal{L}$ has finite elasticity and the membership and MINL for $\mathcal{L}$ are computable in polynomial time, then $\mathcal{L}$ is polynomial time inferable from positive data.

We extend the partial ordering $\preceq$ on $\mathcal{P}$ to a partial ordering $\sqsubseteq$ on $\mathcal{P}^k$. Let $\Pi, T \in \mathcal{P}^k$. We define a binary relation $\sqsubseteq$ on $\mathcal{P}^k$ by $\Pi \sqsubseteq T \iff$ for any $\pi \in \Pi$, there exists $\tau \in T$ such that $\pi \preceq \tau$, and an equivalence relation $\equiv$ by $\Pi \equiv T \iff \Pi \sqsubseteq T$ and $T \sqsubseteq \Pi$. A set $\Pi$ of canonical patterns is of *canonical form* if $\Pi$ contains no $\tau$ such that $\tau \preceq \pi$ for some $\pi \in \Pi$. For any $\Pi \in \mathcal{P}^k$, there uniquely exists $\Pi'$ of canonical form such that $\Pi \equiv \Pi'$. When we identify equivalent sets of patterns from each other, we can think $\sqsubseteq$ as a partial ordering on $\mathcal{P}^k$. By using a set of patterns we define a union of pattern languages, that is, $L(\Pi) = \cup_{\pi \in \Pi} L(\pi)$. We define $L(\emptyset) = \emptyset$. Then, clearly $\Pi \sqsubseteq T \Longrightarrow L(\Pi) \subseteq L(T)$, but the converse does not hold in general.

Hereafter we consider only regular patterns because the membership problem is decidable for the class $\mathcal{RPL}^k$ of at most $k$ unions of regular pattern languages, as well as for $\mathcal{RPL}$. We extend $MINL\_BY\_REFINEMENT$ for $\mathcal{RPL}^k$. By using a refinement operator $MINL\_BY\_REFINEMENT$ finds a syntactically minimal pattern. Therefore, to guarantee the syntactically minimal pattern to be a correct answer for MINL we need a condition that $\tau \preceq \pi \Longleftrightarrow L(\pi) \subseteq L(\tau)$. Although the syntactic relation $\preceq$ coincides with the semantic relation $\subseteq$ in regular pattern languages when $\Sigma$ contains three or more constants, it is not the case for unions of regular pattern languages. However, fortunately, if $\Sigma$ contains enough constants, we can show that $\Pi \sqsubseteq T \Longleftrightarrow L(\Pi) \subseteq L(T)$ for unions of regular pattern languages with bounded number of variables. We denote by $\mathcal{RP}_{(m)}$ the set of regular patterns with at most $m$ variables, and by $\mathcal{RPL}_{(m)}$ the class of their languages.

**Lemma 5.6.** [9] If $\#\Sigma > 2km$, then $\Pi \sqsubseteq T \Longleftrightarrow L(\Pi) \subseteq L(T)$ for any $\Pi, T \in \mathcal{RP}_{(m)}^k$.

First we consider an algorithm that finds a syntactically minimal set of patterns, called a $k$-mmg, and then modify it to work as a correct MINL algorithm.

Let $S$ be a finite set of words. A set $\Pi \in \mathcal{RP}^k$ is called a $k$-*multiple covering* of $S$, if $S \subseteq L(\Pi)$. A set $\Pi \in \mathcal{RP}^k$ is said to be *reduced with respect to* $S$ if $S \subseteq L(\Pi)$ but $S \not\subseteq L(\Pi')$ for any $\Pi' \subsetneq \Pi$. A *maximally common generalization* (*mcg* for short) of $S$ is a pattern $\pi$ such that $S \subseteq L(\pi)$ and for any $\pi' \preceq \pi$, $S \subseteq L(\pi') \Longrightarrow \pi' \equiv \pi$. A *tightest refinement* (*tr* for short) of a pattern $\pi$ *with respect to* $S$ is an mcg $\tau$ of $S$ such that $\tau \preceq \pi$.

**Lemma 5.7.** [9] Given a nonempty set $S$ of words and a pattern $\pi$ such that $S \subseteq L(\pi)$, we can compute a tightest refinement of $\pi$ with respect to $S$ in polynomial time.

**Proof.** Using a complete and polynomial time computable refinement operator, an algorithm similar to $MINL\_BY\_REFINEMENT$ can compute a tightest refinement. □

A $k$-*minimal multiple generalization* ($k$-*mmg*) of $S$ is a set $\Pi \in \mathcal{RP}^k$ such that $S \subseteq L(\Pi)$ and for any $\Pi' \sqsubseteq \Pi$, $S \subseteq L(\Pi') \Longrightarrow \Pi' \equiv \Pi$. A $k$-multiple covering $\Pi$ of $S$ is said to be *tightest* if for each $\pi \in \Pi$, $\pi$ is an mcg of $S - L(\Pi - \{\pi\})$. Clearly any tightest covering of $S$ is of canonical form and reduced with respect to $S$. If $\Pi$ is a $k$-mmg of $S$ and $\Pi$ is of canonical form, then $\Pi$ is a tightest covering of $S$. Furthermore, if $\Pi$ is a tightest covering of $S$ and $\#\Pi = k$, then $\Pi$ is a $k$-mmg of $S$. However, when $\#\Pi < k$, $\Pi$ is not always a $k$-mmg of $S$ even if $\Pi$ is tightest. To explain this phenomena, we introduce the notion of divisibility. Let $\pi$ be a pattern such that $S \subseteq L(\pi)$. For $k > 1$, a $k$-*division of* $\pi$ *with respect to* $S$ is a reduced $k$-multiple covering $\Pi$ of $S$ such that $\#\Pi > 1$ and $\Pi - \{\pi\}$. We say $\pi$ is $k$-*divisible with respect to* $S$ if there exists a $k$-division of $\pi$ with respect to $S$. Now we are ready to characterize $k$-mmg's. We define any pattern is not 1-divisible.

**Lemma 5.8.** [9] Let $S$ be a finite set of words, $\Pi$ be a reduced $k$-multiple covering of $S$. Then $\Pi$ is a $k$-mmg of $S$ if and only if $\Pi$ is a tightest covering of $S$ and any $\pi \in \Pi$ is not $(k - \#\Pi + 1)$-divisible with respect to $S - L(\Pi - \{\pi\})$.

**Lemma 5.9.** [9] Let $\rho$ be a complete refinement operator for $\mathcal{RP}$, $S$ be a nonempty finite set of words, $\pi$ be an mcg of $S$, and $k > 1$. Then $\pi$ is $k$-divisible with respect to $S$ if and only if there exists a set $\Pi \in \mathcal{RP}^k$ such that $\Pi \subseteq \rho(\pi)$, $1 < \#\Pi \leq k$ and $\Pi$ is reduced with respect to $S$.
**Proof.** If part is obvious. Assume that $\{\pi_1, \ldots, \pi_{k'}\}$ is a $k$-division of $\pi$ with respect to $S$ and $1 < k' \leq k$. Since $\pi$ is an mcg of $S$, $\pi_i \prec \pi$ for any $i = 1, \ldots, k'$. Since $\rho$ is a complete refinement operator, for any $i = 1, \ldots, k'$, there exists some $\tau_i \in \rho(\pi)$ such that $\pi_i \preceq \tau_i$. Let $\Pi$ be any subset of $\{\tau \mid \tau = \tau_i \text{ for some } i = 1, \ldots, k'\}$ that is reduced with respect to $S$. Then $\#\Pi > 1$, because $\pi$ is an mcg of $S$ and $\tau \prec \pi$ for any $\tau \in \Pi$. $\square$

**Lemma 5.10.** [9] Let $S$ be a nonempty finite set of words, $\Pi$ be a reduced $k$-multiple covering of $S$. Then we can compute a tightest covering $TC$ of $S$ in polynomial time with respect to total size of $S$.

```
procedure TIGHTEST_COVER(Π, S);
input:   A set Π of patterns and a nonempty set S of words such that
         Π is reduced with respect to S;
output:  A tightest covering TC of S such that TC ⊑ Π;
method:
  begin
    TC := Π;
    while there exist π ∈ TC and τ ∈ ρ(π) such that
         S − L(TC − {π}) ⊆ L(τ) do
      TC := TC − {π} ∪ {τ};
    output TC;
  end
```

**Proof.** Consider the procedure $TIGHTEST\_COVER$. We can prove that $TC$ is reduced with respect to $S$ at every point in the iteration of the while loop. Therefore, the procedure produces a tightest covering if it terminates. Let define $g(TC) = \Sigma_{\pi \in TC}$ $(\min\{size(w) \mid w \in S - L(TC - \{\pi\})\} - size(\pi))$. If $S - L(TC - \{\pi\}) \subseteq L(\tau)$ for some $\pi \in TC$ and $\tau \in \rho(\pi)$, then $g(TC) > g(TC - \{\pi\} \cup \{\tau\})$. Therefore the number of iterations of the while loop is bounded by $g(\Pi)$. It is not hard to see the computing time is bounded by a polynomial. $\square$

From lemma's the above, we can compute a $k$-mmg of $S$ in polynomial time by using the following algorithm.

```
procedure MMG(k, S);
input:   A positive integer k, and a nonempty finite set S of words;
output: A k-mmg of S;
method:
  begin
    Π := TIGHTEST_COVER(S, {x₁});
    Δk := k;
    while  Δk ≥ 2 and there exists π ∈ Π such that
               π is Δk-divisibe with respect to S − L(Π − {π}) do
      begin
        ΔΠ := a Δk-division of π with respect to S − L(Π − {π});
        Π := Π − {π}∪ TIGHTEST_COVER(ΔΠ, S − L(Π − {π}));
        Δk := k − #Π + 1;
      end
    output Π;
  end
```

**Theorem 5.11.** [9]  Given a nonempty set $S$ of words, a $k$-mmg is computable in polynomial time with respect to the total size of $S$.

Any answer of MINL for regular pattern languages is a $k$-mmg, but the converse does not hold in general. From Lemma 5.6, when the alphabet $\Sigma$ has more than $2km$ constants, any $k$-mmg can be used as a correct answer of MINL for the class $\mathcal{RPL}^k_{(m)}$ of unions of at most $k$ languages defined by $m$-variable regular patterns. However, the algorithm we have considered does not work correctly, unless the refinement operator $\rho$ is complete for the restricted class $\mathcal{RP}_{(m)}$ of $m$-variable regular patterns. We define a new refinement operator $\rho_m$ for $\mathcal{RP}_{(m)}$ by modifying $\rho$. A substitution $\theta$ is $m$-*basic* for regular pattern $\pi$ if $\#val(\pi\theta) \leq m$ and $\theta$ satisfies one of the following:

(1)  $\theta = \{x := a\}$ for some $x \in val(\pi)$ and some $a \in \Sigma$.

(2)  $\theta = \{x := yz\}$ for some $x \in val(\pi)$ and some variables $y, z \notin val(\pi)$.

(3)  $\theta = \{x := ax\}$ or $\theta = \{x := xa\}$ for some $x \in val(\pi)$ and some $a \in \Sigma$.

Let define $\rho_m(\pi) = \{\tau \mid \tau = \pi\theta, \theta$ is $m$-basic for $\pi\}$. Then $\rho_m$ is a complete and polynomial time computable refinement operator for $m$-variable regular patterns. Thus, finally we have the following theorem.

**Theorem 5.12.** [9]  The class $\mathcal{RPL}^k_{(m)}$ of unions of $k$ languages defined by $m$-variable regular patterns is polynomial time inferable from positive data.

# 6  Probably Approximately Correct Learning

In this section we discuss the inferability of pattern languages in the sense of Valiant's PAC-learning [45]. In contrast to traditional inductive inference based on "identification in the limit" due to Gold [14] or "learning from minimally adequate teacher

(MAT)" due to Angluin [4], PAC (probably approximately correct) learning is to find an approximation of the target from random sampling, and therefore it has attracted much attention even from the viewpoint of practice. However, it seems that the contributions of studies on theory of PAC-learning are mainly on negative results derived from the theory of computational complexity. Here we introduce a part of the study by Miyano, Shinohara and Shinohara [30] aimed to find learnable classes of languages as general as possible using the framework of elementary formal systems [6, 44], which is a natural extension of pattern languages.

Ko and Tzeng [24] showed that the consistency problem for pattern languages is $\Sigma_2^p$-complete. The consistency problem for a class is to decide whether there exists a language in the class consistent with given positive and negative examples. If the consistency problem is NP-hard, then the class is not polynomial time PAC-learnable under the assumption RP $\neq$ NP. Therefore, we cannot expect any efficient learning for pattern languages. Furthermore, Schapire [38] showed a stronger negative result. Such negative results seem to be quite natural, because even the membership problem for pattern languages is NP-complete [2]. Therefore, we should consider subclasses of pattern languages for which at least the membership problem is computable in polynomial time.

To get a subclass of pattern languages for which the membership problem is computable in polynomial time, we may restrict the total number of variables in patterns. Kearns and Pitt [23] showed that for every fixed $m$ the class $\mathcal{PL}_{(m)}$ of $m$-variable pattern languages is polynomial time PAC learnable from positive and negative examples generated according to any product distribution and arbitrary distribution, respectively. The polynomial time PAC learnability of $\mathcal{PL}_{(m)}$ when all the examples are generated according to any arbitrary distribution is still open.

When we restrict the number of variable occurrences instead of that of different variables in patterns, we get another subclass $\mathcal{PL}_{[m]}$ of pattern languages defined by patterns with at most $m$ variable occurrences. If a pattern $\pi$ defines a language containing a word $w$, then $|\pi| \leq |w|$ and every subword in $\pi$ without variables is a subword of $w$. This property that every constant word appearing in a pattern $\pi$ whose language contains a word $w$ is a subword of $w$ is called "heredity," which is a key to find classes of polynomial time learnable. Therefore, the number of inequivalent languages that are defined by patterns with at most $m$ variable occurrences and contain $w$ is of polynomial order in $|w|$, if we fix $m$ arbitrarily. Thus we can show the polynomial time PAC learnability of this subclass.

## 6.1 Polynomial Time PAC Learnability

This section briefly reviews some necessary notions for PAC learnability due to Valiant [45] according to Natarajan [35].

By $\Lambda$ we denote a finite alphabet used for representing languages. A *representation* for a class $\mathcal{L}$ is a function $R : \mathcal{L} \to 2^{\Lambda^*}$ such that $R(L)$ is a nonempty subset of $\Lambda^*$ for any $L$ in $\mathcal{L}$ and $R(L_1) \cap R(L_2) = \emptyset$ for any distinct $L_1$ and $L_2$ in $\mathcal{L}$. Each element in $R(L)$ is called a *description* for $\mathcal{L}$. The length of a description $d \in R(L)$ is the word length $|d|$ of $d$. We denote the length of the shortest description for $L$ by $l_{min}(L, R)$.

An *example* is an ordered pair $(w, a) \in \Sigma^* \times \{0, 1\}$. An *example for a language* $L$ is a pair $(w, 1)$ if $w \in L$ or $(w, 0)$ otherwise. For a set $S \subseteq \Sigma^* \times \{0, 1\}$ of examples, we define $S_+ = \{w \mid (w,1) \in S\}$ and $S_- = \{w \mid (w,0) \in S\}$. We call a word in $S_+$ a *positive example* and a word in $S_-$ a *negative example*, respectively. For two sets $Y$ and $N$ with $Y \cap N = \emptyset$, we say that a language $L$ is *consistent* with positive examples in $Y$ and negative examples in $N$ if $Y \subseteq L$ and $N \subseteq \Sigma^* - L$. A language $L \in \mathcal{L}$ is *consistent* with a set $S$ of examples if $L$ is consistent with positive examples in $S_+$ and negative examples in $S_-$. For a set $S$ of examples, $l_{min}(S,R)$ is the length of the shortest description in $R$ of any language in $\mathcal{L}$ which is consistent with $S$.

A class $\mathcal{L}$ is *polynomial time learnable* in a representation $R$ if there exist an algorithm $\mathcal{A}$ and a polynomial $poly(\cdot,\cdot,\cdot,\cdot)$ which satisfy the following conditions for any concept $L \in \mathcal{L}$, any real numbers $\varepsilon, \delta (0 < \varepsilon, \delta < 1)$, any integers $n \geq 0$, $s \geq 1$, and any probability distribution $P$ on $\Sigma^{[n]}$:

(a) $\mathcal{A}$ takes $\varepsilon, \delta, n$, and $s$.

(b) $\mathcal{A}$ may call EXAMPLE, which generates examples for $L$, randomly according to $P$.

(c) $\mathcal{A}$ outputs a description $d \in R(H)$ for some $H \in \mathcal{L}$ satisfying $P(L \dot\cup H - L \cap H) < \varepsilon$ with probability at least $1 - \delta$, when $l_{min}(L,R) \leq s$ is satisfied.

(d) The running time of $\mathcal{A}$ is bounded by $poly(1/\varepsilon, 1/\delta, n, s)$.

When $R$ is clear from the context, we simply say that a class $\mathcal{L}$ is polynomial time learnable.

Let $\mathcal{L}$ be a class. We say that $\mathcal{L}$ *shatters* a set $S \subseteq \Sigma^*$ if $\{L \cap S \mid L \in \mathcal{L}\} = 2^S$. The *Vapnik-Chervonenkis dimension* (*VC-dimension* for short) of $\mathcal{L}$, denoted by $VCdim(\mathcal{L})$, is the greatest cardinality of a set that is shattered by $\mathcal{L}$. For an integer $n \geq 0$, we define $\mathcal{L}^{[n]} = \{L \cap \Sigma^{[n]} \mid L \in \mathcal{L}\}$. We say that $\mathcal{L}$ is of *polynomial dimension* if $VCdim(\mathcal{L}^{[n]})$ is bounded by a polynomial in $n$ for all $n \geq 0$.

A representation $R$ for a class $\mathcal{L}$ is *polynomial time computable* if there exist a deterministic algorithm $\mathcal{B}$ and a polynomial $poly$ satisfying (a) and (b):

(a) $\mathcal{B}$ takes as input a word $w \in \Sigma^*$ and a description $d \in \Lambda^*$.

(b) If $d \in R(L)$ for some $L \in \mathcal{L}$, then $\mathcal{B}$ halts in time $poly(|w| + |d|)$ and outputs 1 or 0 according to whether $w \in L$ or not.

Let $\mathcal{L}$ be a class with representation $R$, and $S \subseteq \Sigma^* \times \{0,1\}$ be a finite set of examples. A *fitting* for $\mathcal{L}$ in $R$ is a deterministic algorithm that takes $S$ as input and outputs a description $d \in R(L)$ of some language $L \in \mathcal{L}$ which is consistent with $S$ if any. A fitting is said to be a *polynomial time fitting* if it runs in polynomial time in the length of its input and $l_{min}(S,R)$. A *randomized fitting* for $\mathcal{L}$ in $R$ is a randomized algorithm which takes $S$ as input and outputs a description $d \in R(L)$ of some language $L \in \mathcal{L}$ which is consistent with $S$, if any, with probability greater than $1/2$. A fitting is an *Occam fitting* if there exist a polynomial $poly$ and a real number $0 \leq \alpha < 1$ such that for every input $S$, the output is of length at most $poly(n, l_{min}(S,R))(\#S)^\alpha$, where $n = \max\{|w| \mid (w,a) \in S\}$.

Polynomial time learnability is characterized as follows:

**Theorem 6.1.** (Haussler, et al. [16], Natarajan [34, 35], Blumer, et al. [11]) Let $\mathcal{L}$ be a class and $R$ be a polynomial time computable representation for $\mathcal{L}$.

(1) $\mathcal{L}$ is polynomial time learnable in $R$ if $\mathcal{L}$ is of polynomial dimension and there exists a polynomial time fitting for $\mathcal{L}$ in $R$.

(2) $\mathcal{L}$ is polynomial time learnable in $R$ if there exists a polynomial time Occam fitting for $\mathcal{L}$ in $R$.

(3) $\mathcal{L}$ is polynomial time learnable in $R$ only if there exists a randomized polynomial time fitting for $\mathcal{L}$ in $R$.

## 6.2 Polynomial Time PAC Learning of Pattern Languages

We consider polynomial time PAC learnability of pattern languages. We use patterns themselves as representation. However, $\mathcal{P}$ is not a polynomial time computable representation for $\mathcal{PL}$, because the membership problem for $\mathcal{PL}$ is NP-complete. Therefore we need to restrict pattern languages. The set $\mathcal{RP}$ of regular patterns is a polynomial time computable representation for the class $\mathcal{RPL}$ of regular pattern languages. For any positive integer $m$, we define $\mathcal{P}_{[m]} = \{\pi \in \mathcal{P} \mid \Sigma_{x \in val(\pi)} occ(x, \pi) \leq m\}$ and $\mathcal{PL}_{[m]} = \{L \mid L = L(\pi)$ for some $\pi \in \mathcal{P}_{[m]}\}$. For example, if $\pi = x_1 x_2 x_3$ then $\pi \in \mathcal{P}_{[3]}$ but $\pi \notin \mathcal{P}_{[2]}$. Clearly, $\mathcal{P}_{[m]}$ is a polynomial time computable representation for $\mathcal{PL}_{[m]}$. Note that the difference of $\mathcal{PL}_{[m]}$ from $\mathcal{PL}_{(m)}$.

First we measure the VC-dimension of the class of pattern languages.

**Lemma 6.2.** (Natarajan [34]) A class $\mathcal{L}$ is of polynomial dimension if and only if there exists a polynomial $poly(n)$ such that $\log_2 \#\mathcal{L}^{[n]} \leq poly(n)$ for all $n \geq 0$.

**Lemma 6.3.** [30] The class $\mathcal{PL}$ of pattern languages is of polynomial dimension.
**Proof.** Since $\Sigma^{[n]} \cap L(\pi) = \emptyset$ for any pattern $\pi$ such that $|\pi| > n$, $\mathcal{PL}^{[n]} = \{\Sigma^{[n]} \cap L(\pi) \mid \pi \in \mathcal{P}\} = \{\Sigma^{[n]} \cap L(\pi) \mid \pi \in \mathcal{P}, \pi$ is of canonical form, and $1 \leq |\pi| \leq n\} \cup \{\emptyset\}$. Therefore, $\log_2 \#\mathcal{PL}^{[n]} \leq \log_2 \#\{\pi \in \mathcal{P} \mid \pi$ is of canonical form and $0 \leq |\pi| \leq n\} \leq \log_2 (|\Sigma| + n + 1)^n = n \log_2(|\Sigma| + n + 1)$. From Lemma 6.2, $\mathcal{PL}$ is of polynomial dimension. $\square$

For a class $\mathcal{L}$ with a representation $R$, we consider the following problem:

**Consistency Problem for $\mathcal{L}$ in $R$**
**Instance:** A set of examples $S \subseteq \Sigma^* \times \{0, 1\}$ with $S_+ \cap S_- = \emptyset$.
**Question:** Is there a name $\nu \in R(h)$ of a language $L \in \mathcal{L}$ which is consistent with $S$ ?

If the consistency problem for $\mathcal{L}$ in $R$ is shown NP-complete, we can say that $\mathcal{L}$ is not polynomial time learnable in $R$ under the assumption of RP$\neq$NP, since there is no randomized polynomial time fitting for $\mathcal{L}$ in $R$ by Theorem 6.1 (3).

Unfortunately, the consistency problem is shown NP-complete for regular pattern languages and their unions.

**Theorem 6.4.** [30] The consistency problem for the class $\mathcal{RPL}^k$ of unions of $k$ regular pattern languages is NP-complete for any $k \geq 1$.

**Corollary 6.5.** [30] The class $\mathcal{RPL}^k$ of unions of $k$ regular pattern languages is not polynomial time PAC learnable unless RP = NP.

**Theorem 6.6.** [30] The class $\mathcal{PL}_{[m]}$ of languages, defined by patterns in which the total number of variable occurrences is less than or equal to $m$, is polynomial time PAC learnable for any $m$.

**Proof.** We show a polynomial time fitting for $\mathcal{PL}_{[m]}$ in $\mathcal{P}_{[m]}$. Let $m > 0$ be any integer and $S$ be a finite set of examples. If $S$ contains no positive example, then any word $w \notin S_-$ can be considered as a consistent pattern with $S$. Therefore we assume that $S_+$ contains at least one word. Let $w$ be one of the shortest words in $S_+$, $|w| = n$, and $G = \{\pi \in \mathcal{P}_{[m]} \mid \pi$ is of canonical form, $w \in L(\pi)\}$. Clearly there exists a pattern $\pi \in \mathcal{P}_{[m]}$ consistent with $S$ if and only if there exists a pattern $\pi' \in G$ consistent with $S$. Let $\pi$ be any pattern in $G$. Then, if $\pi$ has a subword $s$ containing no variable, then $s$ is a subword of $w$. Let $G' = \{\pi \in \mathcal{P}[m] \mid \pi$ is of canonical form and any subword $s$ of $\pi$ is a subword of $w\}$. Then, $G \subseteq G'$. The number of subwords of $w$ is bounded by $n(n+1)/2$. Therefore, $\#G' \leq (n(n+1)/2)^{m+1} m^m$. Since we consider $m$ as a constant number, $\#G'$ is bounded by a polynomial in $n$. Clearly, $G'$ can be constructed in polynomial time with respect to $n$. For each pattern $\pi \in G'$, we can check whether $\pi$ is consistent with $S$ in polynomial time with respect to $n$ and the total length of words in $S$. □

# 7 Inconsistent Learning and Others

All the inference algorithms we have dealt with in the preceding sections have to find a consistent hypothesis with given examples. Unfortunately, almost all the related problems to find a consistent hypothesis are computationally very hard for the class of pattern languages. A possible approach, which we have followed, to overcome this computational hardness is to restrict the hypothesis space. Another approach is to abandon some of the requirements for inference algorithms, such as consistency and conservativeness.

## 7.1 Inconsistent Hypothesis

Lange and Wiehagen [26] discussed inference machines that may produce inconsistent hypotheses with a given set of examples. Clearly from the property of pattern languages, any pattern $\pi$ is easily reconstructed from the shortest words of $L(\pi)$. By using this fact, they proposed an inference algorithm that ignores all the examples but the shortest ones. The following illustrates their inference algorithm, where $LCG(\pi, w)$ is the least common generalization of a pattern $\pi$ and a word $w$, which is uniquely and easily obtained when $|\pi| = |w|$.

The polynomial time inferability of the class $\mathcal{PL}_{(m)}$ of $m$-variable pattern languages is still open. In polynomial time inference, we require the inference machine to work consistently and conservatively. Lange [27] reported that $\mathcal{PL}_{(m)}$ is polynomial time inferable from positive data by a consistent but not conservative inference machine. The membership problem for $\mathcal{PL}_{(m)}$ is computable in polynomial time. Therefore, when a hypothesis $\pi$ produced by *INCONSISTENT_PATTERN_INFER* contains at

```
procedure INCONSISTENT_PATTERN_INFER;
input:   an infinite sequence w_1, w_2, ... of words;
output: an infinite sequence π_1, π_2, ... of patterns;
method:
  begin
      π_1 := w_1;
      for i := 2 to ∞ do
         begin
            if |w_i| < |π_{i-1}| then
                π_i := w_i
            else if |w_i| > |π_{i-1}|
                π_i := π_{i-1}
            else
                π_i := LCG(π_{i-1}, w_i);
            output π_i
         end
  end;
```

most $m$ variables, we can check the consistency of $\pi$ with all the examples seen before in polynomial time. If the number of variables in $\pi$ does not exceed $m$ and $L(\pi)$ contains all the examples, then we can output $\pi$, otherwise output the most general pattern "$x_1$" that is always consistent. Note that such an inference machine does not work conservatively.

## 7.2  Monotonic Inference

Jantke [21] introduced the monotonicity in inductive inference and discussed the difference of several kinds of monotonicity. *Strong monotonic* inference should produce larger and larger hypotheses. *Weak monotonic* inference should keep monotonicity as long as produced hypotheses are consistent with examples. In other words, weak monotonicity is nothing less than conservativeness. As we have already seen, the class of pattern languages is weak monotonically inferable from positive data. However, Jantke proved that the class of pattern languages is not strong monotonically inferable from positive data.

Lange and Zeugmann [28] discussed the influence of the choice of representation to the inferability. In some situation, inference machine which may take hypotheses from a larger space can work more efficiently. For example, they proposed an inference algorithm that uses a finite set of patterns as a description of the intersection of pattern languages. More precisely, their algorithm outputs the set of all the patterns consistent with given examples. Clearly the algorithm consistently and strong monotonically identifies any pattern from positive data. Furthermore, the algorithm does not need to remember examples as long as it remembers the last hypothesis. Such a manner of inference algorithm is said to be *iterative*. Combining Lange and Zeugmann's idea with Angluin's pattern automata, we can implement an inference algorithm that produces every hypothesis in polynomial time and infers one-variable pattern languages in a strong monotonic and iterative manner.

## 7.3  Using Queries

Angluin [4] investigated the usefulness of making queries in inductive inference. She formalized query learning as *MAT (minimally adequate teacher) learning*, in that the learner can make two kinds of queries, membership queries and equivalence queries, to the teacher. A *membership query* asks whether a word belongs to the unknown language and an *equivalence query* asks whether a description, like a finite automaton or pattern, represents the unknown language and receives a counterexample when the answer is 'no'. A language $L$ is said to be MAT learnable if a learner produces a correct description of $L$ in polynomial time by asking membership and equivalence queries. Angluin showed that the class of regular languages is MAT learnable.

Angluin [5] showed that any algorithm that learns the class of pattern languages using equivalence, membership, and subset queries must make at least $2^{n-1}$ queries in the worst case, where $n$ is the length of the unknown pattern. Therefore efficient learning of pattern languages in MAT model seems impossible. Angluin also considered the usage of other kind of queries. A *restricted superset query* asks whether a description represents a superset of the unknown language. She proved that pattern languages are identified by using polynomially many restricted superset queries [5].

# 8  Applications

In the preceding sections, we have discussed the inferability of pattern languages from viewpoints of inductive inference from positive data and PAC learning. In this section, we describe several applications of learning algorithms. In applying learning algorithms, the efficiency is very important. First we introduce an application of polynomial time inference of regular pattern languages from positive data to data entry system, which was reported in [40, 43]. In Section 6, we have seen that the class $\mathcal{PL}_{[m]}$ of languages defined by patterns with at most $m$ variable occurrences is polynomial time PAC-learnable. By using Occam fitting we can show that the class $\mathcal{PL}^*_{[m]}$ of finite unions is also polynomial time PAC-learnable. We also introduce experimental results on protein classification problems using the PAC-learning algorithm [7], as well as the $k$-mmg algorithm discussed in Section 5 [13].

## 8.1  A Learning Data Entry System

A data entry system is used for preparing data for database system. Such data are usually assumed to share a common form. Hence the data entry system should make it easy for user to prepare data and for the database system to check the validity of their form.

Here we briefly sketch the idea of learning data entry system. At the stage of data entry, a user may types, for example, some bibliographic data in the following way:

```
$
Author: Angluin, D.
```

```
Title:    Inductive Inference of Formal Languages from
          Positive Data
Journal:  Information and Control, 40
Year:     1980
$
Author:   Gold, E.M.
Title:    Limiting Recursion
Journal:  Journal of Symbolic Logic, 30
Year:     1965
$
  . . .
```

where $ is a special symbol to delimit the bibliographic records. After a few records have been entered, our data entry system will infer or learn a structure of records in the form

$$\mathtt{Author:}_{\sqcup\sqcup}x_1\mathtt{Title:}_{\sqcup\sqcup\sqcup}x_2\mathtt{Journal:}_{\sqcup}x_3\mathtt{Year:}_{\sqcup\sqcup\sqcup\sqcup}x_4,$$

where each of $x_1$, $x_2$, $x_3$ and $x_4$ stands for any string, and the system will successively output the constant parts "$\mathtt{Author:}_{\sqcup\sqcup}$", "$\mathtt{Title:}_{\sqcup\sqcup\sqcup}$", "$\mathtt{Journal:}_{\sqcup}$" and "$\mathtt{Year:}_{\sqcup\sqcup\sqcup\sqcup}$" to prompt the user input. Then the user may only type the data corresponding to $x_1$, $x_2$, $x_3$ and $x_4$.

Clearly such a learning function may be realized as an inference algorithm for regular pattern languages. Shinohara and Arikawa [43] reported some experiments on inference algorithms for regular pattern languages. They compared two algorithms, polynomial time inference algorithms for regular pattern languages and extended regular pattern languages. In experiments, the algorithm for regular pattern languages uses MINL algorithm that finds a regular pattern of maximal length. Therefore, to get a well describing pattern, we need to give examples of short length. On the other hand, the algorithm for extended regular pattern languages uses a refinement operator, and therefore, find more descriptive patterns even when examples are not very much short. Thus, it is very useful to use a refinement operator with some criteria to control nondeterministic choice in the process of MINL calculation.

Nix proposed an application of inductive inference to text editing [36]. In his EBE (editing by example) system, text transformation programs consisting of a pair of patterns are synthesized from input/output examples.

## 8.2   Finding Motifs in Amino Acid Sequences

Genome Informatics is, roughly speaking an area which aims at developing method and tools for analyzing, understanding and designing large molecules such as DNA and proteins with the aid of computer Genome Informatics would be a challenging field for Machine Learning to show its identity and usefulness since it has been generating a lot of problems which should require machine learning technologies. One of the important issues in this field is to establish technologies for discovering knowledge from DNA and amino acid sequences that may provide new directions of investigations for biologists.

This section deals with one such problem, which is to find characteristic features of transmembrane domains of proteins [15, 18] from amino acid sequences. Most approaches to this problem have been by means of biophysical analysis of amino acid residues [17] while our approach is based on concept learning from examples.

The applicability of concept learning largely depends on the representation of concepts. Logic programs have been used for various knowledge representations in Genome Informatics. For instance, Muggleton et al. [32] gave an interesting approach to protein secondary structure prediction by inductive logic programming. On the other hand, "motifs" of functional domains are usually described with patterns, which are words containing variables. Such motifs have been compiled in the PROSITE database [10]. Therefore patterns are more natural representations for functional domains than logic programs. Thus we can directly handle amino acid sequences with patterns.

In PAC learning model, the class of languages defined by patterns with at most m variable occurrences is polynomial time PAC learnable. Here we use the finite unions of *four-variable regular pattern languages*. Although the class of finite unions is not of polynomial dimension, we can construct a polynomial time Occam fitting using an approximation algorithm for weighted set cover problem [12], in a similar way to [11]. For more details the reader should be referred to [30].

The class of unions of at most $k$ languages defined by $m$-variable regular patterns is polynomial time inferable from positive data. We also apply the polynomial time inference algorithm of unions of regular pattern languages to the same problem.

### 8.2.1 Membrane proteins and PIR database

The primary structure of a protein is described as a sequence of amino acid residues of 20 kinds. One of the important problems in Genome Informatics is to discover rules for predicting functions of proteins by analyzing their amino acid sequences.

Figure 8.1 shows an example of an amino acid sequence of a membrane protein of a Norway rat. There is a tendency to assume that a membrane protein has transmembrane domains each of which constitutes an $\alpha$-helix structure generating the membrane. The protein in Figure 8.1 has four transmembrane domains. The reported length of a transmembrane domain is not large, usually, 20 ~ 30. If a sequence corresponding to a transmembrane domain is found in a protein, the probability that it is a membrane protein will get larger. Therefore it is important to identify transmembrane domains in amino acid sequences.

These amino acid sequences have been compiled in the PIR database[37] together with their additional information such as functions.

In applying our learning strategy to this problem, we regard the sequences of transmembrane domains as positive examples. The PIR database contains the amino acid sequences with FEATURE field where transmembrane domains are indicated.

For example, in Figure 8.1 the transmembrane domains of the amino acid sequence $w$ are indicated by intervals 19~41, 101~123, 133~156, 195~ 218. Then the substrings $w[19..41]$, $w[101..123]$, $w[133..156]$, and $w[195..218]$ are taken as positive examples.

The number of all the positive examples from the PIR database is 689. As negative examples, we use amino acid sequences without any overlap with transmembrane domains. Since the length of a positive example is 20~30, we randomly choose sequences of length around 30 for negative examples. We collect the same number of negative examples.

```
FEATURE
    19-41                      #Domain transmembrane
    101-123                    #Domain transmembrane
    133-156                    #Domain transmembrane
    195-218                    #Domain transmembrane
SEQUENCE
                  5         10         15         20         25         30
      1 M D V V N Q L V A G G Q F R V V K E P L G F V K V L Q W V F
     31 A I F A F A T C G S Y T G E L R L S V E C A N K T E S A L N
     61 I E V E F E Y P F R L H Q V Y F D A P S C V K G G T T K I F
     91 L V G D Y S S S A E F F V T V A V F A F L Y S M G A L A T Y
    121 I F L Q N K Y R E N N K G P M M D F L A T A V F A F M W L V
    151 S S S A W A K G L S D V K M A T D P E N I I K E M P M C R Q
    181 T G N T C K E L R D P V T S G L N T S V V F G F L N L V L W
    211 V G N L W F V F K E T G W A A P F M R A P P G A P E K Q P A
    241 P G D A Y G D A G Y G Q G P G G Y G P Q D S Y G P Q G G Y Q
    271 P D Y G Q P A S G G G G Y G P Q G D Y G Q Q G Y G Q Q G A P
    301 T S F S N Q M
```

**Figure 8.1.** An amino acid sequence of a membrane protein containing four transmembrane domains.

A hydropathy plot [25] has been used generally to predict transmembrane domains from primary sequences. Instead of dealing with twenty symbols of amino acids, we classify these symbols into three classes by the hydropathy indices of amino acids [25]. More precisely, we transform symbols by Table 8.1.

| Amino Acids | Hydropathy | | | New Symbol |
|---|---|---|---|---|
| A M C F L V I | 1.8 | ~ | 4.5 | * |
| P Y W S T G | −1.6 | ~ | −0.4 | + |
| R K D E N Q H | −4.5 | ~ | −3.2 | − |

**Table 8.1.** Transformation rules

This transformation from 20 symbols to 3 symbols reduces the search space of hypotheses. The sequence in Figure 8.2 is the result of this transformation from the sequence in Figure 8.1.

As is seen, this transformation makes the characteristics of a transmembrane domain more vivid. Figure 8.3 gives some of the sequences obtained by this transformation from the transmembrane domains chosen from our 689 examples.

We denote by *POS* and *NEG* the sets of these positive and negative examples converted by Table 8.1, respectively. Fortunately, *POS* and *NEG* do not have any overlaps.

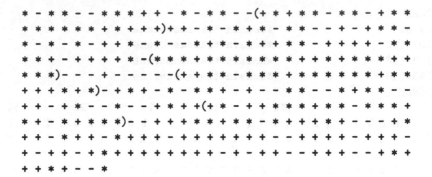

**Figure 8.2.** The sequence obtained by the transformation, where trans-mem-brane domains are indicated by parentheses.

| Positive examples | Negative examples |
|---|---|
| ++*+*+***+*-**+**-+ | *+------**-------*-+-*** |
| +++**+***-**+****+*+***+ | -+++-++--+***-+-*-* |
| +**+*****+** | ****+*-*-*+-++++- |
| +*+*****+****-*****-* | **---**+****++-*---**--* |
| ****+*+*+***+++***-**+* | +**-+*--*+*+-++-**+*+-*-**+- |
| ++-****+*+***+*++***+-+ | ****+-*+-++-+***+-+*+*++ |
| **+**+********+***** | -+*-*+--+*+*-**--**+-*++ |
| *******+*+*+*+*-**** | -*---+-+-+*-+*++--+**** |
| ***+*********+***** | -+--**---+-*-++-+*-**+*+-- |
| **+*****-++*-+***+** | +-+++*-*+*+***---**-**+++- |

**Figure 8.3.** Positive and negative examples

## 8.3 Experiments by PAC learning algorithm

As a hypothesis space, we use the class of finite unions of extended regular pattern languages defined as

$$\{L_\varepsilon(\pi_1) \cup \cdots \cup L_\varepsilon(\pi_k) \mid \pi_i \text{ is a regular pattern in } \Pi \text{ and } k \geq 1\},$$

where $\Pi$ is the set of regular patterns of the following forms:

$$x_1 \alpha_1 x_2,$$

$$x_1 \alpha_1 x_2 \alpha_2 x_3,$$

$$x_1 \alpha_1 x_2 \alpha_2 x_3 \alpha_3 x_4$$

with $\alpha_1, \alpha_2, \alpha_3$ in $\{*, +, -\}^+$.

The reason why we restrict the number of variables to 4 is simply due to the actual time and space required to implement the algorithm.

Our learning algorithm chooses randomly two small sets $pos$ and $neg$ from $POS$ and $NEG$, respectively. Then the sample $S$ defined by $pos$ and $neg$ is given to an input to the learning algorithm. This process is repeated until a good hypothesis is found. In our experiments, the size of $pos$ and $neg$ vary from 5 to 20.

### Finding patterns from positive training examples

The first approach we take to this problem is to find a collection of regular patterns which covers almost all positive training examples and excludes almost all negative training examples.

Table 8.2 shows the good hypotheses and their success rates that our learning system has produced.

### Finding patterns from negative training examples

We are also interested in collections of regular patterns which exclude positive examples and cover negative examples. That is to say, we use transmembrane domains as negative examples, and nontransmembrane domains as positive examples. Table 8.3 shows the results.

As is seen, hypotheses (N1) and (N2) are very small and the success rates for both positive and negative examples are quite good. From these observations, we can say that the approach from negative examples is much better than that from positive examples in the last section.

In the experiments of learning regular patterns, we met with quite satisfactory results on identification of transmembrane domains in amino acid sequences from positive and negative data. We have also taken another approach to this problem by learning decision trees over regular patterns [8, 39]. In comparison, since the algorithm for finding decision trees is much more efficient than that in this paper, we met a better performance in time and accuracy in the experiments, while the algorithm in [8, 39] is not fully analyzed and the accuracy of outputs is not theoretically guaranteed.

| Patterns | Positive | Negative |
|---|---|---|
| $x_1$*****$x_2$ | 72.6% | 10.2% |
| accuracy | 72.6% | 89.8% |

(P1)

| Patterns | Positive | Negative |
|---|---|---|
| $x_1$+***+$x_2$ | 38.6% | 9.6% |
| $x_1$*+*$x_2$***+$x_3$ | 80.4% | 19.7% |
| accuracy | 82.1% | 76.2% |

(P2)

**Table 8.2.** Collections of regular patterns covering positive examples and excluding negative examples that was produced by our learning algorithm from 10 positive (transmembrane domain) and 10 negative (nontransmembrane domain) training examples. The second (third, resp.) column shows the percentage of the positive (negative, resp.) examples that the pattern in the first column covers. The last row shows the accuracy for positive examples and negative examples.

| Pattern | Positive | Negative |
|---|---|---|
| $x_1$--$x_2$ | 7.4% | 87.7% |
| accuracy | 92.6% | 87.7% |

(N1)

| Pattern | Positive | Negative |
|---|---|---|
| $x_1$--$x_2$ | 7.4% | 87.7% |
| $x_1$++-$x_2$ | 7.0% | 53.3% |
| accuracy | 87.7% | 95.1% |

(N2)

**Table 8.3.** Collections of regular patterns covering nontransmembrane domains and excluding transmembrane domains. 10 positive and negative training examples are used.

## 8.4 Experiments by $k$-mmg algorithm

Here we describe some experimental results on the transmembrane problem using $k$-mmg algorithm which finds a minimal unions of at most $k$ regular pattern languages containing a given set of positive examples. Since examples taken from PIR database naturally contain much noise, we take a similar approach to the experiments by PAC learning algorithm. We randomly choose a small subset *pos* of *POS*, feed it to the $k$-mmg algorithm, and evaluate the accuracy by using *POS* and *NEG*. Unlike the PAC learning algorithm used in the previous section, the $k$-mmg algorithm works on raw data as well as transformed data according to the hydropathy index. Thus, the $k$-mmg algorithm works very efficiently.

Table 8.4 shows one of the results obtained from raw amino acid sequences by using the $k$-mmg algorithm, whose accuracy is lower than those by PAC learning. When examples are transformed according to hydropathy index, the $k$-mmg algorithm finds hypotheses with higher accuracy as shown in Table 8.5.

| Patterns | Positive | Negative |
|---|---|---|
| $x_1Ix_2ALx_3$ | 18.1% | 8.3% |
| $x_1Ix_2LGx_3$ | 17.3% | 10.1% |
| $x_1IFx_2Lx_3$ | 14.3% | 4.0% |
| $x_1ILx_2Vx_3$ | 22.6% | 7.5% |
| $x_1LLx_2Lx_3$ | 41.7% | 13.0% |
| accuracy | 70.6% | 67.4% |

**Table 8.4.** A collection of three-variable regular patterns found as a 5-mmg for randomly chosen 25 positive examples without transformation.

| Patterns | Positive | Negative |
|---|---|---|
| $x_1-**+x_2+**+****x_3$ | 1.1% | 0.3% |
| $x_1+***x_2+***x_3$ | 60.0% | 9.0% |
| $x_1******x_2**x_3$ | 47.7% | 4.8% |
| $*+*+***+-*+*+**+*+**$ | 0.1% | 0.0% |
| $**x_1+***x_2*+x_3$ | 29.8% | 5.2% |
| accuracy | 83.3% | 85.8% |

**Table 8.5.** A collection of three-variable regular patterns found as a 5-mmg for randomly chosen 50 positive examples with transformation according to the hydropathy index.

# References

[1] Aho, A.V. and Corasick, M.J.: Efficient string matching: An aid to bibliographic search, *Communications of the ACM* **18**, 333-340, (1975).

[2] Angluin, D.: Finding common patterns to a set of strings, In Proceedings of the 11th Annual Symposium on Theory of Computing, 130-141, (1979). (Journal of Computer and System Sciences 21, 46-62, (1980))

[3] Angluin, D.: Inductive inference of formal languages from positive data, *Information and Control* 45, 117-135, (1980).

[4] Angluin, D.: Learning regular sets from queries and counterexamples, *Information and Control* 75, 87-106, (1987).

[5] Angluin, D.: Queries and concept learning, *Machine Learning* 2, 319-342, (1988).

[6] Arikawa, S., Shinohara, T. and Yamamoto, A.: Learning elementary formal systems, *Theoretical Computer Science* 95, 97-113, (1992).

[7] Arikawa, S., Kuhara, S., Miyano, S., Shinohara, A. and Shinohara, T.: A learning algorithm for elementary formal systems and its experiments on identification of transmembrane domains, In Proceedings of the Twenty-Fifth Hawaii International Conference on System Sciences, Vol.I, 675-684, (1992).

[8] Arikawa, S., Miyano, S., Shinohara, A., Kuhara, S., Mukouchi, Y. and Shinohara, T.: A machine discovery from amino acid sequences by decision trees over regular patterns, *New Generation Computing* 11, 361-375, (1993).

[9] Arimura, H., Shinohara, T. and Otsuki, S.: Finding minimal generalizations for unions of pattern languages and its application to inductive inference from positive data, In Proceedings of STACS'94, Caen, *Lecture Notes in Computer Science* 775, Springer-Verlag, 649-660, (1994).

[10] Bairoch, A.: PROSITE: A dictionary of sites and patterns in proteins, *Nucleic Acids Research* 19, 2241-2245, (1991).

[11] Blumer, A., Ehrenfeucht, A., Haussler, D., and Warmuth, M.: Learnability and the Vapnik-Chervonenkis dimension, *Journal of the ACM* 36, 929-965, (1989).

[12] Chvatal, V.: A greedy heuristic for the set covering problem, *Mathematics of Operations Research* 4, 233-235, (1979).

[13] Fujino, R.: Learning Unions of Extended Regular Pattern Languages from Positive Data and Its Application to Discovering Motifs in Proteins, Master Thesis, Department of Artificial Intelligence, Kyushu Institute of Technology, (1994).

[14] Gold, E.M.: Language identification in the limit, *Information and Control* 10, 447-474, (1967).

[15] Hartmann, E., Rapoport, T.A., and Lodish, H.F.: Predicting the orientation of eukaryotic membrane-spanning proteins, In Proceedings of the National Academy of Science of the United States of America 86, 5786-5790, (1989).

[16] Haussler, D., Kearns, M., Littlestone, N., and Warmuth, M.: Equivalence of models for polynomial learnability, In Proceedings of the First Workshop on Computational Learning Theory, 34-50, (1988).

[17] von Heijine, G.: A new method for predicting signal sequence cleavage sites, *Nucleic Acids Research* **14**, 4683-4690, (1986).

[18] von Heijine, G.: Transcending the impenetrable: how proteins come to terms with membranes, *Biochimica et Biophysica Acta* **947**, 307-333, (1988).

[19] Ibarra, O.H.: On two-way multihead automata, *Journal of Computer and System Sciences* **7**, 28-36, (1973).

[20] Jantke, K.P. and Beick, H.R.: Combining postulates of naturalness in inductive inference, *Electron. Informationsverarb. Kybern.* (EIK) **17**, 465-484, (1981).

[21] Jantke, K.P.: Monotonic and non-monotonic inductive inference of functions and patterns, In Proceedings of the 1st International Workshop on Nonmonotonic and Inductive Logic, *LNCS* **543**, Springer-Verlag, 161-177, (1991).

[22] Jiang, T., Salomaa, A., Salomaa, K. and Yu, S.: Inclusion is undecidable for pattern languages, In Proceedings of the 20th International Colloquium, ICALP'93, *Lecture Notes in Computer Science*, Springer-Verlag, 301-312, (1993).

[23] Kearns, M. and Pitt, L.: A Polynomial-time algorithm for learning k-variable pattern languages from examples, In Proceedings of the Second Annual Workshop on Computational Learning Theory, 57-71, (1989).

[24] Ko, K. and Tzeng, W.: Three $\Sigma_2^p$-complete problems in computational learning theory, *Computational Complexity* **1**, 269-310, (1991).

[25] Kyte, J. and Doolittle, R.: A simple method for displaying the hydropathic character of protein, *Journal of Molecular Biology* **157**, 105-132, (1982).

[26] Lange, S. and Wiehagen, R.: Polynomial time inference of arbitrary pattern languages, *New Generation Computing* **8**, 361-370 (1991).

[27] Lange, S.: A note on polynomial-time inference of k-variable pattern languages, In Proceedings of the 1st International Workshop on Nonmonotonic and Inductive Logic, *LNCS* **543**, Springer-Verlag, 178-183, (1991).

[28] Lange, S. and Zeugmann, T.: Monotonic versus Nonmonotonic Language Learning, In Proceedings of the 2nd International Workshop on Nonmonotonic and Inductive Logic, *LNCS* **659**, Springer-Verlag, 254-269, (1993).

[29] Maier, D.: The complexity of some problems on subsequences and supersequences, *Journal of the ACM* **25**, 322-336, (1978).

[30] Miyano, S., Shinohara, A. and Shinohara, T.: Which classes of elementary formal systems are polynomial-time learnable?, In Proceedings of the 2nd Workshop on Algorithmic Learning Theory, 139-150, (1991).

[31] Motoki, T., Shinohara, T. and Wright, K.:   The correct definition of finite elasticity: corrigendum to identification of unions, In Proceedings of the 4th Annual Workshop on Computational Learning Theory, 375, (1991).

[32] Muggleton, S., King, R., and Sternberg, M.:   Using logic for protein structure prediction, In Proceedings of the Twenty-Fifth Hawaii International Conference on System Sciences, Vol.I, 685-696, (1992).

[33] Mukouchi, Y.:   Containment problems for pattern languages, *IEICE Transactions on Information and Systems* **E75-D**, 420-425, (1992).

[34] Natarajan, B.:   On learning sets and functions, *Machine Learning* **4**, 67-97, (1991).

[35] Natarajan, B.:   *Machine Learning - A Theoretical Approach*, Morgan Kaufmann Publishers, (1991).

[36] Nix, R.P.:   Editing by example, *ACM Trans. Program. Lang. Syst* **7**, 600-621, (1985).

[37] PIR.:   Protein identification resource, National Biomedical Research Foundation, (1991).

[38] Schapire, R.:   Pattern languages are not learnable, In Proceedings of the Third Annual Workshop on Computational Learning Theory, 122-129, (1990).

[39] Shimozono, S., Shinohara, A., Shinohara, T., Miyano, S., Kuhara, S., and Arikawa, S.:   Finding alphabet indexing for decision trees over regular patterns: an approach to bioinformatical knowledge acquisition, In Proceedings of the Twenty-Sixth Hawaii International Conference on System Sciences, Vol.I, 763-773, (1993).

[40] Shinohara, T.:   Polynomial time inference of pattern languages and its applications, Proceedings of the 7th IBM Symposium on Mathematical Foundations of Computer Science, 191-209, (1982).

[41] Shinohara, T.:   Polynomial time inference of extended regular pattern languages, RIMS Symposia on Software Science and Engineering, Kyoto, 1982, Proceedings, *Lecture Notes in Computer Science* **147**, Springer-Verlag, 115-127, (1983).

[42] Shinohara, T.:   Inferring unions of two pattern languages, *Bulletin of Informatics and Cybernetics* **20**, 83-88, (1983).

[43] Shinohara, T. and Arikawa, S.:   Learning data entry systems: An application of inductive inference of pattern languages, Research Report 102, Research Institute of Fundamental Information Science, Kyushu University, (1983).

[44] Smullyan, R.M.:   *Theory of Formal Systems*, Princeton University Press, Princeton, New Jersey, (1961).

[45] Valiant, L.: A theory of the learnable, *Communications of the ACM* **27**, 1134-1142, (1984).

[46] Wagner, R.A. and Fischer, M.J.: The string-to-string correction problem, *Journal of the ACM* **21**, 168-173, (1974).

[47] Wright, K.: Identification of unions of languages drawn from an identifiable class, In Proceedings of the 2nd Annual Workshop on Computational Learning Theory, 328-333, (1989).

[48] Zeugmann, T., Lange, S. and Kapur, S.: Characterizations of monotonic and dual-monotonic language learning, (to appear in *Information and Computation*).

# Inductive Learning
# of Recurrence-Term Languages
# from Positive Data

Phil Watson*

HTWK Leipzig

FB Mathematik und Informatik

PF 66

04251 Leipzig

### Abstract

We show that the class of languages generated by (basic) recurrence-terms
is inferable in the limit from positive data, and that such learning may be consistent and conservative, though not in general strong monotonic. This class of
languages has neither of the properties of finite thickness and finite elasticity
usually used to prove inferability from positive data, so our proof method is the
explicit construction of a tell-tale function for the class of recurrence-term languages. Recurrence-terms are of interest because they generate many sequences
arising from divergent cases of Knuth-Bendix completion.

*Keywords*: Inductive inference from text; recurrence-term languages.

## 1   Introduction and Motivation

Recurrence-terms were introduced by Chen, Hsiang and Kong [CHK90] as a means
of coding a countably infinite sequence of first order terms (equivalently, first order
rewrite rules, for the symbol → can be regarded as just another operator) into a finite
form from which an arbitrary member of the sequence can be effectively recovered.
Recurrence-terms were developed particularly as a means of expressing solutions to
divergent cases of Knuth-Bendix completion [KB70], a problem currently enjoying the
attention of many researchers in formal methods ([TW93] includes a recent survey of
this field). We note in passing that recurrence-terms are a particularly promising
approach to this problem, and have a number of nice features such as an effective
algorithm for matching a first order term with a recurrence-term, so that rewriting
with recurrence-term rules is possible. In [Wa92] extended classes of recurrence-terms
were defined with greatly increased expressive power and it was shown that examples
of divergent sequences arising from specification languages such as LOTOS [ISO88]

---

*Now at Department of Computing, University of Bradford, Bradford BD7 1DP, United Kingdom
(P.R.Watson@comp.brad.ac.uk)

may often be generated by recurrence-terms. Also recurrence-terms may serve as a class of programs in the related problem of program synthesis.

The above named work in many cases leaves the most difficult part of the problem of solving divergence unaddressed: namely, how to identify the infinite sequence of rules being generated by completion from the finite initial segment available to us at any given time. Some partial attempts were made in [CHK90] towards generating recurrence-terms from finite sets of terms. Inductive inference from text has been proposed [TJ89] [La89] as a means of solving this problem and is the approach we adopt here. All in all, we consider that the question of inductive inference of recurrence-term languages from text is well motivated, and this is the problem we address in Section 3. In Section 5 we consider possible future extensions of our results.

# 2 Definitions and Notation

In this section we recap briefly the necessary background in inductive inference and term rewriting which we expect will be familiar to most readers (in particular, detailed understanding of Knuth-Bendix completion will *not* be necessary here). We then spend rather more time on the definitions and notation required by recurrence-terms, illustrating them with examples, as we expect these will be less familiar to most readers.

## 2.1 Inductive inference from text

We will sketch the main ideas of inductive inference from text (inductive inference from informant will not concern us here). The reader is directed to [AS83] for a thorough survey of the field.

*Inductive inference* is a model of learning that proceeds by hypothesizing (guessing) a general rule describing an infinite data flow, which is fed piece by piece to the learning agent, which we represent as a machine.

An *inductive inference machine* or IIM is a Turing machine with at least two distinguished states. When the machine is in one of these states it is requesting input, and when in the other, it is producing output. Inputs will be words (later terms) over a countably infinite alphabet (later signature) $\Sigma$. A set of words over $\Sigma$ is called a *language*. A class of recursive languages $L_1, L_2, ..., L_n, ...$ is called an indexed family of recursive languages, or an *indexed recursive family*, for short, if there exists a recursive function $f$ such that for all positive integers $j$ and words $w$ we have $f(j, w) = 1$ if $w \in L_j$, and $f(j, w) = 0$ otherwise. If the sequence of inputs consists in the limit of a language $L$ then we say the sequence forms a *text* for $L$.

We call each discrete output a *hypothesis*, and interpret it as a finite description (an index for a grammar, say, or a rule or a program) of a language, over some *hypothesis space*.

If after a certain time an IIM $M$ only ever outputs the same hypothesis $i$, then we say the machine *converges* to $i$. If $M$ converges to $i$ on input of a text for $L$, and $i$ is a description of $L$ in the chosen hypothesis space, then we say $M$ *learns* (equivalently *infers*) $L$ *in the limit from text* (equivalently, *from positive data*). If $M$ learns every $L_i$ in the indexed recursive family $C = L_1, L_2, ...$ then we say $M$ learns $C$ in the limit from text, and we write $C \in LIM - TXT$.

We say $M$ works *consistently* (and learning is consistent) if each hypothesis output by $M$ describes a language containing all the data input to $M$ so far. We say $M$ works *conservatively* (and learning is conservative) if a new hypothesis $H_{j+1}$ differs from the previous hypothesis $H_j$ only in the case that since output of $H_j$ there has been some input which is not contained in the language described by $H_j$.

## 2.2 Terms and rules

Our definitions in this section are the standard ones to be found throughout the literature.

We will write $\mathcal{N}$ for the set of non-negative integers $\{0, 1, 2, ...\}$ and $\mathcal{N}^+$ for the set of positive integers $\{1, 2, ...\}$. Throughout we will write $=$ to mean syntactic identity, as it will never be necessary to refer to any particular equational theory. Identity up to some given equivalence relation will be written $\simeq$. We will write $\subseteq$ for subset inclusion, and $\subset$ for proper subset inclusion.

A signature $\Sigma$ is a set of pairs $(f, n)$ of *operators* and their arities. By convention our operators will be prefix. The arity $n \in \mathcal{N}$ tells how many arguments the appropriate operator takes. A *ground term* (over $\Sigma$) is defined to be either $f$ where $(f, 0) \in \Sigma$ (such an operator $f$ will sometimes be called a *constant*) or a tree of the form $f(t_1, ..., t_n)$, for some $n$, where $(f, n) \in \Sigma$ and $t_1, ..., t_n$ are ground terms. The set of all ground terms over $\Sigma$ is written $T_\Sigma$.

Let $\mathcal{X}$ be a countable set of variables. A (general) *term* over $\Sigma, \mathcal{X}$ is either a variable $x \in \mathcal{X}$, a constant $c \in T_\Sigma$ or a tree of the form $f(t_1, ..., t_n)$, for some $n$, where $(f, n) \in \Sigma$ and $t_1, ..., t_n$ are terms. The set of (general) terms over $\Sigma, \mathcal{X}$ is written $T_\Sigma(\mathcal{X})$.

A *substitution* is a function mapping $\sigma : \mathcal{X} \to T_\Sigma(\mathcal{X})$ such that $\sigma(x) = x$ for all but finitely many $x \in \mathcal{X}$. The set of all $x$ for which $\sigma(x) \neq x$ is called the domain of $\sigma$, written $Dom(\sigma)$, and the set of all $t \in T_\Sigma(\mathcal{X})$ such that for some $x \in Dom(\sigma)$ we have $\sigma(x) = t$ is called the range of $\sigma$, written $Ran(\sigma)$. We may represent a substitution $\sigma$ by a finite set of ordered pairs $\{x_1 \to t_1, ..., x_n \to t_n\}$ where $Dom(\sigma) = \{x_1, ..., x_n\}$ and $(\forall x_i : 1 \le i \le n)\sigma(x_i) = t_i$.

A *variable renaming substitution* $\sigma$ has the additional property that $Ran(\sigma) \in \mathcal{X}$ and $(\forall x, y \in \mathcal{X})[x = y$ iff $\sigma(x) = \sigma(y)]$. A substitution $\sigma$ is *ground* if $Ran(\sigma) \subseteq T_\Sigma$. We reserve $\phi$ as the name of the substitution with empty domain, and also as the name of the empty set. Meaning will be clear from context.

Every substitution may be extended to a mapping from $T_\Sigma(\mathcal{X})$ to $T_\Sigma(\mathcal{X})$ (and will usually be regarded as such). Application of a substitution to an arbitrary term $t \in T_\Sigma(\mathcal{X})$ is written $t\sigma$ and is defined as follows. If $t \in \mathcal{X}$ then $t\sigma = \sigma(t)$. Otherwise $(t = f(t_1, ..., t_n)$ for some $n \in \mathcal{N})$ $t\sigma = f(t_1\sigma, ..., t_n\sigma)$. We call $t\sigma$ an *instance* of $t$.

The set of *positions* in $t \in T_\Sigma(\mathcal{X})$ is written $Pos(t)$ and defined as follows. $\epsilon$ (sometimes called root) is a position in $t$. If $t = f(t_1, ..., t_i, ..., t_n)$ for some $n \ge 1$, and $p$ is a position in $Pos(t_i)$ then $i.p$ is a position in $t$, where . is concatenation. For most purposes we may drop the $\epsilon$ from the end of positions. If $p, q \in Pos(t)$ then we write $p \le q$ if $p$ is $\epsilon$ or $p$ is an initial substring of $q$. We write $p < q$ if $p \le q$ and $p \neq q$. If neither $p \le q$ nor $q \le p$ holds then we write $p \| q$. We will sometimes measure the size of $t$, written $|t|$, by $|Pos(t)|$.

The set of *subterms* of $t \in T_\Sigma(\mathcal{X})$ is defined as follows. $t$ is a subterm of $t$, and if $t = f(t_1, ..., t_n)$ then every subterm of each of the $t_i$ (for $i = 1, ..., n$) is a subterm of $t$. The subterm of $t$ at position $p \in Pos(t)$ is written $t|_p$ and is defined to be $t$ if $p = \epsilon$, and otherwise (case $p = i.p'$ and $t = f(t_1, ..., t_i, ..., t_n)$) to be $t_i|_{p'}$. If $t|_p = f(t_1, ..., t_n)$ then we will sometimes say that the operator at position $p$ (in $t$) is $f$, written $Op(t|_p) = f$.

The term arrived at by replacing the subterm(s) of $t$ at (a set of) position(s) $p$ by $s$ is written $t[p \leftarrow s]$. We write $t[p/s]$ when we wish to emphasize that $s$ is the subterm of $p$ at position(s) $p$. If $p_1, ..., p_n$ is a list of disjoint positions in $t$ we use $t[(\forall i : 1 \leq i \leq n)p_i \leftarrow s_i]$ as a natural abbreviation of $((t[p_1 \leftarrow s_1])[p_2 \leftarrow s_2])...[p_n \leftarrow s_n]$

The set of all variables which occur as subterms of $t$ will be written $Vars(t)$. We may also write $Vars(A)$ where $A$ is a set of terms, with the intention that $x \in Vars(A)$ iff $(\exists t \in A)x \in Vars(t)$.

The *occurrences* of an operator $f$ or variable $x$ in $t$, written $Occ(f, t)$ (respectively $Occ(x, t)$) is the set of all $p \in Pos(t)$ such that $Op(t|_p) = f$ (respectively $\{p \mid t|_p = x\}$). Also write $Occ(f, t, g) = \{p \mid Op(t|_p) = f \wedge (\forall q < p)Op(t|_q) \neq g\}$.

If $t, t' \in T_\Sigma(\mathcal{X})$ then we say $t$ *embeds* $t'$ (written $t \trianglerighteq t'$) if there is one-one mapping $\tau$ from $Pos(t')$ to $Pos(t)$ such that $(\forall p \in Pos(t'))$ $[Op(t'|_{\tau(p)}) = Op(t|_p)]$ and $(\forall p, p' \in Pos(t'))[p \leq p' \Leftrightarrow \tau(p) \leq \tau(p')]$.

A *rewrite rule* over $\Sigma$ takes the form $\rightarrow (l, r)$ where $l, r \in T_\Sigma(\mathcal{X})$ and $Vars(r) \subseteq Vars(l)$. We may regard a set of rewrite rules over a signature $\Sigma$ as just a set of terms over a signature $\Sigma \cup (\rightarrow, 2)$ and thus for our main purpose here (concerning countably infinite sets of terms) there is no difference between a term and a rule.

## 2.3 Recurrence-terms

Recurrence-terms were introduced by [CHK90] and give us a remarkably expressive means of representing some countable sequences of terms in finite form, and in such a way that an arbitrary term in the sequence may be effectively recovered from the recurrence-term. The requirements for a sequence to be expressed by (we say 'generated' by) a recurrence-term concern a certain necessary regularity in the structure of the terms that make up the sequence.

¿From this point on we will use the name *basic recurrence-terms* or RTBs to refer to the class of recurrence-terms defined in [CHK90]. This name was coined by [Wa92] to distinguish the original recurrence-terms from the more powerful classes defined in the latter paper. We consider the extension of our results to the recurrence-terms of [Wa92] in section 5.2.

### 2.3.1 Syntax of basic recurrence-terms

Assume we have a signature $\Sigma$ and a variable set $\mathcal{X}$. We will define a slightly modified signature $\Sigma'$ and variable set $\mathcal{X}'$ as follows by the addition of sufficient symbols to represent the non-negative integers (if not already present), e.g. $(0, 0), (s, 1) \in \Sigma'$, and special symbols $(\diamond, 0)$ and $(\Phi, 3)$. We will call $T_\Sigma(\mathcal{X})$ the set of *first-order terms* to distinguish them from terms involving $\Phi$ and $\diamond$.

We distinguish countably many variables (called *degree variables*) by making them upper case. It is intended that degree variables will only ever be substituted by non-negative integer values.

We depart from our usual prefix notation in the case of $\Phi$, which will have its third argument, typically a degree variable, attached as a subscript. The first argument of $\Phi$ is called the *head* and the second argument of $\Phi$ is called the *tail*.

**Definition 1** *A term in $T_{\Sigma'}(\mathcal{X}')$ with at least one occurrence of $\diamond$ (not at $\epsilon$) and no occurrences of $\Phi$ is called a* pattern.

**Definition 2** *A* generator *is defined to be a term in $T_{\Sigma'}(\mathcal{X}')$ with the additional requirements that:*

- *the operator at position $\epsilon$ is $\Phi$;*

- *the heads of all occurrences of $\Phi$ are (possibly distinct) patterns;*

- *the subscripted arguments of all occurrences of $\Phi$ are (possibly distinct) degree variables;*

- *no degree variable occurs except as a subscripted argument of an occurrence of $\Phi$.*

**Definition 3** *The set of* basic recurrence terms *(RTBs) over a signature $\Sigma$ is inductively defined to be the smallest set containing all of the following:*

- *terms in $T_{\Sigma}(X)$;*

- *generators of the form $\Phi_N(h, t)$ where $t$ is a RTB;*

- *trees of the form $f(t_1, ..., t_n)$ where $(f, n) \in \Sigma$ and $t_1, ..., t_n$ are RTBs.*

**Example 1** A simple example of a RTB over the signature with unary operator $f$ and constant 0 is:

$$\Phi_N(f(\diamond), 0)$$

**Note 1** *We will usually use $H, H', H_1, ...$ to represent arbitrary RTBs, and $G, G', G_1, ...$ to represent arbitrary generators. Lower-case letters $p, q, ...$ will represent positions in a term or RTB. Lower case letters such as $x, y, ...$ will represent first-order variables, while upper-case letters such as $M, N, ...$ will represent degree variables. Often to emphasize the connection between a generator and its (subscripted) degree variable argument, we call a generator of the form $\Phi_N(...)$ an N-generator, and similarly its head is an N-pattern, etc.*

*A useful piece of notation is to subscript each occurrence of $\diamond$ in an N-pattern with the degree variable $N$. There is never any ambiguity about the generator to which an occurrence of $\diamond$ corresponds, and the semantics of RTBs will not be changed by the presence or absence of a subscript, but experience has shown that recurrence-terms are much easier to read when $\diamond$ is annotated in this way.*

*Treating RTBs as simply terms over an enlarged signature allows us to continue to use notation for position, subterms, etc. in the usual way.*

**Definition 4** *Given an RTB $H$, define $Gens(H) = \{H \mid_p : H \mid_p \text{ is a generator}\}$. We write $Dvars(H)$ for the set of all the degree variables occurring in $H$. We write $Dvar(H) = N$ if $H$ is an $N$-generator.*

*Given a generator $G \in Gens(H)$, $Pat(G) = h[p/\diamond]$ where $G = \Phi_N(h[p/\diamond], t)$ for some $N, t$.*

*Then $Pats(H) = \{h[p/\diamond] \mid (\exists G \in Gens(H))Pat(G) = h[p/\diamond]\}$.*

*Let $h \in Pats(H)$ and let $\sigma_1, ..., \sigma_k$ be an arbitrary sequence of variable renaming substitutions with $(\forall i : 1 \leq i \leq k)Vars(h) \subseteq Dom(\sigma_i)$ and $(\forall i, j : 1 \leq i, j \leq k)$ $[i \neq j \Rightarrow Ran(\sigma_i) \cap Ran(\sigma_j) = \phi]$. Then $h^k(t)$ (where $k \in \mathcal{N}$) is defined to be $t$ if $k = 0$ and $h\sigma_k[Occ(\diamond, h) \leftarrow h^{k-1}(t)]$ otherwise. (For the purposes for which we use $h^k$, it will not matter which sequence $\sigma_1, ..., \sigma_k$ is chosen. See Note 2.)*

*The precedence ordering on $Gens(H)$, written $\preceq$, is defined as follows. Let $H \mid_p, H \mid_{p'} \in Gens(H)$. Then $H \mid_p \preceq H \mid_{p'}$ iff $p \leq p'$. We write $H \mid_p \prec H \mid_{p'}$ iff $p < p'$.*

## 2.4 Semantics of basic recurrence terms

A recurrence-term represents a (possibly infinite) sequence of terms. Any term in this sequence can be effectively recovered by a process with two components: *instantiation* and *unfolding*.

Informally, *unfolding* is the process which returns a term from the sequence coded by the recurrence-term. *Instantiation* directs the unfolding process to return that term and no other (up to variable renaming).

### 2.4.1 Instantiation

**Definition 5** *A recurrence-term $H$ is said to be* fully instantiated *if each of the degree variables $(N_1, ... N_m)$ in $Dvars(H)$ has a non-negative integer value assigned to it, in which case we write:*

$$H[N_1 \leftarrow n_1, ..., N_m \leftarrow n_m]$$

*where the $n_i$ are the values so assigned (we say $N_i$ is instantiated to $n_i$). Otherwise $H$ is partially instantiated.*

We note in passing that first-order terms are trivially fully instantiated recurrence-terms.

We call $[N_1 \leftarrow n_1, ..., N_m \leftarrow n_m]$ the *instantiation information*. The order in which the assignments (of values to degree variables) occur in the instantiation information is unimportant. The similarity of our notation for instantiation information to that for subterm replacement will cause no ambiguity, as it will always be clear whether the left hand argument of $\leftarrow$ is a degree variable or a position.

When we need to refer to arbitrary instantiation information we will write $[I]$. By convention we will put instantiation information at the end of a recurrence-term, even when this information only applies to a proper subterm. When we are only interested in an initial segment of the instantiation information we may write $[N_1 \leftarrow n_1, ..., N_m \leftarrow n_m, R]$, where $R$ represents the remainder of the information.

We will frequently have reason to refer to the instantiation of $H$ in which every degree variable is instantiated to 0. This instantiation will be written $H[\bar{0}]$. Similarly the instantiation in which $N$ is instantiated to $n$ and all other degree variables are instantiated to 0 is written $[N \leftarrow n, \vec{0}]$, etc. Another distinguished case will be the *set of all possible instantiations* in which no degree variable in $H$ takes a value greater than $n$, written $[\leq n]$.

**Example 2**

$$H = f(\Phi_N(g(\diamond_N)), \Phi_M(f(c, \diamond_M), c)), \Phi_N(g(\diamond_N), c))[N \leftarrow 3, M \leftarrow 1]$$

*is a fully instantiated recurrence-term over the obvious signature.*

### 2.4.2  Unfolding

**Definition 6** *An* unfolding renaming $\sigma$ *(w.r.t. $N$, the degree variable of a generator in a recurrence-term $H$, so such a substitution will sometimes be called an $N$-unfolding renaming) is a variable renaming substitution $\sigma$ such that*

$$\{x \mid (\exists G)x \in Pat(G) \wedge Dvar(G) = N\} \subseteq Dom(\sigma)$$

*and $Ran(\sigma) \cap Vars(H) = \phi$. We call each $x \in Ran(\sigma)$ a* new variable.

**Definition 7** *Let $H[I]$ be a fully instantiated RTB with $N \in Dvars(H)$ and $[I] = [N \leftarrow n, R]$. Let the set of positions of $N$-generators in $H$ which are minimal with respect to $\prec$ be $\{p_1, ..., p_n\}$ and let the $N$-generator in position $p_i$ be $G_i = \Phi_N(h_i[q_i/\diamond], t_i)$.*

*Then a single* level *unfolding* of the $N$-generators in $H$ (sometimes called an $N$-unfolding of $H$ for short), *using the unfolding renaming $\sigma$, is defined as follows, where $\rightsquigarrow$ may be read as 'unfolds to':*

$$H[I] \rightsquigarrow \begin{cases} H[(\forall i : 1 \leq i \leq n)p_i \leftarrow (h_i\sigma)[q_i \leftarrow \Phi_N(h_i[q_i/\diamond, t'_i])]][N \leftarrow n-1, R] \\ \quad if\ n > 0 \\ H[(\forall i : 1 \leq i \leq n)p_i \leftarrow t'_i][R] \\ \quad if\ n = 0\ and\ [R]\ is\ non\text{-}empty \\ H[(\forall i : 1 \leq i \leq n)p_i \leftarrow t'_i] \\ \quad if\ n = 0\ and\ [R]\ is\ empty \end{cases}$$

*where $t'_i[I']$, for some possibly empty $[I']$, is the term or RTB reached by an $N$-unfolding of $t_i[I]$ using the unfolding renaming $\sigma$ if $N \in Dvars(t_i)$, and $t'_i = t_i$ otherwise.*

Note that the fact that the tail of each $G_i$ minimal w.r.t. $\prec$ is also $N$-unfolded using the same variable renaming $\sigma$ means that all $N$-generators are effectively unfolded simultaneously. The complexity of exactly describing the positions of occurrences of $\diamond$ in $N$-generators which are in the tails of $N$-generators (i.e. not minimal w.r.t. $\prec$) leads us to prefer the above recursive definition.

**Definition 8** *Let $H[I]$ be a fully instantiated recurrence-term such that $Dvars(H) = \{N_1, ..., N_m\}$. If $t \in T_\Sigma(\mathcal{X})$ results from $H[I]$ via some sequence of unfoldings with some sequence of unfolding renamings, we write $H[I] \downarrow = t$, and say $H$* generates $t$.

*The* language generated by $H$, *written $L(H)$, is the set of all terms for which there exists a full instantiation $[I]$ of $H$ such that $H[I] \downarrow = t$. The class of all languages generated by RTBs is called $\mathcal{L}(RTB)$.*

*Finally $H[\leq n] \downarrow = \{H[I] \downarrow \mid [I] \in [\leq n]\}$.*

Note that $H[I]\downarrow$ is unique up to variable renaming, and that in particular whether all $N$-unfoldings precede all $M$-unfoldings, or v.v., or whether they are interleaved, makes no difference to the resulting $H[I]\downarrow$.

**Example 3** *We demonstrate unfolding by generating $H[I]\downarrow$ from a fully instantiated RTB $H[I]$.*

*Let $H = \Phi_N(f(x, \diamond_N), \Phi_M(g(\diamond_M), y))$ and $[I] = [N \leftarrow 2, M \leftarrow 1]$. Then $H[I]$ unfolds as follows:*

$$\Phi_N(f(x, \diamond_N), \Phi_M(g(\diamond_M), y))[N \leftarrow 2, M \leftarrow 1]$$
$$\leadsto f(x_1, \Phi_N(f(x, \diamond_N), \Phi_M(g(\diamond_M), y)))[N \leftarrow 1, M \leftarrow 1]$$
$$\leadsto f(x_1, f(x_2, \Phi_N(f(x, \diamond_N), \Phi_M(g(\diamond_M), y))))[N \leftarrow 0, M \leftarrow 1]$$
$$\leadsto f(x_1, f(x_2, \Phi_M(g(\diamond_M), y)))[M \leftarrow 1]$$
$$\leadsto f(x_1, f(x_2, g(\Phi_M(g(\diamond_M), y))))[M \leftarrow 0]$$
$$\leadsto f(x_1, f(x_2, g(y))) = H[I]\downarrow$$

*Here the unfolding renaming $\sigma = \{x\sigma = x_1\}$ was used at the first unfolding, and $\theta = \{x\theta = x_2\}$ at the second. Subsequent unfoldings either do not use a pattern, or use a pattern with no variables. Note that $y$ is not renamed at any unfolding as it does not appear in the pattern of any generator.*

**Note 2** *The way we have defined the language generated by $H$ means that $L(H)$ is closed under the application of variable renaming substitution. In particular this is consistent with our intention to use RTBs to generate sets of rewrite rules, because the equational theories implemented by two rewrite rule sets $R, R'$ are identical if every rule in $R$ can be obtained from a rule in $R'$ and v.v. by variable renaming.*

**Example 4** *Consider the signature $\Sigma = \{(f, 1), (g, 1), (h, 1)\}$.*
*Let*

$$H = \Phi_N(f(\diamond_N), \Phi_M(g(\diamond_M), y))$$

*and*

$$H' = \Phi_N(f(\diamond_N), \Phi_N(g(\diamond_N), y))$$

*Then $L(H) = \{f^n(g^m(y)) \mid m, n \in \mathcal{N}\}$ and $L(H') = \{f^n(g^n(y)) \mid n \in \mathcal{N}\}$, so $L(H') \subset L(H)$. This simple example gives some indication of the powerful expressiveness of RTBs with multiple occurrences of the same degree variable. In particular, many non-context-free languages may be generated by RTBs.*

## 2.5 Contexts and adjacency

**Definition 9** *The set of contexts in a RTB $H$ is equal to $Pos(H[\vec{0}]\downarrow)$.*

*The context of each subterm $H\!\mid_p$ of $H$ is written $Con(H\!\mid_p)$ and defined as follows. $Con(H) = \epsilon$. If $p = q.n$, where $n \in \mathcal{N}^+$ then we have three cases:*
*(i) $Con(H\!\mid_p) = Con(H\!\mid_q)$ if $n = 2$ and $H\!\mid_q$ is a generator;*
*(ii) $Con(H\!\mid_p) = Con(H\!\mid_q).n$ if (i) does not hold and $p, q$ are not positions in any pattern in $H$;*
*(iii) $Con(H\!\mid_p)$ is undefined otherwise.*

We will find it easier to refer to subterms of a RTB by their contexts rather than by their positions in $H$. This is because the case of two generators with the same context is particularly important for the proofs in the following sections.

**Example 5** *Consider a signature* $\Sigma = \{(g,1),(f,2),(h,1),(c,0)\}$.

$$H = \Phi_N(g(\diamond_N), f(c, g(g(\Phi_L(h(\diamond_L), \Phi_M(g(\diamond_M), c)))))))$$

*is a RTB over this signature. The context of the $N$-generator is $\epsilon$, while the other two generators have equal context, namely 2.1.1.*

The following rather technical section is necessary to define when the sequences of operators generated by the unfolding of a pair of generators $G, G'$ appear 'together' in all terms generated by the given RTB, i.e. the sequence generated by $G$ takes as its argument(s) the sequence generated by $G'$. Naively, this appears to be equivalent to the statement that $G'$ is the tail of $G$, but for the purposes of Section 2.6 this is not the case. The following example shows when we might take $G$ and $G'$ to be 'adjacent' in a non-obvious sense.

**Example 6** *Let $H$ be the RTB $\Phi_N(a(\diamond), \Phi_M(a(a(\diamond)), \Phi_L(a(\diamond), c)))$ over the obvious signature. In any term in $L(H)$, the occurrences of $a(...)$ generated by the three generators are indistinguishable. Thus in particular $L(H) = L(H')$ where $H' = \Phi_N(a(\diamond), \Phi_L(a(\diamond), \Phi_M(a(a(\diamond)), c)))$. We may loosely say that the $M$- and $L$- generators are 'exchangable' and so the $N$- and $L$-generators are 'adjacent', concepts which are formalized below.*

**Definition 10** *Let $H$ be a RTB, and let $G, G'$ be generators in $H$. Then we say $G, G'$ are naturally adjacent if $G'$ is exactly the tail of $G$, or vice versa.*

Our aim in this section is to define concepts of adjacency and exchangeability as follows. We wish to say $G, G'$ are exchangable if and only if swapping $Dvar(G)$ and $Dvar(G')$ and swapping $Pat(G)$ and $Pat(G')$ results in a RTB generating the same language as the original. Further, we want to say that $G, G''$ are adjacent exactly in the case that there exists $G'$ such that $G, G'$ are naturally adjacent, and $G', G''$ are exchangable. This is complicated by the simultaneous unfolding of RTBs (see Section 2.4.2) which rules out exchange in many cases.

**Definition 11** *Let $H$ be a RTB including distinct generators $G_1, ..., G_n, G'_1, ..., G'_n$ for some $n \geq 1$, such that each pair $G_i, G'_i$ are in the same context with (w.l.o.g.) $(\forall i : 1 \leq i \leq n)G_i \prec G'_i$.*

*Say $\{G_1, ..., G_n\}$ and $\{G'_1, ..., G'_n\}$ are exchangeable in $H$ iff either the result of exchanging $Pat(G_i)$ with $Pat(G'_i)$ and $Dvar(G_i)$ with $Dvar(G'_i)$ in $H$ (for every $i : 1 \leq i \leq n$) results in some $H\sigma$ where $\sigma$ is a variable renaming, or $(\forall i : 1 \leq i \leq n$ $\exists h_i, m_i, k_{i,0}, ..., k_{i,m_i}, M_0, ..., M_{m_i}, H')$ such that the following two conditions hold:*

- Structure Condition

$$G_i = G_{i,0} = \Phi_{M_{i,0}}((h_i[p/\diamond])^{k_{i,0}}, G_{i,1})$$

$$G_{i,j} = \Phi_{M_{i,j}}((h_i[p/\diamond])^{k_{i,j}}, G_{i,j+1}) \quad for\,all\ j : 1 \leq j < m_i$$

$$G'_i = G_{i,n} = \Phi_{M_{i,m_i}}((h_i[p/\diamond])^{k_{i,m_i}}, H')$$

- Variable Condition

  For all $i : 1 \leq i \leq n$ the following holds:

$$(\forall G'' \in Gens(H), \forall x \in X)$$
$$[Dvar(G'') = Dvar(G_i) \wedge x \in Pat(G'') \cap Pat(G_i)$$
$$\Downarrow$$
$$(\exists k, \exists p \in Pos(H))[1 \leq k \leq n \wedge H \mid_p = G'' = G_{k,0} \wedge$$
$$(\exists y, \sigma) Pat(G_{k,0})\sigma = Pat(G_{k,m_k}) \wedge Pat(G_{i,0})\sigma = Pat(G_{i,m_i}) \wedge x \to y \in \sigma]$$

Note that from the Definition it is decidable whether $\{G_1, ..., G_n\}, \{G'_1, ..., G'_n\}$ are exchangeable in $H$.

**Lemma 1** Let $H$ be a RTB with $G_1, G_n, G'_1, G'_n \in Gens(H)$ such that $(\forall i : 1 \leq i \leq n) H \mid_{p_i} = G_i \wedge H \mid_{q_i} = G'_i$. Define

$$H' = H[(\forall i : 1 \leq i \leq n)$$
$$p_i.1 \leftarrow Pat(G'_i),$$
$$p_i.3 \leftarrow Dvar(G'_i),$$
$$q_i.1 \leftarrow Pat(G_i),$$
$$q_i.3 \leftarrow Dvar(G_i)]$$

Then if $\{G_1, ..., G_n\}, \{G'_1, ..., G'_n\}$ are exchangeable, we have $L(H) = L(H')$.

The proof is not difficult, but requires a great deal of tedious checking through the conditions of Definition 11, and is omitted.

## 2.6 Aberrant generators

We wish to exclude from consideration three classes of RTBs whose structure is not optimal. In every case, given a RTB which falls into one of the classes below, we can effectively recognize that it belongs to the class in question and replace it with a better structured RTB *which generates the same language*. Thus we lose no expressive power by restricting ourselves in this way; the class of languages we consider is still $\mathcal{L}(RTB)$.

### 2.6.1 Verbosity

**Example 7** Let $\Sigma = \{(h, 2), (c, 0)\}$. Then

$$H = \Phi_N(h(x, h(y, h(z, \diamond))), c)$$

and

$$H' = \Phi_N(h(x, \diamond), \Phi_N(h(y, h(z, \diamond)), c))$$

are RTBs over $\Sigma$ which generate the same language:

$$L(H) = L(H') = \{h(x_1, h(x_2, ..., h(x_{3n}, c)...)) \mid n \in \mathcal{N}^+\} \cup \{c\}$$

Clearly we should prefer the form of $H$ to that of $H'$ in cases like Example 7.

**Definition 12** *Let $G_0 = \Phi_N(h_0, H_0)$ and $G_1 = \Phi_N(h_1, H_1)$ be adjacent generators in $H$. $G_0$ and $G_1$ are verbose if there exists a pattern $h_2$ such that $L(\Phi_N(h_0, \Phi_N(h_1, c))) = L(\Phi_N(h_2, c))$, where $c$ is an arbitrary constant.*

**Lemma 2** *Two $N$-generators $G_0, G_1$ in $H$, with patterns $h_0, h_1$ respectively, are verbose iff all of the following hold:*

- *$G_0, G_1$ are adjacent;*

- *$Vars(h_0) \cap Vars(h_1) = \phi$;*

- *for every $N$-generator $G' \in Gens(H) - \{G_0, G_1\}$,*
  *$(Vars(h_0) \cup Vars(h_1)) \cap Vars(G') = \phi$;*

- *there exists a pattern $h$ and there exist $k, k' \in \mathcal{N}^+$ such that*
  *$h_0 \simeq h^k$ and $h_1 \simeq h^{k'}$ where $\simeq$ is identity up to variable renaming.*

*If we replace $G_0, G_1$ by $G_2 = \Phi_N(h^{k+k'}, t)$, where $t$ is the tail of $G_1$ if $G_0 \prec G_1'$ and the tail of $G_0$ otherwise, we arrive at a RTB $H'$ with $L(H') = L(H)$.*

**Proof**

The 'if' direction is trivial, as is the proof that the language generated is unchanged under the given transformation.

The 'only if' direction is simple given the observation that

$$L(\Phi_N(h_0[p_0/\diamond], \Phi_N(h_1[p_1/\diamond], c))) = L(\Phi_N(h_2, c))$$
$$\Updownarrow$$
$$(\forall n \in \mathcal{N})h_0^n[Occ(\diamond, h_0) \leftarrow h_1^n[Occ(\diamond, h_1) \leftarrow c]] \simeq h_2^n[Occ(\diamond, h_2) \leftarrow c]$$

□

**Lemma 3** *It is decidable whether any two generators $G_0, G_1$ are verbose.*

**Proof**

We may assume $G_0, G_1$ are naturally adjacent. If not, either they are not adjacent and so are not verbose, or by Lemma 1 exchanges may be made to effectively reach a RTB in which generators with the desired heads and degree variables are adjacent. Now we simply test the decidable conditions in Lemma 2. □

Thus we have an effective method to replace a RTB with verbose generators with a RTB with no verbosity and which generates the same language.

## 2.6.2 Redundancy

We may assume we have no verbose generators in any of the RTBs we consider in this Section.

**Example 8** *Let $\Sigma = \{(h, 1), (c, 0)\}$. Then $H = \Phi_N(h(\diamond), c)$ generates the same language as $H' = \Phi_N(h(\diamond), \Phi_M(h(\diamond), c))$.*

Clearly in the example above $H$ is to be preferred to $H'$.

**Definition 13** *All $N$-generators in a RTB $H$ are defined to be* redundant *if $L(H) = L(H[N \leftarrow 0])$.*

The definition immediately gives us a method for replacing $H$ with a better structured RTB - simply replace every $N$-generator by its tail. Note that in Example 8 both the $M$- and $N$-generators in $H'$ can be considered redundant. Clearly it is not our intention to replace them both; replacement of generators by their tails is therefore done one degree variable at a time.

**Lemma 4** *All $N_0$-generators in $H$ are redundant iff there exist degree variables $N_1, N_2, ..., N_n$ where $n \geq 1$, such that there exist a bijection $\gamma$ between $N_0$- and $N_i$-generators $(1 \leq i \leq n)$ and a variable renaming substitution $\sigma$ satisfying the following conditions: $(\forall G, G')$*

- *$G$ is adjacent to $\gamma(G)$;*

- *$(\exists k_0, ..., k_n \in \mathcal{N}^+)[Dvar(\gamma(G)) = N_i \Rightarrow Pat(G) = (Pat(\gamma(G)))^{k_i}]$ where the same sequence of renaming substitutions $\sigma_{i,1}, ..., \sigma_{i,k_i}$ is used for the construction of every $Pat(\gamma(G))^{k_i}$ such that $Dvar(\gamma(G)) = N_i$;*

- *if $Dvar(G) = Dvar(G') = N_0$ and $Dvar(\gamma(G)) \neq Dvar(\gamma(G'))$ then $Vars(Pat(G)) \cap Vars(Pat(G')) = \emptyset$;*

- *if $Dvar(\gamma(G)) = Dvar(\gamma(G'))$ then one of the following holds:*

    1. *$\gamma(G) \prec G \Leftrightarrow \gamma(G') \prec G'$;*
    2. *$Vars(Pat(G)) \cap Vars(Pat(\gamma(G))) = \phi$;*
    3. *$Vars(Pat(G')) \cap Vars(Pat(\gamma(G'))) = \phi$.*

**Proof**
Clearly for any $H, N_0, N_1, ..., N_n$ satisfying the conditions, there are only redundant $N_0$-generators in $H$.

It remains to be shown that all redundant generators satisfy the condition. Suppose $L(H[N_0 \leftarrow 0]) = L(H)$, i.e. $N_0$ is redundant. For any context $p$ which is a context of an $N_0$-generator (call this an $N_0$-context), say with pattern $h$, there must be some means of generating every sequence $h^n$ in that context. Furthermore, this generation of $h^n$ must take place in such a way that every $h^n$ may appear in the context $p$ independently of the sequences generated by $M$-generators, where $M \neq N_0$. This is because $N_0$ is instantiated independently of all other degree variables. Thus (*) $n$ is independent of the instantiation of all degree variables which have generators in positions not adjacent to $N_0$-generators. Otherwise some coordination would arise in the language between the terms which appear in our chosen context $p$, and the terms which appear in some other context, and we would find that $L(H[N_0 \leftarrow 0]) \subset L(H)$, contrary to our assumption of the redundancy of the $N_0$-generators.

Yet the sequence $h^n$ must be generated somehow in the case $[N \leftarrow 0]$, so there exists a variable renaming $\sigma$ and there exists in every $N_0$-context some $N_i$-generator whose pattern is $h'$, where $h$ is the $N_0$ pattern in that context and $h \simeq (h')^k$. Furthermore the $N_0$- and $N_i$-generators are adjacent in every context, so that the position of the generated sequence $h^k$ is preserved w.r.t. the sequences generated by other generators, and from (*) no $N_i$-generators occur other than those adjacent to $N_0$-generators, and we have the required bijection. $\square$

**Lemma 5** *For any $H, N$ it is decidable whether all $N$-generators in $H$ are redundant.*

Proof is immediate based on the decidable conditions in Lemma 4.

### 2.6.3 Rotation

**Example 9** *Let $H = \Phi_N(a(b(\diamond_N)), a(c))$ and $H' = a(\Phi_N(b(a(\diamond_N)), c))$ be RTBs over the obvious signature. Clearly $L(H) = L(H')$. In this case there is no strong reason to prefer either form over the other, but we will opt for $H$ as the better formed RTB.*

**Definition 14** *Let $h[p/\diamond], h'[q/\diamond]$ be patterns such that $Vars(h) \cap Vars(h') = \phi$. Let $\sigma, \sigma'$ be variable renaming substitutions with $Vars(h) \subseteq Dom(\sigma) \cap Dom(\sigma')$. Consider the generator*

$$G = \Phi_N(h[p/h'[q/\diamond]], h\sigma'[p/H])$$

*where $H$ is an arbitrary RTB. Then we call*

$$H' = h\sigma[p \leftarrow \Phi_N(h'[q \leftarrow h[p/\diamond]], H)]$$

*a rotation (or a $< N, \sigma', \sigma, Vars(h) >$-rotation) of $G$, and say that $H'$ is rotated.*

Note that in the definition $G$ must be a generator. The case of rotations of arbitrary RTBs is harder to define as we have to consider variable renamings.

**Definition 15** *Let $H$ be an RTB with $p \neq \phi$ the set of all positions of $N$-generators in $H$. An RTB $H'$ is a rotation of $H$ iff $\exists V \subseteq X$ such that*

$$(\forall q)[[(\forall p' \in p)q \not\leq p'] \Rightarrow (Op(H \mid_q) = Op(H' \mid_q) \vee H \mid_q = H' \mid_q \in X - V]$$
$$\wedge$$
$$(\forall q \in p)[H' \mid_q \text{ is a } < N, \sigma', \sigma, V >\text{-rotation of } H \mid_q]$$
$$\wedge$$
$$(\forall x \in V) \; x \text{ occurs in } H' \text{ only inside patterns, if at all}$$

**Lemma 6** *1. If $H'$ is a rotation of $H$, then $L(H') = L(H)$.*

*2. For any $H'$ it is decidable whether $H'$ is rotated, and if so, a RTB $H$ such that $H'$ is a rotation of $H$ may be effectively constructed.*

Proof is immediate based on Definition 15.

Because we will need to have a degree of certainty about the positions (or contexts, see Section 3.3) of generators, we will exclude all RTBs which are rotations from consideration.

### 2.6.4   Simplifying the structure of RTBs

We have shown that in the three cases of rotated, redundant and verbose generators, we can effectively recognise the given condition, and effectively replace $H$ with a RTB generating the same language as $H$, but which does not have this defect. *From this point on we will assume that all the RTBs we encounter are free from rotation, redundancy and verbosity.*

# 3   Learning RTB languages from positive data

**Lemma 7** $\mathcal{L}(RTB)$ *forms an indexed recursive family based on a list of RTBs without verbosity, redundancy or rotation.*

#### Proof
Consider a signature $\Sigma$ in which for each of the countably many different possible arities $n$, there are countably many operator symbols with arity $n$. In particular there are distinguished operator symbols $\Phi$ with arity 3 and $\diamond$ with arity 0. Our variable set $\mathcal{X}$ has countably many first-order variables and (disjoint) countably many degree variables. It is a trivial matter to construct a Gödel numbering of all RTBs over $\Sigma$.

Clearly every possible RTB language is generated (up to renaming of operators and first-order variables) by some $H \in T_\Sigma(\mathcal{X})$, because for every recurrence-term definable in any signature, there exists a RTB in $T_\Sigma(\mathcal{X})$ which is identical up to renaming of operators and variables. Now the decidability conditions of Lemmas 3, 5 and 6 allow us to 'weed out' RTBs with verbosity, redundancy or rotation and construct a canonical list of RTBs without these defects.

Finally, membership of the languages defined by our recurrence-terms is uniformly decidable as follows. Given an index for some $H$, it is possible to effectively reconstruct $H$. It is shown in [CHK90] that membership of the language generated by a given RTB may be decided by a simple search strategy: all possible instantiations of that RTB are partially ordered in the obvious way ($[N \leftarrow n + 1, R]$ being a child of $[N \leftarrow n, R]$ for all $N$ and for all $n \in \mathcal{N}$) and the search for $t$ in any given branch of the ordering tree is abandoned when a term longer than $t$ is generated in that branch. $\square$

### 3.1   Failure of finite elasticity and finite thickness methods

The standard method of proving that an indexed recursive family of languages may be inductively learned from positive data is to show that the family has one of the two propertie of finite thickness [An80] and finite elasticity [Wr89] [MS90], of which the latter implie the former.

**Definition 16** *Let $\mathcal{C}$ be an indexed recursive family. $\mathcal{C}$ has* finite thickness *if, for all $i \in \mathcal{N}^+$, there exists a finite set $T_i \subseteq L_i$ such that*

$$(\forall j \in \mathcal{N}^+)[T_i \subseteq L_j \Rightarrow L_j \not\subseteq L_i]$$

*$\mathcal{C}$ has* infinite elasticity *if there exist two infinite sequences $A_0, A_1, \dots$ and $R_1, R_2, \dots$ where $(\forall i \in \mathcal{N}^+)R_i \in \mathcal{C}$ and*

$$(\forall k \in \mathcal{N}^+)[\{A_0, A_1, ..., A_{k-1}\} \subseteq R_k \wedge A_k \notin R_k]$$

$\mathcal{C}$ *has* finite elasticity *if it does not have infinite elasticity.*

It was shown in [Wr89] [MS90] that if $\mathcal{C}$ has finite elasticity then $\mathcal{C}$ is inferable in the limit from positive data.

**Lemma 8** $\mathcal{L}(RTB)$ *does not have finite elasticity, and* a fortiori $\mathcal{L}(RTB)$ *does not have finite thickness.*

**Proof**
Proof is by counterexample. Let

$$A_k = \underbrace{a(b(a(b(a(b...a(b(0))...))))}_{2k+2}$$

for all $k \in \mathcal{N}^+$ and let

$$R_k = L(\Phi_{N_1}(a(\diamond), \Phi_{N_2}(b(\diamond), \Phi_{N_3}(a(\diamond), ..., \Phi_{N_{2k}}(b(\diamond), 0)...))))$$

Then every $R_k$ is an RTB language, and for all $k$ we have

$$\{A_0, A_1, ..., A_{k-1}\} \subseteq R_k \text{ but } A_k \notin R_k$$

which suffices to prove the infinite elasticity of $\mathcal{L}(RTB)$ as required by Definition 16. □

We note in passing that $\{A_k \mid k \in \mathcal{N}\}$ is in fact an RTB language (although this is not required by Definition 16) and is generated by $\Phi_N(a(b(\diamond_N)), a(b(0)))$.

We further note that our proof uses (in our definition of the sequence $R_1, R_2, ...$) our ability to use arbitrarily many occurrences of $\Phi$ in a recurrence-term. If for any given $n \in \mathcal{N}$ we define $\mathcal{C}_n$ to be the indexed recursive family of all RTB languages generated by a RTB with no more than $n$ occurrences of $\Phi$, then $\mathcal{C}_n$ has finite elasticity and finite thickness.

## 3.2 Angluin's Theorem

The infinite elasticity of the indexed recursive family of RTB languages forces us to fall back on the weakest possible sufficient condition for learning from text, which is expressed in the following famous result of Angluin.

**Theorem 1** [An80]
Let $\mathcal{C} = L_1, L_2, ...$ *be an indexed recursive family, and let* $\mathcal{D} = D_1, D_2, ...$ *be an effective listing of all finite sets. Then* $\mathcal{C}$ *may be learned consistently and conservatively in the limit from text iff there exists a recursive function* $\rho$ *such that the following two conditions hold:*

- $(\forall i \in \mathcal{N}^+)D_{\rho(i)} \subseteq L_i$

- $(\forall i, j \in \mathcal{N}^+)[D_{\rho(i)} \subseteq L_j \subseteq L_i \Rightarrow L_j = L_i]$

The finite set $D_{\rho(i)}$ is often called a *tell-tale* for $L_i$ (and $\rho$ is called the tell-tale function for $\mathcal{C}$).

In subsequent sections we present a number of technical Lemmas useful for proving our main result, namely that $\mathcal{L}(RTB) \in LIM-TXT$.

Our proof method will be to construct a tell-tale function for $\mathcal{L}(RTB)$. From this point on, $H$ will be an arbitrary RTB without redundancy, rotation or verbosity. The Lemmas will generally take the form of proving that any $H'$ that has a certain relation to $H$ must have certain '$H$-like' properties. In sum, the Lemmas will have the result that any $H'$ which is potentially a counter-example to the tell-tale $T(H)$, i.e. $T(H) \subseteq L(H')$ and $L(H') \subseteq L(H)$, will have so many $H$-like properties that $H' \simeq H$, where $\simeq$ is an equivalence relation that preserves the language generated.

## 3.3 The role of $H[\vec{0}]$

We first state a number of facts concerning $H[\vec{0}]$.

**Lemma 9** (a) $(\forall [I] \neq [\vec{0}]) |H[I]\downarrow| > |H[\vec{0}]\downarrow|$
(b) $(\forall [I])H[I]\downarrow \trianglerighteq H[\vec{0}]\downarrow$
(c) $(\forall H')[H[\vec{0}]\downarrow \in L(H') \subseteq L(H)] \Rightarrow H'[\vec{0}]\downarrow = H[\vec{0}]\downarrow$

**Proof**
(a) and (b) are trivial, but we will prove (c) as it is a particularly useful result.
Suppose $H[\vec{0}]\downarrow \in L(H')$, then $H[\vec{0}]\downarrow = H[I]\downarrow$ for some $[I]$. If $[I] \neq [\vec{0}]$ then we have $H'[\vec{0}]\downarrow \notin L(H)$, as $|H'[\vec{0}]\downarrow| < |H[\vec{0}]\downarrow|$, contrary to (a). $\square$

Lemma 9 gives us our first useful information towards building a tell-tale for $L(H)$. It tells us that by putting $H[\vec{0}]$ in our tell-tale, those parts of any $t \in L(H)$ and $t' \in L(H')$ which are not the result of application of a pattern, must be identical.

## 3.4 Simulation between generators and size of tell-tales

In this section we define a function $f$ which takes an RTB and returns a positive integer $f(H)$, such that

$$T(H) = H[\leq f(H)]\downarrow$$

has all the right properties to be our tell-tale.

To see that this is non-trivial, consider the following example.

**Example 10** *Let* $\Sigma = \{(a,1),(b,1),(c,0)\}$ *be our signature.*

$$H = \Phi_N(a(\diamond_N), \Phi_N(b(\diamond_N), \Phi_M(a(b(\diamond_M)), c)))$$

*is a RTB generating the language* $\{a^n b^n (ab)^m(c) \mid n, m \in \mathcal{N}\}$. *Define a RTB*

$$H' = \Phi_N(a(b(\diamond_N), c))$$

*generating the language* $\{(ab)^n(c) \mid n \in \mathcal{N}\}$. *Clearly* $H[\vec{0}]\downarrow = H'[\vec{0}]\downarrow$ *and* $L(H') \subset L(H)$, *but note in particular that* $H[\leq 1]\downarrow \subset L(H')$, *proving that the bound* $[\leq 1]$ $((\forall H)f(H) = 1)$ *is not always sufficient for our tell-tale function.*

Clearly the problem in examples such as the one above is that certain generators in $H$ (in this case the $M$-generator) can 'simulate' the first $N$-unfolding corresponding to an instantiation $[N \leftarrow 1, R]$.

**Definition 17** *Define the* bounding function $f$ *on the size of tell-tales of RTBs as follows. If $H$ is an arbitrary RTB and $Dvars(H) = \{N_1, ..., N_m\}$ then define $f(H, N_i)$ to be the smallest positive integer $k_i$ such that there exists $[I] = [N_1 \leftarrow n_1, ..., N_m \leftarrow n_m]$ such that*

$$H[I]\downarrow \notin L(H[N_i \leftarrow 0]) \wedge (\forall j : 1 \leq j \leq m)n_j \leq k_i$$

*Then define $f(H) = max\{f(H, N_1), ..., f(H, N_m)\}$ and $T(H) = H[\leq f(H)]$.*

Note that by our non-redundancy assumption for all generators in $H$, $f(H, N_i)$ is always defined and may be found effectively by an exhaustive tree search method. Thus $f(H)$ is a recursive function.

**Note 3** *The key idea here is that if $T(H) \subseteq L(H')$, we have sufficient $N_i$ unfoldings that the sequence of operators produced by repetition of the $N_i$-patterns cannot be simulated by the $N_j$-patterns where $j \neq i$, which ensures the presence in every $N_i$-context in $H'$ of some generator which simulates the $N_i$-generator. By the other conditions on $L(H')$ it will then follow that $H' \simeq H$, where $\simeq$ is identity up to variable renaming.*

We now prove our main technical Lemma, after which the main result of the paper follows without difficulty.

**Lemma 10** *Let $G$ be a generator and $H'$ a RTB over a signature $\Sigma$ and variable set $\mathcal{X}$ such that $G, H'$ are free from redundancy, verbosity and rotation, and:*

- $G[\vec{0}]\downarrow \simeq H'[\vec{0}]\downarrow$;

- $L(H') \subseteq L(G)$;

- $T(G) \subseteq L(H')$.

*where $\simeq$ is identity up to variable renaming.*
*Then*

$$G \simeq H'$$

**Proof**
Proof is by induction on $n$, the number of generators in $G$.
*Base Step*
$n = 0$ Then $\{G\} \simeq \{ G[\vec{0}]\downarrow = L(G) = L(H') \simeq \{H'[\vec{0}]\downarrow\} \simeq \{H'\}$ as required.
*induction Step*
$n = j + 1$. Let $G = \Phi_N(h, H)$. Because $T(G) \subseteq L(H')$ by definition of $T(G)$ we have some $t \in L(H') - L(G[N \leftarrow 0])$. So we have

$$t_k = h^k[Occ(\diamond, h^k) \leftarrow H[N \leftarrow k, R]\downarrow] \in L(H')$$

some $k > 0$, some $[R]$, where the $N$-unfolding renamings $\sigma_1, ..., \sigma_k$ used in unfolding $H$ are identical to those used in constructing $h^k$ from $h$, by the simultaneous unfolding of $N$-generators.

**Sublemma 1** $H'$ *is a generator.*

**Proof**

Recall that we assume $G[\vec{0}] \downarrow = H'[\vec{0}] \downarrow$, while $t_k \in L(H')$, so the sequence of operators $h^k$ is produced by unfolding of the patterns of $H'$.

Suppose $Op(H'|_\epsilon) \neq \Phi$, i.e. we have $H' = s[(\forall i : 1 \leq i \leq l)p_i/G'_i]$, for some $s$ with $Op(s|_\epsilon) \neq \Phi$, where the $G'_i$ are the generators in $H'$ minimal under $\prec$ and the $p_i$ are their positions. Then $h = s\sigma[p_i/h'_i]$ where the $h'_i$ are patterns and $\sigma$ is a variable renaming substitution with $Vars(s) \in Dom(\sigma)$.

Then in order for $H'$ to produce each of the sequences $h^1, ..., h^k$ by unfolding, we must have $(\forall i : 1 \leq i \leq l)$ $Pat(G'_i) = h'_i[Occ(\diamond, h'_i) \leftarrow s[p_i \leftarrow \diamond]]$, Also the tail of each $G'_i$ must be of the form $s[p_i \leftarrow t]\sigma'$ (for some $t$ and where $\sigma'$ is a variable renaming substitution with $Vars(s) \in Dom(\sigma)$) in order to complete the sequence of operators which make up the 'kth' (innermost) $h$. These are exactly the requirements for $H'$ to be a $< N, \sigma', \sigma, Vars(s) >$-rotation, contrary to our assumption that $H'$ is free of rotations, and the Sublemma is proved. $\square$

**Sublemma 2** $Pat(G) \simeq Pat(H')$

**Proof**

Recall that we assume $Pat(G) = h$, and let $Pat(H') = h'$. Because we have $L(H') \subset L(G)$ we must be able to produce $(h')^k$, for any $k$, by unfoldings of $h$, which implies that $h' \simeq h^i$ for some $i \in \mathcal{N}^+$. However, also $h$ is produced by some number of unfoldings of $h'$, since $(\forall[R] \in [\leq 1])G[N \leftarrow 1, R] \downarrow \in T(H) \subseteq L(H')$, so the only possible value for $i$ is 1, and the Sublemma is proved.

The following apparently obvious fact actually requires quite a careful proof.

**Sublemma 3** *Let $H''$ be the tail of $H'$ and recall that $H$ is the tail of $G$. Then $L(H'') \subseteq L(H)$.*

**Proof**

Suppose we have $t = H''[Dvar(H') \leftarrow k, R] \downarrow \notin L(H)$ for some $k, [R]$ such that $|t|$ is minimal in $L(H'') - L(H)$. By the assumption $L(H') \subseteq L(G)$ we must have $t' = h^k[Occ(\diamond, h^k) \leftarrow t] \in L(G)$ where the same sequence of unfolding renamings is used in generating $h^k$ as is used in the $k$ $Dvar(H')$-unfoldings of $t$.

Now, recalling that $Dvar(G) = N$, $(\forall[R'])t' \neq G[N \leftarrow k, R'] \downarrow$, as otherwise we have $t \simeq H[N \leftarrow k, R'] \downarrow$. So we have $t \simeq G[N \leftarrow i, R'] \downarrow$ for some $R'$ and some $i > 0$ with $i \neq k$. Suppose w.l.o.g. that $k > i$ (the case $k < i$ is similar, with $G, H'$ exchanged). Then the $k$-fold repetition of the pattern $h$ in $t'$ means (by our non-rotation assumption) we must have

$$G = \Phi_N(h[p'/\diamond], \Phi_M(h', H_2))$$

where $(h')^{j'} = h$ for some sequence of variable renamings $\sigma_1, ..., \sigma_{j'}$ and $m = j' * (k - i)$ and $[R'] = [M \leftarrow m, ...]$, for some $m > 0$.

We may assume (*) that $Dvar(H'')$ and $Pat(H'')$ cannot be obtained from $Dvar(H)$ $Pat(H)$ by a variable renaming (otherwise find a position in $H''$ where this assumption holds - if none we have $G \simeq H'$ and we are done).

We have three cases, distinguished by the possible occurrences of $N$ elsewhere in $G$. We show that all three lead to a contradiction.

1. $N = M$. Then by Definition 12 the two adjacent $N$-generators in context $\epsilon$ in $G$ are verbose;

2. $N \neq M$ and for every context $p_j$ in $H_2$ in which an $N$-generator occurs, with pattern $h_j$ say, there is an adjacent $M'_j$-generator $G'_j$ say, some $M'_j$, which generates the 'missing' $k - i$ repetitions of the pattern $h_0$. Then we deduce the following about $M'_j$ and $G'_j$:

   - $(Pat(G'_j))^{k_{M'_j}} \simeq h_j$ for some $k_{M'_j} \in \mathcal{N}^+$ where $[M'_j \leftarrow m'_j] \in [R]$ and $m'_j = k_{M'_j} * (k - i)$;

   - no $M'_j$-generator occurs in $H_2$ except adjacent to some $N$-generator and with their patterns in the relation expressed on the line above. (Otherwise the argument of Case 3 applies, replacing $M$ by $M'_j$.)

   Now there exists exactly the kind of bijection between the $N$-generators and the $M, M'_0-, M'_1-, \ldots$ generators that proves the redundancy of all the $N$-generators, by the proof of Lemma 4;

3. $N \neq M$ and there exists a non-empty set of contexts $p_j$ in which a $M$-generator $G'_j$ say, occurs with no adjacent $N$-generator with a pattern of the form $h_j$ where $h_j^{k-i} = Pat(G'_j)^{j'}$. Similarly there exists a context $q$ in which an $N$-generator occurs (with pattern $g$, say) with no adjacent $M$-generator with a pattern from which $g$ can be generated. Now the independent instantiation of $N$ and $M$ will allow us to produce a contradiction.

   Consider $G[\vec{0}]\downarrow, G[M \leftarrow 1, \vec{0}]\downarrow, \ldots, G[M \leftarrow f(G, M), \vec{0}]\downarrow$, which by assumption is a sequence of terms in $L(H')$. Now in the context $p_j$ the sequence of operator repetitions $Pat(G'_j)^i$ (for $i = 1, \ldots, f(G, M)$) occurs. This can only be duplicated in $L(H'')$ by some generator(s), $G'''_j$ say, in context(s) $p_j$ with pattern(s) obtained from $Pat(G'_j)$ by variable renaming. Further, the degree variables of the $G'''_j$ are identical (say $M'$) and occur nowhere else but in this strict bijection with the $M$-generators (or by instantiating the $Dvar(G'''_j)$-generators differently we show $L(H') \not\subseteq L(G)$).

   Recall that we have $G[N \leftarrow i, M \leftarrow m, R_0]\downarrow \simeq H'[Dvar(H') \leftarrow k, R_1]\downarrow$, and $t = H[N \leftarrow i, M \leftarrow m, R_0]\downarrow \notin L(H'')$ some $R_0, R_1$, and $m, i > 0$. Now $s = H[N \leftarrow i, M \leftarrow 0, R_0]\downarrow \in L(H''[Dvar(H') \leftarrow k])$ (by the minimality of $t$). The instantiation of $Dvar(H')$ in $s$ must be unchanged from that used to generate $t$ because an $N$-generator appears in the context $q$ not adjacent to any $M$-generators that can generate its pattern $g$, and only the instantiation of $M$ has changed, so $s|_q$, like $t|_q$, embeds the sequence $g^k$. So $G[N \leftarrow i, M \leftarrow 0, R_0]\downarrow \in L(H'[Dvar(H') \leftarrow k])$, but this is impossible as $G$ begins with $i$ repetitions of $h$ while every term in $L(H'[Dvar(H') \leftarrow k])$ begins with $h^k$, while $k \neq i$.

The Sublemma is proved.

**Sublemma 4** *Let $H''$ be the tail of $H'$ and recall that $H$ is the tail of $G$. Then $H\sigma = H''$ where $\sigma = \{Dvar(G) \rightarrow Dvar(H'), \ldots\}$ is a variable renaming substitution.*

**Proof**

Clearly the three conditions of Lemma 10 apply to $H$ and $H''$ (using Sublemma 3 for the second condition) and $H, H''$ have fewer generators than $G, H'$ so we may apply the induction hypothesis to show that $H \simeq H''$. It only remains to show that the renaming $\sigma$ which is used maps $N$ to $Dvar(H')$ (or possibly $N \notin Dvars(H)$, in which case we extend $\sigma$ to $\sigma \cup \{N \rightarrow Dvar(H')\}$).

Suppose there exists some $q \in Pos(G)$ such that $G|_q = N$ and $H'|_q \neq Dvar(H')$. Then by a similar argument to that used in Case 3 of Sublemma 3, (say $H'|_q = M$) we can say that either

- $M$ occurs exactly once in $H'$. Then $L(H') \not\subseteq L(G)$, contrary to assumption, as $H'[M \leftarrow 1, \vec{0}]\downarrow \notin L(G)$;

- $M$ occurs more than once in $H'$. Then if $Occ(M, H') - Occ(N, G) = q'$ we have $G[N \leftarrow f(G, N), \vec{0}]\downarrow \notin L(H')$ contrary to assumption, as any instantiation of $H'$ which produces the correct sequence of operators $(Pat(G|_q))^{f(G,N)}$ in the contexts in $Occ(N, G)$ must also produce 'unwanted' sequences of operators in the contexts in $q'$.

The parallel case in which there exists some $q \in Pos(H)$ such that $H|_q \neq N$ and $H''|_q = Dvar(H')$ is proved similarly.

Sublemma 4 is proved and the renaming $\sigma$ in Sublemma 4 witnesses the proof of the Lemma. $\square$

**Lemma 11** *Lemma 10 still holds in the case that $G$ is replaced by an arbitrary RTB, $H$.*

**Proof**

Clearly the sequence of operators between $\epsilon$ and any constant leaf or occurrence of $\Phi$ minimal under $\prec$ must be identical in $H$ and $H'$. Also for any variable $x = H|_p$ where $p$ is outside all generators in $H$, we must have $H'|_p = y \in \mathcal{X}$ and $Occ(x, H, \Phi) = Occ(y, H', \Phi)$, for some $y$. Then for each generator of $H$, $H|_q$ say, minimal under $\prec$, we have $H|_q \sigma = H'|_q$, by Lemma 10.

Now it remains to show that the same $\sigma$ works in the case of every such generator. This is achieved by an argument similar to that used in the proof of Sublemma 4, and we omit the details. $\square$

**Lemma 12** *For arbitrary $H, H'$ (even allowing for redundancy, verbosity and rotation), if $T(H) \subseteq L(H') \subseteq L(H)$ then $L(H') = L(H)$.*

**Proof**

The Lemmas of Section 2.6 demonstrate that any counter-example to Lemma 12 proves the existence of a counter-example without redundancy, verbosity, or rotation. Then the result is immediate from Lemmas 9(c) and 11. $\square$

**Theorem 2** $\mathcal{L}(RTB)$ *may be learned from text in the limit by a consistent and conservative IIM.*

**Proof**

Lemma 12 proves the correctness of our tell-tale $T(H)$, for arbitrary $H$. Furthermore, $T(H)$ is computed recursively from $H$. So Angluin's Theorem (our Theorem 1) applies. $\square$

# 4 Impossibility of strong monotonic learning of RTB languages from positive data

In this section we prove the negative result that learning of RTB languages from positive data cannot be strong monotonic.

Of the various ways in which a learning process can be said to make 'increasingly good' guesses (see [LZ93] for some others), the following is the one which fits best with a term rewriting system. If a rewrite rule set is being learned while *simultaneously* a proof is being carried out with the latest guess provided by the inference procedure, strong monotonic learning implies that a proof carried out at an earlier stage of the inference procedure is sound at all later stages.

**Definition 18** [Ja91] [Wi91]

*An inductive inference machine $M$ learns an indexed family of recursive languages $C$ strong monotonically if $M$ learns $C$ and the sequence of hypotheses $G_1, G_2, ..., G_i, ...$ output by $M$ satisfies the condition*

$$(\forall i)L(G_i) \subseteq L(G_{i+1})$$

**Theorem 3** *The class of languages generated by basic recurrence-terms cannot be learned strong monotonically from positive data.*

**Proof**

Consider the language

$$L = \{\underbrace{a(b(a(b(...a(b(0))...))))}_{2i} \mid i \geq 1\}$$

generated by the RTB

$$\Phi_N(a(b(\Diamond)), a(b(0)))$$

over the obvious signature.

Suppose $M$ learns $L(RTB)$ from positive data, and suppose $M$ is fed the obvious text for $L$ which simply presents the terms of $L$ in increasing order of size. Then after some finite number $n$ of terms have been seen (call this part of the text $L_n$), $M$ must output as a hypothesis some RTB $H$ such that $L(H) = L$.

However

$$L_n = \{\underbrace{a(b(a(b(...a(b(0))...))))}_{2i} \mid n \geq i \geq 1\}$$

is also an initial part of a text for the RTB language $L'$ generated by

$$\Phi_{N_1}(a(\Diamond), \Phi_{N_2}(b(\Diamond), \Phi_{N_3}(a(\Diamond), ..., \Phi_{N_{2n-1}}(a(\Diamond), \Phi_{N_{2n}}(b(\Diamond), 0))...)))$$

and furthermore $L \not\subseteq L'$ because for example

$$\underbrace{a(b(a(b(...a(b(0))...))))}_{2n+2} \in L - L'$$

Thus $M$ cannot learn $L'$ strong monotonically from text. $\square$

**Note 4** *Our ability to use an arbitrary number of generators (degree variables) in defining our counterexample is a crucial point in the above proof. The class of languages generated by an RTB with no more than n generators (degree variables) for some fixed bound n is learnable strong monotonically from positive data. Comparison with Lemma 8 leads to interesting conjectures concerning the relationship between finite elasticity and strong monotonic learnability from text.*

# 5 Discussion and Future Work

## 5.1 Learning from text despite infinite elasticity

To the best of the author's knowledge, $\mathcal{L}(RTB)$ is the first class which does not have the property of finite elasticity to be proved to be inductively inferable from text. This is particularly remarkable when the intuitive reading of Definition 16 is considered: a class has finite elasticity if *every* IIM which works consistently and conservatively learns that class. Surely we should expect that there are many classes which are consistently, conservatively learnable for which at least *some* such strategies fail?

Naturally we would like to draw some general conclusions from our proof method, but unfortunately it seems to be deeply rooted in the particular attributes of RTBs. The role of $H[\vec{0}]$, while useful in directing the proof, and the existence of a term which is the 'base' of the language in the strong sense that it is embedded in all terms of the language, does not seem to be crucial. More to the point is the strong structural resemblance between RTBs $H, H'$ such that $L(H) \subseteq L(H')$.

## 5.2 Extending our results

In [Wa92], various classes of recurrence-terms were introduced which strictly improve upon the expressive power of RTBs. We would like to extend our results to include these classes. In the case of the simplest such modification, the class RTD, which allows greater control over the renaming of variables in unfoldings, our proof goes through essentially unaltered. More interesting are the classes RTC and RTP, which allow (respectively) a recurrence-term to make a choice between finitely many patterns at any given unfolding, and patterns which are recurrence-terms instead of merely first-order terms. Various sub-classes of RTPs are also defined. It is shown in [Wa92] that $\mathcal{L}(RTC) \subset \mathcal{L}(RTP)$. The class $\mathcal{L}(RTP)$ is of special interest, because RTPs generate various infinite sequences of rules which arise from divergent Knuth-Bendix Completion procedures running on subsets of equational theories in the semantics of the specification language LOTOS [ISO88].

One well-known class of languages can be characterized as a sub-class of $\mathcal{L}(RTC)$. The class of extended pattern languages [Sh82] (or pattern languages with erasing substitutions), $\mathcal{L}(EP)$ is generated by the sub-class of RTCs which have $n$-way atomic choice, defined as follows. On a signature $\Sigma = \{(a_1, 1), (a_2, 1), ..., (a_n, 1), (EOS, 0)\}$ an atomic pattern is any $a_i(\diamond)$. Thus on this sub-class of RTCs all generators have the same choice between patterns (written $a_1(\diamond)\|...\|a_n(\diamond)$) in the language of RTCs) and only the degree variables are significant. We note that $\mathcal{L}(EP) \natural \mathcal{L}(RTB)$. It is shown in [Wata] that $\mathcal{C}(EP)$ has infinite elasticity but can be inductively learned from text.

For the purpose of applications in term rewriting, characterization of those subclasses of RTBs which may be learned strong monotonically is of interest. This may allow us in turn to characterize some class of term rewriting systems, and hence equational theories, whose divergent cases of KBC can always be solved. An alternative approach, though one less related to our main concern of inductive learning, is to develop unification algorithms for recurrence-terms, a problem on which several researchers are working.

# 6 Conclusions

We have demonstrated the inductive inferability from text by a consistently and conservatively working IIM of the class of languages generated by basic recurrence-terms. This class has neither of the attributes of finite elasticity and finite thickness usually used to prove learnability from text. Recurrence-term languages are significant in the field of term rewriting and their inferability is useful in the solution of many cases of divergence of Knuth-Bendix completion.

**Acknowlegements**

The author thanks his colleagues at HTWK Leipzig for their interest and support during the research reported here. Special mention must be made of the invaluable help of Takeshi Shinohara (now at Kyushu Institute of Technology) who expertly guided the author through the literature on inductive learning.

# 7 References

[An80] D. Angluin, Inductive inference of formal languages from positive data, *Information and Control* 45, 117-135, 1980.

[AS83] D. Angluin, C.H. Smith, Inductive inference: theory and methods, *Computing Surveys* 15, 237-269, 1983.

[CHK90] H. Chen, J. Hsiang, H.-C. Kong, On finite representations of infinite sets of terms, in Proc. of the Second International Workshop on Typed and Conditional Rewrite Systems, Montreal 1990, *Lecture Notes in Computer Science* 516, 100-114, Springer-Verlag, 1990.

[De85] N. Dershowitz, Synthesis by completion, in *Proc. 9th International Joint Conference on Artificial Intelligence*, Los Angeles, CA, 1985.

[DP90] N. Dershowitz, E. Pinchover, Inductive synthesis of equational programs, in *Proc. of AIII-90*, 1990.

[Go67] E.M. Gold, Language identification in the limit, *Information and Control* 10, 447-474, 1967.

[ISO88] International Organisation for Standardisation, *Information processing systems - open systems interconnection - LOTOS - a formal description technique based on the temporal ordering of observational behaviour*, 1988.

[Ja91] K.P. Jantke, Monotonic and non-monotonic inductive inference, *New Generation Computing* 8, 349-360.

[KB70] D. Knuth, P. Bendix, Simple word problems in universal algebra, in J. Leech (Ed.), *Computational Problems in Abstract Algebra*, Pergamon Press, 1970.

[La89] St. Lange, Towards a set of inference rules for solving divergence in Knuth-Bendix completion, in K.P. Jantke (Ed.), Proc. Analogical and Inductive Inference '89, GDR, *Lecture Notes in Computer Science* 397, 304-316, Springer-Verlag, 1989.

[LZ93] St. Lange, T. Zeugmann, Monotonic versus non-monotonic language learning, in G. Brewka, K.P. Jantke and P. H Schmitt (Eds.), Proc. Second International Workshop on Nonmonotonic and Inductive Logics, Reinhardsbrunn 1991, *Lecture Notes in Artificial Intelligence*, 659, 254-269, Springer-Verlag, 1993.

[MS90] T. Motoki, T. Shinohara, Correct definition of finite elasticity, Technical Report RIFIS-TR-CS-29, Kyushu University, 1990.

[Sh82] T. Shinohara, Polynomial time inference of extended regular pattern languages, in Proc. RIMS Symposia on Software Science and Engineering, Kyoto, 1982, *Lecture Notes in Computer Science* 147, 115-127, Springer-Verlag, 1982.

[Sh91] T. Shinohara, Inductive inference of monotonic formal systems from positive data, *New Generation Computing* 8, 371-384, 1991.

[TJ89] M. Thomas, K.P. Jantke, Inductive inference for solving divergence in Knuth-Bendix completion, in K.P. Jantke (Ed.), Proc. Analogical and Inductive Inference '89, GDR, *Lecture Notes in Computer Science* 397, 288-303, Springer-Verlag, 1989.

[TW93] M. Thomas, P. Watson, Solving divergence in Knuth-Bendix completion by enriching signatures, *Theoretical Computer Science* 112, 145-185, 1993.

[Wa92] P. Watson, The expressive power of recurrence-terms, University of Glasgow, Department of Computing Science technical report FM 92-6, 1992.

[Wata] P.Watson, Inductive learning of extended pattern languages from text, to appear.

[Wi91] R. Wiehagen, A Thesis in inductive inference, in J. Dix, K.P. Jantke and P.H. Schmitt (Eds.), Proc. First International Workshop on Nonmonotonic and Inductive Logics, Karlsruhe 1990, *Lecture Notes in Artificial Intelligence*, 543, 184-207, Springer-Verlag, 1991.

[Wr89] K. Wright, Identification of unions of languages drawn from an identifiable class, Proc. 2nd Workshop Comput. Learning Theory, 328-333, 1989.

# Learning Formal Languages Based on Control Sets

Yuji Takada

Institute for Social Information Science (*ISIS*)

FUJITSU LABORATORIES LTD.

140 Miyamoto, Numazu, Shizuoka 410-03, JAPAN

## 1 Introduction

Formal language theory is one of the most useful and well-investigated theories in computer science; it is applied to various concepts in many areas such as software engineering and artificial intelligence. For example, in software engineering, context-free grammars are widely used to develop programming languages such as PASCAL. In syntactic pattern recognition, which is one of interesting fields of artificial intelligence, various types of grammars are used to analyze pictures [10]. In these areas, a systematic approach to the design of practical systems requires the use of procedures capable of finding grammars from given examples. This problem, traditionally referred to as the grammatical inference problem or the inductive inference problem and recently referred to as the computational learning problem, is a central issue because of its machine learning implications; its study leads us to basic methods for machine learning and automatic program synthesis. While the problem of learning regular languages are well investigated and many useful learning algorithms have been developed [6, 10, 13], only small number of results have been obtained so far for larger language classes. This is partially because most learning methods for regular languages are not directly applicable to other language classes.

In this paper, we provide a new learning method for some classes of formal languages. Our method is based on control sets on grammars, which regulate rewriting in grammars. We shall show that for some classes of grammars, with regular control sets, rewriting can be simulated by ones of grammars easier to identify than original grammars. Then for these classes, we examine a divide and conquer strategy; we divide the main learning problem into two subproblems, the problem of identifying those easier grammars and the problem of identifying regular control sets.

We first show a representation theorem for linear languages, which says that a linear language is generated by a minimal (in the sense of the number of nonterminals) labeled linear grammar together with a regular control set over the labels. The representation theorem implies that the problem of learning a linear grammar may be divided into the problem of learning a minimal labeled linear grammar and the problem of learning a regular control set over the labels. In general, this seems not to work well. One of its reasons is that we may not fix a minimal labeled linear grammar and a regular control set over the labels at the same time. We show that a minimal grammar can be fixed for any alphabet and that a regular control set can be fixed for a minimal grammar if the minimal grammar is unambiguous.

From these, we consider two subclasses of linear grammars, *even linear grammars* and *parenthesis linear grammars*. An even linear grammar is a linear grammar whose nonterminal productions are of the form $A \rightarrow uBv$ such that the length of the string $u$ is the same as the one of $v$. The problem of learning even linear languages is reduced to the problem of learning regular languages. In the sequel, together with efficient learning algorithms for deterministic finite automata, we have efficient learning algorithms for even linear languages. A parenthesis linear grammar is a linear grammar whose productions are of the form $A \rightarrow [x]$ where symbols [ and ] are not in $x$. For a parenthesis linear grammar, together with the fact that any parenthesis linear grammar is unambiguous, we have a unique regular control set over the labels of a minimal labeled grammar. Then we show an efficient learning method for minimal parenthesis linear grammars and show that if we have efficient learning algorithms for representations of regular languages then we also have efficient learning algorithms for parenthesis linear grammars. Hence, again together with efficient learning algorithms for deterministic finite automata, we have efficient learning algorithms for parenthesis linear grammars.

The same technique is also applicable to the problem of learning a certain type of parallel rewriting systems, called *equal matrix grammars*. We shall summarize the results on learning equal matrix grammars.

Our technique is more powerful than conventional ones in the sense of an iterative applicability; started from regular languages, by iteratively controlling grammars with languages in one class to yield languages in the next larger class, we may have a hierarchy for which our technique can be applied iteratively. In [23] and [22], we have shown some classes of linear grammars and equal matrix grammars for which this works well. This partially shows that regulated rewriting [7] such as control sets are one of promising way for the learning problem for formal languages.

# 2 Preliminaries

Let $\Sigma$ denote an alphabet and $\Sigma^*$ denote the set of all strings over $\Sigma$ including the null string $\lambda$. $lg(w)$ denotes the length of a string $w$. We denote by $w^R$ a mirror image of a string $w$, i.e., if $w = a_1 a_2 \ldots a_n$, then $w^R = a_n \ldots a_2 a_1$. A *language* over $\Sigma$ is a subset of $\Sigma^*$.

We denote a *nondeterministic finite automaton*, abbreviated NFA, $M$ by a 5-tuple $(K, \Sigma, \delta, q_0, F)$, where $K$ is a finite nonempty set of states, $\Sigma$ is a finite input alphabet, $\delta$ is a transition function from $K \times \Sigma$ to $2^K$, $q_0$ in $K$ is the initial state, and $F \subseteq K$ is the set of final states. The transition function $\delta$ can be extended to a function from $2^K \times \Sigma^*$ to $2^K$ in the usual way. The set accepted by $M$, denoted $L(M)$, is the set $L(M) = \{w \in \Sigma^* \mid \delta(q_0, w) \cap F \neq \emptyset\}$. A *deterministic finite automaton*, abbreviated DFA, is an NFA $M = (K, \Sigma, \delta, q_0, F)$ such that for any $q \in K$ and any $a \in \Sigma$, $\delta(q, a)$ is a singleton, that is, the set $\delta(q, a)$ consists of one element. In the sequel, we write $\delta(q, a) = q'$ instead of $\delta(q, a) = \{q'\}$. A subset $L$ of $\Sigma^*$ is called a *regular language* (*regular set*) over $\Sigma$ if and only if $L$ is accepted by an NFA.

A *linear grammar* $G$ over $\Sigma$ is a 4-tuple $(N, \Sigma, P, S)$. $N$ is a finite nonempty set of symbols called *nonterminals*. We assume $N \cap \Sigma = \emptyset$ and denote $N \cup \Sigma$ by $V$. $P$ is a finite nonempty set of *productions*; each production is of the form

$$A \to uBv \text{ or } A \to u,$$

where $A, B \in N$ and $u, v \in \Sigma^*$. $S$ is a special nonterminal called the *start symbol*.

Let $G = (N, \Sigma, P, S)$ be a linear grammar. We define the relation $\underset{G}{\Longrightarrow}$ between strings in $V^*$. For $x, y \in V^*$, $x \underset{G}{\Longrightarrow} y$ if and only if $x = uAv$, $y = uzv$, and $A \to z$ is a production in $P$ for some $u, v \in \Sigma^*$. Let $x_0, x_1, \ldots, x_n$ be strings in $V^*$. If

$$x_0 \underset{G}{\Longrightarrow} x_1, \ x_1 \underset{G}{\Longrightarrow} x_2, \ \ldots, \ x_{n-1} \underset{G}{\Longrightarrow} x_n,$$

then we denote $x_0 \underset{G}{\overset{*}{\Longrightarrow}} x_n$, which is called a *derivation* from $x_0$ to $x_n$ in $G$.

The *language generated by* $G$, denoted $L(G)$, is the set

$$L(G) \ = \ \{w \in \Sigma^* \,|\, S \underset{G}{\overset{*}{\Longrightarrow}} w\}.$$

A language $L$ is said to be *linear* if and only if there exists a linear grammar $G$ such that $L = L(G)$ holds.

# 3 Learning Models and Results on Regular Languages

In this section, we describe formal definitions of the identification in the limit and learning via queries, and summarize previous results on learning regular languages. In this paper, we mainly consider the *exact learning*, that is, learning algorithms that *exactly* identify the target class. Although we do not consider the approximate learning such as PAC-learning [25], some of our results may be developed under the approximate learning criterion.

Let $\mathbf{L}$ be a class of languages over a fixed alphabet $\Sigma$. A *class of representations for* $\mathbf{L}$ is a language $\mathbf{R}$ (over some alphabet $\Gamma$) such that

1. $\mathbf{R}$ is recursive,

2. each $r \in \mathbf{R}$ denotes a language $\Phi(r)$ in $\mathbf{L}$,

3. there exists an algorithm that on input of any element $e$ of $\Sigma^*$ and representation $r \in \mathbf{R}$, outputs *"yes"* if and only if $e \in \Phi(r)$, and outputs *"no"* if and only if $e \notin \Phi(r)$.

For example, the class of *DFAs* is a class of representations for regular languages.

The *size* of a representation $r$ is simply the length of the string $r$.

An *example* of a representation $r$ is a pair $(e, l)$ where $e \in \Sigma^*$, and $l =$ "+" if $e \in \Phi(r)$, and $l =$ "−" if $e \notin \Phi(r)$. An example $(e, +)$ is called *positive* and $(e, -)$ is called *negative*.

## 3.1 Identification in the Limit

We begin with the identification in the limit introduced by Gold [9]. A *presentation* of a given target representation $r$ in $\mathbf{R}$ is defined to be any infinite sequence of examples such that for every element $e \in \Phi(r)$, the example $(e, +)$ occurs at least once in the sequence, for every element $e \in \Sigma^* - \Phi(r)$, the example $(e, -)$ appears at least once in the sequence, and no other (that is, incorrectly labeled) examples appear in the sequence. A *positive presentation* of $r$ is the same as a presentation of $r$, except that the sequence contains all and *only* the positive examples of $r$.

In this model, a learning algorithm A is given as input an arbitrary presentation written on a read-only input tape. After reading each next example of the presentation, the algorithm A outputs a representation as a conjecture. The learning algorithm A is said to *identify* a representation $r$ *in the limit* if and only if on input of any presentation of $r$, the infinite sequence of representations in $\mathbf{R}$ output by A satisfies the following property: there exists a particular representation $r' \in \mathbf{R}$ such that for all sufficiently large $i$, the $i$-th output of A is $r'$, and furthermore, $\Phi(r') = \Phi(r)$. Thus the sequence of outputs of A must converge to a representation that describes the same language as the target representation. Note that the point of convergence may depend on the particular presentation. The class $\mathbf{R}$ of representations is said to be *learnable in the limit* if and only if there exists a learning algorithm A such that for any representation $r \in \mathbf{R}$, A identifies $r$ in the limit. The class $\mathbf{R}$ is said to be learnable in the limit *from positive examples only* if and only if there exists a learning algorithm that identifies every representation in $\mathbf{R}$ from any positive presentation.

Gold [9] has shown the basic learnability for the class of *DFAs*.

**Theorem 3.1 (Gold [9])** *The class of DFAs is learnable in the limit, and is not learnable in the limit from positive examples only.*

For the polynomial time identification in the limit, although several definitions have been considered up to now (see [13], for example), in this paper, we consider only the *polynomial update time*. The class $\mathbf{R}$ of representations is *learnable in the limit in polynomial time* if and only if there exists a learning algorithm A for $\mathbf{R}$ such that for any representation $r$ of $\mathbf{R}$ of size $n$ and for any presentation of $r$, the time used by the algorithm A between receiving the $i$-th example and outputting the $i$-th conjectured representation is at most $p(n, m_1 + \cdots + m_i)$, where $p$ is a polynomial of two variables and each $m_j$ is the length of the $j$-th example $(1 \leq j \leq i)$.

In contrast with Theorem 3.1, Angluin [3] has shown a subclass of *DFAs* polynomial time learnable in the limit from positive examples only. A *DFA* $M = (K, \Sigma, \delta, q_0, F)$ is said to be *reset-free* if and only if for no two distinct states $q_1$ and $q_2$ do there exist $a \in \Sigma$ and $q_3 \in K$ such that $\delta(q_1, a) = q_3 = \delta(q_2, a)$. A *zero-reversible finite automaton* is a *DFA* such that it has at most one final state and is reset-free.

**Theorem 3.2 (Angluin [3])** *The class of zero-reversible finite automata is polynomial time learnable in the limit from positive examples only.*

However, in the sense of Pitt [13], her learning algorithm does not run in polynomial time.

## 3.2 Learning via Queries

One of common learning methods for improving the computational efficiency is using various types of queries. In the above, we had no assumption on the source presenting examples. Here, we assume that there exists an ideal teacher who can answer questions of a learning algorithm and the learning algorithm gets information from the teacher. We also assume that the teacher always answers correctly; the teacher never makes any mistake. In this sense, the teacher acts as *an oracle* and the learning algorithm acts as an oracle Turing machine.

We consider the following types of queries for learning algorithms, where $r_*$ denotes a target representation that learning algorithms should learn:

1. *Membership queries.* A learning algorithm asks whether or not $e$ is in $\Phi(r_*)$ for any $e \in \Sigma^*$ and a teacher answers *yes* if $e \in \Phi(r_*)$ and *no* if $e \notin \Phi(r_*)$.

2. *Equivalence queries.* A learning algorithm asks whether or not $\Phi(r_*) = \Phi(r)$ for any representation $r \in \mathbf{R}$ and a teacher answers *yes* if $\Phi(r_*) = \Phi(r)$ and *no* otherwise. If the answer is *no*, the teacher also gives the learning algorithm an element $e \in (\Phi(r_*) - \Phi(r)) \cup (\Phi(r) - \Phi(r_*))$. This returned element is called a *counterexample*.

A learning algorithm $\mathbf{A}$ is said to *identify a representation $r$ via types of queries* $Qt_1, \ldots, Qt_n$ if and only if when $\mathbf{A}$ is run with an oracle (teacher) to answer queries on $\mathbf{R}$ whose types are one of $Qt_1, \ldots, Qt_n$, it outputs a representation $r'$ such that $\Phi(r') = \Phi(r)$ and halts. A class $\mathbf{R}$ of representations is said to be *learnable* via types of queries $Qt_1, \ldots, Qt_n$ if and only if there exists a learning algorithm that identifies any representation $r \in \mathbf{R}$ via types of queries $Qt_1, \ldots, Qt_n$.

For the polynomial time learning via queries, we request that not only is the total running time bounded, but the amount of time used at any point is polynomial in the size of counterexamples provided to that point. A class $\mathbf{R}$ of representations is said to be *learnable in polynomial time* via types of queries $Qt_1, \ldots, Qt_n$ if and only if there exists a learning algorithm that identifies any representation $r \in \mathbf{R}$ via types of queries $Qt_1, \ldots, Qt_n$ and, at any point during the run, the time used by the algorithm to that point is bounded by a polynomial $p(n, m)$, where $n$ is the size of $r$ and $m$ is the length of the longest counterexample returned by any query seen to that point in the run.

For the class of *DFAs*, Angluin [5] has shown the following positive result.

**Theorem 3.3 (Angluin [5])** *The class of DFAs is polynomial time learnable via equivalence queries and membership queries.*

As a corollary of this theorem, we have the following.

**Theorem 3.4 (Pitt [13])** *The class of DFAs is polynomial time learnable in the limit via membership queries (and an arbitrary presentation).*

Note that this polynomial time learnability is in the sense of [13].

By explicitly providing additional information concerning the target representation at the outset, we may also have an efficient learning algorithm. Angluin [2] has shown such an efficient learning algorithm for *DFAs*.

Let $M = (K, \Sigma, \delta, q_0, F)$ be a DFA. A *transition* of $M$ is a pair $(q, a)$ where $q \in K$ and $a \in \Sigma$. A transition $(q, a)$ of $M$ is *live* if there exist strings $u, v \in \Sigma^*$ such that $\delta(q_0, u) = q$ and $\delta(q, av) \in F$. We also say that the string $uav$ *exercises* the transition $(q, a)$. A *representative sample* for $M$ is a finite subset $R$ of $L(M)$ such that for any live transition $(q, a)$ of $M$ there exists $w \in R$ that exercises $(q, a)$.

**Theorem 3.5 (Angluin [2])** *The class of DFAs is polynomial time learnable from a representative sample and via membership queries.*

# 4    Control Sets on Linear Grammars

In this section, we show a representation theorem for linear languages. The theorem claims that a linear language is generated by a *minimal* labeled linear grammar with a *regular* control set over the labels, and relates the problem of learning linear languages to the problem of learning regular languages.

**Definition 4.1** A *labeled* linear grammar is a 5-tuple $\mathcal{G} = (N, \Sigma, P, S, \Pi)$ where $G = (N, \Sigma, P, S)$ is a linear grammar and $\Pi$ is a set of symbols (labels), each production being labeled by an element of $\Pi$ (i.e., a single valued map from $\Pi$ onto $P$ is assumed). A labeled production is denoted by $\pi : A \to z$.

For any labeled linear grammar $\mathcal{G} = (N, \Sigma, P, S, \Pi)$, we may say that $\mathcal{G}$ is a labeled linear grammar of the linear grammar $G = (N, \Sigma, P, S)$.

**Definition 4.2** A *minimal* (labeled) linear grammar is a (labeled) linear grammar that has only one nonterminal, that is, the start symbol.

Let $\mathcal{G} = (N, \Sigma, P, S, \Pi)$ be a labeled linear grammar.

**Definition 4.3** We write $x \xRightarrow[\mathcal{G}]{\pi} y$ to mean $y$ is derived from $x$ using the production $\pi$. Let $x_0, x_1, \ldots, x_n$ be strings over $N \cup \Sigma$. If

$$x_0 \xRightarrow[\mathcal{G}]{\pi_1} x_1, \; x_1 \xRightarrow[\mathcal{G}]{\pi_2} x_2, \; \ldots, \; x_{n-1} \xRightarrow[\mathcal{G}]{\pi_n} x_n,$$

then we denote $x_0 \xRightarrow[\mathcal{G}]{\alpha} x_n$, where $\alpha = \pi_1 \pi_2 \cdots \pi_n$, that is called a *derivation from* $x_0$ *to* $x_n$ *with the associate word* $\alpha$ in $\mathcal{G}$.

**Definition 4.4** A subset $C$ of $\Pi^*$ is called a *control set on* $\mathcal{G}$ and

$$L_C(\mathcal{G}) = \{w \in \Sigma^* \,|\, S \xRightarrow[\mathcal{G}]{\alpha} w, \, \alpha \in C\}$$

is called the *language generated by* $\mathcal{G}$ *with the control set* $C$.

**Definition 4.5** A *primitive grammar* of $\mathcal{G}$ is a minimal labeled linear grammar $\mathcal{G}^0 = (\{S^0\}, \Sigma, P^0, S^0, \Pi^0)$ such that $P^0 \supseteq \{\pi^0 : R(\pi, S^0) \,|\, \pi \in \Pi\}$, where $\pi^0 : R(\pi, S^0)$ denotes the production for which all occurrences of nonterminals in $\pi : A \to z$ are replaced by $S^0$.

Let $\mathcal{G} = (N, \Sigma, P, S, \Pi)$ be a labeled linear grammar and $\mathcal{G}^0 = (\{S^0\}, \Sigma, P^0, S^0, \Pi^0)$ be a primitive grammar of $\mathcal{G}$. Then we define a homomorphism $h$ from $\Pi^*$ to $\Pi^{0*}$ such that $h(\pi) = \pi^0$ if and only if $\pi^0 : R(\pi, S^0)$. We also define the NFA $M = (N \cup \{q_f\}, \Pi^0, \delta, S, \{q_f\})$ corresponding to $\mathcal{G}$, where $q_f \notin N$ and $\delta$ is defined as follows;

$$\delta(A, \pi^0) = \{B \mid \pi \in h^{-1}(\pi^0) \text{ and } \pi : A \to uBv\},$$
$$\delta(A, \pi^0) = \{q_f\} \quad \text{if for } \pi : A \to z, \pi \in h^{-1}(\pi^0) \text{ and } z \in \Sigma^*.$$

**Lemma 4.6** For any $w \in \Sigma^*$, any $A \in N$, and any $\alpha \in \Pi^*$, $A \overset{\alpha}{\underset{\mathcal{G}}{\Rightarrow}} w$ if and only if $S^0 \overset{h(\alpha)}{\underset{\mathcal{G}^0}{\Rightarrow}} w$ and $q_f \in \delta(A, h(\alpha))$.

*Proof.* We prove this lemma by an induction on the length of associate words. By definitions of $h$ and $\delta$, $A \overset{\pi}{\underset{\mathcal{G}}{\Rightarrow}} w$ if and only if $S^0 \overset{h(\pi)}{\underset{\mathcal{G}^0}{\Rightarrow}} w$ and $q_f \in \delta(A, h(\pi))$.

Inductively suppose that for any $\alpha \in \Pi^*$ such that $lg(\alpha) \le n$ the assertion holds. If $A \overset{\pi}{\underset{\mathcal{G}}{\Rightarrow}} uBv \overset{\alpha}{\underset{\mathcal{G}}{\Rightarrow}} uwv$, then $S^0 \overset{h(\alpha)}{\underset{\mathcal{G}^0}{\Rightarrow}} w$ and $q_f \in \delta(B, h(\alpha))$ by the inductive hypothesis. Since $\pi : A \to uBv$ is in $P$, we have $B \in \delta(A, h(\pi))$ by the definition of $\delta$. Hence $S^0 \overset{h(\pi)}{\underset{\mathcal{G}^0}{\Rightarrow}} uS^0v \overset{h(\alpha)}{\underset{\mathcal{G}^0}{\Rightarrow}} uwv$ and

$$q_f \in \delta(\delta(A, h(\pi)), h(\alpha)) = \delta(A, h(\pi)h(\alpha)) = \delta(A, h(\pi\alpha)).$$

Conversely, suppose that $S^0 \overset{\pi^0}{\underset{\mathcal{G}^0}{\Rightarrow}} uS^0v \overset{\alpha^0}{\underset{\mathcal{G}^0}{\Rightarrow}} uwv$, $B \in \delta(A, \pi^0)$, and $q_f \in \delta(B, \alpha^0)$. Then $B \overset{\alpha}{\underset{\mathcal{G}}{\Rightarrow}} w$ where $\alpha \in h^{-1}(\alpha^0)$ by the inductive hypothesis. By the definition of $\delta$, there exists $\pi : A \to uBv$ in $P$ and $\pi \in h^{-1}(\pi^0)$, therefore $A \overset{\pi\alpha}{\underset{\mathcal{G}}{\Rightarrow}} uwv$. $\square$

**Lemma 4.7** For any linear language $L$, there exist a minimal labeled linear grammar $\mathcal{G}^0$ and a regular control set $C$ on $\mathcal{G}^0$ such that $L = L_C(\mathcal{G}^0)$ holds.

*Proof.* Let $\mathcal{G} = (N, \Sigma, P, S, \Pi)$ be a labeled linear grammar that generates $L$ and $\mathcal{G}^0 = (\{S^0\}, \Sigma, P^0, S^0, \Pi^0)$ be a minimal labeled linear grammar such that $P^0 = \{\pi^0 : R(\pi, S^0) \mid \pi \in \Pi\}$. Then $\mathcal{G}^0$ is a primitive grammar of $\mathcal{G}$. Let $h$ be a homomorphism from $\Pi^*$ to $\Pi^{0*}$ and $M = (N \cup \{q_f\}, \Pi^0, \delta, S, \{q_f\})$ be the NFA corresponding to $G$ defined in the above way. By Lemma 4.6, for any $w \in \Sigma^*$, $S \overset{\alpha}{\underset{\mathcal{G}}{\Rightarrow}} w$ if and only if $S^0 \overset{h(\alpha)}{\underset{\mathcal{G}^0}{\Rightarrow}} w$ and $q_f \in \delta(S, h(\alpha))$. Hence, for the regular control set $C = L(M)$, $L = L_C(\mathcal{G}^0)$ holds. $\square$

We can also show the converse of Lemma 4.7.

**Lemma 4.8** Let $\mathcal{G}^0$ be a minimal labeled linear grammar and $C$ be a regular control set on $\mathcal{G}^0$. Then $L = L_C(\mathcal{G}^0)$ is a linear language.

*Proof.* Let $\mathcal{G}^0 = (\{S^0\}, \Sigma, P^0, S^0, \Pi^0)$ be a minimal labeled linear grammar and $M = (K, \Pi^0, \delta, q_0, F)$ be an NFA that accepts $C$. From $\mathcal{G}^0$ and $M$, we can define a labeled linear grammar $\mathcal{G} = (K, \Sigma, P, q_0, \Pi)$ and a homomorphism $h$ from $\Pi^*$ to $\Pi^{0*}$ as follows.

1. If $\delta(q_i, \pi^0) \ni q_j$ and $\pi^0 : S^0 \to uS^0v$, then $\pi : q_i \to uq_jv$ is in $P$ and $h(\pi) = \pi^0$.

2. If $\delta(q, \pi^0) \cap F \neq \emptyset$ and $\pi^0 : S^0 \to w$ where $w$ is in $\Sigma^*$, then $\pi : q \to w$ is in $P$ and $h(\pi) = \pi^0$,

By an argument similar to the proof of Lemma 4.7, it is easy to verify that for any $w \in \Sigma^*$, $S^0 \overset{\alpha^0}{\underset{\mathcal{G}^0}{\Longrightarrow}} w$ and $\delta(q_0, \alpha^0) \cap F \neq \emptyset$ if and only if $q_0 \overset{\alpha}{\underset{\mathcal{G}}{\Longrightarrow}} w$ where $\alpha \in h^{-1}(\alpha^0)$. Hence, $L = L_C(\mathcal{G}^0) = L(\mathcal{G})$ is a linear language. $\square$

Combining Lemmas 4.7 and 4.8, we have the following representation theorem for linear languages.

**Theorem 4.9 (Representation theorem)** *For any language $L$, $L$ is a linear language if and only if there exist a minimal labeled linear grammar $\mathcal{G}^0$ and a regular control set $C$ on $\mathcal{G}^0$ such that $L = L_C(\mathcal{G}^0)$ holds.*

From Theorem 4.9, we can define a linear language in terms of a minimal labeled linear grammar and a regular control set on it.

**Definition 4.10** Let $L$ be a linear language. A *skeleton* of $L$ is a minimal labeled linear grammar $\mathcal{G}^0$ such that there exists a regular control set $C$ on $\mathcal{G}^0$ with which $\mathcal{G}^0$ generates $L$.

By Theorem 4.9, for any linear language $L$, there exists a skeleton of $L$, that is, a primitive grammar of a labeled linear grammar $\mathcal{G}$ that generates $L$ is a skeleton of $L$.

Let $\mathcal{G} = (N, \Sigma, P, S, \Pi)$ be a labeled linear grammar. A *transition of $\mathcal{G}$* is a pair $(A, \pi)$ where $A \in N$ and $\pi \in \Pi$. A transition $(A, \pi)$ of $\mathcal{G}$ is *live* if there exists a string $w \in \Sigma^*$ such that $S \overset{\alpha\pi\beta}{\underset{\mathcal{G}}{\Longrightarrow}} w$. We also say that the string $w$ *exercises* the transition $(A, \pi)$.

**Definition 4.11** A *representative sample* for $\mathcal{G}$ is a finite subset $R$ of $L(\mathcal{G})$ such that for any live transition $(A, \pi)$ of $\mathcal{G}$ there exists $w \in R$ that exercises $(A, \pi)$.

Let $R$ be a representative sample for $\mathcal{G}$ and $\mathcal{G}^0$ be a primitive grammar of $\mathcal{G}$. Then it is easy to see that the set $A(R) = \{\alpha^0 \mid S^0 \overset{\alpha^0}{\underset{\mathcal{G}^0}{\Longrightarrow}} w, \ w \in R\}$ is a representative sample for the *DFA $M$* corresponding to $\mathcal{G}$ in the sense of Theorem 4.9.

# 5 Learning Method Based on Control Sets

For the problem of learning linear grammars, the representation theorem (Theorem 4.9) implies that a linear grammar can be identified by identifying a minimal labeled linear grammar and a regular control set on it. From this, we try to use a divide and conquer strategy; we divide the problem of learning linear grammars into two subproblems, the problem of learning minimal linear grammars and the problem of learning regular control sets on them, solve these two subproblems, and check whether we can conquer the main problem by combining two solutions. In this section, we consider the problem of learning linear grammars according to this strategy.

According to our strategy, a learning algorithm for linear grammars may have the following two parts;

1. a learning algorithm for minimal grammars, that identifies a skeleton of an unknown linear language, and

2. a learning algorithm for regular control sets, that identifies a regular control set on the skeleton.

Learning methods for regular languages may be used for the second part.

In learning models under our consideration, a learning algorithm (1) gets strings as examples, (2) outputs strings to make queries, especially membership queries, and (3) outputs representations as conjectures. Then, in order to construct a learning algorithm for linear grammars by combining those two parts, the following three auxiliary tasks are necessary;

- converting a string to associate words by parsing in a skeleton $\mathcal{G}^0$,

- converting an associate word to a string by generating in $\mathcal{G}^0$, and

- constructing a linear grammar from $\mathcal{G}^0$ and a representation of a regular control set.

These tasks are processed by the *front-end processing algorithm*.

Since a skeleton is not always unambiguous, more than one associate words may be converted from a string, and therefore, a method for conversion from strings to associate words and its efficiency seem to depend on skeletons. An algorithm generating strings from associate words may be implemented in an obvious way and its time complexity may be bounded by a polynomial in the length of an input associate word and the size of a skeleton. We have shown the conversion of *NFAs* to linear grammars in the proof of Lemma 4.8. It is easy to verify that it takes time polynomial of the size of an *NFA* and the size of a skeleton. Since any regular expression and any regular grammar can be converted to an *NFA* in polynomial time in the size of each representation and since a *DFA* is a special case of an *NFA*, converting a representation of a regular language to a linear grammar takes time polynomial of the size of the representation of the regular language and the size of a skeleton.

Consequently, a learning algorithm for linear grammars may consist of three parts, a learning algorithm for minimal grammars, a learning algorithm for regular control sets, and the front-end processing algorithm. A configuration of a learning algorithm is illustrated in Figure 1.

In general, for each linear language $L$, there exist more than one skeletons of $L$. However, we first show that for any alphabet $\Sigma$, there exists a minimal labeled linear grammar *fixed for* $\Sigma$ that is a skeleton of any linear language over $\Sigma$. This implies that a linear grammar can be identified by identifying a regular control set on a fixed skeleton, that is, a learning algorithm may not have to consider the subproblem of learning minimal linear grammars.

**Definition 5.1** Let $\mathbf{L}$ be a class of linear languages over an alphabet $\Sigma$. A minimal labeled linear grammar $\mathcal{G}^0$ is said to be *universal* for $\mathbf{L}$ if and only if for any linear language $L$ in $\mathbf{L}$, $\mathcal{G}^0$ is a skeleton of $L$.

As described in the above, for any alphabet $\Sigma$, if there exists a universal grammar then we may not have to consider the subproblem of learning minimal linear grammars. Now we show that for any alphabet $\Sigma$ there exists a universal labeled linear grammar.

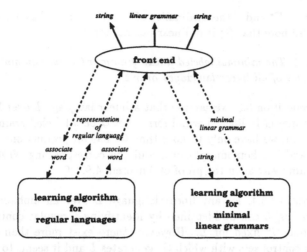

Figure 1: A configuration of a learning algorithm for linear grammars

**Definition 5.2** A linear grammar $G$ is said to be *in linear normal form* if and only if every production of $G$ is of the form

$$S \to \lambda, A \to aB, \ A \to Ba, \ \text{or} \ A \to a$$

where $S$ is the start symbol, $A$ and $B$ are nonterminals, and $a \in \Sigma$.

**Proposition 5.3** *For any linear language $L$, there exists a linear grammar $G$ in linear normal form that generates $L$.*

*Proof.* Without loss of generality, we may assume that any linear language is generated by a linear grammar $G$ that has no production of the form $A \to B$ and has no production of the form $A \to \lambda$ if $\lambda \notin L$. If $\lambda \in L$ then we assume that $G$ has the production $S \to \lambda$, where $S$ is the start symbol.

Let $G' = (N', \Sigma, P', S)$ be a linear grammar that generates $L$. We construct a linear grammar $G = (N, \Sigma, P, S)$ in linear normal form from $G'$ as follows; every nonterminal of $G'$ is in $N$ and each production of the form $A \to aB$, $A \to Ba$, or $A \to a$ in $P'$ is in $P$. If a production of the form $A \to a_1 a_2 \ldots a_k$ $(k \geq 2)$ is in $P'$, then we introduce new nonterminals $C_1, C_2, \ldots, C_{k-1}$ into $N$ and new productions $A \to a_1 C_1$, $C_1 \to a_2 C_2, \ldots, C_{k-1} \to a_k$ into $P$. If a production of the form $A \to a_1 a_2 \ldots a_i B b_1 b_2 \ldots b_j$ is in $P'$, where $i \geq 2$ and $j \geq 0$, or $i \geq 0$ and $j \geq 2$, then we introduce new nonterminals $C_1, C_2, \ldots, C_{i+j-1}$ into $N$ and new productions $A \to a_1 C_1$, $C_1 \to a_2 C_2$, ..., $C_{i-1} \to a_i C_i$, $C_i \to C_{i+1} b_1$, $C_{i+1} \to C_{i+2} b_2$, ..., $C_{i+j-1} \to B b_j$ into $P$. It is easily seen that $S \overset{*}{\underset{G'}{\Rightarrow}} w$ if and only if $S \overset{*}{\underset{G}{\Rightarrow}} w$. Hence, $L(G') = L(G)$. $\square$

Let $\mathcal{G}^u = (\{S^u\}, \Sigma, P^u, S^u, \Pi^u)$ be a minimal labeled linear grammar, where $P^u$ consists of the following productions;

$$
\begin{aligned}
P^u \quad = \quad & \{\pi_L : S^u \to a S^u, \,|\, a \in \Sigma\} \\
\cup \ & \{\pi_R : S^u \to S^u a \,|\, a \in \Sigma\} \\
\cup \ & \{\pi_T : S^u \to a \,|\, a \in \Sigma\} \\
\cup \ & \{\pi_\lambda : S^u \to \lambda\}.
\end{aligned}
$$

Note that $L(\mathcal{G}^u) = \Sigma^*$ and if the cardinality of $\Sigma$ is $m$ then $\mathcal{G}^u$ has $3m + 1$ number of productions. Also note that $\mathcal{G}^u$ is in linear normal form.

**Proposition 5.4** *The minimal labeled linear grammar $\mathcal{G}^u$ over an alphabet $\Sigma$ is universal for the class of all linear languages over $\Sigma$.*

*Proof.* By Proposition 5.3, we assume that a linear language $L$ over $\Sigma$ is generated by a linear grammar $G$ in linear normal form. Let $\mathcal{G}$ be a labeled grammar of $G$. To prove this theorem, we have only to note that $\mathcal{G}^u$ has all productions of a primitive grammar of $\mathcal{G}$ and the homomorphism $h$ and the corresponding NFA to $\mathcal{G}$ can be defined in the same way as in the proof of Theorem 4.9. $\square$

From Proposition 5.4, for any linear language $L$ over an alphabet $\Sigma$, a linear grammar generating $L$ can be identified by identifying a regular control set on the universal grammar $\mathcal{G}^u$ fixed for $\Sigma$. However, there exist more than one (possibly infinite) regular control sets with which $\mathcal{G}^u$ generates $L$ and it seems to be impossible to fix a regular control set on $G^u$ effectively; if we could effectively do so, then the equivalence problem for linear languages could be solvable, but in fact the problem is unsolvable [15]. This implies that in order to make it possible to use the divide and conquer strategy, a skeleton of $L$ should be identifiable and *at the same time*, a regular control on the skeleton can be fixed for $L$. We next show a condition on skeletons so that there exists a unique regular control set.

**Definition 5.5** Let $L$ be a linear language and $\mathcal{G}^0$ be a skeleton of $L$. Then the control set $C = \{\alpha^0 \mid S^0 \overset{\alpha^0}{\underset{\mathcal{G}^0}{\Longrightarrow}} w, w \in L\}$ is said to be *canonical* for $L$.

**Lemma 5.6** *Let $L$ be a linear language and $\mathcal{G}^0$ be a skeleton of $L$. If $\mathcal{G}^0$ is unambiguous, then the canonical control set $C$ is regular and unique, that is, for any two control sets $C$ and $C'$ on $\mathcal{G}^0$, $L = L_C(\mathcal{G}^0)$ and $L =_{C'} (\mathcal{G}^0)$ imply $C = C'$.*

*Proof.* To show that $C$ is unique, assume that $C'$ is another canonical control set such that $L = L_{C'}(\mathcal{G}^0)$ holds. Since $\mathcal{G}^0$ is unambiguous, for any string $w \in L$ the associate word $\alpha^0$ such that $S^0 \overset{\alpha^0}{\underset{\mathcal{G}^0}{\Longrightarrow}} w$ is unique. Then, since $C$ and $C'$ are canonical, $w \in L$ if and only if $\alpha^0 \in C$ if and only if $\alpha^0 \in C'$. Therefore, $C = C'$.

Let $G$ be a linear grammar that has no useless production. Let $\mathcal{G}$ be a labeled linear grammar of $G$ and $\mathcal{G}'$ is a primitive grammar of $\mathcal{G}$. By the assumption and Theorem 4.9, $\mathcal{G}'$ exists. Let $C''$ be a regular control set that the NFA corresponding to $\mathcal{G}$ accepts. Since the construction ensures that $C''$ is canonical, $C = C''$ and therefore $C$ is regular. This completes the proof. $\square$

Hence, for a linear language $L$, if an unambiguous skeleton $\mathcal{G}^0$ of $L$ is found, then a learning algorithm has only to identify the unique canonical regular control set $C$ on $\mathcal{G}^0$. In this case, for any string $w \in \Sigma^*$, if $S^0 \overset{\alpha^0}{\underset{\mathcal{G}^0}{\Longrightarrow}} w$, then $w \in L$ exactly means $\alpha^0 \in C$ and $w \notin L$ means $\alpha^0 \notin C$. If $\alpha^0 \in \Pi^{0*}$ is not an associate word for any derivation in $\mathcal{G}^0$, then $w \notin L$. This implies the following proposition.

**Proposition 5.7** *The problem of identifying a regular control set on an unambiguous minimal labeled linear grammar is reduced to the problem of identifying a regular language.*

In next two sections, we show two subclasses of linear languages for which unambiguous skeletons can be effectively found and therefore we have learning algorithms for them by our divide and conquer strategy.

# 6 Learning Even Linear Grammars

Even linear grammars have been proposed by Amar and Putzolu [1]. The class of even linear languages properly contains the class of regular languages and is properly contained in the class of linear languages.

Radhakrishnan and Nagaraja [14] have presented a learning algorithm for even linear grammars and its application to picture description languages. They have solved the problem in rather specific settings and have not shown the correctness and time complexity of their algorithm.

In this section, we show that the problem of learning even linear languages is reduced to the problem of learning regular languages. We give an algorithm that reduces the learning problem for even linear languages to the one for regular languages. With this, any algorithm for regular languages is applicable to learning even linear languages. Moreover, the correctness and time complexity of a learning algorithm for even linear languages are immediately obtained.

## 6.1 Even Linear Grammars

We begin with the formal definition of even linear grammars.

**Definition 6.1** An *even linear grammar* (abbreviated *ELG*) $G = (N, \Sigma, P, S)$ is a linear grammar such that each production in $P$ is of the form

$$A \to uBv \text{ or } A \to w,$$

where $A, B \in N$, $u, v, w \in \Sigma^*$, and $lg(u) = lg(v)$.

An even linear language is the language generated by an even linear grammar. As we described in the above, the class of even linear languages properly contains the class of regular languages and is properly contained in the class of linear languages.

**Definition 6.2** An *ELG* $G$ is said to be *in even linear normal form* if and only if every production of $G$ is of the form

$$A \to \lambda, A \to a, \text{ or } A \to aBb, \tag{1}$$

where $A$ and $B$ are nonterminals and $a, b \in \Sigma$.

**Proposition 6.3** *For any even linear language $L$, there exists an ELG $G$ in even linear normal form that generates $L$.*

*Proof.* Without loss of generality, we may assume that any even linear language is generated by an $ELG\ G_0 = (N_0, \Sigma, P_0, S)$ that has no production of the form $A \to B$.

Let $A \to axb$ be a production in $P_0$ not having the form (1), where $a, b \in \Sigma$, $x \in (N_0 \cup \Sigma)^*$. We define an $ELG\ G_1 = (N_1, \Sigma, P_1, S)$, where $N_1 = N_0 \cup \{C_1\}$ and $C_1$ is a new nonterminal not in $N_0$, and $P_1$ is obtained from $P_0$ with replacing $A \to axb$ by

$$A \to aC_1b \text{ and } C_1 \to x.$$

Clearly, $L(G_0) = L(G_1)$ and by a finite number of repetition of this procedure the proof is completed. □

## 6.2 Universal Grammars and Canonical Control Sets

Now we show that for the class of even linear languages over an alphabet there exists a universal $ELG$ and an even linear language in the class is generated by the universal $ELG$ with a unique regular control set.

Let $\mathcal{G}_e^u = (\{S^u\}, \Sigma, P^u, S^u, \Pi^u)$ be a minimal labeled $ELG$ such that $P^u$ consists of the following productions;

$$\begin{aligned} P^u = \quad & \{\pi_N^u : S^u \to aS^ub \,|\, a, b \in \Sigma\} \\ \cup \ & \{\pi_T^u : S^u \to a \,|\, a \in \Sigma\} \\ \cup \ & \{\pi_\lambda^u : S^u \to \lambda\}. \end{aligned}$$

Note that for a given alphabet $\Sigma$, $\mathcal{G}_e^u$ is uniquely determined and $L(\mathcal{G}_e^u) = \Sigma^*$. Note also that $\mathcal{G}_e^u$ is in even linear normal form and if the cardinality of $\Sigma$ is $k$ then $\mathcal{G}_e^u$ has $k^2 + k + 1$ number of productions.

**Theorem 6.4** *The minimal labeled ELG $\mathcal{G}_e^u$ over an alphabet $\Sigma$ is universal for the class of all even linear languages over $\Sigma$.*

*Proof.* By Proposition 6.3, we assume that an even linear language $L$ over $\Sigma$ can be generated by an $ELG\ G$ in even linear normal form. Let $\mathcal{G}$ be a labeled grammar of $G$. To prove this theorem, we have only to note that $\mathcal{G}_e^u$ has all productions of a primitive grammar of $\mathcal{G}$ and the homomorphism $h$ and the corresponding *NFA* to $\mathcal{G}$ can be defined in the same way as in the proof of Theorem 4.9. □

Thus, given an $ELG\ G$, we can effectively have an *NFA* that accepts a regular control set on the universal $ELG\ \mathcal{G}_e^u$, and vice versa.

On derivations in the universal $ELG\ \mathcal{G}_e^u$, we have the following lemma.

**Lemma 6.5** *For any alphabet $\Sigma$, the universal ELG $\mathcal{G}_e^u$ over $\Sigma$ is unambiguous.*

*Proof.* This lemma is proved by the induction on the length of strings in $\Sigma^*$. □

By Lemmas 5.6 and 6.5, we have the following lemma.

**Lemma 6.6** *For any even linear language $L$, the canonical control set $C$ such that $L = L_C(\mathcal{G}_e^u)$ is unique and regular.*

Hence we have the following theorem.

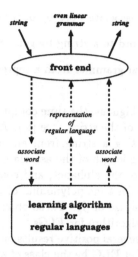

Figure 2: A configuration of a learning algorithm for even linear grammars

**Theorem 6.7** *For any even linear language L, there effectively exists a unique canonical regular control set C on $\mathcal{G}_e^u$ such that $L = L_C(\mathcal{G}_e^u)$ holds.*

From this theorem, we have the following corollaries, which show that the class of even linear languages has similar properties for regular languages.

**Corollary 6.8** *The class of even linear languages is closed under boolean operations.*

**Corollary 6.9** *The following problems are effectively solvable for even linear languages $L_1$ and $L_2$;*

1. $L_1 \subset L_2$,

2. $L_1 = L_2$.

## 6.3    Reduction to Learning Regular Languages

Theorem 6.7 implies that, to identify an *ELG*, a learning algorithm has only to identify its unique canonical regular control set on the universal grammar $\mathcal{G}_e^u$. Hence we have the following theorem.

**Theorem 6.10** *The problem of learning even linear languages is reduced to the problem of learning regular languages.*

*Proof.*    Since the universal grammar $\mathcal{G}_e^u$ is unambiguous, by Proposition 5.7, the theorem follows. □

To construct a learning algorithm for *ELGs*, we have only to prepare the front-end processing algorithm and a learning algorithm for regular languages. A configuration of a learning algorithm is illustrated in Figure 2.

As we mentioned in Section 5, the front-end processing algorithm executes the following three auxiliary tasks;

- converting a string to an associate word by parsing in a universal grammar $\mathcal{G}_e^u$,

- converting an associate word to a string by generating in $\mathcal{G}_e^u$, and

- constructing an even linear grammar from a representation of a regular control set.

We note that, since $\mathcal{G}_e^u$ is unambiguous, the time complexity of parsing a string in $\mathcal{G}_e^u$ is $O(n^2)$, where $n$ is the length of the string (see [8]). As we mentioned in Section 5, the time complexity of generating a string from an associate word in $\mathcal{G}_e^u$ may be bounded by a polynomial in the length of the associate word and the size of $\mathcal{G}_e^u$ that is bounded by the cardinality of the alphabet, and converting a representation of a regular language to an *ELG* takes time polynomial of the size of the representation of the regular language and the size of $\mathcal{G}_e^u$. These observations immediately give the time complexity of a learning algorithm for *ELGs*.

By Theorem 6.10, we have several positive results on learning *ELGs* together with the results on learning *DFAs*. Let **ELG** be the class of all *ELGs* in even linear normal form to which *DFAs* correspond in the sense of Theorem 4.9. Then by Theorem 6.7, **ELG** is a class of representations for the class of even linear languages. We consider the learning problems for the class **ELG**. We immediately have the followings by Theorems 3.3 and 3.4;

**Corollary 6.11** *The class* **ELG** *is polynomial time learnable via equivalence queries and membership queries.*

**Corollary 6.12** *The class* **ELG** *is polynomial time learnable in the limit via membership queries (and an arbitrary presentation).*

By Theorem 3.5, we also have

**Corollary 6.13** *The class* **ELG** *is polynomial time learnable from a representative sample and via membership queries.*

## 6.4   Learning Finite Automata with Output

A learning algorithm for *ELGs* can be used to learn finite automata with output. A finite automaton with output will be used to transduce a regular language to another regular language.

A finite automaton with output is a 7-tuple $M_o = (K, \Sigma, \Delta, \delta, \psi, q_0, F)$, where $K$, $\Sigma$, $\delta$, $q_0$ and $F$ are as in *NFAs*. $\Delta$ is a finite output alphabet and $\psi$ is a mapping from $K \times \Sigma$ to $\Delta$. The output of $M_o$ in response to the input $a_1 a_2 \ldots a_n$ is $\psi(q_0, a_1)\psi(q_1, a_2) \ldots \psi(q_{n-1}, a_n)$, where $q_0, q_1, \ldots, q_n$ is the sequence of states such that $\delta(q_{i-1}, a_i) = q_i$ for $1 \le i \le n$. We note that $M_o$ outputs $\lambda$ on input $\lambda$ and that $M_o$ preserves the length of an input into an output.

Let $M_o = (K, \Sigma, \Delta, \delta, \psi, q_0, F)$ be a finite automaton with output and $G = (K, \Sigma \cup \Delta \cup \{\#\}, P, q_0)$ be an *ELG* such that

1. if $\delta(q, a) = q'$ and $\psi(q, a) = a'$, then $q \to aq'a'$ is in $P$,

2. if $q \in F$, then $q \to \#$ is in $P$.

Then we have the following proposition.

**Proposition 6.14** *For any pair* $(w_i, w_o)$ *in* $\Sigma^* \times \Delta^*$, $\delta(q_0, w_i) \in F$ *and* $\psi(q_0, w_i) = w_o$ *if and only if* $w_i \# w_o^R \in L(G)$.

*Proof.* This is proved by the induction on the length of input-output strings. $\square$

Thus, using a learning algorithm for *ELGs*, a finite automaton with output can also be learned.

# 7 Learning Parenthesis Linear Grammars

The class of languages generated by parenthesis linear grammars, in principle, contains the class of regular languages and is properly contained in the class of linear languages. A parenthesis linear grammar displays derivations in corresponding strings. This implies that a learning algorithm may use supplemental information on derivations of grammars. In this section, we show that our divide and conquer strategy works well for parenthesis linear grammars.

Angluin [4] has presented a learning algorithm for $k$-bounded context-free grammars, where a context-free grammar is $k$-bounded if no production has more than $k$ occurrences of nonterminals in its right hand side (note that a linear grammar is a 1-bounded context-free grammar). If the set of nonterminals of an unknown grammar is given, her algorithm identifies the productions of the grammar. On the other hand, our method only requires structural information (parentheses) of an unknown grammar, then identifies nonterminals of the grammar. Sakakibara [16, 17] has applied learning methods for *DFAs* [3, 5] to tree automata, which are closely related to parenthesis context-free grammars. Although his algorithms are directly applicable to parenthesis linear grammars, our method is more general in the sense that *almost any* learning algorithm for regular languages is applicable to parenthesis linear grammars.

## 7.1 Parenthesis Linear Grammars and Control Sets

Let "[" and "]" be two special symbols not in any alphabet.

**Definition 7.1** Let $G = (N, \Sigma, P, S)$ be a linear grammar. The *parenthesis grammar* of $G$ is a linear grammar $[G] = (N, \Sigma \cup \{[,]\}, P', S)$, where $P'$ is obtained from $P$ by replacing every production $A \to x$ by $A \to [x]$.

A *parenthesis linear grammar*, abbreviated *PLG*, is a parenthesis grammar of a certain linear grammar. For any alphabet $\Sigma$, let $\Sigma_p$ denote the augmented alphabet $\Sigma \cup \{[,]\}$.

A parenthesis grammar $[G]$ is *backwards-deterministic* if and only if no two productions in $[G]$ have the same right hand side.

**Lemma 7.2 (McNaughton [12])** *A backwards-deterministic parenthesis context-free grammar is unambiguous.*

Then it is easy to verify that any minimal labeled *PLG* $[\mathcal{G}]^0$ is backwards-deterministic. Hence, by Lemma 5.6, we have the following.

**Lemma 7.3** *Let* $[\mathcal{G}]$ *be a labeled PLG and* $[\mathcal{G}]^0$ *be a primitive grammar of* $[\mathcal{G}]$. *Then the canonical control set* $C$ *is unique and regular.*

Hence, for a *PLG* $[G]$, if an unambiguous primitive grammar $[\mathcal{G}]^0$ of the labeled grammar of $[G]$ is found, then a learning algorithm has only to identify its unique canonical regular control set $C$ on $[\mathcal{G}]^0$.

## 7.2  Learning Based on Control Sets

A *PLG* in linear normal form is a parenthesis grammar of a linear grammar in linear normal form. In Section 5, we have shown that for any alphabet $\Sigma$, there exists a universal linear grammar (Proposition 5.4). Hence, by Proposition 5.7 and Lemma 7.3, we have the following.

**Proposition 7.4** *The problem of learning PLGs in linear normal form is reduced to the problem of learning regular languages.*

This implies that if information on derivations in linear grammars in linear normal form is available, then the learning problem for linear languages is reduced to the problem for regular languages.

A configuration of a learning algorithm for *PLG*s in linear normal form is the same as the one for *ELG*s illustrated in Figure 2; we have only to prepare the front-end processing algorithm and add it to an algorithm for regular languages. The time complexity of parsing a string in a universal grammar $[\mathcal{G}]^u$ is $O(n^2)$, where $n$ is the length of the string because $[\mathcal{G}]^u$ is unambiguous. The time complexity of generating a string from an associate word in $[\mathcal{G}]^u$ may be bounded by a polynomial in the length of the associate word and the cardinality of the alphabet, and converting a representation of a regular language to a *PLG* in linear normal form takes time polynomial of the size of the representation of the regular language and the size of $[\mathcal{G}]^u$.

Let **NPLG** be the class of all *PLG*s in linear normal form to which *DFA*s correspond in the sense of Theorem 4.9. Then by the representation theorem (Theorem 4.9) and Lemma 7.3, **NPLG** is a class of representations for the class of *PLG*s in linear normal form. We consider the learning problem for the class **NPLG**. We immediately have the followings by Theorems 3.3, 3.4 and 3.5.

**Corollary 7.5** *The class* **NPLG** *is polynomial time learnable via equivalence queries and membership queries.*

**Corollary 7.6** *The class* **NPLG** *is polynomial time learnable in the limit via membership queries (and an arbitrary presentation).*

**Corollary 7.7** *The class* **NPLG** *is polynomial time learnable from a representative sample and via membership queries.*

According to our divide and conquer strategy, a learning algorithm must identify a primitive grammar of a labeled *PLG* in the general case. We next show that for any labeled *PLG* $[\mathcal{G}]$, a primitive grammar of $[\mathcal{G}]$ is efficiently found from given examples.

Let $w$ be a string over the augmented alphabet $\Sigma_p$. Then the set $P(w)$ of labeled productions is defined in the following way (where $S^0$ is a nonterminal).

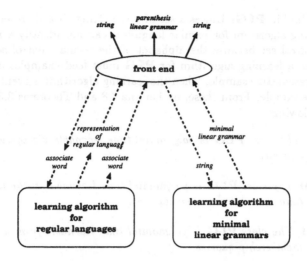

Figure 3: A configuration of a learning algorithm for parenthesis linear grammars

1. If there is no $w' \in \Sigma_p^*$ such that $w = [w']$ then $P(w) = \emptyset$.

2. Suppose that $w$ is a string such that $w = [w']$. If $w' \in \Sigma^*$ then $P(w) = \{\pi : S^0 \to w\}$. If for some strings $u, v \in \Sigma^*$ and $x \in \Sigma_p^*$, $w' = u[x]v$ and $P([x])$ is not empty then $P(w) = P([x]) \cup \{\pi : S^0 \to [uS^0v]\}$. Otherwise, $P(w)$ is empty.

For a set $W$ of strings over $\Sigma_p$, $P(W)$ denotes $\bigcup_{w \in W} P(w)$.

**Lemma 7.8** *If a set $W$ of strings over $\Sigma_p$ is a representative sample for a labeled PLG $[\mathcal{G}]$ then $[\mathcal{G}]^0 = (\{S^0\}, \Sigma_p, P(W), S^0, \Pi^0)$ is a primitive grammar of $[\mathcal{G}]$.*

*Proof.* For each production $\pi : A \to x$ of $[\mathcal{G}]$, if $w \in W$ exercises $(A, \pi)$ then the construction of $P(w)$ ensures that $P(w)$ has $\pi^0 : R(\pi, S^0)$. Since $W$ is a representative sample for $[\mathcal{G}]$, for any production $\pi$ of $[\mathcal{G}]$, there exists an element in $W$ that exercises $\pi$. Hence $[\mathcal{G}]^0$ is a primitive grammar of $[\mathcal{G}]$. $\square$

It is obvious from the construction that there exists an algorithm that constructs $P(w)$ from a given $w$ in polynomial time of the length of $w$. The cardinality of $P(w)$ is also bounded by a polynomial of the length of $w$.

Now we consider the method of learning PLGs using learning algorithms for regular languages. A configuration of a learning algorithm is illustrated in Figure 3. Let $[\mathcal{G}]^0$ be a minimal labeled PLG. The time complexity of parsing a string in $[\mathcal{G}]^0$ is $O(n^2)$, where $n$ is the length of the string because $[\mathcal{G}]^0$ is unambiguous. The time complexity of generating a string from an associate word in $[\mathcal{G}]^0$ is bounded by a polynomial in the length of the associate word and the size of $[\mathcal{G}]^0$, and converting a representation of a regular language to a PLG takes time polynomial of the size of the representation of the regular language and the size of $[\mathcal{G}]^0$.

Let **PLG** be the class of all PLGs to which DFAs correspond in the sense of Theorem 4.9. Then **PLG** is a class of representations for the class of PLGs by the representation theorem (Theorem 4.9) and Lemma 7.3. Let $[\mathcal{G}]$ be a labeled grammar of a *PLG* in **PLG**. Unless a set of given strings is a representative sample for $[\mathcal{G}]$, a learning algorithm for regular languages can not identify a representation of a regular control set because the alphabet of the regular control set is not fully supplied. Hence a learning algorithm for **PLG** must feed examples unless a set of strings is a representative sample. Then the learning algorithm is eventually supplied a representative sample. From these, by Lemma 7.8 and Theorems 3.3, 3.4 and 3.5, we have the followings.

**Corollary 7.9** *The class* **PLG** *is polynomial time learnable via equivalence queries and membership queries.*

**Corollary 7.10** *The class* **PLG** *is polynomial time learnable in the limit via membership queries (and an arbitrary presentation).*

**Corollary 7.11** *The class* **PLG** *is polynomial time learnable from a representative sample and via membership queries.*

## 7.3   Learning Generalized Sequential Machines

A learning algorithm for *PLG*s can be used to learn generalized sequential machines with structural information. A generalized sequential machine will be used to transduce tokens in one programming language to tokens in another programming language.

A *generalized sequential machine*, abbreviated *GSM*, is denoted by a 6-tuple $S_g = (K, \Sigma, \Delta, \delta, q_0, F)$, where K, $\Sigma$, and $\Delta$ are the states, input alphabet, and output alphabet, respectively, $\delta$ is a mapping from $K \times \Sigma$ to finite subsets of $K \times \Delta^*$, $q_0$ is the initial state, and $F$ is the set of final states.

We extend $\delta$ to a function from $K \times \Sigma^*$ to $K \times \Delta^*$ such that for all $q \in K$, $\delta(q, \lambda) = \{(q, \lambda)\}$ and $\delta(q, ua) = \{(p, w) \,|\, w = w_1 w_2$ and for some $p'$, $(p', w_1)$ is in $\delta(q, u)$ and $(p, w_2)$ is in $\delta(p', a)\}$ for all string $u \in \Sigma^*$ and all $a \in \Sigma$.

Any string in the set $\{u \in \Sigma^* \,|\, (p, v) \in \delta(q_0, u)$ and $p \in F\}$ is called an *input* of *GSM* $S_g$, and any string in the set $\{v \in \Delta^* \,|\, (p, v) \in \delta(q_0, u)$ and $p \in F\}$ called an *output* of $S_g$.

Let $S_g = (K, \Sigma, \Delta, \delta, q_0, F)$ be a *GSM*. We construct a linear grammar $G = (K, \Sigma \cup \Delta \cup \{\#\}, P, S)$ as follows, where "#" is a new symbol not in $\Sigma \cup \Delta$. If $\delta(q, a) \ni (q', w)$ then we introduce a production $q \to aq'w^R$ into $P$. For any state $q$ in $F$, we introduce the production $q \to \#$ into $P$.

**Proposition 7.12** *For any $w_1 \in \Sigma^*$ and $w_2 \in \Delta^*$, $\delta(q_0, w_1) \ni (q, w_2)$ and $q \in F$ if and only if $w_1 \# w_2^R \in L(G)$.*

*Proof.*   This is proved by the obvious induction on the length of strings. $\square$

We note that constructing a *GSM* $S_g$ from a linear grammar $G$ in the obvious way takes time polynomial in the size of productions of $G$.

A *GSM* $S_g$ is said to be a *parenthesis GSM* if and only if a linear grammar constructed from $S_g$ by Proposition 7.12 is a *PLG*. Then, using a learning algorithm for *PLG*s, parenthesis *GSM*s can also be learned.

# 8 Learning Equal Matrix Grammars

An equal matrix grammar, introduced by Siromoney [18], is a parallel rewriting system. It is a general extension of a regular grammar and closely related to a multitape automaton, which is a generalization of a finite automaton. Parallel rewriting systems are investigated in several areas such as $L$-systems and Petri nets.

An equal matrix language is a language generated by an equal matrix grammar. The class of equal matrix languages properly contains the class of regular languages and is incomparable with the class of context-free languages.

In previous sections, we have shown a learning method for linear grammars based on control sets and various positive results for subclasses of linear grammars. The same technique used for linear grammars is also applicable to the problem of learning equal matrix grammars. In this section, we shall summarize the results on learning equal matrix grammars; their details are found in [21, 22, 24].

Let $k$ be a positive integer. An *equal matrix grammar of order $k$*, abbreviated $k$-*EMG*, is a $(k + 3)$-tuple $G = (N_1, \ldots, N_k, \Sigma, P, S)$. $N_1, \ldots, N_k$ are finite nonempty pairwise disjoint sets of *nonterminals*. $S$ is not in $N_1 \cup \cdots \cup N_k \cup \Sigma$ and is called the *start symbol*. $P$ is a finite nonempty set of the following three types of *matrix rules*;

1. *initial matrix rules* of the form $[S \rightarrow u_1 A_1 \cdots u_k A_k]$,

2. *nonterminal matrix rules* of the form $[A_1 \rightarrow u_1 B_1, \ldots, A_k \rightarrow u_k B_k]$, and

3. *terminal matrix rules* of the form $[A_1 \rightarrow u_1, \ldots, A_k \rightarrow u_k]$,

where for each $i$ $(1 \leq i \leq k)$, $A_i$, $B_i$ are in $N_i$ and $u_i \in \Sigma^*$.

Let $G = (N_1, \ldots, N_k, \Sigma, P, S)$ be a $k$-*EMG*. We denote $N_1 \cup \cdots \cup N_k \cup \Sigma \cup \{S\}$ by $V$. For any $x, y \in V^*$, $x \underset{G}{\Longrightarrow} y$ if and only if either

1. $x = S$ and $[S \rightarrow y]$ is in $P$ or

2. there exist $u_1, \ldots, u_k$ in $\Sigma^*$, $z_1, \ldots, z_k$ each $z_i$ in $(N_i \cup \Sigma)^*$, and $A_1, \ldots, A_k$ each $A_i$ in $N_i$ such that $x = u_1 A_1 \cdots u_k A_k$ and $y = u_1 z_1 \cdots u_k z_k$, and the matrix rule $[A_1 \rightarrow z_1, \ldots, A_k \rightarrow z_k]$ is in $P$.

We write $x \underset{G}{\overset{*}{\Longrightarrow}} y$ if and only if either

1. $x = y$ or

2. there exist $x_0, \ldots, x_n \in V^*$ such that $x = x_0$, $y = x_n$, and $x_i \underset{G}{\Longrightarrow} x_{i+1}$ for each $i$ $(0 \leq i \leq n - 1)$.

$x \underset{G}{\overset{*}{\Longrightarrow}} y$ is called a *derivation from $x$ to $y$ in $G$*. The *language generated by $G$*, denoted $L(G)$, is the set

$$L(G) = \{w \in \Sigma^* \mid S \underset{G}{\overset{*}{\Longrightarrow}} w\}.$$

A language $L$ is said to be an *equal matrix language of order $k$*, abbreviated $k$-*EML*, if and only if there exists a $k$-*EMG* $G$ such that $L = L(G)$ holds.

Clearly, a 1-*EML* is regular and for $k \geq 2$, the class of $k$-*EMLs* contains some context-sensitive languages; the context-sensitive language $L_{ww} = \{ww \mid w \in \Sigma^*\}$ is a 2-*EML* and for any $k \geq 3$, the context-sensitive language $L_k = \{a_1^n \cdots a_k^n \,|\, n \geq 1,$ each distinct $a_i \in \Sigma\}$ is a *k-EML*. Also, there exists a context-free language that is not a *k-EML* for any $k \geq 1$ [11]; the context-free language $\bigcup_{i>0}\{a^n b^n \,|\, n \geq 1\}^i$ is not a *k-EML* for any $k \geq 1$. The class of *k-EMLs* forms a hierarchy of languages in the class of equal matrix languages [11].

For equal matrix languages, we also have a representation theorem (Theorem 8.2) similar to the one for linear languages; an equal matrix language is generated by a minimal labeled equal matrix grammar with a regular control set over the labels. From this, we again consider the divide and conquer strategy used for linear grammars and consider two subclasses of equal matrix grammars, *even equal matrix grammars* and *structured equal matrix grammars*, which are counterparts of even linear grammars and parenthesis linear grammars, respectively. In the sequel, together with efficient learning algorithms for *DFAs*, we again have various positive results similar to the ones for linear grammars. We shall also show that for any equal matrix language $L$ there exists an equal matrix grammar $G$ such that $L = L(G)$ and the structured grammar of $G$ is identified efficiently from positive examples only.

Corresponding notations such as labeled grammars, derivations with associate words, and languages generated with control sets are defined similarly.

**Definition 8.1** A *minimal* (labeled) *k-EMG* is a (labeled) *k-EMG* such that $N_i$ is a singleton, i.e., $N_i = \{S_i\}$ for every $i$ $(1 \leq i \leq k)$.

For *k-EMLs*, we have a representation theorem similar to the one for linear languages.

**Theorem 8.2 (Representation theorem for *k-EMLs*)** *For any language $L$, $L$ is a k-EML if and only if there exist a minimal labeled k-EMG $\mathcal{G}^0$ and a regular control set $C$ on $\mathcal{G}^0$ such that $L = L_C(\mathcal{G}^0)$ holds.*

An even equal matrix grammar is a general extension of an even linear grammar.

**Definition 8.3** An *even* *k-EMG* $G = (N_1, \ldots, N_k, \Sigma, P, S)$ is a *k-EMG* such that each matrix rule in $P$ is of the form

$$[S \to A_1 \cdots A_k],$$
$$[A_1 \to u_1 B_1, \ldots, A_k \to u_k B_k], \text{ or}$$
$$[A_1 \to w_1, \ldots, A_k \to w_k],$$

where for each $i$, $A_i, B_i \in N_i$, $u_i, w_i \in \Sigma^*$, and $lg(u_1) = \cdots = lg(u_k)$.

A language $L$ is an *even* *k-EML* if and only if there exists an even *k-EMG* $G$ such that $L = L(G)$ holds. Again, an even 1-*EML* is regular and for $k \geq 2$, the class of even *k-EMLs* contains some context-sensitive languages (two context-sensitive languages $L_{ww}$ and $L_k$ described in the above are an even 2-*EML* and an even *k-EML*, respectively).

An even *k-EMG* can be identified by identifying its unique canonical regular control set on a universal grammar fixed for the alphabet. Hence we have the following theorem.

**Theorem 8.4** *The problem of learning even k-EMLs is reduced to the problem of learning regular languages.*

Let **EEMG** be the class of all even $k$-*EMGs* to which *DFAs* correspond in the sense of Theorem 8.2. Then by Theorem 8.2, **EEMG** is a class of representations for the class of even $k$-*EMLs*. We immediately have the followings by Theorems 3.3, 3.4 and 3.5.

**Corollary 8.5** *The class* **EEMG** *is polynomial time learnable via equivalence queries and membership queries.*

**Corollary 8.6** *The class* **EEMG** *is polynomial time learnable in the limit via membership queries (and an arbitrary presentation).*

**Corollary 8.7** *The class* **EEMG** *is polynomial time learnable from a representative sample and via membership queries.*

A structured $k$-*EMG* is a $k$-*EMG* that displays derivations of the grammar in generated strings. This implies that supplemental information on derivations in grammars is available in learning.

Let $\#$ be a special symbol not in any alphabet $\Sigma$.

**Definition 8.8** For any $k$-*EMG* $G = (N_1, \ldots, N_k, \Sigma, P, S)$, the *structured $k$-EMG of* $G$ is a $k$-*EMG* $[G] = (N_1, \ldots, N_k, \Sigma \cup \{\#\}, P', S)$ such that

1. $[S \to \#u_1 A_1 \cdots \#u_k A_k] \in P'$ if $[S \to u_1 A_1 \cdots u_k A_k] \in P$,

2. $[A_1 \to \#u_1 B_1, \ldots, A_k \to \#u_k B_k] \in P'$ if $[A_1 \to u_1 B_1, \ldots, A_k \to u_k B_k] \in P$,

3. $[A_1 \to \#u_1, \ldots, A_k \to \#u_k] \in P'$ if $[A_1 \to u_1, \ldots, A_k \to u_k] \in P$,

where for each $i$ $(1 \leq i \leq k)$, $A_i$, $B_i$ are in $N_i$ and $u_i$ is in $\Sigma^*$.

A *structured $k$-EMG* is a structured $k$-*EMG* of a $k$-*EMG*.

For the problem of learning structured $k$-*EMGs*, we also have the results similar to the ones for parenthesis linear grammars. Let **SEMG** be the class of all structured $k$-*EMGs* to which *DFAs* correspond in the sense of Theorem 8.2. Then **SEMG** is a class of representations for the class of structured $k$-*EMGs*. Then by the similar argument to the one for parenthesis linear grammars, we have the followings.

**Corollary 8.9** *The class* **SEMG** *is polynomial time learnable via equivalence queries and membership queries.*

**Corollary 8.10** *The class* **SEMG** *is polynomial time learnable in the limit via membership queries (and an arbitrary presentation).*

**Corollary 8.11** *The class* **SEMG** *is polynomial time learnable from a representative sample and via membership queries.*

Angluin [3] has introduced *zero-reversible* finite automata and shown that there exists a learning algorithm that identifies any zero-reversible finite automaton in the limit from positive examples only. For $k$-*EMLs*, we can show the following.

**Proposition 8.12** *A $k$-EML $L$ is generated by a minimal $k$-EMG with a regular control set accepted by a zero-reversible automaton.*

Therefore, together with Theorem 3.2, we have the following theorem.

**Theorem 8.13** *For any k-EML L, there exists a k-EMG G such that $L = L(G)$ and the structured k-EMG of G can be identified in the limit from positive examples only.*

Since the update time of Angluin's learning algorithm is bounded by a polynomial in the length of input examples and the number of examples, a constructed learning algorithm using Angluin's one also updates any conjecture in polynomial time in the length of input examples and the number of examples.

# 9  Concluding Remarks

We have shown a learning method for linear grammars and equal matrix grammars. Our method is based on *regular* control sets on grammars and boosts learning algorithms for regular languages up to these larger language classes. One of future researches is to find other classes of languages to which our technique is also applicable.

# References

[1] V. Amar and G. Putzolu. On a family of linear grammars. *Information and Control*, 7:283–291, 1964.

[2] D. Angluin. A note on the number of queries needed to identify regular languages. *Information and Control*, 51:76–87, 1981.

[3] D. Angluin. Inference of reversible languages. *Journal of the ACM*, 29(3):741–765, 1982.

[4] D. Angluin. Learning k-bounded context-free grammars. RR 557, YALEU/DCS, 1987.

[5] D. Angluin. Learning regular sets from queries and counter-examples. *Information and Computation*, 75:87–106, 1987.

[6] D. Angluin and C. H. Smith. Inductive inference : Theory and methods. *ACM Computing Surveys*, 15(3):237–269, 1983.

[7] J. Dassow and G. Păun. *Regulated Rewriting in Formal Language Theory*, volume 18 of *EATCS Monographs on Theoretical Computer Science*. Springer-Verlag, Berlin, 1989.

[8] J. Earley. An efficient context-free parsing algorithm. *Communications of the ACM*, 13(2):94–102, 1970.

[9] E. Gold. Language identification in the limit. *Information and Control*, 10:447–474, 1967.

[10] R. C. Gonzalez and M. G. Thomason. *Syntactic Pattern Recognition: An Introduction*. Addison-Wesley, Reading, Mass., 1978.

[11] O. H. Ibarra. Simple matrix languages. *Information and Control*, 17:359–394, 1970.

[12] R. McNaughton. Parenthesis grammars. *Journal of the ACM*, 14(3):490–500, 1967.

[13] L. Pitt. Inductive inference, DFAs, and computational complexity. In K. P. Jantke, editor, *Proceedings of 2nd Workshop on Analogical and Inductive Inference, Lecture Notes in Artificial Intelligence, 397*, pages 18–44. Springer-Verlag, 1989.

[14] V. Radhakrishnan and G. Nagaraja. Inference of even linear grammars and its application to picture description languages. *Pattern Recognition*, 21(1):55–62, 1988.

[15] A. L. Rosenberg. A machine realization of the linear context-free languages. *Information and Control*, 10:175–188, 1967.

[16] Y. Sakakibara. Learning context-free grammars from structural data in polynomial time. *Theoretical Computer Science*, 76(2):223–242, 1990.

[17] Y. Sakakibara. Efficient learning of context-free grammars from positive structural examples. *Information and Computation*, 97:23–60, 1992.

[18] R. Siromoney. On equal matrix languages. *Information and Control*, 14:135–151, 1969.

[19] Y. Takada. Grammatical inference for even linear languages based on control sets. *Information Processing Letters*, 28(4):193–199, 1988.

[20] Y. Takada. Inferring parenthesis linear grammars based on control sets. *Journal of Information Processing*, 12(1):27–33, 1988.

[21] Y. Takada. Learning equal matrix grammars and multitape automata with structural information. In *Proceedings of the first Workshop on Algorithmic Learning Theory*, 1990.

[22] Y. Takada. Learning even equal matrix languages based on control sets. In M. Nivat, editor, *Parallel Image Analysis, Lecture Notes in Computer Science, 654*. Springer-Verlag, 1992.

[23] Y. Takada. A hierarchy of language families learnable by regular language learners. To appear in *Second International Colloquium on Grammatical Inference*, 1994.

[24] Y. Takada. Learning equal matrix grammars based on control sets. To appear in *International Journal of Pattern Recognition and Artificial Intelligence, Vol.8, No.2*, 1994.

[25] L. G. Valiant. A theory of the learnable. *Communications of the ACM*, 27:1134–1142, 1984.

# Learning in Case-Based Classification Algorithms*

Christoph Globig, Stefan Wess

University of Kaiserslautern, P.O. Box 3049

D-67653 Kaiserslautern, Germany

{globig,wess}@informatik.uni-kl.de

## Abstract

While symbolic learning approaches encode the knowledge provided by the presentation of the cases *explicitly* into a *symbolic representation of the concept*, e.g. formulas, rules, or decision trees, case-based approaches describe learned concepts *implicitly* by a pair $(CB, d)$, i.e. by a set $CB$ of cases and a distance measure $d$. Given the same information, symbolic as well as the case-based approach compute a classification when a new case is presented. This poses the question if there are any differences concerning the learning power of the two approaches. In this work we will study the relationship between the case base, the measure of distance, and the target concept of the learning process. To do so, we transform a simple symbolic learning algorithm (the version space algorithm) into an equivalent case-based variant. The achieved results strengthen the conjecture of the equivalence of the learning power of symbolic and case-based methods and show the interdependency between the measure used by a case-based algorithm and the target concept.

## 1 Introduction

In this paper which is an extended version of (Wess & Globig, 1994) we want to compare two important learning paradigms – the *symbolic* (Michalski, Carbonell, & Mitchell, 1983) and the *case-based* approach (Aha, 1991). As a first step in this direction, Jantke (1992) has already analyzed the common points of inductive inference and case-based learning. The learning task we study is the classification of objects (cases). The aim of a classification task is to map the objects **x** of a universe $U$ to certain concepts $C \subseteq U$, i.e. to subsets of the universe. In the most simple scenario we have to decide the membership problem of a concept $C$, i.e. the universe $U$ is separated in two disjoint subsets $C$ and $\neg C$.

We present a simple symbolic learning algorithm (the Version Space (Mitchell, 1982)) and transform it into a case-based variant. Based on this example we will show that for case-based approaches there exists a strong tradeoff between the set of representable concepts and the minimal number of cases in the case base. Thus for our scenario the used bias must have a comparable strength in both approaches.

---

*The presented work was partly supported by the *Deutsche Forschungsgemeinschaft*, project IND-CBL.

The second important component of a case-based learning system is the case selection strategy, i.e. the method to select appropriate cases for the case base. We study different types of case selection strategies and elaborate relations between the corresponding case-based learning types and relate them to Gold-style language learning (cf. (Gold, 1967)) from positive and both positive and negative examples.

## 1.1 Symbolic Learning

Under the term *symbolic learning*[1] we subsume approaches, e.g. (Michalski et al., 1983), that code the knowledge provided by the presentation of the cases into a *symbolic representation of the concept* only, e.g. by formulas, rules, or decision trees. These learning approaches produce after each presentation of a case a hypothesis formulated in a pregiven (formal) hypothesis language. The aim is to converge against a hypothesis that fulfills a pregiven criterion of correctness.

We will call the phase while the algorithms build their hypothesis *learning phase* and the phase while these hypotheses are used to classify new objects *application phase*. The fundamental problem the symbolic and the case-based approach have to solve during the learning phase is the same. At every moment the system knows the correct classification of a finite subset of the universe only. The knowledge that the algorithm is able to use is incomplete and, therefore, the computed hypothesis needs not to be correct.

Symbolic approaches can be characterized along the following dimensions (Jantke & Lange, 1989):

**Problem class:** For the characterization of a certain algorithm it is important to know the class of problems that it has to solve.

**Presented information:** The learner may get information of different types. It is important to specify, how the presented cases are selected. They may follow an enumeration of all objects or they are drawn according to a given distribution.

**Semantic of the presented information:** The relation between the presented information and the problem class must be specified.

**Hypothesis space:** Like the problem class the class of allowed hypotheses must be characterized. To represent their hypotheses symbolic algorithms may for example use a fragment of the predicate logic.

**Learning algorithms:** For a description of the learning problem the set of allowed learning algorithms must be given. We will demand that the algorithms produce a hypothesis after each presentation.

**Convergence of the sequence of hypotheses:** We have assumed that the learning algorithm produces a hypothesis after each presentation. It must be clarified which hypothesis is identified by a given sequence in the limit.

---

[1]Case-based systems may also use symbolic knowledge. The use of the term "symbolic learning" in this work may therefore be confusing to the reader. But, since the term "symbolic learning" is also used to contrast a special class of learning approaches to systems which use neural networks, we think that the use of the term "symbolic learning" as characterization of these approaches is appropriate.

**Successful learning:** Because of the learning system produces a sequence of hypotheses, there must be a criterion, whether this sequence is a successful learning.

It is important to remember that in symbolic learning cases are not used during the application phase, i.e. to classify new objects. The knowledge provided by the presentation of the cases during the learning phase is completely coded in the symbolic representation of the hypothesis. This compilation process may be seen as a abstraction step.

These terms could also be used to describe case-based algorithms. However, case-based systems have additional characteristical properties that we will describe in the next section.

## 2 Case-Based Learning

Case-based learning (Aha, 1991) applies techniques of nearest neighbor classification (Dasarathy, 1990) in symbolic domains. In case-based learning the learning phase and the application phase are not strictly separated (Kolodner, 1993). The basic idea is to use the knowledge of the known cases *directly* to solve new problems. Direct means that the system does not try to extract the whole knowledge from the case to operate with the extracted knowledge only. All cases (or a subset) are stored and interpreted during the solution of new problems.

Case-based methods solve a given problem in a sequence of steps (Aamodt & Plaza, 1994):

**Retrieve:** In a first step the system tries to retrieve the relevant cases from the case base $CB$. From the cases retrieved in the first step the learner has to select one. We will call this case the *reference case*.

**Reuse:** The reference cases is used to solve the new problem. If the case does not match perfectly the new situation, it has to be adapted. Therefore, the learner must have knowledge which modifications are allowed. This knowledge is tightly related to the domain, where the learning takes place. The complexity of modifications vary from simple parameter changes to the construction of new solutions for parts of the old solution that cannot be reused in the new situation.

**Revise:** If the learner has the ability to evaluate the new solution, a test of the solution will follow. If there arise some problems, the solution must be modified again.

**Retain:** In the learning phase the learner may change its knowledge depending of the feedback of the user. Learning may change all the components of the learner. The easiest way of modification relates to the case base. The new solution can be stored in the case base. If the reference case was not optimal, the methods for the retrieval may be changed.

The following section describes the basic algorithm we want to use for our learning problem.

## 2.1 Basic Algorithm

In the application phase, a case-based system tries to classify a new case with respect to a set of stored cases, the case base $CB$. For simplicity, we consider cases as tuples $(\mathbf{x}, class(\mathbf{x}))$ where $\mathbf{x}$ is a description of the case and $class(\mathbf{x})$ is the classification. Given a new case $(\mathbf{y}, ?)$ with unknown classification, the system searches in the case base $CB$ for the nearest neighbor $(\mathbf{x}, class(\mathbf{x}))$ (or the most similar case) according to a given distance measure $d$. Then it states the classification $class(\mathbf{x})$ of the nearest neighbor as the classification of the new case $(\mathbf{y}, ?)$, i.e. $(\mathbf{y}, class(\mathbf{x}))$. The basic algorithm (Aha, 1991) for a case-based approach is presented in Figure 1.

---

**Basic Algorithm for Case-Based Classification**

1. Define $CB = \{\ \}$ and initialize $d$

2. A new case $(\mathbf{y}, class(\mathbf{y}))$ is presented

3. Find a case $(\mathbf{x}, class(\mathbf{x})) \in CB$ so that $d(\mathbf{y}, \mathbf{x})$ is minimal.

4. If $class(\mathbf{y})$ is unknown, i.e. $(\mathbf{y}, ?)$ then

   (a) State $class(\mathbf{x})$ as classification of $(\mathbf{y}, ?)$, i.e. $(\mathbf{y}, class(\mathbf{x}))$.

   (b) Ask user for the correct classification $class(\mathbf{y})$ of $(\mathbf{y}, ?)$.

5. If $class(\mathbf{y}) = class(\mathbf{x})$
   then $classification := correct$
   else $classification := incorrect$

6. Modify $d$ and/or $CB$ with respect to $classification$.

7. Go to step 2

---

Figure 1: Basic Algorithm for a Case-Based Classifier

From the viewpoint of machine learning, case-based learning may be seen as a *concept formation task* (Richter, 1992). This raises the question how the learned concepts are represented in case-based approaches. Contrary to symbolic learning systems, which represent a learned concept *explicitly*, e.g. by formulas, rules, or decision trees, case-based systems describe a concept $C$ *implicitly* (Holte, 1990) by a pair $(CB, d)$. The relationship between the case base and the measure used for classification may be characterized by the equation:

**Concept = Case Base + Distance Measure**

In analogy to arithmetic this equation indicates that it is possible to represent a given concept $C$ in multiple ways, i.e. there exist several pairs $C = (CB_1, d_1)$, $(CB_2, d_2), \ldots, (CB_k, d_k)$ for the same concept $C$. Furthermore, the equation gives a hint how a case-based learner can improve its classification ability. There are in principle two possibilities to improve a case-based system. The system can

1. learn by changing the case base,

2. learn by changing the measure.

During the learning phase a case-based system (cf. Figure 1) gets a sequence of cases $X_1, X_2, \ldots, X_k$ with $X_i = (x_i, class(x_i))$ and computes a sequence of pairs $(CB_1, d_1), (CB_2, d_2), \ldots, (CB_k, d_k)$ such that $CB_i \subseteq \{X_1, X_2, \ldots, X_i\}$. The aim is to get in the limit a pair $(CB_n, d_n)$ that needs no further change, i.e. $\exists n\ \forall m \geq n\ (CB_n, d_n) = (CB_m, d_m)$, because it is a correct classifier for the target concept $C$.

## 2.2 Remarks

From the above description of the principle work of case-based and symbolic algorithms we can draw the following conclusions immediately.

- Both procedures produce a hypothesis when a new case is presented. Given only input and the classification behavior from the algorithms and the hypotheses, it is impossible to distinguish between the approaches.

- The hypotheses the algorithms produce work differently. The symbolic algorithm builds up its hypothesis by revealing the common characteristics of the examples in a pregiven hypothesis language. The hypothesis describes the relation between an object and the concept. The main component of the hypothesis of a case-based learner is a measure that states the similarity or distance between objects. The measure defines a relation between two objects and is therefore independent from the existence of a concept.

- A main difference between case-based and symbolic algorithms is the representation of the learned concept. The hypothesis produced by a case-based algorithm represents the concept only *implicitly*, while symbolic procedures build up an *explicit* representation of the concept. It is often a non-trivial task to extract a symbolic representation of the concept from a case-base and a measure. Of course, in finite domains the extension of the concept can be determined by classifying all objects of the universe.

- If we abandon the modification of the solutions, we must assume that for all possible solutions a case will be presented and included in the case-base. Without the possibility to modify solutions the case-based learner is unable to produce new solutions.

Based on these characteristics a comparison of the algorithms must clarify the following questions (Globig, 1993).

- How can the hypotheses the different approaches produce be characterized and what is the relationship between the hypotheses of the approaches?

- Which class of problems is learnable by the algorithms? Are there differences in the learning or application phase?

- Are there hints when to prefer an approach?

- How does the algorithms solve typical problems?

The hypotheses the symbolic algorithms build up are predefined by the hypothesis language. We therefore confine ourselves to a characterization of the hypotheses of case-based learners.

# 3 Learning by changing the measure

We now transform a well-known symbolic learner – the Version Space (VS) from (Mitchell, 1982) – in a case-based variant. The Version Space algorithm is a simple and well-known symbolic learning algorithm. Because of its simplicity it is easy to show some properties that hold for many other learning algorithms, for which it would be difficult to prove them.

The case-based variant simulates the symbolic algorithm in the following sense. If an object is classified by the symbolic algorithm, then it is classified equally by the case-based variant.

## 3.1 Symbolic Version Space

The universe $U$ of cases consists of finite vectors over finite value sets $W_i$ ($U = W_1 \times \ldots \times W_n$). We want to decide the membership problem of a certain concept $C$. The concepts to learn fix the value of certain attributes.[2] These concepts $C$ can be described as vectors $(C_1, \ldots, C_n)$, with $C_i = *$ or $C_i = a_{ij} \in W_i$. A case $((a_1, \ldots, a_n), class(\mathbf{a}))$ fulfills the concept $C$, if for all $1 \leq i \leq n$ holds: $C_i = *$ or $C_i = a_i$, i.e. $C_i = *$ is fulfilled by every $x \in W_i$. We further demand that $C_i \neq *$ for at least one $i$.

A concept $C$ is called consistent with a set of cases, if all positive cases, i.e. $class(\mathbf{x}) = +$, of the set fulfill the concept and none of the negative, i.e. $class(\mathbf{x}) = -$, does. A concept $C$ is called more general (more specific) than $C'$ if $C \supset C'$ ($C \subset C'$). The symbolic version space (Mitchell, 1982) solves the learning problem by updating two sets $S$ and $G$ of concepts. $S$ contains the most specific concept that is consistent with the known cases and $G$ includes the most general concepts consistent with the known cases. The task of the symbolic algorithm is to change the sets $S$ and $G$ in order to preserve these properties. Figure 2 shows the algorithm (cf. (Mitchell, 1982)). For simplicity we assume that at first a positive case $a^1$ is given to initialize the sets.

It is important that at every moment all cases subsumed by $S$ are known to be positive, and all cases that are not subsumed by any concept of $G$ are known to be negative. If a case is presented that violates this condition, the target concept is not in the version space. This observation leads to a partial decision function $VS : U \to \{0, 1\}$ that can be used to classify new cases:

$$VS(\mathbf{x}) = \begin{cases} 1 & \text{if } \forall C \in S[C(\mathbf{x}) = 1] \\ 0 & \text{if } \forall C \in G[C(\mathbf{x}) = 0] \\ ? & \text{otherwise} \end{cases}$$

---

[2]These concepts represent the conjunctions of atomic formulas $x_i = a_i$, e.g. *shape = Circle* $\land$ *size = big*.

> **Version Space Algorithm**
>   1. Initialize $G = \{(*, \ldots, *)\}$ and $S = \{a^1\}$.
>
>   2. If the actual case is $(\mathbf{a}, +)$
>      then remove all concepts from $G$ that do not subsume the positive case.
>      Search for the most specific concept $C$ of the version space that subsumes all positive cases and define $S = \{C\}$. If there is no such $C$ define $S = \emptyset$.
>
>   3. If the actual case is $(\mathbf{a}, -)$
>      then remove all concepts from $S$ which are fulfilled by $\mathbf{a}$.
>      For all concepts $\mathbf{g} \in G$ that subsume $\mathbf{a}$, search for the most general specializations that do not subsume $\mathbf{a}$ but all known positive cases.
>      Replace $\mathbf{g}$ by the found concepts.
>
>   4. If $G$ or $S$ is empty or there is a concept $\mathbf{g}$ in $G$ that is more specific
>      than the concept from $S$, then **ERROR**: Not a concept of the version space!
>
>   5. If $S = G$ then **STOP**: Concept $= S$
>      else go to 2.

Figure 2: Algorithm for the symbolic version space

As long as $S \neq G$ holds VS will not classify all cases of the universe. If a case is covered by $S$ but not by $G$ it may belong to the concept $C$ or not. So VS will not return an answer for those cases (this is the semantics of the "?" in the decision function).

### 3.1.1 Example

To illustrate this version space algorithm we present a very simple example. The universe $U$ is $U = \text{shape} \times \text{size} = \{\text{Square, Circle}\} \times \{\text{big, small}\}$. Figure 3 shows the graph of all learnable concepts.

Let us study the changes of $S$ and $G$ during the learning process. If the first positive case is $((Circle, big), +)$ we have:

$$S = \{(Circle, big)\} \quad G = \{(*, *)\}$$

Let the second case be negative $((Square, small), -)$. This forces the algorithm to specialize the concept in $G$. Because all concepts that replace $(*, *)$ must be consistent with the known cases, the most general specialization are $(*, big), (Circle, *)$. So, $S$ and $G$ change to:

$$S = \{(Circle, big)\} \quad G = \{(*, big), (Circle, *)\}$$

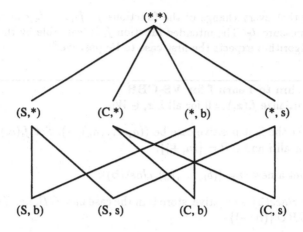

Figure 3: Set of the learnable concepts over $U$

If the third case $((Square, big), +)$ is positive we must generalize the concept in $S$ and specialize the concept in $G$. The only possible concept consistent with the cases is $(*, big)$. $S$ and $G$ turn out to be:

$$S = \{(*, big)\} \quad G = \{(*, big)\}$$

Now $S$ and $G$ are equal and contain only a single concept. The learned concept $C = (*, big)$ is defined totally, i.e. for every case of the universe it is possible to decide whether it fulfills the target concept. If we present more cases, the sets $S$ and $G$ will not change.

## 3.2 Case-Based Version Space

If we analyze the version space algorithm, it is obvious that the main learning task is to distinguish between relevant and irrelevant attributes. We will use this observation to construct a case-based variant VS-CBR of the algorithm of the previous section. An attribute value is called *relevant*, if it is part of the target concept $\mathbf{C} = (C_1, \ldots, C_n)$ $(C_i \in W_i \cup \{*\})$. For every attribute $i$, we define a function $f_i$ that maps $x \in W_i$ to $\{0, 1\}$ with the following definition:

$$f_i(x) = \begin{cases} 1 & : \quad C_i = x \\ 0 & : \quad \text{otherwise} \end{cases}$$

Note that $f_i \equiv 0$ if $C_i = *$. That means the value of the $i$th attribute does not influence the measure of similarity. The functions $f_i$ will be combined to $\mathbf{f}: U \rightarrow \{0, 1\}^n$ $\mathbf{f}((a_1, \ldots, a_n)) = (f_1(a_1), \ldots, f_n(a_n))$. The distance between two cases $a$ and $b$ is then defined using the city-block metric as follows

$$d_{\mathbf{f}}(\mathbf{a}, \mathbf{b}) := |f_1(a_1) - f_1(b_1)| + \ldots + |f_n(a_n) - f_n(b_n)|$$

It is obvious that every change of the functions $f_1, f_2, \ldots, f_n$ causes a change of the underlying measure $d_f$. The intended function $f_i$ is learnable by the algorithm in Figure 4. The algorithm expects the first case to be positive.[3]

---

**Algorithm to Learn f for VS-CBR**

1. Initialize $f_i(x_i) = 0$ for all $i$, $x_i \in W_i$.

2. Let the first positive case be $((a_1, \ldots, a_n), +)$. Set $f_i(a_i) = 1$ for all $i$ and $CB = \{(\mathbf{a}, +)\}$.

3. Get a new case $((b_1, \ldots, b_n), class(\mathbf{b}))$.

4. If $class(\mathbf{b})$ is negative, store $\mathbf{b}$ in the case base $CB$, i.e. $CB := CB \cup \{(\mathbf{b}, -)\}$.

5. If $class(\mathbf{b})$ is positive and $f_i(b_i) = 0$, then let $f_i(x_i) = 0$ for all $x_i \in W_i$ ($f_i$ maps now every value to zero).

6. If there exist two cases $(\mathbf{a}, class(\mathbf{a})), (\mathbf{b}, class(\mathbf{b})) \in CB$ with $d_f(\mathbf{a}, \mathbf{b}) = 0$ and $class(\mathbf{a}) \neq class(\mathbf{b})$ then **ERROR**: The target concept $C$ is not member of the version space.

7. If the concept $C$ is determined then **STOP**: The concept is learned. The classifier $(CB, d_f)$ consists of the case base $CB$ and the measure $d_f$.

8. Go to step 3.

---

Figure 4: Algorithm to learn f for VS-CBR

If the concept is learned, the function **f** and the case base $CB$ are used for classification. Given a new case $(c, ?)$, the set

$$F := \{\mathbf{x} \in CB \mid \forall \, y \in CB \; d_f(\mathbf{x}, c) \leq d_f(y, c)\}$$

is computed. The classification $class(\mathbf{x})$ of the nearest neighbor $(\mathbf{x}, class(\mathbf{x}))$ is then used for the classification of the new case $(c, ?)$. If $F$ contains more than one case with different classifications then $class(\mathbf{c})$ is determined by a fixed strategy to solve this conflict. Different strategies are possible and each strategy will induce its own semantics for VS-CBR.

For example, one conflict solving strategy may state the minimal classification according to a given ordering of the concepts. This strategy is used in the following decision function:

$$\text{VS-CBR}(\mathbf{x}) = \min\{class(\mathbf{y}) \mid \mathbf{y} \in CB \wedge \forall \mathbf{z} \in CB \; d_f(\mathbf{y}, \mathbf{x}) \leq d_f(\mathbf{z}, \mathbf{x})\}$$

To solve the membership problem, we assume that a case $(\mathbf{c}, ?)$ is classified as negative if it has the same minimal distance from a positive and a negative case, i.e.

---

[3]If the first case is not positive, the learner may store all negative cases and start the algorithm, if the first positive case is presented.

$d((\mathbf{a},+),(\mathbf{c},?)) = d((\mathbf{b},-),(\mathbf{c},?))$ is minimal. To achieve this behavior of the classifier the ordering of the concepts must be $" - " < " + "$.

### 3.2.1 Example

Before analyzing the classification ability of VS-CBR in more detail, we illustrate the algorithm by the same simple example we have used for the VS (cf. section 3.1.1). Because the universe has only two dimensions, two functions $f_1 : shape \rightarrow \{0,1\}$ and $f_2 : size \rightarrow \{0,1\}$ are needed. The first positive case $((Circle, big), +)$ is used to initialize the functions $f_1$ and $f_2$.

$$f_1(x) = \begin{cases} 1 & \text{if } x = Circle \\ 0 & \text{otherwise} \end{cases}$$

$$f_2(y) = \begin{cases} 1 & \text{if } y = big \\ 0 & \text{otherwise} \end{cases}$$

$$CB = \{((Circle, big), +)\}$$

The next case of our sequence is $((Square, small), -)$. This new case is stored in the case base.

$$f_1(x) = \begin{cases} 1 & \text{if } x = Circle \\ 0 & \text{otherwise} \end{cases}$$

$$f_2(y) = \begin{cases} 1 & \text{if } y = big \\ 0 & \text{otherwise} \end{cases}$$

$$CB = \{((Circle, big), +), ((Square, small), -)\}$$

Now $(CB, d_f)$ classifies $((Circle, big), +)$ as positive only, because every other case has a distance $\geq 1$ from $((Circle, big), +)$ and $\leq 1$ from $((Square, small), -)$. As third case assume $((Square, big), +)$. Because $f_1(Square) = 0$ holds $f_1$ is defined to be zero for all values. The new case is not stored in the case base.

$$f_1(x) = 0$$

$$f_2(y) = \begin{cases} 1 & \text{if } y = big \\ 0 & \text{otherwise} \end{cases}$$

$$CB = \{((Circle, big), +), ((Square, small), -)\}$$

We may now test the elements of the universe $U$. They are all correctly classified. However, it is not obvious from the algorithm why the learning process can be stopped at this point.

## 3.3 Analysis

Now let us analyze VS-CBR's way of classification in more detail. Positive and negative cases are used differently in VS-CBR during the learning phase:

- Positive cases are used to change $f$, i.e. to adapt the distance measure $d_f$. They will not be stored in the case base (with the exception of the very first positive case).

- Negative cases are stored in the case base $CB$ but do not change the distance measure.

The information that is used by VS to change $S$ and $G$ is used by VS-CBR to change the case base or the distance measure.

It is easy to show that all cases which are classified by the symbolic VS will also be classified correctly by the case-based one. The difference is that the case-based variant VS-CBR computes a classification for every case of the universe (because the distance measure is total) while the symbolic VS classifies only if the proposed classification can be proven to be correct. Otherwise (i.e. the case fulfills a concept from $G$ but not the concept in $S$) it will not produce any classification at all. If we add a test whether the classification of the nearest neighbor is correct to VS-CBR, we can force VS-CBR to produce only certain classifications, too. But this test would more or less be a variant of the original VS algorithm.

We have shown that it is possible to reformulate the Version Space algorithm in a case-based manner so that the case-based variant simulates the symbolic algorithm. As we have seen a case-based learning system consists of two main parts: the case base and the distance measure. Therefore, we want to analyze the implications of the choice of the distance measure and the strategy to select cases for the case base.

## 3.4   Comparing different measures

In this section consequences of the choice of $d$ are drawn. For the rest of section 3 we assume the following scenario:

1. The universe $U$ of cases is finite.

2. We have to decide the membership problem of a certain concept $C$.

3. The distance measure $d$ is total and satisfies the following condition:
   $$\forall \mathbf{a}, \mathbf{b}, \mathbf{x} \in U\, [d(\mathbf{a}, \mathbf{a}) = 0 \land (d(\mathbf{a}, \mathbf{b}) = 0 \Rightarrow d(\mathbf{x}, \mathbf{a}) = d(\mathbf{x}, \mathbf{b}))].$$

Condition 3 has two important consequences: First, the relation $\sim\ \subseteq U \times U$ defined by $\mathbf{x} \sim \mathbf{y} \Leftrightarrow d(\mathbf{x}, \mathbf{y}) = 0$ is an equivalence relation. Second, all members of the equivalence relation must have the same classification because there cannot exist any case to separate them. $|U/\sim|$ is the number of equivalence classes that are induced by $\sim$. So we can state that $d$ is able to represent exactly those concepts $C$ that satisfy $d(\mathbf{x}, \mathbf{y}) = 0 \Rightarrow C(\mathbf{x}) \equiv C(\mathbf{y})$, i.e. the members of an equivalence class must have the same classification.

The measure $d$ is able to distinguish between $2^{|U/\sim|}$ different concepts $C_j$. Each concept can be represented by almost $|U/\sim|$ (appropriate) cases. In other words, in a case-based classifier $(CB, d)$ the measure $d$ defines the set of the learnable concepts and the case base $CB$ selects a concept from this set.

During the learning process the case-based system alters. On one hand, case-based systems $(CB, d)$ use the cases in the case base $CB$ to fill up the equivalence classes induced by the measure $d$. On the other hand, they use the cases to lower the number of equivalence classes by changing the measure $d$. Thereby, the target concept $C$ may be identified by fewer cases. But, a lower number of equivalence classes means that the modified measure $d'$ can distinguish between fewer concepts.

Having this in mind, we can compare case-based systems with respect to two dimensions: *minimality* and *universality*. The first dimension relates to the implicit knowledge that is coded into the used measure $d$. Because we are not able to measure this implicit knowledge directly, we have to look at the size of the case base instead. More knowledge coded in the used measure $d$ will result in a smaller (minimal) size of the case base $CB$ within the classifier $(CB, d)$.

**Definition 1** *The measure $d_1$ is called* better informed *about a concept* $\mathbf{C}$ *than a measure $d_2$ if*[4]

$$\exists CB_1 \subset_{fin} U \quad \forall CB_2 \subset_{fin} U$$
$$[(CB_1, d_1) = \mathbf{C} = (CB_2, d_2) \Rightarrow |CB_1| \leq |CB_2|]$$

The second dimension relates to the set of representable concepts. We must distinguish between the representability and the learnability of a concept. A concept $C$ is called representable by a measure $d$, if there *exists* a finite case base $CB$ such that $(CB, d)$ is a classifier for $C$. A concept $C$ is called learnable by a measure $d$, if there exists a *strategy to build* a finite case base $CB$ such that in the limit $(CB, d)$ is a classifier for the concept.

**Definition 2** *A measure $d_1$ is called* more universal *than a measure $d_2$ iff the set of concepts that are representable by $d_2$ is a proper subset of the set of concepts that are representable by $d_1$.*

Using an universal measure conflicts the minimality of the case base. Reducing the size of the case base, which means to code more knowledge into the measure, usually results in a less universal measure. We can distinguish two extreme situations:

**All knowledge is coded into the case base:** The measure is minimal if and only if the compared cases are identical, i.e.

$$d_{CB}(\mathbf{x}, \mathbf{y}) := \begin{cases} 1 & \text{if } \mathbf{x} \neq \mathbf{y} \\ 0 & \text{if otherwise} \end{cases}$$

The measure $d_{CB}$ is universal because it is able to learn every binary concept $C_i$ in the given universe $U$. But to do so, it needs the whole universe as a case base, i.e. $CB := U$. Thus, the resulting system $(U, d_{CB})$ is universal but not minimal.

**All knowledge is coded into the measure:** The measure is minimal if and only if the classification of the compared cases is identical, i.e. the measure $d_C$ knows the definition of the target concept $C$.

$$d_C(\mathbf{x}, \mathbf{y}) := \begin{cases} 1 & \text{if } (C(\mathbf{x}) \neq C(\mathbf{y})) \\ 0 & \text{if otherwise} \end{cases}$$

Nearly the whole knowledge about the concept is then coded into the measure $d_C$. The case base contains almost one positive case $\mathbf{c}^+$ and one negative case $\mathbf{c}^-$ and is used only to choose between some trivial variations. The measure $d_C$ can only distinguish between four concepts ($C$, $\neg C$, $True$ – i.e. all cases are positive, $False$ – i.e. all cases are negative). Thus, the resulting system $(\{\mathbf{c}^+, \mathbf{c}^-\}, d_C)$ is minimal but not universal.

---

[4] $A \subset_{fin} B$ denotes that $A$ is a finite subset of $B$

We illustrate the contrasting nature of these two aims in Figure 5 by an example. This figure shows different measures $d$ in relation to the minimal size of the case base $CB$ to learn a certain concept $C$ in the relation to the total number of learnable concepts. For the table, we use a universe $U$ of cases that consist of four attributes. Each attribute can take one value out of 16. So, the size of the universe $U$ is 65536. The concept the measures try to learn, fix two attributes out of four.

| Used measure | Minimal size of CB | # Represent. concepts |
|:---:|:---:|:---:|
| $d_{CB}$ | $65536 = 16^4$ | $2^{65536}$ |
| $d_f^1$ | 16 | $65536 = 2^{16}$ |
| $d_f^n$ | 4 | $16 = 2^4$ |
| $d_C$ | 2 | $2^2$ |

Figure 5: Comparing different measures

The universal measure $d_{CB}$ is able to represent all binary concepts, while the minimal measure $d_C$ needs only two cases to represent the learned concept. The other measures in the Figure 5 are between these two extremes. The measures $d_f^1$ and $d_f^n$ are neither maximally universal nor able to represent the concept with a minimal case base. $d_f^1$ is the distance measure computed for VS–CBR after the first case has been presented. In every dimension exactly one value is mapped to 1. The universe $U$ is therefore mapped onto the vertices of a four dimensional cube. $d_f^n$ is the measure used when VS–CBR has learned the concept. It distinguishes only between the two relevant values of the concept and consequently builds up only four equivalence classes.

We can draw the following conclusions from these observations.

- Changing the used measure by coding more knowledge into it means trading universality against minimality.

- In a case-based learner, two processes – reducing the set of the representable concepts (hypothesis space) and increasing the size of the case base – should be performed.

- The last measure in Figure 5 indicates a simple way to reformulate any symbolic algorithm in a case-based manner, i.e. use the actual symbolic hypothesis to construct such a measure and store one positive and one negative case in the case base.

## 3.5 Using extended measures

We have shown that under the assumptions of this section a concept $C$ is representable if and only if $d(\mathbf{x}, \mathbf{y}) = 0 \Rightarrow C(\mathbf{x}) \equiv C(\mathbf{y})$. Whether a concept $C$ is representable by a given distance measure $d$, therefore, depends on the definition of the identity, i.e. the distance $d(\mathbf{x}, \mathbf{y}) = 0$, only. If the concept $C$ is representable by $d$, all other distances may be mapped to any value greater than zero. This poses the question if it does

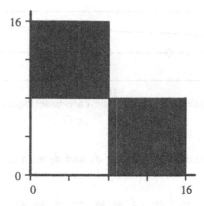

Figure 6: Graphical representation of concept $C$

make any sense to use a distance measure $d$ that maps distances between cases to a greater set of values than $\{0, 1\}$.

The only reason to use a more complex distance measure (in our simple scenario; cf. (Wess, 1993)) is the hope to get more reliable hypotheses before the concept $C$ is learned, i.e. when not all equivalence classes of the measure are filled.

### 3.5.1 Example

To illustrate this, we compare two measures that can learn the same concepts. Let the universe consist of cases with four attributes. The values for each attribute are $\{0, \ldots, 15\}$. So the universe is $U = \{0, \ldots, 15\}^4$. The concept to learn is $C(\mathbf{x})$, $\mathbf{x} := (x_1, \ldots, x_4)$ (cf. Figure 6).

$$C(\mathbf{x}) = 1 \Leftrightarrow (x_2 \geq 8 \wedge x_4 < 8) \vee (x_4 \geq 8 \wedge x_2 < 8)$$

and the distance measures are:

$$d_1(\mathbf{a}, \mathbf{b}) = \begin{cases} 0 & : & \mathbf{a} = \mathbf{b} \\ 1 & : & \text{otherwise} \end{cases}$$
$$d_2(\mathbf{a}, \mathbf{b}) = \sum_i |a_i - b_i|$$

Obviously both measures are able to represent the same concepts in the universe $U$, because $d_i(\mathbf{a}, \mathbf{b}) = 0 \Leftrightarrow \mathbf{a} = \mathbf{b}$. Figure 7 shows the classification rates for the given concept $C(\mathbf{x})$ with case bases of different sizes. To classify more than 90% correctly with the measure $d_1$ more than 52000 cases, are required.

The portion of correctly classified cases grows with the measure $d_2$ while it is nearly constant with measure $d_1$, i.e. $d_2$ of $(CB_2, d_2)$ is a much better informed measure than the $d_1$ of $(CB_1, d_1)$. The difference between the measures $d_1$ and $d_2$ is the significance of the distance value. If $d_1$ measures a distance greater than 0 there is no hint whether the classification of the cases is identical or not. On the other hand, a small distance measured by $d_2$ indicates a high probability that the cases can be equally classified.

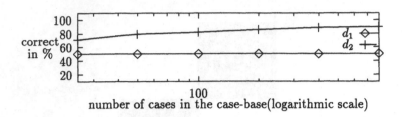

number of cases in the case-base(logarithmic scale)

Figure 7: Classification rate in percent for $d_1$ and $d_2$ with cases bases of different size

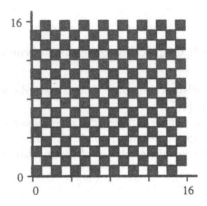

Figure 8: Graphical representation of concept $C_2$

This result does not imply that $d_2$ is the best choice for all concepts (Globig & Wess, 1994). It is possible to define concepts where a small distance between cases implies a high probability for different classification. An example is the following concept (cf. Figure 8):

$$C_2(\mathbf{x}) = 1 \iff ((x_2 \bmod 2 = 0) \wedge (x_4 \bmod 2 = 1)) \vee$$
$$((x_4 \bmod 2 = 0) \wedge (x_2 \bmod 2 = 1))$$

The rate of correct classifications for $d_2$ and concept $C_2$ will be nearly the same as the rate of $d_1$ in Figure 7.

# 4 Learning by changing the case base

In the last section we analyzed some aspects of the choice of the distance measure. In this section we want discuss the influence of the choice of the case selection strategy on the set of the learnable concepts. The example systems of the last section store all presented cases. In this section the measure of similarity is fixed. In (Jantke, 1992)

Jantke has already shown that a case-based system can simulate an inductive learning algorithm if the similarity measure can be changed arbitrarily.

We have done this comparisons in the area of learning indexed families of formal languages (cf. (Angluin, 1980)). This comparison was done by one of the authors together with Steffen Lange. A more detailed description of theses results including the proofs of the theorems can be found in (Globig & Lange, 1994).

The definitions of this section are adapted from the Inductive Inference literature (cf. (Angluin, 1980)). Our target objects are (formal) languages over a finite alphabet $A$. By $A^+$ we denote the set of all non-empty strings over the alphabet $A$. Any subset $L$ of $A^+$ is called a language. We set $\overline{L} = A^+ \setminus L$.

By $\mathbb{N} = \{1, 2, \ldots\}$ we denote the set of all natural numbers. We use $\mathbb{Q}_{[0,1]}$ to denote the set of all rational numbers between 0 and 1. Furthermore, by $card(B)$ we denote the cardinality of set $B$. We write $B \# C$ if $B$, and $C$ are incomparable with respect to inclusion.

There are two basic ways to present information about a language to a learner. We can present positive data only or positive and negative data. These presentations are called *text* and *informant*, respectively. A *text* for a language $L$ is an infinite sequence $t = (s_1, b_1), (s_2, b_2), \ldots$ with $(s_j, b_j) \in A^+ \times \{+\}$ such that $\{s_j \mid j \in \mathbb{N}\} = L$. Let $t[k]$ be the initial sequence $(s_1, b_1), (s_2, b_2), \ldots, (s_k, b_k)$ of $t$. We set $t^+[k] = \{s_j \mid j \leq k\}$. Let $text(L)$ denote the set of all texts of $L$. An *informant* for a language $L$ is an infinite sequence $i = (s_1, b_1), (s_2, b_2), \ldots$ with $(s_j, b_j) \in A^+ \times \{+, -\}$ such that $\{s_j \mid j \in \mathbb{N}, b_j = +\} = L$ and $\{s_j \mid j \in \mathbb{N}, b_j = -\} = A^+ \setminus L$. Let $i[k]$ be the initial sequence $(s_1, b_1), (s_2, b_2), \ldots, (s_k, b_k)$ of $i$. Furthermore, we set $i^+[k] = \{s_j \mid j \leq k, b_j = +\}$ and $i^-[k] = \{s_j \mid j \leq k, b_j = -\}$. By $informant(L)$ we denote the set of all informants of $L$. Without loss of generality we assume that $t[k]$ $(i[k])$ is coded as a natural number that represents the initial segment of the text (resp. informant).

We restrict ourselves to investigate the learnability of indexed families of recursive languages over $A$ (cf. (Angluin, 1980)). A sequence $\mathcal{L} = L_1, L_2, \ldots$ is said to be an *indexed family* if all $L_j$ are non-empty and there is a recursive function $f$ such that for all indices $j$ and all strings $w \in A^+$ holds

$$f(j, w) = \begin{cases} 1 & \text{if } w \in L_j \\ 0 & \text{otherwise} \end{cases}$$

So given an indexed family $\mathcal{L}$ the membership problem is uniformly decidable for all languages in $\mathcal{L}$ by a single function.

**IF** denotes the set of all indexed families.

The following definition is adapted from (Angluin, 1980). We use $f(x) \downarrow$ to denote that a function $f$ is defined on input $x$.

**Definition 3** *Let $\mathcal{L} \in$ **IF**.*
*Then we say $\mathcal{L}$ is* learnable from text *(resp.* learnable from informant*)*
*iff*
$\exists M \in \mathbf{P}\ \forall L \in \mathcal{L}\ \forall t \in text(L)$ *(resp.* $\forall i \in informant(L)$*)*

    (1)  $\forall n \in \mathbb{N}\ M(t[n]) \downarrow$ *(resp.* $\forall n \in \mathbb{N}\ M(i[n]) \downarrow$*)*,

    (2)  $\lim_{n \to \infty} M(t[n]) = a$ *exists (resp.* $\lim_{n \to \infty} M(i[n]) = a$ *exists)*,

    (3)  $L_a = L$.

**LIM.TXT** *(LIM.INF)* *is the set of all indexed families that are learnable from text (informant).*

**P** denotes the set of the unary computable functions.

In order to formalize case-based learnability we have to define the underlying similarity measures. $\sigma : A^+ \times A^+ \to \mathbb{Q}_{[0,1]}$ is called a measure of similarity. $\Sigma$ denotes the set of all totally defined and computable similarity measures.

To define case-based learnability in this setting, we use the so called standard semantics $L_{st}$ (cf. (Jantke & Lange, 1993)).

**Definition 4** *Let $CB \subseteq_{fin} A^+ \times \{+,-\}$ and $\sigma \in \Sigma$ a similarity measure. Furthermore, let $CB^+ := \{s \mid (s,+) \in CB\}$, $CB^- := \{s \mid (s,-) \in CB\}$. Then we say $CB$ and $\sigma$ describe the language $L_{st}(CB,\sigma) = L_{st}(CB^+, CB^-, \sigma) := \{w \in A^+ \mid \exists c \in CB^+ \ (\sigma(c,w) > 0 \wedge \forall c' \in CB^- \sigma(c,w) > \sigma(c',w))\}$.*

**Definition 5** *Let $\mathcal{L} \in \mathbf{IF}$ and $\sigma \in \Sigma$.*
*Then, $\mathcal{L} \in \mathbf{REPR}^+(\sigma)$ iff for every $L \in \mathcal{L}$ there is a $CB^+ \subseteq_{fin} L$ such that $L_{st}(CB^+, \emptyset, \sigma) = L$. Moreover, $\mathcal{L} \in \mathbf{REPR}^{\pm}(\sigma)$ iff for every $L \in \mathcal{L}$ there are $CB^+ \subseteq_{fin} L$ and $CB^- \subseteq_{fin} \overline{L}$ such that $L_{st}(CB^+, CB^-, \sigma) = L$.*
*Let $\mathbf{REPR}^+ := \bigcup_{\sigma \in \Sigma} \mathbf{REPR}^+(\sigma)$ and $\mathbf{REPR}^{\pm} := \bigcup_{\sigma \in \Sigma} \mathbf{REPR}^{\pm}(\sigma)$.*

So $\mathcal{L} \in \mathbf{REPR}^+$ ($\mathcal{L} \in \mathbf{REPR}^{\pm}$) means that there is a $\sigma$ such that $\mathcal{L} \in \mathbf{REPR}^+(\sigma)$ ($\mathcal{L} \in \mathbf{REPR}^{\pm}(\sigma)$).

Based on the classical definitions we define case-based learnability with respect to a certain case selection strategy.

**Definition 6** *An indexed family $\mathcal{L}$ is said to be case-based learnable from text by the case selection strategy $S : \mathbb{N} \to Pot(A^+ \times \{+\})$ iff $\exists \sigma \in \Sigma \ \forall L \in \mathcal{L} \ \forall t \in text(L)$*

$$(1) \quad \forall n \in \mathbb{N} \ CB_n = S(t[n]) \downarrow, \ and \ S(t[n]) \subseteq t^+[n] \times \{+\},$$
$$(2) \quad CB = \lim_{n \to \infty} CB_n \ exists \ and \ CB \ is \ finite,$$
$$(3) \quad L_{st}(CB, \sigma) = L.$$

**Definition 7** *An indexed family $\mathcal{L}$ is said to be case-based learnable from informant by the case selection strategy $S : \mathbb{N} \to Pot(A^+ \times \{+,-\})$ iff $\exists \sigma \in \Sigma \ \forall L \in \mathcal{L} \ \forall i \in informant(L)$*

$$(1) \quad \forall n \in \mathbb{N} \ CB_n = S(i[n]) \downarrow, \wedge S(i[n]) \subseteq (i^+[n] \times \{+\}) \cup (i^-[n] \times \{-\}),$$
$$(2) \quad CB = \lim_{n \to \infty} CB_n \ exists \ and \ CB \ is \ finite,$$
$$(3) \quad L_{st}(CB, \sigma) = L.$$

Here the learner is not allowed to change the measure of similarity during the learning process. Therefore, the learning capability depends on the case selection strategy only.

In the sequel we want to analyze the influence of two dimensions – access to case history and deleting cases form the case base.

**Access to case history:** Is the case selection strategy allowed to store any case that is already presented or has the strategy access to the last one only?

**Deleting cases from the case base:** Is the case selection strategy allowed to delete cases from the case base or does the case base grow monotonically?

With respect to these dimensions we can define types of case selection strategies. Let $CB_k$ be the case base constructed when a learner has seen an initial sequence of length $k$.

**Definition 8** *Let $S$ be a case selection strategy. Then $S$ is said to be of type[5] **MO-LC**, **MO-RA**, **DE-LC**, and **DE-RA**, respectively, iff the corresponding condition holds for all $k \in \mathbb{N}$ ($CB_0 := \emptyset$).*

| | |
|---|---|
| **MO-LC** | iff $CB_{k-1} \subseteq CB_k \subseteq CB_{k-1} \cup \{(s_k, b_k)\}$ |
| **MO-RA** | iff $CB_{k-1} \subseteq CB_k \subseteq \{(s_1, b_1), \ldots, (s_k, b_k)\}$ |
| **DE-LC** | iff $CB_k \subseteq CB_{k-1} \cup \{(s_k, b_k)\}$ |
| **DE-RA** | iff $CB_k \subseteq \{(s_1, b_1), \ldots, (s_k, b_k)\}$ |

We use these abbreviations as prefixes to **CBL.TXT** and **CBL.INF**. For example, $\mathcal{L} \in$ **DE-RA-CBL.TXT** means that there is a case selection strategy $S \in$ **DE-RA** such that $\mathcal{L}$ can be learned by $S$ in the sense of Definition 6.

Strategies of type **MO-RA** and **DE-RA**, respectively, may store multiple cases in a single learning step. If we demand that strategies of both types store at most a single case in every learning step their learning capabilities will not change.

Because many existing systems simply collect all presented cases, we model this approach, too. A case selection strategy $S$ is said to be of type[6] **CA**, if $CB_k = \{(s_j, b_j) \mid j \leq k\}$ for all $k \in \mathbb{N}$.

It is possible that a **CA-CBL.TXT**-strategy leads to a case base of infinite size, for instance, if the language that is described by a text is infinite. So we have to define what it means that such a strategy learns successfully.

**Definition 9** *Let $\mathcal{L}$ be an indexed family. We say $\mathcal{L} \in$ **CA-CBL.TXT** iff*
$\exists \sigma \in \Sigma \; \forall L \in \mathcal{L} \; \forall t \in text(L)$

$$(1) \quad \forall n \in \mathbb{N} \; CB_n = t^+[n] \times \{+\},$$
$$(2) \quad \exists j \in \mathbb{N} \; L_{st}(CB_k, \sigma) = L \text{ for all } k > j.$$

**CA-CBL.INF** *is defined analogously.*

We say $\mathcal{L} \in$ **CA-CBL.TXT** if for all texts of $L$, $(L_{st}(CB_n, \sigma))_{n \in \mathbb{N}}$ converges *semantically.* This is somehow comparable to the notion of convergence underlying the identification type **BC** in Inductive Inference of recursive functions (Angluin & Smith, 1983). All other case-based learning types demand that the sequence $(CB_n)_{n \in \mathbb{N}}$ itself has to converge.

---

[5] *MO* stands for "monotonically", *DE* for "delete", *RA* for "random access" and *LC* for "last case"

[6] *CA* stands for "collect all"

## 4.1 Learning from Text

The two main results concerning case-based learning from text are contained in the following theorem (cf. (Globig & Lange, 1994)).

**Theorem 1**
**LIM.TXT # REPR$^+$**
**LIM.TXT ∩ REPR$^+$ = DE-RA-CBL.TXT**

The first part says, that neither all representable indexed families are learnable nor all learnable families representable. So the lack of learning power of case-based learning from text is due to the lack of representability of indexed families with positive cases. Problems arise when the indexed family contains both finite and infinite languages. Indexed Families that are representable with positive cases only are learnable form text with the most flexible case selection strategy.

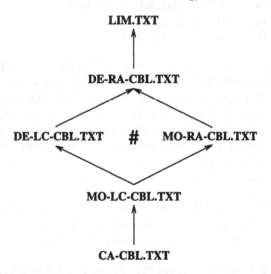

Figure 9: Relationships between the learning types

Figure 9 shows the relationships between the defined case-based learning types. If there is a path from $T_1$ to $T_2$, $T_1$ is a proper subset of $T_2$. The figure indicates that both random access to the already presented cases and the ability to delete cases from the actual case base increase the learning power of a case-based learning system. But neither subsumes the other. Note that even if we allow random access to the presented cases and deleting cases from the case base the full learning power is not reached.

Collecting all cases results not only in a slow system (because of the size of the case base) but also reduces the learning power. This reveals the power of selecting appropriate cases. The more flexible the case selection strategy is, the more classes can be learned.

## 4.2 Learning from Informant

Learning form informant is more powerful than learning from text. It is well known that every indexed family is learnable from informant. The following theorems show that this result is valid for case-based learnability, too.

**Theorem 2**
(1)  **MO-LC-CBL.INF ⊂ IF**
(2)  **MO-RA-CBL.INF = IF**
(3)  **DE-LC-CBL.INF = IF**

**Corollary 1 DE-RA-CBL.INF = IF**

It is not only remarkable that all indexed families are case-based learnable but by comparatively simple selection strategies. While in the text-case even the most flexible case selection strategies were unable to learn all classes in **LIM-TXT** in the informant-case random access or deleting from the case base are enough.

The proof of third equation of Theorem 2 is based on a similarity measure that allows to represent every language of an indexed family using at most two cases.

# 5 Discussion

The symbolic as well as the case-based approach compute a classification when a new case is presented. If only the input and the output of the algorithms are known, we will not be able to distinguish between the symbolic and the case-based approach. The symbolic algorithm builds up its hypothesis by revealing the *common characteristics* of the cases in a predefined *hypothesis language*. The hypothesis describes the *relation between a case and the concept*. One component of a case-based learner is a measure that states the similarity or the distance between cases.

A main difference between case-based and symbolic classification algorithms is the representation of the learned concept (cf. section 2.1). A case-based classifier $(CB, d)$ consists of a case base $CB$ and a measure of similarity $d$. It is possible to represent the same concept $C$ in multiple ways, i.e. by different tuples $(CB_i, d_i)$. But, neither the case base $CB$ nor the measure $sim$ is sufficient to build a classifier for $C$. The knowledge about the concept $C$ is spread to both. Thus, the hypothesis produced by a case-based algorithm represents the concept only *implicitly*, while symbolic procedures build up an *explicit* representation of the learned concept. Often it is a non-trivial task to extract an explicit symbolic representation of the concept from a case base and a measure.

We have shown a method (cf. section 3.4) to reformulate a symbolic learning approach into an equivalent case-based variant. If the problems and the power of case-based and symbolic approaches are similar (Jantke, 1992) as we have seen for our simple scenario (cf. section 3.2), the question arises whether the two approaches can be interchanged in all situations. We assume that we want to get a classifier only and not an explicit description of the concept. In the second case, a case-based system cannot be the appropriate choice. Within this perspective, the symbolic and the case-based approach seem to be interchangeable in the described context. The symbolic approach corresponds to a kind of *compilation process* whereas the case-based approach can be seen as a kind of *interpretation* during run time. Which approach should be used in a concrete situation is a question of an adequate *representation of the previous knowledge*. If previous knowledge contains a *concept of neighborhood* that leads to appropriate hypotheses (like in section 3.5.1), a case-based approach is a good choice. In this scenario we are able to code the neighborhood principle into the used measure. The case-based approach will then produce good hypotheses before the concept is learned, i.e. when not all equivalence classes of the measure are filled.

We have analyzed (cf. section 3.4) the relationship between the measure of similarity, the case base, and the target concept in the described scenario of classification tasks (Globig, 1993). The learning algorithm *needs strong assumptions* about the target concept in order to solve its task with an acceptable number of cases. Assumptions exclude certain concepts from the hypothesis space. Symbolic learners use these assumptions to restrict the language to represent their hypotheses. A case-based learner has to code this assumptions into the measure of similarity. These restrictions of the hypothesis space are called *bias*. (Rendell, 1986) divides the abstraction done by a learning system in two parts: *the bias* (to describe the amount of assumptions), and the *power of the learner*. We have characterized (cf. section 3.4) case-based systems by the *number of learnable concepts* and the *number of cases* they need to identify a target concept. Case-based algorithms use the cases of the case base to fill equivalence classes induced by the measure used. On the other hand, they use the knowledge from the cases to lower the number of equivalence classes by changing the measure. Thereby, the target concept may be identified by fewer cases. The used measure defines the set of the learnable concepts and the cases in the case base select a concept from this set. The *bias* relates to the restriction of the set of learnable concepts induced by the measure of similarity and is therefore comparable to the *degree of universality*. The *minimal size* of the case base reflects the information the learner needs to come to a correct hypothesis, i.e. the power of the learner (Rendell, 1986). Using an universal similarity measure conflicts the minimality of the case base. Reducing the size of the case base, which means to code more knowledge into the measure, usually results in a less universal similarity measure. In section 4 we have seen that if we use a fixed measure of similarity we need advanced case selection strategies to improve the learning power. The knowledge how to select the appropriate cases is of course knowledge about the class of target concepts.

We have stressed that the measure (respectively the way to modify the measure) is the *bias of case-based reasoning*. Without any bias inductive learning is impossible with an acceptable amount of time. Without restrictions of the hypothesis space, neither symbolic nor case-based systems are able to learn even in a finite universe. Because case-based systems are based on a bias that cannot be deduced from the cases, we reject the thesis that case-based classification is more appropriate in situations with a low amount of previous knowledge.

In the last section we studied different types of case-based learning of indexed families from positive data and both positive and negative data with respect to an arbitrary fixed similarity measure. Thereby, we focused our attention on the problem of how the underlying case selection strategies influence the capabilities of case-based learners. As it turns out, the choice of the case selection strategy is of particular importance, if case-based learning from text is investigated. If both positive and negative data are provided, even quite simple case selection strategies are sufficient in order to exhaust the full power of case-based learning.

We conclude that for classification tasks there is no fundamental advantage in the learning power of case-based systems. As we have seen (cf. section 3.5.1) the intelligibleness of the classifications of a case-based system depends on the intelligibleness of the measure of similarity and is therefore not a property of the case-based approach itself. Since the number of cases an algorithm needs to learn a concept is directly related to the size of the hypothesis space, the used bias must have a comparable strength in both approaches. While symbolic approaches use this extra evidential knowledge to restrict the language to represent their hypotheses, the case-based algorithms need it to get appropriate measures of similarity.

# Acknowledgement

We would like to thank M.M. Richter, K.P. Jantke, S. Lange, K.-D. Althoff, and H.-D. Burkhard for many helpful discussions. The study of case selection strategies in Section 4 was done together with Steffen Lange.

# References

Aamodt, A., & Plaza, E. (1994). Case-based reasoning: Foundational issues, methodological variations, and system approaches. *AI Communications*, *7*(1), 39–59.

Aha, D. W. (1991). Case-Based Learning Algorithms. In Bareiss, R. (Ed.), *Proceedings: Case-Based Reasoning Workshop*, pp. 147 – 158. Morgan Kaufmann Publishers.

Angluin, D. (1980). Inductive inference of formal languages from positive data. *Information and Control*, *45*, 117–135.

Angluin, D., & Smith, C. H. (1983). Inductive Inference: Theory and Methods. *Computing Surveys*, *15*(3), 237–269.

Dasarathy, B. (1990). *Nearest Neighbor Norms: NN Pattern Classification Techniques*. IEEE Computer Society Press.

Globig, C., & Lange, S. (1994). On case-based representability and learnability of languages. In Arikawa, S., & Jantke, K. (Eds.), *Algorithmic Learning Theory*, Vol. 872 of *LNAI*, pp. 106–121. Springer-Verlag.

Globig, C. (1993). Symbolisches und Fallbasiertes Lernen. Masters Thesis, University of Kaiserslautern.

Globig, C., & Wess, S. (1994). Symbolic Learning and Nearest-Neighbor Classification. In Bock, P., Lenski, W., & Richter, M. M. (Eds.), *Information Systems and Data Analysis*, Studies in Classification, Data Analysis, and Knowledge Organization, pp. 17–27. Springer Verlag.

Gold, E. M. (1967). Language identification in the limit. *Information and Control*, *10*, 447–474.

Holte, R. S. (1990). Commentary on: PROTOS an exemplar-based learning apprentice. In Kodtratoff, Y., & Michalski, R. (Eds.), *Machine Learning: An Artificial Intelligence Approach*, Vol. III, pp. 128–139. Morgan Kaufmann.

Jantke, K. P. (1992). Case-Based Learning in Inductive Inference. In *Proceedings of the 5th ACM Workshop on Computational Learning Theory (COLT'92)*, pp. 218–223. ACM-Press.

Jantke, K. P., & Lange, S. (1989). Algorithmisches lernen. In Grabowski, J., Jantke, K. P., & Thiele, H. (Eds.), *Grundlagen der Künstlichen Intelligenz*, pp. 246–277. Akademie–Verlag, Berlin.

Jantke, K., & Lange, S. (1993). Case-based representation and learning of pattern languages. In *Proceedings of the 4th International Workshop on Algorithmic learning Theory (ALT'93)*, Vol. 744 of *LNAI*, pp. 87–100. Springer-Verlag.

Kolodner, J. L. (1993). *Case-Based Reasoning*. Morgan Kaufmann.

Michalski, R., Carbonell, J. G., & Mitchell, T. (Eds.). (1983). *Machine Learning: An Artificial Intelligence Approach*, Vol. 1. Tioga, Palo Alto, California.

Mitchell, T. (1982). Generalization as search. *Artificial Intelligence*, *18*(2), 203–226.

Rendell, L. (1986). A General Framework for Induction and a Study of Selective Induction. *Machine Learning*, *1*, 177–226.

Richter, M. M. (1992). Classification and Learning of Similarity Measures. In *Proc. der 16. Jahrestagung der Gesellschaft für Klassifikation e.V.* Springer Verlag.

Wess, S., & Globig, C. (1994). Case-based and symbolic classification – a case study. In Wess, S., Althoff, K.-D., & Richter, M. (Eds.), *Topics in Case-Based Reasoning*, Vol. 837 of *Lecture Notes in Artificial Intelligence*, pp. 65–76. Springer-Verlag.

Wess, S. (1993). PATDEX - Inkrementelle und wissensbasierte Verbesserung von Ähnlichkeitsurteilen in der fallbasierten Diagnostik. In *Tagungsband 2. deutsche Expertensystemtagung XPS-93*, pp. 42–55 Hamburg. Springer Verlag.

# Optimal Strategies -
# Learning from Examples - Boolean Equations

Christian Posthoff

University of The West Indies

Dept. of Mathematics and Computer Science

St. Augustine

TRINIDAD & TOBAGO

cpo@centre1.uwi.tt

Michael Schlosser

Technische Universität Chemnitz-Zwickau

Fakultät für Informatik

D-09107 Chemnitz

GERMANY

msc@informatik.tu-chemnitz.de

**Abstract**

The paper covers a wide range of knowledge acquisition, knowledge engineering and Machine Learning. The main idea is to unify a lot of AI problems using set-theoretic concepts and logical functions.

Many concepts of knowledge-based problem-solving are incorporated into one system which has been based on set-theoretical concepts. This results in a consisting methodology and in a comprehensive set of tools applicable in many fields. The transition between fuzzy and non-fuzzy parts of the problem domain can be realized very flexible supplying a high smartness and a high performance of the constructed model.

Part A of the paper shows the basis for different Machine Learning methods using logical equations. Part B gives a way how to use optimal strategies in order to obtain complete knowledge. A few examples illustrate the method.

## Introduction

Nowadays, many AI conferences show a more or less strong divergency of separate research fields. Roughly spoken, the represented results are deeper and deeper, the concerned fields smaller and smaller. On the other hand, the solution of practical problems very often requires pieces of many theories. Rarely one theory is sufficient and there is still a gap between the set of many theoretical results and the possibility to use the results for a practical problem by one group or even by one person.

Hence, there is a strong demand for methodologies to build consistent models. These methodologies should be applicable in many situations and for many problems in knowledge processing and result in efficient knowledge-based systems. This part of the report has the intention to show how to unify many problem-solving methods on the base of set-theoretical concepts and how to handle precise and fuzzy notions, concepts, ... as flexible as possible.

The authors have designed and partly implemented an interactive system which uses set-theoretical concepts and logical functions. It is able to realize not only the intensively investigated way from the right side to the middle (generalization by different methods of Machine Learning), but also the way from the left side to the middle in Figure 1 (conceptualization of complete knowledge).

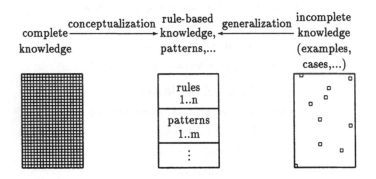

Figure 1: Transformation of Knowledge

Part A of this paper shows the direction from the right side to the middle of Figure 1. Ways to handle the other direction (from the left side to the middle) are given in Part B.

# Part A: Learning from Examples Using BOOLEan Equations

## 1 Set-Theoretical Foundations

There are three ways of representing a set:

1. explicitly: enumeration of the elements

2. implicitly: generation of the elements

3. implicitly: description of the elements by means of properties, attributes, ...

Many AI problems require the creation of one description or the changing between two of these descriptions. Very important for our purposes is the use of the characteristic function (membership function):

Let $M$ be any set, $A \subseteq M$. Then the function $\varphi_A(x)$ with

$$\varphi_A(x) = \begin{cases} 1, & for \quad x \in M, x \in A \\ 0, & for \quad x \in M, x \notin A \end{cases}$$

is the **characteristic function** of $A$ with regard to $M$.

This relation between the subsets of a set and the corresponding characteristic functions is unique:

$$A_1 \neq A_2 \longleftrightarrow \varphi_{A_1}(x) \neq \varphi_{A_2}(x).$$

The characteristic function is able to cover all classification problems (in a wide sense). The isomorphy between set-theoretical and logical operations is well-known[1]:

| Set-theoretic operation | ∩ | ∪ | ⁻ | △ | ◭ |
|---|---|---|---|---|---|
| Logical operation | ∧ | ∨ | ¬ | ⇎ | ∼ |

For instance, the following equations hold:

$$\varphi_{A \cap B}(x) = \varphi_A(x) \wedge \varphi_B(x),$$

$$\varphi_{A \cup B}(x) = \varphi_A(x) \vee \varphi_B(x),$$

$$\varphi_{\overline{A}}(x) = \overline{\varphi_A(x)}.$$

It is supposed that logical functions are well-known.

# 2 Formulation of AI Problems

We always suppose a set of objects, independent of the possibility how to determine the elements, the characteristic functions etc. and formulate important problems set-theoretically. In order to have suitable formulations it is an advantage to build the models onto this foundation.

## 2.1 Single Diagnosis (Classification)

Given: objects described by attributes,
characteristic function $\varphi$.

Find: for any given object $x$, $\varphi(x) = 1$ or $\varphi(x) = 0$ ?

---

[1] The operations are abbreviated as follows:

| | | | | |
|---|---|---|---|---|
| ∩ | intersection | ∧ | conjunction |
| ∪ | union | ∨ | disjunction |
| ⁻ | complement | ¬ | negation |
| △ | symmetrical difference | ⇎ | antivalence |
| ◭ | antisymmetrical difference | ∼ | equivalence |

## 2.2 Multiple Diagnosis (Classification)

Given: objects described by attributes,
characteristic functions $\varphi_1(x)$, $\varphi_2(x)$, ...

Find: for any given object $x$,
$\varphi_1(x) = 1$ or $\varphi_1(x) = 0$ ?
$\varphi_2(x) = 1$ or $\varphi_2(x) = 0$ ?
...

(Imagine the fact that two or more deseases occur simultaneously.)

## 2.3 Configuration, Planning and Design

Given: the description of an object (desired, to be created, to be designed)
by a set of attributes $\{a_1, ..., a_n\}$.

Find: one description of the object by a set of attributes $\{b_1, ..., b_m\}$.

Operations for constructing the new descriptions $\{b_1, ..., b_m\}$ are, for example, parametrization, refinement, combination, optimization, ...

## 2.4 Structuring of Knowledge

Given: a complete enumeration of a set.

Find: description of the set by attributes, rules, patterns,
membership functions.

(For instance endgame databases in chess or checkers, construction of optimal strategies, decision trees.)

## 2.5 Constraints

Given: a set of constraints.

Find: how to include (or exclude) the described sets into (or from)
a problem-solving process?

## 2.6 Learning from Examples

Given: objects,
attributes,
sets (classes),
membership values.

Find: description of each set (e. g. by rules).

## 2.7 Case-Based Reasoning

Given: any sets with certain properties
(e. g. solution of a problem, criteria of optimality).

Find: How does a new object fit into the given sets,
i. e. how can the known properties be used in the new case?

## 2.8 Optimal Strategies

Given: a state space,
set of starting states,
set of final states,
transition rules from one state to another.

Find: the shortest way (or optimal way) from a starting state to a final state.

(Examples: games, configuration, see [PSZ93a] and [Sch92]).

# 3 Learning from Examples

In Learning from Examples, there are several ways in using examples.[2] Here we give only a small view from a wide range of learning methods used in the system which is partly implemented:

- Learning from (only) positive examples
  Starting point is an empty disjunctive normal form (DNF). The input of a (positive) example will cause the addition of a conjunction to the DNF. Using $m$ examples we obtain

$$f = K_1 \vee K_2 \vee \ldots \vee K_m. \qquad (1)$$

  The positive examples are evaluated exactly by $f = 1$, all the $K_i$ being any conjunctions of relevant properties.

- Learning from both positive and negative examples
  In this case we start with two empty DNFs. Positive examples are added to one DNF, negative ones are added to the other. Finally, we obtain the functions

$$f_1 = K_{11} \vee K_{12} \vee \ldots \vee K_{1m_1} \qquad (2)$$

  for the positive examples and

$$f_2 = K_{21} \vee K_{22} \vee \ldots \vee K_{2m_2} \qquad (3)$$

  for the negative examples, respectively.
  All evaluations with $f_1 \not\sim f_2$ are the set of contradictory examples.

---

[2]It should be mentioned that theoretical aspects of Learning from Examples (e. g. by DNF or CNF, respectively) may be credited to VALIANT [Val84]. Here we won't go into the details of the theory of Machine Learning (also called Algorithmic Learning or Computational Learning Theory). The interested reader is referred to [Val84] and to subsequent literature (for an introduction see [AB92]).

For the following chapters of Part A we restrict ourselves to BOOLEan (i. e. binary) functions because they have been intensively investigated. There are a lot of algorithms with BOOLEan functions (such as minimization or transformation of one normal form into another [BS91]). Moreover, BOOLEan functions are suitable to discover redundancies in rule bases [PFRS92].

# 4   The Transition to Logical Equations

The transition to problem-relevant formulations by means of logical equations is possible by various methods, but only some of them are mentioned.

## 4.1   Ternary Data Structures

The objects are described by attributes. The presence or absence of the attributes are notified directly (coded by a conjunction).

| $a_1$ | $a_2$ | $a_3$ | ... | $a_{n-1}$ | $a_n$ |
|-------|-------|-------|-----|-----------|-------|
| 0 | 1 | – | | 1 | 1 |

means, that $a_1$ is not present, $a_2$ is present, $a_3$ is not determined (not observed) and so on.

This leads to powerful object-oriented descriptions useful in any given context. For instance, ways of an automatical verification of knowledge bases are shown in [Sch94].

## 4.2   Advantages

The collection of examples (**learning from examples**) can be understood as learning a disjunctive or a conjunctive normal form. The system realizes
a)   learning from **positive examples**;
b)   learning from **negative examples**;
c)   learning from **both positive and negative examples**.

Learning from examples can completely be embedded into the theory of logical functions that is offering many additional features:

- solving different approaches by the same theory (in corporation of rules, constraints, ...),

- changing between different representations,

- using efficient algorithms and data structures,

- consistency checking, elimination of redundancy,

- using the BOOLEan differential calculus for the qualitative analysis of the problem.

Efficient algorithms for logical functions are only mentioned here - for more information see e. g. [BS91]. The BOOLEan Differential Calculus is represented in [BP81].

## 4.3   Elimination of Rules, Constraints

In many cases it is very useful to eliminate rules in the following way:

the rule

$$f(x_1, ..., x_n) \rightarrow g(x_1, ..., x_n),$$

or abbreviated

$$f(\vec{x}) \rightarrow g(\vec{x})$$

(the most general form of a rule), will be equivalently replaced by the equation

$$\overline{f(\vec{x})} \vee g(\vec{x}) = 1$$

or by the equation

$$f(\vec{x}) \wedge \overline{g(\vec{x})} = 0.$$

In this way, any set of rules can be replaced by a set of equations, and the set of solutions is the set of all objects which are consistent with this set of rules [PFRS92]. Constraints are handled in the same way. If the variables are discrete variables it is again possible to use a binary codification.

# 5   Fuzzification of Classic Logical or Set-Theoretical Concepts

In practice we often have inexact, incomplete, ... (i. e. fuzzy) knowledge. That means we must realize the transitions

crisp knowledge $\Longleftrightarrow$ fuzzy knowledge

in both directions.

The main advantage of set-theoretical concepts is an easy realization of the necessary transitions. All the models remain completely consistent using the following replace-ments:

a) $\Longrightarrow$:
A $\rightarrow$ {0,1} is replaced by A $\rightarrow$ [0,1].

The set-theoretic operations ∧, ∨, ⁻, ... are replaced by fuzzy-logical operations.[3]

b) ⟸:
α-cuts at a certain (problem-dependent) level.

Many essential properties can be defined in both structures and be transformed into each other (equivalence relation, partial ordering, similarity, ...).
Important fuzzy descriptions of sets are **evaluation functions** (in strategic games, diagnosis, evaluation of products, events, plans, configurations, ...).

## Main proposition.

Given any expression describing a logical function, this expression can be understood (and evaluated) in the sense of classical logic <u>as well as</u> in the sense of fuzzy logic.

This is done by replacing the operations ∧, ∨, ⁻, ... with fuzzy-logical operations (selected with respect to the problem) and by replacing {0,1} with any other set (for instance [0,1] or another one).

Hence, the construction of logical equations or the transfer of concepts into the language of logical equations is the main point of the unifying methodology and will be presented by some example concepts.

Logical equations as well as descriptions of examples may be fuzzified (on the right side). In the crisp case the right-hand side of an equation is equal to 1. In the fuzzy case, however, we may distinguish different "classes" of examples. For instance, we may have "very good examples" (i. e. examples which fulfill a given condition very well), "good examples", "more or less good examples",... In this case, we can put the right side of the logical equation equal to $1$, $\frac{3}{4}$, $\frac{1}{2}$,..., respectively. Thus, we obtain fuzzy-logical equations which may be solved by replacing the set-theoretical operations ∧, ∨, ⁻ with fuzzy-logical operations.

## Remark.

An extension of the presented logical calculus could be the use of the changes of the variables. The so-called differential $dx_i$ of a variable $x_i$ describes the change of the variable $x_i$. From a given "old" value of $x_i$ and a value of $dx_i$ the relation

$$x_i^* = x_i \not\sim dx_i$$

---

[3]Mostly used fuzzy-logical operations are defined as follows:

- Conjunction
  Minimum: $(\mu_A \wedge \mu_B)(u) = \min_{u \in U}\{\mu_A(u), \mu_B(u)\}$
  Bounded Difference: $(\mu_A \wedge \mu_B)(u) = \max_{u \in U}\{0, \mu_A(u) + \mu_B(u) - 1\}$
  Algebraic Product: $(\mu_A \wedge \mu_B)(u) = \mu_A(u) \times \mu_B(u)$

- Disjunction
  Maximum: $(\mu_A \vee \mu_B)(u) = \max_{u \in U}\{\mu_A(u), \mu_B(u)\}$
  Bounded Sum: $(\mu_A \vee \mu_B)(u) = \min_{u \in U}\{1, \mu_A(u) + \mu_B(u)\}$
  Algebraic Sum: $(\mu_A \vee \mu_B)(u) = \mu_A(u) + \mu_B(u) - \mu_A(u) \times \mu_B(u)$

- Negation
  $(\neg\mu_A)(u) = 1 - \mu_A(u)$

gives a "new" value $x_i^*$ of $x_i$. $dx_i = 1$ means a change, $dx_i = 0$ a non-change (i. e. constancy) of $x_i$.

Using differentials we may consider equations like

$$f(x_1, x_2, ..., x_n, dx_1, dx_2, ..., dx_n) = 1$$

which not only describe states but also their transitions. Fuzzifying such equations could be a promising field for further investigations.

**Remark.**

For those skilled in the art it is easy to understand that logical functions constructed in any problem field by arbitrary means are also an important starting point for the use of **neural networks** and of **genetic algorithms**. Both ways are under consideration, but here they won't be mentioned furthermore.

# 6   Important Results

The consistent use of BOOLEan (logical) functions and equations is an important way of constructing knowledge-based systems allowing the simultaneous treatment of crisp and fuzzy knowledge within the same formalism.

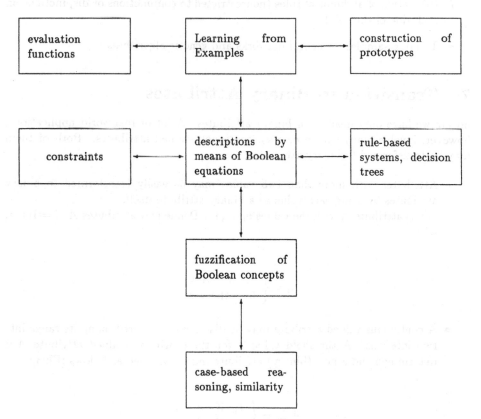

Figure 2: The logical structure of the system

The system realized so far (see Figure 2) allows the construction of knowledge-based systems in many fields.

For the field of **learning from examples** it shows at least the following results:

1. Convenient solutions by using ternary data structures. For more datails see [PFRS92].

2. Consistency checks within the set of samples and during the application ($\Rightarrow$ discussion in the domain).

3. Generalization and specialization of the example set, the constructed rules and the evaluation functions.

4. Construction and verification of missing examples (utilization of stochastic and genetic methods).

5. Elimination of redundancy by minimization.

6. Definition of input and output variables, elimination of intermediate variables, construction of rules, simplification of the original rule set.

7. Utilization of all kinds of rules (nonrestricted to conjunctions or disjunctions on each side of the rule).

8. Training samples for neural networks and genetic algorithms.

# 7 Transition to Binary Attributes

So far we have only dealt with binary attributes. A lot of real-world applications, however, involve many-valued or even continuous-valued attributes. Both of them may be transformed to binary attributes:

- Attributes with more than two values may be easily transformed to binary attributes by using each value as a binary attribute itself.
  Given attribute $A$ with the values $v_1, ..., v_n$. Define new attributes $A_i, i = 1(1)n$, with

$$A_i = \begin{cases} 1, & \text{if} \quad A = v_i, \\ 0, & \text{otherwise.} \end{cases}$$

- A continuous-valued attribute may be discretized by partitioning its range into two intervals. A threshold value $T$ for the continuous-valued attribute $A$ is determined and a new (binary) attribute may be defined as follows [FI93]:

$$A_{new} = \begin{cases} 1, & \text{if} \quad A \leq T, \\ 0, & \text{if} \quad A > T. \end{cases}$$

# Part B: Optimal Strategies and Diagnosis

# 8 Optimal Strategies

## 8.1 Subjective Evaluation

The generation of rules (understandable to human beings) from a given data base is an important object of research in Artificial Intelligence. Its aim is to substitute the objective evaluations inside a database by (observable, computable, evaluable, understandable) attributes (features). This may be compared with the way human beings are handling such problems.

Maybe experts can provide problem-relevant attributes which describe sets of states, assuming the attributes are linked together by conjunction:

$$P = a_1 \wedge a_2 \wedge \dots \wedge a_m.$$

Each possible logical description of a set of states forms a class. Besides other methods, logical functions are only one approach which may immediately be derived from the notion of the characteristic function.

Each classification with more than two classes may be transferred to a sequence of two-class problems.

Using logical descriptions we obtain the following definition of similarity:

**Two states are similar if they fulfill the same logical expression.**

This makes sense because all problems of a class may be solved by the same problem solving method:

"execute $i$ optimal moves." (see chap. 8.2)

In order to use this concept of similarity we need a description of the used sets and we have to ascertain the membership of a certain position to a set.

If this cannot be done exactly, we may choose among various ways. In using conjunctions for instance we have the following definition of similarity:

**Two states are the more similar the more attributes coincide in their logical expressions.**

For instance, the HAMMING distance may be used as a measure.

Very attractive and efficient generalizations are the applications of fuzzy set theory and fuzzy logic, respectively. Thereby the membership to a set is not restricted to the values 0 and 1, but we have a finer graduation, e. g. within the whole interval [0,1]. With the fuzzy approach we may also model the (eventual) membership to more than one set.

**The more similar a state to the states of a certain set is the greater the membership.**

Another way based on the set theory is to use the explicit descriptions by means of attributes. So far, the reflections are more general, because the definition of the attributes that are describing the state is only needed in a second step.

However, once the attributes are fixed (assume $A_1, ..., A_n$) and their domains are known (say $A_i = \{a_{i1}, ..., a_{ik_i}\}$), each element of a set of states may be described by an n-tuple $(a_1, ..., a_n)$. Each $a_i$ is a value of the attribute $A_i$. The whole set of states corresponds to a relation $R \subseteq A_1 \times A_2 \times ... \times A_n$. Now we have further chances to formalize the similarity:

A relation $R$ is a <u>similarity relation</u> if $R$ is <u>reflexive</u> und <u>symmetric</u>.

In the same way, <u>equivalence relations</u> may be used. These relations are reflexive, symmetric and transitive. An equivalence relation causes the division of a set into equivalence classes:

**Two states are similar if they belong to the same equivalence class.**

Because these three properties may be also extended to fuzzy concepts, we obtain fuzzy similarity relations and fuzzy equivalence relations, respectively, as efficient and well-investigated models.

So far we have dealt with a 'state' in a general way. In the following chapters of Part B we will consider games, so we use 'position' synonymously.

## 8.2   The Existence of an Optimal Strategy

It is well-known since 1912 [Zer12] that for finite games like chess or checkers an optimal strategy can be constructed on the base of set-theoretical considerations. Starting with results achieved by STRÖHLEIN [Str70], these ideas led to complete endgame databases for a big number of chess endgames. We use the following notions as a base for further investigations (without detailed proofs or explanations) and refer to the following propositions:

The set $M$ of all possible legal positions[4] p can be partitioned into three disjoint subsets (classes)

$M_W = \{$p: White has a forced win after n plies, $n \geq 0\}$,
$M_B = \{$p: Black has a forced win after n plies, $n \geq 0\}$,
$M_D = M \setminus (M_W \cup M_B) = \{$p: p is drawn $\}$
with $M = M_W \cup M_B \cup M_D$, $M_W \cap M_B = \emptyset$, $M_W \cap M_D = \emptyset$, $M_D \cap M_B = \emptyset$.

For the class $M_W$ (in an analogous way for $M_B$) further partitions are possible resulting in a sequence

$M_W^0, M_W^1, M_W^2, \ldots$ with the following meaning:
$M_W^0$: Black to move, but Black has been checkmated;
$M_W^1$: White to move, checkmate after one ply;
$M_W^2$: Black to move, checkmate after two plies;

...

The actions on the board are forced in the following sense:
if $p \in M_W^{2i}, i = 1, 2, \ldots$, then **each** black move leads to $p' \in M_W^k$ ($k < 2i$, k odd);
if $p \in M_W^{2i+1}, i = 0, 1, 2, \ldots$, then **at least one** white move exists leading to $p' \in M_W^{2i}$.

---

[4]A position p is considered to be legal if it can be obtained from the starting position by legal moves.

An optimal sequence of moves has its corresponding positions successively in $M_W^i$, $M_W^{i-1}$, $M_W^{i-2}$ ..., $M_W^0$.

Analogous reflections are valid for $M_B$.

Therefore, we have: $M_W = M_W^0 \cup M_W^1 \cup \ldots \cup M_W^{nW}$; $M_B = M_B^0 \cup M_B^1 \cup \ldots \cup M_B^{nB}$.

$nW, nB$ are the maximum lengths for a forced winning variation of White or Black, respectively. All sets appearing in this way are finite. Exact values of $nW, nB$ are not known. The repetition of a position and the 50-move-rule are not considered here. Historically, mate positions have been the goal of the construction, this means that the shortest way to a mate position is the criterion of optimality. However, any other exactly defined criterion (maybe a subgoal on the way to mate) can be taken as a base for the construction of similar sets. This existence of an optimal strategy (winning way, problem solution) can be generalized to many AI problems.

The class of draw positions $M_D$ can be partitioned into two subclasses:
$M_D = M_D^0 \cup M_D^1$ with
$M_D^0 = \{p: \textbf{each} \text{ possible move leads again to a position of } M_D\}$;
$M_D^1 = M_D \setminus M_D^0 = \{p: \textbf{at least one} \text{ possible move leads to a position of } M_D\}$;
$M_D^0$ contains the positions which cannot be lost (e. g. KBK, that is King and Bishop against King, KNK, ...); the positions of $M_D^1$ are drawn only potentially. There are moves which can lead to $M_W$ as well as to $M_B$.

We obtain: $M = (M_W^0 \cup \ldots \cup M_W^{nW}) \cup (M_B^0 \cup \ldots \cup M_B^{nB}) \cup (M_D^0 \cup M_D^1)$,
no pair of the sets on the right-hand side having elements in common.

These well-defined sets can now explain exactly the factual meaning of the notion "uncertainty" in chess (and in all similar problems) [Pos92]:

- It is not generally known to which partition of $M$ a given position p belongs.

- In the same way, this fact is not known for all successor positions of the position p.

That means: for optimal play, we need a "diagnostic instrument" which determines the corresponding set $M_W^i$ for a given position p. Then the move to be selected would depend on the index of the successor positions, the best move leading to $M_W^{i-1}$. This will be shown in the following chapter on diagnosis.

Assume White is the stronger side and will win the game. The class $M_W$ may be illustrated in Figure 3. To win the game starting at a given position is equivalent to looking for a shortest path in the graph of Figure 3.

For the set $M$ of all legal positions a half-ordering relation can be defined: So we have

$$p_i \in M_W^i \leq p_j \in M_W^j \quad \text{if and only if} \quad i \leq j,$$

where $p_i \leq p_j$ is to be read as '$p_i$ precedes $p_j$'.

Especially important for further considerations is the strict inequality

$$p_i < p_j \quad \text{if and only if} \quad p_i \text{ is closer to a goal than} \quad p_j,$$

where $<$ is to be read as 'strictly precedes'.

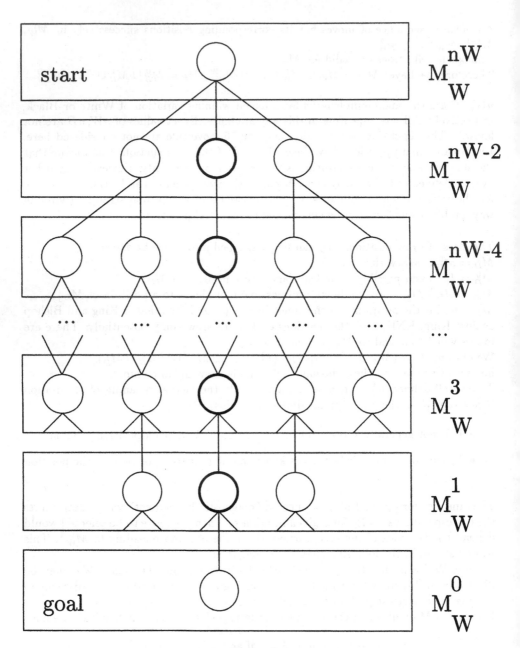

Figure 3:

## 8.3 Diagnosis

HORACEK pointed out that the main defect of classical evaluation functions is the absence of relations among subsequent problem states, an evaluation considers only isolated positions. At least some connection to the initial position is absolutely necessary [Hor84]. In the authors' opinion, though completely equivalent to the statement of HORACEK, the connection of a position to one final position should be preferred. This proposal of connection to the goal is caused by the existence of complete endgame databases based on the optimal strategy (cf. chap. 8.2).

Diagnosis is considered to be a very simple way of an evaluation. In medical and technical diagnosis as well, the class of an object may be determined by its attribute values. The simplest diagnoses are classifications of two classes (two-class problems or dichotomizing problems).

In this way, certain chess endgames have been solved during the last decade. The classification procedures separate one type of situation from another. Their aim is to find rules to classify a given position correctly (see e. g. [Qui83], [MN77]).

In order to give a general outline of the diagnosis in games, subsequently only positions of $M_W$ are considered ($M_B$ is treated analogously).

The membership of a given position may be decided by diagnostic rules (such as decision trees, logical formulae, ...). However, diagnostic rules are not sufficient for practical play in general. A player (the white side) does not only want to know that his present position is in $M_W$, but he likes to know the "best" move that he will stay in $M_W$ and, moreover, he will win "as fast as possible".

The optimal strategy after ZERMELO is useful in this case (cf. chap. 8.2).

Let $d_{max}$ be the maximum distance to mate of the considered endgame. $M_W$ is divided into $d_{max} = (nW + 1)/2$ equivalence classes ($nW$ odd)

$$M_W^1, M_W^3, \ldots, M_W^{nW}$$

with "Mate in d moves", $1 \leq d \leq d_{max}$. Therefore, $d_{max} - 1$ diagnostic rules for $d_{max} - 1$ two-class problems are to be found:

| | |
|---|---|
| rule 1 | separates $M_W^1$ and $M_W \setminus M_W^1$ |
| rule 2 | separates $M_W^3$ and $M_W \setminus (M_W^1 \cup M_W^3)$ |

$$\vdots \tag{4}$$

| | |
|---|---|
| rule d | separates $M_W^{2d-1}$ and $M_W \setminus (M_W^1 \cup \ldots \cup M_W^{2d-1})$ |

$$\vdots$$

| | |
|---|---|
| rule $d_{max} - 1$ | separates $M_W^{nW-2}$ and $M_W \setminus (M_W^1 \cup \ldots \cup M_W^{2d_{max}-3}) = M_W^{nW}$. |

We may obtain the rules (4) by methods of machine learning. [5]

---

[5] One way of discovering rules by decision trees for the endgame KRK (i. e. King and Rook against King) is given in [PSS92].

In this way, all positions with an equal distance to mate (according to ZERMELO) are aggregated and described by a corresponding diagnostic rule. For any position $p \in M_W$, we find the index $i$ in $M_W^i$ by defining the evaluation function

$$f(p) = \min\{i \ : \ p \in M_W^{2i-1}\}. \tag{5}$$

The rules (5) serve as the basis for the "therapy" (see [PSZ93b]). In terms of games 'therapy' and 'optimal play' are synonymous. The following transitions are carried out by a white move in each case

$$M_W^i \longrightarrow M_W^{i-1}, i = nW, nW - 2, \ldots, 1. \tag{6}$$

The positions of $M_W^{i-1}, i = nW, nW - 2, \ldots, 1$, are with Black to move. Black's subsequent best move leads to a position of $M_W^{i-2}, i = nW, nW - 2, \ldots, 1$. $M_W^0$ is the set of all mating positions in which no black move is available.

To determine an optimal move in a given position $p \in M_W^i$, i odd, all successors $p'_j, j = 1(1)k$, are investigated. Using the diagnostic rules (4) again, we select a position $p'_{j1}$ for which

$$p'_{j1} \in M_W^{i-1}$$

holds. (By construction, in $M_W^{i-1}$ all black moves lead to a position of $M_W^{i'}, i' \leq i-2$.) $p'_{j1}$ is not necessarily uniquely determined.

The selection of an optimal white move from position $p \in M_W^i$ leading to $p'_{j1} \in M_W^{i-1}$ may be considered as the therapy in the field of games.

The transitions (7) are related to a *certain* index $i$, that is to a fixed distance to a goal (mate). We should like to know transition rules

$$M_W^i \longrightarrow M_W^{i-1}, \tag{7}$$

holding for *all* $i = 1(1)d_{max} - 1$ or at least for more than one index $i$. For more details see [PSZ93b].

# 9 An Example

## 9.1 The Endgame Database QK

Some years ago, one of the authors created a new endgame database (EDB) to get new results in another field of chess [Sch88] [Sch91]. The generated database differs from usually considered EDBs in one point only, namely that there is a fixed number of immobile pieces on the board (Figure 4).

Figure 4

We note that this somewhat artificial position of black pieces avoids moves of the white King, but it is not a restrictive condition for the EDB construction.

We constructed a data base in which all positions contain white Queen (wQ) and black King (bK) in addition to Figure 4. All positions of the EDB differ from each other only in the placing of wQ and bK. These two chessmen are alone active during the play. For more details see [Sch92].

The main results of this EDB construction (cf. [Sch88]):

- The mating position Qh5/Kh3 is only attainable with the black King inside a region consisting of 8 squares, namely h3, h4, h5, h6, g4, g5, f3, and f4. Outside this region, checkmating the black King on h3 cannot be forced.

  (Other ways to win, e. g. checkmating with King and Queen against King, after capturing the three black pieces need more than 9 moves. They are not considered here.
  The fixed position of Figure 4 might be slightly changed, so that all black pieces are guarded, e. g. White: Kf1; Black: Rg2, Bg1, Bh1, Pf2, g3, h2.)

- If the mating position Qh5/Kh3 is attainable at all, then in at most 9 moves (assuming optimal play).

The small amount of this EDB (2 mobile pieces only; one of them, the black King, restricted to 8 squares only) enables us to write it down completely on one page (see Table below).

The wQ/bK EDB can be used as follows:

1. Choose a WTM position (wQ and bK in additon to Figure 4),

2. Read the corresponding table entry.

For each position of wQ and bK in addition to Figure 4, a table entry contains

number-square[/square ...] if there is a win according to ZERMELO's algorithm, the meaning of the elements is the following
number: number of moves to win (mate),
square: the target square of a wQ move; maybe there are two or more equi-optimal moves.

draw if there is no win according to ZERMELO's algorithm (with mating position Qh5/Kh3).

ill if the position is illegal.

| wQ pos. | bK position | | | | | | | | |
|---|---|---|---|---|---|---|---|---|---|
| | h3 | h4 | h5 | h6 | g4 | g5 | f3 | f4 | any |
| a1 | 3-g7 | 5-e5 | 3-g7 | draw | 4-f6 | draw | 5-e5 | draw | ill or draw |
| a2 | 3-e6/g8 | 4-g8 | 6-e6 | 4-g8 | 7-d5 | 5-f7 | draw | 6-e6 | ill or draw |
| a3 | 5-a6/d6/e7/f8 | 5-e7 | draw | draw | 6-f8 | draw | ill | draw | ill or draw |
| a4 | 5-a6/c6 | ill | 7-e8 | draw | ill | draw | 7-e8 | ill | ill or draw |
| a5 | 1-h5 | 5-e5 | ill | draw | 7-d5 | ill | 5-e5 | draw | ill or draw |
| a6 | 3-e6 | 2-g6 | 6-e6 | ill | 4-f6 | draw | draw | 6-e6 | ill or draw |
| a7 | 3-g7 | 5-e7 | 3-g7 | draw | 8-d7 | 5-f7 | 7-e7 | draw | ill or draw |
| a8 | 3-g8 | 4-g8 | 7-e8 | 4-g8 | 6-f8 | draw | ill | draw | ill or draw |
| b1 | 3-f5 | 2-g6 | 9-h7 | draw | 8-g6 | draw | 9-e1 | draw | ill or draw |
| b2 | 3-g7 | 5-e5 | 3-g7 | draw | 4-f6 | draw | 5-e5 | draw | ill or draw |
| b3 | 3-e6/g8 | 4-g8 | 6-e6 | 4-g8 | 7-d5 | 5-f7 | ill | 6-e6 | ill or draw |
| b4 | 5-b6/d6/e7/f8 | ill | draw | draw | ill | draw | 7-e7 | ill | ill or draw |
| b5 | 1-h5 | 5-e5 | ill | draw | 7-d5 | ill | 5-e5 | draw | ill or draw |
| b6 | 3-e6 | 2-g6 | 6-e6 | ill | 4-f6 | draw | draw | 6-e6 | ill or draw |
| b7 | 3-g7 | 5-e7 | 3-g7 | draw | 7-d5 | 5-f7 | ill | draw | ill or draw |
| b8 | 3-g8 | 4-g8 | 7-e8 | 4-g8 | 6-f8 | draw | 5-e5 | ill | ill or draw |
| c1 | 5-c6/c8/h6 | 5-h6 | draw | ill | draw | ill | 9-e1 | ill | ill or draw |
| c2 | 3-f5 | 2-g6 | 9-h7 | draw | 8-g6 | draw | draw | draw | ill or draw |
| c3 | 3-g7 | 5-e5 | 3-g7 | draw | 4-f6 | draw | ill | draw | ill or draw |
| c4 | 3-e6/g8 | ill | 6-e6 | 4-g8 | ill | 5-f7 | draw | ill | ill or draw |
| c5 | 1-h5 | 5-e5/e7 | ill | draw | 6-f8 | ill | 5-e5 | draw | ill or draw |
| c6 | 3-e6 | 2-g6 | 6-e6 | ill | 4-f6 | draw | ill | 6-e6 | ill or draw |
| c7 | 3-g7 | 5-e5/e7 | 3-g7 | draw | 8-d7/e5 | 5-f7 | 5-e5 | ill | ill or draw |
| c8 | ill | 4-g8 | 6-e6 | 4-g8 | ill | draw | 7-e8 | 6-e6 | ill or draw |
| d1 | 1-h5 | 6-d7/f3 | ill | draw | ill | draw | ill | draw | ill or draw |
| d2 | 5-d6/d8/h6 | 5-h6 | draw | ill | 7-d5 | ill | 9-e1 | ill | ill or draw |
| d3 | 3-f5 | 2-g6 | 9-h7 | draw | 7-d5 | draw | ill | draw | ill or draw |
| d4 | 3-g7 | ill | 3-g7 | draw | ill | draw | 5-e5 | ill | ill or draw |
| d5 | 1-h5 | 4-g8 | ill | 4-g8 | 8-d7/e5 | ill | ill | 6-e6 | ill or draw |
| d6 | 3-e6 | 2-g6 | 6-e6 | ill | 4-f6 | draw | 5-e5 | ill | ill or draw |
| d7 | ill | 5-e7 | 3-g7 | draw | ill | 5-f7 | 7-e7/e8 | 6-e6 | ill or draw |
| d8 | 3-g8 | ill | 7-e8/f6 | 4-g8 | 4-f6 | ill | 7-e7/e8 | draw | ill or draw |
| e1 | 3-e6 | 5-e5/e7 | 6-e6 | draw | 8-e5 | draw | 5-e5 | 6-e6 | ill or draw |
| e2 | 1-h5 | 5-e5/e7 | ill | draw | ill | draw | ill | 6-e6 | ill or draw |
| e3 | 3-e6 | 5-e5/e7/h6 | 6-e6 | ill | 8-e5 | ill | ill | ill | ill or draw |
| e4 | 3-e6/f5 | ill | 6-e6 | draw | ill | draw | ill | ill | ill or draw |
| e5 | 1-h5 | 5-e7 | ill | draw | 4-f6 | ill | 7-e7/e8 | ill | ill or draw |
| e6 | ill | 2-g6 | 7-e8/f6 | ill | ill | 5-f7 | 5-e5 | draw | ill or draw |
| e7 | 3-e6/g7 | ill | 3-g7 | draw | 4-f6 | ill | 5-e5 | 6-e6 | ill or draw |
| e8 | 1-h5 | 2-g6 | ill | 4-g8 | 6-f8 | 5-f7 | 5-e5 | 6-e6 | ill or draw |
| f1 | 3-f5 | 6-f3/f8 | 7-f6 | draw | 4-f6 | 5-f7 | ill | ill | ill or draw |
| f2 | 3-f5 | 6-f3/f8 | 7-f6 | draw | 4-f6 | 5-f7 | ill | ill | ill or draw |
| f3 | 1-h5 | 6-f8 | ill | draw | ill | 5-f7 | ill | ill | ill or draw |
| f4 | 3-f5 | ill | 7-f6 | ill | ill | ill | ill | ill | ill or draw |
| f5 | ill | 2-g6 | ill | draw | ill | ill | ill | ill | ill or draw |
| f6 | 3-e6/f5/g7 | ill | 3-g7 | ill | 6-f8 | ill | ill | ill | ill or draw |
| f7 | 1-h5 | 2-g6 | ill | 4-g8 | 4-f6 | draw | ill | ill | ill or draw |
| f8 | 3-f5/g7/g8 | 4-g8 | 3-g7 | ill | 4-f6 | 5-f7 | ill | ill | ill or draw |
| g1 | ill | ill | ill | ill | ill | ill | ill | ill | ill or draw |
| g2 | ill | ill | ill | ill | ill | ill | ill | ill | ill or draw |
| g3 | ill | ill | ill | ill | ill | ill | ill | ill | ill or draw |
| g4 | ill | ill | ill | 4-g8 | ill | ill | ill | ill | ill or draw |
| g5 | 1-h5 | ill | ill | ill | ill | ill | 5-e5 | ill | ill or draw |
| g6 | 1-h5 | 4-g8 | ill | ill | ill | ill | 7-e8 | 6-e6 | ill or draw |
| g7 | 3-g8 | 2-g6 | 7-f6 | ill | ill | ill | 5-e5 | draw | ill or draw |
| g8 | 3-e6/g7 | 2-g6 | 3-g7 | draw | ill | ill | 7-e8 | 6-e6 | ill or draw |
| h1 | ill | ill | ill | ill | ill | ill | ill | ill | ill or draw |
| h2 | ill | ill | ill | ill | draw | draw | draw | draw | ill or draw |
| h3 | ill | ill | ill | ill | ill | draw | draw | 6-e6 | ill or draw |
| h4 | ill | ill | ill | ill | ill | ill | 7-e7 | ill | ill or draw |
| h5 | ill | ill | ill | ill | ill | ill | ill | draw | ill or draw |
| h6 | ill | ill | ill | ill | 4-f6 | ill | draw | ill | ill or draw |
| h7 | ill | ill | ill | ill | 8-d7/g6 | 5-f7 | 7-e7 | draw | ill or draw |
| h8 | ill | ill | ill | ill | 4-f6 | draw | 5-e5 | draw | ill or draw |

Table: EDB wQ/bK

## 9.2 Combination of Knowledge and Search

According to CLARKE [Cla77], we can solve problems by using both ends of the trade-off axis: the pure algorithmic or the pure descriptive concept, respectively (see also [PSSZ94]).

Using the pure algorithmic concept in our QK example would mean a look-ahead search of 9 moves (17 plies). We can reduce the search by using subgoals, that means parts of the knowledge inside the EDB. The following table shows different numbers of subgoals, the corresponding maximum search depth, the number of positions in the subgoal(s) and the sets according to ZERMELO.

| Number of subgoals | Max. search depth | Number of positions | Sets of EDB |
|---|---|---|---|
| 0 (i. e. brute-force) = algorithmic concept | 9 moves/17 plies | 0 | – |
| 1 | 5 / 9 | 14 | $M_W^8$ |
| 2 | 3 / 5 | 9 | $M_W^6, M_W^{12}$ |
| 4 | 2 / 3 | 26 | $M_W^4, M_W^8, M_W^{12}, M_W^{16}$ |
| 8 (i. e. use of EDB) = descriptive concept | no search (use of complete EDB) | 40 | $M_W^2, M_W^4, ..., M_W^{14}, M_W^{16}$ |

An existing EDB replaces traditional (brute-force) search for a goal, starting at any position, by 1-ply search step by step (using complete knowledge available), see Figure 3. Using subgoals replaces traditional search for a goal, starting at any position, by $(i_j - i_{j-1})$-ply search (using only the knowledge of $Patt_j$, $j = 1, ..., k$), cf. Figure 5.

On one hand, the transition from Figure 3 to Figure 5 reduces the required knowledge, i. e. the number of subgoals (rules, patterns, ...). On the other hand, the amount of search increases, depending on the gap between two successive subgoals. This reflects the well-known compromise between search and knowledge in problem solving.

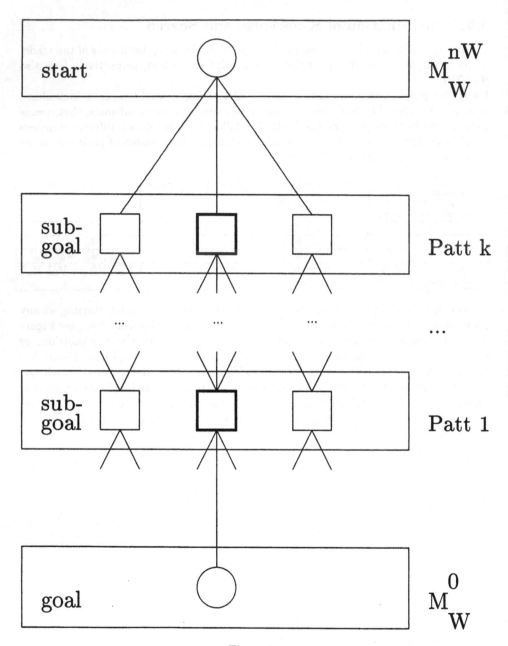

Figure 5:

## 9.3 Generation of Rules

Depthcharts[6] are just right to be transformed into rules. Let us show a very easy example. The depthchart for bK on f4 with BTM

Figure 6

can immediately be transformed into a rule which is appropriate to play the QK problem optimally:

```
if   (bK on f4 and wQ can move to e6)
then win for White (more exactly: Mate in 6 moves) by moving wQ to e6
else draw
```

In chess jargon this reads as follows:

> "With the black King on f4 White can only win by moving his Queen to
> e6. Otherwise Black can draw."

In this way depthcharts (and so finally the whole EDB) may be transformed into a set of rules which represent chess knowledge about a restricted domain.

## 9.4 Conceptualization of the Knowledge by Using Patterns

Until now we have used exact knowledge, i. e. exact descriptions of the sequence of subgoals. Now we show how to use inexact descriptions.

Patterns are relevant to AI in general, for the evaluation of game positions in particular (e. g. in chess [Kur77] [Ste84] [Hee84]).

> A pattern is defined to be any property (relation) concerning some pieces
> on the board which may be present or absent. In chess patterns are often
> "geometrically" defined.

Certain patterns may occur in a game more than once depending on the index $i$ (i. e. distance to a goal). Examples are simple chess endgames, such as KRK [Mic77] [Sei86], KPK [BC80], KBNK [Kor84], QK [Sch88].

---

[6]Depthchart is a technique for expressing in a concentrated visual form the content of a database under consideration.
A depthchart for an n-men endgame is a chess diagram showing (n-1) men in well-defined positions. The notion of depthcharts was introduced by J. ROYCROFT [Roy86]. The n-th piece is free to be located on any of the unoccupied squares. The number recorded in the square is the distance-to-mate (or win). Such depthcharts may serve as heuristics to discover strategies [HvdHS89].
In our EDB n=2 holds.

One typical pattern which occurs more than once in QK is shown in Figure 7. wQ and bK have a distance of a Knight's move (named $Patt_{QK}$). This pattern was discovered by a decision tree using the relative distance between King and Queen as an attribute.

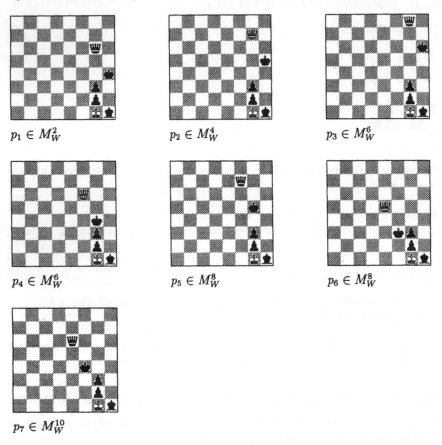

$p_1 \in M_W^2$ $p_2 \in M_W^4$ $p_3 \in M_W^6$

$p_4 \in M_W^6$ $p_5 \in M_W^8$ $p_6 \in M_W^8$

$p_7 \in M_W^{10}$

Figure 7

Among all the positions of Figure 7 having a fixed distance of wQ and bK we can extract subsets of positions which have an additonal property in common (e. g. bK's distance to the edge, bK's distance to a certain square, etc.).

$p_1 \in M_W^6$ $p_2 \in M_W^4$ $p_3 \in M_W^2$

Figure 8

The three positions of Figure 8 may be described as follows:

$$p_1 : Patt_{QK} \wedge bk\_on\_h\text{-}file \wedge dist(bk, square(h3)) = 3,$$
$$p_2 : Patt_{QK} \wedge bk\_on\_h\text{-}file \wedge dist(bk, square(h3)) = 2, \tag{8}$$
$$p_3 : Patt_{QK} \wedge bk\_on\_h\text{-}file \wedge dist(bk, square(h3)) = 1.$$

The three positions are ordered as follows:

$$p_1 > p_2 > p_3. \tag{9}$$

Only one part of the description (8) is variable and responsible for the different distances from the goal.

If we like to identify a certain position p, we look for a pattern first (in the example above $Patt_{QK}$). Next we search for the index $j$ such that

$$j = \min\{i \; : \; Patt_{QK} \wedge bk\_on\_h\text{-}file \wedge dist(bk, square(h3)) = i\}. \tag{10}$$

Rule (10) reflects a combination of patterns and distances to a goal, in this particular case h3 being the goal square.

In general, each position is a member of some set $M_W^i$, so the patterns $Patt_j$ can be numbered and ordered:

$$Patt_{l_1} < Patt_{l_2} \quad \text{if and only if} \quad Patt_{l_1} \in M_W^{l_1}, Patt_{l_2} \in M_W^{l_2}, l_1 < l_2. \tag{11}$$

These patterns $Patt_{i_j}$ are now used for realizing a suboptimal strategy; we no longer look for an exact description of the sequence $M_W^i, M_W^{i-1}, M_W^{i-2}, ...$, but only for the sequence $Patt_j, Patt_{j-1}, Patt_{j-2}, ...$

This way is only suboptimal. It is not necessarily the shortest one in the sense of ZERMELO (mate as goal), but the number of subgoals is reduced, the subgaols are understandable.

Another example is shown in Figure 9.

 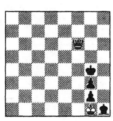 

$p_1 \in M_W^{10}$  $p_2 \in M_W^6$ $\qquad\qquad p_3 \in M_W^2$

Figure 9

## 9.5 Hierarchical Classification

The complete EDB may be classified according to the outcome of the game (win and draw in our example). Using a hierarchical sequence of decision trees, we will finally find a small region for the black King in which mate may be forced:

1. Initial situation: black King in all legal positions on the board.

2. A first decision tree shows that there is no win with the black King on the a- to e-file (Figure 10a), i. e. the leftmost five files of the board are a drawing zone for the black King. Thus, a new binary attribute (K1<6, suitable to the problem under consideration) was found.

3. Considering the remaining positions, another decision tree gives a second drawing zone: 7th and 8th rank (see Figure 10b).

4. The next step cuts off another region shown in Figure 10c.

Therefore, only the residual squares of the black King (i. e. inside the 8-square region) are relevant for this endgame. This result was already given in chapter 9.1.

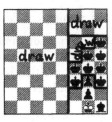

Figure 10a        b                c

Decision trees (parts only):

```
K1                      K2                      K1
=1 --> 0 (313)          =8 --> 0 (118)          =6
=2 --> 0 (303)          =7 --> 0 (114)             and K2
=3 --> 0 (295)          =6 ...                            =6 --> 0 (34)
=4 --> 0 (291)          =5 ...                            =5 --> 0 (34)
=5 --> 0 (293)          =4 ...                            ...
=6 ...                  =3 ...                  =5
=7 ...                  =2 ...                     and K2
=8 ...                  =1 ...                            =6 --> 0 (39)
                                                          ...

                                                ...
```

New rules (using new attributes):

```
IF K1<6                 IF K2>6                 IF (((K1=6) AND (K2 in [5,6]))
THEN class=0            THEN class=0               OR ((K1=5) AND (K2=6)))
ELSE ...               ELSE ...                THEN class=0
                                               ELSE ...
```

Definition of attributes and classes:
K1 - King-file
K2 - King-rank
Q1 - Queen-file
Q2 - Queen-rank
class 0 - draw
class 1 - win
(number) - number of cases in the leaf

Using decision trees, we have found new attributes which are relevant for the considered endgame.

We have generated the decision trees with LEARNER [Naj92].

## 9.6 Finding Heuristic Rules

In general, heuristic rules do not describe exactly the same knowledge like the original data base. Often those rules are much easier than the original ones by dropping special cases (exceptions). On one hand easy rules are much more comprehensible to human beings, on the other hand they may provide wrong results in exceptional cases. There is the classical trade-off between comprehensibility and exactness or between completeness and simplicity in problem solving.

Heuristic rules may be obtained by pruning exact decision trees. Let us show an example.

From Figure 10a (i. e. from the corresponding decision tree) we can derive a simple heuristic rule for White:

"The black King must not enter the drawing zone (files a to e inclusive)."

This heuristics means for practical play:

If the black King is on the f-file, the white Queen must guard the corresponding squares on the e-file,
or, much simpler (but not fully equivalently), the Queen must occupy a safe square on the e-file.

The heuristic above does not work in each case. For example, if the black King is on f4, then the Queen moving to, say, e1 cannot prevent the black King from proceeding to f5 or g5 (into the drawing zone).

# 10  Other Applications

ZERMELO's algorithm (i. e. the method above of going backwards from a goal state) may be immediately transferred to other problem solving methods, such as configuration and planning [PS94]. Starting at a configuration or a plan (or their descriptions) carried out so far, one can take back the last decision etc. until we reach a possible starting point. We can store the intermediate description as well as the reason (i. e. the conditions) for the selected decision. By interaction with experts or by observing and analyzing examples, it is possible to complete the decision tree step by step.

As we can see from computer chess, we are able to manage problems with a high complexity. Engineering problems, however, often have a much lower complexity.

The longer such a system is used in a certain domain the better is its performance. The obtained intermediate descriptions are still incomplete. They always correspond to a set of configurations (or plans) which are still possible in this situation.

So we have another approach for practical problems. If we have found partial solutions, we have to look for the intermediate set which will fit best. We can use any definition of similarity (in the range from identity up to fuzzy evaluations). All these concepts may be directly put down to the membership to the corresponding sets, either in the classical crisp sense or in the fuzzy-logical sense. This means that case-based reasoning starts with putting the actual problem into a decision tree, and then we can continue, according to this tree.

# References

[AB92]    M. Anthony and N. Biggs. *Computational Learning Theory. An Introduction*. Cambridge University Press, Cambridge, 1992.

[BC80]    D. F. Beal and M. R. B. Clarke. The Construction of Economical and Correct Algorithms for King and Pawn against King. In M. R. B. Clarke, editor, *Advances in Computer Chess 2*, pages 1–30, Edinburgh, Scotland, 1980. Edinburgh Univ. Press.

[BP81]    D. Bochmann and Chr. Posthoff. *Binäre dynamische Systeme*. Akademie-Verlag, Berlin, 1981.

[BS91]    D. Bochmann and B. Steinbach. *Logikentwurf mit XBOOLE, Algorithmen und Programme*. Verlag Technik GmbH, Berlin, 1991.

[Cla77]   M. R. B. Clarke. A Quantitative Study of King and Pawn against King. In M. R. B. Clarke, editor, *Advances in Computer Chess 1*, pages 108–118, Edinburgh, Scotland, 1977. Edinburgh Univ. Press.

[FI93]    U. M. Fayyad and K. B. Irani. Multi-Interval Discretization of Continuous-Valued Attributes for Classification Learning. In *13th International Joint Conference on Artificial Intelligence*, pages 1022–1027, San Mateo, 1993. Morgan Kaufmann Publ.

[Hee84]   A. Heeffer. Automated Acquisition of Concepts for the Description of Middle-Game Positions in Chess. Technical Report No. TIRM-84-005, The Turing Institute, 1984.

[Hor84]   H. Horacek. Some Conceptual Defects of Evaluation Functions. In T. O'Shea, editor, *Proc. ECAI-84*. Elsevier Science Publishers B.V., 1984.

[HvdHS89] I. S. Herschberg, H. J. van den Herik, and P. N. A. Schoo. Verifying and Codifying Strategies in the KNNKP(h) Endgame. *ICCA Journal*, 12(3):144–154, 1989.

[Kor84]   J. Korst. Het genereren van regels voor schaak eindspelen ofwel eind-spelen, moeilijker dan je denkt! Master's thesis, Technische Universität Delft, Delft, 1984.

[Kur77]   R. Kurz. *Musterverarbeitung bei der Schachprogrammierung*. PhD thesis, Universität Stuttgart, Stuttgart, 1977.

[Mic77]   D. Michie. King and Rook against King: Historical Background and a Problem on the Infinite Board. In M. R. B. Clarke, editor, *Advances in Computer Chess 1*, pages 30–59, Edinburgh, Scotland, 1977. Edinburgh Univ. Press.

[MN77]     R. S. Michalski and P. Negri. *An Experiment on Inductive Learning in Chess End Games*, pages 175–192. Halstead Press, Ellis Horwood, Chichester, UK, 1977.

[Naj92]    O. Najmann. *Techniques and Heuristics for Acquiring Symbolic Knowledge from Examples*. PhD thesis, Universität - Gesamthochschule -, Paderborn, 1992.

[PFRS92]   Chr. Posthoff, C. Friedrich, D. Rätz, and O. Schumann. Zur Compilation von Wissensbasen. PROKON-Memo Nr. 1, TU Chemnitz, 1992.

[Pos92]    Chr. Posthoff. Fuzzy Logics - New Concepts for Computer Chess? In H. J. van den Herik and V. Allis, editors, *Heuristic Programming in Irtificial Intelligence 3. The Third Computer Olympiad*, pages 88–101. Ellis Horwood, 1992.

[PS94]     Chr. Posthoff and M. Schlosser. Mengentheoretische Grundlagen für optimale Strategien beim Planen und Konfigurieren. In R. Bergmann, J. Paulokat, A.-M. Schoeller, and H. Wache, editors, *Proc. 8. Workshop "Planen und Konfigurieren", Kaiserslautern, 18.-19. April 1994*, pages 186–189. Universität und DFKI Kaiserslautern, 1994.

[PSS92]    Chr. Posthoff, M. Schlosser, and R. Staudte. Wissensdarstellung und - verarbeitung in strategischen Spielen. Preprint Nr. 218, Juni 1992, TU Chemnitz, 1992.

[PSSZ94]   Chr. Posthoff, M. Schlosser, R. Staudte, and J. Zeidler. Transformations of Knowledge. In H. J. van den Herik, I. S. Herschberg, and J. W. H. M. Uiterwijk, editors, *Advances in Computer Chess 7*, pages 177–202, Maastricht, The Netherlands, 1994. University of Limburg.

[PSZ93a]   Chr. Posthoff, M. Schlosser, and J. Zeidler. Optimal strategies. In *Proc. First European Congress on Fuzzy and Intelligent Technologies (EUFIT'93), Aachen, September 7-10*, pages 643–644, Aachen, 1993.

[PSZ93b]   Chr. Posthoff, M. Schlosser, and J. Zeidler. Search vs. Knowledge? - Search and Knowledge! In *Proc. 3rd KADS Meeting, March 8-9 1993*, pages 305–326, Munich, 1993. SIEMENS AG, Corporate Research and Development.

[Qui83]    J. R. Quinlan. *Learning Efficient Classification Procedures and their Application to Chess End Games*, pages 463–482. Morgan Kaufmann, Los Altos, Cal., 1983.

[Roy86]    A. J. Roycroft. GBR Class 0023. *EG*, 6(83):12–15, 1986.

[Sch88]    M. Schlosser. Computers and Chess Problem Composition. *ICCA Journal*, 11(4):51–55, 1988.

[Sch91]    M. Schlosser. Can a Computer Compose Chess Problems? In D. F. Beal, editor, *Advances in Computer Chess 6*, pages 117–131, Chichester, UK, 1991. Ellis Horwood.

[Sch92]   M. Schlosser. A Test-Bed for Investigations in Machine Learning. Gosler-Report No. 18, TH Leipzig, October 1992.

[Sch94]   O. Schumann. *Darstellung und Verarbeitung regelorientierter Wissensbasen mittels BOOLEscher Gleichungen.* PhD thesis, TU Chemnitz-Zwickau, FB Informatik, Chemnitz, April 1994.

[Sei86]   R. Seidel. Deriving Correct Pattern Descriptions and Rules for the KRK Endgame by Deductive Methods. In D. F. Beal, editor, *Advances in Computer Chess 4*, pages 19–36, Oxford, UK, 1986. Pergamon Press.

[Ste84]   D. Steinwender. Bewertungsfunktionen in Schachprogrammen. Master's thesis, Fachbereich Informatik, Universität Hamburg, Hamburg, 1984.

[Str70]   T. Ströhlein. *Untersuchungen über kombinatorische Spiele.* PhD thesis, TU München, München, 1970.

[Val84]   L. G. Valiant. A Theory of the Learnable. *Communications of the ACM*, 27(11):1134–1142, 1984.

[Zer12]   E. Zermelo. Über eine Anwendung der Mengenlehre auf die Theorie des Schachspiels. In *5. Int. Mathematikerkongreß*, volume 2, pages 501–504, Cambridge, 1912.

# Feature Construction during Tree Learning

Gerhard Mehlsam and Hermann Kaindl

Siemens AG Österreich

PSE

Geusaugasse 17, A—1030 Vienna, Austria

kaih@siemens.co.at

Wilhelm Barth

Technische Universität Wien

Inst. f. Computergraphik

Karlsplatz 13/186, A—1040 Vienna, Austria

barth@eichow.una.ac.at

### Abstract

This paper addresses the "problem of new terms" in the context of learning decision trees using the approach based on ID3. We discuss an algorithm for efficiently constructing new features from given primitive features and relate it to *constructive induction*. In our approach, feature construction is integrated with selecting a (new) feature for building the decision tree in *one* process. Hence, appropriate features are constructed *during* tree generation. The representation of constructed features is based on sets. While the search space of possible features is *exponential*, we use a geometric interpretation to show that this algorithm provides *linear* time and space complexity. Moreover, we show that it finds features with *optimal* value for the tree construction procedure of ID3. Results of experiments are reported, and besides of considerations related to the size of the generated trees we also discuss the important issue of how comprehensible these trees are. In particular, we are interested in the intelligibility of the discovered features.

## 1 Introduction

In the sub-field *machine learning* of *artificial intelligence*, so-called learning by example plays a prominent role. For long, *empirical* learning of a "rule" which generalizes a given set of examples dominated this area. One of the first approaches was called CLS by Hunt *et al.* [6], which was designed to learn decision trees for tasks of classifying examples into "concepts". This approach has strongly influenced later work, in particular the well-known ID3 of Quinlan (see e.g. [16] and [17]).

The basis is a universe of *objects* which are described in terms of *attributes* (often synonymously called *features*) taking certain *values*. Each object belongs to one of a set of mutually exclusive *classes*. The task is to develop a *decision tree* that can determine the class of any object from its feature values.

Of course, compared to the more recently developed methods for *analytic* learning (mainly *explanation-based generalization* or *learning* (EBG or EBL), see e.g. [13]), *empirical* learning like that in ID3 utilizes very little domain knowledge. However, it should be clear that the complex features which are normally used for tests in the decision trees represent very important knowledge for making the trees tractable.

While humans with sufficient knowledge about the domain in question can provide appropriate features after serious work, machines themselves usually cannot. This was recognized as the "problem of new terms". Michalski [11] called the approach for constructing new features automatically *constructive induction*. Recently, also the names *constructive deduction* [12], *constructive compilation*, and *feature construction* [8] have been used for variations of the general theme, especially in order to denote whether induction is actually involved or not.

There may be different goals for constructing new features. Since the primitive features used for describing the instances would lead to very large trees for classification tasks of realistic size, there is actually a need for more appropriate features in order to achieve smaller trees. Also the process of tree generation is much easier then. Another point is the issue of intelligibility of the generated trees for humans. While too large trees will typically be difficult to understand, unfortunately also small ones are not necessarily intelligible.

While it is clear that for real practicability also for the process of constructing useful features a large amount of domain knowledge is necessary, we investigate here an approach of "discovering" them. (Combination with methods like those described by Matheus [7] is possible, however.) This approach is implemented in a system called FEACON, which was used for experiments. While the methods described are fairly general, for these experiments the domain of the chess ending KPK (king and pawn against king) was chosen. We also use it as a running example for explaining our approach.

First, we describe the basic representation used, which resembles approaches used in the systems CART [3] and ASSISTANT (see [2] and [4]). While to our best knowledge this approach has not yet been related to feature construction, we show how it fits into the general framework of Matheus and Rendell [8]. As a matter of fact, this approach to feature construction has to cope with an exponential search space. Then we discuss an algorithm of CART [3] with *linear* time and space complexity which can be applied to a wide variety of such problems. We use a geometric interpretation to show that it finds *optimal* features in the sense defined below. Thereafter, we present some experimental results of using this algorithm. Finally, we discuss our approach and relate it to the literature.

Major part of this paper is based on part of the first author's doctoral dissertation [9], where more details can be found.

# 2   Basic Representation

While CLS of Hunt *et al.* is restricted to binary tests of the form "attribute $A$ has value $A_i$", Quinlan's ID3 also involves tests of multi-valued attributes. However, the usual evaluation function for selecting the attribute-based test (using information theory and introduced by ID3) tends to favor attributes with many values. This was observed by Kononenko *et al.* experimenting with ASSISTANT, and Quinlan [18] analyses this problem in more abstract terms. Since a bias is introduced this way, ASSISTANT uses a "subset criterion". A multi-valued attribute is "binarised" by partitioning its value set $S$ into two subsets $S_L$ and $S_R$ so that each subset is treated as one value of the resulting binary attribute. In subsequent tests these subsets can be partitioned further. Unfortunately, a set with $n$ values has $2^n$ subsets, and even when removing trivial and symmetric subsets, there are still $2^{n-1} - 1$ different ways of partitioning [17]. The splits of "categorial" variables in CART are performed in the same way.

Now let us fit this approach into the framework for feature construction of Matheus and Rendell [8]. Let $\mathcal{F}$ be the set of (primitive) *features* given. Ideally, these would be the ones used to describe the instances. Another view of a "primitive" feature is related to its complexity and its ease of being evaluated (cf. the *operationality criterion* of EBG). *Constructive operators* are applied to $\mathcal{F}$, resulting in a set of new features. Since the representation of a constructed feature in ASSISTANT and in FEACON is a *set*, the constructive operator used is the "inclusive or": $or(binary, binary)$. It is usually applied several times in sequence during one step of feature construction.

However, the nominal features with multiple values (more than two) first have to be converted into Boolean expressions. As an example of a primitive feature in KPK, let $F$ be the position of the white king within the range of 64 squares. The conversion results in 64 Boolean expressions of the form $equal(F, F_i)$. It is interesting to note, that this is reminiscent to the binary tests of CLS.

In the approach we adopt, however, these expressions are not directly used for the tests in the tree. They only serve as the basis for constructed features, which are more conveniently viewed as sets of feature values. For instance, $\{F_i, F_j, F_k\}$ can be constructed by $or(or(equal(F, F_i), equal(F, F_j)), equal(F, F_k))$. In KPK such a set can represent some "critical squares", each of which is equivalent for a given piece.

Since the resulting tests are still binary, actually there are two complementary subsets constructed. This view of construction is dual to the one of "partitioning" or "splitting" described in [2]. We prefer still another view for the description of our algorithm. Beginning with the given set $S = S_R$ and its empty complement $S_L$, one element is removed from $S_R$ and put into $S_L$, in effect "moving" it from $S_R$ to $S_L$. This way the question which binary features to combine using the $or$-operator—or equivalently which partition to chose—can be reformulated to the question of which element to move. Besides of the more convenient way of looking at the problem in terms of a geometric interpretation (presented below), it has the technical advantage of allowing for incremental (and therefore cheaper) computations.

Consequently, binarisation can be viewed as a special case of feature construction. Of course, the latter is in general more ambitious, and besides of using several constructive operators other aspects can be involved as well. However, the special case of binarisation still deserves special attention. In fact, it can very efficiently provide useful results, while the general case is usually intractable.

# 3  Feature Generation

Matheus and Rendell [8] and Pagallo [15] propose iterations of tree learning and feature construction. Our approach integrates more tightly in constructing features *during* tree generation. In our system FEACON, we integrated selecting a feature for generating the decision tree and creating this feature into *one* process. First, features are constructed using the method described below. Immediately thereafter these features are used for the normal procedure of test selection in ID3. Currently, features are always generated from the primitive features given. This approach could be extended to also build upon generated ones.

Using the values of a given nominal feature as a basis, a space of features to be constructed is defined as described above. This space is traversed by systematically moving elements from one set to the other. The evaluation is done using the information-based function of ID3 itself. Due to certain properties of this function it is possible to find a feature in this space with minimal value of this function without backtracking. The key idea is to order the elements appropriately before "moving". While Breiman *et al.* [3] present similar results, we emphasize the algorithmic aspect and a geometric interpretation.

First, we describe an algorithm for feature construction in the context of *single-concept learning*, i.e. there is only a distinction between positive and negative instances, or between two classes.

Due to the exponential search space of features and sets with a typical cardinality of 64 (the number of chess squares) or larger (up to 225 in our experiments), no blind algorithm can do a complete search within reasonable time. A heuristic best-first search for a feature with an optimal value requires too much storage (and still too much time). In such a situation, some sort of hill-climbing often serves as a last resort. A straight-forward approach is to determine at each step the element which results in the best evaluation when moved, and to proceed by moving an element from one set to the other as long as there is improvement. While such a procedure can efficiently find solutions (features), there is no guarantee that they are optimal (in any sense), due to the well-known disadvantages of hill-climbing (in particular getting stuck on local minima). Moreover, even if the procedure does not stop when there is no immediate improvement, sub-optimal solutions may be found.

We tried to have a closer look on the properties of the information-based function. The formula for the *expected information requirement* $E_F(a, b)$ after testing a feature $F$ in the decision tree can be written as follows, for the case of 2 classes $A$ and $B$ (*single-concept learning*) and 2-valued features. This function is to be minimized, and $a$ and $b$ are the numbers of objects which show up the feature $F$.

$$
\begin{aligned}
E_F(a, b) \;=\; & \tfrac{1}{n_A + n_B} \cdot \big( (a + b) \cdot \log_2(a + b) - a \cdot \log_2(a) - b \cdot \log_2(b) + \\
& + (n_A - a + n_B - b) \cdot \log_2(n_A - a + n_B - b) - \\
& - (n_A - a) \cdot \log_2(n_A - a) - (n_B - b) \cdot \log_2(n_B - b) \big)
\end{aligned}
$$

$a$ ... number of objects of class $A$ in the left branch

$b$ ... number of objects of class $B$ in the left branch

$n_A$ ... total number of objects of class $A$ in the left and in the right branch together (constant)

$n_B$ ... total number of objects of class $B$ in the left and
in the right branch together (constant)

There actually exists a property of $E_F$ which allows for a very efficient method of finding features with optimal value. It can probably best be understood using a geometric interpretation of the function and the procedure of moving elements. Therefore, see Fig. 1 for a plot of an example. It indicates that values become smaller the closer they are to the boundary. This is indeed an important property, since it implies that there are no minima at an inner point of a closed area.

Now let us relate this to a geometric interpretation of our approach of moving elements from one set to the other. Each element of such a set (i.e., a binary feature) has associated with it a certain number of objects of class $A$ and a certain number of objects of class $B$ (which show up this feature). Hence, it corresponds to a point in the $a,b$-plane (see also Fig. 2). If several such elements are in a set, the numbers of their associated objects are summed up, and the whole set again corresponds to a point. Consequently, we can visualize the procedure of adding (removing) an element from (to) a set as moving from one point in the $a,b$-plane to another. We connect two such points by a straight line. The whole procedure of adding the elements of one set ($S_R$) to the other ($S_L$, which is initially empty) can be visualized as a polygonal line.

Note, that the dual procedure of moving the elements from set $S_L$ to the initially empty set $S_R$ is represented by another polygonal line which is symmetric to the opposite one (see Fig. 2). Related to this is the obvious property $E_F(a,b) = E_F(n_A - a, n_B - b)$, implying that symmetric points have the same value of $E_F$.

The key idea is now to identify a closed polygon which contains all points in the $a,b$-plane corresponding to subsets. In fact, it is easy to see that this can be achieved in the following way. If at each step the element with the straight line of steepest ascent is chosen, no point above this line can correspond to a subset. Symmetrically, the opposite part of the polygon is found by going back along the steepest descent.

This polygon determines a closed area of those points which actually correspond to subsets and hence can be achieved by moving elements. If the conjecture stated above is true (it is, as the proof sketch below shows) the minimum value of $E_F$ in this area is on the boundary. Due to the symmetry it occurs (at least) twice, and more precisely at those points of the polygon where the direction changes. The following algorithm $X$ uses these properties for efficiently finding features with optimal value.

**Definition.** A constructed feature $F$ is $E_F$-*optimal* if its associated value $E_F$ is minimal compared to the competing features. □

Although this optimality of a feature does not necessarily imply that its use results in a decision tree of minimal size, this definition is reasonable in the sense that ID3 selects features for tests according to the same criterion.

**Algorithm X.** Before actually moving elements, they are ordered according to their corresponding quotient $b/(a + b)$. Then they are actually moved in this order, and each time an element has been moved, $E_F$ is computed for the resulting partition. This procedure does not stop on its route until all the elements have been moved. A partition with the minimal value of $E_F$ found corresponds to an $E_F$-optimal feature. □

**Proposition 1.** Algorithm $X$ has *linear* time and space complexity. □

This proposition is obviously true, and it is also worth noting that the actual computations performed are even less than those for hill-climbing. However, it is less obvious that this algorithm also finds $E_F$-*optimal* features, minimizing $E_F$ as its evaluation function. Especially, this depends on the properties of $E_F$. Therefore, we state some propositions below and sketch their proofs (more elaborate proofs can be found in [9]).

**Lemma.** The function $E_F(a, b)$ is concave in the whole domain $0 < a < n_A$, $0 < b < n_B$. This is equivalent to

$$2 \cdot E_F(a, b) \geq E_F(a + x, b + y) + E_F(a - x, b - y)$$

for every $a, b, x, y$, as long as all arguments are in the domain.

*Proof sketch:* $x$ and $y$ determine $s$ and $\alpha$ by $x = s \cdot \cos \alpha$ and $y = s \cdot \sin \alpha$. We can prove that $\frac{d^2 E_F}{ds^2} \leq 0$ holds for all angles $\alpha$. From this the stated inequality follows directly. $\square$

**Proposition 2.** For any part of the $a,b$-domain surrounded by a polygon the function $E_F(a, b)$ takes its minimum only on the polygon itself, more precisely on the vertices.

*Proof sketch:* The lemma shows that along any straight line through $(a, b)$ the function $E_F(a, b)$ decreases in the one or in the other direction (or remains constant). Consequently, there is no local minimum at an inner point of the domain. This also holds for the edges of the polygon with the exception of the vertices. Therefore, all the local minima are on the vertices, hence also the global minimum. $\square$

**Proposition 3.** Algorithm $X$ finds an $E_F$-optimal feature, i.e., a subset corresponding to a partition with minimal value of $E_F$.

*Proof sketch:* Algorithm $X$ builds the subset representing the constructed feature by adding one element after each other. At each step, it takes the element associated with the steepest ascent. The sequence of straight lines constructed this way lies above all points corresponding to subsets. The polygonal line as constructed by algorithm $X$ is above the center of symmetry of $E_F$. Together with its symmetric "dual" it constructs a complete polygon. The points of all other partitions lie strictly within this boundary. According to Proposition 2, the minimum is at a vertex of this polygon, and it is consequently found by algorithm $X$. $\square$

Since a key point in this argumentation is that $E_F$ is a concave function, the question may arise, why the hill-climbing approach mentioned above (without the specific ordering mechanism) does *not* work for guaranteeing $E_F$-optimality. In order to answer this, it is necessary to note that the arguments $a$ and $b$ denote numbers of objects in class $A$ and $B$, respectively. The hill-climbing approach tries to minimize the information content related to a one-ply look-ahead of moving one element. Movement of an element, however, may add an arbitrary number of associated objects of both classes, in effect allowing for large "jumps" in the space of $a$ and $b$. Additionally, the direction of such a jump may be different from the direction chosen by algorithm $X$. Moreover, the hill-climbing procedure may proceed along some sequence of straight lines not visiting all vertices visited by algorithm $X$. Therefore, without the possibility of backtracking (taking back some element) it may miss the optimum. Moreover, suboptimal features may also be constructed due to stopping at a local minimum on the boundary.

Having found an efficient procedure for the case of two classes, the question arises whether algorithm $X$ can be generalized for *multi-concept learning*, i.e. making the distinction between more than two classes. Analogously to the considerations in the 2-dimensional space, the principal arguments should also be valid in an $n$-dimensional space defined by $n$ classes. Therefore, such a generalization should be possible in principle. However, the exact method is not clear yet, and such a procedure would again be rather costly. After all, a search in a space with $n - 1$ dimensions would be necessary.

Hence, the straight-forward way of transforming the multi-concept learning problem into a sequence of single-concept learning problems is a pragmatic way to do it. Unfortunately, this approach does not guarantee optimal solutions, even though all the single-concept problems are solved by algorithm $X$.

# 4  Experimental Results

Due to lack of space, we can only give a qualitative summary here. Quantitative data and an elaborate discussion can be found in [9]. For the experiments a data base containing complete and reliable information on the chess ending KPK (king and pawn against king) was generated and used. For instance, the work by Beal and Clarke [1] can be seen as an indication that the task of generating decision rules for classification of such endgame positions has been a challenge for humans. Moreover, they used much chess knowledge in their approach of designing such rules "by hand". In addition to the problem of whether a position is a win or a draw (*single-concept learning*), we also made experiments with our approach for the more difficult problem of determining the number of moves to a (possible) win, given "optimal" play of both sides (*multi-concept learning*). It might be interesting to compare human results on the latter task, for which they probably have much less knowledge available since in chess practice it is usually not important to win in a minimal number of moves.

We provided the program with simple features (of chess positions), and restricted these to *static* features (i.e., using none which would require search in the problem space). The most simple ones are the *absolute* positions of the pieces on the board (given as the codes of the squares they are located). Possible features to be created from these are sets of squares, e.g. lines, rows, or arbitrary regions, and even unions of different regions. Additionally, the *relative* positions of the pieces have been used (i.e., coding the distances, which amounts to providing additional knowledge). For further experiments also distances to specific (key) squares were taken into account, and finally schemata of the form "piece $A$ is closer to square $x$ than piece $B$", with $A$ and $B$ fixed, while $x$ was a variable parameter to be determined automatically by the machine. When only providing such simple features to the original ID3, the given problem is intractable within practical time and space limits. The same is true for applying the subset criterion with an exponential search.

For the reported experiments we always had the system learn complete information, hence there was *no induction* involved. Moreover, for reasons of simplicity we did not employ the iterations with "windows" of ID3. The primary measure for comparison is the number of nodes in the generated decision trees. 14 example problems of varying difficulty based on KPK were defined, fixing the position of the pawn on specific squares. From these, 7 are single- and 7 multi-concept learning problems, depending on whether the number of moves to a (possible) win is taken into account. To give an idea of the relative difficulty (for the machine), the factors in tree size between corresponding pairs of problems varied between 1.6 up to about 4 (using only the absolute positions of the pieces as given features).

Generally, with more complicated features given initially, better features could be constructed, and the trees became smaller, but not as much as could have been expected. The given procedure can already create reasonable trees with only the absolute positions of the pieces as a given primitive feature, which is readily available from the instance descriptions. Using all the features described above, the decision tree generated for the complete KPK domain had a total number of 733 nodes, or 366 internal nodes with associated decisions using constructed features. This is only larger by a factor of 7.6 than the best known decision procedure created manually (see [1]), which uses 48 much more complicated criteria, and these represent a lot of domain knowledge especially provided by the human creators.

In addition to the size of the generated trees, an important point is also how intelligible they are to humans. There are many factors involved, such as the branching of the trees, of course also their size, the intelligibility of the features used for the tests, and their distribution within the trees. While Shepherd [20] conjectures that multi-branching trees may have an advantage in this regard over binary trees, Cestnik et al. [4] report that due to binarisation the trees became smaller and for this reason also more intelligible to human experts. A potential problem with this approach is that the parts of the original multi-valued feature may appear "scattered" to humans, when they occur in various subsets distributed over the whole tree. Of course, the general issue of comprehensible trees deserves further attention. We were particularly interested in the aspect, how intelligible the discovered *features* are.

Careful inspection of some of the generated trees revealed both features corresponding to known chess concepts as well as features which could not be interpreted by us. From this experience, we realized more and more that this interpretation of discovered features is strongly related to "matching" them with already existing domain knowledge. While we do not claim that every feature constructed here is really important, apparently there are many of them worth a closer look. In general, if a discovered feature is not known by the human user, it may be useful for him to learn the underlying concept. For this purpose the system should be able to present examples via an appropriate user interface. Such procedures have some potential of "creativity". For instance given the primitive features described above, FEACON (re-)discovered the "rule of the square". (Since no generalization is done yet, it is discovered and represented for each position of a pawn anew.)

## 5  Discussion and Related Work

While Michalski [11] investigated constructive induction in the framework of AQ11, Quinlan [16] made first attempts with ID3 discovering patterns from statistics of a complete set of instances and generalizing these patterns. Bratko and Kononenko [2] employed binarisation using set partitioning, but they did not present an efficient method for doing it with larger sets. Interestingly, the relationship of this approach to feature construction has not been mentioned before. Quinlan [18] made extensive experiments with it, but lacking an efficient method only small sets could be handled.

For this reason, in ASSISTANT a hill-climbing approach is used for features with more than four values, and exhaustive search is performed for fewer values [4].

Similar work was performed independently by Breiman *et al.* [3] in the context of *classification* and *regression trees* (CART). As a matter of fact, in this book no reference is made to [6] and [16]. Conversely, the ASSISTANT group and Quinlan were obviously unaware of important results in [3]. In fact, also our work reported here was performed without knowledge of the CART system. Nevertheless, binarisation is reminiscent of the method of dealing with "categorial" variables in this system. Moreover, a major result in [3] essentially proves our proposition 3. While their proof is more general, our geometric interpretation appears to be much more understandable. In addition, our lemma shows that the information theoretic function so often used in tree learning systems in the field of AI in fact has the required property.

Matheus and Rendell [8] provide a general framework for feature construction, and we have shown how the subset approach fits into it. Now let us briefly discuss, how our system relates to the four aspects they have identified. First, FEACON has no explicit step for *detection* of when construction is required. Due to the linear complexity of the employed algorithm $X$ the method of construction is very efficient, and it may be more costly to try detecting the need than just doing it. Since FEACON uses only one constructive operator, the question of constructor *selection* boils down to the question of which operands to chose. Again, this is very efficiently done by this algorithm without the need for domain knowledge (though it could be included). Currently, there is no *generalization* of selected constructors in FEACON.

Finally, for *evaluation* of the new features, FEACON uses the same criterion as it does for deciding which feature to select as a test during tree formation. Hence, this evaluation is fully compatible to the process it is designed to support. Moreover, it is specific for the part handled at each node, since it is performed *during* tree generation. This way it can avoid potential disadvantages of evaluating features according to their utility on the entire training set. This latter issue is discussed for the system CITRE by Matheus and Rendell [8], since this system performs iterations of tree learning and feature construction.

In both CITRE and the system FRINGE by Pagallo [15], iterations of tree learning and feature construction are used to achieve trees that are *less tall*. In FEACON, feature construction is done *during* tree learning in order to achieve *less bushy* trees. Hence, combinations of these approaches appear to be both easy from an algorithmic view as well as useful in adding the effects. In particular, Pagallo reports on using FRINGE in Boolean domains, which are constructed from multiple values by FEACON. Moreover, an integration of the approach of Matheus [7] into FEACON would be useful as a means to include domain knowledge.

In fact, there exist many more systems doing some form of feature construction, for instance Muggleton's DUCE [14], Rendell's PLS0 [19], MIRO by Drastal *et al.* [5], and a system by Watanabe and Elio [21]. While these appear to be not so directly related to our approach, still considerations on combining the ideas will be useful. Finally, the geometric interpretation using "inverted spaces" by Mehra *et al.* [10] may help in this respect.

# 6 Conclusion

We put the "subset criterion" (as used in CART and ASSISTANT and now in FEA-CON) into the framework for feature construction of [8]. Due to the combinatorial explosion inherent in this approach, an efficient method is necessary to make it practicable for sets of realistic size. Algorithm $X$ constructs $E_F$-optimal features efficiently with *linear* time and space complexity. While we have experimented with it in the KPK subdomain of chess, its general applicability is only determined by the following conditions. The nominal features must have a finite number of values greater than two, and a concave evaluation function (like the common information-based one) must be used. (For instance, ASSISTANT has been applied for medical and technical diagnostic tasks.) When more than two classes are to be distinguished, optimal solutions are not guaranteed, but the method can still serve as a very efficient means of handling the single-concept problems involved in solving the multi-concept learning problem.

We have not studied the effects of *induction* in this context (i.e., the performance on "unseen cases"), since this had already been done by Quinlan [18]. The results from theses experiments as well as the experience reported from the use of ASSISTANT suggest that the accuracy is improved by binarisation, which is related to the reductions of the size of the generated decision trees. Algorithm $X$ allows to do it efficiently. Still it may be useful to study the effect of using $E_F$-optimal vs. non-optimal features on the accuracy. Also the influence of noisy data would be of interest.

Moreover, *generalization* of discovered features is an interesting issue here. The already achieved results as well as these extensions are to be seen as steps towards fully automatic generation of decision trees, which should be based only on (primitive) features as given for the description of the instances. There should be no need for hand-crafted features, though the inclusion of domain knowledge in some form will be necessary for larger problems.

# References

[1] D. F. Beal and M. R. B. Clarke. The construction of economical and correct algorithms for king and pawn against king. In M. R. B. Clarke, editor, *Advances in Computer Chess 2*, pages 1–30. Edinburgh University Press, Edinburgh, U.K., 1980.

[2] I. Bratko and I. Kononenko. Learning diagnostic rules from incomplete and noisy data. In B. Phelps, editor, *Interactions in Artificial Intelligence and Statistical Method*, pages 142–153. London, England, 1986.

[3] L. Breiman, J.H. Friedman, R.A. Olshen, and C.J. Stone. *Classification and Regression Trees*. Wadsworth, Belmont, 1984.

[4] B. Cestnik, I. Kononenko, and I. Bratko. ASSISTANT 86: A knowledge-elicitation tool for sophisticated users. In I. Bratko and N. Lavrac, editors, *Progress in Machine Learning*, pages 31–45. Sigma Press, Wilmslow, England, 1987.

[5] G. Drastal, G. Czako, and S. Raatz. Induction in an abstraction space: A form of constructive induction. In *Proceedings of the Eleventh International Joint*

*Conference on Artificial Intelligence*, pages 708–712, Detroit, MI, August 1989. Morgan Kaufmann.

[6] E. B. Hunt, J. Marin, and P. T. Stone. *Experiments in Induction*. Academic Press, New York, NY, 1966.

[7] C. J. Matheus. Adding domain knowledge to SBL through feature construction. In *Proceedings of the Eighth National Conference on Artificial Intelligence*, pages 803–808, Boston, MA, July/August 1990. AAAI, AAAI Press and MIT Press.

[8] C. J. Matheus and L. A. Rendell. Constructive induction on decision trees. In *Proceedings of the Eleventh International Joint Conference on Artificial Intelligence*, pages 645–650, Detroit, MI, August 1989. Morgan Kaufmann.

[9] G. Mehlsam. Automatisches Erzeugen von Klassifikationskriterien. Doctoral dissertation, Technische Universität Wien, Vienna, Austria, August 1989.

[10] P. Mehra, L. A. Rendell, and B. W. Wah. Principled constructive induction. In *Proceedings of the Eleventh International Joint Conference on Artificial Intelligence*, pages 651–656, Detroit, MI, August 1989. Morgan Kaufmann.

[11] R. S. Michalski. Pattern recognition as rule-guided inductive inference. *IEEE Transactions on Pattern Analysis and Machine Intelligence*, PAMI-2(4):349–361, July 1980.

[12] R. S. Michalski and Y. Kodratoff. Research in machine learning: Recent progress, classification of methods, and future directions. In Y. Kodratoff and R. S. Michalski, editors, *Machine Learning: An Artificial Intelligence Approach, Volume III*, chapter 1, pages 3–30. Morgan Kaufmann, San Mateo, CA, 1990.

[13] T. M. Mitchell, R. M. Keller, and S. T. Kedar-Cabelli. Explanation-based generalization: A unifying view. *Machine Learning*, 1:47–80, 1986.

[14] S. Muggleton. Duce, an oracle based approach to constructive induction. In *Proceedings of the Tenth International Joint Conference on Artificial Intelligence*, pages 287–292, Milan, Italy, August 1987. Morgan Kaufmann.

[15] G. Pagallo. Learning DNF by decision trees. In *Proceedings of the Eleventh International Joint Conference on Artificial Intelligence*, pages 639–644, Detroit, MI, August 1989. Morgan Kaufmann.

[16] J. R. Quinlan. Learning efficient classification procedures and their application to chess end games. In R. S. Michalski, J. G. Carbonell, and T. M. Mitchell, editors, *Machine Learning: An Artificial Intelligence Approach*, chapter 15, pages 463–482. Tioga, Palo Alto, CA, 1983.

[17] J. R. Quinlan. Induction of decision trees. *Machine Learning*, 1:81–106, 1986.

[18] J. R. Quinlan. Decision trees and multi-valued attributes. In J. E. Hayes, D. Michie, and J. Richards, editors, *Machine Intelligence 11*, chapter 13, pages 305–318. Clarendon Press, Oxford, England, 1988.

[19] L. A. Rendell. Substantial constructive induction using layered information compression: Tractable feature formation in search. In *Proceedings of the Ninth International Joint Conference on Artificial Intelligence*, pages 650–658, Los Angeles, CA, August 1985. Morgan Kaufmann.

[20] B. A. Shepherd. An appraisal of a decision tree approach to image classification. In *Proceedings of the Eighth International Joint Conference on Artificial Intelligence*, pages 473–475, Karlsruhe, FRG, August 1983. Morgan Kaufmann.

[21] L. Watanabe and R. Elio. Guiding constructive induction for incremental learning from examples. In *Proceedings of the Tenth International Joint Conference on Artificial Intelligence*, pages 293–296, Milan, Italy, August 1987. Morgan Kaufmann.

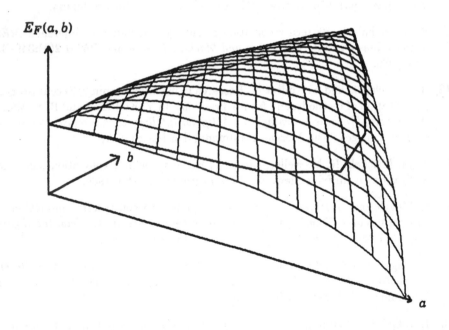

Figure 1: A plot of the function $E_F(a, b)$

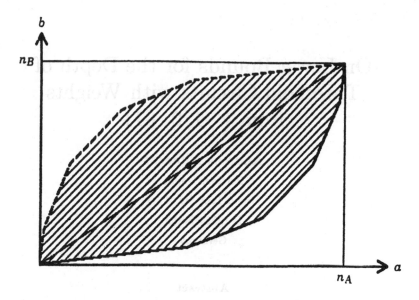

Figure 2: Area of the points corresponding to subsets

# On Lower Bounds for the Depth of Threshold Circuits with Weights from $\{-1, 0, +1\}$

Andreas Albrecht

BerCom GmbH

Bruno-Taut-Str. 4 - 6

D-12524 Berlin

Germany

## Abstract

We consider boolean threshold circuits of polynomial size and constant depth. The threshold gates are of unbounded fan-in and with weights from $\{-1, 0, +1\}$. We introduce the notation of sharp bounded density and prove that boolean functions $f_n(\tilde{x})$ satisfying this property cannot be realized by threshold circuits of depth two with weights from $\{-1, 0, +1\}$. Furthermore, some properties of threshold circuits are discussed resulting in lower bounds of depth four.

## 1 Introduction

Threshold circuits are closely connected to neural nets and the interest in constant depth circuits results, besides the importance for seperating complexity classes, from the small depth of real nets of neurons (which contain, however, also feedback edges). By *Maass, Schnitger*, and *Sontag* [16] it was shown that constant depth sigmoid circuits of polynomial size with polynomially bounded weights compute the same class of boolean functions as the corresponding threshold circuits; there is only a difference for constant size circuits.

In order to characterize boolean functions which can be realized by constant depth circuits of polynomial size, the relation to other complexity classes is investigated, e.g. to $\mathcal{NC}^1$ -the family of boolean circuits with bounded fan-in, gate number $n^{O(1)}$, and depth $O(\log n)$. For a deeper analysis of $\mathcal{NC}^1$ the class $\mathcal{AC}$ was introduced, representing languages accepted by polynomial size, constant depth circuits consisting of NOT gates and unbounded fan-in AND and OR gates. The subclass of circuits with constant depth $O(1)$ is denoted by $\mathcal{AC}^0$.

As a first result *Furst/Saxe/Sipser* [11] proved that parity cannot be computed by circuits from $\mathcal{AC}^0$. J. Håstad [14] obtained a lower bound $\Omega(\log(n)/\log\log(n))$ for the depth of circuits from $\mathcal{AC}$ realizing the parity function $\oplus_{i=1}^n x_i$. A. Hajnal et al. [13] separated subclasses from $\mathcal{TC}^0$ of small depth; in particular, they showed that the inner product mod 2 of two binary vectors of length n, the function $f(\tilde{x}, \tilde{y}) =$

$x_1y_1 \oplus x_2y_2 \oplus ... \oplus x_ny_n$, belongs to depth-three circuits from $\mathcal{TC}^0$, but not to depth-two circuits. In [22] $A.C.\ Yao$ has shown that languages accepted by monotone depth $k$ threshold circuits require exponential size for depth $2 \cdot k$ circuits from $\mathcal{AC}^0$. In contrast to lower bounds $E.\ Allender$ [3] proved that any language accepted by depth k $\mathcal{AC}^0$ circuits is accepted by depth-three threshold circuits of size $n^{O(\log^k n)}$.

Another direction is to study the computational power of different sets of basic functions. $A.\ Razborov$ [17] has shown that circuits of constant depth built by a polynomial number of gates from { PARITY, AND, OR, NOT } do not suffice to compute the MAJORITY function. $R.\ Smolensky$ [19] extended $Razborov$'s method to show that an $\mathcal{AC}^0$ circuit with $MOD_p$ gates cannot realize the $MOD_q$ function if $p$ and $q$ are distinct primes. The next step was to allow $\mathcal{AC}^0$ circuits with PARITY and $MOD_m$ gates for various moduli $m$. This class is denoted by $\mathcal{ACC}$. $A.C.Yao$ [23] proved the first nontrivial upper bounds on the power of $\mathcal{ACC}$ circuits; $Beigel/Tarui$ [8] improved these bounds and showed that each set in $\mathcal{ACC}$ is accepted by a family of deterministic depth three threshold circuits of size $2^{(\log n)^{O(1)}}$. $Allender/Gore$ [5] have shown that computing the permanent cannot be realized by uniform circuits (that means, the structure can be easily recognized) of constant depth and subexponential size.

We consider boolean circuits of polynomial size with threshold gates of unbounded fan-in, where the gates are restricted to realize threshold functions with weights from $\{-1, +1\}$. That type of circuits is an important class in the theory of neural network synthesis, see e.g. [20]. In [12] $Goldmann/Håstad/Razborov$ proved that the depth $d$ class with arbitrary weights is contained in depth $d + 1$ with small weights. The present paper is based on the methods and results from [13], [1], and [2].

## 2  Basic Notations

The set of all n-ary boolean functions is denoted by $\mathcal{B}_n$. We consider threshold circuits whose basic functions are from the set

$$\mathrm{TF}_{bin}^s := \{h : \exists[\tilde{w}, \vartheta]\,(\tilde{w} \in \{-1, 0, +1\}^s \wedge h(\tilde{\sigma}) = 1 \Leftrightarrow \sum_{i=1}^s w^i \cdot \sigma_i \geq \vartheta\,)\},$$

where $\vartheta \in \mathbf{N}[-(s+1), +(s+1)]$. The inputs to the circuits are from $X_n := \{x_0, ..., x_{n-1}\}$ because of the transformation $-1 \cdot x_i = -1 + 1 \cdot (1 - x_i) = -1 + 1 \cdot \bar{x}_i$. The corresponding class of sequences $F = \{f_n\}_{n=1}^\infty$ of functions $f_n \in \mathcal{B}_n$ which are realized by threshold circuits consisting of a polynomial number $n^{O(1)}$ of gates (functions from $\mathrm{TF}_{bin}^s$, $s \leq n^{O(1)}$, $n = 1, 2, ....$) with unbounded fan-in is denoted by $\mathcal{TC}_{bin}$. If for $F = \{f_n\}_{n=1}^\infty \in \mathcal{TC}_{bin}$ exists a constant $k$ as a universal upper bound for the depth of all circuits $C_1, C_2, ..., C_n, ...$, we say that $F$ is realized by bounded depth threshold circuits. The class of sequences $F$ having bounded depth circuits is denoted by $\mathcal{TC}_{bin}^0$. Given the subsets $W \subseteq \{-1, 0, +1\}^s$ and $T \subseteq W \times \mathbf{N}[-(s+1), +(s+1)]$, we denote $\tau := |\,T\,|$ and $\mathrm{TF}(T) \subseteq \mathrm{TF}_{bin}^s$ is the corresponding subset consisting of $g_1, ..., g_\tau$.

We consider at first the case of depth-two circuits $C_n \in \mathcal{TC}_{bin}^0$, where the input gates of $\{C_n\}_{n=1}^\infty$ are from $\mathrm{TF}(T)$, that means $s := n$, and the output gate is of fan-in $\tau$; $C_n$ realizes $f_n$. For $g_i$ we denote

$$a(i) := |\,\{w_j^i : w_j^i = +1\,\}\,| \quad \text{and} \quad b(i) := |\,\{w_j^i : w_j^i = -1\,\}\,|.$$

Therefore, each function $g_i(\tilde{\sigma})$ is defined by an inequality

$$(1) \qquad \sigma_{l_1} + \sigma_{l_2} + \dots + \sigma_{l_{a(i)}} \geq \vartheta_i + \sigma_{r_1} + \sigma_{r_2} + \dots + \sigma_{r_{b(i)}}.$$

For $\tilde{\sigma} \in \{0,1\}^n$ we set $\| \tilde{\sigma} \| := \sum_{i=1}^n \sigma_i$.

Let $C_n^2$ from a sequence of $\mathcal{TC}_{bin}^0$ denote a circuit of depth 2. The output gate $G_o$ has p inputs with positive weights, q inputs with negative weights, and the threshold is $\vartheta_o$, p + q = $\tau$. We transform the output gate $G_o$ to a threshold gate $G_1$ with $\vartheta_1 = \vartheta_o + q$ and the q input gates with a negative weight are transformed to the opposite inequalities where the thresholds $\vartheta_i$ are changed to $-(\vartheta_i - 1)$. These transformations can be performed also for circuits with a depth larger than two; for each intermediate gate one has to consider an individual subcircuit. Therefore, one obtains

**Lemma 1** *Circuits from $\mathcal{TC}_{bin}^0$ having $n^{O(1)}$ gates can be transformed to polynomial size threshold circuits of the same depth where only the input gates may have negative weights.*

In the following we assume that all threshold circuits from $\mathcal{TC}_{bin}^0$ are transformed in accordance to Lemma 1.

By $\mathcal{G} := \{ g_i, i = 1, \dots, \tau \}$ we denote the set of input gates of $C_n^2$. Furthermore, let $\chi^{\tilde{\alpha}}(g)$ be the characteristic function on $\mathcal{G}$ with respect to $\tilde{\alpha}$, that means $\chi^{\tilde{\alpha}}(g) = 1 \iff g(\tilde{\alpha}) = 1$. We use the notations $\mathcal{V}_n^m := \{ \tilde{\alpha} \mid \| \tilde{\alpha} \| = m \}$ and $Q := \{ \tilde{\alpha} \mid \tilde{\alpha} \in \mathcal{V}_n^m \text{ and } f(\tilde{\alpha}) = 1 \}$. Furthermore, we set $P := \mathcal{V}_n^m \setminus Q$ and denote $q := | Q |$, $p := | P |$. Let $\vartheta_1$ be the threshold of the output gate of $C_n^2$. As in [13] we consider the following inequalities :

$$\sum_{\tilde{\alpha} \in Q} \sum_{i=1}^{\tau} \chi^{\tilde{\alpha}}(g_i) \geq q \cdot \vartheta_1, \quad \sum_{\tilde{\beta} \in P} \sum_{i=1}^{\tau} \chi^{\tilde{\beta}}(g_i) \leq p \cdot (\vartheta_1 - 1).$$

From both inequalities we obtain

$$(2) \qquad \sum_{i=1}^{\tau} \left[ \frac{1}{q} \cdot \sum_{\tilde{\alpha} \in Q} \chi^{\tilde{\alpha}}(g_i) - \frac{1}{p} \cdot \sum_{\tilde{\beta} \in P} \chi^{\tilde{\beta}}(g_i) \right] \geq 1.$$

With respect to $Q$ we suppose that

$$(3) \qquad | Q | \in [\frac{2^n}{n^{O(1)}}, \binom{n}{m} - \frac{2^n}{n^{O(1)}}]$$

is satisfied. That means, the number of essential variables cannot be reduced significantly compared to $n$. We are especially interested in sets $Q$ having a distribution in the whole set $\{0,1\}^n$ which induces that the negative part in (2) dominates the part defined by $Q$.

For this reason we consider partitions of $X_n = \{x_0, x_2, \dots, x_{n-1}\}$ into three sets $X^1$, $X^2$, and $X^3$, where $| X^1 | = l$, $| X^2 | = r$, and $| X^3 | = k := n - l - r$. The corresponding to $X^i$ parts of $\tilde{\alpha} \in \{0,1\}^n$ are denoted by $\tilde{\alpha}^i$, $i = 1, 2, 3$; furthermore, we set $\| \tilde{\alpha}^1 \| = a$, $\| \tilde{\alpha}^2 \| = b$, and $\| \tilde{\alpha}^3 \| = c$. Given a gate $g(\vartheta) \in \mathcal{G}$ with the threshold $\vartheta$, we have

$$\sum_{a+b+c=m} \sum_{a \geq \vartheta + b} \binom{l}{a} \cdot \binom{r}{b} \cdot \binom{n-l-r}{m-a-b}$$

tuples $\tilde{\alpha}$ from $V_n^m$ with $\chi^{\tilde{\alpha}}(g) = 1$; the set of $\tilde{\alpha} \in V_n^m$ satisfying $a \geq \vartheta + b$ for fixed $a$ and $b$ is denoted by $R(a, b)$. Finally, we denote for a given partition of $X_n$

(4) $$M(a, b) := R(a, b) \cap Q.$$

We introduce the following notation :

**Definition 1** *The sequence* $\mathcal{Q} = \{Q_n\}_{n=1}^{\infty}$, *where* $Q_n \subseteq V_n^m$, *is called to represent functions of sharp bounded density, iff for any* $\varphi(n) \longrightarrow \infty$ *there exists a function* $\psi(n) \longrightarrow \infty$ *such that for any partition* $[X^1, X^2, X^3]$ *and arbitrary conditions* $a \geq \vartheta + b$ *satisfying*

(5) $$|\, R(a, b)\, | \geq n^{\varphi(n)}$$

*it holds*

(6) $$\frac{p}{q} \leq \frac{|\, R(a, b)\, | - |\, M(a, b)\, |}{|\, M(a, b)\, |} \cdot (1 + \frac{1}{n^{\psi(n)}}).$$

We will illustrate the definition by two examples :
At first we consider a simple special case of division where Definition 1 is not satisfied. For an even $n$ and natural numbers $N$, where $2^{n/2} - 1 \leq N$ and $\|\, \tilde{\sigma}_N\, \| = \frac{n}{2}$, we take the subset $Q$ of numbers divisible by an odd number $u = 2 \cdot t + 1$, $t \geq 1$ : $f_n^u(\tilde{\sigma}) = 1 \iff \sum_{\sigma_i = 1} 2^{i-1} = D \cdot u$. In more detail we consider only $u = 3$. An arbitrary number $2^j$ can be represented by $2^j = V \cdot 3 + (-1)^j$. That means, we have the residue 1 for an even $j$ and the residue 2 for an odd $j$. Given a partition $[X^1, X^2, X^3]$, one has to distinguish between the odd and even variables in $X^i$. If we take $a$ variables from $X^1$ equal to 1, we denote by $a^0$ the variables with an even index, by $a^1$ the variables with an odd index; $b^\eta$ and $c^\eta$ are the corresponding values for $X^2$ and $X^3$. Thus, if $\tilde{\sigma} \in Q_{f_n^3}$, we have

(7) $$a^0 + b^0 + c^0 + 2 \cdot (a^1 + b^1 + c^1) = D \cdot 3.$$

That means, $f_n^3$ represents a symmetric function with the characteristic numbers $\|\, \tilde{\alpha}\, \| \equiv 0 \mod 3$. Applying the representation from [13], one obtains a depth two circuit for $f_n^3$. On the other hand, threshold functions where $X^1$ represents only even numbered variables and $X^2$ only variables with an odd index do not satisfy Definition 1.

The second example concerns the inner product $f(\vec{x}, \vec{y}) = x_1 y_1 \oplus x_2 y_2 \oplus \ldots \oplus x_n y_n$. This function can be realized by circuits of depth three, cf. [13]. We try to prove

$$\frac{p_n}{q_n} \geq (1 + \frac{1}{n^{O(1)}}) \cdot \frac{|\, R_n(\vartheta)\, | - |\, M_n(\vartheta)\, |}{|\, M_n(\vartheta)\, |}$$

for the particular threshold function $x_1 + \ldots + x_n \geq y_1 + \ldots + y_n$, where $\vartheta = 0$ and $m = n$. Obviously, (5) is satisfied. We try to show

$$p_n \cdot |\, M_n(0)\, | + q_n \cdot |\, M_n(0)\, | - q_n \cdot |\, R_n(0)\, | + \frac{1}{n^{O(1)}} \cdot |\, M_n(0)\, | \cdot q_n$$

$$\geq \frac{1}{n^{O(1)}} \cdot |\, R_n(0)\, | \cdot q_n.$$

The particular values are defined by

$$p_n = \binom{2 \cdot n}{n} - q_n, \quad \text{where}$$

$$q_n = \sum_{s=0}^{\frac{n-2}{4}} \binom{n}{2 \cdot s + 1} \cdot \binom{n - 2 \cdot s - 1}{n - 4 \cdot s - 2} \cdot 2^{n-4 \cdot s-2};$$

$$|M_n(0)| = \sum_{s=0}^{\frac{n-2}{4}} \binom{n}{2 \cdot s + 1} \sum_{i=\frac{n-4 \cdot s-2}{2}}^{n-4 \cdot s-2} \binom{n - 2 \cdot s - 1}{i} \cdot \binom{n - i - 2 \cdot s - 1}{n - i - 4 \cdot s - 2};$$

$$|R_n(0)| = \sum_{j=\frac{n}{2}}^{n} \binom{n}{j}^2.$$

From the previous condition we obtain the stronger inequalities

$$(p_n + q_n) \cdot |M_n(0)| - q_n \cdot |R_n(0)| \geq \frac{1}{n^{O(1)}} \cdot |R_n(0)| \cdot q_n;$$

$$(8) \qquad \frac{\binom{2 \cdot n}{n}}{|R_n(0)|} \cdot |M_n(0)| - q_n \geq \frac{1}{n^{O(1)}} \cdot q_n.$$

Therefore, we obtain for $a := 2 \cdot s + 1$

$$(9) \qquad \sum_{a} \binom{n}{a} \left[ \frac{\binom{2 \cdot n}{n}}{|R_n(0)|} \cdot \sum_{i=\frac{n-2 \cdot a}{2}}^{n-2 \cdot a} B(s,i) - A(s) \right] \geq \frac{1}{n^{O(1)}} \cdot q_n,$$

where

$$A(s) = \binom{n - a}{n - 2 \cdot a} \cdot 2^{n-2 \cdot a} \quad \text{and} \quad B(s,i) = \binom{n - a}{i} \cdot \binom{n - i - a}{n - i - 2 \cdot a}.$$

We consider at first $B(s) := \sum_{i=\frac{n-2 \cdot a}{2}}^{n-2 \cdot a} B(s,i)$ :

$$B(s) = \binom{n - a}{\frac{n}{2} - a} \cdot \binom{\frac{n}{2}}{a} + ... + \binom{n - a}{n - 2 \cdot a} \cdot \binom{a}{a}$$

$$= \binom{n - a}{\frac{n}{2} - a} \cdot \binom{\frac{n}{2}}{a} \cdot \left[ 1 + \frac{1}{([\frac{n}{2} - a]^2 - 1)} + ... + \right.$$

$$\left. + \frac{1}{([\frac{n}{2} - a]^2 - 1) \cdot ... \cdot ([\frac{n}{2} - a]^2 - [\frac{n}{2} - a - 1]^2)} \right]$$

$$> \binom{n - a}{\frac{n}{2} - a} \cdot \binom{\frac{n}{2}}{a} \cdot \sum_{m=0}^{\frac{n}{2}-a-1} \frac{1}{t^m} \quad \text{for } t := ([\frac{n}{2} - a]^2 - 1).$$

Building the sum for the geometric progression, we obtain

$$B(s) > \binom{n - a}{\frac{n}{2} - a} \cdot \binom{\frac{n}{2}}{a} \cdot \frac{n^2 - 4 \cdot a + 4 \cdot a^2 - 8}{n^2 - 4 \cdot a + 4 \cdot a^2 - 4} \cdot \left( 1 - \frac{1}{([\frac{n}{2} - a]^2 - 1)^{\frac{n}{2}-a}} \right).$$

Furthermore, we consider

$$
\begin{aligned}
|R_n(0)| &= \sum_{j=\frac{n}{2}}^{n} \binom{n}{j}^2 \\
&= \binom{n}{\frac{n}{2}}^2 \cdot \left[ 1 + (1 - \frac{2}{n+2})^2 + \ldots + \right.
\end{aligned}
$$

(10)
$$
\left. + (1 - \frac{2}{n+2})^2 \cdot \ldots \cdot (1 - \frac{2 \cdot n - 2}{2 \cdot n + 2})^2 \right]
$$

$$
< \binom{n}{\frac{n}{2}}^2 \cdot \sum_{m=0}^{\frac{n}{2}} t^m \quad \text{for} \quad t = \left( \frac{n}{n+2} \right)^2
$$

$$
= \binom{n}{\frac{n}{2}}^2 \cdot \frac{n^2 + 2 \cdot n + 4}{2 \cdot n + 4} \cdot \left( 1 - \left( \frac{n}{n+2} \right)^n \right)
$$

$$
< \binom{n}{\frac{n}{2}}^2 \cdot \frac{n^2 + 2 \cdot n + 4}{2 \cdot n + 4}.
$$

According to the *Stirling*-Formula

$$
\sqrt{2 \cdot \pi \cdot n} \cdot \left( \frac{n}{e} \right)^n < n! < \sqrt{2 \cdot \pi \cdot n} \cdot \left( \frac{n}{e} \right)^n \cdot e^{\frac{1}{12 \cdot n}}
$$

we have for $n \geq n_0$

$$
\frac{\binom{2 \cdot n}{n}}{|R_n(0)|} > \frac{\sqrt{\pi \cdot n}}{2} \cdot \frac{1}{e^{\frac{1}{3 \cdot n}}} \cdot \frac{2 \cdot n + 4}{n^2 + 2 \cdot n + 4}.
$$

Now, we take into account

$$
\frac{\binom{n-a}{\frac{n}{2}-a} \cdot \binom{\frac{n}{2}}{a}}{\binom{n-a}{n-2 \cdot a}} = \binom{n - 2 \cdot a}{\frac{n}{2} - a}.
$$

Thus, (9) can be transformed to

$$
\sum_{a} \binom{n}{a} \cdot \binom{n-a}{n-2 \cdot a} \cdot 2^{n-2 \cdot a} \times
$$

$$
\times \left[ \frac{\binom{n - 2 \cdot a}{\frac{n}{2} - a}}{2^{n-2 \cdot a}} \cdot O(\frac{1}{\sqrt{n}}) \cdot \left( 1 - \frac{1}{([\frac{n}{2} - a]^2 - 1)^{\frac{n}{2} - a}} \right) - 1 \right]
$$

$$
\geq \frac{1}{n^{O(1)}} \cdot q_n.
$$

Again the *Stirling*-Formula is applied (w.l.o.g. we assume $a < \frac{n}{2}$):

$$
\sum_{a} \binom{n}{a} \cdot \binom{n-a}{n-2 \cdot a} \cdot 2^{n-2 \cdot a} \times
$$

$$
\times \left[ O(\frac{1}{\sqrt{n}} \cdot \frac{1}{\sqrt{n - 2 \cdot a}}) \cdot \left( 1 - \frac{1}{([\frac{n}{2} - a]^2 - 1)^{\frac{n}{2} - a}} \right) - 1 \right]
$$

$$
\geq \frac{1}{n^{O(1)}} \cdot q_n.
$$

For $a \leq a_0 < \frac{n}{2}$ the value on the left side is defined by $q_n \cdot O(\frac{1}{n})$, and (8) is true for sufficiently large $n$. That means, the function $f(\vec{x}, \vec{y})$ satisfies the inequality 2, but does not satisfy Definition 1. As already mentiones above, the inner product $f(\vec{x}, \vec{y})$ cannot be realized by threshold circuits of depth two.

In fact, we consider sequences of threshold gates $g_n$, sequences of partitions $[X_n^1, X_n^2, X_n^3]$ e.t.c. But for simplicity we will speak about only a particular gate, partition and so on. Furthermore, we consider Definition 1 w.l.o.g. mainly for particular values of $m$; that means, we will use Definition 1 for arbitrary $m \in [\gamma(n), n-\gamma(n)]$ only if it is necessary.

# 3   Local Properties of Depth-two Circuits

Now, we consider arbitrary sequences representing functions of sharp bounded density:

**Theorem 1** *If $F = \{f_n\}_{n=1}^\infty$ is defined by a sequence $\mathcal{Q}$, $Q \subseteq \mathcal{V}_n^m$, representing functions of (modified) sharp bounded density, then $F$ cannot be realized by depth-two circuits from $TC_{bin}^0$.*

**Proof :** We denote by $\mathcal{G}'$ the set of gates $g_i$ satisfying $| R(a, b) | < n^{\varphi(n)}$ for the corresponding to $a$ and $b$ tuples from $Q'$; $\varphi(n)$ is a slowly growing function depending on F (w.r.t. Definition 1); the set $\mathcal{G}''$ is for gates and tuples with $| R(a, b) | \geq n^{\varphi(n)}$. The sum from (2) is divided into two parts :

$$\sum_{g_i \in \mathcal{G}'} \left[ \frac{1}{q} \cdot \sum_{\tilde{\alpha} \in Q'} \chi^{\tilde{\alpha}}(g_i) \right] + \sum_{g_j \in \mathcal{G}''} \left[ \frac{1}{q} \cdot \sum_{\tilde{\alpha} \in Q''} \chi^{\tilde{\alpha}}(g_j) - \frac{1}{p} \cdot \sum_{\tilde{\beta} \in P} \chi^{\tilde{\beta}}(g_j) \right] \geq 1.$$

For the first part of the left side we take the upper bound $\frac{n^{\varphi(n)}}{q}$. The second part corresponds in our notation for a single $j$ to

$$\sum_{a+b+c=m} \left[ \frac{1}{q} \cdot | M(a, b) | - \frac{1}{p} \cdot \left( | R(a, b) | - | M(a, b) | \right) \right].$$

The right side of inequality (6) is applied to each $g_j \in \mathcal{G}''$, and we obtain the upper bound

$$\left[ \sum_{g_j \in \mathcal{G}''} m^3 \cdot \frac{1}{p} \cdot \sum_{\tilde{\beta} \in P} \chi^{\tilde{\beta}}(g_j) \right] \cdot \frac{1}{n^{\psi(n)}}.$$

Thus, the inequality turns to the condition $\dfrac{n^{\varphi(n)} + O(1)}{q} + \dfrac{n^{O(1)}}{n^{\psi(n)}} \geq 1$. But $q$ is a hyperpolynomial number (we take $\varphi(n)$ such that $\dfrac{n^{\varphi(n)}}{q} \to 0$), and we obtain a contradiction for sufficiently large $n$.

q.e.d.

# 4  Analyzing Threshold Circuits of Depth Three

Because of Lemma 1 the circuits $C_n^3$ have starting from the second level only gates with positive weights. Let $e_0$ denote the output gate of $C_n^3$; $\tau(e_0) = n^{O(1)}$ is the number of inputs to $e_0$. The gates $h_1, \ldots, h_{\tau(e_0)}$ are connected to $e_0$, and $H_i^\sigma$ is the set of input tuples producing the output $\sigma$ at $h_i$. As before we set $q := | Q |$ and $p := | P | = | V_n^m \setminus Q |$. We make the following observation :

**Lemma 2** If $C_n^3$ realizes $f_n$ from $Q$, then there exists a gate $h_{j_0}$ such that $| H_{j_0}^1 | \geq O(\frac{q}{n^{O(1)}})$ and

(11)
$$\frac{| H_{j_0}^1 \cap Q |}{| H_{j_0}^1 \cap P |} \geq \frac{q}{p} \cdot \left(1 + \frac{p}{| H_{j_0}^1 \cap P | \cdot n^{O(1)}}\right).$$

**Proof :** To the output gate $e_0$ of $C_n^3$ the inequality (2) is applied, however, with respect to the functions $h_j$ of depth two. As in Theorem 1, the sum is divided into two parts, where for the first part we have $| H_j^1 | < \frac{q}{\tau(e_0)}$. Now, if we assume

$$\frac{1}{q} \cdot | H_j^1 \cap Q | - \frac{1}{p} \cdot | H_j^1 \cap P | < \frac{1}{\tau(g_0) \cdot n^3}$$

for all $h_j$ from the second part, $j \in \{1, \ldots, \tau(g_0)\}$, then we obtain a contradiction to (2).

q.e.d.

We take a single input gate $g := g_{i_0}$ of $h := h_{j_0}$ representing a hyperpolynomial number of tuples from $H^1 := H_{j_0}^1$. We assume that $g$ has the properties required in Definition 1; otherwise the input gates of $h$ could not realize $O(\frac{q}{n^{O(1)}})$ elements of $Q$. We use the notations $G^1[Q] := G^1 \cap Q$ and $G^1[P] := G^1 \cap P$ for $g := g_{i_0}$. Let $z(\tilde\sigma) := | \{g_i : g_i(\tilde\sigma) = 1, 1 \leq i \leq \tau(h)\} |$ be the number of input gates $g_i$ of $h$ equal to 1 on $\tilde\sigma$. With respect to arbitrary intersections

$$\mathcal{I}(s) := \left(G^1[Q] \cup G^1[P]\right) \cap G_{i_1}^1 \cap \ldots \cap G_{i_s}^1$$

we try to show that tuples $\tilde\sigma$ with $z(\tilde\sigma) \geq \vartheta(h)$ are distributed within $G^1[Q]$ and $G^1[P]$ according to the relation $\frac{q}{p}$.

At first some rough considerations : The gate $g$ defines the partition $[X^1, X^2, X^3]$, where $l$ variables are on the "left side" and $r$ variables are on the "right side". Let $[X_j^1, X_j^2, X_j^3]$ denote a partition defined by some $g_{i_j}, 1 \leq j \leq s$.
Starting from $\tilde\sigma$, we try to characterize tuples $\tilde\eta$ generated from $\tilde\sigma$ by exchanging values of variables equal to 1 and 0 that are satisfying a defined number of threshold inequalities of input gates. With respect to tuples $\tilde\eta$, *critical* configurations occur only if $\tilde\sigma$ defines an equation for the input gate $g$. We assume w.r.t. $g$ the equality $a = b + \vartheta$ for the particular $\tilde\sigma \in \mathcal{I}$. If $a' = b' + \vartheta_j$ is satisfied for $g_{i_j}$, we consider $X^1 \cap X_j^2$ in more detail (for exchanging the values 1 and 0 w.r.t. variables from $X^1 \cap X_j^2$) and

assume w.l.o.g. $X^3 = X_j^3$ (for this case the principal considerations are the same as for $X^3 \neq X_j^3$). Because of $\tilde{\sigma} \in \mathcal{I}$, the tuple $\tilde{\sigma}$ assigns the value 1 at least to the same number of variables from $X^2 \cap X_j^2$ compared to variables from $X^1 \cap X_j^2$. If we have e.g. $|X^2 \cap X_j^2| = |X^1 \cap X_j^2| = 1$, the case $x^2 = x_j^1 = 0$ and $x^1 = x_j^2 = 1$ is excluded. That means, the assignment of variables from $X^1 \cap X_j^2$ defines the possible values of variables from $X^2 \cap X_j^1$.

The gate $g = g_{i_0}$ has to realize at least $\frac{|H^1|}{n^{O(1)}}$ tuples from $H^1$. The maximal number of tuples $\tilde{\sigma}$ satisfying $g$ for fixed $a$, $b$, and $c$ is $\binom{l}{a} \cdot \binom{r}{b} \cdot \binom{h}{c}$. If we assume, that there exist constants $c_1, c_2, c_3 > 1$ such that $a \leq \frac{l}{c_1 \cdot 2}$, $b \leq \frac{r}{c_2 \cdot 2}$, $c \leq \frac{h}{c_3 \cdot 2}$ (or inequalities in the other direction with $c_i < 1$), then the product of binomial factors cannot achieve $2^n/n^{O(1)}$ because of $l + r + h = n$. That means, $g$ cannot realize the required number of tuples from $H^1$. Therefore, w.l.o.g. we suppose that $b \approx \frac{r}{2} \pm O(\log n)$ and that $\binom{r}{b}$ is the largest of the three factors, that means $\binom{r}{b} \geq \frac{2^{\frac{1}{3} \cdot n}}{n^{O(1)}}$.

Now, in more detail : We take a fixed partial assignment $\tilde{\alpha}$ to a subset of variables from $X^1$ (in order to ensure $a = b + \vartheta$, $\tilde{\gamma}$ for $X^3$ is also fixed) and consider the possible assignments $\tilde{\beta}$ to variables of $X^2$ such that there exists $\mathcal{I}[\tilde{\beta}]$ built by at least $s$ gates. We denote

$$U(s) := U_s(g) := \{\tilde{\beta} : g(\tilde{\alpha}\tilde{\beta}\tilde{\gamma}) = 1 \;\; and \;\; \exists \, \mathcal{I}[\tilde{\beta}](s-1) \neq \emptyset\}.$$

For pairs $[\tilde{\beta}_1, \tilde{\beta}_2] \in V := U \times U$ we try to build from $\mathcal{I}[\tilde{\beta}_1]$ and $\mathcal{I}[\tilde{\beta}_2]$ an intersection $\mathcal{I}'$ of at least $s$ gates for an intermediate (w.r.t. $\tilde{\beta}_1$ and $\tilde{\beta}_2$) assignment $\tilde{\beta}'$. We denote by $\Delta$ the number of variable positions where $\tilde{\beta}_1$ differs from $\tilde{\beta}_2$; the corresponding set of variables is denoted by $\mathcal{D} := \mathcal{D}[\tilde{\beta}_1, \tilde{\beta}_2]$ (only for $g$ we know that $\mathcal{D} \subseteq X^2$). We take $x, y \in \mathcal{D}$ where $x = 1$, $y = 0$ on $\tilde{\beta}_1$ and $x = 0$, $y = 1$ on $\tilde{\beta}_2$. Now, we change $(x, y)$ to $x = 0$, $y = 1$ for $\mathcal{I}[\tilde{\beta}_1]$ and to $x = 1$, $y = 0$ for $\mathcal{I}[\tilde{\beta}_2]$. There are only three critical configurations for the gates of $\mathcal{I}[\tilde{\beta}_1]$ where the output of a gate can alter from 1 to 0 :

$$\ldots + x \;\; \geq \;\; y + \ldots + \vartheta_{i_j};$$
$$\ldots \;\; \geq \;\; y + \ldots + \vartheta_{i_j};$$
$$\ldots + x \;\; \geq \;\; \ldots$$

The same is true for $\mathcal{I}[\tilde{\beta}_2]$ for exchanged positions of $x$ and $y$. Let $t_i := t_i(x, y)$ denote the number of critical gates (where indeed the output changes from 1 to 0) for $\tilde{\beta}_i$, $i = 1, 2$. For a particular pair $(x, y)$, $x, y \in \mathcal{D}$, a critical gate of $\mathcal{I}[\tilde{\beta}_2]$ cannot be a critical gate for $\mathcal{I}[\tilde{\beta}_1]$ and vice versa.

In the case, that for almost all pairs $[\tilde{\beta}_1, \tilde{\beta}_2]$ there exists an intermediate tuple $\tilde{\beta}'$ satisfying $\mathcal{I}[\tilde{\beta}'](\vartheta(h) - 1) \neq \emptyset$, then Definition 1 can be applied to the set of tuples $\tilde{\beta}$ (this follows from recursive applications to pairs $[\tilde{\beta}_1, \tilde{\beta}']$, $[\tilde{\beta}', \tilde{\beta}_2]$ etc.). Based on this observation we introduce a restricted type of depth-two threshold circuits. Let $U' \subseteq U(\vartheta)$ denote the set of tuples $\tilde{\beta}$ such that $|\mathcal{I}[\tilde{\beta}](\vartheta - 1)| \geq n^{\alpha(n)}$, where $\alpha(n) \to \infty$.

**Definition 2** *The sequence $\{\mathcal{C}_n^2\}_n$ of depth-two threshold circuits from $TC_{bin}^o$ is called a homogeneous sequence, iff for all input gates $g$ satisfying $|G^1| \geq \frac{|H^1|}{n^{O(1)}}$ it holds $\frac{|U'(g)|}{|U(g)|} \geq (1 - \frac{1}{n^{\xi(n)}})$, $\xi(n) \to \infty$.*

Circuits of depth three realized by homogeneous sequences of depth two are also called homogeneous sequences (of depth three).

Hence, for homogeneous sequences (circuits) the dominating part of pairs $[\tilde{\beta}_1, \tilde{\beta}_2]$ (related to the remaining part by a factor $(1 - \frac{1}{n^{\xi(n)}})$) can be used to produce intermediate assignments $\tilde{\beta}'$ (applying the same procedure to the new constructed intermediate assignments). That means, it is possible to apply Definition 1 to the sets of tuples $\tilde{\sigma}$ defined by intersections $\mathcal{I}$, where $\mathcal{I}$ is built by at least $\vartheta$ gates. Thus, we have the relation $\frac{q}{p} \cdot (1 + \frac{1}{n^{\beta(n)}})$ for the tuples of $G^1[Q]$ and $G^1[P]$. Therefore, we obtain

**Lemma 3** *If $h$ is realized by a homogeneous circuit and $g_i$ is an input gate representing a hyperpolynomial number of tuples from $H^1 \cap Q$, then*

$$(12) \qquad \frac{\mid G^1[Q] \cap H^1 \mid}{\mid G^1[P] \cap H^1 \mid} \leq \frac{q}{p} \cdot (1 + \frac{1}{n^{\xi(n)}})$$

*is satisfied, where $\xi(n) \to \infty$ is a (slowly) growing function.*

It seems to be possible to remove the restriction concerning homogeneous sequences of depth-two circuits : Given the input gate $g$ and the $\binom{r}{b}$ tuples $\tilde{\beta}$, we consider for any of the remaining input gates $g_i$ the part of $G^1$ which is realized also by $g_i$ ($\tilde{\alpha}, \tilde{\beta}$ are fixed). The gate $g_i$ has a defined distribution of variables from $X^2$; that means, if $g_i$ realizes less than (approximately) $\frac{1}{2} \cdot \mid G^1 \mid$, then there exists a number of input gates realizing the remaining part of $G^1$ (in some sense a complementary set of gates). Therefore, if $g_i$ is a critical gate for $\tilde{\beta}_1$ and the pair of variables $(x, y)$, we can try to replace $g_i$ by one of the gates realizing the remaining part of $G^1$. The problem is to ensure that a complementary gate is used only once with respect to $\tilde{\beta}_1$ and $(x, y)$. As a consequence of Lemma 2 and Lemma 3 one obtains

**Theorem 2** *Sequences $F = \{f_n\}_{n=1}^\infty$ representing functions of sharp bounded density cannot be realized by homogeneous depth-three circuits from $TC_{bin}^\circ$.*

**Proof :** We suppose that $f_n$ has a realization by circuits of depth three and consider in more detail the function $h$ from Lemma 2. Because of Lemma 3 we know that the gates realizing $h$ with $\mid G^1 \mid = \frac{|H^1|}{n^{O(1)}}$ satisfy the conditions of Definition 1. Therefore, we obtain a contradiction to Theorem 1 w.r.t. to the function $h$.

q.e.d.

That means, if $Q$ can be realized by depth three circuits, there exist threshold gates such that a relatively large fraction of tuples from $R(a, b)$ satisfies the same threshold equalities. In other terms, it is possible to cover all tuples $f_n(\tilde{\sigma}) = 1$ by a polynomial number of input gates having at least a fraction of $\frac{p}{q} \cdot (1 + \frac{1}{n^a})$ tuples $\tilde{\sigma}$. These properties can be used e.g. for learning procedures of functions having depth three circuits. For example, it would be interesting to apply the quasi-polynomial learning algorithm from [21] to depth-three threshold circuits, where the relation $\frac{p}{q} \cdot (1 + \frac{1}{n^a})$ of *negative* and *positive* examples is exploited w.r.t. the corresponding greedy algorithm. It seems to be possible to apply Theorem 2 (in a slightly changed form) to the operation of division $div_{n,k}(\tilde{\alpha}, \tilde{\beta})$ indicating that $\tilde{\alpha}$ is divisible by $\tilde{\beta}$. It remains to show

that for arbitrary subsets of $u$ and $v$ variables and fixed values $\alpha$, $\beta$ for the other $(n - u - v)$ variables the ratio of all pairs $2^u \cdot \binom{v}{m_2}$ to the number of divisions with residue zero is nearly the same as for the $\binom{u}{m_1} \cdot \binom{v}{m_2}$ pairs with a fixed norm $m_1$ and $m_2$. That means, one has to show that for $\binom{u}{m_1}$ integers $N$ (with fixed values outside of $u$ variables) the number of residue zero divisions by $l := \binom{v}{m_2}$ integers $y_1, y_2, \ldots y_l$ is approximately equal to $\binom{u}{m_1} \cdot \left(\frac{1}{y_1} + \frac{1}{y_2} + \ldots + \frac{1}{y_l}\right)$.
This problem can be reduced to the following equations

$$(2^{x_i} - 1) \cdot R_i = a \cdot y_i, \ i = 1, \ldots, l,$$

where $x_i$ is the smallest period for residues appearing in divisions of $N' = 2^b$ by $y_i = 2^{c_1} + \ldots + 2^{c_{m_2}}$, $2^b > y_i$ and $c_1 > \ldots > c_{m_2}$. The value $R_i$ is defined by $R_i := 2^{c_1+1} - y_i$. If for almost all $y_i$ the period $x_i$ is relatively large (compared to $u$ and $v$), then for a fixed $y_i$ the number of residue zero divisions is mainly defined by a single $N$ and the shifted values of $2^{d_1} + \ldots + 2^{d_{m_1}}$ (if the shifted value fits into the $u$ variable positions).

**Conjecture** *The function $div_{n,k}(\tilde{\alpha}, \tilde{\beta})$ cannot be realized by $TC_{bin}^o$ circuits of depth three.*


# 5  Concluding Remarks

For threshold circuits with binary weights we described a method for obtaining lower bounds for the depth which is based on local properties of the function. It would be interesting to find further extensions of this method in order to separate depth-bounded complexity classes within the complexity class $\mathcal{NC}^1$. For example, in [8] and [5] reductions to circuits of constant depth three and two are proved, resulting in circuits of a hyperpolynomial size. For the case of nonuniform circuits it is not known whether a hyperpolynomial number of gates is necessary or not.
Further work will be directed on the application of the relation $\frac{p}{q} \cdot (1 + \frac{1}{n^a})$ to learning procedures. The polynomial value $n^a$ can be used as a parameter during the learning process ($a = 1, 2, \ldots$). The aim is to find at least quasi-polynomial learning algorithms for depth-three circuits from $TC_{bin}^o$, where a uniform distribution of positive and negative examples is assumed.
The presented approach cannot be extended immediately to circuits of depth five or a larger depth, because after the first decomposition (from depth four to depth three) it seems to be difficult to ensure the relation $\frac{p}{q} \cdot (1 \pm \frac{1}{n^{\varphi(n)}})$ for the decomposition from depth three to depth two.
We think that lower bounds for threshold circuits provide a better insight into the computational power of organic neural nets.


# References

[1] A. Albrecht. On the complexity of learning circuits. *IIR*, 5(12):29 – 35, 1989.

[2] A. Albrecht. On bounded-depth threshold circuits for pattern functions. In Proc. of The International Conference on Artificial Neural Networks; *ICANN'92*, pages 135 – 138, Brighton, 1992.

[3] E. Allender. A note on the power of threshold circuits. Technical Report TR-5, Univ. of Würzburg, Inst. of Informatics, July 1989.

[4] E. Allender and V. Gore. On strong separations from $AC^0$. In *Proc. 8th International Conference on Fundamentals of Computation Theory (FCT '91), Lecture Notes in Computer Science*, volume 529, pages 1 – 15. Springer-Verlag, 1991.

[5] E. Allender and V. Gore. A uniform circuit lower bound for the permanent. Technical report, Rutgers University, Dept. of Computer Science, 1992.

[6] D.A. Barrington. Quasipolynomial size circuit classes. In *Proc. 7th IEEE Structure in Complexity Theory Conference*, pages 86 – 93, 1992.

[7] D.A. Barrington and D.Thérien. Finite monoids and the fine structure of $NC^0$. *J. Assoc. Comput. Mach.*, 35:941 – 952, 1988.

[8] R. Beigel and J. Tarui. On ACC. In *Proc. 32nd IEEE Symposium on Foundations of Computer Science*, pages 783 – 792, 1991.

[9] J. Bruck. Harmonic analysis of polynomial threshold functions. *SIAM Journal on Discrete Mathematics*, 3(2):168 – 177, 1990.

[10] J. Bruck and R. Smolensky. Polynomial threshold functions, $AC^0$ functions and spectral norms. In *Proc. of the 31st IEEE Symp. on Foundations of Computer Science*, pages 632 – 641, 1990.

[11] M. Furst, J.B. Saxe, and M. Sipser. Parity, circuits, and the polynomial-time hierarchy. In *Proc. 22nd IEEE Symp. on Foundations of Computer Science*, pages 260 – 270, 1981.

[12] M. Goldmann, J. Håstad, and A. Razborov. Majority gates vs. general weighted threshold gates. In *Proc. 7th IEEE Structure in Complexity Theory Conf.*, 1992.

[13] A. Hajnal, W. Maass, P. Pudlak, M. Szegedy, and G. Turan. Threshold functions of bounded depth. In *Proc. 28 IEEE Symp. on Foundations of Computer Science*, pages 99 – 110, 1987.

[14] J. Håstad. Almost optimal lower bounds for small depth circuits. In *Proc. of the 18th ACM Symp. on Theory of Computing*, pages 6 – 20, 1986.

[15] J. Håstad and M. Goldmann. On the power of small-depth threshold circuits. In *Proc. of the 31st IEEE Symp. on Foundations of Computer Science*, pages 610 – 618, 1990.

[16] W. Maass, G. Schnitger, and E. Sontag. On the computational power of sigmoid versus boolean threshold circuits. In *Proc. of the 32nd IEEE Symp. on Foundations of Computer Science*, pages 767 – 776, 1991.

[17] A.A. Razborov. Lower bounds on the size of bounded depth networks over a complete basis with logical addition; in Russian. *Mathem. Zametki*, 41:598–607, 1987.

[18] K.-Y. Siu and J. Bruck. On the power of threshold circuits with small weights. *SIAM Journal on Discrete Mathematics*, 4(3):423 – 435, 1991.

[19] R. Smolensky. Algebraic methods in the theory of lower bounds for boolean circuit complexity. In *Proc. of the 19th ACM Symp. on Theory of Computing*, pages 77 – 82, 1987.

[20] Ph. Treleaven. Neurocomputers. Technical Report CS-RN-89-8, University College London, 1989.

[21] K. Verbeurgt. Learning DNF under the uniform distribution in quasi-polynomial time. In *Proc. of the $3^{rd}$ Annual Workshop on Computational Learning Theory*, pages 314 – 326, 1990.

[22] A.C. Yao. Circuits and local computation. In *Proc. of the 21st ACM Symp. on Theory of Computing*, pages 186 – 196, 1989.

[23] A.C. Yao. On ACC and threshold circuits. In *Proc. 31st IEEE Symposium on Foundations of Computer Science*, pages 619 – 627, 1990.

# Structuring Neural Networks and PAC-Learning

Eberhard Pippig*

HTWK Leipzig

Dept. of Informatics

P.O.Box 66 04251 Leipzig, Germany

eberhard@informatik.th-leipzig.de

### Abstract

There is investigated the problem of structuring neural networks. This is a crucial task in designing neural networks similar to the corresponding task of designing modular software systems. We propose a particulary new approach of invoking inductive inference techniques for recognizing regularities in the partially given relation to be implemented and for proposing a prestructured net. Furthermore there will be given some mathematical foundations of the choosen approach in form of some convergence theorems by using the back-propagation strategy. Finally we show some connections to the field of PAC-Learning.

## 1  Introduction

The present article deals with an artificial intelligence approach to structuring neural networks. Roughly spoken, we propose to invoke certain inductive learning ideas for prestructuring neural networks by processing only incomplete information about the desired behaviour.

It is out of the scope of the present article to give an introduction into neural networks or inductive inference. For both areas, there are excellent introductions and surveys. Especially for neural networks, there is a huge amount of recent literature. We restrict ourselves to the classical paper [MP43] and to the recent books [Arb87] and [RM86]. For inductive inference, there is the distinguished survey paper [AS83]. The foundations of PAC-Learnability are presented in the paper [Val84].

Neural networks provide a framework for efficiently implementing solutions for a remarkably large class of problems. Given a problem to be attacked, designing an appropriate neural network is a task similar to the problem of developing software

---

*This work has been supported by the German Ministry for Research and Technology (BMFT) under grant no. 01 IW 101.

for a classical problem of computer applications. Scientists and engineers are faced to similar problems. As in classical software engineering, there is a fundamental gap between the problem to be solved and formal tools for its solution. Even if the problem is completely formalized, it is still a difficult task to transform this specification into an operational form. The intention of the present article is to provide some new ideas for bridging the gap from formal problem descriptions to neural networks implementing appropriate solutions.

We consider Boolean relations with different input and output attributes as complete formal specifications for problems to be solved by neural networks. It is particularly typical for applications of neural networks that problem descriptions are usually incomplete. Formally spoken, one may imagine a target relation which is not given explicitly. Instead of this, one has a certain subrelation available, and the task is to design a neural network implementing the whole relation as good as possible. For relating our approach to this general situation, we sketch it in an abstract manner by the following figure:

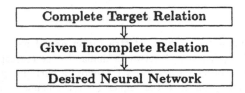

Figure 1: The general situation

Inductive inference denotes a wide area of investigations dealing with learning from usually incomplete information (cf. [AS83], [Jan89]). We propose to bridge the gap from an incomplete specification to a desired neural network by applying inductive inference rules to the incomplete information provided. The result shall be described as a formula or a set of formulae which have to be transformed into a neural network. It is interesting, that it turns out that this way is a generalization of the classical approach to transform some completely given relation via some propositional normal form into an equivalent network (see below). The scenario proposed may be illustrated as follows:

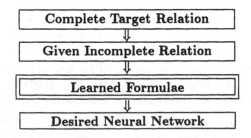

Figure 2: The scenario

It is obvious from the generality of the approach, that learning formulae by inspecting incomplete information can not always yield the desired result because the information presented could be far too incomplete. However, our experiments below show that our approach succeeds in a remarkable number of cases.

The key idea is to look for some functional dependencies between input and output attributes. We will demonstrate some advantages of prestructuring nets by investigating a frequently used relation.

Finally, we show some connections to the area of PAC-Learning. One can transform and modify some methods of approximative learning to justify our structuring approach.

## 2    Notions and Notations

We adopt the standard notions and notations of classical propositional logic. Because we consider the behaviour of a neural network as a Boolean relation, i.e. a relation over $\{0, 1\}$ , we need some elementary concepts of the classical relational data base theory (cf. [FV84] in this regard).

Since relations are understood as the descriptions of the desired behaviour of some neural net, there are distinguished input and output attributes resp. columns. We always denote input attributes by $\mathbf{x}$, sometimes specified by some further index. Analogously, output attributes are called $\mathbf{y}$ which may be indexed.

We consider a subset $\mathbf{B}$ of the set of all Boolean relations of the following kind:

$$B \in \mathbf{B} \quad \leftrightarrow \quad B : \{0, 1\}^n \to \{0, 1\}^m$$

$$\text{where} \quad y_i = B_i(x_1, ..., x_n) \qquad i = 1, ..., m$$

In particular, we call elements of any relation tuples (i.e. rows, if one arranges the relation as a table) and denote them usually by $\mathbf{t}$.

If $\mathbf{z}$ is any attribute name (i.e. the name of a column in the table), the value of the tuple $\mathbf{t}$ in the column $\mathbf{z}$ is denoted by $\mathbf{t}.\mathbf{z}$.

**Definition 1**    A **vector-valued functional dependency** $F : \{0, 1\}^r \to \{0, 1\}^l$ is a mapping from some input attributes to some output attributes:

$$(y_{j_1}, ..., y_{j_l}) = F(x_{i_1}, ..., x_{i_r})$$

where $\{i_1, ..., i_r\} \subset \{1, ..., n\}$ and $\{j_1, ..., j_l\} \subseteq \{1, ..., m\}$.

**Definition 2**    A **functional dependency** $f : \{0, 1\}^r \to \{0, 1\}$ is a mapping from a proper subset of the inputs to one output attribute:

$$y_k = f(x_{i_1}, ..., x_{i_r}) \text{ where } \{i_1, ..., i_r\} \subset \{1, ..., n\} \text{ and } k \in \{1, ..., m\}.$$

Concerning data dependencies, the reader is directed again to [FV84]. We are particularly interested in functional dependencies.

# 3 The Structuring Approach

Neural networks may be considered from different viewpoints. It turns out that for the investigations on hand, it is quite helpful to consider neural networks as massively parallel computers. It will be sufficient to interpret neural nets as computing devices for implementing Boolean functions, i.e. we abstract from a finer interpretation of output values in the interval [0,1] . We adopt the corresponding results because they provide us with a canonical method for structuring neural networks in dependence on knowledge about the relation to be implemented. More precisely, the canonical method allows to find a neural network implementing any Boolean relation exactly, provided the target relation is effectively given. Our approach exceeds this canonical methodology in some respect: First, we are mainly interested in processing incomplete information about some relation to be implemented. The incompleteness of the given information seems to be the crux of real applications. In particular, the task to process incomplete knowledge motivates our attempt to invoke inductive inference techniques. Second, as usual in connectionists work, we do not try to find always an implementation being absolutely correct. A sufficiently good approximation will do it. There is an obvious tradeoff between the incompleteness of information processed and the accuracy of the result obtained.

It is a well known result that even quite simple types of neural networks are able to compute any Boolean function (cf. [Arb87]). This can be immediately extended to implementing Boolean relations. To obtain this result, it is sufficient to use as processors simple threshold elements which are propagating the value **1** if the weighted sum of inputs reaches or exceeds their threshold. They are propagating **0** otherwise. The key idea is to find simple elementary nets for representing any basis of Boolean functions, e.g. {not , and , or }. We exemplify a solution for the logical **and** here:

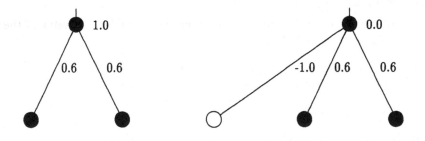

Figure 3: The logical **and**

Both elementary nets implement the logical conjunction **and** , where the processor element contains its threshold. The right hand version has a bias indicated as a white circle. Usually, a bias is a particular input node representing the fixed value **1**. A bias allows to use uniform threshold values within a whole net. For simplicity, we are using **0** as the uniform threshold in all nets containing a bias.

Thus, one may implement any Boolean function by representing it in terms of the assumed basis (say, as canonical disjunctive normal form called CDNF, e.g.) and implementing this normal form directly by means of the elementary nets found. This applies to Boolean relations similarly. We illustrate this scenario as follows:

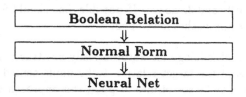

Figure 4: The normalform scenario

If a neural net has been derived from a Boolean relation via its CCNF (canonical conjunctive normal form) or CDNF using the elementary nets introduced above, we call it the corresponding CCNF net and CDNF net, respectively.

Naturally, there is a couple of similar approaches. For example, one may drop the internal nodes for implementing the negation in CCNF resp. CDNF nets by only changing weights locally. However, it is always quite difficult to find effective neural nets for given Boolean relations. In the scenario explained above, the normal form may grow exponentially in dependence on the number of occurring variables. Consequently, the resulting net may become considerably large. But this is no surprise. Because of its expressiveness, neural networks are inheriting all known undecidability and complexity problems (cf. [Jud87]).

Following the scenario above, one processes complete information and generates a complete net correctly implementing the Boolean relation to be processed. In case the information provided is no longer complete, one may be immediately unable to find a correct implementation. In this case, one should not overestimate weights of edges constructed. Moreover, it may be even reasonable to consider only the derived structure and to learn appropriate weights by training the net as usual in connectionists work. Therefore, in the case of incompleteness of the information presented, we call the synthesis (design) of a neural network along a scenario as the one above rather prestructuring than implementation.

Prestructuring turns out to be a version of implementing neural networks under some more realistic conditions. We propose in the sequel the new scenario of prestructuring in some respect.

1. One should allow to process only incomplete information about the target Boolean relation to be implemented.

2. Doing so, one needs to specify

(a) the type of knowledge to be deduced from the partial relation inspected as well as

(b) the type of formulae to be constructed for reflecting the dependencies recognized.

3. Doing so, one needs rules for transforming formulae into nets and net structures, respectively.

4. Doing so, one needs to explore the power and applicability of the approaches developed under 2. and 3. above. If possible, one should formally characterize the power of the approaches developed.

This will result in a methodology for automatically prestructuring neural networks by learning properties of the target relation to be implemented inductively. As incomplete information may be sometimes to poor, this approach may fail. Therefore, one should always imagine a semiautomatic process, where the methodology proposed offers a prestructuring of a network to be synthesized. In case, the information processed although being incomplete led to a sufficient solution, human intervention is not necessary. Otherwise, the offered prestructuring may be understood as a proposal to the engineer which may be used in several ways. One may add more information for provoking the system to make a better proposal, or one may refine the automatically generated proposal by hand.

We are going to illustrate the approach by means of a small but sufficiently expressive example. Motivating the example is out of the scope of this article. If the reader has some basic knowledge about information encoding, (s)he may know about Gray code. This is a way of binary encoding natural numbers which has some information-theoretic advantages over standard dual code. The key property of Gray code is that the encodings of subsequent numbers differ in exactly one bit. For a better understanding we present the first tuples of this relation.

| Number | Standard Binary Code | | | | | | | | Gray Code | | | | | | | |
|---|---|---|---|---|---|---|---|---|---|---|---|---|---|---|---|---|
| $n$ | $x_7$ | $x_6$ | $x_5$ | $x_4$ | $x_3$ | $x_2$ | $x_1$ | $x_0$ | $y_7$ | $y_6$ | $y_5$ | $y_4$ | $y_3$ | $y_2$ | $y_1$ | $y_0$ |
| 0 | 0 | 0 | 0 | 0 | 0 | 0 | 0 | 0 | 0 | 0 | 0 | 0 | 0 | 0 | 0 | 0 |
| 1 | 0 | 0 | 0 | 0 | 0 | 0 | 0 | 1 | 0 | 0 | 0 | 0 | 0 | 0 | 0 | 1 |
| 2 | 0 | 0 | 0 | 0 | 0 | 0 | 1 | 0 | 0 | 0 | 0 | 0 | 0 | 0 | 1 | 1 |
| 3 | 0 | 0 | 0 | 0 | 0 | 0 | 1 | 1 | 0 | 0 | 0 | 0 | 0 | 0 | 1 | 0 |
| 4 | 0 | 0 | 0 | 0 | 0 | 1 | 0 | 0 | 0 | 0 | 0 | 0 | 0 | 1 | 1 | 0 |
| 5 | 0 | 0 | 0 | 0 | 0 | 1 | 0 | 1 | 0 | 0 | 0 | 0 | 0 | 1 | 1 | 1 |
| 6 | 0 | 0 | 0 | 0 | 0 | 1 | 1 | 0 | 0 | 0 | 0 | 0 | 0 | 1 | 0 | 1 |
| 7 | 0 | 0 | 0 | 0 | 0 | 1 | 1 | 1 | 0 | 0 | 0 | 0 | 0 | 1 | 0 | 0 |
| 8 | 0 | 0 | 0 | 0 | 1 | 0 | 0 | 0 | 0 | 0 | 0 | 0 | 1 | 1 | 0 | 0 |

Table 1:

We consider the task of designing a neural network implementing the transformation from standard binary code into Gray code for ASCII characters. For instance,

the desired net should transform the ASCII code **01000000** of the question mark
"?" into **01100000**. Both the CCNF and the CDNF net would be huge, as each
one is the conjunction resp. disjunction of 128 terms being elementary disjunctions
resp. conjunctions of 8 atomic literals (variables being either negated or not).

We are invoking two extremely simple rules for prestructuring. These rules will yield
a remarkably small prestructured neural network able to be trained for implementing
the desired relation.

---

### Elementary Dependency 1

If there is an output attribute **y** and an input attribute **x** such that for all tuples
**t** of the relation presented it holds **t.y = t.x**, that means we have a functional
dependency **y = f(x)**, then construct the formula **x → y** .

---

The validity of such a dependency may be checked by moving output columns over
the input part of the target relation. We are dropping implementational details here.

---

### Elementary Dependency 2

If there is an output attribute **y** and an input attribute **x** such that for a set of
tuples **Q** and for all tuples **t** in **Q** it holds **t.y = t.x**, and furthermore, if there is an
attribute **x'** such that **Q** contains exactly all tuples **t** of the relation satisfying the
condition **t.x' = 0**, then construct the formula **x & x' → y** .

---

Note that there are several versions of these rules which work similarly. For example,
one may substitute **t.y = t.x** by **t.y ≠ t.x** in both cases. It is also possible to replace
**t.x' = 0** by **t.x' = 1** .

---

### Elementary Structuring Rule 1

The formula **x → y** is implemented by an edge from the input node **x** to the output
node **y**. No other edge leads to **y**.

---

We illustrate the resulting elementary nets for both rules by the figure 5 below.

---

### Elementary Structuring Rule 2

The formula **x & x' → y** is implemented by one hidden node **z** and five edges. From
both input nodes **x** and **x'**, there are edges to **z** as well as to **y**. From **z** there is an
additional edge to the output node **y**. Both **y** and **z** may get an edge from the bias.
No other edges lead to **y** and **z**.

---

The following figure shows the result of prestructuring a net by processing the relation

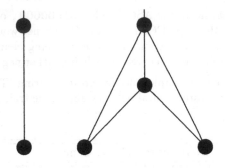

Figure 5: Simple nets

which describes the transformation of standard binary code of one byte into Gray code. If one considers this relation, there are some obvious dependencies of input and output attributes. We can establish the identity of the first input attribute and the first output attribute, that means $x_7 = y_7$. Moreover, one may easily recognize that certain neighbouring inputs are determining corresponding outputs as indicated by the following dependency: $y_i = f(x_i, x_{i+1})$, $(i = 1...7)$. Using the rules described above, we get the following net:

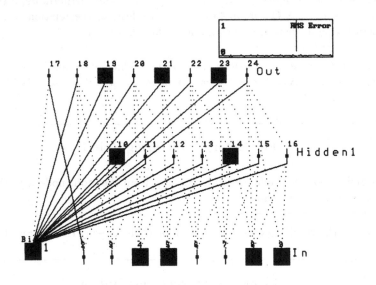

Figure 6: Gray-Code

Our investigations were supported by experiments using the network simulator **Neu-ralWorks Professional II Plus**. During the training phase, we used the backpropagation algorithm as learning strategy and a sigmoid function as transfer function. The error was cumulated, i.e. we worked with the cumulated delta rule. Other parameters of the learning rule have been chosen variabel. The reader is directed to [RM86] for the corresponding mathematical concepts in neural network theory.

The net in Fig. 6 is able to learn the above relation correctly after a training with approximately 200,000 examples. During this, the net has been fed in single instances randomly. The net shown in the Figure above reflects particular input and output values, where large and small squares indicate the values **1** and **0**, respectively. In the upper right corner, the error between desired and current output is represented graphically. In dependence on the application requirements, the training phase can be finished when this error reaches some given error estimate. We have chosen the value **0.1**, for instance.

Throughout our introductory example we assumed the completeness of the relation presented just for simplifying the approach. As a side effect, we could demonstrate that our methodology proposed may result in remarkably efficient implementations compared to standard approaches (consider the CDNF net, e.g.). In the sequel, we will put emphasis on the incompleteness of information processed. Already in the case of our introductory example, one may find subrelations of the target relation which would yield exactly the same result although presenting only incomplete information.

For this purpose, we consider the following subrelation consisting of eight instances:

```
0 0 0 0 0 0 0 0    0 0 0 0 0 0 0 0
1 1 1 1 1 1 1 1    1 0 0 0 0 0 0 0
1 0 1 0 1 0 1 0    1 1 1 1 1 1 1 1
0 1 0 1 0 1 0 1    0 1 1 1 1 1 1 1
1 0 0 1 1 0 0 1    1 1 0 1 0 1 0 1
1 1 0 0 1 1 0 0    1 0 1 0 1 0 1 0
0 0 1 1 0 0 1 1    0 0 1 0 1 0 1 0
0 1 1 0 0 1 1 0    0 1 0 1 0 1 0 1
```

In the learning phase, these instances are offered to the prestructured net in Figure 6 as well as to a net with the same neuron topology and fully connections between neurons in different layers. Both nets have learned this subrelation without any problem after a sufficient number of presentations of the training set. Afterwards, our prestructured net was able to reproduce the whole relation, i.e. it correctly recognizes the other 248 input/output examples which were not presented in the training set. In contrast, the fully connected net was not able to handle the complete relation correctly. After the training phase, the full connected net was tested with some instances not contained in the training set. Figure 7 illustrates the result of such a test.

For the current input **0 1 0 0 0 1 0 0**, the vector **0 1 1 0 0 1 1 0** is a correct output instead of **0 1 0.2 1 0.2 1 0.2 1**. This example shows that the fully connected net makes remarkable errors although its connection set contains the connection set of the prestructured (in our sense) net. Since the fully connected case

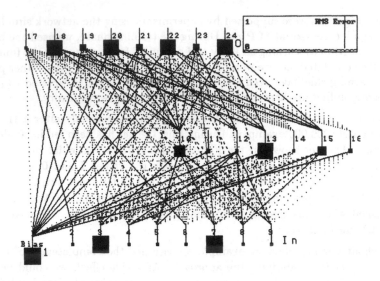

Figure 7: Gray-Code full connected

has more degrees of freedom, this net is not able to find a feasible solution for the weight vector. Moreover, the backpropagation strategy provides a local minimum of the error surface. This is a well known mathematical founded disadvantage of such optimization methods more precise discussed later.

We can expand this relation to $n = 2^k$, $k > 3$ inputs and obtain a net with $n - 1$ units in the hidden layer. Let the number of weights one has to adjust be a measure for the complexity of the net. Then we get the following statements.

Let n be the number of inputs/outputs for Gray code, Num(n) be the number of weights. We consider three different net types:

1) Layer connected System

$$Num(n) > 2n(n - 1) = 2n^2 - 2n$$

2) Fully connected System

$$Num(n) = 2n(n - 1) + n^2 = 3n^2 - 2n$$

3) Prestructured System

$$Num(n) = 2(n - 1) + (n - 1) + 2(n - 1) + 1 = 5n - 4$$

By neglecting the bias connections, we obtain a linearly growth of the number of weights with respect to the number of inputs of our approach. For the other two kinds of nets, this growth is at least quadratic.

The advantages of the present approach may be resulted in:

- **more efficient structures as in the heuristical case,**
- **better learning results compared to layer connected or fully connected systems,**
- **recognition from relations by means of incomplete information.**

It is easy to verify that our method is not a universal method. Therefore, one should know in which cases it is helpful to apply structuring rules. An answer to this question requires more theoretical investigations of the rules introduced in [JP92]

Within the next section we discuss some mathematical aspects of our methodology.

# 4 Mathematical Foundations

The main reason for the renaissance in the domain of neural networks was the introduction and validation of the generalized delta-rule by David Rumelhart and Geoffrey Hinton in 1985 [RM86]. This allowed an expansion of the failed perceptron to universal feed forward nets and provided a foundation of the backpropagation strategy.

Some remarks about this method. In general, the backpropagation algorithm was introduced to handle the following optimization problem. We have to minimize an objective function without restrictions, i.e. we must solve the free optimization task:

$$E(g_1, ..., g_r) = \sum_{i=1}^{n} E_i(g_1, ..., g_r) \rightarrow \min.$$

$$E_i(g_1, ..., g_r) = \frac{1}{2} \sum_{j=1}^{k} (T_{ij} - a_{ij}(g_1, ..., g_r))^2.$$

Within the problem description above, we use the following abbreviations:

$E$ - objective function (sum of differences between desired and current value over all output neurons and all training examples)

$E_i$ - subobjective function for the i-th training set

$r$ - number of adjustable weights

$n$ - number of given training samples

$k$   -   subobjective function for the i-th training set

$g_l$   -   l-th weight

$T_{ij}$   -   desired output of the j-th output neuron for the i-th sample

$a_{ij}$   -   current output of the j-th output neuron for the i-th sample by the momentary weight distribution

In the sequel we use an usually sigmoid function as activation function **a**, i.e.:

$$a(x) = F_\theta(x) = (1 + e^{-(\frac{x-\theta}{T})})^{-1}$$

with T=1. For the i-th training sample, we set

$$E = \frac{1}{2} \sum_{j=1}^{k} (T_{ij} - a_{ij})^2.$$

Now we want to give a validatity of some simple structuring rules. The proofs for the lemmata and theorems will be leave out. They may be found elsewhere [Pip92].

**Rule 1** (Logical Identity)

Assume any Boolean relation. If one input attribute **x** is equivalent to an output attribute **y**, then implement a direct connection between this two attributes in the target neural network.

## Mathematical Foundation

As mentioned above, we use the backpropagation algorithm as learning strategy with a sigmoid function $F_\theta$ as transfer function.
Let us consider the error function $E^1(g)$ (g is the weight to be learned between x and y).

$$E^1(g) = \frac{1}{2} \sum_{i=1}^{2} (T_i - a_i(g))^2 = \frac{1}{2}((1 - F_\theta(g))^2 + F_\theta(0)^2).$$

By $T_j$ we denote the teaching input (**0** or **1**), $a_j$ designates the actual activation of the output neuron.

## Lemma 1

For every $\varepsilon > 0$ $(\varepsilon < \frac{1}{2})$, exists a $\theta \epsilon R$ with $\lim_{g \to \infty} E^1(g) < \varepsilon$.

This Lemma is required for our first theorem.

**Theorem 1**    For any $\varepsilon > 0$, exists a $\theta$ such that there is a sequence of step widths for which the backpropagation algorithm produces a sequence of weights $g^0, g^1, ...$ with the property: for all initial values $g^0$, exists a $k' \epsilon R$ with $E^1(g^k) < \varepsilon$ for all $k > k'$.

For logical negation, we obtain similar results.

**Rule 2** (Logical Negation)

Assume any Boolean relation. If one input attribute **x** is equivalent to the negation of an output attribute **y**, then implement a direct connection between this two attributes in the target neural network.

## Mathematical Foundation

In this case, the error function $E^2(g)$ has the following form

$$E^2(g) = \frac{1}{2}((1 - F_\theta(0))^2 + F_\theta(g)^2).$$

## Lemma 2

For every $\varepsilon > 0$ $(\varepsilon < \frac{1}{2})$, exists a $\theta \epsilon R$ with $\lim_{g \to -\infty} E^2(g) < \varepsilon$.

**Theorem 2** For any $\varepsilon > 0$, exists a $\theta$ such that there is a sequence of step widths for which the backpropagation algorithm produces a sequence of weights $g^0, g^1, \ldots$ with the property: for all initial values $g^0$, exists a $k' \epsilon R$ with $E^2(g^k) < \varepsilon$ for all $k > k'$.

Finally, in this section we will investigate a further form of connections, the logical independence.

**Rule 3** (Logical Independence)

If an output attribute is independent from all input values then connect this neuron with the bias element.

## Mathematical Foundation

As an error function $E_3(g)$ we obtain:

$$E^3(g) = \frac{1}{2} F_\theta(g)^2.$$

**Lemma 3** It values

$$\lim_{g \to -\infty} E^3(g) = 0$$

and $E^3(g)$ is strictly monotonous increasing.

**Theorem 3** For the error function $E^3$ and for an arbitrary starting point $g^0$ backpropagation produces a sequence of weights $g^0, g^1, \ldots$ with the property: there exists a $k' \epsilon R$ with $E^3(g^k) < \varepsilon$ for all $k > k'$.

By application of the structuring rules the statements outlined above guarantee that the backpropagation algorithm works successful. This is valid for arbitrarily starting points of weights and threshold values.

It seems impossible to find such mathematical foundations for more complicated structuring rules like the **elementary structuring rule 2** in **section 3**. The reason is, that in such cases the error function has not such necessary properties like convexity. So there is no hope to find always a global minimum with the backpropagation algorithm.

# 5 PAC-Learnability

In this section we want to confront our approach to the field of PAC-Learning. Therefore, we need at first the definition of the consistence of a set of tuples with a functional dependency.

**Definition 3**    A functional dependency

$$y_k = f(x_{i_1}, ..., x_{i_r})$$

is called **consistent** with a set of tuples T, iff

$$\forall t^h, t^j \epsilon T \quad \text{holds}: \quad \forall l (1 \le l \le r \mid x_{i_l}^h = x_{i_l}^j) \Rightarrow y_k^h = y_k^j.$$

**Example 1**    $B = \{(x_1, x_2, y)\} = \{(0,1,1), (0,0,0), (1,0,1), (1,1,1)\} \subset \{0,1\}^3$. Consider furthermore the functinal dependency $y = f(x_1)$. Then the set $\{(0,1,1), (1,0,1), (1,1,1)\}$ is consistent with f while $\{(0,1,1), (0,0,0)\}$ is inconsistent with f.

There exists an efficient implementation of an algorithm to test consistence of a functional dependency with a set of tuples [AT92]. We consider in the next the PAC-Learnability of a functional dependency. Therefore we define the error, that a set T of tuples is consistent with a functional dependency $f$. $p(t)$ denotes the probability that we pick an element of T as an example with respect to a probability distribution D.

**Definition 4**    For a set of tuples T, a probabilistic distribution D and a functional dependency f, the error $\varepsilon(T, D, f)$ is defined as

$$\varepsilon(T, D, f) = \sum_{t \epsilon V} p(t)$$

where V satisfies the following conditions:

(1)    f is consistent with $T \backslash V$

(2)    $\sum_{t \epsilon V} p(t)$ is  the minimum among such sets that satisfy the condition (1).

For illustration we consider the following example.

**Example 2**  $B = \{t^1, ..., t^{10}\} = \{(0,0,0,0,0), (0,0,0,1,0), (0,0,1,0,0), (0,0,1,1,0),$
$(0,1,0,1,0),(0,1,1,0,1),(0,1,1,1,1),(1,0,1,0,0),(1,0,1,1,1),(1,1,1,1,0)\}$ where each $t^i$ has the
form $(x^i_1, ..., x^i_4, y^i)$.
Let $D = \{0.1, 0.1, 0.1, 0.1, 0.1, 0.1, 0.1, 0.1, 0.1, 0.1\}$ be a probabilistic distribution and
$y = f(x_2, x_3)$ a functional dependency, then we can choose $V_1 = \{t^3, t^4, t^6, t^7, t^8\}$
and $V_2 = \{t^9, t^{10}\}$ satisfying condition (1) of Definition 4. That means, one obtains
$\varepsilon(T, D, f) = \sum_{t \in V_2} p(t) = 0.2$ .

Now, we want to consider the problem to infer a set of all the functional dependencies
consistent with the whole data from example tuples in a PAC manner. For further
information see [AT92].

There exists a simple algorithm enumerating all functional dependencies. However, it
seems to be very difficult to develop a polynomialtime algorithm, because the number
of functional dependencies is exponential.

Let us consider this number in our approach:

$$numfd = m \cdot \sum_{i=1}^{n} \binom{n}{i} < m \cdot 2^n.$$

**Theorem 4**   The number of examples required to infer a set of (vector valued)
functional dependencies FS such that $\varepsilon(T, D, FS) \le \varepsilon$ is satisfied and that all the
functional dependencies consistent with the whole tuples are included by FS with the
probability at least $1 - \delta$ is

$$O\left(\left(\frac{m \cdot 2^n}{\varepsilon}\right) \cdot \sqrt{ln\left(\frac{m \cdot 2^n}{\delta}\right) \cdot \sqrt{s}}\right), \qquad \text{where} \quad s = |T|.$$

Here $\varepsilon(T, D, FS)$ means the error with respect to consistency of T with a set of
functional dependencies FS. To define this error, we have to replace $f$ by $\forall f \epsilon FS$ in
Definition 4 (1).

**Remark 1**   For a single valued set of functional dependencies, we obtain obviously
the estimation

$$O\left(\left(\frac{2^n}{\varepsilon}\right) \cdot \sqrt{ln\left(\frac{2^n}{\delta}\right) \cdot \sqrt{s}}\right)$$

for the number of required examples depending from the input number and the cardinality of the tuple set.

To verify the connections to structuring neural networks let us consider the following
example:

**Example 3**    Consider the dual multiplication    $x_1x_2 \cdot x_3x_4 = y_1y_2y_3y_4$    with the data set:

$$
\begin{array}{cccc\ \ cccc}
0\ 0\ 0\ 0 & 0\ 0\ 0\ 0 \\
0\ 0\ 0\ 1 & 0\ 0\ 0\ 0 \\
0\ 0\ 1\ 0 & 0\ 0\ 0\ 0 \\
0\ 0\ 1\ 1 & 0\ 0\ 0\ 0 \\
0\ 1\ 0\ 1 & 0\ 0\ 0\ 1 \\
0\ 1\ 1\ 0 & 0\ 0\ 1\ 0 \\
0\ 1\ 1\ 1 & 0\ 0\ 1\ 1 \\
1\ 0\ 1\ 0 & 0\ 1\ 0\ 0 \\
1\ 0\ 1\ 1 & 0\ 1\ 1\ 0 \\
1\ 1\ 1\ 1 & 1\ 0\ 0\ 1 \\
\end{array}
$$

We have to remark, that this is only the asymmetric subrelation. There is the following set $fs$ of functional dependencies:

$y_1 = f_1(x_1, x_2)$

$y_2 = f_2(x_1, x_3)$    (exception input  1 1 1 1 )

$y_3 = f_3(x_2, x_3)$    (exception inputs  1 0 1 1    and    1 1 1 1 )

$y_4 = f_4(x_2, x_4)$

We compute the set V from **Definition 4** as:

$$V = \{(1, 0, 1, 1, 0, 1, 1, 0), (1, 1, 1, 1, 1, 0, 0, 1)\}$$

This set corresponds to the tuples 9 and 10 from our data set. It reflects exactly the exceptions. Furthermore, it holds $\varepsilon(T, D, fs) = 0.2$.

Let $h_1$ be the number of hidden units corresponding to our structuring rules with respect to $T\backslash V$, $h$ the number of all hidden units of a subnetwork which are necessary to realize a Boolean subrelation with respect to a set of functional dependencies fs.

**Lemma 4**    Assuming V contains no subset consistent with $fs$. Then it holds:

$h \geq h_1 + \#V.$

**Remark 2**    $h = h_1 + \#V + r$, where r depends from the expected accuracy.

**Example 4**    For dual multiplication from Example 3 we obtain: $h = 4 + 2 + r$ with $r = 0$ for $RMS - Error \leq 0.1$.

# 6  Conclusions

Let us summarize some essential aspects which may direct further investigations.

First, it seems to be reasonable to develop more complex structuring rules. But, like mentioned it is very difficult or even impossible to proof their correctness. The main difficulties will consist in the fast growth of the complexity of the error functions and the mathematical problems influenced by this fact.

Second, it is quite important to formally investigate the learnability of Boolean relations from incomplete information. Obviously, this question is much more general. We hope that we can find some way to characterize that, for certain types of Boolean relations, there exist characteristic sets of good examples. Good examples means that this set of examples form a training set which allows to learn the complete relation, correctly.

Third, we want to apply some results in the field of PAC-Learnability to characterize the necessary network size and the number of requisite training examples. Besides, it is useful to embed the class of error backpropagation nets into a PAC-Learnability problem as object class. That means, we have to consider the problem, is the class of this nets PAC-learnable.

# References

[Arb87] M.A. Arbib. *Brains, Machines, and Mathematics*. Springer Verlag, second edition, 1987.

[AS83] D. Anguin and C.H. Smith. Inductive inference: Theory and methods. *Computing Surveys*, 15(3):237–269, 1983.

[AT92] T. Akutsu and A. Takasu. On pac-learnability of functional dependencies. In S. Doshita, K. Furukawa, K.P. Jantke, and T. Nishida, editors, *Algorithmic Learning Theory*, volume 743 of *Lecture Notes in Artifical Intelligence*, pages 229–239, 1992.

[FV84] R. Fagin and M.Y. Vardi. The theory of data dependencies - an overview. In J. Paredeans, editor, *Automata, Languages and Programming*, volume 172 of *Lecture Notes in Computer Science*, pages 1–22, 1984.

[Jan89] K.P. Jantke. Algorithmic learning from incomplete information: Principles and problems. In J. Dassow and J. Kelemen, editors, *Machines, Languages, and Complexity.*, volume 381 of *Lecture Notes in Computer Science*, pages 188–207. Springer Verlag, 1989.

[JP92] K.P. Jantke and E. Pippig. Inductive inference for structuring neural networks i: The approach. GOSLER Report 01/92, THL, January 1992.

[Jud87]   J.S. Judd. *Complexity of Connectionist Learning with Various Node Functions*. PhD thesis, Dept. Computer and Informations Science, University of Massachusetts, July 1987.

[MP43]   W.S. McCulloch and W. Pitts. A logical calculus of the ideas immanent in nervous activity. *Bull. Math. Biophysics*, 5:115–133, 1943.

[Pip92]   E. Pippig. Inductive inference for structuring neural networks ii: First results. GOSLER Report 12/92, THL, July 1992.

[RM86]   D.E. Rumelhart and J.L. McClelland. *Parallel Distributed Processing.*, volume I and II. MIT Press, 1986.

[Val84]   L.G. Valiant. A theory of the learnable. *Comm. ACM*, 27(11):1134–1142, 1984.

# Inductive Synthesis of Rewrite Programs

Ulf Goldammer*

HTWK Leipzig

FB Mathematik und Informatik

PF 66

04251 Leipzig

ulf@informatik.th-leipzig.de

## Abstract

First the existence and learnability of rewrite programs representing certain infinite, canonical ground rewrite systems (consisting of input/output examples as rewrite rules) is investigated. The second part contains an experimental synthesis algorithm for rewrite programs which is based on the instantiation and combination of simple (rewrite) program schemes.

## 1 Motivation

Rewrite programs, as defined in the sequel, are finite sets of rewrite rules such that for an arbitrary (input) term without variables any sequence of reductions using these rules yields a unique, irreducible (output) term. Deductive approaches to the synthesis of rewrite programs from equational specifications were initiated by DERSHOWITZ [Der82, Der85], further elaborated for instance in [Red89, DP90, Bel91, DR93]. These methods are based on (restricted versions of) KNUTH-BENDIX-completion procedures to generate the rewrite rules of the programs, and they share the problem to handle the possibly diverging behaviour of the procedure. This is done, deductively, by searching and inductively *proving* (again based on completion techniques) appropriate lemmas (rewrite rules) such that the completion procedure eventually terminates and the synthesis stops successfully. Another approach to handle the divergence problem (in general) is based on *learning in the limit*, by an inductive inference algorithm [Gol67], a finite, convergent set of rewrite rules which can equivalently replace the potentially infinite, convergent rewrite system generated by the completion procedure, as proposed by THOMAS and JANTKE [TJ89]. That means the inductive inference algorithm will provably output, after processing a finite, but in general non-predictable amount of the rules, the desired finite replacement and will not change this hypothesis anymoore when processing more rules. In a combined approach the deductive and the inductive learning methods can supplement each other, improving both the search for lemmas and hypotheses and also inductive proof algorithms.

---

*This work has been supported by the German Ministry for Research and Technology (BMFT) under grant no. 01 IW 101.

In this paper we are dealt with the learning approach. However the problem under consideration is a purely inductive synthesis of rewrite programs from certain examples of their input and output terms. The main motivation for this is the observation that a means to synthesize "simple" auxialary programs just from input/output examples can be very useful both in the deductive as well as in the learning approach. At least the latter case needs an explanation.

Given a rewrite systems $R$ to be completed and an infinite, convergent rewrite system $R^\infty$ of persisting rules generated by a KNUTH-BENDIX-completion of $R$, the finite replacement $R'$ of $R$ should be convergent, may be based on a larger signature than $R$, and it must exactly preserve the equalities between ground terms defined by $R$ ($R'$ is a *conservative enrichment* of $R$, when rules are considered as equations). One of the methods to construct $R'$ proposed in [TJ89] is based on replacing infinitely many rules in $R^\infty$ by a single rule which *exactly generalizes* the replaced rules. Considering a rewrite rule as a term with outermost operator $\rightarrow$, a term $t_0$ exactly generalizes a set $S = \{t_1, t_2, t_3, \ldots\}$ of terms if $\mathcal{G}(t_0) = \mathcal{G}(t_1) \cup \mathcal{G}(t_2) \cup \mathcal{G}(t_3) \cup \ldots$, where $\mathcal{G}(t)$ denotes the set of all ground instances of a term $t$. If $S$ indeed contains exactly all ground instances of some term, then learning this term from elements of $S$ is simple[1], and solves the problem to exactly generalize $S$. Besides this, the work contains also proposals to enrich $R$ conservatively such that $R^\infty$ becomes just the set of all ground instances of finitely many rewrite rules. According to these ideas LANGE [Lan89] developed a set of inference rules for the construction of such enrichments and for the generalization of sequences of rules or terms. For short, the basic idea is to identify varying terms $t_1, t_2, t_3, \ldots$ at constant positions in a sequence of rules and to construct a convergent rewrite system $R''$ such that each of the terms has a normalform which corresponds (according to its position in the sequence) to an initial part of a particular enumeration of *all* ground instances of just one single term, for instance

1. $t_1 \downarrow_{R''} = H(o, b_1, \ldots, b_n)$
2. $t_2 \downarrow_{R''} = H(c(o), b_1, \ldots, b_n)$
3. $t_3 \downarrow_{R''} = H(c(c(o)), b_1, \ldots, b_n)$

$\vdots$

where $t \downarrow_{R''}$ denotes the unique normalform of a term $t$ with respect to $R''$, $b_1, \ldots, b_n$ are the same terms in all rules, $H$ is a new operator and $o, c(o), c(c(o)), \ldots$ are irreducible terms of a new sort. $R''$ is added to $R$ ($R \cup R''$ is a conservative enrichment of $R$ by construction), and a restart of the completion procedure yields the sequence with the desired normalforms. If this succeeds for *all* varying subterms in a sequence of rewrite rules and for the continuation of the sequence to any length then a generalized rule can easily be constructed. For instance, if the sequence is finally

1. $H_1(o, b_1, \ldots, b_n) \rightarrow H_2(o, b'_1, \ldots, b'_n)$
2. $H_1(c(o), b_1, \ldots, b_n) \rightarrow H_2(c(o), b'_1, \ldots, b'_n)$
3. $H_1(c(c(o)), b_1, \ldots, b_n) \rightarrow H_2(c(c(o)), b'_1, \ldots, b'_n)$

---

[1] However, some peculiarities of the underlying signature may cause difficulties, see [TJ89].

$$\vdots$$

i. $H_1(c^i(o)), b_1, \ldots, b_n) \rightarrow H_2(c^i(o), b'_1, \ldots, b'_n)$

$$\vdots$$

then the rule

$$H_1(x, b_1, \ldots, b_n) \rightarrow H_2(x, b'_1, \ldots, b'_n)$$

(where $x$ is a variable and $b_1, b'_1, \ldots, b_n, b'_n$ are the same terms in all rules) generalizes exactly the rules of the sequence. Moreover, the completion process will terminate if this sequence is exactly what it would produce when continued (otherwise the whole process can be iterated). If the terms $t_1, t_2, t_3, \ldots$ are instances of some term $t$ such that $t_1 = t\sigma_1, t_2 = t\sigma_2, t_3 = t\sigma_3, \ldots$, then the construction starts with

1. $t \rightarrow H(o, x_1, \ldots, x_n)$   ($x_1, \ldots, x_n$ are the variables of $t$)

and other rules of $R''$ must ensure that

1. $H(o, x_1, \ldots, x_n)\sigma_1 \downarrow_{R''} = H(o, b_1, \ldots, b_n)$
2. $H(o, x_1, \ldots, x_n)\sigma_2 \downarrow_{R''} = H(c(o), b_1, \ldots, b_n)$
3. $H(o, x_1, \ldots, x_n)\sigma_3 \downarrow_{R''} = H(c(c(o)), b_1, \ldots, b_n)$

$$\vdots$$

The construction does not refer to $R$, therefore $R''$ can cause new sequences of rules to be generated by the completion procedure. Now the problem above can be reformulated as the synthesis of a rewrite program from the input/output examples

1. $f_H(x_1, \ldots, x_n)\sigma_1 \downarrow_{R''} = H(o)$
2. $f_H(x_1, \ldots, x_n)\sigma_2 \downarrow_{R''} = H(c(o))$
3. $f_H(x_1, \ldots, x_n)\sigma_3 \downarrow_{R''} = H(c(c(o)))$

$$\vdots$$

which is an instance of the more general synthesis problem defined in the sequel (where arbitrary right-hand sides are allowed).

In Section 3 we define some concepts to describe such synthesis problems and we are dealt with the existence and learnability of corresponding rewrite programs. In Section 3 we describe a simple experimental synthesis algorithm. Although this algorithm works correctly and can synthesize programs for quite complicated looking sequences of input/output examples in practice, its main purpose is to be a framework for the (experimental) study of a particular approach, namely the synthesis based on instantiation and combination of simple (rewrite) program schemes which describe concepts of growth of terms. The schemes presented here are based on slightly generalized versions of some recurrence relations used in [Lan89] and [Gol92] and are meant to be a starting point to find more interesting schemes (we outline some ideas in this regard). From our point of view it seems reasonable to have the schemes available as building blocks for the construction of rewrite programs and to separate them from the synthesis algorithm in order to study their properties, based on the theory of term rewriting systems.

# 2   Preliminaries

We adopt the standard notions and notations for term rewriting systems (cf. [DJ90, Klo92] for comprehensive surveys), and merely recap some of them to clarify our notations, together with some theorems from the literature which are used in the subsequent sections. Some familiarity with term rewriting systems is assumed. The neccessary notions from the theory of inductive inference (cf. [AS83] for an introductory survey) will be defined in Section 3. $\mathbb{N}$ denotes the set of natural numbers $0, 1, \ldots$

In the sequel all *signatures* $\Sigma$ are assumed to be *finite, finitary, heteregeneous* (however, we have only one sort sometimes). That is, a signature is the set $\{(f_i, \alpha_\Sigma(f_i)) \mid 1 \le i \le n\}$ build upon some finite, disjoint sets $op_\Sigma = \{f_1, \ldots, f_n\}$ of *operator* symbols and $sorts_\Sigma = \{s_1, \ldots, s_m\}$ of *sort* symbols, and a total *arity* function $\alpha_\Sigma : op_\Sigma \to (sorts_\Sigma)^+$ such that every $s \in sorts_\Sigma$ occurs in a word of the range of $\alpha_\Sigma$. For every operator $f \in op_\Sigma$ with $\alpha_\Sigma(f) = s_{k_1} \ldots s_{k_n} s_{k_{n+1}}$, $|f|_\Sigma = n$ denotes the number of arguments of $f$, $s_{k_{n+1}}$ is called its *target sort* and $\alpha_\Sigma(f)_{|i}$ is $s_{k_i}$ for $1 \le i \le n + 1$. $\alpha_\Sigma(f)$ is also written as $(f : s_{k_1} \ldots s_{k_n} \to s_{k_{n+1}})$. $f$ is called a *constant* if $|f|_\Sigma = 0$. For an arbitrary $\Sigma$, $\Sigma \setminus f$ is the signature $\Sigma \setminus \{(f, \alpha_\Sigma(f))\}$ if $f \in op_\Sigma$, and $\Sigma$ otherwise. We always assume that $\Sigma$ allows at least one ground term for every sort.

The set of well-formed (first-order) terms over a signature $\Sigma$ with $sorts_\Sigma = \{s_1, \ldots, s_m\}$ and a family of disjoint, countable sets of sorted *variables* $X = X_{s_1} \cup \ldots \cup X_{s_m}$ is denoted by $T(\Sigma, X)$. Usually we denote terms by $p, q, r, s, t$ and variables by $x, y, z, u, v, w$, all possibly with indexes and/or dashes. $T_s(\Sigma, X)$ denotes those terms of sort $s \in sorts_\Sigma$. The set of terms without variables, called *ground* terms, is denoted by $T(\Sigma)$ and $T_s(\Sigma)$ accordingly. We omit the sort index whenever it is clear from the context. As mentioned we require for any signature considered in the sequel that there is at least one ground term for every sort. For every term $t \in T(\Sigma, X)$, $sort(t)$ denotes its sort, $var(t)$ the set of variables from $X$ contained in $t$, $t_{|p}$ the subterm at position $p$ in $t$ and $t[t']_p$ the term obtained from $t$ by replacing $t_{|p}$ by $t'$, for some position $p$ in $t$ and term $t'$ of sort $sort(t_{|p})$. A term is called *linear* if the same variable occurs at most once in this term. The *depth* of a term is defined recursively: the depth of constants and variables is 0, and the depth of all other terms is one more than the maximum of the depths of its proper subterms. In a term $f(t_1, \ldots, t_n)$, $f$ is the *root* or *outermost* operator, accordingly for constants. Substitutions to variables and terms are defined as usual, as well as the property of a substitution to be a unifier of two terms. For some term $t$, we denote the substitution $\sigma$ of variables $x_1, \ldots, x_n \in var(t)$ by terms $t_1, \ldots, t_n$ by $[x_1 \leftarrow t_1, \ldots, x_n \leftarrow t_n]$ and the result of applying $\sigma$ to $t$ by $t\sigma$. $t\sigma$ is called an *instance* of $t$ and a *ground instance* if $t\sigma$ is a ground term. A term $t$ *overlaps* a term $s$ if $t$ is unifiable (after renaming of variables) with a subterm $s'$ of $s$ and $s'$ is not a variable. Two terms overlap if at least one of them overlaps the other. For instance, let $x$ and $y$ be variables, then $y$ overlaps $f(x)$, $g(f(x))$ and $f(g(x))$ mutually overlap, and $x$ and $y$ as well as $f(x)$ and $g(x)$ do not overlap.

In our notation of terms we abbreviate repetitions of subsequent unary operators by an exponential notation, such that $f^0(t) = t$ and $f^{i+1}(t) = f(f^i(t))$. Furthermore, for any operator $f$ with $|f| = n \ge 1$ a bold face notation $\mathbf{f}(t_1, \ldots, t_n)$ means that $f$ is the root operator but does not occur elsewhere in this term.

An element of $T(\Sigma, X) \times T(\Sigma, X)$, written as $l \rightarrow r$, is called *(rewrite) rule* (over $T(\Sigma, X)$). We only consider rewrite rules where $var(r) \subseteq var(l)$ and $l \notin X$. For a rewrite rule $q = (l \rightarrow r)$, $lhs(q) = l$ is called the *left-hand side* and $rhs(q) = r$ the *right-hand side* of $q$. $q$ is called *ground* if $l$ and $r$ are ground. Two distinct rewrite rules *overlap* if their left-hand sides do, and a rule is *self-overlapping* if its left-hand side overlaps a proper subterm of itself. A rewrite rule $q$ is *left-linear* if $lhs(q)$ is linear, *right-linear* if $rhs(q)$ is linear and *linear* if both cases apply. $q$ is called *non-erasing* if $var(lhs(q)) = var(rhs(q))$.

A set $R$ of rewrite rules over some set $T(\Sigma, X)$ of terms is called a *term rewriting system* (or just rewrite system, over $\Sigma$). $R$ is called *ground, left-linear, right-linear, linear* and *non-erasing*, respectively, if all its rules have this property. $R$ is *overlapping* if it has overlapping or self-overlapping rules, otherwise *non-overlapping*. By $lhs(R)$ and $rhs(R)$ we denote the sets of left-hand sides and right-hand sides over all rules in $R$, respectively. The *(standard) rewrite relation* $\rightarrow_R$ of $R$ is defined by: $t \rightarrow_R t'$ (for terms $t$ and $t'$) iff there is a position $p$ of $t$, a rule $l \rightarrow r$ in $R$ and a substitution $\sigma$ for the variables in $l$ such that $t_{|p} = l\sigma$, and $t' = t[r\sigma]_p$. In this case $t_{|p}$ is called a *redex* for the rule. An *innermost* redex for a rule of $R$ is a redex which does not properly contain another redex. $\rightarrow_R^*$ denotes the transitive-reflexive closure of $\rightarrow_R$. With respect to $R$, a term $t$ is *irreducible* or in *normalform* if there is no term $t'$ such that $t \rightarrow_R t'$. The elements of the set $\{t' \mid t \rightarrow_R^* t' \wedge t' \text{ is irreducible}\}$ are called the normalforms of $t$. In case a term $t$ has exactly one normalform then the latter is denoted by $t \downarrow_R$. A *derivation* of $t$ is a sequence $[t, t', t'', \ldots]$ of terms from $T(\Sigma, X)$ such that $t \rightarrow_R t' \rightarrow_R t'' \rightarrow_R \ldots$. We say that $t$ can be *reduced* or *rewritten* to any element in the derivation. An *innermost derivation* is a derivation where each element (excluding the last, if any) can be rewritten to its successor using only innermost redexes. A (finite) derivation with an irreducible last term is called *normalizing derivation* and we also say that $t$ can be *normalized* to this last term.

$R$ as well as $\rightarrow_R$ is called

- *(strongly) terminating* if no term has a infinite derivation with respect to $R$

- *weakly terminating* if every term has at least one normalform with respect to $R$

- *confluent for some set* $Q \subseteq T(\Sigma, X)$ if $\forall t_0, t_1, t_2 \in Q$ :
  $(t_0 \rightarrow_R^* t_1) \wedge (t_0 \rightarrow_R^* t_2) \Rightarrow \exists t_3 \in T(\Sigma, X) : (t_1 \rightarrow_R^* t_3) \wedge (t_2 \rightarrow_R^* t_3)$,
  where we omit the qualification for $Q = T(\Sigma, X)$, and say *ground-confluent* for $Q = T(\Sigma_R)$,

- *convergent* (or *complete*) if $R$ is terminating as well as confluent,

- *ground-convergent* if $R$ is terminating as well as ground-confluent,

- *canonical* if $R$ is convergent and for all rules $l \rightarrow r$ of $R$, $r$ is irreducible with respect to $R$ and $l$ is irreducible with respect to $R \setminus \{l \rightarrow r\}$,

- *orthogonal* if $R$ is non-overlapping and left-linear .

A *constructor system (CS)* is a rewrite system $Q$ over $\Sigma_Q$ such that $\Sigma_Q = \Sigma_C \cup \Sigma_D$, $op_{\Sigma_D} \cap op_{\Sigma_C} = \emptyset$, and for every left-hand side $f(t_1, \ldots, t_n)$ of a rule in $Q$, $f \in op_{\Sigma_D}$ and $t_1, \ldots, t_n \in T(\Sigma_C, X)$. When saying that $Q$ is a CS then we refer to the *constructors* and *defined operators* for a specification of $\Sigma_C$ and $\Sigma_D$, respectively (note that an operator occuring only at right-hand sides can belong, arbitrarily, either to the constructors or to the defined operators).

We will use several results from the literature to show termination for rewrite systems and collect them here.

**Theorem P1 (Middeldorp and Toyama [MT91])**[2]. Let $R_1$ and $R_2$ be two convergent CS with the sets $C_1$ and $C_2$ of constructors and the sets $D_1$ and $D_2$ of defined symbols, respectively. Let $D_1 \cap D_2 = D_1 \cap C_2 = D_2 \cap C_1 = \emptyset$. Then $R_1 \cup R_2$ is convergent.

**Theorem P2 (Bachmair and Dershowitz [BD86])**. Let $R_1$ and $R_2$ be two rewrite systems over some set $T$ of terms. Suppose that $R_1$ is left-linear, $R_2$ is right-linear, and there is no overlap between left-hand sides of $R_1$ and right-hand sides of $R_2$. Then, the combined system $R_1 \cup R_2$ is terminating if, and only if, $R_1$ and $R_2$ both are.

**Theorem P3 (O'Donnell [O'D77])**. Let $R$ be orthogonal. Then: $R$ is weakly innermost terminating if and only if $R$ is (strongly) terminating.

Here, *weakly innermost terminating* means that every term has a normalizing innermost derivation.

**Theorem P4 (Church [Chu41], cf. [Klo92])**. Let $R$ be orthogonal and non-erasing. Then: $R$ is weakly terminating if and only if $R$ is (strongly) terminating.

For sequences (of arbitrary elements) $S = [a_i]_{i=0,1,\ldots}$ or $S = [a_i]_{i=1,2,\ldots}$ we use this notation: $S(k) = a_k$, $S[k]$ is the restriction of $S$ to the first subsequent elements up to (and including) $a_k$, $|S|$ is the length (number of elements) for finite $S$ and $a \in S$ if $a$ is an element of $S$. For a sequence $S$ of rewrite rules $lhs(S)$ and $rhs(S)$ denote the sets of all left-hand and right-hand sides of rules in $S$, respectively.

# 3 Rewrite definitions and rewrite programs

## 3.1 Rewrite definitions and their representation by rewrite programs

A particular class of rewrite systems has a very intuitive interpretation as a means to perform computations since the latter is just the normalization of arbitrary ground terms to a unique result.

---

[2]The original theorem is much stronger since both systems may share defined symbols under certain conditions.

**Definition 3.1.** A *rewrite program* is a finite, ground-confluent and terminating rewrite system[3] $P$ over a signature $\Sigma_P$. $\mathcal{RP}$ denotes the class of all rewrite programs together with their signatures.

The viewpoint from which the following considerations are taken is operational. We want to synthesize rewrite programs which represent infinite, canonical ground rewrite systems, and the first requirement to a rewrite program $P$ which represents such a rewrite system $R$ is that for any (ground) rule $(t \to t') \in R$, $t \downarrow_P$ must be $t'$. It were too restrictive to have also the requirement that any term irreducible with respect to $R$ should be irreducible with respect to $P$ as well. Even quite simple systems $R$ (also of the particular form considered in the sequel) had no representing rewrite program, as, for instance, the system

0. $f(0) \to 0$
1. $f(s(s(0))) \to s(0)$
2. $f(s(s(s(s(0))))) \to s(s(0))$

$\quad \vdots$

i. $f(s^{2i}(0)) \to s^i(0)$

$\quad \vdots$

There is no rewrite program such that the terms $f(0), f(s(s(0))), \ldots$ were reducible but the terms $f(s(0)), f(s(s(s(0)))), \ldots$ not. Therefore the (less restrictive) second requirement to $P$ is that it just provides a means to decide whether a term is reducible with respect to $R$. That means, in particular, $lhs(R)$ has to be a decidable set of terms. Then, by the supposed existence of $P$, it also follows that the rules of $R$ are a decidable set of pairs of terms. This operational view differs from a view where one is interested merely in the equational knowledge given by $R$, and it is the background to define a particular class of infinite, canonical ground rewrite systems to be identified in the limit by an inductive synthesis algorithm.

**Definition 3.2.** Let $R$ be a infinite ground rewrite system over $\Sigma_R$ such that

1. The sets $\{(l,r) \mid l,r \in T(\Sigma_R) \wedge (l \to r) \in R\}$
   and $\{l \mid l \in T(\Sigma_R) \wedge l \in lhs(R)\}$ are both decidable.

2. Every rule has the form $\mathbf{f}(t_1, \ldots, t_n) \to t_{n+1}$,
   where $n \geq 1$ and $t_i \in T(\Sigma_R \backslash f)$ for $i = 1, \ldots, n+1$.

3. The left hand sides of rules in $R$ are pairwise distinct.

---

[3]In the literature there are also more general definitions for *rewrite programs*, for instance based on the notion of ordered rewriting (cf. [DJ90, DR93]). However, in this paper we prefer the simplest concept according to our motivation and the synthesis ideas in the second part.

Then $R$ is called a *rewrite definition* (for $f$)[4]. Furthermore the class of all rewrite definitions together with their signatures is denoted by $\mathcal{RD}$.

By $T^f(\Sigma_R)$ we denote the set

$$\{t \mid t \in T(\Sigma_R) \wedge \exists t_1, ..., t_n \in T(\Sigma_R) : t = f(t_1, ..., t_n)\}$$

of all *possible left-hand sides* of $R$.

Obviously, a rewrite definition is a non-overlapping and terminating constructor system. We use rewrite programs to represent rewrite definitions as follows.

**Definition 3.3.** Let $R$ be a rewrite definition over $\Sigma_R$, $\Sigma_C = \Sigma_R \backslash f$ and $n = |f|_{\Sigma_R}$. A rewrite system $P$ over $\Sigma_P$ *represents* $R$ if and only if

1. $P \in \mathcal{RP} \wedge \Sigma_R \subseteq \Sigma_P$

2. $\forall (l \to r) \in R : l \downarrow_P = r$

3. $\forall t \in T(\Sigma_C) : t \downarrow_P = t$

4. $\forall t \in T^f(\Sigma_R) \backslash lhs(R) : t \downarrow_P \notin T(\Sigma_C)$

Furthermore we say that $P$ *minimally* represents $R$ if additionally the condition

5. $\exists u \in T(\Sigma_P) \, \forall t \in T^f(\Sigma_R) \backslash lhs(R) : t \downarrow_P = u$

holds, or that $P$ *conservatively* represents $R$ if additionally the condition

5. $\forall t, t' \in T^f(\Sigma_R) \backslash lhs(R) : t \neq t' \Rightarrow t \downarrow_P \neq t' \downarrow_P$

holds.

To formulate that all rewrite definitions have a representing rewrite program we use the following

**Definition 3.4.**

1. $\mathcal{RD}_{RP} = \{R \mid R \in \mathcal{RD} \wedge \exists P \in \mathcal{RP} : P \text{ represents } R\}$

2. $\mathcal{RD}_{OCS,m} =$
   $\{R \mid R \in \mathcal{RD} \wedge (\exists P \in \mathcal{RP} : P \text{ minimally represents } R \text{ and}$
   $P \text{ is an orthogonal constructor system})\}$

3. $\mathcal{RD}_{OCS,c} =$
   $\{R \mid R \in \mathcal{RD} \wedge (\exists P \in \mathcal{RP} : P \text{ conservatively represents } R \text{ and}$
   $P \text{ is an orthogonal constructor system})\}$

---

[4]From now on, we require that a rewrite definition has indeed this particular symbol $f$, just to avoid the notational overhead.

In fact, orthogonal rewrite programs which are (additionally) constructor systems suffice to represent rewrite definitions.

**Theorem 3.1.** $\mathcal{RD} = \mathcal{RD}_{RP} = \mathcal{RD}_{OCS,m} = \mathcal{RD}_{OCS,c}$ .

*Proof.* For an arbitrary rewrite definition $R$ we construct a rewrite program $P$ which has, among others, the new operators $0, s, \omega, \tau$ and $f'$, and "works" as follows: for any term $t = f(t_1, \ldots, t_k) \in lhs(R)$ the term $\omega(t)$ will be normalized to a term $c = s^i(0)$, then the term $f'(c)$ will be normalized to a term $c' = s^j(0)$ and finally the term $\tau(c')$ will be normalized (decoded) to a term in $T(\Sigma_R \setminus f)$. The construction is done for the single-sorted case but the extension to heterogeneous signatures by adding sorted variants for the encoding and decoding operators $\omega$ and $\tau$ is straightforward. A construction in [BT80] is the main argument of the proof.

Let $R \in \mathcal{RD}$ and $\Sigma_R$ be given. Let $op_{\Sigma_R}$ consist of constants $c_1, \ldots, c_m$ ($m \geq 1$ by assumption) and non-constant operators $g_1, \ldots, g_n$ ($n \geq 1$ since no element of $lhs(R)$ is a constant). Let $\{f', f'', 0, s, \omega, \pi, \mu_1, \mu_2, \tau, \tau', p_1, \ldots, p_l, q_1, \ldots, q_{l'}, h_1, \ldots, h_{l''}\}$ be a set of pairwise distinct operators not in $op_{\Sigma_R}$. Furthermore let $k_{c_i}$ denote terms $s^i(0)$ for $1 \leq i \leq m$, and let $k_{g_i}$ denote terms $s^{m+i}(0)$ for $1 \leq i \leq n$. These terms are used to "encode" the operators of $\Sigma_R$ ($0$ is left out). Using the additional new operators we define three rewrite systems $P_\omega$, $P_\tau$ and $P_R$, and put them together in order to construct $P$. In the sequel we omit parentheses for unary operators where this improves readability.

First an arbitrary *pairing function* (cf. [MY74] for a definition and for the example function below) $pair : \mathcal{N}^2 \to \mathcal{N}$ is choosen such that for all $x, y \in \mathcal{N}$, $(x > 0) \Rightarrow (x < pair(x, y))$ and $(y > 0) \Rightarrow (y < pair(x, y))$. An example is $pair(x, y) = 2^x(2y + 1) - 1$.

Second, let $P_\omega = \emptyset$ initially, and add

1. $\omega(c_i) \to \pi(k_{c_i}, 0)$ for $i = 1, \ldots, m$

2. for $i = 1, \ldots, n$, with $j = |g_i|$
   $\omega(g_i(x)) \to \pi(k_{g_i}, \omega x)$ if $j = 1$
   $\omega(g_i(x_1 \ldots, x_j)) \to \pi(k_{g_i}, \pi(\omega x_1, \ldots, \pi(\omega x_{j-1}, \omega x_j) \ldots))$ if $j \geq 2$

At this point $P_\omega$ is terminating since every rule removes an operator from $op_{\Sigma_R}$ from a term being reduced. Then add to $P_\omega$ an orthogonal CS $P_\pi$ with constructors $\{0, s\}$ and with defined symbols $\{\pi, p_1, \ldots, p_l\}$ such that $P_\omega$ remains terminating, and such that for all $x, y \in \mathcal{N}$, $\pi(s^x(0), s^y(0)) \downarrow_{P_\pi} = s^{pair(x,y)}(0)$.

For the example function, $pair(x,y) = 2^x(2y+1)-1$, $P_\pi$ as below has all required properties:

3. $\pi(x,y) \to p_1(s(0),y,0,x)$

4. $p_1(w,s(y),z,x) \to p_1(s(s(w)),y,z,x)$

5. $p_1(w,0,0,s(x)) \to p_1(w,0,s(x),0)$

6. $p_1(w,0,s(z),x) \to p_1(0,w,z,x)$

7. $p_1(s(w),0,0,0) \to s(p_1(w,0,0,0))$

8. $p_1(s(0),0,0,0) \to 0$

Rule 4 computes $w := 2y+1$, then $w$ will be doubled $x$ times. Rules 7 and 8 are equivalent to $p_1(s(w),0,0,0) \to w$ (the splitting simplifies termination arguments), that is they subtract 1 from $w$, which is the result.

The essential argument to show termination for this system is a lexicographic comparision of the arguments of $p_1$ in reversed order. $P_\omega$ together with these rules is terminating since both systems are terminating and the left-hand sides of $P_\omega$ and the right-hand sides of 3.–8. are linear and mutually non-overlapping, therefore Theorem P2 can be applied.

Third, let $P_\tau = \emptyset$ initially, and add

1. $\tau(x) \to \tau'(\mu_1(x), \mu_2(x))$,

2. $\tau'(k_{c_i}, 0) \to c_i$ for $i = 1, \ldots, m$

3. for $i = 1, \ldots, n$, with $j = |g_i|$,
   $\tau'(k_{g_i}, y) \to g_i(\tau y)$ if $j = 1$
   $\tau'(k_{g_i}, y) \to g_i(\tau\mu_1(y), \tau\mu_2(y))$ if $j = 2$
   $\tau'(k_{g_i}, y) \to g_i(\tau\mu_1(y), \tau\mu_1\mu_2(y), \ldots, \tau\mu_1\mu_2^{j-2}(y), \tau\mu_2^{j-1}(y))$ if $j \geq 3$

At this point $P_\tau$ is terminating (see below). Then add to $P_\tau$ an orthogonal CS with constructors $\{0, s\}$ and with defined symbols $\{\mu_1, \mu_2, q_1, \ldots, q_{l'}\}$ such that $P_\tau$ remains terminating, and such that for all $x, y \in \mathcal{N}$, $\mu_1(s^{pair(x,y)}(0))\downarrow_{P_\mu} = s^x(0)$ and $\mu_2(s^{pair(x,y)}(0))\downarrow_{P_\mu} = s^y(0)$.

In $P_\mu$ given below for the example function $pair$ the inverse operators $\mu_1$ and $\mu_2$ are defined using the same structure for the "essential" rules 4, 5 and 6:

4. $\mu_{1,2}(z) \to q_{1,2}(0,0,s(z))$

5. $q_{1,2}(x,y,s(s(z))) \to q_{1,2}(x,s(y),z)$

6. $q_{1,2}(x,s(y),0) \to q_{1,2}(s(x),0,s(y))$

7. $q_1(x,s(y),s(0)) \to q_1(x,y,s(0))$

8. $q_1(x,0,s(0)) \to x$

9. $q_2(s(x),y,s(0)) \to q_2(x,y,s(0))$

10. $q_2(0,y,s(0)) \to y$

Rule 5 computes $y := z/2$, and rule 6 counts how often this can be repeated if the result was even, and it also "restarts" rule 5. Rules 7 and 8 are equivalent to $q_1(x,y,s(0)) \to x$ (the splitting simplifies termination arguments, similiarly for rules 9 and 10).

Termination of this system can be proved using, for instance, a polynomial interpretation with $\theta(\mu_{1,2}(u)) = 4\theta(u) + 5$, $\theta(q_{1,2}(u,v,w)) = 2\theta(u) + 7\theta(v) + 4\theta(w)$, $\theta(s(u)) = \theta(u) + 1$ and $\theta(0) = 0$. Since the union $P'_\tau$ of $P_\tau$ and these rules is orthogonal and non-erasing we only need to show that $P'_\tau$ is weakly terminating, from which termination follows due to Theorem P4.

We describe a strategy to normalize an arbitrary term $t$. Let $P''_\tau$ be $P'_\tau$ without the rules from 3. $P''_\tau$ is clearly terminating, and step (a) is the normalization of $t$ to some $t'$ using $P''_\tau$. $t'$ contains, if at all, only redexes for (the rules from) 3. Step (b) is the choice of an innermost redex for 3. (at some position $p$) and its (one-step) reduction using a rule from 3. (thus, the subterm matched by $y$ is irreducible w.r.t. $P'_\tau$), followed again by a normalization w.r.t. $P''_\tau$ (all new redexes for rules of $P''_\tau$ are below $p$). This yields new redexes below $p$ for some rule of 3. only if $y$ has matched a subterm of the form $s^i(0)$, and in this case each new redex has the form $\tau'(s^{j_1}(0), s^{j_2}(0))$ and can be removed by the same steps beginning with (b) below $p$ since $j_1, j_2 < i$ due to the monotonicity of $pair$. After all the subterm at $p$ is irreducible, and another redex for 3. can be choosen and removed beginning with (b) again. That means eventually all redexes for 3. will be removed and an irreducible term is obtained.

---

The signatures of both systems are constructed as extensions of $\Sigma_R$ in the obvious way for the new operators. Both systems are terminating and consist of non-overlapping, left-linear rules only, hence they are convergent and orthogonal. $P_\omega$ is a CS with constructors $\{0, s, c_1, \ldots, c_m, g_1, \ldots, g_n\}$ and defined symbols $\{\omega, \pi, p_1, \ldots, p_l\}$, and $P_\tau$ is a CS with the same constructors and defined symbols $\{\tau, \tau', \mu_1, \mu_2, q_1, \ldots, q_{l'}\}$. Their union $P_0$ is therefore a convergent CS due to Theorem P1, and it is also orthogonal. According to the construction, we have that

1. $\forall t \in T(\Sigma_R)\, \exists i \in \mathcal{N} : \omega(t)\!\downarrow_{P_0} = s^i(0) \wedge i \neq pair(0,0)$

2. $\forall t, t' \in T(\Sigma_R) : \omega(t)\!\downarrow_{P_0} = \omega(t')\!\downarrow_{P_0} \Leftrightarrow t = t'$

3. $\forall t \in T(\Sigma_R) : \tau(\omega(t))\!\downarrow_{P_0} = t$

4. $\tau(s^{pair(0,0)}(0))\!\downarrow_{P_0} \notin T(\Sigma_R)$

(which can easily be shown based on inspection of the systems, simple inductive arguments and properties of pairing functions; we omit the details).

Finally we construct the rewrite system $P_R$. Because of 1. and 3. above the set

$$R' = \bigcup_{l \to r \in R} (\omega(l)\!\downarrow_{P_0}, \omega(r)\!\downarrow_{P_0})$$

consists of pairs of terms t build solely from $s$ and 0 such that $\tau(t)\!\downarrow_{P_0} \in T(\Sigma_R)$, and the function $\mathcal{F}_{R'} : \mathcal{N} \to \mathcal{N}$ with

$$\mathcal{F}_{R'}(x) = \begin{cases} pair(0,0) & : \quad if \\ & \quad \forall z \in \mathcal{N} : (s^x(0), s^z(0)) \notin R' \\ min\{y \mid (s^x(0), s^y(0)) \in R'\} & : \quad otherwise \end{cases}$$

is total recursive since both $lhs(R)$ and $R$ are recursive sets. A procedure for $\mathcal{F}_{R'}$ can compute, for every $x \in \mathcal{N}$, $\tau(s^x(0))\!\downarrow_{P_0}$, check whether this is a term $t = \mathbf{f}(t_1, \ldots, t_n) \in T(\Sigma_R)$ and, in case it is, apply a decision procedure for $t \in lhs(R)$. If $t \in lhs(R)$ then, with a generator for the rules of $R$, it finds a rule $t \to r \in R$ and computes $\omega(r)\!\downarrow_{P_0} = s^y(0)$. If $t \notin lhs(R)$ then $y = pair(0,0)$. Now we build $P_R$ such that

1. $\{f', 0, s, h_1, \ldots, h_{l''}\}$ are the only operators occuring in $P_R$.

2. $P_R$ is a convergent, orthogonal CS with constructors $\{0, s\}$.

3. $\forall x \in \mathcal{N} : f'(s^x(0)) \downarrow_{P_R} = s^{\mathcal{F}_{R'}(x)}(0)$.

A particular construction scheme how to do this, for an arbitrary total recursive function over the natural numbers (which $\mathcal{F}_{R'}$ is), can be found in [BT80], where the main theorem is essentially based on this method. Therefore we omit the details and consider $P_R$ to be given.

Since $P_0$ and $P_R$ do not have common operators except $0$ and $s$, which belong to their constructor sets, $P' = P_0 \cup P_R$ is a convergent CS due to Theorem P1, and since constructor symbols are not the root symbol of a left-hand side in a CS-rule, the union of the orthogonal systems $P_0$ and $P_R$ is again a non-overlapping system, hence orthogonal.

We analyze the normalforms of terms $\tau f'(\omega f(t))$, for $t \in T(\Sigma_R)$, under $P'$. $P'$ is confluent, thus an arbitrary order of reduction of subterms can be choosen. Since $f(t) \in T(\Sigma_R)$, $\omega f(t) \downarrow_{P'}$ is some term $s^k(0)$, and $f'(s^k(0)) \downarrow_{P'}$ will be $\omega(r) \downarrow_{P'}$ if there is some rule $f(t) \to r \in R$. Thus the whole term has the normalform $r$ if there is a rule $f(t) \to r \in R$. On the other hand, if there is no such $r$, then $f'(s^k(0)) \downarrow_{P'}$ is $s^{pair(0,0)}(0)$, and $\tau(s^{pair(0,0)}(0)) \downarrow_{P'} \notin T(\Sigma_R)$.

Therefore, it remains to force the introduction of this term in order to have a representing rewrite program for $R$, and this can be done by replacing all occurences of $f$ in $P'$ by the new operator $f''$ and the construction

$$P = P' \cup \{ f(x_1, \ldots, x_a) \to \tau f'(\omega f''(x_1, \ldots, x_a)) \}$$

where $a = |f|_{\Sigma_R}$. $P$ is again an orthogonal CS, and it is also terminating (in an innermost derivation of any term no rule of $P'$ can produce new occurences of $f$, and the new rule deletes one; termination follows due to Theorem P3), hence $P$ is convergent. Furthermore $P$ cannot reduce terms from $T(\Sigma_R \setminus f)$ since there is no rule with an appropriate operator at the root of the left-hand side. Therefore $P$ is a rewrite program which minimally represents $R$ with $u = \tau(s^{pair(0,0)}(0))$ according to Definition 3.3, and this proves $\mathcal{RD} = \mathcal{RD}_{RP} = \mathcal{RD}_{OCS,m}$. From the definition of $R'$ follows $i \neq j$ for all $(s^i(0), s^j(0)) \in R'$. By replacing the result $pair(0,0)$ in the definition of $\mathcal{F}_{R'}$ by $x$ and the same line of construction as above $P$ becomes therefore a rewrite program which conservatively represents $R$ (for $f(t) \in T(\Sigma_R)$ and $f(t) \notin lhs(R)$, $\tau f'(\omega f(t)) \downarrow_{P'}$ is then $f(t)$), hence also $\mathcal{RD} = \mathcal{RD}_{OCS,c}$. $\square$

## 3.2 The synthesis of rewrite programs for rewrite definitions from positive descriptions

The problem investigated in the sequel is the synthesis (in the limit) of a rewrite program $P$ for an arbitrary rewrite definition $R$ from some class $\mathcal{U} \subseteq \mathcal{RD}$, given $\Sigma_R$ and (stepwise) more and more elements of $R$. Since $\Sigma_P$ must contain $\Sigma_R$ we can restrict the problem to classes $\mathcal{U} \subset \mathcal{RD}$ with a common signature for all rewrite definitions. Therefore we assume from now on, simplifying the notation, that all rewrite definitions of $\mathcal{RD}$ have some common signature which is also contained in the signatures of all programs in $\mathcal{RP}$. Two programs in $\mathcal{RD}$ are considered the same modulo renaming of sorts, operators or variables. First some further notions will be defined to describe the problem more precisely. We consider a particular notion of learnability of rewrite definitions adopting an inductive inference approach [Gol67, AS83].

**Definition 3.5.** Let $R \in \mathcal{RD}$. A sequence $S = [S(0), S(1), \ldots]$ of rewrite rules is called

1. *positive description* of $R$ if $S(0) \cup S(1) \cup \ldots = R$, and

2. *full description* of $R$ if $S(0) \cup S(1) \cup \ldots = R \cup R^{\not\rightarrow}$, where $R^{\not\rightarrow} = (T^t(\Sigma_R) \setminus lhs(R)) \times T(\Sigma_R \setminus f)$ and every rule in $S$ is marked as *positive rule* or *negative rule* according to whether it belongs to $R$ or not (to indicate this we use "$\not\rightarrow$" instead of "$\rightarrow$" for negative rules).

The class of all positive descriptions of $R$ is denoted by $\mathcal{S}_R^+$, and the class of all full descriptions of $R$ by $\mathcal{S}_R$.

**Definition 3.6.** Let $U \subseteq \mathcal{RD}$, and let $M$ be some effective procedure, called *inductive inference machine (IIM)*. Then $U$ is said to be *RP-learnable by $M$ in the limit from positive descriptions* [5] if and only if the following holds:

$\forall R \in U, \forall S \in \mathcal{S}_R^+,$

1. $\forall n \in \mathcal{N} : M(S[n])$ *is defined* $\wedge M(S[n]) \in \mathcal{RP}$
2. $\exists m \in \mathcal{N}, \forall n \in \mathcal{N} :$
   $(n \geq m) \Rightarrow M(S[n]) = M(S[m]) \wedge M(S[m])$ *represents* $R$

Furthermore, U is called RP-learnable from positive descriptions if and only if such a $M$ exists.

In the sequel we are also dealt with variants of this definition obtained by replacing $\mathcal{S}_R^+$ by some other set $I$ and refer to this variants by saying that $U$ is RP-learnable (by $M$) *from I*.

Based on these notions we restate the synthesis problem as an RP-learnability problem. However, some well-known facts from the theory of inductive inference imply that this synthesis problem must be restricted in order to solve it successfully.

**Proposition 3.1.** $\mathcal{RD}$ is neither RP-learnable from positive nor from full descriptions.

*Proof sketch.* Let $R \in \mathcal{RD}$ and $n = |f|_{\Sigma_R}$. $R$ defines the recursive language $L = \{t_1, \ldots, t_n \mid f(t_1, \ldots, t_n) \in lhs(R)\} \subseteq T(\Sigma_R \setminus f)^n$. A rewrite program representing $R$ can be used to compute the characteristic function for $L$. Thus, the synthesis

---

[5] Some of the qualifications will be omitted if clear from the context.

problem for full descriptions is equivalent, in the terminology of inductive inference of formal languages, to learning a characteristic function of an arbitrary recursive language from an (arbitrary) informant (the left-hand sides of a full description), which is not possible [Gol67]. For positive descriptions the same holds since they are contained in full descriptions (cf. also the construction of $\mathcal{P}_0$ below). □

A synthesis algorithm which learns a class of rewrite definitions according to our definition must output rewrite programs. Therefore it is natural to make the assumption that the algorithm can check a finite rewrite system in this regard by some recursive procedure and to restrict the problem class such that every rewrite definition has a rewrite program correctly recognized as such by this procedure. This is considered next.

**Definition 3.7.** A *ground-convergence prover* CP is an effective procedure with the following properties:

1. Given a (finite) rewrite system and its signature as input, CP always halts with output 0 or 1.

2. If the input is a (finite) rewrite system and its signature, then CP outputs 0 if the system is not terminating or not ground-confluent.

For any ground-convergence prover CP we denote by $\mathcal{RP}_{CP}$ the class $\{R \mid R \in \mathcal{RP} \wedge CP(R, \Sigma_R) = 1\}$ of all rewrite programs correctly recognized by $CP$, and by $\mathcal{RD}_{CP}$ the class of all rewrite definitions with a representing rewrite program in $\mathcal{RP}_{CP}$.

*Remark.* According to Theorem 3.1, there are also confluent (and even orthogonal) rewrite programs for all elements of $\mathcal{RD}$. Therefore it is also reasonable to consider ground-convergence provers which just test termination based on known methods [Der87] and merely test confluence for terminating candidates (based on local confluence). If only orthogonal rewrite programs are considered then termination is the only problem to be solved by the ground-convergence prover[6]. Therefore we could equally well consider just termination provers instead of ground-convergence provers.

Even under the restriction of $\mathcal{RD}$ by some ground-convergence prover many simple classes remain to be not RP-learnable from positive descriptions. For instance, let $CP$ be some ground-convergence prover and let $\mathcal{P}_0 \subseteq \mathcal{RP}_{CP}$ be defined as follows, according to a theorem in [Gol67]:

$$\mathcal{P}_0 = \{f(x) \to x\} \cup P_0 \cup P_1 \cup \ldots \cup P_i \cup \ldots, \text{ where } P_i =$$

$$\{ \ f(x) \to h(x, x = s^i(0))$$
$$h(x, false) \to x$$
$$s(x) = s(y) \to x = y$$
$$0 = s(y) \to false$$
$$s(x) = 0 \to false \ \}$$

---

[6]Hence from Theorem 3.1 and Propositions 3.1 and 3.3 (below) follows the undecidability of termination for orthogonal constructor systems (which is known even for orthogonal one-rule systems [Dau89])

If $\mathcal{RD}_{CP}$ contains all rewrite definitions (with operators $0, s, f$ only) representable by programs from $\mathcal{P}_0$ then the class can not be learned: assume an IIM $M$ can learn the class, then a positive description $S$ for $\{f(x) \to x\}$ can be constructed (using $M$) such that $M$ changes its output infinitely many often on $S[1], S[2], \dots$. This is possible by first leaving out some single rule $f(s^k(0)) \to s^k(0)$ until $M$'s output would stabilize on $P_k$ (or some equivalent, representing program), then include the rule and leave out some other instead, and so on. Thus we have

**Proposition 3.2.** There exists a ground-convergence prover $CP$ such that $\mathcal{RD}_{CP}$ is not RP-learnable from positive descriptions.

*Proof sketch.* cf. GOLD [Gol67]. □

However, full descriptions suffice to learn rewrite programs recognizable by a ground-convergence prover.

**Proposition 3.3.** For every ground-convergence prover $CP$, $\mathcal{RD}_{CP}$ is RP-learnable from full descriptions.

*Proof sketch.* This is an application of the *identification by enumeration* idea [Gol67]. Since $\mathcal{RP}_{CP}$ is recursively enumerable[7], an IIM $M$ , applied to the input $S[n]$ for some $S \in \mathcal{S}_R$ and $n \geq 0$, can output the first rewrite program $P$ in its enumeration $E(n)$ of $\mathcal{RP}_{CP}$ which is a consistent hypothesis, in the sense that $l \downarrow_{M(S[n])} = r$ for every positive rule $l \to r \in S[n]$ and $l \downarrow_{M(S[n])} \neq r$ for every negative rule $l \not\to r \in S[n]$. Since no full description of a rewrite definition is contained in a full description of another rewrite definition proper stabilization of this output is ensured. □

Depending on the class to be learned, and in particular if we consider rewrite definitions embedded in the output of some diverging KNUTH-BENDIX-completion procedure, it might be possible to construct full descriptions from positive descriptions using additional information or properties of the rewrite system being completed, or it might be the case that no rewrite definition of the class to be learned is properly contained in another of that class. Instead of more general characterizations we give some specific examples for such cases. Particular scenarios of this kind can be found in Subsection 3.3.

**Proposition 3.4.** Let $CP$ be a ground-convergence prover and $U \subseteq \mathcal{RD}_{CP}$. Suppose that for all $R \in U$ one of the following conditions holds:

1. $lhs(R) = T^t(\Sigma_R)$ , or

2. All rules in $R$ have pairwise distinct right-hand sides and $rhs(R)$ contains all terms of $f$'s target sort.

---

[7]Starting from $\Sigma_R$, all candidates from $\mathcal{RP}_{CP}$ can be generated by constructing, for $n = 1, 2, \dots$ all signatures resp. rewrite systems with at most $n$ additional (new) sorts and operators (with at most $n$ arguments), terms of maximal depth $n$ and at most $n$ rules, modulo renaming of new symbols. Using $CP$ the rewrite systems being not ground-convergent can be ruled out.

Then $U$ is RP-learnable from positive descriptions.

*Proof sketch.* If 1 applies to some $R$ then $R$ is not properly contained in any other rewrite definition from $U$. If 2 applies and $R$ is a proper subset of some $R' \in U$ then $R'$ does not meet 2 (some right- hand side must be repeated) but meets 1. Using $CP$ an IIM $M$ can generate the class $E$ of rewrite programs consistent with the input rules $S[n]$ (cf. proof sketch of Proposition 3.3). Along with $E(n)$, $M$ can also generate the terms $t \in T^f(\Sigma_R)$. To avoid the stabilization on a hypotheses representing a too general rewrite definition it is then sufficient to output, as long as the right-hand sides of $M$'s input rules are pairwise distinct, only such programs $P$ from $E(n)$ that the normalforms of the $n$ generated terms $t$ with respect to $P$, restricted to those in $T(\Sigma_R \backslash f)$, are pairwise distinct. $\square$

Another learnability criterion is related to simple properties of positive descriptions.

**Proposition 3.5.** For every ground-convergence prover $CP$, (any subclass of) $\mathcal{RD}_{CP}$ is RP-learnable from positive descriptions $S$ which have one of the following properties, for all rules $S(i) = l_i \to r_i$ $(i \in \mathbb{N})$ in $S$:

1. $depth(l_i) \leq depth(l_{i+1})$

2. $depth(r_i) < depth(r_{i+1})$

3. $max(depth(l_i), depth(r_i)) \leq max(depth(l_{i+1}), depth(r_{i+1}))$

4. $min(depth(l_i), depth(r_i)) < min(depth(l_{i+1}), depth(r_{i+1}))$

where $depth(t)$ denotes the depth of a term $t$.

*Proof sketch.* In all four cases an IIM $M$ with input $S[n]$ can determine whether the conditions 1–4 hold for $S[n]$ or not, and it can generate, depending on this test and on $S[n]$, the set $R^- = (T^f(\Sigma_R) \times T(\Sigma_R \backslash f)) \backslash R$, (as set of negative rules). $R^-$ consists of the set of all negative rules of a full description for $R$ and the set $(lhs(R) \times T(\Sigma_R \backslash f)) \backslash R$. The rest follows as for Proposition 3.3 since the negative rules from the latter set can be used in the same way as those in the former for the computation of consistent hypotheses. $\square$

*Remark.* If it is required to learn minimally or conservatively representing rewrite programs for rewrite definitions then the previous propositions still hold accordingly (with Definition 3.7 changed). Any non-learnability result clearly also holds. Any learnability result also holds because an IIM can generate, along with the number $n$ of input rules, all possible left-hand sides of a rewrite definition and check its hypotheses $P$ additionally with respect to the condition that the normalforms of the generated terms with respect to $P$, restricted to those not in $T(\Sigma_R \backslash f)$, are either all the same or pairwise distinct, respectively.

Finally we discuss a more strategic application of the Propositions 3.4 and 3.5. For any $U \subseteq \mathcal{RD}$ two new classes $U_1, U_2 \subset \mathcal{RD}$ can be constructed by splitting any $R \in U$

according to the scheme

| $R =$ | $R_1 =$ | $R_2 =$ |
|---|---|---|
| 1. $l_1 \to r_1$ | 1. $l_1 \to o$ | 1. $f(o) \to r_1$ |
| 2. $l_2 \to r_2$ $\longrightarrow$ | 2. $l_2 \to c(o)$ and | 2. $f(c(o)) \to r_2$ |
| 3. $l_3 \to r_3$ | 3. $l_3 \to c(c(o))$ | 3. $f(c(c(o))) \to r_3$ |
| $\vdots$ | $\vdots$ | $\vdots$ |

(where $o$ is a constant of a new sort *counter* and $c$ is a new operator with arity (*counter* $\to$ *counter*)) and collecting rewrite definitions $R_1$ and $R_2$ according to the scheme into $U_1$ and $U_2$, respectively. Both classes can be learned from positive descriptions if appropriate ground-convergence provers can be found, as shown, and a program for $R$ can be constructed by combining programs for $R_1$ and $R_2$ in the obvious way (for an example see the synthesis algorithm in Section 3). If the problem with $U$ is "essentially" the relations between left- and right-hand sides of its rewrite definitions then this might be helpful in order to learn this "essential" part (for instance, the example class constructed via $\mathcal{P}_0$ has a trivial relationship between left- and right-hand sides and would be inessential from this point of view). The other way around we take this as an argument to concentrate on finding synthesis algorithms for classes as $U_1$ and $U_2$. The algorithm presented in Section 3 is based on these considerations.

## 3.3 Generating rewrite definitions from finite rewrite systems

Rewrite definitions can be embedded in the output of a diverging KNUTH-BENDIX-completion procedure. They can also be generated by systematic instantiation and simplification (by a given rewrite system) of particular rewrite rules. We give an example for both cases.

Given a groundconfluent, terminating rewrite system $B$ (without operator $f$) and a rewrite rule $f(t_1, \ldots, t_n) \to t_{n+1}$, a rewrite definition can be obtained by rewriting, for all systematically generated ground instances of the rule, both of its sides to their normalform. For instance, let $B$ consist of the rules

1. $x + 0 \to x$

2. $x + s(y) \to s(x + y)$.

Then the rules

$$( f(x, x + y) \to true ) [x \leftarrow s^i(0), y \leftarrow s^j(0)] \downarrow_B \quad (i, j \in \mathbb{N})$$

form a rewrite definition specifying (in the obvious way) a predicate for the relation $\leq$ over $\mathcal{N}$. The instantiation may also be done via a completion procedure. For instance, the ground rules (in normalform) generated by a KNUTH-BENDIX-completion procedure applied to $B \cup \{f(x + x) \to x\}$ are the rewrite definition

1. $f(s^{2i}(0)) \to s^i(0) \ (i \in \mathcal{N})$

specifying a function to compute the half of even natural numbers. Based on these examples and Propositions 3.4 and 3.5 it is easy to see how quite interesting classes of rewrite definitions can be defined which are RP-learnable from the generated rules.

An interesting example related to condition 1 of Proposition 3.4 is a rewrite definition for Ackermann's function $A$, consisting of the rules

1. $f(s^i(0), s^j(0)) \to s^{A(i,j)}(0) \ (i, j \in \mathcal{N})$

(henceforth called *graph* of the function). This system consists just of the ground rules (in normalform) generated by a KNUTH-BENDIX-completion procedure[8] applied to the system

1. $g(0) \to 0$

2. $g(s(x)) \to s(g(x))$

3. $f(g(x), g(y)) \to A(x, y)$

4. $A(0, w) \to s(w)$

5. $A(s(v), 0) \to A(v, s(0))$

6. $A(s(v), s(w)) \to A(v, A(s(v), w))$,

where only the last 3 rules define $A$. In fact, the completion procedure can generate the graph of an arbitrary total recursive function $\mathcal{F} : \mathcal{N} \to \mathcal{N}$ since it is possible (cf. the proof of the main theorem in [BT80]) to define a convergent system $B'$ such that $F(s^x(0)) \downarrow_{B'} = s^y(0) \Leftrightarrow \mathcal{F}(x) = y$. All to do in order to obtain the graph for $\mathcal{F}$ via some completion procedure is to replace the definition of Ackermann's function above by (a properly renamed version of) $B'$ (and rule 3 by $f(g(x)) \to F(x)$ ).

# 4 An experimental inductive synthesis algorithm for rewrite programs

## 4.1 The synthesis approach

One major motivation for the development of our algorithm, which learns rewrite programs from positive descriptions of rewrite definitions according to the presentation in Section 3, was to provide a framework for experiments, in order to discover inspirating phenomena. The algorithm has two distinguished components: a set of program schemes and a simple strategy to combine them. The main reason for this is our intuition that the rewrite rules generated by a diverging KNUTH-BENDIX-completion procedure have in many "practically" interesting cases a somehow regular structure which can be easily described in terms of some basic concepts for the growth of terms. Thus it seems reasonable to have a representation of such concepts as building blocks

---

[8]All generated "critical pairs" can be oriented in a way such that the graph is obtained.

for rewrite programs. The synthesis algorithm is *experimental* from at least two points of view. First we did some work to implement it's basic mechanisms as a computer program, using TLPS ([Gri93]). Second since we are going to undertake practical experiments with new program schemes and their combinations, taking advantage of the simple modularity of the algorithm.

For simplicity it is assumed here that there is only one sort in the signatures of the rewrite definitions to be learned. In a sense, this is *not* a simplification since one might use the encoding and decoding techniques from the proof of Theorem 3.1 to achieve this situation (and, moreover, to have only three operators) and then construct an appropriate final rewrite program with decoding rules. Clearly, structural information about the terms in the example rules would be lost and the synthesis would become more complicated in many cases. On the other hand, such an encoding could equally well *induce* certain structural information and in fact this seems to be related to the well-known problem to choose a "good translation" to solve a problem. This is, in a sense, also the basic technique applied in the synthesis algorithm described here, according to the ideas in [TJ89] and [Lan89], as already mentioned.

The synthesis is based on the splitting scheme discussed in the previous section. That means two rewrite programs are synthesized independently, one for the left-hand sides and one for the right-hand sides of the input rules, and then put together. First we define some program schemes, called *encoding* and *decoding* systems. These schemes are not maximal in the sense that we strongly restrict their structure based on implementational considerations (not discussed here). However, we describe them based on some unifying concepts and arguments.

Throughout this section we adopt special conventions for some operators and sorts. Special *counter-sorts*, denoted by $counter_i$ $(i = 1, \ldots)$, are used to contruct certain signatures and rewrite systems. Every sort $counter_i$ has the *counter-operators* $(o_i : \to counter_i)$ and $(c_i : counter_i \to counter_i)$, and if these operators are contained in a rewrite system then the terms $c^j(o)$ $(j \in \mathbb{N})$ are all irreducible and every term of sort $counter_i$ has a normalform $c^j(o)$ for some $j \in \mathbb{N}$ with respect to this system. Also dashed and non-indexed variants of the counter-sorts and -operators are used. If (sub)terms with a counter-operator at root are displayed then they are of the corresponding counter-sort, which in this case is (implicitly) assumed to be a sort of the signature under consideration. For any sort also a set of variables should be provided, however this is not done explicitly as long as no confusion about sorts of variables can arise. Moreover, details about sorts involved are mostly suppressed if clear from the context.

## 4.2 Encoding and decoding systems

Encoding and decoding systems are itself rewrite programs establishing a *one-to-one* and *onto* correspondence between certain infinite sequences of ground terms and all ground instances of a particular, single term. For their presentation variables are denoted by $u, v, w, x, y, z$, (arbitrary) terms by $b, p, q, r$ and $t$, and natural numbers by $i, j, k, l, m$ and $n$ (all possibly with indexes and dashes).

**Definition 4.1.** An *encoding system* $E$ is a finite, ground-convergent rewrite system with a designated *encoding operator* $H$ such that $|H| \geq 2$ and $\alpha(H)_{|1}$ is a counter sort. $E$ *encodes* a single ground term $t$ if $t$ does not contain $H$ and there is a *basis* of ground terms $b_1, \ldots, b_n$ and an *index* $j \in \mathbb{N}$ such that

$$t \downarrow_E = \mathbf{H}(c^j(o), b_1, \ldots, b_n)$$

$E$ does not encode two distinct ground terms to the same normalform. $E$ *encodes* a sequence $[t_0, \ldots, t_i, \ldots, t_k]$ of ground terms if it encodes all its terms such that every $t_i$ has the index $i$. $E$ is called an encoding system *for* a ground term and sequences thereof if the conditions above hold, respectively.

**Definition 4.2.** An encoding system of *type 1* is a <u>non-overlapping</u>, <u>non-erasing</u> and <u>right-linear</u> rewrite system $E_1$ of the following form:

1. $q_0 \rightarrow H(c^m(o), x_1, \ldots, x_n)$

2. if $m > 0$ :

$q_1 \rightarrow \mathbf{H}(o, p_{11}, \ldots, p_{1n})$

$\vdots$

$q_m \rightarrow \mathbf{H}(c^{m-1}(o), p_{m1}, \ldots, p_{mn})$

3. $\mathbf{H}(c^m(w), r_1, \ldots, r_n) \rightarrow H(c^{m+1}(w), y_1, \ldots, y_n)$

where $1 \leq n$ and $0 \leq m$, $H$ is the encoding operator, for $1 \leq i \leq n$ and $1 \leq j \leq m$ at least one $r_i$ is not a variable, $p_{ji}$ is a proper subterm of $q_j$, and neither $r_i$ nor $q_j$ nor $q_0$ contain an operator given in the scheme.

We refer to the rules of 1 and 2 as *introduction rules* of the system.

**Proposition 4.1.** $E_1$ is convergent and does not encode two distinct ground terms to the same normalform. Furthermore, there is an effective procedure which for any given sequence $S$ of at least two ground terms outputs all encoding systems of type 1 with at most $|S|$ rules for that sequence and stops then.

*Proof sketch.* $E_1$ is obviously terminating, and non-overlapping by definition, hence convergent. The inverse system of $E_1$ (i.e. all rules reversed, note: $E$ is non-erasing) is a non-overlapping, terminating rewrite system, and can be used to "unencode" any encoded ground term uniquely since the term does not contain $H$ and its normalform has $H$ as root operator but nowhere else (by Definition 3.1). Therefore two distinct ground terms cannot be encoded to the same normalform. Second, in a system which encodes a given sequence $S$ of at least two ground terms, $r_1, \ldots, r_n$ and $q_0, \ldots, q_m$ must not contain an operator not contained in any ground term of $S$, and their depth is limited by the maximal depth of the terms of $S$, as well as $n$, and $m \leq |S|$. Therefore only finitely many, convergent systems remain as candidates, which can all be checked  by normalizing the terms of the sequence. $\square$

Systems of this type can be used to capture recurrence relations characterized by fixed substitutions, contexts and permutations. For instance, the sequence

$$[ f(0,0) , f(s(0),0) , f(s(0),s(0)) , f(s^2(0),s(0)) , f(s^2(0),s^2(0)) ]$$

is encoded by the system

1. $f(x,y) \rightarrow H(o,x,y)$
2. $H(w,s(x),y) \rightarrow H(c(w),y,x)$

with one and the same basis for all terms, and the sequence

$$[ f(g(s(0))), f(g(g(s(s(0))))), f(g(g(g(s(s(s(0))))))) ]$$

is encoded by the system

1. $f(g(x)) \rightarrow H(o,x)$
2. $H(w,g(x)) \rightarrow H(c(w),x)$

with the bases $s(0), s(s(0))$ and $s(s(s(0)))$.

**Definition 4.3.** A *decoding system* $D$ is a finite, ground-convergent rewrite system with a designated *decoding operator* $G$ such that $|G| \geq 2$ and $\alpha(G)_{|1}$ is a counter sort. $D$ *decodes* a single ground term $t$ if $t$ does not contain $G$ and there is a *basis* $b_1, \ldots, b_n$ of ground terms and an *index* $j \in \mathbb{N}$ (of $t$) such that

$$t = G(c^j(o), b_1, \ldots, b_n) \downarrow_D$$

$D$ *decodes* a sequence $[t_0, \ldots, t_i, \ldots, t_k]$ of ground terms if every $t_i$ can be decoded with index $i$. $D$ is called an decoding system *for* a ground term and sequences thereof if the conditions above hold, respectively.

The following is a (somewhat simplified) dual version of Definition 3.2.

**Definition 4.4.** A decoding system of *type 1* is a non-erasing, left-linear rewrite system $D_1$ of the following form:

1. $G(c(w), y_1, \ldots, y_n) \rightarrow G(w, r_1, \ldots, r_n)$
2. $G(o, x_1, \ldots, x_n) \rightarrow q$

where $1 \leq n$, $G$ is the decoding operator, for $1 \leq i \leq n$ at least one $r_i$ is not a variable and neither $q$ nor $r_i$ contain an operator given in the scheme.

**Proposition 4.2.** $D_1$ is convergent. Furthermore, there is an effective procedure which for any given sequence of at least two ground terms outputs all decoding systems of type 1, each together with all bases for every term of the sequence, and stops then.

*Proof sketch.* $D_1$ is obviously terminating and also non-overlapping, hence convergent. Furthermore, if $D_1$ decodes a sequence $S = [t_0, ..., t_i, ..., t_k]$ of at least two ground terms, then $q$ and $r_1, \ldots, r_n$ must not contain an operator not contained in any term of $S$, and their depth (as well as $n$) is limited by the maximal depth of the terms of $S$. Therefore only finitely many, convergent systems remain as candidates, and for each it can be checked whether it decodes $S$ for the following reasons. None of the $t_i$ must contain $G$ (by Definition 3.3) and every $t_i$ must therefore be an instance of $q$. The choice of rules to normalize $\mathbf{G}(c^i(o), b_1, \ldots, b_n)$, for some basis $b_1, \ldots, b_n$, to $t_i$ is uniquely determined and depends only on $i$. Since $D_1$ is non-erasing (the only basis) $b_1, \ldots, b_n$ can be found, given $t_i$ and $i$, by reducing $t_i$, with that choice in reversed order and with the direction of the rules reversed (where $q$ is instantiated to $t_i$) $i + 1$ times. If this is possible for all $t_i$ then a candidate decodes the sequence, otherwise not, and also all bases for the terms have been constructed. $\square$

For instance, the sequence

$$[\, f(0,0),\ f(s(0), s(0)),\ f(s(s(0)), s(s(0)))\,]$$

is decoded by the system

1. $G(c(w), x) \to G(w, s(x))$

2. $G(o, x) \to f(x, x)$

with the same basis 0 for all terms.

**Definition 4.5.** An encoding system of *type 2* is a <u>non-overlapping</u>, <u>non-erasing</u> rewrite system $E_2$ which contains a decoding system $D_1$ of type 1. $E_2 \setminus D_1$ is <u>right-linear</u> and has the form

1. $q \to H(o, o', x_1, \ldots, x_n)$

2. $\mathbf{H}(w, c'(v), r_1, \ldots, r_n) \to H(w, v, y_1, \ldots, y_n)$

3. $\mathbf{H}(w, o', r_1, \ldots, r_n) \to H(c(w), G(w, c'^m(o')), y_1, \ldots, y_n)$

where $1 \le n$ and $m \in \mathbb{N}$, $H$ is the encoding operator, for all $(1 \le i \le n)$ at least one $r_i$ is not a variable, neither $q$ nor $r_i$ contain an operator given in the scheme, and $G$ is the decoding operator of $D_1$.

We refer to $D_1$ as the *associated* decoding system of $E_2$ and to rule 1 as the *introduction rule* of the system.

**Proposition 4.3.** $E_2$ is convergent and does not encode two distinct ground terms to the same normalform. Furthermore, there is an effective procedure which for any given sequence of at least three ground terms outputs all encoding systems of type 2 for that sequence and stops then.

*Proof sketch.* $E_2$ is non-overlapping and obviously terminating (note that any ground instance of $G(w, c'^m(o'))$ is reducible only by rules of $D_1$ and has a normalform not containing $G$ since $\alpha(H)_{|2}$ is a counter sort), hence convergent. The (uniquely determined) choice of rules to normalize a ground term $t$ encoded by $E_2$ with a given index $j$ and basis $b_1, \ldots, b_n$ can be traced back using $D_1$ from $j$ and $b_1$ alone (note that $E_2$

is non-erasing), and this allows to "unencode" $t$ from $t \downarrow_{E_2}$. Therefore no two distinct encoded ground terms can have the same normalform under $E_2$. Second, if $E_2$ encodes a sequence $S$ of at least three ground terms, then $q$ and $r_1, \ldots, r_n$ must not contain an operator not contained in the terms of $S$, and their depth (as well as $n$) is limited by the maximal depth of the terms in $S$. The terms decoded by $D_1$ directly control (via the occurences of $c'$) the number of possible applications of rule 2. Therefore their depth is also limited as soon as all others are fixed, and only finitely many suitable sequences of $|S| - 1$ terms decoded by $D_1$ remain to be considered. Proposition 3.2 says that for all (with at least two elements) some decoding system can be found, if it exists. Therefore only finitely many, convergent systems remain as candidates and can all be checked by normalizing the terms of the sequence. $\square$

**Definition 4.6.** A *decoding system of type 2* is a non-erasing, left-linear rewrite system $D_2$ which contains a decoding system $D_1$ of type 1. $D_2 \setminus D_1$ has the form

1. $G(c(w), o', y_1, \ldots, y_n) \rightarrow \mathbf{G}(w, G'(w, c'^m(o')), r_1, \ldots, r_n)$

2. $G(w, c'(v), y_1, \ldots, y_n) \rightarrow \mathbf{G}(w, v, r_1, \ldots, r_n)$

3. $G(o, o', x_1, \ldots, x_n) \rightarrow q$

where $1 \leq n$ and $m \in \mathbb{N}$, $G$ is the decoding operator, for $1 \leq i \leq n$ at least one $r_i$ is not a variable, neither $q$ nor $r_i$ contain an operator given in the scheme, and $G'$ is the decoding operator of $D_1$.

We refer to $D_1$ as the *associated* decoding system of $D_2$.

**Proposition 4.4.** $D_2$ is convergent. Furthermore, there is an effective procedure which for any given sequence of at least three ground terms outputs all decoding systems of type 2, each together with all bases for every term of the sequence, and stops then.

*Proof sketch.* $D_2$ is non-overlapping and terminating (cf. termination remark for Proposition 3.3), hence convergent. Second, if $D_2$ decodes a sequence $S = [t_0, \ldots, t_i, \ldots, t_k]$ ($k \geq 2$) of ground terms, then $q$ and $r_1, \ldots, r_n$ must not contain an operator not contained in any term of $S$, and their depth (as well as $n$) is limited by the maximal depth of the terms in $S$. The same holds, as with encoding systems of type 2, for the terms decoded by $D_1$. Therefore only finitely many, convergent systems remain as candidates, and for each it can be checked whether it decodes $S$ for the following reasons. None of the $t_i$ must contain $G$ (by Definition 3.3) and every $t_i$ must therefore be an instance of $q$. The choice of rules to reduce $\mathbf{G}(c^i(o), b_1, \ldots, b_n)$, for some basis $b_1, \ldots, b_n$, to $t_i$ is uniquely determined and depends only on $i$ and $b_1$. $b_1$ is limited in depth by the maximum of depths of terms in $S$ (due to rule 2). Since $D_2$ is non-erasing $b_2, \ldots, b_n$ can be found, given $t_i$, $i$, $D_1$ and one of the finitely many $b_1$ fixed, by reducing $t_i$, with that choice of rules in reversed order and with the direction of the rules reversed, where $q$ is instantiated to $t_i$ and the second argument of $G$ is ignored. If this is possible for all $t_i$ then a candidate decodes the sequence, otherwise not, and also all bases for the terms have been constructed. $\square$

For instance, the sequence

$$[\, f(0)\,,\ f(s(0))\,,\ f(s^4(0))\,,\ f(s^9(0))\,,\ f(s^{16}(0))\,]$$

is encoded by the system

1. $f(x) \rightarrow H(o, o', x)$

2. $H(w, c'(z), s(x)) \rightarrow H(w, z, x)$

3. $H(w, o', s(x)) \rightarrow H(c(w), G(w, o'), x)$

4. $G(c(w), y) \rightarrow G(w, c'(c'(y)))$

5. $G(o, y) \rightarrow y$

and it is decoded by the system

1. $G(c(w), o', x) \rightarrow G(w, G'(w, o'), s(x))$

2. $G(w, c'(z), x) \rightarrow G(w, z, s(x))$

3. $G(o, o', x) \rightarrow f(x)$

4. $G'(c(w), y) \rightarrow G'(w, c'(c'(y)))$

5. $G'(o, y) \rightarrow y$

In both cases all terms have the common basis $(o', 0)$ and rules 4 and 5 are the associated decoding systems.

Two distinct systems can encode or decode the same sequence of terms with a common basis. A simple example is $S = [f(s^i(0), s^i(0))]_{i=1,\ldots,n}$, which is encoded by the systems $\{f(x, x) \rightarrow H(o, x),\ H(w, s(x)) \rightarrow H(c(w), x)\}$ as well as by $\{f(x, y) \rightarrow H(o, x, y),\ H(w, s(x), s(y)) \rightarrow H(c(w), x, y)\}$. The latter might look like an overgeneralization, however enlarging $S$ with any element of

$$[f(s^i(0), s^j(0))]_{i=1,\ldots,\ j=1,\ldots}$$

which is not in $S$ will change the encoding bases.

The schemes of type 1 and 2 presented here can easily be extended. For instance encoding systems of type 2 can be equipped with additional rules in the style of type 1 systems, the right-linearity of the encoding systems can be dropped, more arguments for the encoding and decoding operators could be allowed etc. A wider step is to incorporate particular (also synthesis-) algorithms to define associated decoding systems, for instance to find functions $\mathcal{F}$ over the natural numbers (from some class, say integer polynomials in $x$) and corresponding definitions such that the "given" instances $G(c^x(o), b)$ have the "right" normalform $c^{\mathcal{F}(x)}(o)$. With the initial definition $G(w, o) \rightarrow o$ an encoding system must encode the terms just to increasing indexes, this gives the neccessary values for $x$ and $y$ (the difference from one index to the next, minus 1). For instance, to encode the sequence

$$[f(0),\ f(s(o)),\ f(s^4(0)),\ f(s^{15}(0))]$$

a definition for $G$ would be $G(w, o) \rightarrow w*w*w+w$, together with standard definitions for addition, subtraction and multiplication. Furthermore, the schemes can be easily interweaved to obtain more complex structures. A simple combination based on type 1 systems is:

1. $q \rightarrow H(o, o', o'', p_1, \ldots, p_n)$

2. $H(w, c'(u), v, r_1, \ldots, r_n) \rightarrow H(w, u, v, x_1, \ldots, x_n)$

3. $H(w, o', c''(v), r_1'', \ldots, r_n'') \rightarrow H(w, o', v, y_1, \ldots, y_n)$

4. $H(w, o', o'', r_1, \ldots, r_n) \rightarrow H(cw, G(w, b_1), G'(w, b_2), z_1, \ldots, z_n)$

However, all this is a tradeoff between the problem to find a system efficiently and the power of one single system. It is a matter of further work to find "interesting" encoding (and decoding) systems, in particular schemes which are not restricted to the primitive-recursive style of the definitions presented (for instance by letting associated decoding systems "use" also terms to be encoded as arguments and the encoding system itself for computations, recursively). In the sequel we suppose the basic schemes as well as some algorithm to find corresponding systems according to the propositions as given.

## 4.3 The synthesis algorithm

The input for the synthesis algorithm $A$ is a finite initial subsequence $S[n] = S(0) \cup S(1) \cup \ldots \cup S(n)$ of a positive descriptions $S \in S_R^+$, for some $R \in \mathcal{RD}$ and $n \in \mathbb{N}$. For each $n = 0, 1, \ldots$ $A$ outputs a rewrite program, called hypothesis, and furthermore $A$ "knows of" its last hypothesis (for $S[n-1]$) and also of $\Sigma_R$. First $A$ checks its last hypotheses, the rewrite program $P$. This is done by normalizing all left-hand sides in $S[n]$ using $P$. If this yields the corresponding right-hand sides for all rules then the last hypothesis is maintained and is also the new, otherwise another hypothesis $P$ is constructed. For this construction of $P$ the new operators $H, H_0, H_1, \ldots, G, G_0, G_1, \ldots$ as well as new counter operators $o_1, c_1, c_1', o_1', o_2, c_2, \ldots$ are used (i.e. none of them ever occurs in an input sequence). $P$ (if successfully constructed) has then three parts:

1. $P_l$ is a rewrite program normalizing $lhs(S(i))$ to $H(c^i(o))$, for $0 \leq i \leq n$.

2. $P_r$ is an rewrite program normalizing $G(c^i(o))$ to $rhs(S(i))$, for $0 \leq i \leq n$.

3. The rule $H(w) \rightarrow G(w)$.

$P_l$ and $P_r$ are synthesized separately by the subprocedures $syn_l$ and $syn_r$, respectively, and build as chains of encoding and decoding systems of type 1 and 2.

Before $A$ is described in more detail we give an example of how it proceeds with the sequence $S = [f(s^{i \times i}(g^i(0))) \rightarrow g^i(s^i(0))]_{i=0, \ldots, n}$, for some $n \geq 2$ in order to compute a (completely new) hypotheses $P$. Let $lhs(S[n])$ be $l_0, \ldots, l_n$ and let $rhs(S[n])$ be $r_0, \ldots, r_n$. Let $i$ range from 0 to $n$.

1. Start with $P_l = \emptyset$

2. $l_0, \ldots, l_n$ cannot be encoded with a common basis and a single introduction rule by an encoding system (of type 1 or 2).

3. Therefore the next step is the construction of all possible systems which encode $l_0, \ldots, l_n$ using a single introduction rule, based on the available schemes. No system of type 1 can be found, however there is one of type 2 which encodes the sequence with the bases $[0, \ldots, g^n(0)]$.

   (a) $f(x) \rightarrow H_1(o_1, o'_1, x)$
   (b) $H_1(w, o'_1, s(x)) \rightarrow H_1(c_1(w), G_1(w, o'_1), x)$
   (c) $H_1(w, c'_1(z), s(x)) \rightarrow H_1(w, z, x)$
   (d) $G_1(c_1(w), y) \rightarrow G_1(w, c'_1(c'_1(y)))$
   (e) $G_1(o_1, y) \rightarrow y$

4. Using these rules, the terms $l_i$ are normalized to $H(c_1^i(o_1), o'_1, g^i(0))$ for further operation, and the rules are added to $P_l$.

5. The new sequence has several encoding systems with a single introduction rule, but all overlap with $P_l$. Therefore systems with two introduction rules are checked. One of type 1 is found with a common basis for all terms:

   (a) $H_1(o_1, o'_1, 0) \rightarrow H_2(o_2, o_1, 0)$
   (b) $H_1(c_1(x), o'_1, g(y)) \rightarrow H_2(c_2(o_2), x, y)$
   (c) $H_2(c_2(w), c_1(x), g(y)) \rightarrow H_2(c_2(c_2(w)), x, y)$

   These rules are added to $P_l$.

6. Since now $l_i \downarrow_{P_l}$ is $H_2(c_2^i(o_2), o_1, 0)$ the rule $H_2(w, o_1, 0) \rightarrow H(w)$ is added to $P_l$ and the synthesis for $P_l$ is finished.

7. $P_r$ is set to $\emptyset$ initially. $r_0, \ldots, r_n$ cannot be decoded with a common basis (by a system of type 1 or 2). But there exist a decoding system of type 1 which decodes the sequence:

   (a) $G_3(c_3(w), x) \rightarrow G_3(w, g(x))$
   (b) $G_3(o_3, x) \rightarrow x$

8. The (only) bases computed for $r_0, \ldots, r_n$ are $0, \ldots, s^n(0)$. The rules are added to $P_r$ and $r_0, \ldots, r_n$ are replaced by the terms from which they are decoded: $G_3(c_3^i(o_3), s^i(0))$.

9. The new sequence $G_3(c_3^i(o_3), s^i(0))$ can be decoded by a system of type 1 with a common basis $(o_3, 0)$ for all terms. The system is:

   (a) $G_4(c_4(w), v, x) \rightarrow G_4(w, c_3(v), s(x))$
   (b) $G_4(o_4, v, x) \rightarrow G_3(v, x)$

   These rules are added to $P_r$. Since now $G(c_4^i(o_4)) \downarrow_{P_r}$ is $r_i$ the rule $G(w) \rightarrow G_4(w, o_3, 0)$ is constructed using the common basis $(o_3, 0)$ and also added to $P_r$. The synthesis of $P_r$ is done.

10. Finally $P_l$, $P_r$ and the rule $H(w) \to G(w)$ are put together forming $P$. $c_2$ and $o_2$ are replaced by $c_4$ and $o_4$, respectively (and $\alpha(H_0)_{|1}$ by $\alpha(G_0)_{|1}$, accordingly), in all rules.

11. $A$ stops.

The finally synthesized rewrite program is therefore:

1. $f(x) \to H_1(o_1, o'_1, x)$
2. $H_1(w, o'_1, s(x)) \to H_1(c_1(w), G_1(w, o'_1), x)$
3. $H_1(w, c'_1(z), s(x)) \to H_1(w, z, x)$
4. $G_1(c_1(w), y) \to G_1(w, c'_1(c'_1(y)))$
5. $G_1(o_1, y) \to y$
6. $G_1(o, y) \to y$
7. $H_1(o_1, o'_1, 0) \to H_2(o_4, o_1, 0)$
8. $H_1(c_1(x), o'_1, g(y)) \to H_2(c_4(o_4), x, y)$
9. $H_2(c_4(w), c_1(x), g(y)) \to H_2(c_4(c_4(w)), x, y)$
10. $H_2(w, o_1, 0) \to H(w)$
11. $H(w) \to G(w)$
12. $G_3(c_3(w), x) \to G_3(w, g(x))$
13. $G_3(o_3, x) \to x$
14. $G_4(c_4(w), v, x) \to G_4(w, c_3(v), s(x))$
15. $G_4(o_4, v, x) \to G_3(v, x)$
16. $G(w) \to G_4(w, o_3, 0)$

This system is a (conservatively) representing rewrite program for the rewrite definition

$$\bigcup_{i=0,\dots} \{ f(s^{i \times i}(g^i(0))) \to g^i(s^i(0)) \}.$$

We restrict our attention to $syn_l$ ($syn_r$ is quite similiar and is shortly discussed afterwards) since this is the more important part according to our motivation. The input for $syn_l$ is the sequence $lhs(S[n]) = L = [l_0, \dots, l_n]$ and $\Lambda$ calls $syn_l$ with the arguments $(0, L, \emptyset, \emptyset)$ and $\Sigma_R$ (not mentioned explicitly as an argument). By $L \downarrow_Q$ we denote the sequence obtained from $L$ by normalizing all elements with respect to a ground-convergent rewrite system $Q$, and by $\|L\|_{\Sigma_R}$ we denote the sum over all terms in $L$ of the number of operators from $op_{\Sigma_R}$ in a term.

**Construction 3.1.** $syn_l(k, L, P_0, P_l)$

1. If $P_l \neq \emptyset$ then return else goto 2

2. *If $k = 0$ then goto 3.*
   *Let $m = |H_k| - 1$.*
   *If $L = [H_k(c_k^i(o_k), b_1, \ldots, b_m)]_{i=0,\ldots,n}$ for some ground terms $b_1, \ldots, b_m$*
   *then : $P_l = P_0 \cup \{H_k(w, b_1, \ldots, b_m) \to H(w)\}$, and return*
   *else : goto 3.*

3. *Construct all encoding systems $E$ (of type 1 or 2) for $L$ with encoding operator $H_{k+1}$, counter operators out of $\{o_{k+1}, c_{k+1}, o'_{k+1}, c'_{k+1}, \ldots\}$ and (if any) associated decoding systems with decoding operator $G_{k+1}$, such that systems with lower number of introduction rules are built first and among them those which encode $L$ with a common basis are constructed first, and further such that*

   (a) *$E$ and $P_0$ do not overlap*

   (b) *$\|L \downarrow_E\|_{\Sigma_R} < \|L\|_{\Sigma_R}$*

   (c) *$E$ has at most $|L|$ rules*

   *Forall these systems $E$, in the order of their construction,*
   *do: $syn_l(k+1, L \downarrow_E, P_0 \cup E, P_l)$*

4. *Return.*

*Analysis sketch.* Because of (b) and since all possible encoding systems in step 3 can be generated finitely, according to the propositions for encoding and decoding systems, the whole procedure must terminate. If step 3 yields some $E$ which encodes $L$ with the same basis for all terms, then step 2 terminates all computations without further changes to $P_l$. On the other hand, if this never happens then $P_l$ is finally empty. Furthermore, $L \downarrow_E$ is defined since $E$ is convergent, as shown. Let $syn_l$ terminate with nonempty $P_l$, and let it consist of the encoding systems $E_1, \ldots, E_j, \ldots, E_k$, constructed in that order, where $E_j$ has the encoding operator $H_j$. For simplicity, let $E_{k+1}$ denote the single rule containing $H$, let $H_{k+1}$ denote $H$ and let $H_0$ denote $f$. Further denote $L$ by $L_0$ and $L \downarrow_{E_1} \ldots \downarrow_{E_j}$ by $L_j$, for $1 \leq j \leq k+1$. We call the operators $H_j$, $0 \leq j \leq k+1$, the *used encoding operators*.

First we argue that $P_l$ is a rewrite program. For $0 \leq j \leq k+1$ all terms in $L_j$ have $H_j$ as root operator but do not contain any further used encoding operator. Accordingly, all rules of $P_l$ have the form

$$\mathbf{H_j}(\ldots) \to \mathbf{H_j}(\ldots) \text{ or}$$

$$\mathbf{H_{j-1}}(\ldots) \to \mathbf{H_j}(\ldots) \text{ or}$$

$$\mathbf{G_j}(\ldots) \to \mathbf{G_j}(\ldots) \text{ or}$$

$$\mathbf{G_j}(\ldots) \to q,$$

where $1 \leq j \leq k+1$, $q$ is of a counter-sort and $q$ does neither contain some $H_j$ nor some $G_j$. Suppose a derivation of some term $t$ by $P_l$. Only subterms of $t$ with some $H_j$ or $G_j$ at root can be reduced. The number of subterms with some $H_j$ at root does not increase since $P_l$ without associated decoding systems is right-linear and the latter can reduce only subterms completely built of counter-sorted subterms. For any reduced subterm with $H_j$ at root, either $j$ is increased by a reduction up to the maximum $k + 1$, or it remains constant. In both cases eventually only rules from a single system of $E_1, \ldots, E_{k+1}$ can be applied (which are all terminating, clearly including $E_{k+1}$). The associated decoding systems alone are obviously terminating, hence $P_l$ is terminating. Additionally, condition (a) ensures that $P_l \setminus E_{k+1}$ is non-overlapping. The only candidate for an overlapping were the left-hand side of $E_{k+1}$ and a left-hand side of $E_k$ with $H_k$ at root, but this would be a contradiction to the fact that $E_k$ encodes the terms of $L_k$ with the common basis used to construct $E_{k+1}$. Therefore $P_l$ is non-overlapping, hence convergent. That means $P_l$ is a rewrite program.

Furthermore, since all terms of $L_0$ are stepwise normalized during the construction to those in $L_k$ using rules of the convergent system $P_l$ and since all terms in $L_k$ are reducible by $E_{k+1}$ we have that $L\downarrow_{P_l} = [H(c_k^i(o_k))]_{i=0,\ldots,n}$.

Let $t$ and $t'$ be two distinct ground terms which have a singular $f$ as root operator but do not contain any further used encoding operator. Now we argue that $t$ and $t'$ do not have the same normalform with respect to $P_l$. This follows from the fact that, due to the structure of the non-overlapping rules of $P_l$ as schematized above, $t\downarrow_{P_l} = (t\downarrow_{E_1} \cdots \downarrow_{E_l})$ and $t'\downarrow_{P_l} = (t\downarrow_{E_1} \cdots \downarrow_{E_{l'}})$, for some $l, l' \leq k + 1$. If $l \neq l'$ then clearly their normalforms are distinct. In the opposite case this follows from the property of every $E_j$ to not encode distinct ground terms to the same normalform (which has been shown for the encoding systems) and from the fact that $E_{k+1}$ is non-erasing. $\square$

Since $syn_r$ is not presented we assume

$$R = \bigcup_{i=0,\ldots} \{S(i) \to c^i(o)\}$$

and consider as output of $A$ the rewrite program $P$ obtained by replacing $H(w)$ in $P_l$ by $w$. Let let $c$ and $o$ denote $c_k$ and $o_k$ in $P$, repectively. Again, suppose $syn_l$ applied to $S[n]$ terminates with nonempty $P_l$, and suppose further that $A$ will not change its hypothesis $P$ for any $S[m]$ with $m > n$. In this case $P$ conservatively represents $R$ for the following reasons. If $A$ maintains $P$ then for every $i \in \mathbb{N}$ there is some $t \in lhs(R)$ such that $t\downarrow_P = c^i(o)$, and moreover there is one and only one such term (cf. Analysis of Construction 3.1). Thus $P$ then defines via the normalization of terms of $lhs(R)$ a one-to-one and onto mapping from $lhs(R)$ to $\{c^i(o) | i \in \mathbb{N}\}$. If a term $t \in T^f(\Sigma_R) \setminus lhs(R)$ is reducible by $P$ then its normalform contains some $H_j$ ($1 \leq j \leq k$). In this case as well as if $t$ is not reducible by $P$ we have $t\downarrow_P \notin T(\Sigma_R \setminus f)$, and the normalform of any such two distinct terms with respect to $P$ is distinct (either only one contains $f$, or the terms are both not reducible by $P$, or otherwise their normalforms differ as shown in the Analysis of Construction 3.1). This establishes conditions 2, 4 and 5 of Definition 3.3, and conditions 1 and 3 follow easily by construction of $syn_l$ (we skip the details). All these arguments are collected by the

**Proposition 4.5.** $A$ (without $syn_r$) is correct.

*Proof sketch.* See above. $\square$

$syn_r$ works similiar to $syn_l$. The main difference is that $P_r$ is built from decoding systems only and the input terms are not normalized but replaced by new terms (to be generated in further steps), which are contructed from decoding bases as demonstrated in the introductory synthesis example.

As with the definition of the rewrite program schemes we have the synthesis algorithm restricted to the essential mechanisms. For instance we did not consider that finitely many "exeptional" rules of $R$ can easily carried over to $P$ (by "reserving" some ground instances of $H(w)$ in $P_l$), and our strategy to generate all possible encoding systems in step 3 of $syn_l$ might be changed in several ways. Also the class of rewrite definitions learnable by $A$ will not be characterized here. We just add two remarks. The first is that for positive descriptions of rewrite definitions of this class it cannot be decided from initial subsequences whether a hypothesis (rewrite program) is already a representing rewrite program for the rewrite definition. This follows from the structure of encoding systems of type 1 which can "take care for exceptional input rules" at the beginning of a positive description by sufficiently large values for $m$ in Definition 3.2. The second remark is that a rewrite program for the graph of Ackermann's function, as discussed in Subsection 3.3, cannot be learned by the algorithm, even with the suggested local improvements for the program schemes, as long as the primitive-recursive style of the schemes is maintained.

# 5 Conclusions

We have seen that rewrite definitions can be represented by rewrite programs and that such programs can be learned from positive descriptions of rewrite definitions under certain (exemplary) circumstances. At least three major problems arise in view of our motivation to consider a purely inductive synthesis of rewrite programs. The first is to extend rewrite definitions by allowing non-ground rules. The second is how to incorporate (properties of) rewrite systems used to generate rewrite definitions into the learning process, based on appropriate sufficient conditions for the RP-learnability of classes of rewrite definitions, and the third regards to the development of a useful theory for rewrite program schemes.

# 6 Acknowledgements

The author thanks Steffen Lange and Klaus P. Jantke for many helpful discussions and hints.

# References

[AS83]   Dana Angluin and Carl H. Smith. A Survey of Inductive Inference: Theory and Methods. *Computing Surveys*, 15:237–269, 1983.

[BD86]   Leo Bachmair and Nachum Dershowitz. Commutation, transformation, and termination. In *Proceedings of the Eighth International Conference on Automated Deduction, Oxford, England*, volume 230 of *Lecture Notes in Computer Science*, pages 5–20. Springer, 1986.

[Bel91]  Francois Bellegarde. Program transformation and rewriting. In R. Book, editor, *Proceedings of the Fourth International Conference on Rewriting Techniques and Applications, Como, Italy, April 1991*, volume 488 of *Lecture Notes in Computer Science*, pages 226–239. Springer, Berlin, 1991.

[BT80]   J. A. Bergstra and J. V. Tucker. A characterization of computable data types by means of a finite equational specification method. In J. W. de Bakker and J. van Leeuwen, editors, *Proceedings of the Seventh International Colloquium on Automata, Languages and Programming*, volume 85 of *Lecture Notes in Computer Science*, pages 76–90. Springer, Amsterdam, 1980.

[Chu41]  A. Church. The calculi of lambda conversion. In *Annals of Mathematics Studies*, volume 6. Princeton University Press, 1941.

[Dau89]  M. Dauchet. Simulation of Turing machines by a left-linear rewrite rule. In N. Dershowitz, editor, *Proceedings of the Third International Conference on Rewriting Techniques and Applications, Chapel Hill, NC, April 1989*, volume 355 of *Lecture Notes in Computer Science*, pages 109–120. Springer, Berlin, 1989.

[Der82]  Nachum Dershowitz. Applications of the Knuth–Bendix completion procedure. In *Proc. of the Seminaire d'Informatique Theorique, Paris, December 1982*, pages 95–111, 1982.

[Der85]  Nachum Dershowitz. Synthesis by Completion. In *Proc. 9th Intern. Joint Conference on Artificial Intelligence, Los Angeles*, pages 208–214, 1985.

[Der87]  Nachum Dershowitz. Termination of rewriting. *Journal of Symbolic Computation*, 3(1&2):69–115, 1987.

[DJ90]   Nachum Dershowitz and Jean-Pierre Jouannaud. Rewrite Systems. In J. van Leeuwen, editor, *Formal Models and Semantics. Handbook of Theoretical Computer Science*, volume B, pages 243–320. North-Holland, Amsterdam, 1990.

[DP90]   Nachum Dershowitz and Eli Pinchover. Inductive synthesis of equational programs. In *AAAI-90, Proceedings, Eighth National Conference on Artificial Intelligence*, pages 234–239. MIT Press, 1990.

[DR93]   Nachum Dershowitz and Uday S. Reddy. Deductive and Inductive Synthesis of Equational Programs. *Journal of Symbolic Computation*, 15(5&6):467–494, 1993.

[Gol67] E Mark Gold. Language identification in the limit. *Information and Control*, 14:447–474, 1967.

[Gol92] Ulf Goldammer. A method for the inductive synthesis of rewrite programs based on KNUTH-BENDIX-completion techniques. GOSLER Report 06/92, Technische Hochschule Leipzig, FB Mathematik & Informatik, February 1992.

[Gri93] Gunter Grieser. TLPS - a term rewriting laboratory (not only) for experiments in automatic program synthesis. GOSLER Report 22/93, HTWK Leipzig (FH), FB Informatik, Mathematik & Naturwissenschaften, December 1993.

[Klo92] J.W. Klop. Term Rewriting Systems. In S. Abramsky, Dov. M. Gabbay, and T. S. E. Maibaum, editors, *Handbook of logic in computer science*, volume 1, pages 1–116. Oxford University Press, New York, 1992.

[Lan89] Steffen Lange. Towards a Set of Inference Rules for Solving Divergence in Knuth-Bendix completion. In Klaus P. Jantke, editor, *Analogical and Inductive Inference, AII'89*, volume 397 of *Lecture Notes in Artificial Intelligence*, pages 304–316. Springer-Verlag, 1989.

[MT91] Aart Middeldorp and Yoshihito Toyama. Completeness of Combinations of Constructor Systems. In R. Book, editor, *Proceedings of the Fourth International Conference on Rewriting Techniques and Applications, Como, Italy, April 1991*, volume 488 of *Lecture Notes in Computer Science*, pages 188–199. Springer, Berlin, 1991.

[MY74] Michael Machtey and Paul Young. *An Introduction to the General Theory of Algorithms*. North-Holland, 1974.

[O'D77] M. J. O'Donnell. *Computing in Systems Described by Equations*, volume 58 of *Lecture Notes in Computer Science*. Springer, 1977.

[Red89] Uday S. Reddy. Rewriting Techniques for Program Synthesis. In N. Dershowitz, editor, *Proceedings of the Third International Conference on Rewriting Techniques and Applications, Chapel Hill, NC, April 1989*, volume 355 of *Lecture Notes in Computer Science*, pages 338–403. Springer, Berlin, 1989.

[TJ89] Muffy Thomas and Klaus P. Jantke. Inductive inference for solving divergence in Knuth-Bendix completion. In K.P. Jantke, editor, *Analogical and Inductive Inference*, Lecture Notes in Artificial Intelligence 397, pages 288–303. Springer-Verlag, 1989.

# T$_{\text{L}}$PS –
# A Term Rewriting Laboratory (not only) for Experiments in Automatic Program Synthesis

Gunter Grieser

HTWK Leipzig

FB Mathematik und Informatik

PF 66

04251 Leipzig

gunter@informatik.th-leipzig.de

### Abstract

There exists many approaches to solve divergence at Knuth-Bendix Completion procedure. One way is to use ideas of inductive inference. T$_{\text{L}}$PS provides a tool for implementing such inference rules. The problem is shown by a simple example and an idea to solve it. Some requirements which a system for its implementation should fullfil are expressed. The introduced small rule is implemented stepwise to show the use of T$_{\text{L}}$PS. Lastly the approach of T$_{\text{L}}$PS is discussed.

## 1 Overview

The problem to finitely represent the infinitely many rewrite rules produced by a diverging Knuth-Bendix Completion of a term rewriting system is the object of current research. This has many applications, for instance in the fields of automatic theorem proving and automatic program synthesis. Here we will present a tool which has been successfully applied for experiments belonging to the latter field, in particular to the synthesis of term rewriting programs. Although we will not go into full details about this approach, we'll mention them as far as they explain certain properties of our tool. Nevertheless we believe that our system can be useful whenever experiments have to be done which involve computations with and sophisticated manipulations of term rewriting systems.

This paper is not intended to be an exhaustive system description. First a simple problem is discussed to which our tool can be applied if experiments are desired. Then we use a particular program synthesis example to give a taste and to demonstrate the power of our tool. This is done, from the user's point of view, by a stepwise implementation of a fairly complicated inference rule. The inference rule itself has been taken from [Go], where a set of such rules is presented. This work, in turn, is strongly based on [Th/Ja] and [La/Ja], where ideas were developed to infer finite replacements for the outcome of a diverging completion process within the framework of Inductive Inference.

To develop such inference rules, to test them with practical problems, to find counter-examples etc. a computer based test bed is highly desirable. Experiments 'by hand' would be very cumbersome.

The goal is to provide a convienient high level language which allows complicated operations on term rewriting systems (and terms). Our tool T$_{L}$P$^{S}$ is a prototype. Thus the language it provides has no syntactic sugar, it looks like LISP. Also it is a compromise between compactness, computational efficiency and effort of implementation. One of our targets was to prove that this kind of user interface is quite appropriate here. T$_{L}$P$^{S}$ has many features which should ease the fast implementation and application of things like the inference rules mentioned above.

# 2  Notions and Notations

We adopt all the standard notions and notations for (first order) terms and term rewriting systems. Let $F$ and $X$ be sets of function symbols and variables, respectively. Then $T(F, X)$ denotes the set of all first order terms over $F$ and $X$. A term rewriting system (TRS, for short) is a set of rewrite rules $l \to r$, where $l$ and $r$ are terms and all variables in $r$ occur in $l$. A term $t$ is reducible to $t'$ by TRS $R$, written as $t \longrightarrow_R t'$, iff there exists a rule $l \to r \in R$, a subterm $s$ of $t$ and a substitution $\sigma$ such that $l\sigma = s$ and $t'$ is $t$ with $s$ replaced by $r\sigma$.

$\longrightarrow_R^*$ is the reflexive and transitive, $\longleftrightarrow_R^*$ the reflexive, transitive and symmetric closure of $\longrightarrow_R$.

A term $t$ is in normal form with respect to TRS $R$ iff it is irreducible, that means no term $t'$ exists such that $t \longrightarrow_R t'$. A TRS $R$ is terminating if there is no infinite rewrite sequence. It is confluent, iff for all terms $t \longrightarrow_R^* t_1$ and $t \longrightarrow_R^* t_2$ implies the existence of a term $t'$ such that $t_1 \longrightarrow_R^* t'$ and $t_2 \longrightarrow_R^* t'$. It is ground confluent if this property holds for all ground terms.

Confluence of a terminating TRS $R$ can be decided by a class of algorithms known as Knuth-Bendix Completion procedures. In case of nonconfluence such procedures generate 'critical pairs' (two different normal forms of one term) which are useful to construct an equivalent confluent system (while keeping $\longleftrightarrow_R^*$ unchanged).

In order to find critical pairs, two rules are overlapped in the following way: The left-hand side of a rule is unified with a nonvariable subterm of the left-hand side of (another) rule. The resulting term is reducible by the two used rules. A critical pair is obtained if the normal forms of the two derived terms are different. In this case $R$ is obviously not confluent and a new rule built from this pair might be added to the system to solve this problem.

A finite, terminating and ground confluent TRS will be understood as a program.

Two programs $R$ and $R'$ are said to be equivalent with respect to $F$ (written $R =_F R'$) iff for all $t, t' \in T(F, \emptyset)$: $t \longleftrightarrow^*_R t'$ iff $t \longleftrightarrow^*_{R'} t'$ ($R'$ is called a conservative extension of $R$).

The antiunifier of two terms is defined as follows:
$t_1 \diagup\!\!\!\!\diagdown t_2 =_{def} t$ iff 1. $\exists \sigma : t\sigma = t_1$
$\qquad\qquad\qquad\qquad$ 2. $\exists \sigma : t\sigma = t_2$

# 3 Motivation

Term rewriting systems are often an elegant way to operationalize equational knowledge. Equations can be oriented into rules and after this it is necessary to check the new rewrite system for termination and confluence. In practice termination seems to be a less difficult problem than confluence, and in many cases the Knuth-Bendix-Completion for a system succeeds. If not, then it often produces a potentially infinite set of rewrite rules which has an easily discovered regularity.

**example 1:**

$\qquad$ **TRS1:** $\qquad$ (A1) $\qquad$ f(g(X)) $\qquad\qquad \rightarrow$ $\quad$ o
$\qquad\qquad\qquad\qquad$ (A2) $\qquad$ g(s(X)) $\qquad\qquad \rightarrow$ $\quad$ s(g(X))

The term $t = f(g(s(o)))$ can be reduced to $o$ by (A1). ($s = t, \sigma = \{X/s(o)\}$) On the other hand, applying the rule (A2) leads to $f(s(g(o)))$. ($s = g(s(o)), \sigma = \{X/o\}$) Both terms are in normal form with respect to $TRS1$. Obviously $TRS1$ is not confluent.

Overlapping the rules (A1) and (A2) yields the term $f(g(s(X)))$. This can be reduced either by (A1) to $o$ or by (A2) to $f(s(g(X)))$. Appending this rule $f(s(g(X))) \rightarrow o$ to $TRS1$ leads to a normal form for $t$: $o$.
But the resulting TRS is not yet confluent. New overlapping steps are possible between $(A2)$ and the last rule added. This process can be repeated infinitely many times:

$\qquad$ **TRS2:** $\qquad$ (B1) $\qquad$ f(g(X)) $\qquad\qquad \rightarrow$ $\quad$ o
$\qquad\qquad\qquad\qquad$ (B2) $\qquad$ g(s(X)) $\qquad\qquad \rightarrow$ $\quad$ s(g(X))
$\qquad\qquad\qquad\qquad$ (B3) $\qquad$ f(s(g(X))) $\qquad\; \rightarrow$ $\quad$ o
$\qquad\qquad\qquad\qquad$ (B4) $\qquad$ f(s$^2$(g(X))) $\qquad \rightarrow$ $\quad$ o
$\qquad\qquad\qquad\qquad$ (B5) $\qquad$ f(s$^3$(g(X))) $\qquad \rightarrow$ $\quad$ o
$\qquad\qquad\qquad\qquad$ (B6) $\qquad$ f(s$^4$(g(X))) $\qquad \rightarrow$ $\quad$ o
$\qquad\qquad\qquad\qquad$ (B7) $\qquad$ f(s$^5$(g(X))) $\qquad \rightarrow$ $\quad$ o
$\qquad\qquad\qquad\qquad\qquad\qquad\qquad\qquad\qquad\qquad$ $\vdots$

In such cases one could try to characterize the regularity of the new rules and to capture this sequence by finitely many rewrite rules.

In other words, for a given TRS $R$ consisting of infinitely many rules an equivalent finite $R'$ has to be found.

$\qquad$ The first idea here is to generalize the sequence $(B3), (B4), \ldots$ by the new rule $f(s(X)) \rightarrow o$.

**TRS3:**       (C1)      f(g(X))      $\rightarrow$    o
                      (C2)      g(s(X))      $\rightarrow$    s(g(X))
                      (C3)      f(s(X))      $\rightarrow$    o

$TRS3$ is confluent, but it is not equivalent to $TRS2$. For example, the term $f(s(o))$ is reducible by $TRS3$ to $o$, but not by $TRS2$. Now new equalities exist, the new system is an overgeneralisation. Obviously it is too simple an idea to simply replace the sequence by its syntactic generalization.

In general the rules (considered as terms) obtained by the completion procedure have a rich structure. For example, the number of occurrences of function symbols on the left- and right-hand side may depend on each other or may depend on the position in the term and so on.

The regularity of the rules in $TRS2$ can be described by
$(Bi+2)$      $f(s^i(g(X)))$      $\rightarrow$      o.
If it is possible to express this by rewrite rules, then the whole sequence could be replaced by those rules.

Is it possible to find a single term such that its instances are exactly the terms $s^i(X)$ ?

An inspection of the sequence shows that the number of occurences of $s$ plays no role. Here is a new idea:

**TRS4:**       (D1)      f(g(X))      $\rightarrow$    o
                      (D2)      g(s(X))      $\rightarrow$    s(g(X))
                      (D3)      f(s(g(X)))      $\rightarrow$    o
                      (D4)      f(s(s(X)))      $\rightarrow$    f(s(X))

This system seems to be closer to the original sequence than $TRS3$. But the definition of $f$ is changed, now for instance the term $f(s(s(o)))$ is reducible to $f(s(o))$. $TRS2$ and $TRS4$ are not yet equivalent. Obviously other ideas are needed.

Enrichment of the signature and introduction of a new operator $h$ is a further possibility (and sometimes necessary) to meet the goal. $h$ should be defined such that the side effects discussed above do not occur (note that equivalence is considered with respect to the original set $F$).

First: divert the computation to the new operator $h$: $f(s(X)) \rightarrow h(X)$.
Second: the number of occurences of $s$ does not matter: $h(s(X)) \rightarrow h(X)$.
After all create the appropriate normal form : $h(g(X)) \rightarrow o$.

**TRS5:**       (E1)      f(g(X))      $\rightarrow$    o
                      (E2)      g(s(X))      $\rightarrow$    s(g(X))
                      (E3)      f(s(X))      $\rightarrow$    h(X)
                      (E4)      h(s(X))      $\rightarrow$    h(X)
                      (E5)      h(g(X))      $\rightarrow$    o

Now the desired effect has been obtained, although no definition of the initial symbols is changed. The reduction of $f(s(o))$ leads to $h(o)$ (which means, that

$f(s(o))$ was irreducible with respect to the original system, since its new normal form contains a new operator). The programs $TRS2$ and $TRS5$ are equivalent with respect to the original function set $F$.

What has happened? A regularity of a structure of a sequence has been analysed and was translated into rewrite rules.
Does the idea of enriching the signature work in general? Is it possible to find a generalization on the basis of this kind of syntactic analysis?

## example 2:

Let's do further experiments with another TRS which is similar to $TRS1$:

**TRS6:**

| | | |
|---|---|---|
| (F1) | $f(g(X))$ | $\rightarrow$ o |
| (F2) | $g(s^2(X))$ | $\rightarrow$ $s^2(g(X))$ |

Knuth-Bendix-Completion generates :

**TRS7:**

| | | |
|---|---|---|
| (G1) | $f(g(X))$ | $\rightarrow$ o |
| (G2) | $g(s^2(X))$ | $\rightarrow$ $s^2(g(X))$ |
| (G3) | $f(s^2(g(X)))$ | $\rightarrow$ o |
| (G4) | $f(s^4(g(X)))$ | $\rightarrow$ o |
| (G5) | $f(s^6(g(X)))$ | $\rightarrow$ o |
| (G6) | $f(s^8(g(X)))$ | $\rightarrow$ o |
| (G7) | $f(s^{10}(g(X)))$ | $\rightarrow$ o |

$$\vdots$$

This sequence was is similar to that for $TRS2$. The idea from above also works in this case:

**TRS8:**

| | | |
|---|---|---|
| (H1) | $f(g(X))$ | $\rightarrow$ o |
| (H2) | $g(s^2(X))$ | $\rightarrow$ $s^2(g(X))$ |
| (H3) | $f(s^2(X))$ | $\rightarrow$ $h(X)$ |
| (H4) | $h(s^2(X))$ | $\rightarrow$ $h(X)$ |
| (H5) | $h(g(X))$ | $\rightarrow$ o |

The reason is that each rule at $TRS7$ has in a certain sense a 'constant distance' from its neighbour, which is used in (H4).

## example 3:

But not all TRS are such simple-structured. Little modifications of $TRS1$ lead to a quite different behaviour.

**TRS9:**

| | | |
|---|---|---|
| (I1) | $f(g(X))$ | $\rightarrow$ o |
| (I2) | $g(s(X))$ | $\rightarrow$ $k(s(g(X)))$ |
| (I3) | $k(s(X))$ | $\rightarrow$ $s^2(k(X))$ |

Knuth-Bendix-Completion outputs

**TRS10:**   (J1)   $f(g(X))$                      $\rightarrow$   o
       (J2)   $g(s(X))$                      $\rightarrow$   $k(s(g(X)))$
       (J3)   $k(s(X))$                      $\rightarrow$   $s^2(k(X))$
       (J4)   $f(s^2(k(g(X))))$              $\rightarrow$   o
       (J5)   $f(s^6(k^2(g(X))))$            $\rightarrow$   o
       (J6)   $f(s^{14}(k^3(g(X))))$         $\rightarrow$   o
       (J7)   $f(s^{30}(k^4(g(X))))$         $\rightarrow$   o
       (J8)   $f(s^{62}(k^5(g(X))))$         $\rightarrow$   o

$$\vdots$$

This time the growing occurs simultaneously at two positions having a special relationship: $f(s^{h(i)}(k^i(g(X))))$, where $h(i) = \sum_{j=1}^{i} 2^j$. One way to generalize this sequence is to 'invent' the power and the sum functions, i.e. to introduce the corresponding new operators.

Of course, the power of this approach depends on the difficulty to define the new operators.

What to do if the new operators do not solve the problem, but introduce new sequences to be captured ?

Here we are concerned with an inductive process. The initial task is changed due to the addition of rewrite rules and after this it simply restarts. This will be repeated until the problem is solved.

Inductive Inference is a field dealing with algorithmic learning from possibly incomplete information. The term 'learning' is interpreted in the sense that an object (here TRS) is said to be learned iff after finitely many steps the hypothesis will not be changed any more and correctly describes the object to be learned. This property of a learning algorithm is independent from what is known about the correctness of any particular hypothesis it produces.

With ideas of Inductive Inference in mind some learning rules have been developed by [Th/Ja], [La/Ja] and [Go] to solve divergence problems of the Knuth-Bendix Completion. In essence these learning rules work similarly to the method discussed in example 1. Of course, an input sequence need not be drawn from a completion process, it could be taken from any potentially infinite sequence of rewrite rules. The inference rules recognize certain regularities within these sequences and describe them by introducing and defining new operators.

Because these synthesis rules each cover a fairly large class of regularities, they are accordingly complex. On the other hand such rules are specified mathematically and with some operational background. There should be no problem to translate them into some programming language. This is particulary desirable because the inference rules are the object of current research and they are used for computer experiments. Although the theoretical work is the main line of research in this case, practical investigations are one of the main sources here. Experiments allow the study of special syntactic phenomena, they can give counter-examples or inspiration to new ideas.

But what kind of system use? Which properties a prototyping tool should have?

# 4 Requirements for a prototyping system

In principle an implementation of the ideas discussed above is possible with each programming language.

Working close to a lower machine level has several disadvantages. Quick modification of rules would become quite cumbersome and the programs would be fairly large and hard to manage.

Thus a language is to be prefered which offers sufficiently powerful statements related to this world of terms and TRS. That means powerful data structures have to be provided. It should possess basic operations on terms and rewrite systems similar to those needed in the discussion of the examples above.

A prototyping system like this one should be interactive, it should have good possibilities for editing objects, undoing calculation steps and recording the interactions.

The system should have only a few but powerful basic functions and an easy but sufficient syntax. It should be free of details like data representation, data types, their conversion and so on, to be user-friendly and easy to learn. Nevertheless it must remain fast and handy.

# 5 The programming system $T_{I\!I}P^S$

$T_{I\!I}P^S$ provides its own programming language. It is particular adapted to work with terms and TRS.

Beside the usual control structures the most useful operations with rewrite systems are available as basic functions, for instance substitution, unification, Knuth-Bendix Completion and reduction.

$T_{I\!I}P^S$ is based on LISP and has a functional language. Roughly, statements are written as terms which are evaluated by an 'innermost' strategy in order of their appearance.

There is some special notation for function calls which makes their names easier to remember and which proves to be quite powerful. It looks like a relational notation, which will be explained by an example.

> Investigating the following operation of substitution: $t_1\sigma=t_2$ (*), several questions are imaginable:
>
> 1. Is this equation true for fixed $t_1$, $t_2$ and $\sigma$? $\implies$ Use as predicate given all arguments: `substitute(t`$_1$`,`$\sigma$`,t`$_2$`)`.
>
> 2. Does any substitution $\sigma$ exist such that (*) becomes true? $\implies$ Use as predicate with $\sigma$ ignored: `substitute(t`$_1$`,_,t`$_2$`)`.
>
> 3. Which substitution fulfils (*) for fixed $t_1$ and $t_2$? $\implies$ Use as function to compute the substitution: `substitute(t`$_1$`,`**c**`,t`$_2$`)`.
>
> 4. What is the result of applying $\sigma$ to $t_1$? $\implies$ Use as function to compute the third argument: `substitute(t`$_1$`,`$\sigma$`,`**c**`)`.

5. Given $t_2$ and $\sigma$. Which terms give $t_2$ under this substitution ? $\implies$
Use as a function to compute the first argument: **substitute(@,$\sigma$,$t_2$)**.

(Here one problem comes up: There may be a lot of terms fulfilling (*), for instance the term consisting of the variable X only would always work. Further agreements are necessary to define the computed result, for example the 'most special' of all possible terms.)

$$\vdots$$

All this is related to the idea "substitution". Instead of providing a lot of single functions (which would be harder to remember), T$_I$P$^S$ has this simple convention for all basic functions.

A particular selection is made by using appropriate arguments and special characters (_ and @) with some identifier which represents a class of functions.
This way an intuitive programming style is supported and formal descriptions can be more easily translated into the T$_I$P$^S$-language.

Beside this there exist a couple of data types needed to work in this world of terms and TRS. Every object has a fixed type. On the other hand every argument of a function must be of a fixed, predefined type. Type checking and type conversion are done automatically in T$_I$P$^S$. Normally the user is not involved here.

These and many other features will be explained now by an example. It consists of the user's implementation of an inference rule for the method developped in example 1.

# 6 Programming in T$_I$P$^S$

Given a sequence of rules $l_1{\rightarrow}r_1$, ..., $l_n{\rightarrow}r_n$, it has to be checked whether or not the sequence has the required regularity and the corresponding generalization rules should be created.

What does 'the required regularity' mean?

(C-a) All functions need to be unary.

(C-b) The right-hand sides of all rule are the same: $\forall i \in \{2\ldots n\} : r_i = r_1$.

(C-c) The left-hand sides have a constant growth in the sense that given $s_i = l_i$ ↙
↘$l_{i+1}$ (i=1...n-1), a regularity similar to that of the the initial sequence can be observed, formally: (i) $\exists \delta \; \forall i \in \{1 \ldots n-2\} : s_i \delta = s_{i+1}$.
This means the 'distance' between two subsequent terms is constant.

The second condition is then: (ii) $\exists \sigma \; \forall i \in \{1 \ldots n-1\} : s_i \sigma = l_i$.

This is what we feel to be 'regular growth' of the input sequence.

Now we describe the inference step, namely the rules to be introduced:

(I-a) First introduce the new operator: $s_1{\rightarrow}h(X)$. (Let h be a new symbol).

(I-b) The second rule is to decrease the term to be reduced by the constant distance, which is represented as $\delta : h(X)\delta \rightarrow h(X)$.

(I-c) If the 'inner rest' — represented as $\sigma$ — remains, then it can be reduced to the original right-hand side: $h(X)\sigma \rightarrow r_1$.

This is the complete inference rule to be implemented.

At the beginning an implementation for (C-b) is discussed: $\forall i \in \{2 \ldots n\} : r_i = r_1$ $\implies$ `forall(rule, seq, equal(right(rule),right(nth(1,seq))))`. (The input sequence to be generalized will be stored at the variable **seq**.)

> **forall**(x:*raw*, domain:*list*, condition:*raw*, result:*boolean*)
> is an iteration test function. The first argument **x** must be a symbol and is used as the name of a variable. It can be used in the **condition**. The term *raw* means that this argument has a special meaning: it is not evaluated. The third argument **condition** has this same property. It must be a $T_HP^S$-statement. This statement is executed for every element of the **domain**. The **result** of the function is true if for all evaluations its result is true. Normally the statement above has to be written as `forall(rule, seq, equal(...,...), ©)`: "What is the result of this application?". The case that the @ occurs as last argument applies very often. Then the @ can then be omitted.
>
> **equal**(a:*all*, b:*all*, result:*boolean*)
> This function compares two objects **a** and **b** of arbitrary type (*all*). Normally only objects of the same type can be compared. Therefore a conversion to the 'least common' type is done. The meaning of 'equality' depends on the type. For instance, two terms are equal iff they are identical up to consistent renaming of variables.
>
> **right**(rule:*rule*, term:*term*)
> This function extracts the right-hand side of a rule. In the statement above the right-hand sides are computed and compared by **equal**. The statement `right(rule,right(nth(1,seq)))` has the same effect. Now the outermost **right** is used as a predicate, the inner one as a function.
>
> **nth**(i:*number*, list:*list*, x:*all*)
> This finds the i-th element from a list, starting the counting at 1.
>
> The type conversion transforms an object to the type specified by the function's argument list. For example, the first argument of **right** is not of type **rule** - it will be converted to this type. The conversion of the type **list-of-rules** gives the first rule of this list. This shows that for our purpose the nth-statement would not be necessary. `equal(right(rule),right(seq))` would have the same effect .

Thus the statement above can be rewritten as
`forall(rule, seq, right(rule,right(seq)))`.

If this test gives true then the $s_i$ can be computed:
`s=for2(ri, rj, seq, superterm(left(ri),left(rj)))`.

**for**(x:raw, domain:*list*, command:raw, result:*list*)
Similar to **forall**, there is the function **for**. In this case the variable **x** is
successively bound to all elements of **domain** and the T$_\text{I}$PS-command is executed.
The results are collected into **result**. This list is the result of the statement.
For example, **for(i,'(1,2,3),i + 1)** $\implies$ **(2,3,4):list-of-numbers**.

**for2**(x:raw, y:raw, domain:*list*, command:raw, result:*list*)
This is provided to handle the respective neighbours of a list within one operation. First, **x** is bound to the first element of **domain** and **y** to its successor. At
every step the variables are set to their respective successors. So the length of
the resulting list is shorter by one than that of domain: *list*. For example,
**for2(i,j,'(1,2,3),i + j)** $\implies$ **(3,5):list-of-numbers**.

**superterm**(t$_1$:*term*, t$_2$:*term*, term:*term*)
is the implementation of the relation $\bigwedge$.

**set**(variable:raw, value:*all*)
stores the **value** at the **variable**. This function can be abbreviated by the
term **variable = value**. **Variable** can be an arbitrary symbol, which is used
as the name of the variable. It is considered as global if it is undeclared so far.
Every T$_\text{I}$PS-object can be stored at a variable, for example rewrite systems can
be stored at variables too.

The result of this statement is a list of the respective antiunifiers stored at the variable
s.

This can be used to compute the substitutions $\sigma$ and $\delta$. They are computed from the
first pair and then tested against the full sequence:

```
sigma=substitute(nth(1,s), @, left(nth(1,seq)));
delta=substitute(nth(1,s), @, nth(2,s));
and( forall(i, [1, length(s)],
                substitute(nth(i,s), sigma, left(nth(i,seq))) ),
     forall2(ti, tj, s, substitute(ti,delta,tj)) )
```

(Subsequent statements are seperated by semicolon or full stop.)

**substitute**(t$_1$:*term*, $\sigma$:*substitution*, t$_2$:*term*)
This function was discussed in a previous section: $t_2=t_1\sigma$. Here it is used both
as a function to compute the substitution and as a predicate to test it.

**and**(a:raw, b:raw, r:*boolean*)
This is the logical and. The first statement is evaluated. The second is evaluated
iff the result was true. The final result is true iff both statements have been
evaluated to true.

**[i,j]** is a macro to abbreviate special lists of numbers. It expands to a list
of numbers from **i** to **j** with a step width of one. For example: **[1,5]** $\implies$
**(1,2,3,4,5):list-of-numbers**.

From the conditions to be tested (C-a) is left. Several approaches are possible to test
whether a function is unary . A direct function does not exist. One way is to use the
possible subterm positions of this term:

```
forall(rule, seq, forall(pos, tree-domain(left(rule)),
                          forall(i, pos, i < 2) ))
```

A position of a subterm of a term is a (listed) description of the way to this subterm. In T$_\text{I}$P$^\text{S}$ the description is a list of integers.

The number i in this list means to go to the i-th argument of the function. For example, the subterm of f(a,g(h(X,b),c)) at position (1) is a, at (2,1,2) it is b. There exists a function to compute all possible positions of subterms of a term: **tree-domain**(term:*term*, td:*list-of-positions*)
which may be used to provide the necessary information.

If the conditions (C-a) ... (C-c) hold then the created rules must be appended:

```
append-rule(nth(1,s),'h(X));
append-rule(substitute('h(X), delta), 'h(X));
append-rule(substitute('h(X), sigma), right(nth(1,seq)))
```

> **append-rule**(left:*term*, right:*term*, trs:*trs*)
> appends the rewrite rule left→right to trs.
> The nth-statements at the lines above could be dropped due to the automatic type conversion.

All those single steps are summarized now to define a new T$_\text{I}$P$^\text{S}$-function:

```
1 defun(syntactic-analysis,
2     ((seq, list-of-rules), (trs, trs), (new-trs, trs)), (
3   (new-trs, (), (1, r, s, sigma, delta, hx), (
4     l=for(rule, seq, left(rule)),
5     r=for(rule, seq, right(rule)),
6     s=for2(li, lj, l, superterm(li, lj)),
7     sigma=substitute(s, ¢, l),
8     delta=substitute(s, ¢, nth(2,s)),
9     if( and( and(forall(li, l, forall(p, tree-domain(li),
10                                     forall(i, p, i < 2) )),
11                forall(ri, r, right(seq,ri) ),
12              and(forall(i, [1, length(s)],
13                              substitute(nth(i,s),sigma,nth(i,l)) ),
14                forall2(ti, tj, s, substitute(ti,delta,tj)) ) ),
15       block(( hx=build-term('h,var(s)),
16             append-rule(s, hx, trs),
17             append-rule(substitute(hx, delta), hx, trs),
18             append-rule(substitute(hx, sigma), r, trs) )),
19       message("Not generalizable by this inference rule") ) )) ),
20   "This function generalizes a sequence of potentially
21     infinitely many rules with a certain regularity." );
```

> **defun**(name:*raw*, args:*raw*, definition:*raw*, doc:*string*)
> allows the user to define a new function **name**. **Args** is a list of pairs, consisting of argument names and their required data types. All arguments need to be specified. The function above, **syntactic-analysis**, has three: **seq**, **trs** and **new-trs** (line 2). **Seq** is the input sequence to be checked and **trs** the initial TRS. Finally **new-trs** represents the system produced by the inference rule.

A documentation string can be included (lines 20,21) and displayed with the statement help('syntactic-analysis).

The definition itself is contained in **definition** (lines 3...19). This is, in turn, a list of single definitions. Every element of this list is a declaration of a subfunction. Several subfunctions are selected by the special characters _ and @. Therefore the positions of these characters must be specified in every subdefinition. The first element is the name of an argument to be replaced by the @. The function is used like a predicate when given the empty list (() or nil).

In a function call several underlines can appear. Thus the second element of the definition list is a list of argument names to be replaced by the underline. All names appearing at these two positions must be argument names occuring at **args**.

The                                                                      subfunction defined for the example starts by calling **syntactic-analysis**($a_1$,$a_2$,@) or **syntactic-analysis**($a_1$,$a_2$), for short.

A list of local variables can be declared for every subfunction. This can be done by specifying it as the third element of the definition list. In the example the symbols 1 ...**hx** are declared as local variables.

The next element of this list is a list of the statements to be executed at run time, seperated by comma (lines 4...19).

First the input sequence is divided into its left- and right-hand sides, stored at the variables 1 and r, respectively (lines 4,5). This is done to simplify the handling of the original list. At line 6 the list of antiunifiers is computed. The two substitutions result from the first elements of their corresponding lists. Now the conditions (C-a), (C-b) and (C-c) are tested (at lines 9/10, 11 and 12...14, respectively) and depending on the result an error message is printed (line 19) or the new rules (I-a)...(I-c) are added to the original TRS (15...18).

**if**(condition:*boolean*, then:*raw*, else:*raw*, result:*all*)
executes either the **then** or the **else** statement depending on the **condition**. Statements can be combined to a single statement by:
**block**(list:*raw*)
Due to the writing style in T$_L$P$^S$ this must be written as block(($a_1$,...,$a_n$)).

Often the term 'h(X) appears in the conclusions (I-a)...(I-c). It is stored at the variable **hx**.

**build-term**(functor:*term*, arguments:*list-of-terms*, term:*term*)
constructs and divides a **term** from and to its parts **functor** and **arguments**, respectively.

Now we are ready to use the new inference rule for experiments.

This is a protocol of an experiment with the TRS of example 1:

Execute the file containing the definition of the inference rule:
```
TLPS> load('analysis)
-> syntactic-analysis : ALL
```
Load the TRS of the first example and its overlapping sequence:

```
TLPS> trs1=load('example1)
-> current TRS: example1.trs (#1)
{1}  f(g(X)) --> o
{2}  g(s(X)) --> s(g(X))
 : TRS


TLPS> seq1=load('ex1_seq)
-> current TRS: ex1_seq.trs (#2)
{1}  f(s(g(X))) --> o
{2}  f(s^2(g(X))) --> o
{3}  f(s^3(g(X))) --> o
{4}  f(s^4(g(X))) --> o
{5}  f(s^5(g(X))) --> o
 : TRS
```

Apply the function to example 1:

```
TLPS> syntactic-analysis(seq1,trs1)
-> current TRS: example1.trs (#1)
{1}  f(g(X)) --> o
{2}  g(s(X)) --> s(g(X))
{3}  f(s(X0)) --> h(X0)
{4}  h(s(X0)) --> h(X0)
{5}  h(g(X)) --> o
 : TRS
```

The resulting system is the same (modulo variable renaming) as TRS5. The inference rule correctly reflects our ideas.

This is another test with example 2:

```
TLPS> syntactic-analysis(seq6,trs6)
-> current TRS: example2.trs (#3)
{1}  f(g(X)) --> o
{2}  g(s^2(X)) --> s^2(g(X))
{3}  f(s^2(X0)) --> h(X0)
{4}  h(s^2(X0)) --> h(X0)
{5}  h(g(X)) --> o
 : TRS
```

This is the same as TRS8.

```
TLPS> syntactic-analysis(seq9,trs9)
Not generalizable by this inference rule
-> false : BOOLEAN
```

The inference rule, applied to TRS9, says that the needed regularity can not be found. The result of the application is false.

Thus the rule can be embedded in other function calls like this:
```
if(t=syntactic-analysis(seq,trs), t, try-other-way(seq,trs)).
```

In summary, the application of the implemented inference rule to the three examples from the first section leads to the desired results in all cases.

# 7 Discussion

We discuss aspects of the implementation of the inference rules given in [Go]. For more complex projects like this, particularly in the framework of program synthesis experiments, we have several levels of benefit depending on the level of implementation effort.

1. The verification of results, i.e. applying a given rule by completely specifying all parameters, is possible.

2. The computation of certain parameters (resp. solutions) of an inference rule becomes possible while others need to be given.

3. The application of an inference rule is possible in the sense that it is fully implemented – no need to provide partial solutions via parameters.

4. The most successful rule from a set of given inference rules can be discovered.

5. The choice between various rule systems becomes possible.

At present we can benefit from the implementation at level 3 while rule systems (point 5) are still the object of current research.

Does $T_{\!L}P^S$ meet the discussed requirements ? We feel it does.

The system is fitted to the world of terms and TRS. There are many powerful functions for complex manipulations of such objects. The translation of formal descriptions of such manipulations was fairly convenient even in complex cases. The basic functions were sufficiently powerful and easy to use in real life experiments. Its not necessary to think about data representation because terms and TRS are basic types in $T_{\!L}P^S$.

Nevertheless the work with $T_{\!L}P^S$ is work with a programming language and has all its disadvantages. The structuring by brackets may be difficult. On the other hand the interactive change both of data and of programs is quite helpful. Function names are intuitive and the **help**-function substantially shortens the initial training time. The concept of accessing similar functions with one and only one name proved to be very elegant, but also has disadvantages: when writing a new function definition one has (in general) to define additional subfunctions. In this case a relational programming language would have many advantages.

Among the $T_{\!L}P^S$- components which are not the topic of this overview there is a debugger which supports the development of functions resp. TRSs and a recorder which stores all input and output of computations for later evaluation.

Currently we are starting to use $T_{\!L}P^S$ for other problems which are quite different from the implemention of inference rules dealing with TRSs but are, of course, also concerned with terms.

# 8 References

[Th/Ja] Thomas, M. and Jantke, K.P.: Inductive Inference for solving Divergence in Knuth-Bendix Completion, Lecture Notes in AI, Vol. 397, Springer-Verlag, 1989, pp. 288-303

[La/Ja] Lange, St. and Jantke, K.P.: Inductive Completion for Transforming of Equational Specifications, Lecture Notes in Comp. Sci., Vol. 534, Springer-Verlag, 1991, pp. 117-140

[Go] Goldammer, U.: A method for the inductive synthesis of rewrite programs based on Knuth-Bendix-Completion Techniques, GOSLER Report 06/92

[Gr] Grieser, G.: $T_I P^S$ – Eine Einführung

# GoslerP - A Logic Programming Tool for Inductive Inference *

Hans-Rainer Beick and Ventsislav Stankov

Humboldt University of Berlin

Institute of Informatics

10099 Berlin, Germany

### Abstract

This paper starts from the following task: Logic programming is to be connected with a declarative concept of database changes. The theory of inductive inference is considered as the domain of application. Learning processes are characterized by hypothetical knowledge and by permanent changes of this knowledge. Finally, the target consists in the creation of GoslerP, a tool of logic programming, which is usable for the modelling of knowledge based learning processes and the implementation of learning algorithms. GoslerP is an extension of Prolog. At the end of the paper, the new possibilities for learning are demonstrated by a first simple application.

## 1   The Logical Approach of Grabowski

The ideas formulated in Grabowski (1991) and (1992) are the starting point of this project. In these papers, a logic programming language is described in which the database changes are declarative. In Prolog for instance, as the most known logic programming language, database changes are realized in a non-declarative way. Grabowski mainly refers to the following papers:

• Hill / Lloyd (1988), for a many-sorted meta-level language and a declarative concept for database changes. But here, updates must be performed on idle programs only, self-updates of running object-level programs are not possible. The approach of Grabowski allows them.

• Iline / Kanoui (1987), Koschmann / Evans (1988), Mellender (1988), and Grabowski / Müller (1990), for declarative programming with modules, objects, or reusing components, partly without giving declarative semantics for them.

• Chen (1987), for named databases as objects.

In Hill / Lloyd (1992), the logic programming language Gödel is described, "which is intended to be a declarative successor to Prolog. ... In particular, Gödel has declarative replacements for Prolog's *var*, *nonvar*, *assert*, and *retract*. Gödel is a strongly

---
*The work has been supported by the German Ministry for Research and Technology (BMFT) within the joint project GOSLER (no. 413-4001-01 IW 101 D).

typed language, ... based on many-sorted logic ... ." (page i) "In Gödel, the computation rule is partly specified by DELAY declarations and the pruning of the search
tree is specified by the Gödel commit." (page 12)

A database considered in an abstract sense is a set of formulas and subbases. Formulas and named databases are objects of different sorts, in addition to objects of other
sorts like names, goals, and answers. Now, the change of a database is described by
constructors, for instance in the following way:

> assert : database × formula → database,
> retract : database × formula → database.

These operators are programmable in a declarative way, by using metaprogramming:

demo(OldBase, assert(Formula), yes, asserted(OldBase,Formula)).
demo(OldBase, retract(Formula), yes, retracted(OldBase,Formula)).

The predicate "demo(OldBase, Goal, Answer, NewBase)" is defined on arguments
of the sorts database × goal × answer × database. The first and second argument
should be instantiated by the current database and by a goal, for instance for a
database change. The last arguments give the results, an answer 'yes' or 'no' and the
new database.
The database change is not really executed like in Prolog. The change is only recorded
in a term over a fixed signature by constructors like assert( _ ) and retract( _ ). Then
for the derivation of a goal, it has to be fixed which formulas hold and which do not. A
goal not using the new metapredicates is transfered to the predicate "reduce/4", which
again calls the predicate "demo/4". That means that compositions of declarative and
non-declarative goals are possible in an arbitrary way.

demo(OldBase, Goal, Answer, NewBase) :-
        reduce(OldBase, Goal, Answer, NewBase).

reduce(OldBase, Goal, Answer, NewBase) :-
        formula(OldBase, (Head :- Body)),
        rename_and_unify(Goal, Head, Body, Answer1),
        instantiate(Body, Answer1, Goal1),
        demo(OldBase, Goal1, Answer2, NewBase),
        combine_answer(Answer1, Answer2, Answer).

The program "formula(Base,Formula)" is to generate all formulas containing in the
given base. Here, answers are variable subsitutions, 'yes' is the identical substitution,
and "combine_answer" makes the superposition of substitutions.
Especially, it holds:

formula(asserted(Base, Formula), Formula ).
formula(asserted(Base, Formula1 ), Formula) :-
        formula(Base, Formula).
formula(retracted(Base, Formula1), Formula) :-
        formula(Base, Formula),
        Formula1 \ = Formula.

The operational semantic of "retract" differs from Prolog. Here, "retract(Clause)" means: Retract all clauses unifiable with the given! This semantic is more convenient for knowledge processing. Further, "retract(C)" is always succeeded, if C is a correct clause, contrary to Prolog.

In the second step, a structuring of the database is made possible. There are operators

$$new : database \times name \rightarrow database,$$
$$delete : database \times name \rightarrow database,$$

which allows the creation and the removing of subbases. The metaprograms look like:

demo( OldBase, new(Name), yes, named(OldBase,root,Name)).

demo( OldBase, delete(Name), yes, deleted(OldBase,Name)) :-
    object(OldBase, Name, Base).
demo( OldBase, delete(Name), yes, OldBase) :-
    notobject(OldBase, Name, Base).

Here, 'root' is a constant describing the content of an empty database. The program always works in only one database, in the current database. Only the formulas of this base are used for the goal reduction. For instance, formulas of a subbase are not used. The predicate "object(OB,N,SB)" tests if there is a subbase SB with the name N in the base OB, and the predicate "notobject(OB,N,SB)" tests if there is no subbase SB with the name N.

At the beginning, the current database is the whole base. The predicate "with N do G" makes the subbase with the name N to the current base, but only for the derivation of the goal G.

demo( OldBase, with N do Goal, Answer, named(OldBase,Base2,N)) :-
    object(OldBase, N, Base),
    demo(Base, Goal, Answer, Base2).

Further predicates for managing databases are described, like a copy predicate, "cover(N)", and "uncover(N)". They make it possible to transmit the content from one base to another.

demo( OldBase, N2 := N1 \ N3, Answer, named(OldBase,Base3,N2)) :-
    object(OldBase, N1, Base1),
    object(Base1, N3, Base3).

demo( OldBase, N2 \ N3 := N1 , Answer,
        named(OldBase, named(Base2,Base1,N3), N2)) :-
    object(OldBase, N1, Base1),
    object(OldBase, N2, Base2).

demo( OldBase, cover(N) , Answer, named(OldBase,OldBase,N)).

demo( OldBase, uncover(N) , Answer, uncovered(OldBase,N)) :-
    object(OldBase, N, Base).

The base "uncovered(OldBase,N)" is got from the base OldBase by removing the subbase N and adding all formulas and subbases of N to OldBase, except the subbases for which the name is already used in OldBase.

In the abstract approach of Grabowski, a lot of questions are open. For instance, when do we get the answer 'no', how is the backtracking organized, what do happen with the database changes in backtracking? Moreover, the term structure is very complex.

# 2  The Target from the Learning Theory

In inductive inference, one of the sources and components of the algorithmic learning theory, the following learning approach is considered:

A class of objects is given. Objects may be formal languages, automatons, special functions, or another things, depending on the concrete world of the learning process. Successively, more and more information about one object is given. The information can be a pair of an input and an output, a word belonging to the language or not, or similar things. The information sequence must be complete, in the limit.

Now, an algorithm is wanted, which constructs a hypothesis from the information, given at the moment. The hypothesis is a description in a fixed language with a fixed semantic, for instance a Gödel number, a grammar, a pattern, or a program. In the learning process, a sequence of hypotheses is constructed, depending on the increasing information. In this sequence, there exists a point from which the same hypothesis is always constructed. This hypothesis must be a correct description of the given object. It is also said that the sequence of the hypotheses converges on a correct description. In Angluin/Smith (1983) and Jantke/Beick (1981), a survey of inductive inference is given.

In our project, knowledge based algorithmic learning is investigated. The property "knowledge based" means for us, that all elements of the learning process like the information, the hypothesis, and the background knowledge are separated knowledge bases.

Which properties should a logic programming language have, which is designed for such a knowledge based learning?

• The language has to be object oriented. Special parts of the database are integrated into objects. It is possibly to manage these objects. In our modelling of learning, the information, the hypothesis, and the background knowledge are packed in different objects.

• This object orientation allows to manage simultaneously different hypothyses.

• In the learning process, there are two different kinds of knowledge. The background knowledge is considered as a correct and fixed knowledge, never changed in the learning process. In most learning approaches, the information about the objects which are to be learned has the same character. But here, new information is always added to the knowledge during the process.

On the other side, the knowledge of the hypothesis can be changed later. So, it seems to be useful to introduce two different kinds of knowledge in our logic programming language, connected with two different mechanism of changing. The changing of hypothetical knowledge is to be totally integrated into the derivation process. A knowledge change is taken back during the backtracking. Therefore, the controlling of the construction of the hypothesis can be embedded in the controlling of the derivation, in some cases. A change of the real knowledge has to be independent of the backtracking. For instance, if a hypothesis has been constructed, is tested for compatibility with a new information, and has to be changed, then the information should be preserved.

• By the partition into real and hypothetical knowledge, new possibilities are obtained: real knowledge can be superposed by hypothetical knowledge, by the help of a hypothetical "assert" and "retract". The real knowledge is unchanged, but the influence of the knowledge is changed, in the sense of the hypothetical changing. This is usable for algorithms working on a set of facts so that every element is used exactly one time.

# 3   The Main Ideas of GoslerP

The language for specification and implementation of GoslerP is Prolog, in the main parts. There are good experiences from the artificial intelligence in prototyping with Prolog. The programs are relatively short and easy to make. Moreover, the knowledge is described by clauses, and Prolog is clause-based. In addition, the participants of the project have their own experiences from applications of Prolog.

There exists applications of Prolog in the learning Theory. For instance in Beick (1989), the description of functions by terms in a fixed signature and algebra is learned from input–output–pairs of the function. Moreover, Prolog programs are also used as hypotheses ( Shapiro (1981), Ishikato / Arikawa / Shinohara (1992) ).

First, a new logic programming languages was to be developed, with declarative database changes and without some other non-declarative elements. Only for implementation, Prolog was to be used. But for applications of the language, such elements like 'cut' and 'not' are important. Both arguments led us to the decision that Prolog is to be conveniently and optionally extended by a declarative database concept.

This decision opened a new possibility which is the kernel idea of GoslerP today:

## The Partition of the Database into Two Parts

The database managed by GoslerP is divided into two complexes:
• the primary base with the database changing operations "assert" and "retract" and
• the metabase with the operations "metaAssert" and "metaRetract".

Both complexes differ in essential points. So, a different changing of the database is possible.

Especially, the difference between real and hypothetical knowledge can be realized. The primary base contains all the real knowledge and the programs of the algorithms. For this base, the Prolog database is used, with the built-in predicates "assert" and "retract" for the changings. Hence, the change of the primary base does not depend on the derivation of the goals. It is not cancelled by backtracking. In the learning process, this database change describes the knowledge aquisition. For testing a hypothesis, new information about the object which is to be learned, is added. This information stays, also if, in the case of backtracking, the hypothesis is rejected and a new hypothesis is constructed.

The metabase contains the hypothetical knowledge. A change of the metabase subordinates to the derivation process. It is cancelled in backtracking back before the change. But, if a goal on the top level, containing a metabase change, is succeeded, then the change is final, because there is no backtracking. On the other hand, the metabase is easily changeable, not only by "metaAssert" and "metaRetract". Such changes can also be canceled.

Further main ideas of GoslerP are:

## The Hierarchical Structuring of Both Bases

Like in Grabowski (1991,1992), clauses and databases are considered as objects of different sorts. An object database is an ordered sequence of objects of the sorts databases and clauses. Every object of the sort database is connected with a name, so that two subbases of one base have different names. In view of databases, a hierarchical structure is possible, parallelly in the primary and the metabase. In the metabase, there exists a third sort of objects, the 'retracted clauses', which also can belong to the database.

## A Meta–Interpreter as Manager

Like in Grabowski too, a meta-interpreter manages the metabase. Moreover, he organizes the interaction with the user and the controlling of the derivation. Big efforts are made, that using GoslerP does not differ from using Prolog, apart from the new possibilities.

## The Integrated Focus Principle

GoslerP always works in one and only one database of the primary base and in one and only one database of the metabase. These bases are called current bases or bases at which the focus points. Working in one and only one base means that changes are only possible in this base and that only subbases, clauses (and perhaps retracted clause) of this base are used, in the derivation.

There is a predicate "withDo(N,G)", which puts the focus to the subbase with the name N, but only for the derivation of the goal G. After that, the focus goes back, automatically.

The target was to create an intergrated focus in both bases. For it, some agreements are necessary:

(1) Before starting the meta-interpreter, a structured primary base with an current subbase is possible.

(2) The meta-interpreter has only access to the current primary base at the moment of calling the meta-interpreter. This base can already be structured. On the other hande, the metabase is without structure, in most cases. But the user can start with a structured metabase, if he wants.

(3) The simplest way of an integrated focus is an integrated structure of both bases. But that means, that there is unnecessary structure.

The way of GoslerP is very hesitant. A subbase can exist only in the primary base or only in the metabase. A subbase which exists only in the metabase is considered as an existing but empty subbase of the primary base. On the other hand, if a subbase exists only in the primary base and the focus is to point at it, then the subbase is automatically created in the metabase.

(4) The focus of the current primary base is divided into two parts: the absolute part at the moment of starting the meta-interpreter and the relative part, which is the real focus for the meta-interpreter. The relative part is called metafocus and agrees with the focus of the metabase.

(5) Finally, it is fixed, when the focus of the primary base is really changed. The changing is done at the moment, when the meta-interpreter really changes or uses the subbase, not automatically with the predicate "withDo". For instance, derivating the goal "withDo(a, (!,p(X),write(X)))", the foculs only points at the subbase 'a' for derivating the subgoal "p(X)".

## The High Declarativity of the Metaprogramming

The programs of the meta-interpreter are purely declarative, in big parts. Especially that means, that only a small number of Prolog built-in predicates is used. These predicates are besides standard predicates. That also gives a high independence of the the concrete Prolog version. In the implementation of GoslerP, all possibilities of the concrete Prolog are used. A complete renunciation of all built-in predicates is not possible. Concretely, we use them in the following parts:

• for the input and the output

• Twice we need an intervention in the resolution derivation, by cut and "not(G)" (often "\+(G)" written).

• Such testing predicates like "var(X)", "nonvar(X)", "atom(X)", "X==Y", "X\=Y" (for X and Y are not unifiable) and conversion predicates like "functor(Term,Name,Arity)" and "X=..L" are necessary.

Alltogether, the meta-interpreter, restricted on the metabase, realizes logic programming with "and", "or", cut, "not", "call", "metaAssert", "metaRetract", and a hierarchical structuring of the database, nearly declaratively. Moreover, the cut is programmed from the outside, without using internal dates of Prolog.

This part of the Prolog extension is programmed in Prolog. For structuring the primary base, programs in C are used. Here, a programming in Prolog is also possible, by simulation of the wished behaviour in Prolog. (Instead off adding the clause "H:-B" to the subbase a, you can add the clause "subobjekt(a,(H:-B)) :- true." to the database.) But here, the extended Prolog interpreter is not to be overloaded, for a higher effectivity.

## The Representation of the Metabase by a List

The metabase is to be managed by the meta-interpreter in a parameter. The whole metabase and all subbases are described by lists. The name of the base stands at the head of the list. The tail of the list is the content of the base, consisting of subbases, clauses, and retracted clauses.

A clause "H:-B" is represented as "(H,B)", and a retracted clause by "#(H,B)." The name 'metaRoot' is generally used for the whole metabase. The elements of the list standing at the front are younger than the elements standing at the back. This is important, if a clause and an unifiable retracted clause belong to the base. Then, the retracted clause erases only an older unifiable clause of the metabase and the unifiable clauses of the primary base.

# 4  The Structuring of the Primary Base

The structuring of the primary base depends on the used version of Prolog and has a clearly operational character. Our implementation is done in SICStus-Prolog 0.7 for workstations. SICStus-Prolog manages the work with the built-in predicates and the user defined predicates in so called hash tables, which enable the using of the different programs. User defined predicates are always dynamic and not compiled in GoslerP. (A compilation is possible in SICStus-Prolog.) A new empty database is created by the creation of a new hash table. At the beginning, the table contains the references to the built-in predicates only. Every hash table can be extended by consulting files or by adding clauses.

That means, that the different bases are parallel hash tables. This elementary extension is programmed in C.

Now, the top level interpreter is extended so, that the switching from one to another base is possible. Here, the hierarchical arrangement of the different bases is organized.

Starting GoslerP, there exists only one empty base denoted by 'root'. That means, that 'root' is also the current (primary) base. The following predicates allow the construction and the structuring of the primary base:

**"create(N)"**: This predicate fails only then, if N is a not permissible name for a database. Permissible names are atoms. If N is correctly instantiated and there is no subbase with the name N, then a new subbase N of the current base is created. If N is not instantiated, a new name is generated firstly and then a subbase with the generated name is created.

**"new(N)"** works like "create(N)", but it also fails if a subbase with the instantiated name N already exists.

**"exist(N)"** decided for instantiated N whether a subbase of the current base with the name N exists or not. For non-instantiated N, all names of subbases of the current base are successively generated.

**"delete(N)"** is only successful if N is instantiated with the name of a subbase of the current base. Then this subbase is erased, together with all its subbases.

**"empty"** erases all subbases and clauses of the current object.

**"withDo(P,G)"** puts the focus to the subbase described by the path P, but only for the derivation of the goal G. The goal G is derivated on a lower level than the goal "withDo(P,G)". For instance, the answer of the goal "withDo(a,!), fail; true." is 'yes' if a subbase with the name 'a' exists. (The answer of "!, fail; true." is 'no'.). After the derivation of "call(G)", the focus goes back, automatically. It is successful if and only if P is instantiated with a path of an existing database and if the derivation of G in this database is successful.

Which paths are possible?

- P can be the name of a subbase of the current base.
- P can be a list of permissible names. Then

"withDo([ ],G)" means "call(G)" (the focus is not changed),

"withDo([N],G)" means "withDo(N,G)",

"withDo([N|Tail], G)" means "withDo(N, withDo(Tail,G))".

- A list $[N_0, ..., N_n]$ of at least two elements can also be written $N_0\backslash...\backslash N_n$.

"P \\ G" is another notation for "withDo(P,G)."

Moreover, "**create($N_0\backslash$ ... $\backslash N_{n+1}$)**" or "**create([$N_0$,...,$N_{n+1}$])**" stands for "create($N_0$), withDo($N_0$, create([$N_1$,...,$N_{n+1}$])", "create([N])" for "create(N)", and "create([ ])" for "true".

Then, "**new($N_0\backslash$ ... $\backslash N_{n+1}$)**" or "**new([$N_0$,...,$N_{n+1}$])**" means "create($N_0$), withDo($N_0$, new([$N_1$, ..., $N_{n+1}$]))", "new([N])" means "new(N)", and "new([ ])" means "fail".

"**delete($N_0\backslash$ ... $\backslash N_{n+1}$)**" or "**delete([$N_0$,...,$N_{n+1}$])**" is another notation for "withDo([$N_0$, ..., $N_n$], delete($N_{n+1}$))", "delete([N])" for "delete(N)", and "delete([ ])" for "fail".

Last, "**exist($N_0\backslash$ ... $\backslash N_{n+1}$)**" or "**exist([$N_0$,...,$N_{n+1}$])**" stands for "exist($N_0$), withDo($N_0$, exist([$N_1$, ..., $N_{n+1}$]))", "exist([N])" for "exist(N)", and "exist([ ])" for "true".

There exists fine differents when the variables in the paths can be free or not. For instance, all variables in "create" can be free. But all variables in "delete" have to be correctly instantiated. If there is an uncorrect element in the path, then the goal fails, but all changes before are preserved.

"**copy(P1,P2)**" is successful if and only if the path P1 correctly decribes a database DB1 and the path P2 contains only premissible names. Firstly, a database DB2 with the path P2 is created, in the sense of "create". Then, die content of the database DB1 is added to DB2. Subbases with same names are overwritten.

(In Grabowski, there exists predicates "cover(N)" and "uncover(N)". They are similar to "copy([ ],N)" or "copy(N,[ ])".)

Further predicates for changing a primary base are "assert(Clause)", "retract(Clause)", and "consult(File)" from Prolog. Also such predicates like "listing" and "clause(Head,Body)" can be used, in relation to the current base.

"**focus(F)**" gives the focus of the current database, in relation to the database 'root'. [ ] denotes the whole base, [a,b] denotes the subbase b of the subbase a of the whole base, for instance.

"**structure(S)**" gives a overview of the structure of the current database, as a list.
• The structure [N] describes that the current database has the name N and no sub-bases.
• [N, $L_1$, ... , $L_n$] means that the current database has the name N and the subbases with the structures $L_1$, ..., $L_n$. You can also use this predicate for initializing the metabase with the same structure like the primary base.

# 5 The Construction of the Meta–Interpreter

## 5.1 The External Frame

The predicate of the external frame is "**meta(Base)**". It has the following program:

```
meta(OldBase) :-
      input(Goal, ListOfVariables),
      demo(OldBase, [ ], Goal, NewBase, Answer),
      output(Answer, ListOfVariables),
      nextStep(NewBase, Answer).

nextStep(NewBase, stop).
nextStep(NewBase, Answer) :-
      notStop(Answer),
      meta(NewBase).

notStop(yes).
notStop(no).
notStop(cutNo).
```

In "meta/1", the argument is instantiated. [ ] describes the metafocus which is the empty list on the top level of the meta-interpreter.
The predicate "**input(Goal, ListOfVariables)**" organizes the input of a correct goal and puts the list of the names of the variables together, for the correct output.
The predicate "**output(Answer, ListOfVariables)**" works like in Prolog. In the case of Answer = 'no' or Answer = 'cutNot', the output is only 'no'. In the case of the answer 'yes' and a non-empty list of variables of the goal, the interpreter shows a solution and waits for an input. If the input is ';' the next solution is looked for. In the other positive cases, only the word 'yes' is written.
The programs of both predicates depends on the concrete Prolog, on the built-in predicates and on the possibility of using the top level programs.
The metapredicate "**stop**" closes the meta-interpreter.
There are some calls for the meta-interpreter possible, for instance "**meta**" and "**metaInit**":

```
meta :-
      meta([metaRoot]).
```

```
metaInit :-
      structure([Name|Tail]),
      meta([metaRoot|Tail]).
```

The starting metabase is empty, in the first case, or has the same structure like the current primary database. Now the meta-interpreter manages the derivations and the database changes in the primary and in the metabase.

## 5.2  The External Kernel Predicate

For a correct operational semantic of the cut in relation to "and" and "or" in complex goals like in Prolog, the predicate "**demo(OldBase, Focus, Goal, NewBase, Answer)**" is used. Here, complex goals can have the following external functor:

- ',' / 2 ('and'),
- ';' / 2 ('or'),
- ! / 0 (cut),
- commonCall / 1,
- withDo / 2 (also \\ / 2 written),
- not / 1,
- stop / 0.

The other goals are called simple goals.

The correct derivation of complex goals is not easy to realize without internal Prolog dates. We use four parameters for the internal control, namely 'yes', 'no', 'cutNo', and 'stop'. The control is done by the argument "Answer".

```
demo(Base, Focus, Goal, Base, stop) :-
      nonvar(Goal),
      unifying(Goal, stop).

demo(Base, Focus, Goal, Base, yes) :-
      nonvar(Goal),
      unifying(Goal, !).
demo(Base, Focus, Goal, Base, cutNo) :-
      nonvar(Goal),
      unifying(Goal, !).

demo(OldBase, Focus, (Goal1,Goal2), NewBase, Answer) :-
      nonvar(Goal1),
      nonvar(Goal2),
      renameTerm( (Goal1,Goal2), (Goal10, Goal20) ),
      demo(OldBase, Focus, Goal10, NewBase1, Answer1),
      notNo(Answer1),
      demoAnd(Answer1, NewBase1, Focus, Goal20, NewBase2, Answer),
      notNo(Answer),
      ifThenUnifying(Answer , (Goal1,Goal2), (Goal10,Goal20)),
      ifThenElseUnifying(Answer, OldBase, NewBase2, NewBase).

demo(OldBase, Focus, (Goal1;Goal2), NewBase, Answer) :-
```

```
        nonvar(Goal1),
        nonvar(Goal2),
        demo(OldBase, Focus, Goal1, NewBase1, Answer1),
        demoOr(Answer1, OldBase, NewBase1, Focus, Goal2, NewBase, Answer),
        notNo(Answer).

demo(OldBase, Focus, commonCall(Goal), NewBase, Answer) :-
        nonvar(Goal),
        demo(OldBase, Focus, Goal, NewBase, Answer),
        ( negative(Answer1), !,
        ; positive(Answer1)
        ),
        forgetTheCut(Answer1,Answer).

demo([N1|Tail1], Focus, withDo(Name,Goal), [N1|Tail2], Answer) :-
        atom(Name),
        member([Name|Tail3], Tail1),
        append(Focus,[Name], Focus1),
        demo([Name|Tail3], Focus1, commonCall(Goal), [Name|Tail4], Answer),
        notNo(Answer),
        replace(Tail1, [Name|Tail3], [Name|Tail4], Tail2).
demo([N1|Tail1], Focus, withDo(Name,Goal), [N1,[Name|Tail3] | Tail2], Answer) :-
        atom(Name),
        notMember([Name| _ ], Tail1),
        withDo(Focus,exist(Name)),
        append(Focus, [Name], Focus1),
        demo([Name], Focus1, commonCall(Goal), [Name|Tail3], Answer),
        notNo(Answer).
demo(OldBase, Focus, withDo(List,Goal), NewBase, Answer) :-
        nonvar(List),
        unifying(List, [ ]),
        demo(OldBase, Focus, commonCall(Goal), NewBase, Answer),
        notNo(Answer).
demo(OldBase, Focus, withDo(List,Goal), NewBase, Answer) :-
        nonvar(List),
        unifying(List, [N|Tail]),
        demo(OldBase, Focus, withDo(N, withDo(Tail,Goal)), NewBase, Answer).
demo(OldBase, Focus, withDo(Path,Goal), NewBase, Answer) :-
        transformToList(Path,List),
        demo(OldBase, Focus, withDo(List,Goal), NewBase, Answer).
demo(OldBase, Focus, Path \\ Goal, NewBase, Answer) :-
        demo(OldBase, Focus, withDo(Path,Goal), NewBase, Answer).

demo(Base, Focus, not(Goal), Base, Answer) :-
        nonvar(Goal),
        demo(Base, Focus, commonCall((Goal,!,fail;true)), Base1, Answer),
        notNo(Answer).
```

```
demo(OldBase, Focus, Goal, NewBase, yes) :-
     nonvar(Goal),
     demo(OldBase, Focus, Goal, NewBase).

demo(OldBase, Focus, Goal, NewBase, Answer) :-
     nonvar(Goal),
     allowed(Goal),
     demo(OldBase, Focus,
          commonCall((commonClause(Head,Body),Body)),
          NewBase, Answer),
     notNo(Answer).

demo(Base, Focus, Goal, Base, no).
```

The control parameter 'stop' says that the meta-interpreter is to be closed. It is a dominant parameter and passes through the whole complex goal. There are no further substitutions of variables and no further changes of the database. The answer 'stop' is only got if the goal was **"stop"**.

Simple goals get the answer 'yes', if a new solution is found. If there exists only a finite number of solutions, the answer 'no' is given after the last solution, but only one time. Then, the predicate "demo/5" fails for the goal.

A goal, which gets the answer 'no', causes no substitutions of variables and no changes of the metabase. The same holds for the answer 'cutNo'.

The cut produces the answers 'yes'. In backtracking then, the answer 'cutNo' is got. This parameter is also dominant and passes through the whole complex goal, apart from the "commonCall" where the 'cutNo' is transformed to 'no' and further backtracking for negative answers is prevented by a Prolog cut. On the top level, further backtracking for the answer 'cutNo' is prevented by the predicate "output/2".

In a goal **"(G1,G2)"**, the answer for G1 is generated firstly, after a renaming of all variables. If the answer is 'no', so the answer for "(G1,G2)" is also 'no', using the last clause of "demo/5". In the other cases, the predicate "demoAnd" produces the answer for "(G1,G2)". For the answers 'stop' or 'cutNo', it is done without derivation of the goal G2. If the answer for G2 is 'no' then the next solution of G1 is looked for in backtracking. In the other cases, the answer for G2 is also the answer of "(G1,G2)". Only in the case of a positive answer for "(G1,G2)", that means 'yes' and 'stop', the substitutions of the variables and the changes of the metabase are really done, by the predicates **"ifThenUnifying"** and **"ifThenElseUnifying"**. This care is necessary. G1 can produces the answer 'yes' and G2 the answer 'cutNo', for instance. Then, the answer for "(G1,G2)" has to be also 'cutNo' and no substitutions and no changes are allowed.

The predicate **"renameTerm(T1,T2)"** renames all variables in the term T1 into variables with new names and gets the term T2. It is programmable with using built-in predicates like "X == Y" and "X =.. L", for instance.

```
demoAnd(yes, NewBase1, Focus, Goal20, NewBase, Answer) :-
     demo(NewBase1, Focus, Goal20, NewBase, Answer).
```

demoAnd(cutNo, Base, Focus, Goal20, Base, cutNo).
demoAnd(stop, Base, Focus, Goal20, Base, stop).

ifThenUnifying(Answer, Term1, Term2) :-
    negative(Answer).
ifThenUnifying(Answer, Term, Term) :-
    positive(Answer).

ifThenElseUnifying(Answer, Term1, Term2, Term1) :-
    negative(Answer).
ifThenElseUnifying(Answer, Term1, Term2, Term2) :-
    positive(Answer).

For a goal "(G1;G2)", the answer for G1 is produced firstly. This answer is the answer of the whole goal, if it is not 'no'. In the case 'no', the answer for G2 is generated and taken as the answer for "(G1;G2)". The predicate "demoOr" organizes it.

demoOr(yes, OldBase, NewBase1, Goal2, NewBase1, yes).
demoOr(cutNo, OldBase, NewBase1, Goal2, OldBase, cutNo).
demoOr(stop, OldBase, NewBase1, Goal2, NewBase1, stop).
demoOr(no, OldBase, NewBase1, Goal2, NewBase, Answer) :-
    demo(OldBase, Goal2, NewBase, Answer).

For a goal "commonCall(G)", the goal G is derivated by the predicate "demo/5". If it gets a negative answer, further backtracking is prevented by a Prolog cut. Like by the predicate "call" in Prolog, the cut is taken onto a lower level. For instance, the goal "call((!, fail)); true." is successful, in opposite to "!, fail; true." Here, the metaprograms are not purely declarative.

The predicate "withDo(P,G)" puts the focus to the databases with the path P, for derivating the goal "commonCall(G)". The current situation of the focus is record-eded in the parameter Focus. It is the relative focus, in relation to the current primary base at the moment of starting the meta-interpreter. The connection to the primary base is only made by the predicate "withDo(Path,Goal)" of the extended Prolog.
Free variables in the path are not allowed. If a subbase with a name not exists in the current metabase but exists in the current primary base, it is automatically created in the metabase. A focus in the form $N_1 \backslash ... \backslash N_n$ is transformed into the form $[N|1, ..., N_n]$, by the predicate "transformToList". The transformation is only successful if there are only atoms and non-instantiated variables. For instance, the path 'a\X' is transformed to the list [a,X].
The predicate "replace(L,X,X1,L1)" replaces the element X in the list L at the first occurence by X1 and gets the list L1.
"notMember(X,L)" is only successful if X cannot be unified with an element of L. There is no instantiation of variables.

transformToList(Path,List) :-
    nonvar(Path),

```
        unifying(Path, Path1 \ Path2 ),
        transformToList1(Path2, [ ], List2),
        transformToList1(Path1, List2, List).

transformToList1(N, List, [N|List]) :-
        atom(N).
transformToList1(N, List, [N|List]) :-
        var(N).
transformToList1(Path, List1, List) :-
        nonvar(Path),
        unifying(Path, Path1 \ Path2 ),
        transformToList1(Path2, List1, List2),
        transformToList1(Path1, List2, List).

replace([X|Tail], X, Y, [Y|Tail]).
replace([X1|Tail], X, Y, [X1|Tail1]) :-
        X1 \ = X,
        replace(Tail, X, Y, Tail1).

notMember(X, [ ]).
notMember(X,[Y|Tail]) :-
        X \= Y,
        notMember(X,Tail).
```

The **"not(G)"** realizes negation as failure and can also be reduced to the "commonCall". Then, the using of the built-in predicates is organized. It is done by the predicate "demo/4". This predicate has no parameter for control answers and is described in the next subsection.

At last, it is desribed how "demo/5" works with user defined predicates. Here, **"commonClause(Head,Body)"** is a metapredicate which generates for a given Goal G all valid clauses "Head:-Body" of the current primary base and the current metabase whose head can be unified with G, described in the next subsection.
The predicate **"allowed"** secures that this part of the program is not used also for the built-in predicates. This is necessary. Otherwise, an infinite cycle would be possible. Here in "allowed", the second non-declarative place of the metaprogram is.
The user has to take another name for his predicate as the names of a built-in predicate with the same arity, if he wants that the clauses are used in the derivation process.

```
allowed(Goal) :-
        not systemPredicate(Goal).

systemPredicate(!).
systemPredicate(stop).
systemPredicate(','( _ , _ )).
systemPredicate(';'( _ , _ )).
systemPredicate(commonCall( _ )).
```

systemPredicate(withDo( _ , _ )).
systemPredicate(not( _ )).
systemPredicate(Term) :-
     prologBuilt_in(Term).
systemPredicate(Term) :-
     metaBuilt_in(Term).

The predicates **"prologBuilt_in"** and **"metaBuilt_in"** lists all other built-in predicates, usable by "demo/4", in the same way like above. The predicate "focus" is taken as a metapredicate. The following predicates are used above:

notNo(yes).
notNo(cutNo).
notNo(stop).

positive(yes).
positive(stop).

negative(no).
negative(cutNo).

forgetTheCut(yes,yes).
forgetTheCut(no,no).
forgetTheCut(cutNo,no).
forgetTheCut(stop,stop).

unifying(T,T).

## 5.3  The Inner Kernel Predicate

The predicate **"demo(OldBase, Focus, Goal, NewBase)"** organizes the realization of the most built-in predicates of Prolog and of the meta-interpreter.

demo(OldBase, Focus, Goal, NewBase) :-
     prologBuilt_in(Goal),
     withDo(Focus,Goal).

Now, the predicate "focus" is fited to meta-interpreter.

demo(Base, Focus, focus(F), Base) :-
     focus(F1),
     append(F1, Focus, F).

For technical reasons, there exists also a program for "withDo" in "demo/4". But it is hidden for the user.

demo(Base, Focus, withDo(P,G), NewBase) :-
     demo(Base, Focus, withDo(P,G), NewBase, yes).

The metapredicates are described in the next subsection.

## 5.4   The Definition of the Main Metapredicates

The definition of the metapredicates is realized in the frame of the predicate "demo/4", the inner kernel predicate.

demo(Base, Focus, metaBase(Base), Base).

demo([N|OldContent], Focus, metaNewBase([N1|NewContent]),
      [N|NewContent]) :-
    correctContent(NewContent).

demo([N|Content], Focus, metaAssert((H:-B)), [N,(H,B)|Content]) :-
    correctClause((H:-B)).

demo([N|Content], Focus, metaRetract((H:-B)), [N,#(H,B)|Content]) :-
    correctClause((H:-B)).

correctContent([ ]).
correctContent([ [N|Tail1] | Tail]) :-
    correctBase([N|Tail1]),
    notMember([N| _ ], Tail),
    correctContent(Tail).
correctContent([(H,B)|Tail]) :-
    correctClause((H:-B)),
    correctContent(Tail).
correctContent([#(H,B)|Tail]) :-
    correctClause((H:-B)),
    correctContent(Tail).

correctBase([N|Content]) :-
    atom(N),
    correctContent(Content).
correctClause((Head:-Body)) :-
    nonvar(Head),
    nonvar(Body).

"metaBase(L)" generates the current metabase, in the list representation. "metaNewBase(L)" overwrites the content of the old metabase with the content of a new metabase. Some tests of correctness of the new base are done. "metaAssert((Head:-Body))" adds a new clause, written as '(Head,Body)' to the current metabase, directly behind the name of the base. The head and the body have to be instantiated. Further tests of correctness are not made. Prolog has to accept the term (Head:-Body). The notation "Head." is also possible for "Head:-true". "metaRetract((Head:-Body))" adds a restricted clause, written as '#(Head,Body)', to the current metabase, also directly behind the name. The head and the body have to be instantiated too.

demo(Base, Focus, commonClause(Head,Body), Base) :-

```
        demo(Base, Focus, steadyClause(Head,Body), Base).
demo(Base, Focus, commonClause(Head,Body), Base) :-
        demo(Base, Focus, metaClause(Head,Body), Base).

demo(Base, Focus, steadyClause(Head,Body), Base) :-
        withDo(Focus, clause(Head,Body)),
        notMember(#(Head,Body), Base).

demo([Name|Content], Focus, metaClause(Head,Body), [Name|Content]) :-
        nonvar(Head),
        metaClause(Content, Head0, Body0),
        renameTerm( (Head0,Body0), (Head1,Body1) ),
        unifying( (Head1,Body1), (Head,Body) ).

metaClause(Content, Head, Body) :-
        metaClause(Content, [ ], Head, Body).

metaClause([(H,B)|Tail], List, Head, Body) :-
        metaClause(Tail, List, Head, Body).
metaClause([(Head,Body)|Tail], List, Head, Body) :-
        notMember(#(Head,Body), List).
metaClause([#(H,B)|Tail], List, Head, Body) :-
        metaClause(Tail, [#(H,B)|List], Head, Body).
metaClause([[N1|Tail1]|Tail], List, Head, Body) :-
        metaClause(Tail, List, Head, Body).
```

"**commonClause(Head,Body**" calles "steadyClause(Head,Body)" or "meta-Clause(Head,Body)".

"**steadyClause(Head,Body)**" successively produces all valid clauses of the current primary base, whose head is unifiable with Head. For calling this metapredicate, Head has to be instantiated. A clause "H:-B" of the primary base is valid if and only if there exists no retracted clause "#(H1,B1)" in the parallel metabase so that (H,B) and (H1,B1) can be unified.

"**metaClause(Head,Body)**" successively generates all valid clauses of the current metabase, whose head is unifiable with Head. For calling this metapredicate, Head has to be instantiated too. A clause "H:-B" of the metabase is valid if and only if there exists no younger retracted clause #(H1,B1) in the same base so that (H,B) and (H1,B1) can be unified. A (retracted) clause C1 is younger than a clause C2, if C1 stands in the list describing the metabase before C2. Older clauses are generated earlier than younger.

"**metaClause(Content,Head,Body)**" generates all valid clauses Head :- Body containing in Content. For avoiding instantiations in Content, Head and Body should be not instantiated.

The next predicates enable the structuring of the metabase. The operational semantic is to be like the semantic of the parallel predicates of the primary base, in the successful case. Here is a list of the names of the predicates described in the following:

- "metaCreate(P)"
- "metaNew(P)"
- "metaDelete(P)"
- "metaExist(P)"
- "metaEmpty"
- "metaCopy(P1,P2)"

```
demo([N|Tail], Focus, metaCreate(Name), [N,[Name]|Tail]) :-
      var(Name),
      newName([N|Tail], Name).
demo(Base, Focus, metaCreate(Name), Base) :-
      nonvar(Name),
      member([Name| _ ], Base).
demo([N|Tail], Focus, metaCreate(Name), [N,[Name]|Tail]) :-
      atom(Name),
      notMember([Name| _ ], Base).
demo(Base, Focus, metaCreate(List), Base) :-
      nonvar(List),
      unifying(List, [ ]).
demo(OldBase, Focus, metaCreate(List), NewBase) :-
      nonvar(List),
      unifying(List, [N]),
      demo(OldBase, Focus, metaCreate(N), NewBase).
demo(OldBase, Focus, metaCreate([N1,N2|Tail]), NewBase) :-
      atom(N1),
      nonvar(Tail),
      demo(OldBase, Focus, metaCreate(N1), NewBase1),
      demo(NewBase1, Focus, withDo(N1, metaCreate([N2|Tail]), NewBase).
demo(OldBase, Focus, metaCreate(Path), NewBase) :-
      transformToList(Path, List),
      demo(OldBase, Focus, metaCreate(List), NewBase).


demo([N|Tail], Focus, metaNew(Name), [N,[Name]|Tail]) :-
      var(Name),
      newName([N|Tail], Name).
demo([N|Tail], Focus, metaNew(Name), [N,[Name]|Tail]) :-
      atom(Name),
      notMember([Name| _ ], Tail).
demo(OldBase, Focus, metaNew(List), NewBase) :-
      nonvar(List),
      unifying(List, [N]),
      demo( OldBase, Focus, metaNew(N), NewBase ).
demo(OldBase, Focus, metaNew([N1,N2|Tail]), NewBase) :-
      atom(N1),
      nonvar(Tail),
      demo(OldBase, Focus, metaCreate(N1), NewBase1),
      demo(NewBase1, Focus, withDo(N1, metaNew([N2|Tail]), NewBase).
demo(OldBase, Focus, metaNew(Path), NewBase) :-
```

```
        transformToList(Path, List),
        demo(OldBase, Focus, metaCreate(List), NewBase).

demo(OldBase, Focus, metaDelete(Name), NewBase) :-
        atom(Name),
        retract(OldBase, [Name|Tail], NewBase).
demo(OldBase, Focus, metaDelete([N]), NewBase ) :-
        atom(N),
        demo(OldBase, Focus, metaDelete(N), NewBase).
demo(OldBase, Focus, metaDelete([N1,N2|Tail]), Base) :-
        atom(N1),
        demo(OldBase, Focus, withDo(N1, metaDelete([N2|Tail]), NewBase).
demo(OldBase, Focus, metaDelete(Path), NewBase ) :-
        transformToList(Path, List),
        demo(OldBase, Focus, metaDelete(List), NewBase).


demo(Base, Focus, metaExist(Name), Base) :-
        var(Name),
        member([Name|Tail], Base).
demo(Base, Focus, metaExist(Name), Base) :-
        atom(Name),
        member([Name| _ ], Base).
demo(Base, Focus, metaExist(List), Base) :-
        nonvar(List),
        unifying(List, [ ]).
demo(Base, Focus, metaExist(List), Base) :-
        nonvar(List),
        unifying(List,[N]),
        demo(Base, Focus, metaExist(N), Base).
demo(Base, Focus, metaExist([N1,N2|Tail]), Base) :-
        nonvar(Tail),
        demo(Base, Focus, metaExist(N1), Base),
        demo(Base, Focus, withDo(N1, metaExist([N2|Tail]), Base).
demo(Base, Focus, metaExist(Path), Base) :-
        transformToList(Path, List),
        demo(Base, Focus, metaExist(List), Base).


demo([N| _ ], Focus, metaEmpty, [N]).


demo(OldBase, Focus, metaCopy(Path1, Path2), NewBase) :-
        demo(OldBase, Focus, withDo(Path1, metaBase([N1|Tail1]), OldBase),
        demo(OldBase, Focus, metaCreate(Path2), NewBase1),
        demo(NewBase1, Focus, withDo(Path2, metaBase([N2|Tail2])),
                NewBase1)
        uniting(Tail2, Tail1, Tail),
        demo(NewBase1, Focus, withDo(Path2, metaNewBase([N2|Tail])),
                NewBase).
```

The predicate "**newName(Base,N)**" generates successively new names for a new subbase of the metabase Base. "**retract(List,X,List1)**" is only successful if X can be unified with an element of List. List1 is created from List by erasing the first of these elements. "**uniting(L1,L2,L)**" unites the lists L1 and L2 into L. But elements of L1, which have the form [X|Tail] and it exists an element [X|Tail1] of L2, are erased.

retract([X|Tail], X1, Tail) :-
    unifying(X,X1).
retract([X1|Tail], X, [X1|Tail1]) :-
    X \ = X1,
    retract(Tail, X, Tail1).

uniting([ ], List, List).
uniting([X|Tail], List1, [X|List]) :-
    X \= [N1|Tail],
    uniting(Tail, List1, List).
uniting([[N1|Tail1]|Tail], List1, List) :-
    member([N1|Tail2], List1),
    uniting(Tail, List1, List).
uniting([[N1|Tail1]|Tail], List1, [[N1|Tail1]|List]) :-
    notMember([N1|Tail2], List1),
    uniting(Tail, List1, List).

## 5.5 Further Metapredicates

As a service for the user, there are some further metapredicates.
The predicate "**metaFocus(F)**" gives the information about the current focus, relatively to the focus at the moment of starting the meta-interpreter. The starting focus you can get by **startingFocus(F)**".

demo(OldBase, Focus, metaFocus(Focus), NewBase).
demo(OldBase, Focus, startingFocus(F), NewBase) :-
    focus(F).

"**metaListing**" and **metaListing(Term)**" list the valid clauses of the current metabase, in a form like "listing" in Prolog. The predicates "**steadyListing**" and "**steadyListing(Term)**" do the same for current primary base.

"**metaRealize**" transforms the hypothetical knowledge into real knowledge. That means, that the following is done, beginning at the oldest part of the metabase:
• A clause "(H,B)" is added by "assert((H:-B))" to the parallel primary base.
• A restricted clause "#(H,B)" causes the erasing of all unifiable clauses of the parallel primary base.
• A subbase [N|Tail] is also added, in the sense of "create(N),withDo(N,metaRealize)".

demo([N|Content], Focus, metaRealize, [N|Content]) :-

realize(Focus,Content).

realize(Focus, [ ]).
realize(Focus, [(H,B)|Tail]) :-
      realize(Focus, Tail),
      withDo(Focus, assert((H:-B))).
realize(Focus), [#(H,B)|Tail]) :-
      realize(Focus, Tail),
      withDo(Focus, retractAll((H:-B))).
realize(Focus, [[N|Tail1] | Tail]) :-
      realize(Focus,Tail).
      withDo(Focus, (create(N)), realize([N], Tail1))).

retractAll((Head:-Body)) :-
      clause(Head,Body),
      retract((Head:-Body)),
      fail.
retractAll( _ ).

"**metaStructure(L)**" generates the structure of the current metabase, in the same form as "structure(L)" for the primary base.
"**metaSave(File)**" stores the whole primary and metabase into an ASCI data file.
"**metaAttach(File)**" adds the stored primary and metabase into the current base.
"**metaDebug**" switches a mode on in which some diagnostic reports are given.
"**metaNoDebug**" switches the mode again off.

# 6    A Session with GoslerP

In the following, an example session with GoslerP is described. The inputs of the user are written in bold type, the outputs of the computer in normal type. Remarks are given in brackets.
At the beginning, a structured database is constructed.

% **goslerP**
| ?- **meta.**

meta ?- **create(a\b1).**
yes

meta ?- **metaCreate(a\b2).**
yes

meta ?- **a\b1 \\ assert((p(a):-true)).**
yes

meta ?- **a\b1 \\ assert((p(X):-q(X)).**
X = _ 231 → .
yes

meta ?- a\b1 \\ metaAssert((p(a1):-true)).
yes
(Here, the metabase 'a\b1' is automatically created, because there is a primary base
'a\b1'.)

meta ?- a\b1 \\ metaRetract((p(X):-true)).
X = _ 321 → .
yes

meta ?- a\b1 \\ metaAssert((p(b):-true)).
yes

meta ?- a\b1 \\ metaAssert((q(c):-true)).
yes

In the second step, the structure and the content of the database is to be illustrated.

meta ?- structure(L).
L = [root,[a,[b1]]] → .
yes

meta ?- metaStructure(L).
L = [metaRoot,[a,[b1],[b2]]] → .
yes

meta ?- exist(N1\N2).
N1 = a
N2 = b1 → .
yes

meta ?- metaExist(N1\N2).
N1 = a
N2 = b2 → ;

N1 = a
N2 = b1 → ;
no

meta ?- a\b1 \\ listing.
p(a) :- true.
p( _ 123 ) :- q( _ 123).
yes

meta ?- a\b1 \\ metaListing.
p(b) :- true.

q(c) :- true.
yes
("metaListing" lists only the valid clauses of the current metabase. Therefore, the
clause "p(a1):-true." is not written.)

meta ?- a\b1 \\ steadyListing.
p( _ 123) :- q( _ 123).
yes
("steadyListing" lists only the valid clauses of the current primary base. Hence,
"p(a):-true." is omitted, because of the goal "metaRetract((p(X)):-true))".)

meta ?- metaBase(L).
L = [metaRoot,[a,[b1,(q(c),true),(p(b),true),'#(p(_213),true)],[b2]]]
→ .
yes

In the third part, the different possibilities of derivations is illustrated.

meta ?- a\b1 \\ p(X).
X = c → ;
X = b → ;
no

meta ?- a\b1 \\ call(p(X)).
X = a → ;
no

meta ?- a\b1 \\ metaCall(p(X)).
X = b → ;
no

This predicate "metaCall(Goal)" is not contained in GoslerP, but it is easy to be
programmed in GoslerP, if the goal does not use the "metaFocus" and the "focus"
predicates. Only the clauses of the metabase and all built-in predicates are used, for
the derivation.

metaCall(Goal) :-
        metaNew(Base),
        not(exist(Base)),
        metaCopy([ ], Base),
        Base \\ metaDelete(Base),
        Base \\ commonCall(Goal),
        metaDelete(Base).

# 7 A First Application in Learning Theory

In this section, a general scenario is described, usable for all learning processes, working with "generating and testing" algorithms. We use the following concrete world for learning:

• Let L be a formal language over a finite alphabet, for instance over {a,b}, and W(L) the set of all non-empty words over L. The words are described as atoms in GoslerP.

• A computable similarity predicate "near(X,Y)" for words is given. It should be reflexive.

• The language is to be learnt by text instruction. This means, that all words belonging to L are successively given. At the beginning, a lot of clauses should be contained in a subbase 'information' of the primary base, in the form "fact(Number,Word):-true.". The facts are consequently numbered from 1 to the end. All Words belong to L. Later, new examples of words are got and also stored in 'information', with correct numbers.

• The hypothesis is to be a finite case base CB, a set of words. The case base CB describes the following language:

L(CB) = { x ∈ W(L) | ∃y ∈ CB near(y,x) }.

The case base is stored in a subbase 'hypothesis' of the metabase, by clauses of the form "caseBase(Word):-true.".

Our learning is done by "identification by enumeration" (Gold 1967). Successively, all possible case bases are generated from the given examples and tested with the given examples. (Because of the reflexivity, there is a case base so that every example is similar to a case.)

The learning process can be so modelled in GoslerP:

## The Generating of the Hypothesis

For choosing the cases for the case base, a fact is choosen firstly. Then, the case base is filled with facts of lower numbers. Described by the numbers of the facts, the cases bases are generated in the following order:

{1}, {2}, {1,2}, {3}, {1,3}, {2,3}, {1,2,3}, {4}, {1,4}, {2,4}, ... .

The cases belonging to the numbers stand in the same order in the database 'hypothesis'.

"count(1,N)" generates all integers 1, 2, 3, ... , successively. "permissible(N)" tests whether a fact with the number N exists or not. For generating the case base, an erasing of clauses is not necessary. The non-needed cases are omitted in backtracking, automatically.

```
generate :-
      count(1,Number),
      (      not permissible(Number),
             !, fail
      ;      information \\ fact(Number,Word),
             fill(Number),
             hypothesis \\ metaAssert((caseBase(Word):-true))
      ).
```

```
count(N,N).
count(M,N) :-
      M1 is M+1,
      count(M1,N).

permissible(N) :-
      information \\ fact(N, _ ).

fill(N) :-
      information \\ fact(N1,Word),
      (      N >= N1,
             !, fail
      ;      fill(N1),
             metaAssert((caseBase(Word):-true))
      ).
```

## The Frame of the Process

A manager of the learning process organizes the interaction in the process. The user can wish the following tasks:

- The hypothesis is accepted. (okay)
- A further hypothesis is to be found which is also consistent with the given examples! (next)
- The learning process is to fail and the initial conditions are to be restored! (back) That do not include the information.
- Further tests are to be done! (test) If the current hypothesis has to be rejected, then a new hypothesis is to be generated, automatically and by using also the new information.

```
learn :-
      prepare,
      generate,
      test,
      manage(Parameter),
      ( Parameter = okay
      ; Parameter = back, !, fail
      ).

prepare :-
      create(information),
      metaCreate(hypothesis),
      readTheInitialInformation.

test :-
      information \\ fact( _ , Fact),
      test(Fact,no),
      !, fail.
test.
```

```
test(Fact,yes) :-
      hypothesis \\ caseBase(Case),
      near(Case,Fact),
      !.
test(Fact,no).

manage :-
      repeat,
      writeTheActualHypothesis,
      askWhatToDo(Answer),
      ( Answer = okay, Parameter = okay
      ; Answer = back, Parameter = back
      ; Answer = next, !, fail
      ; Answer = test, furtherTest(Result), Result=no, !, fail
      ).

furtherTest(Result) :-
      AskForTheNextFact,
      read(Fact),
      information \\ storeTheInformation(Fact),
      test(Fact,Result).
```

The predicate "test(F,Result)" tests whether the current hypothesis is consistent with the fact F. The result can be 'yes' or 'no'. Together with "generate", both predicates are the interfaces between the program and the concrete world of learning. The other predicates do not depend on the concrete situation.

The example should demonstrate the following advantages of programming in GoslerP:

• Complicated processes can easy be programmed. The both types of databases, together with the different possibilities of changing, allow a compressed style with less parameters.

• The construction and reconstruction of databases can be embedded in the derivation process. For instance, we can use only "metaAssert". The omitting of the clauses is automatically done in backtracking. A dual tackling with "metaRetract" is possible.

# References

D. ANGLUIN / C.H. SMITH (1983) : Inductive inference : Theory and methods. Computing Surveys 15, 237 - 269.

H.-R. BEICK (1989) : Enumerative learning from examples in a fixed algebra. Fifth Conference of Program Designers, Eötvös Lorand University, Proceedings Vol I p. 27 - 32, Budapest.

M. CARLSON / J. WIEN (1992) : SICStus - Prolog User's Manual. (Version 0.7) Swedish Institute of Computer Science, Kista.

W. CHEN (1987) : A theory of modules based on second order logic.
Proc. IEEE Int. Symp. Logic Programming, 24 - 33.

W.F. CLOCKSIN / C.S. MELLISH (1981) : Programming in PROLOG.
Springer-Verlag.

U. GESKE (1988) : Programmieren mit Prolog.
Akademie-Verlag Berlin.

E.M. GOLD (1967) : Languages indentification in the limit.
Information and Control 10, 447 - 474.

H.-J. GOLTZ / H. HERRE (1990) : Grundlagen der Logischen Programmierung.
Akademie-Verlag Berlin.

J. GRABOWSKI (1991) : Declarative semantics for changing objects : A metaprogramming approach.
Informatik-Preprint, FB Informatik, Humboldt-Universität zu Berlin.

J. GRABOWSKI (1992) : Metaprograms for change, assumptions, objects, and inheritance.
GOSLER Report 09/92, Fachbereich Mathematik und Informatik, TH Leipzig.

J. GRABOWSKI / W. MÜLLER (1990) : Introduction to PROPEL (Version 1.0).
Informatik-Preprint, FB Informatik, Humboldt-Universität zu Berlin.

P.M. HILL / J.W. LLOYD (1988) : Meta-programming for dynamic knowledge bases.
CS-88-18, Department of Computer Science, University of Bristol.

P.M. HILL / J.W. LLOYD (1992) : The Gödel programming language.
CSTR-92-27, Department of Computer Science, University of Bristol.

H. ILINE / H. KANOUI (1987) : Extending logic programming to object programming : The system LAP.
Proc. IJCAI 87, 34 - 39, Morgan Kaufmann.

H. ISHIKATO / H. ARIKAWA / T. SHINOHARA (1992) : Efficient inductive inference of primitive Prologs from positive data.
Algorithmic Learning Theory '92, Springer-Verlag, LNAI 743, 135 - 146.

K.P. JANTKE / H.-R. BEICK (1981) : Combining postulates of naturalness in inductive inference.
Journal of Information Processing and Cybernetiks (EIK) 17, 465 - 484.

T. KOSCHMANN / M.W. EVANS (1988) : Bridging the gap between object-oriented and logic programming.
IEEE Software, 5(4), 36 - 42.

F. MELLENDER (1988) : An integration of logic and object-oriented programming.
SIGPLAN Notices, 23(10), 102 - 186.

E.Y. SHAPIRO (1981) : Inductive inference of theories from facts.
Technical Report 192, Computer Science Department, Yale University.

R. WIEHAGEN (1978) : Zur Theorie der algorithmischen Erkennung.
Diss.B, Sektion Mathematik, Humboldt-Universität zu Berlin.

# INDEX OF AUTHORS

# Springer-Verlag
# and the Environment

We at Springer-Verlag firmly believe that an international science publisher has a special obligation to the environment, and our corporate policies consistently reflect this conviction.

We also expect our business partners – paper mills, printers, packaging manufacturers, etc. – to commit themselves to using environmentally friendly materials and production processes.

The paper in this book is made from low- or no-chlorine pulp and is acid free, in conformance with international standards for paper permanency.

# Lecture Notes in Artificial Intelligence (LNAI)

# Lecture Notes in Computer Science